THE COMMON LAW OF INTELLECTUAL PROPERTY

This collection of essays was written in honour of David Vaver, who recently retired as Professor of Intellectual Property and Information Technology Law and Director of the Oxford Intellectual Property Research Centre at the University of Oxford. The chapters, written by some of the world's leading academics, practitioners and judges in the field of intellectual property law, take as their starting point the common assumption that the patent, copyright and trade mark laws within members of the 'common law family' (Australia, Canada, Israel, Singapore, South Africa, the United Kingdom, the United States and so on) share some sort of common tradition. The contributors examine, in relation to particular topics, the extent to which such a shared view of the field exists in the face of other forces that are producing divergence. The chapters discuss, inter alia, issues concerning court practices, the medical treatment exception, non-obviousness and sufficiency in patent law, originality and exceptions in copyright law, unfair competition law, and cross-border goodwill and dilution in trade mark law.

The Common Law of Intellectual Property

Essays in Honour of Professor David Vaver

Edited by
Catherine W Ng
Lionel Bently
and
Giuseppina D'Agostino

·HART·
PUBLISHING
OXFORD AND PORTLAND, OREGON
2010

Published in the United Kingdom by Hart Publishing Ltd
16C Worcester Place, Oxford, OX1 2JW
Telephone: +44 (0)1865 517530
Fax: +44 (0)1865 510710
E-mail: mail@hartpub.co.uk
Website: http://www.hartpub.co.uk

Published in North America (US and Canada) by
Hart Publishing
c/o International Specialized Book Services
920 NE 58th Avenue, Suite 300
Portland, OR 97213-3786
USA
Tel: +1 503 287 3093 or toll-free: (1) 800 944 6190
Fax: +1 503 280 8832
E-mail: orders@isbs.com
Website: http://www.isbs.com

British Library Cataloguing in Publication Data
Data Available

ISBN: 978-1-84113-970-8

Typeset by Compuscript Ltd, Shannon
Printed and bound in Great Britain by
TJ International Ltd, Padstow, Cornwall

Foreword

When Lionel Bently asked me to write this, I confess that my first reaction was 'Damn, another bloody festschrift. There should be a law against them.' That, I discover in my regular email discussions with other European judges, is a perfectly normal reaction. The German judge apologised for this German disease which has now spread around the world. The Dutch judge was not willing to go so far as to agree that capital punishment should be imposed on criminals such as Lionel. We settled on life imprisonment. But more than that was needed. The initial idea was hard labour. But that was too crude. We hit upon something more fitting: that the criminal be required to write a piece for a festschrift every week.

Of course, despite my initial reaction, I could not say 'no'. Nor indeed did I want to. For this is something that I need to do to honour and praise David Vaver. But what could I write about? A Foreword is not quite an essay. Nor, on the other hand, is it a publisher's blurb. Lionel said the volume would be loosely linked to a theme: whether it is useful to think that there is a shared tradition among the common law countries. I thought I could say a little about that and perhaps say something about the main essays of the volume. I was accordingly sent the essays to read over the summer. I did not think I would enjoy this—sitting with a glass of pink wine in the Mediterranean sun is not normally the moment for reading this sort of stuff. Yet I did (both), and enjoyed it immensely.

Before I say why, I wish to identify what at first seems a stark omission from these essays. That sounds like I am about to launch into a criticism. But I am not. It is just that in the nature of things, the missing topic would not be covered. That missing topic is, of course, David Vaver himself, the man, the person. So I thought that before I turned to the essays and their theme, I would do a little to rectify that.

I begin in a roundabout way (because I wanted this to be recorded somehow, and I know David would like it too) by how I came to know him. It started with a letter in about 1996 or 97 from a man I'd never heard of called John Barron. He said he was Master of an Oxford College called St Peter's. I'd never heard of that either. He said he had a problem and an idea. Would I meet him for lunch at the Reform Club? So I did. The problem was that through the initiative of one of its law dons, then nearing retirement, St Peters had obtained and used a very generous gift from a Japanese company to create a library of intellectual property law books. John Barron said it was hardly ever used. What John wanted to know was whether the library was any good, because if it was he had the idea about bringing it into use.

So would I come to look at it? I did, and, as it says in Genesis, I 'saw that it was good'. John said he wanted to bring IP to Oxford and to make St Peter's College the place for it. The library would be the hook. Through his genius he brought that to pass, centring this important subject in little St Peter's.

Critical to the success of the task was getting someone really good to develop it. I had no useful ideas. IP expertise in academia was a problem (the attractions of practice were so great that academia was short; besides there was, perhaps still is, a school of academic lawyers which says that things like intellectual property are too practical to be proper academic subjects). Cornish was at Cambridge. QMC had some good professors already tied up. MacQueen would never leave Scotland and Bently had yet to emerge. Who could be found for Oxford?

John Barron pressed on regardless. And the first time I heard of David was from Hugh Laddie. Hugh phoned to say he had just been on the appointment committee and that they had had no difficulty whatever. It was to be this chap called David Vaver, a New Zealander who had spent most of his working life in Canada. Hugh enthused. The next year David arrived at Oxford, to a welcoming college under the wise guidance of John Barron.

When I eventually met David I at once saw why the selection process had been easy. John Barron had struck gold. David was, and is, immensely learned. But he wears it lightly. The first two things that strike you about him are his humour (described as 'wry', in a footnote in the Rothstein/Holderman Floyd/Pickard chapter) and his balanced view of the subject. But the more you get to know him, the more his sheer warmth of personality endears. David is someone you enjoy being with, whether it is having a dinner (a good wine is in his case essential) or trying to solve some knotty problem of IP law.

Coming as he did from North America he could easily have been infected with the then prevailing disease of IPitis ('some intellectual property is a good thing, so more will be better and even more even better'). But he had none of that. Instead one found, as one still finds, an immense sense of balance. The big question for David is and always has been, where is the rational, the sensible, place to draw the line between too much and too little. That in a sense, is the question which faces a judge too.

It helps judges to have academics like David. There is a temptation in some academics to get too theoretical. David simply has never been so. He has always written for the practical side of law. That is why judges cite him so often. Mr Justice Roger Hughes has even found out how often: 9 times in the Supreme Court, seven in the Federal Appeal Court, seven in the Federal Court and 24 in the Provincial Courts (appellate and first instance). And that is only Canada. And only in IP. One wonders how the Canadian judges manage when Vaver has not said something relevant. I cannot think of any academic author who has been cited more.

As far as Oxford is concerned, he did what was expected. And a lot more. The Oxford IP Centre (which now of course includes that St Peter's IP library which started it all) has become important. It is on the IP map. And as part of the Faculty of Law of Oxford University. Moreover, David invented the Oxford International IP moot—there is nothing else like it in the world of IP; only the Jessup International Law moot competition is older and better known. Oxford and St Peter's were lucky to have David.

I will make him blush no more and turn to the essays. There is not a dud amongst them. What struck me was their total originality. They come from around the common law world. The contributors include judges from two Supreme Courts, of Canada and South Africa, and a host of other top players—a fact which again tells you a lot about David: how many other law professors could induce such contributions? True it is that some authors have drifted somewhat afar from the common law theme (Henry Carr, for instance, obviously still sore about losing, eloquently explains why my judgment in *Unilin* was not only wrong, but so obviously so) but no matter. They are all worth a read.

Let me comment on them lightly. Hector MacQueen begins, with a subject I had never thought about before—the merger of Scots IP into UK IP as a common UK market grew from smaller markets. It is a valuable tale—not merely as a historical record, but as a parallel to our own European common market. We are attempting a similar merger across Europe, albeit, because legislation is involved, it is not so judge-led as was the way in Scotland. Nonetheless, the same sort of compromises of judicial traditions are, and will increasingly be, involved. Next there is Kathy Bowrey's insightful examination of originality in copyright. I am not sure I agree with her conclusions—for instance, that Australia has been hampered by the notion of a monolithic Anglo common law. What should it have done differently? And is there much point in a very distinct IP law for a country of Australia's size? And is it really the case that modern Australian judges are less astute in trying to draw that difficult line between too little and too much than were their predecessors?

Moving on from history, one comes to the section on procedure. I say no more about Henry Carr's bit. The next chapter is joint and from three distinguished judges in their respective countries. It is about the conduct of a patent trial in Canada, the US and the UK. What would strike an outsider (eg a civil lawyer) is how much they have in common—and how much they are beset by the great problem of legal costs. Sadly, but unsurprisingly, none of the authors could come up with any ideas about that. Fiddling at the edges will not be enough. Only if we severely restrict and modify the common law method of long open trials with lots of cross-examination and discovery can anything be done. Whether common law users—also imbued with the tradition of the common law—really want that change is not clear. I doubt that US users do—they are besotted with jury trial. And even in the

UK, in, but on the edge of, Europe, there is great fear of too great a departure from the common law way of doing things. Roger Hughes' sparkling piece gives a delightful view of the Canadian way of doing things—particularly recognising that there is a real practical difference between big and little IP cases.

Turning to patents, Tina Piper begins with brilliant and insightful view of the medical methods exception and its history. I never knew most of the things she has unearthed—the hostile view of the medical establishment to patents, the fascinating way in which the Canadian and UK medical professions interacted in the inter-war years due to the insulin patent, and the irrational way in which the exception began. She postulates that UK common law might have abolished it altogether but for the enshrinement of the exception by the EPC in 1977. She might be right—we shall never know. I think policy-makers would do well to get rid of the exception. It serves no rational purpose, and removes the patent incentive from an area calling for research. Next there is Graham Dutfield's controversial view that synthetic biology patents for whole organisms have gone too far. I confess I do not agree with him, save that some biotech patents probably have too broad a scope. His basic postulate is founded on the fact that too little is known about whole organisms. But basic science has never mattered for patent law. If you devise something new and useful, and tell people how to make or do it, it does not matter if you explain it all by phlogiston theory or have no explanation at all. All that matters is that it works. Ann Monotti's piece about inventive step is a clear description of how judges in Australia and the UK have turned a simple basic question—is it obvious?—into a distinct branch of metaphysics. She points out that the approach has diverged in the two countries, that Australia currently has made it particularly complicated and has a unique and idiosyncratic prior art basis provided by section 7(3) of its Act. She is surely right to say that Australia should come into line with the international system of worldwide prior art, and probably right in saying that the courts in Australia have gone too far in limiting obviousness challenges. Finally on patents, Siva Thambisetty takes on the hardest task of all. She addresses what I regard as the most fundamentally difficult area of patent law, sufficiency of disclosure and its relationship to claims of undue width. Her piece analyses with clarity how Australian and UK courts have tried to cope with the problem in different ways. It is not surprising that she does not identify a clear picture in either country (or in the EPO). A clear intellectual basis has yet to emerge—and may never do so.

Copyright follows, though of course Kathy Bowrey's piece could have come here too. Burton Ong starts with that recursive problem: what if a work re-creates an earlier work? Is it original so that it can have a copyright? There are different answers in the common law world. His conclusion, that if enough work is involved, it should do, makes a lot of sense. The next contribution is from Israel, where there is a new Copyright Act replacing the late, great, 1911 Act. Lior Zemer suggests that the departure from the strict and limited fair use exceptions of that Act (and of subsequent UK Acts) is a good thing. It gives the judges more wiggle room, but even though there are factors to be considered, I myself feel uncomfortable with too much of that. 'Fairness' is woolly—and rather alien to the common law. Civil law is full of it.

Christopher Wadlow starts off the trade marks/unfair competition section by considering the reception by other common law courts of the *International News* case of the US Supreme Court. It is a fascinating survey of the common law's struggle to try and find the elusive line. And how that line is different in different common law countries. Graeme Dinwoodie, now sitting in Oxford in what was David's Chair, gives a masterly survey of the limits of registered trade marks as found in the US, the UK and Europe. Kelly Gill shows how local considerations have fashioned local views about the protection of extra-territorial goodwill. He ranges over the entire common law world. He was too late to comment on the Malaysian case of *McDonald's v McCurry*—a case which, I am bound to say, I might have decided the other way on the grounds of the get-up used by the defendants, not just the name. Louis Harms writes a characteristically elegant demolition of the idea of trade mark dilution—ending with a postscript damning the ECJ's decision in *L'Oréal*. I expect he is glad he has not got to apply it in South Africa.

Before ending this Foreword I will, as I was asked, give my own view about the theme of a monolithic common law of IP. What I say is borne out of experience, rather than research. That experience is now a bit long. But it has enabled me to go to most of the major common law jurisdictions (the big omission is African common law countries, especially South Africa), to have appeared as counsel in several (Australia, Singapore, Hong Kong) and to have met many judges and practitioners from many countries. My first comment is this—that the common law way of thinking is pervasive. I have long said you can take a good barrister (advocate) from one common law country and, with but a little help about the local rules, put him or her before the court of another: a barrister is a barrister is a barrister. My second comment is this: the courts of different common law countries do not always agree on detailed rules, the British Empire is no more and the legislation has diverged. But still apparent in most is the common law's scepticism of monopoly. Such scepticism I do not find in most of my civil law colleagues. Of all the common law countries, it is the US which has diverged most—almost to the point of having a sui generis system. Some there, eg Justice Scalia, even think that it is so sui generis that American courts should forget the rest of the world. That is far from the common law way of looking at things.

Lionel asked another question: Do I pay more attention to a judgment of a common law judge than to that of a civil law judge? I cannot say that

I do. But generally these days I will be considering the same legislation as the civil law judge, whereas the common law judge from outside the EU will be working on the basis of a different law. Also, and this is of some importance, civil law judges in Europe have, at least in the case of some countries, started to become more 'common law' like. They refer to previous decisions and to cases in other countries in much the same way as we do. Case law governs them as much as it governs us. And with globalisation of trade comes the globalisation of IP law. So the laws of all nation states or regions will converge more and more: the common law (and civil law) will become less and less individually distinct.

Robin Jacob
The Royal Courts of Justice,
September 2009

Contents

Patents

Copyright

Trade Marks and Unfair Competition

Conclusion

List of Contributors

Lionel Bently is the Herchel Smith Professor of Intellectual Property Law and Director of the Centre for Intellectual Property and Information Law at the University of Cambridge (www.cipil.law.cam.ac.uk). He is also a Professorial Fellow of Emmanuel College, Cambridge. He is co-author (both with B Sherman) of *Intellectual Property Law* (Oxford, OUP, 2001; 2nd edn, 2004; 3rd edn, 2008) and *The Making of Modern Intellectual Property Law – The British Experience, 1760–1911* (Cambridge, CUP, 1999) and is co-authoring (with T Aplin and S Malynicz) the second edition of *Gurry on Breach of Confidence: The Law of Trade Secrets and Confidentiality* (Oxford, OUP).

Kathy Bowrey was appointed as a Professor to the Faculty of Law, University of New South Wales, Sydney in 2007. Her publications primarily relate to intellectual property and information technology regulation, reflecting a broad range of interests pertaining to socio-legal history, media and cultural studies, and legal theory.

Her current research projects include a consideration of the relevance of copyright's categories to the emerging global mass entertainment markets, and a critical analysis of calls for cultural exceptions in intellectual property concerning indigenous intellectual and cultural property and sui generis rights.

Henry Carr practises in all fields of intellectual property, with a particular concentration on patent, trade mark and computer law litigation.

Recent cases of significance in which he appeared include *Procter & Gamble v Reckitt Benkiser* (Community Designs); *L'Oreal v Bellure* (trade marks and unfair advantage); *L'Oreal v eBay* (liability of eBay for trade mark infringements in respect of goods sold on its site); *Kelly v GE Healthcare* (compensation for invention of outstanding benefit) and *Dr Reddys v Eli Lilly* (selection patents).

He is a Deputy High Court Judge of the Chancery Division, and Deputy Chairman of the Copyright Tribunal, UK.

Giuseppina D'Agostino has been an Associate Professor since July 2010 at Osgoode Hall Law School, York University, Canada and is the Founder and

Director of IP Osgoode, Osgoode's Intellectual Property and Technology Programme. Before her appointment, she joined the Department of Canadian Heritage through the Federal government's Recruitment of Policy Leaders programme. She completed her doctoral and masters studies with distinction at the University of Oxford where she was a Lecturer and recipient of various scholarships including an SSHRC fellowship. She is a Research Associate of the Oxford Intellectual Property Research Centre and previously was an associate at a large firm. Her book, *Copyright, Contracts, Creators* is forthcoming (Edward Elgar, 2010).

Graeme B Dinwoodie is the Professor of Intellectual Property and Information Technology Law at the University of Oxford. He is also Director of the Oxford Intellectual Property Research Centre, and a Professorial Fellow of St Peter's College. Prior to taking up the IP Chair at Oxford, Professor Dinwoodie was a Professor of Law and Director of the Programme in Intellectual Property Law at the Chicago-Kent College of Law. He has also previously taught at the University of Cincinnati College of Law and the University of Pennsylvania School of Law, and from 2005–09 held a Chair in Intellectual Property Law at Queen Mary College, University of London. In 2008, Professor Dinwoodie was awarded the Pattishall Medal for Excellence in Teaching Trademark and Trade Identity Law by the International Trademark Association.

Graham Dutfield is Professor of International Governance at Leeds University School of Law. His research on intellectual property crosses several disciplines, including law, history, politics, economics and anthropology. More general scholarly interests include the law, science and business of technical innovation from the enlightenment to the present, especially in the life sciences. His books include *Global Intellectual Property Law*, *Innovation Without Patents* (both with U Suthersanen), and *Intellectual Property, Biogenetic Resources and Traditional Knowledge*. His expanded second edition of *Intellectual Property Rights and the Life Science Industries*, now subtitled *Past, Present and Future*, was published in 2009 by World Scientific.

Christopher Floyd has been a Judge of the Chancery Division of the High Court in London, a nominated Judge of the Patents Court and a Chairman of the Competition Appeal Tribunal since 2007. He practised in intellectual property law from chambers at 11 South Square, Gray's Inn from 1975 until 2007, becoming Queen's Counsel in 1992. Whilst in practice he was a Deputy Chairman of the Copyright Tribunal (1995–2007), Chairman of the Intellectual Property Bar Association (1999–2004) and a Recorder (2000–07). His main field of practice was in patents and he appeared in a number of leading cases in that field.

Kelly Gill is a partner with Gowling Lafleur Henderson, LLP (Toronto, Canada). Mr Gill's practice specialises in trade mark, copyright, patent and misleading advertising litigation, including related rights and opinion work. Mr Gill has appeared before the Supreme Court of Canada as counsel for the Law Society in the leading Canadian copyright decision of *CCH Ltd v The Law Society of Upper Canada*, and also the Federal Court of Appeal, the Federal Court Trial Division, the Ontario Court of Appeal, Superior Court and Divisional Court. Mr Gill is the author of numerous publications, including the leading Canadian trade mark text, *The Canadian Law of Trade-Marks and Unfair Competition.*

Louis Harms is the Deputy President of the Supreme Court of Appeal of South Africa and has been an appeal judge since 1991. He graduated cum laude from the University of Pretoria (Law) and holds an honorary doctorate from the University of the Free State. After academia, he spent 20 years as a trial lawyer specialising in intellectual property law. He also served on the committee responsible for the current Patents Act, chaired the committee responsible for the Trade Marks Act, the Designs Act and the updating of the Copyright Act in South Africa, and vice-chaired the Assembly of the Paris Convention (1995–97), inter alia, on the international stage. He has published and presented widely on intellectual property and other law subjects.

James F Holderman has been the Chief Judge of the Northern District of Illinois since 1 July 2006. He has been a US District Judge in Chicago since 1985 and has served by designation on judicial panels of the US Courts of Appeals for the Seventh Circuit in Chicago and for the Federal Circuit in Washington, DC. During his more than 20 years on the bench, he has presided over numerous cases in all areas of federal jurisdiction. Before his judicial appointment, he was a partner in the law firm of Sonnenschein Nath & Rosenthal and earlier an Assistant United States Attorney in Chicago.

Roger T Hughes was appointed Federal Court Judge in Canada, and ex officio, member of the Federal Court of Appeal in 2005, and appointed a Judge of the Court Martial Appeal Court of Canada in 2006. He was educated at Queen's University, Canada (BSc 1963) and University of Toronto (LLB 1966), called to the Bar of Ontario (1968) and Alberta (1976), and appointed Queen's Counsel (1984) while at Sim, Hughes, Ashton & McKay and Sim & McBurney (1969–2005) in Toronto, Canada. He has published and presented extensively on court practice and procedure, patent, trade mark and copyright laws, and media and entertainment law.

Robin Jacob has been Lord Justice of Appeal at the Court of Appeal for England and Wales since 2003. He was called to the Bar (Gray's Inn), and then appointed Junior Counsel to the Treasury in Patent matters (1976–81), Queen's Counsel (1981), High Court Judge (Chancery Division) for England and Wales (1993–2003).

Hector MacQueen is Professor of Private Law at the University of Edinburgh. He has also held visiting appointments at Cornell University and Stetson University College of Law in the USA and the University of Utrecht in the Netherlands. He was the first Director of the AHRC Research Centre in Intellectual Property and Technology Law (SCRIPT) at Edinburgh. He is a Fellow of both the British Academy and the Royal Society of Edinburgh, and is Vice-President (Humanities) of the latter. In September 2009 he was appointed as a Scottish Law Commissioner. Copyright and design law are his principal areas of interest in intellectual property.

Ann Monotti is Professor and Associate Dean (Postgraduate Studies) in the Monash University Law Faculty. She was a partner in legal practice for a number of years before entering academia in 1991. Ann has both honours and master's degrees in law from the University of Melbourne and her Monash University PhD was awarded for the book of which she is principal author: *Universities and Intellectual Property, Ownership and Exploitation* (Oxford, OUP, 2003). She wrote the patents, confidential information and plant breeder's rights chapters in *Australian Intellectual Property Law* (Cambridge, CUP, 2008). Her current research focuses on patents and intellectual property issues in universities.

Victor Nabhan is a former Professor of Law at Laval University Law School. He has studied law in Lebanon, France and the USA. He has also taught as a guest professor in a number of universities in Europe and the Middle East. He is the president of ALAI (Association littéraire et artistique internationale). He acted as a consultant to WIPO and UNESCO as well as to a number of countries on the revision of their copyright legislation. He is presently a freelance consultant and professor, and is counsel at the law firm of Kimbrough et Associés in Paris.

Catherine W Ng is a Lecturer at the University of Aberdeen, School of Law, and the Director for Post-Graduate Research Training there. She completed her DPhil at the University of Oxford, where her thesis written under Prof. Vaver's supervision was awarded the first British Brands Group Prize. She then completed her research fellowship at L'Institut de hautes études internationales et du développement in Geneva, Switzerland. Her research interests remain focused on trade mark and related laws. She is currently a research associate at the Oxford Intellectual Property Research Centre and a research affiliate at IP Osgoode, York University, Canada.

Burton Ong is an Associate Professor at the Faculty of Law of the National University of Singapore where he teaches contract law, intellectual property law and competition law. He received his legal education at the National University of Singapore and Oxford University, where he was awarded the Lee Kuan Yew Gold Medal and Vinerian Scholarship respectively, as well as at Harvard Law School. He is a Fellow of the IP Academy in Singapore, where he has designed and conducted copyright and patent law programmes for lawyers, legal officers, corporate counsel and intellectual property professionals.

Kathryn Pickard is a practising barrister who specialises in intellectual property law. She has a scientific background, having studied natural sciences before graduating in Law from Clare College, University of Cambridge. Kathryn later read for the BCL at Brasenose College, University of Oxford. She has been a tenant at 11 South Square, Gray's Inn, since 2004 and regularly appears in patent actions in the High Court of England and Wales.

Tina Piper is an Assistant Professor at McGill's Faculty of Law and Research Director of the Centre for Intellectual Property Policy. She completed her DPhil at the University of Oxford as a Rhodes Scholar under Prof. David Vaver's supervision and is a Research Associate of the Oxford Intellectual Property Research Centre.

Staniforth (Sam) Ricketson is a Professor of Law at the University of Melbourne and also practises at the Victorian Bar in the areas of intellectual property (copyright, patents, trade marks and designs) and trade practices and corporations law. Prior to November 2000, he was the Sir Keith Aickin Professor of Commercial Law at Monash University, and before this held various teaching and research positions at the Universities of Melbourne and London.

He has written and published widely in the area of intellectual property, including a commentary on international copyright co-authored with Jane Ginsburg of Columbia Law School. He is a former President of the Intellectual Property Society of Australia and New Zealand and was a member of the Commonwealth Copyright Tribunal from 1984 to 1998. Most recently, he served as a part-time member of the Victorian Law Reform Commission (2001–2010).

Marshall Rothstein was called to the Manitoba Bar in 1966, and practised administrative law and litigation (primarily transportation and competition law) at Aikins, MacAulay & Thorvaldson (1966–92). He was appointed Queen's Counsel in 1979. He has also lectured on transportation law at the

University of Manitoba, Faculty of Law and the Bar Admission Course at the Law Society of Manitoba. He chaired the Commission on Compulsory Retirement (Manitoba) and Ministerial Task Force on International Air Policy (Canada). He was appointed judge to the Federal Court, Trial Division (1992–99), Court Martial Appeal Court (1992–2006), Competition Tribunal, (1993–99), Federal Court of Appeal (1999–2006), and has been a judge at the Supreme Court of Canada since 1 March 2006.

Sivaramjani Thambisetty is a Lecturer in intellectual property law at the London School of Economics. She holds a BA LLB from the National Law School of India, and a BCL and DPhil from the University of Oxford. Her doctorate on biotechnological inventions was supervised by Professor David Vaver. Her current research interests include the comparative protection of new technologies, the politics of patent law and institutionalism and its effect on the quality of patent law. She has been consulted by the UK Commission on Intellectual Property Rights and the Strategic Advisory Board on Intellectual Property, among others.

Christopher Wadlow is a Professor at the Norwich Law School, and a member of the ESRC Centre for Competition Policy, both at the University of East Anglia, where he is the programme leader of the LLM in Information, Technology and Intellectual Property Law. His main research interests are the international law of intellectual property, patents, and unfair competition. He is probably best known as the author of *The Law of Passing-off: Unfair Competition by Misrepresentation*, now in its third edition. He previously worked for international law firm Simmons & Simmons in its London office, specialising in international intellectual property litigation. The support of the Economic and Social Research Council (UK) is gratefully acknowledged.

Lior Zemer is a Lecturer in law at the Radzyner School of Law, Interdisciplinary Centre Herzliya, Israel. Lior also serves as a regular Visiting Professor at Boston University School of Law. He previously taught in the faculties of law at the Universities of Leicester and Birmingham in the UK and at Osgoode Hall Law School, York University, Canada. Lior is the author of *The Idea of Authorship in Copyright* (Ashgate, 2007).

Table of Cases

Australia

Benelux Countries

Canada

European Patent Office

European Union

Germany

Hong Kong

India

Ireland

Israel

Malaysia

Mauritius

Netherlands

New Zealand

South Africa

Singapore

Trinidad

United Kingdom

United States of America

Table of Legislation

Australia

British Guiana

Canada

Fiji

Germany

St Helena

Hong Kong (now SAR of the People's Republic of China)

India

Israel

Jamaica

New Zealand

South Africa

Singapore

Sri Lanka (at the relevant time Ceylon)

United Kingdom

United States of America

Table of EU Legislation

Table of International Instruments

Introduction

1

Emerging Divergences in the Common Law of Intellectual Property

An Overview

LIONEL BENTLY, CATHERINE W NG
and GIUSEPPINA D'AGOSTINO

THE CHAPTERS IN this collection, written in honour of David Vaver by friends, colleagues and former students, all relate to intellectual property and the common law. The idea of the 'common law' is understood primarily to refer to the family of legal systems of the so-called 'common law countries'—including, Australia, Hong Kong, India, the Republic of Ireland, Israel, Malaysia, New Zealand, Singapore, and the United States, as well as bi-jural Canada, and the common law hybrids, Scotland, South Africa, and Sri Lanka—which historically have adopted, in whole or part, the laws of England or Great Britain.[1] In our field, the various statutory intellectual property regimes of copyright, design and patents in these common law countries typically trace their origins back to the Statute of Anne 1710,[2] the British Calico Printers Acts of the late eighteenth century (1787),[3] and, of course, the Statute of Monopolies of 1624.[4]

[1] Much of David Vaver's work compares and contrasts developments in intellectual property law within the common law system.

[2] An Act for the Encouragement of Learning by Vesting the Copies of Printed Books in the Authors or Purchasers of such Copies, 8 Anne c 19 (1710). As Kathy Bowrey argues in ch 3, this tracing of history back to Britain often results in a real neglect of distinctive features of each country's own legal history.

[3] An Act for the Encouragement of the Arts of Designing and Printing Linens, Cottons, Calicoes and Muslins by vesting the Properties thereof in the Designers, Printers and Proprietors for a Limited Time, 27 Geo III c 38 (1787). Renewed and made permanent by Acts of 1789, 29 Geo III c 19 and 1794, 34 Geo III c 23.

[4] An Act Concerning Monopolies and Dispensation with Penal Laws and Forfeitures Thereof, 21 Jac I c 3 (1624).

In addition, we also use common law in its more traditional, technical sense,[5] as referring to legal actions that have been developed through the courts of both law and equity: in the field of intellectual property these include 'common law copyright' in unpublished works, the law of passing off and 'common law trade mark', the law of confidence, the law of injurious falsehood, and (to the extent that they exist) laws of privacy, misappropriation and unfair competition.[6]

The commonality of this common law of intellectual property, understood in both senses, seems latterly to have become increasingly fractured. Paradoxically, in an era where intellectual property laws are usually characterised as undergoing global 'convergence' and where diversity is being sacrificed to international standardisation at a high level,[7] the intellectual property laws of the common law countries seem to be diverging. In the field of common law proper, different approaches are being taken for example to the basic components of the action for passing off, such as goodwill and misrepresentation, with some common law countries starting to open up the action into something akin to a law of misappropriation or unfair competition. In the field of statutory rights, divergences are emerging in fundamental concepts of copyright and patent law, such as 'originality', 'fair use', 'patentable subject matter' and 'inventive step'. The chapters in this collection explore these divergences, and attempt to offer explanations for them.

EMERGING DIVERGENCES

In general, the chapters support the thesis of growing divergence in the approaches taken by the courts and legislatures of the various common law countries. Gill, for example, charts the divergence in understandings of the localisation of goodwill, noting that while most of the common

[5] Ch 15, Dinwoodie.

[6] D Vaver, 'Reforming Intellectual Property Law: an obvious and not-so-obvious agenda: the Stephen Stewart Lecture for 2008' (2009) 2 *Intellectual Property Quarterly* 143, 154 ('Our IP laws are a product of our history. Apart from the occasional hiccup and exception such as for trade secrets and passing off, there has been no common law of IP since the end of the 18th century. IP rights depend on legislation.') But, as both Bowrey, ch 3, and Dinwoodie, ch 15, suggest, the relationship between statutory intellectual property rights and common law is rather more complicated: what was developed at common law has often been incorporated within legislative regimes, and what is contained in legislation has often been so limited as to require elaboration by judges using the common law. See also D Vaver, 'Canada's Intellectual Property Framework: A Comparative Overview' (2004) 17 *Intellectual Property Journal* 125, 150 (acknowledging the role of courts in copyright).

[7] D Vaver, 'Need Intellectual Property be Everywhere? Against Ubiquity and Uniformity?' (2002) 25 Dalhousie Law Journal 1 (noting current trend toward 'one world, one law'). See also, D Vaver, 'Copyright in Canada: The New Millennium' (1997) 12 IPJ 120 (predicting that there will be no 'Canadian' copyright law).

law countries recognise 'international goodwill', English courts have not done so.[8] Ong and Ricketson identify divergences in applying the concept of originality as between Australia, Canada, the United Kingdom and the United States, where a range of concepts have been recognised: 'sweat of the brow', 'skill and judgment', 'intellectual creation' and 'minimal creativity'. Zemer identifies different approaches to exceptions, with Israel and Singapore recently adopting open-ended, flexible, defences (akin to the 'fair use' defence under US law), whereas other countries in the common law system retain, albeit with variations of detail, the narrow, purpose-limited, 'fair dealing' defences. Dutfield describes different approaches in relation to the patentability of life forms, which are excluded from protection in Canada, but protectable in both the United Kingdom and the United States.[9] Piper, similarly, explains how 'methods of medical treatment' are excluded by statute from patentability in the United Kingdom, and by case law in Canada and New Zealand, while Australia has no such common law or statutory exception. Monotti details important differences in the approach taken to the assessment of inventive step in Australia and the United Kingdom, observing at a general level that it is easier to demonstrate non-obviousness in Australia than in the United Kingdom. Thambisetty elucidates divergent approaches to the disclosure required of a patentee (from the 'best mode' standard operative in Australia, Canada, New Zealand, and the United States, to the seemingly lesser standard of mere 'enablement' in the United Kingdom), and the relationship between disclosure and claim breadth (in particular, the idea of 'fair basis' contained in Australian patent law, and the case law of the House of Lords in *Biogen* and *Lundbeck*). The combined contributions of Rothstein, Holderman, Floyd and Pickard, as well as Hughes, highlight the various differences in court procedure in the UK, Canada and the US that underpin significant divergences in the conduct of a patent trial. Carr raises questions about how *res judicata* would apply across the interface between the UK and EU jurisdictions. The cumulative effect of the chapters is to make a strong case that the approaches taken in the common law countries are anything but common.

[8] See also *Hotel Cipriani Srl v Cipriani (Grosvenor St) Ltd* [2010] EWCA 110 (esp at para 93, where Lloyd LJ notes the 'considerable divergence of view as between different common law jurisdictions.').

[9] See also D Vaver, 'Invention in Patent Law: A Review and a Modest Proposal' (2003) 11 *International Journal of Law and Information Technology* 286 (describing different ways in which jurisdictions, including US, EPC, Australia, Canada and New Zealand, define patentable 'invention'). And, cf, *Joos v Commissioner of Patents* [1972] HCA 38 per Barwick CJ (para 25) ('Whilst the decisions of the Tribunal of the United Kingdom are not binding on this Tribunal, there is no reason to think that the law with respect to the grant of letters patent for inventions should be any less liberal in Australia than that which obtains in the United Kingdom; and, although there is no imperative that it should be, the desirability of such law being the same in both countries is readily acceptable.')

EXPLANATIONS FOR DIVERGENCES

These chapters also provide explanations for these divergences. Some of these are more obvious than others.

Perhaps the most obvious explanation lies in the fact that most of these jurisdictions, once colonies of England or (after the 1707 Union between England and Scotland) Britain,[10] are now sovereign, so their courts and legislatures are able to determine their own course as best they see fit, no longer needing the approval of the Colonial Office, or the guidance of the Privy Council.[11] The various jurisdictions have, in Zemer's words, thrown off their 'old legal chains'.[12] In the case of the United States, this independence is very long-standing, and whilst the courts and commentators of the United States often looked to English authorities,[13] particularly in the nineteenth century, divergences nevertheless began to emerge.

One important cause of divergence between Britain and the United States has been the United States Constitution, and the limitations it provided to federal intellectual property legislation. In the late nineteenth century, these Constitutional limitations led to a significant divergence in the field of trade marks, as a result of the Supreme Court's decision[14] holding that the eighth clause of section 8 of the first article[15] did not empower Congress to establish a trade marks registry. As Dinwoodie describes, this meant that US federal trade mark law retained its character as a body of case law,

[10] Nevertheless it was English rather than Scottish law that was taken to the settled colonies.

[11] Appeals from Canada and India were abolished in 1949, those from South Africa in 1950, those from Australia in 1986, and those from New Zealand in 2003. The Privy Council still hears appeals from Jersey, Guernsey, the Isle of Man, as well as Antigua and Barbuda, Bahamas, Barbados, Belize, Cook Islands and Niue (Associated States of New Zealand), Grenada, Jamaica, St Christopher and Nevis, Saint Lucia, Saint Vincent and the Grenadines, Tuvalu, the Republic of Trinidad and Tobago, the Commonwealth of Dominica, Kiribati, Mauritius, Anguilla, Bermuda, British Virgin Islands, Cayman Islands, Falkland Islands, Gibraltar, Monserrat, Pitcairn Islands, St Helena and the Turks and Caicos Islands.

[12] Ch 13, Zemer, 284.

[13] On trade marks see eg FH Upton, *A Treatise on the Law of Trade Mark with a Digest and Review of the English and American Authorities* (Albany, Weare C Little, Law Bookseller, 1860). Cox stated in the preface to his 1881 *A Manual of Trade-Mark Cases Comprising Sebastian's Digest of Trade-Mark Cases* that 'Whatever of virtue there may be in this compilation is to be credited to the intelligence and industry of the English author. The American editor has attempted only to supplement the original text, and to adapt it to the wants of the American reader.' R Cox *A Manual of Trade-Mark Cases Comprising Sebastian's Digest of Trade-Mark Cases* (Boston, Houghton, Mifflin and Company, 1881) iii.

[14] *Trade-mark Cases* 100 US 82 (1879).

[15] The clause gives Congress power 'to promote the Progress of Science and useful Arts, by securing for limited Times to Authors and Inventors the exclusive Right to their respective Writings and Discoveries'. Justice Miller stated in *Trade-mark Cases* 100 US 82, 93–94 (1879): 'Any attempt, however, to identify the essential characteristics of a trade-mark with inventions and discoveries in the arts and sciences, or with the writings of authors, will show that the effort is surrounded with insurmountable difficulties.'

with rights grounded in use of a mark in commerce under the third clause (the 'Commerce Clause') of the same section of the Constitution, when other countries from the common law system adopted registration-based systems of protection.[16] The Constitutional limitations are felt elsewhere: as Ricketson describes, in the US Supreme Court's characterisation of the originality requirement in copyright law as demanding minimal creativity, and, as Rothstein, Holderman, Floyd and Pickard explain, in relation to the right to a jury trial in US patent law,[17] a consideration which informs many of the procedural differences between the US and other common law jurisdictions which have long since abandoned jury trials in most, if not all, civil actions.

For the most part, the judicial and legislative independence of the different common law countries has allowed for divergences in intellectual property to emerge in response to concrete differences in social and economic circumstances. As Kathy Bowrey emphasises, at least one judge from the Australian High Courts has urged his colleagues to sever the 'apron strings' and develop a common law 'for Australia best suited to its conditions and circumstances'.[18] Similarly, in the context of the common law of passing off, the Supreme Court of India recently explained:[19]

> While English cases may be relevant in understanding the essential features of trade mark law but when we are dealing with the sale of consumer items in India, you have to see and bear in mind the difference in situation between England and India. Can English principles apply in their entirety in India with no regard to Indian conditions? We think not. In a country like India where there is no single common language, a large percentage of population is illiterate and a small fraction of people know English, then to apply the principles of English law regarding dissimilarity of the marks or the customer knowing about the distinguishing characteristics of the plaintiff's goods seems to overlook the ground realities in India.

Moreover, the fact that the common law countries constitute today a multitude of sovereign decision-makers also allows for divergences to emerge *for their own sake*. Just as different courts within a single jurisdiction can take divergent but equally reasonable approaches, only for an appellate court to be required to prefer one approach over another, so different common law courts or legislatures can take divergent approaches to precisely

[16] Congress shall have power 'to regulate Commerce with foreign Nations, and among the several States, and with the Indian tribes'.

[17] Reflecting the Seventh Amendment to the US Constitution.

[18] Ch 3, Bowrey, 52.

[19] *Cadila Healthcare Limited v Cadila Pharmaceuticals Limited* AIR 2001 SC 1952, 2001 (2) SCR 743.

the same legal problems. In so doing, they may merely be expressing their freedom.[20]

Another explanation for growing divergence amongst common law countries is that the various common law nations, scattered across the globe, have come to operate within regional trading (and, in some cases, law-making) arrangements that introduce divergences: British and Irish intellectual property law has undergone repeated modification in order to meet the requirements of European harmonisation, while the common law of confidentiality,[21] as well as various aspects of procedure, have developed in response to the principles of the European Convention on Human Rights. As Ricketson explains, European harmonisation explains the different approach of the UK to 'originality' of databases, and, to a certain extent, the North American Free Trade Agreement among the US, Canada and Mexico explains Canada's approach to the same issue.[22] Monotti likewise sees the United Kingdom's ratification of the European Patent Convention as 'a defining time for divergence' between British and Australian patent law, introducing as it did 'some radical differences' from the Australian law.[23] This move, in part, explains divergences in the approaches to patenting of higher life forms, as the EPC required the United Kingdom to abandon the standard for inherent patentability of 'manner of new manufacture', which goes some way to explaining the differences in the responses of the United Kingdom and Canada to the *OncoMouse* patent.[24] According to Thambisetty, UK adherence to the EPC is also the major reason for the divergences in approach between British and Australian courts to questions of 'sufficiency' of disclosure. Such regional harmonisations have impacts further afield. Harms identifies the origins of the South African laws protecting trade marks against dilution in EC harmonisation, itself modelled, it seems on Benelux law.[25]

Moreover, as the trading influence of the United States has displaced that of Great Britain, the intellectual property laws of Singapore and Australia

[20] Ch 13, Zemer.

[21] For a discussion of the development of the right of privacy and publicity in Europe under the influence of Art 8 of the Convention, see D Vaver, 'Recent Trends in European Trademark Law: of Shape, Senses and Sensation' (2005) 95 *Trade Mark Reporter* 895, 907 et seq. See also D Vaver 'Does IP have Personality?' in N Whitty and R Zimmermann (eds) *Rights of Personality in Scots Law: a Comparative Perspective* (Dundee, Dundee University Press, 2009).

[22] Vaver 'Need Intellectual Property be Everywhere?' (n 7) (with 'significant sections' of NAFTA, US law replaced Canadian law).

[23] Ch 9, Monotti, 178.

[24] *Harvard College v Canada (Commissioner of Patents)* [2002] SCC 76, discussed generally by Dutfield in Ch 8; *Harvard/OncoMouse* [1990] EPOR 4; [1991] EPOR 525; [2003] OJEPO 473; T 315/03 (TBA) [2005] EPOR 31.

[25] See also *Century City Apartments v Century City Property Owners* (57/09) [2009] ZASCA paras 25 and 26 in respect of the South African and UK legislative histories regarding geographical names.

have been modified to implement free trade agreements with the United States[26] (rather than, as previously, to echo changes effected in Great Britain).[27] One effect of this is that there is now a range of different terms in operation for copyright in sound recordings: these are protected as original works in the United States, with the consequence that protection lasts for 70 years after the death of the author, or, in the case of a work-made-for-hire, 95 years. As a result of the free trade agreement, Singapore and Australia protect such recordings for 70 years;[28] while in the United Kingdom and Ireland the term remains 50 years (as under the 1911 Act, though with minor modifications effected during European harmonisation).[29] Although there is no requirement to do so, these free trade arrangements may well also have prompted Singapore to take advantage of all available flexibilities, and thus to move from the British 'fair dealing' approach to the US 'fair use', while Israel has (as Zemer describes) adopted the US lead in recognising a 'fair use' defence to copyright infringement.

Other explanations offered by the essayists are more subtle. Gill attributes increasing divergences to different 'societal goals and norms'.[30] While many jurisdictions within the common law family now extend their protection of the goodwill in a trade mark to traders beyond their jurisdictions, English law on the issue remains contentious. Gill argues that extraterritorial goodwill has been recognised in those countries which border with other jurisdictions with the same language and a similar culture.[31] In other jurisdictions, such as Australia, the time for this recognition came when the transportation and telecommunication industries had advanced to connect nearby countries which share a language and a similar culture. In the cases of India and South Africa, for example, the time came when freer trade became a part of the state policy. Although England has long engaged in trade with its Continental neighbours, these neighbours do not share a language or a similar culture. England's ambiguous position on the law (which co-exists with a registry system conferring UK-wide protection), according to Gill, reflects on the one hand England's sense of 'physical and cultural isolation', and on the other hand its 'prominence in global affairs in which

[26] See eg D Vaver 'Unconventional and Well-Known Trade Marks' [2005] *Singapore Journal of Legal Studies* 1, 2 ('We cannot ignore international pressure in this respect. Left to itself, Singapore's trade mark law would look quite different from what it is today. Singapore's view of what its national interest dictates is not the same as that dictated by others, to some extent the world community through the World Trade Organisation ('WTO'), but especially through more free trade agreements with the European Union ("EU") and the United States.')

[27] www.ustr.org/trade-agreements/free-trade-agreements.

[28] Singapore-US Free Trade Agreement (May 6, 2003) art 16.4(4)(b); Australia-US Free Trade Agreement (Washington, 18 May, 2004) ch 17, art 17.4(4).

[29] Directive 2006/116/EC, art 3(2) (codifying and replacing Directive 93/98/EEC).

[30] Ch 16, Gill, 355.

[31] *Orkin Exterminating Co Inc v Pestco Co of Canada Ltd* (1985) 5 CPR(3d) 433, at 450 (Ont CA).

business and cultural influence will inevitably flow across its physical borders.'[32]

PERSISTING COMMONALITY

While there are many divergences in detail as between the common law countries, there are also very large areas of common practice or approach. These are not merely 'residual' areas, the historically shared norms that have yet to be altered.[33] Rather, a number of the contributors to the volume highlight that the 'special bond' of common law countries continues to be important to the development of the law by courts and legislatures.

Monotti, for example, not only carefully analyses the differences between Australian and British law on inventive step, but notes how the Australian policy-makers continue to look to the United Kingdom and the United States when considering reform.[34] If divergences amongst common law countries represent 'laboratories', they are ones in which the results of the experiments can be assumed to be equally valid. 'Transplanting' a legal innovation from the United Kingdom or the United States into Australia, for example, risks fewer dangers than transplanting law from a civil legal system with different procedures, decision-making processes and so on. Thus, as Zemer shows, Israel may 'borrow' the idea of fair use from the United States in order to introduce flexibility into the copyright system.

There is plenty of evidence that this phenomenon—looking to each other's laws as guides to reform—is widely shared amongst the common law countries: that Britain will now look to Australia for guidance, just as Australia might look to Britain. Two examples, not drawn from this collection, will suffice. The first comes from the UK debates over the introduction of a freedom of information law, something with which Australia, New Zealand and Canada all had experience. When debating the exclusion of 'trade secrets' from material that would be disclosed under the proposed British FOIA,[35] the Government spokesman, David Lock, specifically referred to the Federal Court of Australia in *Searle Australia Property Ltd v Public Interest Advocacy Centre*.[36] As if to highlight the continued self-referentiality within the common law, *Searle* itself had referred to the

[32] Ch 16, Gill, 357.

[33] Although Thambisetty claims: '[i]t is only the common history that ensures in the face of significant diversity in patent disclosure requirements ... that the quid pro quo of the patent bargain endures in the spirit of the common law.' Ch 16, Thambisetty, 217.

[34] Ch 9, Monotti.

[35] *Hansard*, House of Commons, Standing Committee B (February 1, 2000).

[36] *Searle Australia Property Ltd v Public Interest Advocacy Centre* [1992] 108 ALR 163.

definition of 'trade secret' contained in *Lansing Linde v Kerr*, a decision of the Court of Appeal of England and Wales.[37]

A second example of British imitation can be found in the bureaucratic structures for law reform: when establishing the Strategic Advisory Board on Intellectual Property in 2008, the British Government explicitly copied Australia's approach to IP law reform, the Advisory Council on Intellectual Property (which has been in operation since 1994); in turn, calls have been made in Canada for just such an advisory body to be established.[38]

If the legislators continue to find guidance, and comfort, from the experiences of other common law jurisdictions, it is not surprising that judges should also do so. While British courts certainly do not *follow* the decisions of other common law courts, they frequently find useful guidance in them.[39] This is so even in relation to matters where there is no common legislative history, such as the issue of the protection of technological measures. In this area, different common law countries have enacted different statutory regimes in order to implement international obligations contained in the WIPO Internet Treaties of 1996. Nevertheless, the English Court of Appeal referred approvingly to the Australian High Court, when adopting its *reasoning* that the technological features of computer games which so-called 'mod-chips' were designed to overcome were indeed measures that were designed to prevent access to or copying of copyright-protected material.[40] Ong's contribution to this volume assumes that the common law remains a coherent resource of reasons, principles and policies from which courts can pull appropriate solution to cases before them. He argues that 'lurking beneath the jurisprudential surface' of British and US copyright law, where divergences may be seen to exist, one can identify 'a common framework of principles and policies' addressing the specific problem of derivative and restorative works. 'At the end of the day' he observes, 'both [the British and the US] copyright regimes share a common interest in ... developing a coherent concept of originality' with which to address the

[37] *Lansing Linde v Kerr* [1991] 1 All ER 418.

[38] G D'Agostino, 'Canadian Copyright's Just Three Things' *The Hill Times* (2 November 2009) 30 discussing the establishment of such an advisory board among other recommendations presented to the Canadian government's Toronto Roundtable Copyright Consultation in Toronto on August 27, 2009.

[39] See also Kitchin J in *Football Association Premier League v QC Leisure* [2008] FSR (32) 789, para 228–29 (referring approvingly to the conclusion of Emmett J in *Australian Video Retailers Assn v Warner Home Video* (2001) 53 IPR 242 that when a film embodied on a DVD is played, the RAM of a DVD player at no single point reproduces a 'substantial part' of the film).

[40] *R v Higgs* [2009] 1 WLR 73 referring approvingly to the decision of the Federal Court of Australia in *Stevens v Kabushiki Kaisha Sony Computer Entertainment Inc* (2005) 21 ALR 448.

issue of recreative derivative works. Formal divergences then are simply inevitable moments on the journey to 'just and fair' legal solutions.

Other chapters highlight deeper structures that may inform common approaches amongst common law countries, something we might describe as 'legal cultures'. Two contributors, in particular, identify a common reaction to 'legal transplants' such as 'unfair competition' or 'trade mark dilution' that are viewed as originating in civil law jurisdictions or thinking.[41] Wadlow's description of the reaction to *International News Services v Associated Press*[42] emphasises how much the common law courts have preferred 'case-by-case analogy over grand theory and far reaching principles.'[43] *INS* thus was rejected in Australia and the United Kingdom, and treated as increasingly anomalous within the US common law. Similarly, Harms argues that, despite its legislative underpinning, common law courts are resisting implementation of the concept of dilution within trade mark law. Harms finds the basis for protection against blurring without consumer confusion in the civilian principle that an act *contra bonos mores* which injures another creates liability in delict.[44] In contrast, he argues that the action for passing off is premised upon the source-identification function of trade marks. He concludes: 'Absent an identifiable public interest dimension, courts naturally would not be too keen to make factual findings that fail to serve such (or any) real interest.'[45] Even though trade mark dilution provisions now appear in varying degrees in trade mark laws within the common law family, as Harms and Dinwoodie note in their chapters, judges continue to find them difficult to reconcile with the core common law principle that underpins trade mark law, the 'common societal goals and norms' that Gill underlines in his chapter.

Piper's essay, too, counters an assumption that the commonality of the 'common law' is merely a matter of common 'positive laws', but her emphasis is on linkages operating outside of the legal field. Examining

[41] Note Vaver's observations on the reception of moral rights in the United Kingdom: D Vaver, 'Moral Rights: Yesterday, Today and Tomorrow' (1999) 7 *International Journal of Law & Information Technology* 270, 272 (attributing the difficult reception of moral rights into UK law in part to terminology, and in part to their association with a particular normative vision of copyright, and observing: 'A new right may be introduced and treated more sympathetically in a jurisdiction where it resembles existing rights, or flows logically from accepted principles, than where it is a completely new transplant into inhospitable soil.') Vaver goes on to argue that, once it is understood that moral rights can be justified on grounds that are familiar to the common law, the tendency to resist their introduction should be reduced. See also D Vaver, 'Authors' Moral Rights and the Copyright Law Review Committee's Report: W(h)ither Such Rights Now?' (1988) 14 *Monash University Law Review* 284, 291 (describing as 'nothing short of astonishing' the majority's description of moral rights as 'alien' and 'foreign' to the common law system, and observing that Canadian, Indian and Israeli law, as well as some states in the US, already protected moral rights, and that legislation was pending in the UK).

[42] *International News Services v Associated Press* 248 US 215, 39 S Ct 68, 63 L Ed 211 (1918).

[43] Ch 14, Wadlow, 329.

[44] Ch 17, Harms, 385.

[45] Ch 17, Harms, 390.

the emergence of the exception from patentability of methods of medical treatment, she argues that 'professional communities', as well as legal ones, have shaped the content of the common law. Moreover, she observes that these 'professional communities' may well 'transcend national boundaries',[46] emphasising the close links between the British Medical Association and the Canadian Medical Association. Piper's essay highlights the way in which the introduction of the exclusion of 'methods of treatment' from patentability under British law reflected a 'legal articulation of what the [British] medical profession aspired to achieve'[47] at the time, but that through the twentieth century those aspirations changed, in part via connections with the Canadian medical profession. The implication of this is that divergences at the level of formal law might be mediated through common reception by or amongst linked professional groups.

CONCLUSION

If the chapters in this volume are correct, and there is a discernible growth in legal divergence amongst countries in the 'common law system', is this a problem? As those who argue for harmonisation repeatedly tell us, legal variation inevitably adds unwanted complexity for those involved in international or transnational trade or business. In order to be able to be certain of one's legal position, anybody proposing to offer services may well need to understand the various legal specificities in multiple countries. Such legal advice is specialised, and inevitably expensive. In turn, the cost of accessing such legal expertise is likely to be a greater burden on smaller enterprises. Legal variation carries real (transaction) costs for business, and thus for competitiveness, with the ultimate loser being the consumer.[48]

The growth in divergence amongst the common law system also deprives lawyers and courts of resources on which they have traditionally relied. In particular, lawyers can no longer assume that case law in one common law country is a guide to the law in another common law jurisdiction. A good example of this is the difficult question of the potential liability of those who provide services, by way of internet access, 'peer-to-peer

[46] Ch 7, Piper, 143.
[47] Ch 7, Piper, 145.
[48] Even sceptics acknowledge these benefits (though they doubt claims as to the extent of such costs, as well as the possibility of their elimination). See, for example, Gerhard Wagner, 'The Virtues of Diversity in European Private Law' in Jan Smits (ed), *The Need for a European Contract Law* (Groningen, Europa Law Publishing, 2005) 1, 4 ('It should not be disputed that a European Civil Code would produce considerable benefits, as it would work to save transaction costs. The crucial question is not whether this is so but what the costs of these savings are and whether the savings outweigh the costs or vice versa. However, many proponents of harmonization keep celebrating the virtues of a European Civil Code without ever acknowledging the price tag associated with these.')

software' or web sites, which are used by others to copy or make available copyright-protected content. Although the acts of users are widely assumed to be infringing reproductions, doubt exists as to the potential liability of the service provider, who merely provides the means that can (and in many cases will) be used to infringe. In most of the common law countries, particularly those that have built on the Copyright Act 1911, such liability is likely to depend on the meaning of the term 'authorisation'. In the United Kingdom, 'to authorise' has been interpreted to mean 'to grant or purport to grant' the right to do an act.[49] In contrast, in Australia, 'to authorise' has been said to mean 'to sanction, countenance or approve'.[50] Moreover, the Australian legislature has specified that whether 'authorisation exists' depends on a range of factors.[51] These divergences in approach raise difficult questions as to whether Australian case-law[52] would be applicable in the UK, Canada, New Zealand and so on. Although the High Court of England and Wales[53] recently referred to Australian case-law, suggesting that the principles applicable in both jurisdictions remain the same,[54] considerable uncertainty inevitably remains as to whether this is in fact the case. The question as to what actions on the part of the service providers would amount to 'authorisation' under UK law (or indeed, the law of Canada, India, New Zealand and so on) still remains somewhat unclear.[55]

[49] *CBS Songs v Amstrad Ltd* [1988] 2 All ER 484.

[50] *Moorhouse v University of New South Wales* [1976] RPC 151 (High Court of Australia).

[51] Copyright Act 1968 s 101(1A) (Commonwealth of Australia), as amended by the Copyright Amendment (Digital Agenda) Act 2000.

[52] In *Universal Music v Sharman License Holdings Ltd* [2005] FCA 1242 (5 September 2005) the Federal Court of Australia has held that the supplier of peer-to-peer software had 'authorised' infringement of copyright in sound recordings, because the provider encouraged such infringement (exhorting its users to 'Join the Revolution'), did nothing to prevent (for example by using filtering technology) and, indeed, depended on such infringement. However, in *Roadshow Films Pty Ltd v iiNet Limited (No 3)* [2010] FCA 24 (4 February 2010) Cowdroy J found that an Internet service provider did not provide the 'means' of infringement by extending the infringers an 'invitation' to commit any such acts. Rather, it provided a legitimate communication facility, one that was neither intended nor designed to authorise infringement, and that it was only by customer use of a certain peer-to-peer software that copyright infringements took place. Although the decisions in these two cases relate to quite different factual circumstances, the tenor of the decisions is quite different, with Cowdroy J adopting a much narrower view of when liability was to be imposed. *Roadshow* is under appeal.

[53] *Twentieth Century Fox Film Corporation v Newzbin Limited* [2010] EWHC 608 (Ch) (29 March 2010) (Kitchin J) (holding that a website allowing users to download films had authorised its users to infringe copyrighted movies).

[54] ibid para. 95. Note also para 102 (where Kitchin J said that the defendant had not merely 'sanctioned, countenanced or approved' the infringement but had purported to grant the authority to use copyright material—thus utilising both the 'British' and 'Australian' standards of 'authorisation'.)

[55] In Canada, for instance, *SOCAN v Canadian Association of Internet Providers* 2004 SCC 45, [127–28] requires a demonstration that the defendant did '[g]ive approval to; sanction; permit; favour, encourage' and 'could be inferred in a proper case but would all depend on the facts.'

The chapters in the collection also suggest that there are some limits to the divergences amongst common law countries. Some limits are attributable to shared attitudes to the interpretation of language, to statutory drafting, to judicial procedure, to modes of adducing evidence. Some limits to divergence derive from shared ideas about legal and political policy, such as the benefits of free competition. Some limits derived from continued practices of copying, imitation, and influencing one another's laws. These tendencies are doubtless reinforced by the existence of a common working language (English), and the ready availability of legal information systems (Lexis, Westlaw, as well as the free services such as WorldLII ('a new online "home" for Commonwealth law'[56]) and in earlier days, the wide circulation of the *Reports of Patent Cases* among common law jurisdictions, which continues today). At a judicial level, it remains common for 'common law judges' to appear at conferences together, whether at the Fordham International Intellectual Property Conference,[57] or the IP Academy in Singapore.[58] The market for legal academics also seems to reinforce the 'commonality' of the common law: one need only think of the likes of Professor David Vaver himself, a New Zealander who worked in Canada and the United Kingdom, but was a frequent guest in the common law countries of Australia, Singapore, the United States and South Africa.

Other limits to divergence come from outside the specificities of the common law system. The most obvious of these are the very international standards that lead people to talk of global convergence in the field of intellectual property. Although many common law countries now benefit from a political and legal sovereignty which they once lacked, they frequently do not possess economic muscle in international law-making, and thus find that the freedom provided by formal sovereignty is in fact heavily curtailed by these realities. In his essay on divergences in the interpretation of 'originality' in copyright law, Ricketson investigates whether these divergences can be reconciled by reference to the international copyright framework, and, indeed, suggests that a 'sweat of the brow' standard goes beyond that envisaged by the Berne Convention. However, in contrast with some commentators, most notably Daniel Gervais,[59] Ricketson does not view this as rendering a 'sweat' standard incompatible with Berne, but rather as hav-

[56] G Greenleaf, P Chung, and A Mowbray 'WorldLII: a new home for Commonwealth law online' (28 February 2003) www2.austlii.edu.au/~graham/publications/2003/Cth_Conference/WorldLII_Cth_final.html.

[57] At Fordham's annual conferences, US judges Randy Rader and Pauline Newman have mingled with British judges such as Pumfrey J, Laddie J, and Jacob LJ.

[58] The IP Academy's 'Global Forum of Intellectual Property' has featured Andrew Phang J (from Singapore), Laddie J (from the UK), and Gummow J (from Australia).

[59] D Gervais, 'The Compatability of Skill and Labour Originality with the Berne Convention and TRIPs Agreement' [2004] *European Intellectual Property Review* 75.

ing consequences in terms of the application of Berne requirements such as 'national treatment'. Ricketson's contribution does, however, suggest that he is attracted to international intellectual property law as a mechanism to control divergences in the development of intellectual property norms within the common law system.

Some have suggested that even without formal international law-making, other mechanisms operate effectively to constrain divergence. One such notion could be that of 'international ethics'—globally shared views as to what is fair or unfair. Such an idea could explain how courts from a range of distinct jurisdictions (civil and common law) with very different legal norms have responded in similar ways to common issues, such as peer-to-peer file-sharing, the use of trade marks as key-words in advertising or the liability of internet auction sites which are used to sell counterfeit goods. In relation to peer-to-peer software, for example, it is remarkable how courts in Australia, Korea, the Netherlands, and the United States have largely identified common factors that underpin liability: in particular, whether a defendant's business model depends on infringement and they have done nothing to prevent such infringement from occurring.[60] More sceptical onlookers might think that these common responses say less about a common international morality, and owe more to the systematic way in which global actors—here various agents for the global record and film industries—have presented their cases in different fora. But, whatever the reason, the similar outcomes may allay some of the anxieties of anyone worried about the development of divergences at the level of 'formal law': 'formal law' may be less important than what judges around the world were fed (literally, or metaphorically) for breakfast, or, perhaps, dinner.

Professor Vaver would likely not share such anxieties. He is on record as celebrating legal diversity in the field: 'more varied intellectual property laws should be considered virtues and not vices.'[61] Legal variation should be celebrated because it reflects the right of every sovereign country to fashion its laws in its own ways, and according to its own traditions, and its own perceptions of what legal philosophers call the 'good life'. This does not imply that common law countries should not continue to look to each other's experiences for guidance. Legal variation should also be considered valuable because it enables experimentation with different policies, different modes of regulation, and so on. For example, Canada, which is in the midst of copyright reform in an effort to ratify the 1996 WIPO Internet

[60] *Metro-Goldwyn-Meyer Studios Inc v Grokster* 125 S Ct 2764 (2005); *Stichting Bescherming Rechten Entertainment Industrie Nedereland, Brein v Mininova BV* (26 August 2009) (District Court of Utrecht).

[61] Vaver, 'Need Intellectual Property be Everywhere?' (n 7) 1.

Treaties, is considering closely the copyright frameworks with respect to technological measures already implemented by Australia, the UK, and the US.[62] One may wonder whether, had there been more variation in approach, more could have been learned.

[62] Bill C-60, *An Act to Amend the Copyright Act*, 1st Sess, 38th Parl, 2005, died on the order paper on 29 November 2005 when Parliament was dissolved due to a non-confidence motion and an election was called; Bill C-61, *An Act to Amend the Copyright Act*, 2nd Sess, 39th Parl, 2008 (First Reading 12 June, 2008) died on the order paper on 17 September 2008 when Parliament was dissolved again due to an election call. Both Bills would have introduced significant amendments to Canada's Copyright Act, especially in relation to technological protection measures.

Historical Perspectives

2

Intellectual Property and the Common Law in Scotland c1700–c1850

HECTOR L MACQUEEN*

THIS CHAPTER SEEKS to chart, in a tentative and preliminary way, some of the main staging posts along the route by which the Scots law of intellectual property came to be largely subsumed within a United Kingdom legal framework in the period between roughly 1700 and 1850.

THE 1707 UNION AND THE STATUTE OF ANNE

The origins of a United Kingdom intellectual property law lie in the two critical moments which created the United Kingdom: first, the Union of the Crowns in 1603, under which King James VI of Scotland inherited the English throne and became King James I of England; and second, the Treaty and Acts of Union in 1707. While the 1603 Union left in place two separate kingdoms, each under a Crown which for the next century simply happened both to be held by the same person, Articles I and II of the 1707 Union created a single united kingdom and Crown of Great-Britain. Article III provided for a single Parliament, while Article IV established a legal framework for a single market with full freedom of trade between Scotland and England.

Article VI stated that:

> ... all parts of the United Kingdom, for ever, from and after the Union, shall have the same Allowances, Encouragements and Drawbacks, and be under the same Prohibitions, Restrictions, and Regulations of Trade ... [T]he Allowances, Encouragements, and Draw-backs, Prohibitions, Restrictions, and Regulations of Trade ... settled in England, when the Union commences, shall, from and after the Union, take place throughout the whole United Kingdom.

* I am grateful to Gillian Black, John Cairns, Tomas Gomez-Arostegui and Alastair Mann for various forms of assistance.

But this drive for a single market was not thought to make necessary the general unification of the laws and legal systems of England and Scotland. The existence and jurisdiction of the Scottish Court of Session and High Court of Justiciary were preserved 'in all time coming'. But appeals from the Scottish courts to the House of Lords in its judicial capacity became firmly established, although nothing was said of this in the Union Articles; this would later have significant effect in the development of intellectual property rights in Scotland. Under Article XVIII Scots law itself was to 'remain in the same force as before', albeit 'alterable by the Parliament of Great-Britain'. This was however qualified in various ways by other provisions in the Article. '[T]he Laws concerning Regulation of Trade ... [were] to be the same in Scotland, from and after the Union, as in England'. Article XVIII also sought to regulate the Parliamentary power to alter Scots law: only with 'the Laws which concern public Right, Policy, and civil Government' might the object of the change be to make the law 'the same throughout the whole United Kingdom', whereas 'no Alteration [might] be made in Laws which concern private Right, except for evident Utility of the Subjects within Scotland'.[1]

An early manifestation of the power of the Parliament of Great Britain under Article XVIII was the Statute of Anne 1710, which introduced the concept of literary property and applied throughout the United Kingdom. Before the 1707 Union, the Scottish copyright system was based upon government grants to publishers, underpinned by the royal prerogative, of exclusive privileges to print and import particular works.[2] Authors too could apply for such privileges.[3] The Scottish Privy Council provided both the granting body to which application for privileges was made, and the forum in which disputes about the scope of the privileges were determined. The grants were increasingly in standardised forms, and typically provided for a 19-year period of exclusivity, as well as search powers for the right-holder to root out infringing copies.

This system was however undermined as an immediate consequence of the 1707 Union, when the Scottish Privy Council was abolished by statute from 1 May 1708.[4] This event provided a reason for introducing in 1709 what became the Statute of Anne; in this respect at least, some form of exclusivity to replace what had just been lost was for the 'evident utility' of Scottish authors and publishers if it was not actually a matter of 'public right' to make the grant of literary privilege uniform throughout the newly united kingdom.[5]

[1] For discussion of the meanings of public and private right see JD Ford, 'The Legal Provisions in the Acts of Union' (2007) 66 *Cambridge Law Journal* 106, 108–18; JW Cairns, 'The Origins of the Edinburgh Law School: the Union of 1707 and the Regius Chair' (2007) 11 *Edinburgh Law Review* 300, 313–26.

[2] A Mann, *The Scottish Book Trade 1500–1720* (East Linton, Tuckwell Press, 2000) ch 4.

[3] Ibid 113–14.

[4] Union with Scotland (Amendment) Act 1707, 6 Anne c 40, s 1.

[5] Mann (n 2) 123.

The Scottish dimension was certainly provided for in the 1710 Act. The Court of Session was given jurisdiction 'if any person or persons incur the penalties contained in this Act, in that part of Great Britain called Scotland'; the deposit of copies of registered works was required in the libraries of the Faculty of Advocates and the four Scottish universities via the Stationers' Company; and book price regulatory powers in Scotland were given to the Lord President, the Lord Justice General,[6] the Lord Chief Baron of the Scottish Exchequer and the Rector of the College (i.e. University) of Edinburgh.

THE POST-UNION SCOTCH PATENT

The impact of the 1707 Union upon the grant of letters patent for invention has been much less studied than its effect on copyright. In England, long before 1707, letters patent were regularly granted under the king's Great Seal as an exercise of the royal prerogative in favour of the 'true and first inventors' of 'new manufactures', giving them the exclusive monopoly right to work or make their inventions for up to 14 years. The practice was recognised as lawful under the Statute of Monopolies 1623, which had declared the grant of monopolies otherwise to be 'utterly void and of none effect'. The position in pre-1707 Scotland is much less clear, although the Scottish Crown certainly did grant monopolies of various kinds and durations under the Great Seal of the kings of Scots. Typically, however, these were not for inventions so much as the protection and support of those speculatively investing in the exploitation of the country's natural resources or the establishment in Scotland of industries already well-known elsewhere.[7] There was no Scottish equivalent to the Statute of Monopolies, although in 1641 an Act 'dischargeing monopolies' was passed by a Parliament openly hostile to royal prerogative, especially in matters of religion and worship, and in consequence determined to clip the wings of King Charles I as much as possible in order to subject him to a binding covenant with his people.[8] The 1641 Act referred to the 'great hurt and prejudice sustained by sundry of his majesty's lieges by the monopolies used and exacted within this kingdom' and ordained 'all ... patents ..., purchased or to be purchased, for the benefit of particular persons in prejudice of the public to cease and be ineffectual in all time coming.'[9] After the Restoration, however, the Scottish Parliament rescinded all previous legislation purporting to restrict the royal

[6] The offices of Lord President and Lord Justice General were at this time held by different persons; they were merged in one person from 1836 on.

[7] See I Whyte, *Scotland before the Industrial Revolution: an Economic and Social History c.1050–c.1750* (London, Longmans, 1995) 274–79, 288–90.

[8] See generally M Lynch, *Scotland: A New History* (London, Century, 1991) 265–73.

[9] KM Brown et al (eds), *The Records of the Parliaments of Scotland to 1707* (St Andrews, 2007), accessible at www.rps.ac.uk, 1641/8/192.

prerogative,[10] leaving the regulation of monopolies under letters patent to the common law and custom.

Later in the eighteenth and nineteenth centuries, the conventional wisdom amongst Scots lawyers was that, while monopolies were prohibited at common law,[11] Article VI of the 1707 Union had had the effect of legitimating patents for inventions and applying the Statute of Monopolies in Scotland, thus making the law on the subject the same in both kingdoms.[12] The accuracy of this belief can only be determined from a more thorough investigation of the grant of patents in Scotland both before and after 1707 than is possible in this chapter. The Act of Union made provision for a Great Seal of the United Kingdom in its Article XXIV, but also laid down that there should be a royal seal in Scotland for 'Offices, Grants, Commissions, and privat Rights within that Kingdom'. To take effect in Scotland patents had to be sealed with this Scottish Seal, and there continued to be separate Scottish (or Scotch, as they were more commonly known by the nineteenth century) and English patents after 1707, with no room for single grants taking effect across the whole United Kingdom. This would remain the position until the Patent Law Amendment Act 1852, which abolished separate Scottish and English (and Irish) patents, and replaced them with a patent for the whole of the United Kingdom. Until then, however, Scottish patents for inventions were expressed to have effect 'in that part of the realm of Great Britain known as Scotland'. There was, however, nothing to stop inventors in each jurisdiction applying for patents in both parts of the realm, and this seems to have been common (although by no means universal) practice by the beginning of the nineteenth century.[13]

Scottish practice in relation to the grant of patents for inventions began to develop significantly after the Union. Between 1712 and 1852 the 'paper' register of the Great Seal was used to record 'an increasing number of patents for inventions'.[14] The 'paper' (as distinct from 'parchment') register

[10] Ibid, 1661/1/16.

[11] Andrew McDouall, Lord Bankton, *An Institute of the Laws of Scotland* (Edinburgh, 1751) I, xix, 11 (also available in a reprint as vols 41–43 in the Stair Society series, edited with an introduction by WM Gordon); GCH Paton (ed), *Baron David Hume's Lectures 1786–1822* (6 vols, Edinburgh, Stair Society, 1939–58) vol 4, 60–61; GJ Bell, *Principles of the Law of Scotland* (1st edn, Edinburgh, 1829; 4th edn (the last produced by Bell), Edinburgh, 1839), § 1348. Hume's lectures, last delivered in the 1821–22 academic session and unpublished until the 20th century, nonetheless had considerable contemporary influence.

[12] See eg *Roebuck and Garbett v Stirlings* (1774) 3 Pat 346, 348; GJ Bell, *Commentaries on the Mercantile Jurisprudence of Scotland*, 7th edn (Edinburgh, 1870) vol 1, 105. The 7th edition has been used, since it reprints the text of the 5th edition of 1835, the last produced by Bell himself. The work first began to be published in 1800. See also Bell, *Principles* (n 11) § 1349; *Neilson v Househill Coal and Iron Co* (1842) 4 D 470, 475. Cf Hume, *Lectures* (n 11) vol 4, 61.

[13] HI Dutton, *The Patent System and Inventive Activity during the Industrial Revolution 1750–1852* (Manchester, Manchester University Press, 1984) 35.

[14] *Guide to the National Archives of Scotland (Scottish Record Office)* (Edinburgh, Stair Society, 1996) 84.

had been established as long before as 1596, to be a record of temporary or redeemable rights, with the parchment register being thenceforward reserved for grants in perpetuity, typically of land. Applications for patents were made through the Home Office in London, a warrant under the royal sign manual authorising the grant to pass the great seal. An application for a Scottish patent would be remitted to the Lord Advocate (the Scottish Law Officer equivalent to the English Attorney General) for an opinion on whether a patent might lawfully be granted. If the opinion was favourable, then the warrant was issued and the grant would pass the Seals.[15] It seems unlikely that this entailed any difference between Scottish and English law and practice on patent grants, however. By the beginning of the nineteenth century, if not well before, the normal period of the grant was 14 years, as in England, and the grantee had to lodge a detailed specification of the invention in the Scottish Chancery within four months. A post-1750 increase in Scots patent grants[16] can almost certainly be linked to the Industrial Revolution in Scotland.[17] Inward investment from England was important in this development,[18] and it is possible that the growth in use of patents in Scotland from 1750 was triggered by English patentees moving to protect their Scottish ventures also.[19]

The importance of keeping the substance of patent law the same each side of the border must have been reinforced by such developments. In the first reported Scottish patent case, *Roebuck and Garbett v Stirlings*, which reached the House of Lords in 1774,[20] the House of Lords upheld the interlocutors of the Court of Session to the effect that a patent obtained for an invention in Scotland was invalidated by proof of previous use in England, even although there was no convincing evidence of such use in Scotland. Patent litigation did not really take off in Scotland until after 1800,[21] but numerous decisions thereafter up to 1850 make clear the continuing sense of the Scottish courts that, despite the split between Scottish and English patents, the law was essentially a unity north and south of the border, with a uniform approach to patent questions generally appropriate.

[15] See further Hume, *Lectures* (n 11) vol 4, 62, and Bell, *Commentaries* (n 12) vol 1, 105. For the costs see Dutton, *Patent System* (n 13) 35.

[16] *Guide to the National Archives* (n 14) 88–89.

[17] See generally CA Whatley, *The Industrial Revolution in Scotland* (Cambridge, Cambridge University Press, 1997).

[18] TM Devine, *The Scottish Nation 1700–2000* (London, Penguin, 1999) 116.

[19] See *Roebuck and Garbett v Stirlings* (1774) 3 Pat 346, where the appellant patentees were English entrepreneurs. On Roebuck and Garbett, see Whyte, *Scotland before the Industrial Revolution* 305; Whatley, *Industrial Revolution* 29; 'Roebuck, John, bap 1718–1794', *Oxford Dictionary of National Biography* (Oxford, Oxford University Press, 2004).

[20] *Roebuck and Garbett v Stirlings* (1774) 3 Pat 346.

[21] Hume, *Lectures* (n 11) vol 4, 62, cites four unreported patent infringement cases between 1800 and 1804, which appear to be the earliest known after the *Roebuck and Garbett* case in 1774.

This was not merely a matter of referring to English decisions and treatises like those of Collier, Davies, Godson and Webster, common though this was in Scottish cases and writing on the subject.[22] Unity cut to the very heart of substantive patent law on the issues of inventiveness, novelty and prior publication.[23]

So in *Brown v Kidston & Waters*[24] in 1852, a Scottish patentee's widow was refused interdict against parties alleged to be infringing the patent, because the patentee had also obtained an English patent in January 1840, some 10 months before the Scottish grant, while a description of the invention had also been published in various journals, particularly the August 1840 issue of the *Mechanics Magazine* (which circulated in both jurisdictions). The interdict sought was granted at first instance by the Lord Ordinary, who held that the grant of a patent was evidence of a prima facie entitlement and thought it a 'hypercritical plea' to argue that publication of an invention in a magazine annulled a Scottish patent when there was no evidence that the invention had actually been used in Scotland. But on a reclaiming motion this was overturned by the Second Division, upholding the respondents' argument that the Scottish patent, being subsequent to publication of the invention, was invalid. Even if England was technically a foreign legal system, publication in that jurisdiction could not be irrelevant in determining the novelty of an invention in Scotland. Publication in England was for the benefit not only of the people of England but also of the whole of the United Kingdom. A party seeking interdict (as distinct from damages) was not able to proceed unless his title was free from prima facie objections. Lord Cockburn was the most trenchant member of the Second Division, and his language hints at not only a degree of covert anti-English but also anti-patent sentiment in the decision:

> Had the patentee wished to secure his patent in Scotland, he should have taken it out there. But instead of this, he took it out in England only, although he knew that he could not get it without publishing his invention to all and sundry. He neglects to stop the ears and mouths of the people of Scotland by a patent; and then, when he afterwards wants one, he says, 'I published this invention only in England, and you in Scotland had no right to hear.' I give no opinion upon the merits, but I am clear that this is not a case for interdict.[25]

A predisposition towards as unified an approach as possible also became apparent in questions about procedure, pleading and evidence in patent

[22] See eg *Hadden v Pirie & Co* (1823) 2 S 423 (NS 376); *Wilson v Black* (1847) 10 D 1; *Templeton v Macfarlane Brothers* (1847) 10 D 4, revd (1848) 10 D 796; as well as cases cited elsewhere in this article.

[23] The precedent of *Roebuck* nevertheless had to be reaffirmed as late as 1841 (*Brown v Annandale* (1841) 3 D 1189), despite its import being made clear in Bell, *Commentaries* (n 12) vol 1, 107–8.

[24] *Brown v Kidston & Waters* (1852) 14 D 826.

[25] (1852) 14 D 826, 829.

cases. From the decision of the House of Lords in *Astley v Taylor* in 1821 on,[26] it became standard practice in Scotland, as it already was in England, for patent infringement actions to be heard before a civil jury, although this mode of trial or proof had only been introduced to Scotland in 1815 and patent actions were not listed amongst the causes which by statute from 1819 had to be taken before jurors as well as a judge. This jury court procedure required the court to set out the issues to be determined by the jury, and practice evolved from the formulations initially laid down in the *Astley* case. In *Neilson v Househill Coal and Iron Co*[27] in 1842, the issue initially proposed on the question of the validity of the pursuer Neilson's patent was, 'whether N was the true and first inventor of the said *machinery and apparatus* for which the said letters-patent were granted' (emphasis supplied); this was said to be the standard way of expressing such issues in Scotland. But the pursuer objected and argued that the issue should be 'whether N was the true and first inventor of the *invention* for which the said letters-patent were granted' (emphasis again supplied). Neilson's basic point was that the scope of his patent, which was 'for the improved application of air to produce heat in furnaces', and of considerable importance in iron manufacture, extended beyond the machinery by which the effect was achieved. He claimed that his form of issue was the recognised English form of pleading on this point, with the advantage that it could be used whether the patent was for machinery, a process or a principle of art and manufacture. It would also, of course, help give a wide scope to his patent if the jury found for him. The issue finally approved by the court—'Whether thc invention, as described in the said letters-patent and specification, is not the original invention of the said N?'—went most of the way with Neilson's arguments.

Neilson's knowledge of English pleading and procedure probably owed something to the knowledge built up as a result of parallel proceedings in England on the English patent for his invention.[28] Similarly the pursuer in *Russell v Crichton*[29] held parallel Scottish and English patents, and in a Scottish infringement action requested the court to follow English practice illustrated from his own previous actions south of the border,[30] by ordering

26 *Astley v Taylor* (1821) 1 Shaw's App Cas 54.

27 *Neilson v Househill Coal and Iron Co* (1842) 4 D 470.

28 See *Neilson v Harford* (1841) 11 LJ Ex 20. For Neilson's further reported litigations in defence of his Scottish patent, see *Neilson v Househill Coal and Iron Co* (1842) 4 D 1187 (six-day jury trial); (1842) 5 D 86 (bill of exceptions rejected by Second Division); (1843) 2 Bell's App Cas 1 (House of Lords, reversing Second Division in part and ordering retrial); also *Baird & Co v Neilson* (1842) 1 Bell's App Cas 219 (House of Lords); *Neilson v Baird & Co* (1843) 6 D 51 (nine-day jury trial, bill of exceptions rejected by First Division).

29 *Russell v Crichton* (1837) 15 S 1270. On James Russell see Dutton, *Patent System* (n 13) 74, 136, 157, 162, 181, 182.

30 As cited in the report, the English cases were *Russell v Cowley and Dickson*, Repertory of Arts (Law Reports), vol XVII, p 168; *Russell*, Nov 21, 1834, Crompton, Neesom and Roscoe's Reports, vol 1, 64.

an inspection of the defender's works by persons of skill. Despite the defender's argument that the inspection would deprive its own secret manufacturing processes of their value, the First Division ordered the inspection, holding that without such a procedure patents might be infringed with impunity. Safeguards were put in place for the defender: the inspection was to be of both parties' works at the sight of the sheriff and in presence of each party's solicitor, with the viewers also being charged not to use any private information obtained except for the purpose of giving evidence. Again, however, remaining abreast of English practice was clearly important for the court.[31]

There were, however, technical obstacles in the way of a completely unified and uniform approach to patents across the United Kingdom. Possibly the problem that arose in *Grover, Baker & Co v Hunter & Barr*[32] was relatively easy to overcome. Here an English domiciliary had taken out a Scottish patent and assigned it to a manufacturer in the USA, using the English form of an indenture or collateral deed, signed only by the patentee. The assignees obtained an interim interdict against alleged infringers in Glasgow, despite arguments that they had not shown a good title to the patent under Scots law; the answer, that no formal proof of title was required in interim interdict proceedings, along with the observation that the deed would have provided good title in English law and the provision of caution (a guarantee) by the assignees, was upheld by the Court of Session.

More complex were the cases which arose from the patents legislation passed by the Parliament of Great Britain in 1835 (Lord Brougham's Act) and 1852 (the Patent Law Amendment Act). One of the many points in *Neilson v Househill Coal and Iron Co* concerned the defender's attempt, after the parties' written pleadings and the jury issues had been finally adjusted to go to trial, to lodge a note of objections under section 5 of the 1835 Act, stating, inter alia, that Neilson was not the first and true inventor and that the invention was known and publicly practised both in Scotland and England prior to the date of the letters-patent. This the defender proposed to prove by witness at the trial. The trial judge refused to allow this step, however, and was affirmed, first by the Second Division and then by the House of Lords. Section 5 of the 1835 Act, it was held, was intended to fit into English pleading and procedure only, and had no application to the very different Scottish system.

Despite its abolition of separate patents north and south of the border, the Patent Law Amendment Act 1852 was much more careful than its 1835 predecessor to take explicit account of the Scottish legal system. So for example where Lord Brougham's Act of 1835 referred only to the English

31 For subsequent interdict proceedings see *Russell v Crichton* (1837) 16 S 1155.
32 *Grover, Baker & Co v Hunter & Barr* (1854) 26 Sc Jur 543 (First Division).

procedure of *scire facias* as the means of invalidating a patent, section 43 of the 1852 Act made clear (presumably for the avoidance of doubt) that:

> proceedings in Scotland to repeal letters patent are to be actions of reduction at the instance of Her Majesty's Advocate, or at the instance of any other party having interest with the concurrence of Her Majesty's Advocate, which concurrence Her Majesty's Advocate is authorized and empowered to give upon just cause shown only.[33]

But the 1852 Act nevertheless ran into trans-jurisdictional difficulties in *Knox v Paterson*.[34] Under section 1 of the 1835 Act a patentee or his assignee could enter a disclaimer or alteration of the patent specification having obtained the consent of an appropriate Law Officer for the jurisdiction in which the patent applied: the Attorney General in England, the Lord Advocate or the Solicitor General for Scotland north of the border, and the Attorney General and Solicitor General in Ireland. The 1852 Act continued the procedure for the new United Kingdom patent, but the statutory language failed to make clear whether the patentee now needed the consent of the Law Officers for all three jurisdictions, or the consent of any one of them, or the consent of the Law Officers for the territory in which the patentee was domiciled. Having enjoyed pointing up the infelicities of the drafting of the 1852 Act, the Court of Session, perhaps rather limply, took the common sense line that the Attorney General's consent was enough and that the patentee had no need to seek the leave of the Lord Advocate or the Solicitor General for Scotland as well. But given the centralisation of the patent system as a whole in London, the effect of the decision must have been to eliminate any residual role the Scottish Law Officers might still have had—probably to their considerable relief.

PLACING PATENTS AND COPYRIGHT IN THE FRAMEWORK OF SCOTS LAW

As patents for invention grew in practical significance from 1750 on, so writers on Scots law were compelled to take cognisance of them, and put these rights within the general structures of their expositions, which were of course usually based on Civilian systematics. For this purpose patents were usually yoked together with copyright. In 1751 Andrew McDouall (Lord Bankton) placed a brief discussion of the two rights in his chapter on 'Permutation and Sale', referring to them as 'exclusive privileges' limiting the general freedom of commerce along with rules privileging markets and

33 For a decision on this section, holding the Lord Advocate's concurrence invalid unless he had actually applied his mind to the question before giving it, see *Gillespie v Young* (1861) 23 D 1357.

34 *Knox v Paterson* (1857) 20 D 40.

fairs, and criminal provisions on selling of counterfeit drink and the use of false weights and measures.[35] He also noted that grants to 'the inventors of new manufactures, or authors of books, securing to them the sole benefit of the same' did not fall foul of the common law's prohibition on monopolies, being 'in vertue of statute' (presumably the Statute of Monopolies and the Statute of Anne, although Bankton does not name them specifically) and 'limited to a certain period of years, after which they determine'.[36] Lord Kames likewise treated patents and copyright as an aspect of the regulation of commerce in his *Principles of Equity*, first published in 1760,[37] and observed that the only lawful monopolies were those granted for the public good. Patents for inventions and copyright for books, 'limited to a time certain', were examples: 'the profit made in that period is a spur to invention: people are not hurt by such a monopoly, being deprived of no privilege enjoyed by them before the monopoly took place; and after expiry of the time limited, all are benefited without distinction.'[38]

Later writers discussed patents and copyright, not within the law of personal rights or obligations, or in conjunction with aspects of market regulation, but rather as part of the law of real rights or property (using that word in a very broad generic sense).[39] The concept of 'exclusive privilege' as a form of real right began to develop. Lecturing on jurisprudence to moral philosophy students at Glasgow University in the 1760s, Adam Smith analysed the four real rights of the civil law: property (ie in its more precise meaning of ownership), servitude, pledge and inheritance, and argued that the last of these could only be considered as a distinct real right in the context where the heir was preparing to take up his right following the death of the previous proprietor, since his privilege to inherit excluded the right of any others who would be heirs after him. On this analogy, 'all other exclusive priviledges [*sic*] have the same title, and appear evidently as well as it to be real rights'.[40] Some exclusive privileges, such as inheritance, or that of the hunter to the pursuit of his prey, were founded on natural reason, but 'the greatest part ... are the creatures of the civil constitutions of the country'; and amongst them were to be placed patents for inventions and copyright.[41]

David Hume, Professor of Scots Law at Edinburgh 1786–1822, in his lectures likewise categorised patents and copyright as 'instances of the real

[35] On the civil protection of trade marks in this period, see further below, p 42.

[36] Bankton, *Institute* (n 11) I, xix, 11.

[37] H Home, Lord Kames, *Principles of Equity* 3rd edn, (Edinburgh, 1778) Book II Chapter III.

[38] Ibid vol 2, 99.

[39] For the doctrine of real rights in Scots law at this time, see Hume, *Lectures* (n 11) vol 2, 2–3

[40] Adam Smith, *Lectures on Jurisprudence* (Oxford, Oxford University Press, 1979) 82.

[41] Ibid 82–83.

right of Exclusive Privilege', which he seems to have conceived of as an 'exclusive title ... to perform a certain operation ... for and within a certain territory of land, and to draw the profit attached to that operation'. Any other person presuming to perform the operation was guilty of 'usurpation ... infringement of the exclusive privilege', and the holder was entitled to vindication, meaning that the right was 'thus marked with all the characters of a proper legitimate and real right'.[42] Other examples included the trading monopolies and privileges of royal burghs, merchant guilds and incorporated crafts.

George Joseph Bell, Hume's successor in the Edinburgh Chair from 1822 to 1837, also treated patents and copyrights as real rights, or as 'estates available to creditors',[43] but more or less abandoned the concept of 'exclusive privilege' in favour of seeing the rights as ones of property, albeit in a somewhat opaque passage suggesting that the right of ownership was less than full-blown:

> The right to enjoy the benefit of a useful invention, or literary composition, seems to rest securely on the great foundation on which property depends; namely, occupancy, with skill, labour, expense and intellectual exertion, employed in the acquisition of production. But a more narrow view has been taken of this matter, and instead of considering the invention or the composition as itself the subject of property, it has been held that, as the purchase of the individual machine, or book gives the power of imitating or of copying it, either such copy or the original may be sold, and so copies multiplied to make gain. With this view, in the case of discoveries in the useful arts, concurs the interest which the public has to prevent the undue raising of prices, and restraining of industry and improvement, according to the caprice or self-interest of monopolists. The Legislature has therefore interposed, on the one hand to secure for a certain but limited time, to the authors of useful inventions, or of literary compositions, a monopoly of sale and profit; and on the other to protect the interests of the public.[44]

On patents specifically, Bell added elsewhere:

> The right is useful as property in these respects: 1. It secures to the patentee the profits of the sale of the thing invented. 2. The privilege may be assigned in whole or in part. The patent generally bears a restriction not to be communicated to more than five. But the whole privilege may be sold.[45]

The inter vivos transferability of patents and copyrights was certainly a significant point of difference from many of the other forms of exclusive privilege mentioned by Smith and Hume.

[42] Hume, *Lectures* (n 11) vol 4, 38 (exemplified with thirlage and inheritance rights).

[43] Bell, *Commentaries* (n 12) vol 1, 103.

[44] Bell, *Principles* (n 11) § 1348. Bell's *Commentaries* (n 12) refers to the 'exclusive privilege of patent or copyright' in a sub-heading (at 120).

[45] Bell, *Commentaries* (n 12) 105.

Hume and Bell both clearly, and without much discussion, considered patents and copyrights to be incorporeal rights. Hume also raised, without answering, the question of whether the rights were to be considered as heritable rather than moveable rights;[46] that is to say, as rights that passed on the death of the holder to that person's heir-at-law rather than to that part of the deceased's estate which would be administered by executors and could be bequeathed by will subject to the legal rights of the deceased's descendants and surviving spouse. In 1832 John Shank More, an advocate later to be Bell's successor in the Scots Law Chair at Edinburgh, argued that the rights were heritable,[47] his approach being based on the heritability of rights (such as pensions and annuities) with a tract of future time—'rights of such a nature that they cannot be at once paid or fulfilled by the debtor, but continue for a number of years, and carry a yearly profit to the creditor while they subsist, without any relation to any capital sum or stock'[48]—and the fit between this definition and patents and copyrights. Bell appeared to accept the analogy in his *Commentaries*, with one consequence being that the rights could only be attached by the process against heritage known as adjudication;[49] the forms of attachment for moveables, in particular arrestment, were not available to the holder's creditors. But the analysis was not consistently maintained throughout Bell's writings, for his *Principles* brought the substantive treatment of the rights under the general heading 'Property in moveables' and a further sub-heading 'Of incorporeal moveable subjects'.

While copyrights were finally declared to be moveable property in the Copyright Act 1842,[50] the question of classification of patents was not settled for Scots law until *Advocate-General v Oswald*[51] in 1848. In this case about duty payable on legacies, the Exchequer Court held that patents were moveable property, rejecting the arguments about rights with a tract of future time. The Court's view was based upon the terms of the patent grant, which was expressly made, not just to the patentee, but also to his executors, administrators and assigns. The leading judgment was delivered by Lord Murray:

> Subjects, however, become heritable or moveable according to their destination. Where that is clear it is decisive. ... I must confess, that after the evidence we have

46 Hume, *Lectures* (n 11) vol 4, 565.
47 JS More, *Notes on Stair* (Edinburgh, 1832) cxli (Note R(4)).
48 The definition of Erskine, *Institute* (n 11) II, 2, 6.
49 Bell, *Commentaries* (n 12) vol 1, 110–11. See also *Principles* (n 11) § 1480.
50 Section 25.
51 *Advocate-General v Oswald* (1848) 10 D 969. This case also arose from the Neilson patent (above, pp 27–28), and reflects its ultimate financial success in various settlements of 1843 and 1844, for which see the ODNB article 'Neilson, James Beaumont (1792–1865)'. The decision is only grudgingly accepted by More in his *Lectures on the Law of Scotland* (Edinburgh, 1864) vol 1, 452.

> had in this case, it seems to me very difficult to trace any resemblance between the profits arising from the exclusive privileges conferred by a patent, and those arising from a pension or annuity. There is, perhaps, no trade of which the returns are more uncertain and precarious than the profits arising from a patent. A great many patents produce nothing; and sometimes the expenses of enforcing the exclusive right exceed the returns. I cannot, therefore, acknowledge the resemblance between the profits which may arise from a patent and a yearly annuity or feudal estate. ... [T]he terms of the warrant and letters patent ... make it clear, beyond the possibility of dispute, that every such Scotch patent is a moveable right, which goes to executors.[52]

Doubtless a further factor in the Court's conclusion in *Oswald*, however, was its observation that patent rights were classified as personal rather than real property in English law.

LITERARY PROPERTY IN SCOTLAND AND THE BATTLE OF THE BOOKSELLERS

We may now turn back to the history of copyright in Scotland. Although the Stationers' Hall registration requirements of the Statute of Anne might have made life more difficult for Scottish publishers and authors, in practice Scottish publications seem to have been frequently entered in the register throughout the eighteenth century, so the barriers were not insuperable, at least for those with resources and good prospects of literary success.[53] In the mid-eighteenth century, however, London and Scottish publishers and booksellers fell into conflict over a number of issues about literary property. The issues first arose from the making, import and export by the Scots of cheap reprints of works with subsisting registrations in Stationers' Hall, where the question was whether the Statute's very limited sanctions against infringement—forfeiture of the infringing publications and payment of one penny for every infringing sheet, half going to the Crown, the other to the person suing—could be supplemented by the remedies of interdict (Scottish equivalent of the injunction), claims to the infringer's profits, and damages. The most elemental question of all, however, was about works whose term of protection under the Statute of Anne had expired, or which had never been registered. Was there still subsisting in the work a common law right which could be invoked to prevent it becoming freely available to all for the purposes of republication?

From the start, the answers given to these questions by the Court of Session differed fundamentally from those of the English judiciary.

[52] (1848) 10 D 969, 978–79.

[53] Mann, *Scottish Book Trade* 123–24; RB Sher, *The Enlightenment and the Book: Scottish Authors and their Publishers in Eighteenth-Century Britain, Ireland, and America* (Chicago, Chicago University Press, 2006) 243–44.

Where the London booksellers succeeded in persuading the Court of Chancery to grant injunctions and order infringers to disgorge their profits,[54] the Scottish judges ultimately refused to supplement the Statute of Anne in this way in the case of *Midwinter v Hamilton*,[55] decided in 1748. An appeal to the House of Lords failed, not by upholding the court below, but by finding instead that the action 'was improperly and inconsistently brought' because the appellants had illegitimately cumulated non-statutory with statutory remedies, as well as suing several defenders in one claim when the points at issue against each were about separate and distinct books and rights therein. The case was remitted back to the Court of Session, but no further litigation ensued there.[56] Dr McDougall comments that 'from the middle of the century until 1774 ... the strategy of the London booksellers was to let well enough alone north of the border and to take action only in England or the English courts';[57] but these English actions might be against English provincial booksellers selling Scottish reprints.[58] Henry Home, counsel for the Scottish booksellers in *Midwinter* and later appointed to the bench as Lord Kames, referred to his past triumph at the bar in his monumental *Principles of Equity*, implicitly criticising the English equity courts, in arguing that statutes granting monopolies, like the Statute of Anne, should not be extended in equity: 'monopolies or personal privileges cannot be extended by a court of equity; because that court may prevent mischief, but has no power to do any act for enriching any person, or making him *locupletior*, as termed in the Roman law.'[59]

The Scottish courts maintained this refusal to extend the remedial structure of the Statute of Anne, whether through the common law or equity, until the beginning of the nineteenth century,[60] when the House of Lords in

[54] See R Deazley, *On the Origin of the Right to Copy: Charting the Movement of Copyright Law in Eighteenth-century Britain (1695–1775)* (Oxford, Hart Publishing, 2004) 57–69, 137–38; T Gomez-Arostegui, 'What History Teaches Us about Copyright Injunctions and the Inadequate Remedy-at-Law Requirement' (2008) 81 *University of Southern California Law Review* 1197.

[55] *Midwinter v Hamilton* 1748 Mor 8295; Deazley, *Right to Copy* 116–32. Note also Bankton, *Institute* (n 11) I, xix, 12. Bankton's publishers were the booksellers who would feature in the major Scottish copyright cases of the period, Alexander Kincaid and Alexander Donaldson; for their partnership see Sher, *Enlightenment and the Book* (n 53) 311–16.

[56] *Millar v Kincaid*, unreported; see Deazley, *Right to Copy* (n 55) 130–32.

[57] W McDougall, 'Copyright Litigation in the Court of Session, 1738–1749, and the Rise of the Scottish Book Trade' (1971–87) 5 *Transactions of the Edinburgh Bibliographical Society* 2, 9.

[58] J Feather, *Publishing, Piracy and Politics: An Historical Study of Copyright in Britain* (London, Mansell, 1994) 83.

[59] Kames, *Equity* 1st edn (Edinburgh, 1760) 185. The statement, or something close to it, reappears in subsequent editions (2nd edn, 1767, 265–66; 3rd edn, 1778 (last prepared by Kames himself) vol 2, 126). Later editions reproduce the text of the 3rd.

[60] See *Payne and Cadell v Anderson and Robertson* 1787 Mor 8312 (where however interdict and damages were granted on the basis that the defenders had committed the wrong of counterfeiting the pursuers' book; see further below, n 111).

Cadell v Robertson, a Scottish appeal about the rights in a book not registered at Stationers' Hall, overturned the view of the Court of Session that no action was competent in such a case.[61] Lord Chancellor Eldon observed that the Statute was 'uniformly administered ... in this country',[62] and cited the 1798 King's Bench decision in *Beckford v Hood*[63] as deciding that unregistered authors nevertheless had the rights given by the Statute and could obtain injunctions and damages for infringement. Eldon added:

> The judges in Scotland say truly, that they ought not to decide as the judges in England decide, unless they decide rightly and according to the law of Scotland. On the other hand, we may say, that if the judges in Scotland have not decided right, they are not to be followed; and in my own view, they have misunderstood the meaning of the statute in this instance.[64]

It was presumably by way of silent comment on this passage that its reporter provided as an appendix the text of the judicial opinions in an earlier Scottish case not mentioned by Lord Eldon, *Hinton v Donaldson*,[65] decided in 1773. There, as is now well known, nine out of 10 Court of Session judges altogether held that literary property, or copyright, had no existence in relation to published works except under the Statute of Anne. There was no such thing as copyright at common law in Scotland. The court refused to follow the contrary decision handed down by the Court of King's Bench in 1769, *Millar v Taylor*.[66] It also anticipated by a year the reversal of *Millar v Taylor* by the House of Lords' decision in *Donaldson v Beckett*.[67]

As Ronan Deazley has pointed out, however, the arguments supporting the decision in *Hinton v Donaldson* have a flavour quite distinct from those in *Donaldson v Beckett*, flowing from the powerful Civilian influence on Scottish legal thinking. Professor Deazley draws attention to 'three central tenets' in the opinions of the Court of Session judges: 'a common law copyright was deemed to have no foundation either in the law of nature, or the

[61] *Cadell v Robertson* (1811) 5 Pat 453. For the Court of Session pleadings, see Session Papers, Advocates Library, Edinburgh, vol 52 (Hume Collection), no 5. Note that George Joseph Bell was counsel for the pursuers in the Court of Session.

[62] (1811) 5 Pat 453, 504.

[63] *Beckford v Hood* (1798) 7 D&E 620.

[64] (1811) 5 Pat 453, 504.

[65] *Hinton v Donaldson* 1773 Mor 8307; more fully at 5 Br Supp 508; and most fully of all at 5 Pat 505 and in J Boswell, *The Decisions of the Court of Session upon the Question of Literary Property in the Cause John Hinton of London, bookseller, against Alexander Donaldson and John Wood, booksellers in Edinburgh and James Meurose, bookseller in Kilmarnock* (Edinburgh, 1774). Quotations and citations below are from this last source.

[66] *Millar v Taylor* (1768) 4 Burr 2303.

[67] *Donaldson v Beckett* (1774) 4 Burr 2408, 2 Bro PC 129. See further RS Tompson, 'Scottish Judges and the Birth of British Copyright' 1992 JR 18; Deazley, *Right to Copy* (n 55) 191–210; B Sherman and L Bently, *The Making of Modern Intellectual Property Law* (Cambridge, Cambridge University Press, 1999) 11–42.

law of nations, nor was any vestige of such a right to be found in the law of Scotland.'[68] In an as yet unpublished paper that my colleague Professor John Cairns has kindly shared with me, however, Professor Deazley's point is elaborated and reshaped in so far as it distinguishes the law of Scotland from the law of nature or the law of nations.[69] Professor Cairns points out that for the Scots lawyer, the 'common law' was closely linked to European ideas of the *ius commune* as the *ius gentium*, Roman law and, ultimately, the *ius naturale*. Natural law was not something separate from, but was rather the foundation of Scots law.[70] Its content was to be determined by looking at what men in general understood and accepted, as well as the laws of other peoples and nations—the *ius gentium*. As Lord Gardenston put it, 'the most substantial and convincing evidence of what is really just and rational, in a matter of public concern to all countries, is the concurring sense of nations.'[71] For this purpose, the law of England could of course be considered, but if that law was the only system to recognise a right of literary property outside statutory provision or the grant of a special privilege, then it was not very powerful support for the existence of such a right in Scots law. The absence of any previous reference to such a right in Scots law was also evidence that it was not a natural right, readily comprehended by all; indeed in Lord Gardenston's words again, 'property, when applied to ideas, or literary and intellectual compositions, is perfectly new and surprising'.[72]

A further point of significance in the *Hinton* opinions can be more readily identified as a result of our earlier discussion of the distinction drawn by contemporary jurists such as Adam Smith and, a little later, David Hume: between the real right of property—outright ownership—and the real right of exclusive privilege.[73] Several of the judges in *Hinton v Donaldson* refer to this distinction. Thus Lord Auchinleck distinguished prerogative from property and criticised 'blending the notions arising from privileges and patents with a common-law right, which is quite erroneous'.[74] The Lord

[68] Deazley, *Right to Copy* (n 55) 185. Natural law was seriously discussed in the English cases *Tonson v Collins* (1761) 1 W Bl 301 and *Millar v Taylor* (1769) 4 Burr 2303: see DJ Ibbetson, 'Natural Law and Common Law' (2001) 5 Edin LR 4, 11–12.

[69] JW Cairns, 'Natural Law and Copyright in Eighteenth-century Scotland', unpublished draft.

[70] Note also Lord Alva's comment, reflecting another aspect of a more positivistic if also traditional understanding of the place of Roman law in the structure of Scots law: 'the Roman law, which our statute-book teaches us to acknowledge by the name of the common law of this ancient kingdom; in which the ideas of literary property do not seem to have been objects of attention in any considerable degree' (Boswell, *Decisions* (n 65) 32).

[71] Ibid 22.

[72] Ibid 25.

[73] See above, pp 30–31.

[74] Boswell, *Decisions* (n 65) 5.

Justice Clerk, Lord Glenlee, recognised that 'every civilized state in modern times has introduced exclusive privileges for authors'; but, he said:

> this suggests no idea of an original property in the author; on the contrary, it is inconsistent with it: for if such property previously existed in the author, how should it have occurred to sovereigns, meaning to encourage authors, to limit the endurance of the author's right to a certain term of years; which is the case of all letters patent known in the different states of Europe.[75]

For Lord Kames, 'the meaning of property, in the laws of all nations, is a right to some corporeal subject, that can be possessed, that can be transferred from hand to hand, that goes to heirs, that may be stolen or robbed, and that may be demanded by a real action, termed *rei vindicatio*.'[76] But the right claimed by the pursuer was not to any corpus that could be possessed or stolen. He continued:

> *Ergo*, it is not property. Taking it in all views, no more can be made of it than to be a privilege or monopoly, which intitles the claimant to the commerce of a certain book, and excludes all others from making money by it. The important question then is, from what source is this monopoly derived, a monopoly that endures for ever, and is effectual against all the world? The act of Queen Anne bestows this monopoly upon authors for a limited time upon certain conditions. But our legislature, far from acknowledging a perpetual monopoly at common law, declares that it shall last no longer than a limited time.[77]

Lord Gardenston thought that the 'concurring sense of nations' showed that the nature of an author's right was 'no more than a temporary privilege'[78] and not one of property. Lord Alva's opinion is also to be understood as distinguishing privilege from property:

> By the common law of this country, or any other country, where there is not a restriction upon natural liberty understood, either *tacito populi suffragio*, or by express statute, there is no antecedent property vested in an author, or his heirs, or assigns, further than what relates to the *ipsum corpus* of the MS: that this property, in so far as it exists, is merely a creature of civil society and refined policy, and consequently will go no further than it is expressly established by custom or statute: but we have no custom or common law for it here; and therefore it can go no further with us than it is carried by the statute.[79]

Another way in which the judicial arguments draw upon the idea of exclusive privilege to reject the claim of property is in their observation that the author of a book might be analogised with the inventor of a useful machine who, however, had no property right apart from the monopoly of a patent

[75] Ibid 15.
[76] Ibid 18.
[77] Ibid 18.
[78] Ibid 22.
[79] Ibid 32.

granted under the royal prerogative.[80] Indeed, the existence of such a perpetual property right in inventors would be deeply damaging to society and commerce; Lord Kames commented darkly that 'it would be in the power of inventors to deprive mankind of both food and raiment'.[81]

For present purposes, a final important feature of the opinions in *Hinton v Donaldson* is that most were careful to distinguish between unpublished and published books. With the former, the judges were much more ready to recognise the existence of a property right. So for example Lord Auchinleck: 'It is agreed by all, that while the book is not published, whether the work be in the author's head or his cabinet, it is absolutely his, and no man can deprive him of it';[82] and similarly the Lord Justice Clerk: 'Before publication this copy-right in the author exists, and must have all the effects of property in every nation.'[83] As the sole dissentient judge, Lord Monboddo, pointed out,[84] however, they did not explain what happened to this property right upon publication of the work. Lord Kames, Lord Gardenston, Lord Coalston and Lord Alva also recognised a pre-publication property right, albeit on the basis of the ownership of the manuscript on which the work was recorded, rather than anything more abstract or incorporeal. But the two latter judges also recognised what Lord Coalston termed 'full power'[85] and Lord Alva an 'interest'[86] over, respectively, one's 'own ideas' or the 'productions of [one's] own brain'. In both cases the judges were careful to distinguish this power or interest from property, but did not otherwise seek to define what if any legal effects arose from it. Further, to the eye of the modern copyright lawyer, they and their fellow judges failed in their discussion of property rights to distinguish adequately between ideas, forms of expression and the physical record of the work in question.[87]

The issues thus raised in *Hinton v Donaldson* about unpublished works quickly became a matter for decision in the Court of Session in relation to private correspondence.[88] In *Dodsley v McFarquhar*[89] in 1775, letters written

[80] See the opinions of the Lord Justice Clerk (Boswell, *Decisions* (n 65) 15), Lord Kames (ibid 18–19), Lord Gardenston (ibid 23–24), Lord Coalston (ibid 29), and Lord President Dundas (ibid 33). See also Lord Monboddo's dissent at ibid 12.

[81] Boswell, *Decisions* (n 65) 19.

[82] Ibid 3.

[83] Ibid 14.

[84] Ibid 10.

[85] Ibid 28.

[86] Ibid 32.

[87] For contemporary uncertainty on these issues in England see Sherman and Bently, *Making of Modern Intellectual Property Law* (n 67) 15–42.

[88] For insightful discussion of contemporary social attitudes towards personal correspondence see K Williamson, 'The Emergence of Privacy: Letters, Journals and Domestic Writing', in I Brown et al (eds), *Edinburgh History of Scottish Literature Volume 2: Enlightenment, Britain and Empire 1707–1918* (Edinburgh, Edinburgh University Press, 2007).

[89] *Dodsley v McFarquhar* 1775 Mor 8308; more fully at ibid, *Literary Property* (n 65) Appendix, 1.

by the Earl of Chesterfield to his son Philip Stanhope were, after the death of the two men, sold by the addressee's widow to a London publisher who published them with the consent of the Earl's executors. Before giving that consent, however, the executors had obtained from the Lord Chancellor in England an injunction against publication. The book was registered in Stationers' Hall. The publishers were held entitled to an interdict against an unauthorised reprint by Edinburgh printers and booksellers, arguments that the Statute of Anne conferred no express right upon an author's representatives after his death, and that neither the recipient nor the widow had such rights of property in the letters as would enable them to publish, being rejected by the court. While the recipient and then the widow might own the manuscripts, there was at least an implied prohibition of publication; and in some of the letters there was an express statement that they should remain secret. With regard to this latter point, the court seems to have accepted the counter-argument that it was for the sender's representatives to take the point about obligations of secrecy, not those who sought to give the material further public circulation. But the court does not seem to have relied upon any notion that the sender retained any right of property in the letters, whether in reference to the original manuscripts or their content.

The next case was *Cadell and Davies v Stewart*, decided in 1804.[90] Six years after the death of the poet Robert Burns in 1796, a Glasgow publisher projected the publication of a volume of his letters to Agnes McLehose, a close friend whom he addressed as 'Clarinda' (dubbing himself 'Sylvander'). Clarinda, the publisher claimed, consented to the publication.[91] London and Edinburgh booksellers who had acquired rights to all Burns' works and also had the concurrence of the Burns family successfully sought interdict to stop the publication. Their argument, put forward by George Joseph Bell advocate, and based on English authorities such as *Pope v Curl*[92] and *Duke of Queensberry v Shebbeare*,[93] was that an addressee such as Clarinda acquired only a limited property right in a letter, with no right to use it in any other way than as manuscript. No reconciliation was attempted between this limited property right and the traditional Scots law view of ownership as the most absolute of all rights, capable of being vested in only one person at a time. But, crucially, the concurrence of the Burns family also enabled a further argument, based on their interest in preventing injury to

[90] *Cadell and Davies v Stewart* 1804 Mor, Literary Property Appendix, 13. More details can be obtained from the Session Papers available in the Advocates Library, Edinburgh: see vol 52 (Hume Collection) no 6 (including a handwritten note of the judges' opinions, possibly by Hume himself); vol 65 (Blair Collection) no 13; vol 114 (Campbell Collection) nos 2–3; and Faculty Collection February 1804-July 1804 no 166.

[91] Doubt as to the reality of her consent emerges from the pleadings for Cadell and Davies as found in the Session Papers, but the court did not need to make any findings on the matter.

[92] *Pope v Curl* (1741) 2 Atk 342.

[93] *Duke of Queensberry v Shebbeare* (1758) 2 Eden 329.

Burns' character and reputation. The respondent argued that the recipient had full and unfettered property in the letters, and even if their publication was detrimental to Burns' reputation, that could not restrict the owner's legal use of her property. Breach of confidence was an argument of morality, not law: 'whoever intrusts any secret, or makes any communication to another, commits himself in some measure to the discretion of his friend, and he can never hope, by means of a suspension and interdict, to prevent him from telling the secret.'[94] The court's opinions are not reported, but the reporter noted 'little difference of opinion upon the Bench'[95] and summarised the decision as follows:

> The ground upon which the Court seemed to pronounce the decision was, That the communication in letters is always made under the implied confidence that they shall not be published without the consent of the writer, and that the representatives of Burns had a sufficient interest, for the vindication of his literary character, to restrain this publication.[96]

Discussing these cases alongside the English authorities in his lectures, Hume observed that 'it seems obvious that letters are written and conveyed under the implied condition of not being published without the consent of the writer, who in that respect has certainly no intention of transferring the property of what he writes'.[97] But although Bell thought that 'unpublished compositions are property at common law; and the publication of them is an invasion of the rights of the owner',[98] he also argued that the basis of the Scottish decisions on the publication of private letters specifically was not the same as the English cases on the subject:

> The law of England and that of Scotland proceed on different grounds in denying the right to publish letters. In England, it is on the ground of property alone; in Scotland, on the ground chiefly of a just and expedient interference for the protection of reputation.[99]

The argument was reiterated in more detail in Bell's *Commentaries*:

> In Scotland, the Court of Session is held to have jurisdiction, by interdict, to protect not property merely, but reputation, and even private feelings, from outrage and invasion. ... By the publication of such effusions, confidential, careless, unthinking of consequences, a man may be wounded in the tenderest part; his literary reputation hurt; his character traduced. It is, accordingly, the understood

[94] *Cadell and Davies v Stewart* 1804 Mor, Literary Property Appendix, 16.
[95] Ibid 16.
[96] Ibid 16. The contemporary note of the judicial opinions in Session Papers, vol 52 (Hume Collection) no 6, shows the judges rejecting property arguments.
[97] Hume, *Lectures* (n 11) vol 4, 68.
[98] Bell, *Principles* (n 11) § 1356.
[99] Ibid.

> or implied condition of the communication, the implied limitation of the right conferred, that such communications are not to be published.[100]

Bell also noted that 'doubts seem to be entertained in England, whether letters falling into the hands of the assignees of bankrupts could be secured from publication by injunction'. 'With us,' he wrote, 'I think, there would be no such doubt.'[101]

Bell's distinction between an author's right of property in an unpublished work and a letter-writer's entitlement to control publication of the letter to protect reputation was largely borne out in the limited subsequent case law. An 1855 jury case held the writer of a letter to a newspaper editor for publication entitled to withdraw it before publication, albeit without reference to Bell.[102] In 1881 the Second Division discharged an interdict against publication of personal correspondence (while noting that there might be a remedy after publication if injury was caused thereby); but the judges, although thinking the rules to be the same in England and Scotland, cited Bell and were clear that there was no property, literary or otherwise, in the letters.[103] Four years later, in the great case of *Caird v Sime*,[104] which concerned the unauthorised publication of the lectures of the Professor of Moral Philosophy at Glasgow University, the judges of the Whole Court of Session were virtually unanimous in declaring that the author of an unpublished work had a right of property in his work, citing mainly the English authorities on the matter and in particular *Abernethy v Hutchinson*,[105] *Prince Albert v Strange*,[106] and *Jefferys v Boosey*.[107] This view was upheld in the House of Lords, where the leading speech was given by the Scottish Law Lord, Watson.[108] But all were clear that this property right was not copyright, and that it ceased upon publication. How this might be reconciled with the Scots law concept of property—ownership—as single, undivided and indefinite in duration was, however, never addressed.

CONCLUSION

Only the most general of conclusions may be offered from this sketchy survey of its subject, based as it is almost entirely on printed formal legal

100 Bell, *Commentaries* (n 12) vol 1, 111–12.
101 Ibid 112. See also ibid 114, for more expansive use of interdict in Scotland than would be possible with injunctions in England.
102 *Davis v Miller and Fairly* (1855) 17 D 1166.
103 *White v Dickson* (1881) 8 R 896.
104 *Caird v Sime* (1885) 13 R 23. Only Lord Shand of the 13 consulted judges rejected the property analysis.
105 *Abernethy v Hutchinson* (1825) 1 H & TW 28.
106 *Prince Albert v Strange* (1849) 1 M&G 25.
107 *Jefferys v Boosey* (1854) 4 HLC 815.
108 *Caird v Sime* (1887) 14 R (HL) 37.

sources. A significant Scottish dimension is apparent in the development of what we would now call intellectual property in the United Kingdom after the Union of 1707. With both patents and copyright under the Statute of Anne, however, that Scottish dimension was always seen in the context of the single market created by the Union; this was occasionally reinforced by the House of Lords in cases such as *Roebuck and Garbett v Stirlings*, *Cadell v Robertson*, and *Astley v Taylor*, as well as by the legislature. In Scotland itself there were also issues about how to understand these developing rights within the systematics of Scots law, in particular the doctrine of real rights. While this did not prevent the development of a unified substantive patent law for the United Kingdom long before the abolition of separate Scots and English patents in 1852, there were significant effects in the debate about the existence of rights at common law, beyond grants made under the royal prerogative or by virtue of United Kingdom legislation. The effects were not limited to the literary property arena. The notions of protecting reputation and privacy rather than rights of property also helped from early in the nineteenth century to go well beyond an existing *ius commune* idea of the professionally entrusted secret that could not be disclosed by the recipient,[109] to follow the English development of a concept of a right to protect confidentiality, preventing or sanctioning the taking and use or disclosure of another's confidential information.[110] Similarly the unauthorised use of badges of another's trading identity and reputation, successfully challenged in 1787 using the analogy of the *crimen falsi*,[111] and seen by Bell as resting on 'tak[ing], without authority, the advantage of [the pursuer's] personal character and credit as an artist',[112] would provide the platform from which Scots law would move in the second half of the nineteenth century to use the English concept of passing off (reinforced by the statutory protection of trade marks available throughout the United Kingdom from 1875). But in both common law developments it generally remained clear (as it did not with literary property) that their basis in Scots law was in personal rights, whether by way of delict or contract, and not in any form of property in the confidential information or the badges of identity.[113] It was, however,

[109] See J Blackie, 'The History of Personality Rights in Scots Law', in N Whitty and R Zimmermann (eds), *Rights of Personality in Scots Law* (Dundee, Dundee University Press, 2009) section 2.2.5.

[110] *Kerr v Duke of Roxburgh* (1822) 3 Murr 126, said by the judge to be 'the first case of the kind in this country' (141). See also *Newton v Fleming* (1846) 8 D 677, revd (1848) 6 Bell 175, *AB v CD* (1851) 14 D 177, and Blackie, 'Personality Rights' (n 109) section 2.3.6.

[111] *Payne and Cadell v Anderson and Robertson* 1787 Mor 8312.

[112] Bell, *Commentaries* (n 12) vol 1, 111, citing *Wilkie v McCulloch* (1823) 2 S 413 (interdict to prevent representation that ploughs manufactured under inspection or by authority of pursuer who had invented, but not patented, new kind of plough). See also *Edinburgh Correspondent Newspaper* (1822) 1 S 407 (protection of newspaper title).

[113] See EM Clive, 'The Action for Passing Off: Its Scope and Basis' 1963 JR 117; Scottish Law Commission Memorandum No 40, *Confidential Information* (1977).

always a comfort for the Scottish courts that here, as with patents and copyright, the results produced by this different approach were generally in line with those that would be reached in England. The United Kingdom was the inescapable backcloth to the development of intellectual property law; and for Scots law that did indeed mean, to adjust the metaphor first coined by Pierre Trudeau, being on stage with an elephant.

3

On Clarifying the Role of Originality and Fair Use in Nineteenth Century UK Jurisprudence

Appreciating 'the humble grey which emerges as the result of long controversy'*

KATHY BOWREY

ANY INQUIRY INTO intellectual property and the notion of a monolithic common law applicable throughout the Commonwealth, is most immediately challenged by difficult questions about the methodology we use to discover 'the law'. The task is made more difficult given that, for most of the twentieth century, the conservative legal training on offer in Australia erased and suppressed most of the important political questions about the origins and legitimacy of our inherited system of law. Sir Anthony Mason, (Chief Justice High Court 1987–95) noted that in the 1940s, when he began to study law at the University of Sydney, with the exception of constitutional law, the law taught was the common law of England.[1] Bruce Kercher notes nothing much had changed with his legal education in the 1970s: 'English decisions were simply adopted as if they were Australian. There was little if any consideration as to whether Australian law had any distinctive qualities.'[2]

* With thanks to Catherine Bond, Ronan Deazley, Lionel Bently, Michael Handler, Brad Sherman and Peta MacGilvray.

[1] Sir A Mason, 'An Australian Common Law?' in M Chanock and LA Marks (eds), *Cross Currents: Internationalism, National Identity and Law* (Bundoora, Vic, La Trobe University Press, 1995).

[2] B Kercher, *An Unruly Child. A History of law in Australia* (Sydney, Allen & Unwin, 1995) ix. Likewise Jeremy Finn notes: '... it is little wonder that many Australasians ... were indoctrinated with the idea that "legal history" was essentially something that happened in England ... the books which were available were either English (and by and large English legal

Likewise, Sam Ricketson notes:

> The inclination of Australian lawyers to follow English precedents cannot be explained as just a version of the cultural cringe ... Even if the judges had shared that Anglophile vision, it would not necessarily follow that they would simply copy English law ... [However] for most of the twentieth century, Australian lawyers simply accepted that there was one unitary common law across the empire, passed down from above in a system of strict precedent ... This reflects recognition of the UK as the summit of judge made law.[3]

Throughout the Commonwealth, common law judges have, across the years, 'adopted' particular nineteenth century precedents as if the particular selection was in fact representative of a unitary common law. However as is well known, in looking at precedent there can be significant creativity and selection, claiming only what one hopes to find and rendering invisible whatever does not fit the preconceived view and need to legitimate today's decision.[4] There is a degree of unavoidability to this political dimension to law. Any coherent legal history requires some imposition of order on the subject. However arguably, copyright law presents an especially difficult state of affairs.

Detailed, scholarly historical inquiry into copyright is a relatively recent endeavour. Books have emerged that look at the broader jurisprudence,[5] and the politics of nineteenth century legislative reforms.[6] However serious engagement with any broad sweep of copyright case authority beyond the question of copyright 'origins' and the legacy of *Donaldson v Beckett* (1774)[7] remains exceedingly rare. It is only quite recently that there has been a renewed interest in the considering past case law more expansively.[8]

Generally speaking, we actually know very little about the state of the law from which our 'precedents' have been plucked. Given this reality, this chapter seeks to open up discussion and debate about the use of precedent. The role of originality and fair use in UK nineteenth century case

histories ignore the British Empire); or partial in coverage or dated or bad- or any combination thereof' in J Finn, 'A Formidable Subject: Some Thoughts on the Writing of Australasian Legal History' (2003) 7(1) *Australian Journal of Legal History* 53.

[3] S Ricketson, 'Australia and International Copyright Protection', in MP Ellinghaus, AJ Bradbrook, AJ Duggan (eds) *The Emergence of Australian Law* (Sydney, Butterworths, 1989) 166.

[4] N Duxbury, *The Nature and Authority of Precedent* (Cambridge, Cambridge University Press, 2008).

[5] B Sherman and L Bently, *The Making of Modern Intellectual Property Laws* (Cambridge, Cambridge University Press, 1999).

[6] C Seville, *Literary Copyright Reform in early Victorian England* (Cambridge, Cambridge University Press, 1999).

[7] *Donaldson v Beckett* 1 Eng Rep 837; 4 Burr 2408, 98 Eng Rep 257 (1774).

[8] R Deazley, *Rethinking Copyright: History, Theory, Language,* (Cheltenham, Edward Elgar, 2006); I Alexander, *Copyright and the Public Interest in the 19th Century*, (Oxford, Hart Publishing, 2010); HT Gomez-Arostegui, 'What History Teaches Us About Copyright Injunctions and the Inadequate-Remedy-at-Law Requirement' (2008) 81 *Southern California Law Review* 1197.

law forms the basis of the inquiry. I consider why the nineteenth century cases and treatises failed to clearly identify what the author owns of 'right', and the implications for the criterion of originality and for determining infringement today. Rather than assume that the common law of the UK was, once, 'one unitary common law across the empire', that subsequently fractured or morphed with the influence of the UK dissipating in face of the dominance of the US or legal internationalism, it is argued that in case law, the common law was never treated as monolithic.

That this was once well appreciated can be seen from the opening of Scrutton's 1883 tome:

> 'The question of Copyright, like most questions of civil prudence, is neither black nor white, but grey'. (Macaulay's Speeches, p110)
>
> ... we have through all the storm to bear in mind that the truth is not the black or white ... but the humble grey which emerges as the result of long controversy.[9]

Scrutton's treatise sought to rise above this fray with recourse to a scientific approach to law, justified by an Austinian Utilitarianism:

> Utilitarianism is the groundwork of the science and art of legislation, and that therefore the justification of any particular law, the reason which justifies its enactment, is the ultimate benefit to result to the community from its conformity to such a law.[10]

This led to his conclusion that 'The Fundamental Question of Copyright Law is: Is it desirable in the interests of the community that the State should create and protect property in literary productions or the results of intellectual labour?'[11]

By way of contrast, Copinger's earlier treatise had began: 'copyright may be defined as the sole and exclusive liberty of multiplying copies of an original work or composition ...What property can be more emphatically a man's own than his literary works?'[12]

However even Copinger, a most ardent advocate for the common law right of the author,[13] goes on to acknowledge that:

> In order to acquire a copyright in a work it is necessary that it should be original ... [However] Over this vast *field it is impossible to erect an unvarying general rule,* which can be fitted to all cases and capable of determining whether a particular work exhibits the degree of originality necessary to a valid copyright.[14]

[9] Sir TE Scrutton, *The Laws of Copyright: an examination of the principles which regulate literary and artistic property in England and other Countries* (London, J. Murray, 1883) §1, 1–2.

[10] Ibid §4, 4.

[11] Ibid §5, 5.

[12] WA Copinger, *The Law of Copyright in Works of Literature and Art* (London, Stevens and Haynes, 1870) 1, 5.

[13] See Deazley (n 8) 75–78.

[14] Copinger (n 12) 20 (emphasis supplied).

Copinger retreats from his opening 'black and white' statement of absolute rights in original works to a safer shade of grey. For example, he suggests that rules about originality should be capable of adaptation to the objects of their labours,[15] and, with regard to what constitutes piracy he concludes: 'In many cases the line of demarcation is so loosely and indifferently drawn, that arrival at a just conclusion is a matter of difficulty.'[16]

Despite very different politics and jurisprudence that lead to marked distinctions in approach to the subject of copyright and to legal reasoning, both eminent authors[17] are unwilling or unable to deduce clear principles that clarify legal boundaries with regard to what was actually protected by the 'author's right' and what constitutes an infringement. This leads to my deeper consideration of what Macaulay and Scrutton meant by referring to copyright as a 'grey subject'. Grey is a neutral tone that comes from mixing black and white, and thus an allusion to the balancing of rights. It is clear that this is what Macaulay meant.[18] However, we also refer to our brains as 'grey matter' and associate the colour grey with the wisdom that is supposed to come with age, experience and the passing of time. My broader motivation in reflecting upon the 'humble grey that emerges from long controversy' is to try and bring into the light the wisdom of nineteenth century copyright scholars in resisting a monolithic approach to the subject, and the potential relevance of this history to controversies over originality, compilations and copyright's limits today.

Appreciating the complexity of this history matters because it has, of late, become common to refer to nineteenth century positions in order to authorise very contemporary readings of the scope of protection awarded to original compilations in copyright. In the nineteenth century the notion of fair use had a much larger role to play, leading to a relative consideration of the original efforts and corresponding markets of the plaintiff and defendant. Further as Scrutton infers, consideration of the good served by our laws and, co-relatively, determining the wrong of 'piracy', involved an assessment of benefit to the community in conferring protection. By invoking history today, whilst ignoring these key points, we erase the wisdom of nineteenth century considerations of the need for 'balance'.

[15] Ibid 21.

[16] Ibid 84.

[17] Copinger's treatise was in its second edition by 1881, growing from an original 437pp to 956pp. Scrutton's text of 353pp was awarded the Yorke Prize Essay of the University of Cambridge in 1882.

[18] He went on to say: 'The system of copyright has great advantages, and great disadvantages; and it is our business to ascertain what these are, and then to make arrangement under which the advantages may be as far as possible secured; and the disadvantages as far as possible excluded.' *Speeches of the Honourable T.B. Macaulay M.P.* (London, Longman, Brown, Green and Longmans, 1854) 232.

There is nothing to suggest that a 'loss' of consideration of the public interest was ever intended. Rather it has come about as a consequence of codification and legislative drafting enacted in the twentieth century with quite different reasons in mind. This raises complex questions about the use precedent in copyright and legal methodologies, given that:

> To be a lawyer in Australia is, in a sense, to be a legal historian. It is an escapable feature of the common law that we live our lives in the presence of the great legal spirits of the past and their cases.[19]

SOME RESERVATIONS DISMISSED

It could be considered that debate about the historical justification for copyright, the status of the common law right and its more limited positive expression in eighteenth and nineteenth century law is currently so conflicted and politicised[20] that making authoritative reference to the law's origins and purpose is fraught with difficulty. It could also be that the nineteenth century legislation was so deficient, and decisions were so inconsistent or incoherent, that it is possible to read the law in support of any manner of contrary propositions. Judicial technique in discerning and applying 'legal principles' could have been so poorly applied, or used methodologies so many and varied, that drawing any universal conclusions about the reason and logic of nineteenth century law may be unwise.

But if any of the above propositions are true, this raises fundamental questions affecting all and any use of precedent in copyright law today. At what point can one confidently presume that an authoritative path was established and clear principles (either black or white) were crystallised? If this is taken to have occurred, when did that come to pass? How was it justified, and with reference to what kind or form of legal reasoning or other authority? A longstanding judicial (and scholarly) failure to doubt the relevance and authority of precedent for well over a century suggests we need to consider the role and lessons of nineteenth century case law differently.

Can we minimise potential problems in reading the common law by adopting a utilitarian Austinian approach, as Scrutton desired? This would suggest discerning the logic of copyright law by recourse to the community interest as defined by the state.

[19] Justice M Kirby, 'Living with Legal History in the Courts' (2003) 7(1) *Australian Journal of Legal History* 17.

[20] See R Deazley, *On the Origin of the Right to Copy* (Oxford, Hart Publishing, 2004); J Ginsburg, 'Une Chose Publique'? The Author's Domain and the Public Domain in Early British, French and US Copyright Law' (2006) 65 *Cambridge Law Journal* 636–70; K Bowrey and N Fowell, 'Digging up fragments and building IP franchises' (2009) 31 *Sydney Law Review* 185.

The problem with this approach is that the British and Australian Acts are too poverty-stricken as resources to be of much assistance. There is scant reference to legislative objective, principle or public purpose(s) in all our copyright legislation. Putting to one side the 'pre-modern'[21] matrix of subject-specific seventeenth and eighteenth century legislation and confining our consideration to the modern legislation, none of this law—from the Copyright Act 1905 (Cth), Copyright Act 1911 (UK), Copyright Act 1912 (Cth) to the Copyright Act 1968 (Cth)—purports to set a new path for determining the nature and scope of literary copyright. Legislative reform was not claimed as necessary to 'resolve' past confusion about the fundamental nature and scope of the rights, or to inscribe significantly new precepts or legal principles in relation to the old subject matter.[22] Rather justifications for the new laws have been far more conservative and primarily confined to redressing the past pre-modern organisation of the law through codification.[23] To the extent that Commissions identified disagreement as to copyright's purpose and scope, state wisdom was to leave it unchanged. As such, a utilitarian reading of positive law only returns you to the case law and judicial interpretation of 'state' or 'community interest'.

It is true that the Berne Convention for the Protection of Literary and Artistic Works (1886) and the Berlin Convention of 1908[24] provided significant impetus to reconsider the rights awarded. These instruments influenced the drafting of the 1905 Act (Cth) to a minor degree,[25] and the UK 1911 Act especially in relation to translations, abridgments, abolition of formalities and duration. However, the text of the 1911 Act was also crafted with a view to fostering uniformity across the Empire, affirming UK law and requiring minimal changes to the domestic law across the Empire.[26] In Australia the Berne Convention has only been considered as

[21] As described by Sherman and Bently (n 5).

[22] Of course the provisions regarding the new technologies and subject matter poses a somewhat different case. See also *Copyright Owners Reproduction Society Ltd v EMI (Australia) Pty Ltd* [1958] HCA 54; (1958) 100 CLR 597.

[23] For example, the Royal Commission Report of 1878 begins: 'The first observation which a study of the existing law suggests is that its form, as distinguished from its substance is bad. The law is wholly destitute of any sort of arrangement, incomplete, often obscure, and even when it is intelligible upon long study, it is in many parts so ill-expressed that no one who does not give such study to it can expect to understand it.' See Royal Commissioners' Report (1878), *Primary Sources on Copyright (1450–1900)*, eds L Bently and M Kretschmer. Available at www.copyrighthistory.org.

[24] The Convention for the Protection of Literary and Artistic Works (Berlin Act, 1908) extended the Berne Convention in recognising new subject matter such as photography, film and sound recordings, and also rights of translation, adaption and arrangement of music.

[25] Compare for example, Art 5 of the revised 1896 Berne Convention and s 30 of the Copyright Act 1905 (Cth). Thanks to Catherine Bond for this point.

[26] As was noted in the House of Commons debates, 'the delegates were very emphatic on the line of uniformity of Copyright throughout the Empire ... The basis of the Imperial Conference, and the Bill founded on its deliberations is that while we leave to the self governing Dominions liberty to legislate for themselves, we offer them the greatest possible

requiring reconsideration of the scope of our traditional rights minimally, and for most of the twentieth century, very inconsistently.[27] Whilst Berne is discussed knowledgeably in Parliamentary debates,[28] there is uncertainty as to the significance of the Berne Convention as a relevant source of Australian law to be found in our case law.

The influence of the Berne Convention on statutory interpretation of the 1911 Act (UK) is noted in *Sands & McDougall Pty Ltd v Robinson* (1917). While Isaacs J notes 'the international origin of the [1911] Act affords considerable aid in understanding it'[29] he then goes on to affirm the signatories were not attempting to affect pre-1911 UK law in regard to key concepts such as originality.[30] It is also worth noting that when there is debate about Australia's international obligations it has become common to refer to the external affairs power under section 51(xxix) as the authority for the necessary reform, not to the power to make laws with respect to the copyright (as informed by the Berne Convention) under section 51(xviii).[31]

It may well be that until relatively recently, Australia has been unable to consider the longer-term implications of Berne as a significant legal authority because that would have necessitated a more far-reaching and uncomfortable discourse about the nature of our 'sovereign' legal order, impossible within the embrace of Empire. Whilst nationalist historians have asserted that with Federation, we defiantly cut the apron strings and rejected the bonds of the British connection, the reality is that as a matter of business and trade, Australia remained closely tied to Britain throughout

inducement to accept the Imperial Act as a model, and to differ from it as little as possible, by offering reciprocal advantages.' Mr Buxton, The debate on the Second Reading, Hansard HC vol XXIII, 2594. See also LCF Oldfield, *The Law of Copyright* (London, Sydney, Calcutta, Butterworth & Co, 1912) Part 1.

[27] Australia was bound by Berne from 1887 as it was declared to apply to the colonies. We became signatories in our own right in 1928. The Spicer Committee referenced the Berne Convention, as well as the significance of the Berlin (1908) and Brussels revisions (1948) and the Universal Copyright Convention (1952). However the Copyright Law Review Committee, *Report on Moral Rights* (1988) debated whether we were Berne compliant, and the minority report considered whether moral rights were an 'alien concept' to the Australian system of property rights. See also Sam Ricketson, 'Australia and International Copyright Protection', in Ellinghaus, et al (n 3); S Ricketson, 'The Berne Convention: The Continued Relevance of an Ancient Text', in D Vaver and L Bently (eds), *Intellectual Property In The New Millennium: Essays In Honour Of William R. Cornish* (Cambridge, Cambridge University Press, 2004) 217–33.

[28] For example, whilst the Berne Convention is introduced as the motivation behind the 1911 Act (UK), 'The first principle laid down by the British Act is that copyright is an Imperial matter ... The majority of the countries of Europe ... are in the Berne Convention, and the protection of this Act would extend to our authors and artists in all of the countries which are in the Convention ... we have the power of the British Empire behind us when we ask for anything which is just and fair from another country.' See Senator McGregor, Second Reading Speech of the Copyright Bill, Hansard 1912 vol LXIV 1334–35.

[29] *Sands & McDougall Pty Ltd v Robinson* [1917] 23 CLR 49, 54.

[30] This is discussed further below.

[31] Thanks to Catherine Bond for these points.

most of the twentieth century.[32] In terms of legal education, we had regard to embracing abstractions about the unitary legal order, such as the appeal to the supremacy of the UK Parliament and the authority of British nineteenth century precedent. It needs to be recalled that it was only in 1974 that it was recognised that the Australian High Court might be in a better position than the Privy Council to determine whether the High Court should adhere to or depart from an earlier decision. It would take the Australia Act 1986 to complete the untying of these apron strings, by ending the inclusion into Australian law of British Acts of Parliament and abolishing all remaining constitutional provision for appeals from Australian courts to the Privy Council in London. It was as recent as 1987 that Sir Anthony Mason began to talk about 'in the tradition of continuity, *developing* an Australian common law, that is, a common law for Australia best suited to its conditions and circumstances' (emphasis added).[33]

Historically we have been so preoccupied with the importance of the authority and continuity of the common law that there has been scant consideration of the process of translation of UK copyright law to local circumstances. Self-doubt, insecurity and/or uncertainty about when we gained the right to define Australian common law has led to considerable scholarly neglect of colonial legal history in particular, even though there were distinctive colonial copyright laws and interesting reflections on nineteenth century UK law.[34] For example, Routledge v Low (1868)[35] held that to qualify for protection under the 1842 Act, a work actually had to be first published in the UK. This created serious problems for the emerging colonial publishing industry, as works first published outside the UK were left unprotected in the colonies and in their markets abroad. Though subsequent Acts extended protection to works first published in any British Possession, or certain foreign countries, as England began to enter into international agreements there remained confusion about the status of literary works first published in the colonies, and concerns over copyright in subject matter beyond literary works. Melbourne artists, artisans and manufacturers petitioned Parliament seeking protection for productions first made in the colonies. Victoria passed a general copyright law in 1869, South Australia in 1878, New South Wales in 1879 and Western Australia

[32] S Ward, *Australia and the British Embrace: The Demise of the Imperial Ideal* (Carlton, Vic, Melbourne University Press, 2001); D Schreuder and S Ward, (eds) *Australia's Empire,* (Oxford, New York, Oxford University Press, 2008).

[33] Mason (n 1) 81.

[34] The most significant work completed to date is Catherine Bond, 'Mapping Australia's Copyright Commons' (PhD work in progress, UNSW). See also Lionel Bently, 'Copyright and the Victorian Internet. Telegraphic Property Laws in Colonial Australia' (2004) 38 *Loyola of Los Angeles Law Review* 71. Post-Federation see also Catherine Banks, 'Lost in Translation: A History of Moral Rights in Australian Law' (PhD, Griffith University, 2005).

[35] *Routledge v Low* (1868) LR 3 HL 100.

in 1895. These local laws co-existed alongside rights in particular subject matter conferred by different Imperial statutes. Colonial case law also discussed the existence and merit of common law copyright and associated property rights alongside interests conferred by statute.[36] However, notwithstanding this, when it comes to discussing the origin of Australian law, for most of the twentieth century Australian lawyers have overwhelmingly remained fixated on the UK common law. For most of the twentieth century we accessed Australian legal authority, including international obligation, through the legacy of Empire.

It is because of this reality that this chapter is also preoccupied with UK common law, leaving consideration of Australia's legal distinctiveness to a later time. In relation to nineteenth century UK copyright, my concern is to explore whether the inherited common law was really as unitary, clear or as certain as has generally been presumed.

The following section suggests that the order of the law, and consequently the relevance of precedent, was much more thorny than has been appreciated. It is uncritical reliance on overarching symbolic references such as the unitary authority of the common law that has allowed the true diversity and wisdom of nineteenth century approaches to copyright to be subverted and neglected. Understanding the complexity of nineteenth century UK case law is fundamental to understanding the long history of controversies surrounding copyright. As such, grappling with its difficulty should not be avoided. It is only by appreciating this past that we can critically understand the significance and values that inform citation of precedent today.

THE NINETEENTH CENTURY CASES

Creativity Distinguished from Originality

If the question asked was: 'Are certain kinds of factual or informational works, that lack creative inputs, altogether excluded from copyright protection?', the courts usually answered that such works qualify for protection. Wood VC sums up the rationale well:

> Copyright was considered for the highest purposes of society in every country as necessary to be secured to those who contributed to civilisation, refinement, or instruction of mankind, and extended in this country, if not elsewhere, to every description of work, however humble it might be, even to the mere collection of

[36] Molesworth J said: 'This is a kind of property which a peculiar state of society has brought into existence for the first time. The plaintiffs have a clear property in that for which they give a price, and from which they obtain a profit, and the defendant appears to have been habitually interfering with that property by publishing, without paying for it, that which they [the plaintiffs] have procured by a large outlay.' *Wilson v Rowcroft* (1873) 4 AJR 57, 61. See also *Wilson v Luke* (1875) 1 VLR (E) 127; *Broadhurst v Nicholls* (1903) 3 SR (NSW) 147.

> the abodes of persons and to streets and places; and labour having been employed upon subjects even of that class, no one had a right to avail himself of it.[37]

To answer otherwise would be to endorse 'reaping without sowing'. For example, in *Collis v Cater* the defendant conceded copying, but argued that a 'dry list' of products for sale comprised in a chemist's catalogue, was not protected. North J noted:

> The question is whether a man has a right to appropriate to himself without payment or recognition in any way what it has cost his neighbour expense and trouble to make out. In my opinion, he has not.[38]

Other commonly cited cases that express this view include *Matthewson v Stockdale*,[39] *Roworth v Wilkes*,[40] *Jarrold v Houlston*,[41] *Scott v Stanford*,[42] *Walter v Steinkopff*[43] and *Leslie v Young*.[44] However it is wrong to conclude from this that the plaintiff had any absolute right to protection of skill and labour. Piracy was not determined by a finding of copying alone. Large and unacknowledged takings were inherently suspect, but even that was not necessarily sufficient to determine the wrong because notwithstanding the taking, the use may have been considered as fair.

There is a strong endorsement of an absolutist 'reaping without sowing' position in *Kelly v Morris*.[45] This case involved a postal directory, where the defendant used the entries from the plaintiff's work as the basis of his own directory. He hired clerks to independently verify names and addresses were correct, but acknowledged that clerks sent to verify entries had been negligent and simply ticked as correct the plaintiff's entries instead and these were then cut and pasted by the defendant into his work. In finding a copyright infringement had occurred, Sir W Page Wood VC said,

> He must map the milestones for himself. He is not entitled to take one word of the information previously published without independently working out the matter for himself.[46]

However the view that 'he must not take one word' is very much at odds with the weight of nineteenth century case law.

While *Kelly v Morris* was supported in *Morris v Ashbee*,[47] both of these decisions were substantially pared down in *Morris v Wright*. Of the opinion

[37] *Spiers v Brown* [1858] Ch 6 WR 352, 352.
[38] *Collis v Cater* 78 LT 613 [Ch 1898] 615.
[39] *Matthewson v Stockdale* 33 Eng Rep 103 [Ch 1806].
[40] *Roworth v Wilkes* 107 Eng Rep 889 [KB 1807].
[41] *Jarrold v Houlston* [1857] 3 K7J 708.
[42] *Scott v Stanford* (1867) LR 3 Eq 718.
[43] *Walter v Steinkopff* [1892] 3 Ch 489.
[44] *Leslie v Young* [1894] AC 335 HL.
[45] *Kelly v Morris* [1866] Law Rep 1 Eq 697.
[46] Ibid, 701.
[47] *Morris v Ashbee* [1868] 7 Eq 34.

in *Kelly v Morris* that 'the Defendant could not take a single line of the Plaintiff's directory for the purpose of saving himself labour and trouble in getting this information', Giffard LJ said:

> I cannot doubt that [this passage] goes beyond what the law authorizes, and beyond the decision of the Lord Chancellor and myself in the late case of *Pike v Nicholas*.[48]

Sir Giffard LJ went on to say that the defendant is not precluded from using the plaintiff's work as the reference point to start the defendant's work. It is perfectly legitimate to use that as a guide and then compile another work with reference to the original work. However the relevant inquiry is not about the effort or input by the plaintiff in creating the first work and protecting that, but is directed to assessing the legitimacy of the use of the work by the defendant.

Unprotected Works

There is also a line of authority that suggests some works do not qualify for protection at all for want of originality. For example, in *Leslie v Young & Sons* Lord Herschell suggests:

> The mere publication in any particular order of the time-tables which are to be found in railway guides and the publications of the different railway companies could not be claimed as a subject-matter of copyright. Proceedings could not be taken against a person who merely published that information which it was open to all the world to publish and to obtain from the same source.[49]

This view was endorsed in *Cramp Ltd v Frank Smythson Ltd,* with Viscount Simon suggesting that:

> There would, indeed, as it seems to me, be considerable difficulty in successfully contending that ordinary tables which can be got from, or checked by, the postal guide or the Nautical Almanac are a subject of copyright as being an original literary work. One of the essential qualities of such tables is that they should be accurate, so that there is no question of variation in what is stated. The sun does in fact rise, and the moon set, at times which have been calculated ... There is so far no room for taste or judgment. ... There was no feature of them which could be pointed out as novel or specially meritorious or ingenious from the point of view of the judgment or skill of the compiler. [50]

With *Leslie v Young* the discussion went to an assessment of the independent labour of the plaintiff and the defendant, with an emphasis that in these kinds of compilation cases there would need to be a substantial appropriation to justify proceedings. However in *Cramp & Sons v Smythson*,

[48] *Morris v Wright* [1870] LR Vol 5 279, 285.
[49] *Leslie v Young & Sons* [1894] AC 335 (HL) 340.
[50] *Cramp Ltd v Frank Smythson Ltd* [1944] AC 329, 336.

referring to the principles of the 1911 Act, and endorsing the need to consider the 'fact and degree' of originality, both Viscount Simon LC and Lord Macmillan suggest that commonplace and factual information would be exceedingly difficult to protect, notwithstanding how convenient or useful the information might be.[51]

Arguably the Australian case *Victoria Park Racing and Recreation Grounds Co Ltd v Taylor* follows this line of authority. Protection was denied to the compilation of horse racing details written on a display board on the grounds. Dixon J argued:

> some original result must be produced. This does not mean that new or inventive ideas must be contributed. The work need show no literary or other skill or judgment. But ... the material for the board consists in the actual allotment of places and other arrangements made by the plaintiff's company's officers in respect of the horses. To fit in on the notice board the names and figures which will display this information for a short time does not appear to me to make an original literary work.[52]

Likewise Latham CJ said:

> The law of copyright does not operate to give any person an exclusive right to state or to describe particular facts. A person cannot by first announcing that a man fell off a bus or that a particular horse won a race prevent other people from stating those facts.[53]

In *Victoria Park* the creation of the facts did not give rise to proprietary rights to that information. Similar cases that deny protection range from simple lists of competitors, to more complex 'facts', such as starting prices and betting odds.[54]

Notwithstanding these decisions,[55] awarding some level of protection to very pedestrian subject matter does not trouble the majority of nineteenth century cases. The more important and controversial question was what level of protection is deserved?

Abridgments

Abridgments were accepted as legitimate in the eighteenth century because they were 'stand alone' works of benefit to readers:

[51] In support they cite *Macmillan & Co Ltd v K & J Cooper* (1923) LR 51 Ind App 109; 93 LJ (PC) 113.

[52] *Victoria Park Racing and Recreation Grounds Co Ltd v Taylor* (1937) 58 CLR 479, 511.

[53] Ibid, 498.

[54] See S Ricketson, *The Law of Intellectual Property* (Sydney, Law Book Co, 1984) [5.19], *Chilton v Progress Printing & Publishing Co* [1895] 2 Ch 28 (CA); *Smith's Newspapers Ltd v The Labour Daily* (1925) 25 SR (NSW) 593; *Greyhound Racing Association Led v Shallis* [1923–28] MacG Cop Cas 370 (Ch D); *Odham Press Ltd v London & Provincial Sporting News Agency Ltd* [1935] Ch 672.

[55] There are additional nineteenth century UK examples available.

> The design of an abridgment is to benefit mankind by facilitating the attainment of knowledge ...[56]

This position was refined in the nineteenth century. David Vaver notes that 'the mantle of "benefactor to mankind, by assisting in the diffusion of knowledge" largely slipped off the abridger's shoulders by the early 20th century'.[57] He argues that non-infringing abridgments were confined to published literary and dramatic works, the question being resolved to whether the abridgement was a merely colourable piracy or 'fair'.[58]

Interestingly, Vaver's analysis extended to abstracts. He cites two decisions from the colonial Victorian court. This is arguably the first ever reference to Australian colonial law in academic literature where our law is treated as if it were a relevant authority beyond the borders of that colony.[59]

Fair Use

The majority of nineteenth century cases were not ungenerous in awarding protection to original works, but the bulk of the inquiry turns on what is 'fair use' and a 'legitimate taking'.

Formulations of this test include:

In relation to road maps:

> That part of the work of one auther [*sic*] is found in another, is not of itself piracy, or sufficient to support an action; a man may fairly adopt part of the work of another : he may so make use of another's labours for the promotion of science, and the benefit of the public: but having done so, the question will be, Was the matter taken used fairly with that view (to the promotion of science and benefit of the public) and without what I may term the animus furandi?[60]

With respect to descriptions of antiquity:

> The question upon the whole is, whether this is a legitimate use of the Plaintiff's publication in the fair exercise of a mental operation, deserving the character of an original work.[61]

In a case involving appropriation of coal statistics:

> The general principles guiding the Court in cases of this description could hardly be found better stated than in the works of Mr Justice Story in *Folsom v Marsh*,

[56] Samuel Johnson, as cited in D Vaver, 'Abridgements and Abstracts: Copyright Implications' [1995] 5 EIPR 225; Ricketson (n 54)[5.57].

[57] Vaver, ibid 226, citing *Tinsley v Lace* [1864] 1 H & M 747, 754.

[58] I return to his analysis below.

[59] There is also, of course, the encyclopaedic and extraordinarily rich book by Ricketson (n 54).

[60] *Cary v Kearsley* 170 Eng Rep 679 [KB 1802].

[61] *Wilkins v Aiken* [1810] 17 Ves Jun 424 at 426. Cited as authority in *Bramwell v Halcomb* [1836] 3 My & Cr 736.

> cited in Mr *Palmer Phillips'* Treatise on Copyright:- "In short, we must, in deciding questions of this sort, look to the nature and objects of the selections made, and the degree to which the use may prejudice the sale, or diminish the profits, or supercede the objects, of the original work."[62]

The earliest expression of 'fair use' is probably in *Sayres v Moore*.[63] Apart from the other above-mentioned cases, other formulations stressing the significance attached to producing a new work include *Carnan v Bowles*,[64] *Mawman v Tegg*,[65] *Martin v Wright*,[66] *D'Alamaine v Boosey*,[67] *Spiers v Brown*,[68] *Leslie v Young & Sons*,[69] *Hanfstaengl v Baines*,[70] *McCrum v Eisner*.[71]

Recently some authors have suggested that the fair use defence was created by the courts and then confined throughout the latter course of the nineteenth century.[72] However given the bounty of references to its role throughout the entire century, there is little evidence in support of there having been a significant policy shift away from fair use. Copinger for example, says of the 'Principles by which piracy is judged',

> The inquiry in most cases, is not, whether the defendant has used the thoughts, conceptions, information and discoveries promulgated by the original, but whether his composition may be considered a *new work*, requiring invention, learning and judgment, or only a mere transcript of the whole or parts of the original, with mere colourable variations.[73]

His second and third editions restate this original formulation. Likewise Scrutton states the principle regulating infringement as this:

> Whenever a substantial part of an author's copyright work is reproduced without his authority, whether alone or in conjunction with new matter, whether by the same or a different channel to the original, so as to damage the sale of such original work, and thus lessen the original author's return for his work, such reproduction is an infringement of copyright.[74]

There does not appear to be any critical reference to 'fair use' or suggestion that its role need be pared back in these treatises at all. There is however

[62] *Scott v Stanford* [1867] LR Vol 3 718, 722. Citations omitted.
[63] *Sayres v Moore* 102 Eng Rep 139n [KB 1785].
[64] *Carnan v Bowles* 29 Eng Rep 45 [Ch 1786].
[65] *Mawman v Tegg* [1826] 2 Russ 385.
[66] *Martin v Wright* 58 Eng Rep 605 (Ch 1833).
[67] *D'Alamaine v Boosey* 160 Eng Rep 117 [Ex 1835].
[68] *Spiers v Brown* [1858] 6 WR 352.
[69] *Leslie v Young & Sons* [1894] AC 335 HL.
[70] *Hanfstaengl v Baines* [1895] AC 20.
[71] *McCrum v Eisner* [1918] 87 LJ Ch 99.
[72] See R Burrell and A Coleman, *Copyright Exceptions: The Digital Impact* (Cambridge, Cambridge University Press, 2005) 253–55.
[73] Copinger (n 12) 87.
[74] Scrutton (n 9) §52, 52–53.

confirmation that the relevant inquiry is into a comparison of the market for the two works.

With fair use there was more involved than simply equating 'originality' with the plaintiff's effort and protecting that contribution. A finding of 'piracy' was reserved for the cases where there was no public interest being served by the defendant's taking. The pirate was one whose copying failed to bring forth a 'new work'. As the servile copy would generally be sold cheaper than the plaintiff's work, with a significant part of the associated labour costs having been paid for by the plaintiff, it imperiled access to new works, by providing a disincentive for further investment in such productions. For servile copies, there was little benefit to the public to be gained from re-publication by another source. But where the defendant had produced more than a servile copy, the assessment was far more complicated. This is why so many of the nineteenth century cases discuss the effect of the alleged piracy on the market for the original work. If the works were in competition, it was highly likely that the copying would be deemed unfair. But if there was another purpose in play, the defendant's taking may have been excused.[75]

In the nineteenth century the copyright balance between protection and access was not seen as simply a case of arbitrating between competing private rights. It was not simply a matter of determining if a substantial part had been taken. When sensitivity to private property claims might be expected to be uppermost in judicial minds, it was not axiomatic that protection of original effort or investment would be the paramount concern. Deciding what was to be protected, and what use of another's work was permitted, involved broad considerations into the social purpose served by copyright. These policy factors influenced how the line between protection and legitimate use was drawn.

Some case analysis, such as Vaver's aforementioned analysis of abridgment and Ronan Deazley's recent work on derivatives,[76] suggests that over the nineteenth century greater weight was given to protection of the plaintiff's rights, and a corresponding subordination of concern for fair use. As the century progressed, takings were more likely presumed to have a significant market impact, and as such be considered as piracy. I do not dispute this interpretation. There are clearly many authorities that support

[75] See eg *Roworth v Wilkes* [1807] 1 Camp 94 (notion of 'substitute work'); *Mawman v Tegg* [1826] 2 Russ 358 (distinction between a new work and robbing the former author); *D'Almaine and Another v Boosey* [1835] 1 Y & C Ex 297 (adaptation of music); *Bell v Whitehead* [1839] Ch 8 LJ (NS) Ch 141 (taking justified as criticism); *Scott v Stanford* [1867] LR Vol 3, 718 (prejudice to sales); *Spiers v Brown* [1857] Ch 6 W R 352 (unacknowledged taking but different result achieved and alterations not colourably made).

[76] R Deazley, 'Breaking the Mould? The Radical Nature of the Fine Art Copyright Bill 1862' in R Deazley, M Kretschmer and L Bently (eds) *Privilege And Property: Essays On The History Of Copyright* (Cambridge, Open Book, 2009).

this conclusion, especially in relation to the more pedestrian copyright subject matter. However I think one needs to take care to separate the formulation of the test of infringement, from the application of it. As noted in relation to the early treatises, as late as the 1890s, fair use and the notion of public interest broadly described, have significant presence and apparent work to do in relation to the formulation of the legal test for piracy.

The importance of reference to the public interest in assessing the nature of the right and wrong can be seen from *Walter v Lane*. This case is particularly important because, as a consequence of its unusual facts, the central issue in the case was whether intellectual effort is a prerequisite for copyright protection of a work.[77]

The case involved whether copyright could subsist in a speech given by Lord Rosebery, where the speaker had not sought to protect his oratory. A journalist from *The Times* newspaper had transcribed Lord Rosebery's speech. *The Times* claimed to own copyright in the speech by virtue of a copyright arising from the act of transcribing it. They sought to restrain another publisher from copying 'their' text. Unlike the usual circumstance of competition between an originator of an expression and an alleged copier, here the issue is that of bare subsistence of copyright. If the transcription of another's speech gives rise to a copyright, the defendant has no legal excuse for copying it verbatim.

Walter v Lane has been recently interpreted as supporting the proposition that intellectual effort is not a requirement for copyright.[78] However, drawing this conclusion from the case is problematic.

Lord Halsbury reasoned that the particular words of the Copyright Act 1842[79] awarded protection to the producer of a written composition. The statute was not interested in 'the proprietary right of every man to his own literary compositions'. If copyright was not about 'authors' and their natural entitlements, it did not matter that the reporters simply recorded another's speech.[80] Lord Halsbury and Lord Davey then agreed that, by way of analogy to other copyright cases, if a person who compiled a street directory could be an author, so could a reporter. To find otherwise would sanction 'reaping without sowing'.

Lord James of Hereford thought something more than 'mere mechanical transcribing' was necessary for protection, but through the art of shorthand an intellectual component had been present in the reporter's copy of the speech. The reporter was more than a mere scribe, and so his work should

[77] *Walter v Lane* [1900] AC 539 (HL). Hereafter *Walter.*

[78] *Telstra Corporation Ltd v Desktop Marketing Systems Pty Ltd* [2001] FCA 612 [55]: 'the view of the majority of the Lords shows that intellectual effort was not regarded as a requirement for copyright'.

[79] Copyright Act 1842 (5 & 6 Vict c 45).

[80] *Walter* (n 77), 547–48.

be protected. Lord Brampton also agreed that the reporter's skill went beyond the mere mechanical operation of writing. Lord Robertson however, thought there had been little more than accurate transcribing in this case and that this was insufficient to protect the reporter's work.

In terms of addressing the principle of whether an intellectual input was necessary in copyright or not, three of the five judges (two majority, one minority view) actually thought intellectual effort was required in copyright. This was noted by Isaac J in *Sands & McDougall Pty Ltd v Robinson*.[81] In discussing the significance of *Walter*, his Honour rejected the defendant's contention that 'inventive skill' in terms of requiring novel and distinctive features was now required, as a consequence of acceding to the Berne Convention.

Walter also addressed the various policy objectives of copyright law. Halsbury LC noted that, in addition to the 'grievous injustice' that would follow if the defendant were permitted to appropriate 'what has been produced by the skill, labour and capital of another',[82]

> An importer of a foreign inventor is for the purpose of patent laws an inventor, and, as Lord Broughton said in *re Berry's patent*, there were 'two species of public benefactors—the one, those who benefit the public by their ingenuity, industry, and science and invention and personal capability; the other, those who benefit the public without any ingenuity or invention of their own, by the appropriation of the results of foreign inventions. Now the latter is a benefit to the public incontestably' ... I might paraphrase Lord Broughton's language by asking whether those who preserve the memory of spoken words, which are assumed to be of value to the public, are not entitled to a merit analogous to that which Lord Broughton attributes to the importer of foreign inventions?[83]

Lord Brampton also felt a copyright was justified so that the wisdom of Lord Rosebery, who had chosen not to publish his own speech, would be made available to the public.

Here the text deserves protection, as of natural right flowing from *The Times'* expenditure of labour, but also because such protection supports the public interest, as determined by the conventions of that time.[84] 'Appropriations' are legally sanctioned or not, depending upon the status of the source of the work and the public benefits that flow from the appropriation. In this case, *The Times* is to be rewarded for recording for posterity 'speeches being of great interest to the public'.[85]

[81] *Sands & McDougall Pty Ltd v Robinson* (1917) 23 CLR 49, 54.
[82] *Walter* (n 77), 545.
[83] *Walter* (n 77), 549.
[84] For a lengthier discussion see K Bowrey, 'Don't Fence Me In: The Many Histories of Copyright' (SJD thesis, University of Sydney, 1994), ch 6, 'The judicial construction of author as owner'.
[85] Lord James of Hereford, *Walter* (n 77), 553.

Thus the decision to protect the author's private right or not remained largely a matter of public policy. Protection was justified in the name of the national economic and social good served. It is this sense of 'balance', measured with respect to an assessment of how the public interest is best served, that has largely been lost in the retelling of the nineteenth century law today.

Why the Confusion over Case Law Principles?

Most of the nineteenth century case law revolves around claims for injunctive relief.[86] Decisions do not usually clearly separate out statements of law and findings of fact. Further, in relation to any inquiry into piracy, Copinger affirms 'so entirely must each case be governed and regulated by the particular circumstances attending it, that *any general rule on the subject must be received with extreme caution*' (emphasis added).[87]

Whilst the question of infringement frequently entailed a balanced consideration of the original efforts of both parties in a marketplace for informational works, the facts were often incomplete.

In many of the cases it was felt that the available evidence did not permit award of an injunction, or sustain maintaining the original injunction, because there had been no clear identification of the exact extent and context of the taking. As more was often needed to succeed than simply averting to the presence of some taking of the plaintiff's work in the work of the defendant's, and because it was commonly argued that there should be no enjoining of publication of the parts that were the defendant's original work, the matter was very often sent for arbitration or to common law juries.[88] From that point on, legal records do not reveal how matters were ultimately resolved.

These factors make appreciating the subtlety of the nineteenth century court difficult. However the problems are compounded when these cases are approached with twentieth century jurisprudential constructions in mind. It is no wonder that the older cases appear confusing or uncertain about the role of originality once originality comes to be constructed as primarily a 'subsistence' issue and infringement is dissociated from consideration of the defendant's originality.

[86] For an interesting discussion of the historical role of injunctions in literary property see Gomez-Arostegui (n 8).

[87] WA Copinger, *The Law of Copyright in Works of Literature and Art: including that of the drama, music, engraving, sculpture, painting, photography, and ...* 3rd edn (London, 1893) 193.

[88] See for example, *Mawman v Tegg* [1826] 2 Russ 358; *Jarrold v Houston* [1857] Ch 3 Kay & J 707.

The Unanticipated Change Effected Through Legislative Drafting

One of the biggest changes to the role of originality comes about as a consequence of the rewriting of the Copyright Act 1911 (UK). As noted above, this codification was not heralded as bringing any substantial change to the law. However in the new legislation, originality came to be considered as a requirement in its own right: copyright subsists in every *original* literary work.[89] This formulation directs the question of originality to the plaintiff's efforts alone.

The 1911 Act's shift from fair use to enumerated fair dealing rights compounds the problem. Whilst Burrell notes that while the evidence of what the 1911 fair dealing provisions were supposed to achieve is limited, it 'suggests that Parliament did not intend the introduction of the fair dealing provision to mark the start of a more restrictive or less flexible approach to the copyright exceptions.'[90] It was supposed to be a codification of existing law, and not a strategic reorganisation of basic precepts that shifted the copyright balance. But the outcome of these legislative reforms was that, as a matter of statutory interpretation, the originality requirement slowly came to be read as a question of subsistence of right and as a reference to the plaintiff's work alone, and then there is a separate consideration as to whether the defendant had any available 'defences'.

We now understand originality as primarily a requirement of the plaintiff and no longer see it as involving the relational issues of the past. Further our test has come to be much more narrowly defined:

> The originality which is required relates to the expression of the thought. But the Act does not require that the expression must be in an original or novel form, but that the work must not be copied from another work—that it should originate from the author.[91]

In keeping with the move toward a more positivistic and objective approach to law, the attempt was to define originality without reference to the original work's value in scientific or aesthetic terms. The answer which suggested itself to the judge was to focus on the 'material fact' of the creation of an expression by the plaintiff, drawing on the significance of the act of making the writing, and not tying that to a requirement for any special manner of writing. That in this case the exam papers drew on the common stock of

[89] Originality had been a requirement under the Sculpture Copyright Act 1814, 54 Geo III, c 56; Copyright Designs Act 1842, 5 & 6 Vict, c 100; and the Fine Arts Copyright Act 1862, 25 & 26 Vict, c 68. See R Deazley, 'Commentary on Fine Arts Copyright Act 1862', in L Bently and M Kretschmer (eds), *Primary Sources on Copyright* (1450–1900) (www.copyrighthistory.org, 2008) [10].

[90] 'All that is done here is to make a plain declaration of what the law is and to put all copyright works under the same wording': Hansard HL 1911, vol X col 117; Burrell (n 72) 257.

[91] *University of London Press Ltd v University Tutorial Press Ltd* [1916] 2 Ch 601.

knowledge and were commonplace did not mean they were not protected. The plaintiffs had not copied them from anywhere, but had written them themselves. Thus they were entitled to protection of an original literary work. Originality is now largely dispensed with as a question of subsistence of copyright, judged without reference to the significance or intrinsic value of the plaintiff's expression to the world at large. This approach means that 'originality' ends up being a reference mainly to what it is not. It does not require inventiveness, novelty, high creativity and so on.

The historic significance of originality as a relational concept and as involving questions of public policy begins to be lost from this point. Consideration of the defendant's work now only appears in the context of defences to infringement—in relation to whether or not an alleged taking of the plaintiff's work is 'substantial', given the changes that the defendant may have made to that work. It also comes to be accepted that the originality of the defendant in creating a new work is no obstacle to a finding of infringement.[92]

The statutory construction of the plaintiff's rights and copyright 'exceptions' in the 1911 Act has placed the defendant at a much greater disadvantage than in the nineteenth century. However there is nothing to suggest that this was considered to be a likely or desired outcome of the codification.

An additional level of disadvantage to the defendant was then imposed by the Copyright Act 1956 (UK) and followed by the Copyright Act 1968 (Cth). It was negatively commented on by the Spicer Committee 1959[93] that, compared with the Copyright Act 1911 (UK) (in force in Australia by virtue of the Copyright Act 1912 (Cth)), the drafting of the 1956 Act had created an unprecedented focus on the enumerated 'exclusive rights' of the owner. This drafting change 'directs the mind *to the* infringer—to the things which must not be done without the owner's consent—rather than to the owner and what is comprised in his ownership'.[94]

Subsequently in calculating the merits of awarding protection, the formulation of originality from *University of London Press Ltd v University Tutorial Press Ltd* has come to take on a quite different policy implication. The phrase 'that the work must not be copied from another work—that it should originate from the author' has now come to be read not only in terms of assessing the subsistence of copyright in the plaintiff's work. It has come to influence consideration of the status of the defendant's work. This leads to the endorsement of the *University of London* test in *Ladbroke (Football) Ltd v William Hill (Football) Ltd* that 'as regards infringement … I think

[92] *A-One Accessory Imports Pty Ltd v Off Road Imports Ltd* (1996) 34 IPR 306.
[93] Copyright Law Review Committee, *Report to Consider what Alterations are Desirable in Copyright Law of the Commonwealth* (Commonwealth of Australia, 1959).
[94] Ibid [24].

there is much wisdom in the reference by Peterson J to the 'rough practical test that what is worth copyright is prima facie worth protecting'.[95]

This development heralds the arrival of, historically speaking, a very significant change in copyright policy. What started out in *University of London Press* as a definition of originality that primarily addressed the status of the plaintiff's original work, has ended up literally framing the defendant's effort. This shift signifies a revival of the previously discredited position of *Kelly v Morris*.[96] It is worth noting that the High Court recently strongly criticised this development.[97]

Notwithstanding that, originality is now mainly considered in terms of assessing the plaintiff's work, and in terms of a far more limited inquiry than would have occurred in the nineteenth century. This was not a consequence of a deliberate policy shift behind the legislation concerning the comparative weight to be accorded to the defendant's efforts. It was not the case that the originality of the plaintiff was to be considered as a more important issue than the defendant's originality. It comes from the logic produced by the structure of the twentieth century statutes, combined with judicial anxiety in assessing the respective 'worth' of the plaintiff's and the defendant's products. The reason we need to better appreciate the legal history of the nineteenth century is to remain alert to the implications of what probably seemed like relatively innocuous changes to the wording of legislation engineered by copyright functionaries, with no political authority to transform the fundamental character of the law.

SOME IMPLICATIONS

When originality and infringement used to appear together as a matter of the legal inquiry, policy considerations in drawing the balance either way were transparent. The originality of one party was generally considered in light of the originality of the other. The worth of both efforts was considered in relation to each other, and reference to the community interest often explicitly informed that evaluation. With the new reordering and apparent separation into originality then infringement in the twentieth century, there is a policy shift in support of the plaintiff's often meagre claims to originality, at the expense of an equal consideration of the defendant's claim.

[95] *University of London Press Ltd* (n 91) quoted with approval in *Ladbroke (Football) Ltd v William Hill (Football) Ltd* [1964] 1 WLR 273, 279 (Lord Reid), 288 (Lord Hodson), 293–94 (Lord Pearce).

[96] [1866] Law Rep 1 Eq 697.

[97] *Network Ten Pty Ltd v Channel Nine Pty Ltd* [2004] HCA 14; 27 TCL 16/3; 218 CLR 273; 205 ALR 1; 78 ALJR 585 [14–17]; *IceTV Pty Limited v Nine Network Australia Pty Limited* [2009] HCA 14 [31], [70].

Of even greater consequence than this unaccountable weighting in favour of one of two competing private rights, is the loss of a space for a proper judicial consideration of the public interest in drawing the balance between protection and access. A fair consideration of the pre-eminent policy issue in copyright, the public interest in creating the rights, is pre-empted by the presumption of the public good in protecting the plaintiff's effort under the auspices of 'originality'. In this context it is difficult to address broader justifications for accessing and reproducing part of a plaintiff's work in terms beyond the specifics of the actions of the defendant and the narrow confines of our fair dealing provisions.

This major shift in the politics of the law remains obscured by the continuing emphasis on the requirement that originality be tested as a matter of 'fact and degree'. By using this empirical explanation for decisions, past cases can continue to be explained and differentiated with reference to their specific facts, rather than having to confront their different politics. Further the suggestion remains that some works may still be rejected because of the minimal effort involved, when this is most unlikely to be the case.

It is possible to dress up the most unlikely contributions as meaningful in copyright terms, because of the failure to set a benchmark against which the plaintiff's contributions can be assessed. For example in the Australian case *Kalamazoo*, Thomas J says of accounting forms, which until recently had never been considered in the industry as worthy of protection:

> ... whilst I refuse to find that the authors showed great skill, I do find that their preparation required a degree of concentration, care, analysis, comparison, and a certain facility in using and adapting the altered forms to a composite one-write system. In each use, some awareness of contemporary developments and the marketability of such forms played a part in their creation. Looking at each system as expressed, there is sufficient originality of expression, shape and content to comprise an original literary work.[98]

If identifying a market, initiating product development and overseeing a very pedestrian execution of the stages essential for manufacturing the particular product can form a significant part of the 'originality' of the compilation work and hence justify its protection, it is hard to think how any commodity could fail the test, outside of apparent negligence in design. If the test really were one of 'fact and degree', the benchmark would refer to the ordinary practice in that industry. But even in *Kalamazoo*, Thomas J sought to bolster the merits of protection by claiming that these blank accounting forms 'in the end, ... have their own character, their own form of expression, and in a sense tell their own story to the user'.[99] Uncertain

[98] *Kalamazoo (Australia) Pty Ltd v Compact Business Systems Pty Ltd* (1985) 5 IPR 213, 237.

[99] *Kalamazoo* (n 98), 238. See also K Bowrey, 'The Outer Limits of Copyright Law' (2001) 12(1) *Law and Critique* 1–24.

that something so pedestrian really deserved protection, he resorted to a rather incredulous assertion that blank forms inherently conveyed meaningful expression.

Interestingly, in the recent High Court decision *IceTV*,[100] concerning copyright in television programme guides, there is no mention of *Kalamazoo*. The court did however emphasise the importance of connecting the original authorial contribution to the form of expression of the copyright work, and as such business considerations would need to impact on the specific form of expression adopted. It was noted:

> Rewarding skill and labour in respect of compilations without any real consideration of the productive effort directed to coming up with a particular form of expression of information can lead to error. The error is of a kind which might enable copyright law to be employed to achieve anti-competitive behaviour of a sort not contemplated by the balance struck in the Act between the rights of authors and the entitlements of the reading public.[101] (Footnote omitted.)

However there is scant treatment altogether of authorities on originality in *IceTV*: 'in the light of the admission of Ice that the Weekly Schedule was an original literary work, this is not an appropriate occasion to take any further the subject of originality in copyright works.'[102] As such, *IceTV* offers little direct guidance for reconciling difficulties over precedent and the requirement of originality, as touched on above.

Indirectly, the High Court's focus on the *plaintiff's originality* as part of the test of infringement does move the spirit of Australian law closer toward half of the deliberation that may have occurred in infringement proceedings in the nineteenth century. In this case, a low level of skill and labour led to limited protection being available to headings and facts as laid out in the Channel Nine programme guides and the circumstances did not support a finding of infringement. Inter alia, *IceTV* also offers some grounds for optimism with the acknowledgement of the importance of recognising:

> the longstanding theoretical underpinnings of copyright legislation. Copyright legislation strikes a balance of competing interests and competing policy considerations. Relevantly, it is concerned with rewarding authors of original literary works with commercial benefits having regard to the fact that literary works in turn benefit the reading public.[103] (Footnote omitted.)

However 'balance' is presumed implicit in the application of existing copyright tests rather than serving as an overarching criteria or limit to rights.

[100] *IceTV Pty Limited v Nine Network Australia Pty Limited* [2009] HCA 14. An earlier version of this chapter was cited in the amicus submission by Australian Digital Alliance (No S415 of 2008). The decision has been subsequently applied. See *Telstra Corporation Ltd v Phone Directories Company Pty Ltd* [2010] FCA 44. On Appeal.

[101] French CJ, Crennan and Kiefel JJ, *IceTV* (n 100) [52].

[102] Gummow, Hayne and Heydon JJ, *IceTV* (n 100) [88].

[103] French CJ, Crennan and Kiefel JJ, *IceTV* (n 100) [24].

As such, 'balance' remains present in the life of the law, but with no need to articulate what the public interest specifically comprises or how 'balance' is maintained in any given scenario.

CONCLUSION

It remains common for judges and copyright scholars alike to delve into the past and claim nineteenth century case law in support of contemporary readings of originality criterion. References to the nineteenth century law are used by academics to justify twenty-first century rejections of fair use doctrine,[104] and to ground claims about the erosion of the public domain.[105] This reflection on the nineteenth century case law suggests that unless significant care is taken, use of nineteenth century precedent will only lead to obfuscation, hiding a significant legal transformation that took hold in copyright across the twentieth century.

It could be argued that the nineteenth century approach was so different to what we now know, that it should not be relied upon today as authority in copyright at all. However were we to read this history in this way, it would create impossibly difficult and fundamental questions about the origins of our law. Whilst superficially we could turn to the 1911 Act, this legislation did not intend to break with the past. It was not subsequently interpreted as if it instated new principles, rights or interests. To pragmatically invent a new origin in order to distance us from an inconvenient historical record, brings forth serious questions about the role and relevance of the common law altogether.

For Australians, the presumption of a monolithic Anglo common law has led to a suppression of interest in and understanding of our colonial legal history. It has contributed to a culture where we have failed to take full ownership of the development of our common law. It has led to the stifling of discussion about the public interests at stake in copyright. For these reasons we need to move far beyond de-politicised abstractions about the continuity of the common law and more openly debate the value of precedent today. This creates a challenge—to address the forgotten wisdom of our legal history, we need to critically reconsider the sources of law and the methodologies appropriate to Australian legal reasoning in the twenty-first century. We need to redefine a legal culture that is no longer embraced or held together by Empire, but one that is appropriate to a nation that is self-consciously and actively part of the global marketplace. This does not require abandonment of the common law, nor of legal continuity, but it does require judges and scholars to reason differently to how many do now.

[104] Burrell and Coleman (n 72) 253ff.

[105] Deazley (n 8).

The 'humble grey' of the nineteenth century was, on the whole, much more reflective about the issues at stake in copyright than we are in case law today. They were much more willing to confront the relativity of interests, the balance to be struck, and most importantly, to consider the community interest to be served by protection and in gaining access to new works and products. Losing this discourse was, it would seem, something no one deliberately sought to bring about in the twentieth century. Thus what remains to be considered is our ability, and our responsibility, to redress this undesirable development.

Court Practices

4

The Relationship between UK Common Law and the European Systems in the Context of Res Judicata

HENRY CARR

INTRODUCTION

THE DOCTRINE OF *res judicata* is a common law development, founded upon basic policy considerations. Where a litigant has fought and lost, there should not be an opportunity to re-litigate an issue which was, or ought to have been, raised and decided in that litigation. Otherwise, the successful party would be required to fight the same battle again, and the unsuccessful party would be given a second bite of the cherry. This is not only unfair to the successful litigant, but also contrary to the efficient administration of justice. These considerations are counterbalanced by the need to ensure that the opposite party is not prevented from being heard unless this is a just result. Further, the principles of *res judicata* cannot displace a statutory scheme which contemplates re-litigation of issues in different proceedings.

These competing arguments are easy to express. However, the law of *res judicata* is far from simple. It has become bedevilled by difficult classifications of different types of *res judicata*—cause of action estoppel, issue estoppel and abuse of process. This difficulty is compounded in patent and trade mark cases, where it is necessary to reconcile the common law principles, not only with domestic legislation, but also with the international conventions, directives and regulations which such legislation is intended to implement.

This chapter considers the interplay between the international conventions and EU directives specific to intellectual property, and the domestic common law principles. It is submitted that the results of recent UK decisions in this area may be regarded as lacking consistency. It is also suggested that, in relation to the application of *res judicata* in patent cases, the UK may be out of step with other EU member states, and other common law jurisdictions.

The problem arises from two recent decisions of the Court of Appeal, *Special Effects v L'Oreal SA*[1] and *Unilin Beheer BV v Berry Floor NV*.[2] In *Special Effects*, L'Oreal SA unsuccessfully opposed in the Trade Marks Registry an application for the trade mark SPECIAL EFFECTS. It chose not to appeal the decision of the Hearing Officer, and the mark proceeded to grant. About two and a half years after the conclusion of the opposition, L'Oreal SA and its UK affiliate were sued for infringement of the SPECIAL EFFECTS registration. They denied infringement and claimed in the alternative that if the mark was infringed, then it was invalid. In support of invalidity, they sought to raise the same grounds as had been rejected in the opposition proceedings. The Court of Appeal decided that *res judicata* did not apply. A key part of the Court's reasoning was that the co-existence in the Trade Marks Act 1994 of provisions for opposition before grant, and for a declaration of invalidity after grant, had the result that the opposition proceedings were inherently not a final decision on the validity of the granted registration. In other words, the statute showed an intention to exclude the principles of *res judicata*. The Court relied on recent decisions of the Federal Court of Australia, where the same conclusion had been reached under a similar legislative regime.

In *Unilin* a European patent (UK) had been found valid and infringed by the High Court and the Court of Appeal. However, the first defendant's holding company, Berry Finance NV, was an opponent in EPO proceedings concerning the validity of the European patent which were pending before the Board of Appeal[3]. Accordingly the defendants submitted that validity could not be *res judicata*, since it had not been finally determined. However, the Court of Appeal decided:

1. that the question of validity (and resulting issues of infringement if the opposition resulted in amendment) had been finally determined by the UK courts, and was therefore *res judicata*; and
2. any revocation or limitation of the European patent (UK) by the Technical Board of Appeal in the EPO would be irrelevant to the award of damages or an account of profits in the UK action.

[1] *Special Effects v L'Oreal SA* [2007] RPC 15.

[2] *Unilin Beheer BV v Berry Floor NV* [2007] FSR 25.

[3] The defendants contended that there was no relevant distinction between Berry Finance NV and the first defendant. Berry Finance NV had guaranteed any damages or profits that might have been awarded against the first defendant. As further recorded by the judge at first instance, the first defendant was treated by the parties as if it were an opponent in the EPO.

This judgment sits uneasily with the *Special Effects* case. The Patents Act 1977 and the European Patent Convention contemplate two routes to invalidating a European patent, either in domestic proceedings, or in the EPO. Neither is mutually exclusive, and both can be taken simultaneously. Accordingly, until both routes have been exhausted, it appears contrary to the intention of the legislation to conclude that the validity of the European patent has been finally determined. As a matter of reality, validity has not been finally determined whilst the European opposition is continuing. Further, it may be suggested that the decision has a surprising and unjust consequence. If an opposition succeeds in the EPO, the patent is retrospectively revoked in all designated Convention countries. Yet in the UK, the patentee can be awarded damages in respect of infringement of a property right which is deemed never to have existed. This may be regarded as inconsistent with the grant of a 'basket' of rights, intended to have the same effect in all designated jurisdictions. The result is unlikely to promote a consistent approach with other European jurisdictions, where the EPO is seen as the supreme and final arbiter of the validity of European patents.[4]

THE *SPECIAL EFFECTS* CASE

At first instance,[5] Chancellor Morritt held, in determining certain preliminary issues, that both defendants were precluded by cause of action estoppel and issue estoppel from challenging the validity of the SPECIAL EFFECTS registered trade mark in their defence and counterclaim to infringement. He considered that the issue of validity of the mark, and the sub-issue of its distinctiveness, had already been raised and decided in the opposition proceedings, and there was no reason why L'Oreal should be allowed to relitigate those matters.

Accordingly, the appeal raised the fundamental question of whether participation in an opposition to an application for registration prior to grant precluded challenges to validity by the opponent in respect of the granted registration; and if so, whether this bar extended to prevent defendants to infringement actions from putting validity in issue by way of defence to infringement. In reaching his conclusions, the Chancellor relied on a decision of Richard Arnold QC[6] sitting as a Deputy Judge of the High Court in *Hormel Foods Corpn v Antilles Landscape Investments NV.*[7] It was held in *Hormel* that a decision of the Registrar in opposition proceedings was

[4] This is why national proceedings may be stayed pending final conclusion of the EPO opposition. In this regard, see eg *Unilever plc v Frisa NV* [2000] FSR 708, 713.

[5] [2006] RPC 33.

[6] Now Mr Justice Arnold.

[7] *Hormel Foods Corpn v Antilles Landscape Investments NV* [2005] RPC 28.

capable of founding a plea of *res judicata*, since it was a court of competent jurisdiction.[8] Furthermore, it was final, in that it could not be revised by the court or tribunal which gave the decision.[9]

However, the facts of *Hormel* were unusual, and L'Oreal argued that the case was distinguishable from *Special Effects*. In *Hormel*, the claimant sought a declaration of invalidity in respect of a granted trade mark in the High Court. However, it had previously sought a declaration of invalidity in respect of the same granted registration in the Registry, which application had failed.[10] The judge decided that cause of action estoppel applied because the same cause of action, ie validity of the granted registration, existed in both sets of proceedings. In reaching this decision, he expressly excluded participation in oppositions from the scope of his reasoning. At paragraph 95 he stated:

> For the avoidance of doubt, I should make it clear that I am not considering the position where a person who has unsuccessfully opposed the registration of a trade mark then applies for a declaration of invalidity.

A fortiori he was not considering the position of a party who sought to raise invalidity by way of defence to an allegation of infringement of a trade mark.

The *Hormel* decision is strongly criticised in the latest edition of *Kerly on Registered Trade Marks*.[11] The authors are astute to point out that the *Hormel* decision does not extend to preclude challenges to validity of registered trade marks as a result of opposition proceedings, and their criticisms may be regarded as having particular force if that extension were to be made. In *Special Effects*, L'Oreal contended that the appeal should succeed irrespective of whether *Hormel* was rightly decided. Alternatively, they contended that *Hormel* was wrongly decided.

History of Opposition Proceedings

The possibility of preventing an application for a trade mark from proceeding to grant by opposition before the Registrar was first introduced by section 69 of the Trade Marks Act 1883 and the procedure was altered by the amending Act of 1888. The ability to oppose applications was continued in section 14 of the Trade Marks Act 1905 and section 18 of the Trade Marks

[8] As explained in Spencer Bower, Turner and Handley, *The Doctrine of Res Judicata*, 3rd edn (London, Butterworths) paragraphs 21–25.

[9] Ibid paragraph 167.

[10] *Hormel* (n 7) [1] and [11].

[11] *Kerly's Law of Trade Marks and Trade Names*, 14th edn (London, Sweet & Maxwell, 2005) §§10-016 to 10-020. There is a typographical error in §10-018 at the fourth line on p 283; it should read '... there was no reason why the same should **not** apply to trade marks.'

Act 1938. Oppositions are now provided for by section 38 of the Trade Marks Act 1994.

Over the last 125 years, oppositions have provided a relatively low-cost forum in which to oppose the grant of registrations. They constitute a part of the Registrar's jurisdiction concerning the administration of trade mark applications prior to grant, a position shared by other Commonwealth jurisdictions, such as Canada and Australia. Until *Special Effects*, no defendant had ever been precluded from raising validity in infringement proceedings as a result of unsuccessful participation in an opposition.[12]

The Legislative Framework

Oppositions to applications for registration may be brought under section 38(2) of the 1994 Act. In contrast to applications for revocation and declarations of invalidity of the granted registration, oppositions may only be brought in the Registry prior to grant (*cf* sections 46(4), 47(3) with section 38(2) of the 1994 Act). Section 47(3) deals with declarations of invalidity after grant, and provides as follows:

> (3) An application for a declaration of invalidity may be made by any person, and may be made either to the registrar or to the court, except that:
>
> (a) if proceedings concerning the trade mark in question are pending in the court, *the application must be made to the court*; and
>
> (b) if in any other case the application is made to the registrar, he may at any stage of the proceedings refer the application to the court.
>
> (Emphasis added.)

Section 47 of the 1994 Act implements Articles 3 and 4 of the First Council Directive 89/104. Those Articles provide that certain signs/trade marks 'shall not be registered or if registered shall be liable to be declared invalid.' As Kerly points out,[13] there is no residual discretion under section 47. If one of the grounds of invalidity is made out, then the registration must be declared invalid.[14] This reflects the public interest in removal of invalid marks from the Register.

[12] There were very few attempts to assert *res judicata* as a result of opposition proceedings. The issue arose in *The Matter of Three Trade Marks of Kenrick and Jefferson* (1911) 28 RPC 45 where a motion to expunge three marks on the basis of the same and additional grounds raised in the opposition was held not to be *res judicata*. By contrast, in *Hunt's Application* (1911) 28 RPC 302 it was contemplated (obiter) that the applicant for registration might not be able to bring a further application for the same trade mark after the first application had been successfully opposed, but this was not directed to a challenge to validity of the granted trade mark. On the facts of that case, the second application was allowed to proceed.

[13] *Kerly's Law of Trade Marks and Trade Names* (n 11) §§10-021 to 10-024.

[14] The only qualification to this is the saving provision whereby acquired distinctiveness can be relied upon to defeat inherent non-distinctiveness.

From those provisions, the following conclusions may be drawn:

1. Pre-grant opposition proceedings are exclusively a matter for the Registrar. By contrast, if a declaration of invalidity is raised in infringement proceedings, the application must be made to the court. That is because the Registry has no jurisdiction over infringement proceedings or validity issues arising in infringement proceedings, and reflects the legislative policy that only the court can make decisions on validity in the context of infringement claims.
2. The statute provides that any person may apply for a declaration of invalidity. Persons who have opposed the application for the mark are not excluded. Furthermore if the grounds are made out at the behest of any such person, expungement of the registration is mandatory.
3. If *res judicata* applied in the circumstances of *Special Effects*, then the decision of the hearing officer in the opposition would mean that the court could not make a decision in the infringement action as to the validity of the registration, since the defendants would be precluded from raising any such issue. This may be seen as contrary to the intention of the statute. Furthermore, a class of persons, namely, opponents and any companies in the same group, would be precluded from seeking declarations of invalidity, and the court could not expunge the registration even if one of the mandatory grounds of invalidity could be made out. This, submitted L'Oreal, was contrary to the statute and the Directive which it implements.

There are significant differences between an application for a trade mark and a granted registration, which are evident on the face of the statute. In particular, the exclusive rights of the trade mark owner referred to in sections 9 and 10 of the 1994 Act only apply if the mark is registered, and can only be exercised after registration. Furthermore, section 2 provides as follows:

> 2–(1) A registered trade mark is a property right obtained by the registration of the trade mark under this Act and the proprietor of a registered trade mark has the rights and remedies provided by this Act.
>
> (2) No proceedings lie to prevent or recover damages for the infringement of an unregistered trade mark as such; but nothing in this Act affects the law relating to passing off.

In summary, an application for a trade mark gives no right to commence infringement proceedings unless and until it proceeds to registration. In that event, proceedings may be commenced, and the rights of the proprietor have effect from the date of registration which, in accordance with section 40(3) of the 1994 Act, is deemed to be the date of filing of the application (see also section 9(3) of the 1994 Act).

Further recognition of these differences is shown by section 72 of the 1994 Act, which creates a presumption of validity in relation to registered trade marks, which does not apply to applications, or oppositions to applications. This different treatment of granted trade marks makes sense, since at this stage the mark has passed through the process of registration, and a granted property right has come into existence.

Differences between Registry and High Court Proceedings

Information as to the nature of registry proceedings, including opposition proceedings, is given by the Registry's Tribunal Practice Notices.[15] In particular:

1. There is no automatic or standard disclosure in opposition proceedings, and any disclosure of documents is not common.
2. Costs of opposition proceedings are not intended to compensate parties for the expense to which they have been put. Rather, an award of costs is intended to represent only a contribution to that expense (typically around £2000). The Registry considered changing this policy but decided not to do so on the basis that 'it provides a low cost tribunal for all litigants, but especially unrepresented ones and SMEs and builds in a degree of predictability as to how much proceedings before the Comptroller, ... may cost them.'

In *Bessant and others v South Cone Incorporated*,[16] the Court of Appeal noted that hearing officers are usually very experienced in the practicalities of trade mark registrations, but are not normally qualified lawyers. Furthermore, orders for cross-examination of deponents are permissible in opposition proceedings but have been rare in the past (although there may be a trend to such orders becoming rather less rare).

In summary, opposition proceedings serve a useful function as a relatively low cost route for preventing unmeritorious applications from proceeding beyond the application stage to registration. It is important to note that such proceedings do not determine the rights of parties to use any mark, and cannot result in an award of an injunction or damages. The Registrar has no power to hear infringement proceedings. Hence, the effort and resources devoted to opposition proceedings are proportionate to the nature of those proceedings and what is at stake.

Consequences of the First Instance Judgment in *Special Effects*

If the first instance judgment were correct, then a party who had unsuccessfully opposed an application (and any company in the same group) would not be able to raise invalidity by way of defence to infringement

[15] TPN1-2/2000.
[16] *Bessant and others v South Cone Incorporated* [2003] RPC 5.

proceedings. This means that the nature of opposition proceedings would change completely. The most likely consequence is that they would be ignored and fall into disuse on the basis that losing carried too great a risk. A larger proportion of invalid trade marks would be likely to proceed to registration, and remain on the Register unless High Court proceedings were commenced to remove them. Alternatively, full pleadings, disclosure, witness statements, cross-examination and trials would need to be conducted in opposition proceedings, as in the High Court (but before a hearing officer experienced in the practicalities of trade mark applications who is unlikely to be a qualified lawyer). Accordingly, the same resources would have to be devoted to them as to High Court proceedings, but with no adequate compensation in costs. Further, opposition proceedings in the Registry are fundamentally unsuited to litigation on such a scale.

The above reasoning assumes that *res judicata* would only apply in respect of UK opposition proceedings. But this is not correct. If the judgment at first instance were right, then it will follow that opposition proceedings in other jurisdictions could give rise to cause of action and issue estoppel. It is settled law that a foreign judgment can give rise to such estoppels.[17] So an opposition in eg the Office of Harmonisation for the Internal Market (OHIM) could prevent the unsuccessful opponent from defending itself against allegations of infringement in UK proceedings by putting validity in issue.

The consequences of the judgment extend even further. The point may be illustrated by way of an example:

> A applies for a trade mark; B opposes on the basis of section 5(4)(a) of the 1994 Act, ie that use of the trade mark by A would constitute passing off. The opposition succeeds and in the absence of disclosure or cross-examination the hearing officer finds that such use would constitute passing-off. In practice an appeal can only succeed if there is an error of law or principle.[18] B then sues A in the High Court for passing-off. When A seeks to defend itself, B seeks summary judgment on the basis that the issue of passing-off has already been decided and the matter is *res judicata*. An injunction and damages are then awarded against A on the basis of a Registry decision made by a non-lawyer who has no power to grant such relief. This consequence seems fundamentally unjust.

Res Judicata and the Effect of Statute

In *Daejan Properties Ltd v Mahoney*,[19] the Court of Appeal considered whether the common law doctrine of estoppel was capable of creating

[17] Spencer Bower, *The Doctrine of Res Judicata* (n 8) §197.
[18] *South Cone* (n 16) [28]–[29].
[19] *Daejan Properties Ltd v Mahoney* [1995] 2 EGLR 75.

a statutory tenancy where the statutory conditions for such a tenancy were not made out. Sir Thomas Bingham MR (as he then was) held as follows:[20]

> Since the appellant could not became a statutory tenant by an agreement not satisfying para. 13, the landlords cannot be estopped from denying that the appellant is in law a statutory tenant. Parliament having clearly prescribed the way in which a statutory tenancy can arise or be transmitted, a statutory tenancy cannot arise or be transferred in any other way and the judge quite rightly held that an estoppel cannot have the effect of giving rise to a state of affairs which would indirectly confer on the court a jurisdiction denied by Parliament.[21]

In summary, the common law doctrine of estoppel could not override the scheme of the statute.

The relationship between statute and the common law was considered further by the House of Lords in *Thrasyvoulou v Secretary of State for the Environment*[22] in which Lord Bridge said:, at 289:

> The doctrine of res judicata rests on the twin principles which cannot be better expressed than in terms of the two Latin maxims 'interest reipublicae ut sit finis litium' ['it is in the interest of the state that litigation be finite'] and 'nemo debet bis vexari pro una et eadem causa' ['no one should be twice troubled for one and the same cause']. These principles are of such fundamental importance that they cannot be confined in their application to litigation in the private law field. They certainly have their place in the criminal law. In principle they must apply equally to adjudications in the field of public law. In relation to adjudications subject to a comprehensive self-contained statutory code, the presumption, in my opinion, must be that where the statute has created a specific jurisdiction for the determination of any issue which establishes the existence of a legal right, the principle of res judicata applies to give finality to that determination *unless an intention to exclude that principle can properly be inferred as a matter of construction of the statutory provisions*.'[23] (Emphasis added.)

Further, it is settled law that provisions of domestic law may not be relied on to frustrate the mandatory provisions of an EU Directive. This is clear from the judgment of the ECJ in *R v Secretary of State for Transport ex p Factortame*:[24]

> 20. The Court has also held that any provision of a national legal system and any legislative, administrative or judicial practice which might impair the effectiveness of Community law by withholding from the national court having

[20] [1995] 2 EGLR 75, 77F.
[21] Note that in *Daejan* it was held that the landlords by their representation were estopped from denying that the appellant and her mother would be treated by them as if they were joint statutory tenants.
[22] *Thrasyvoulou v Secretary of State for the Environment* [1990] 2 AC 273.
[23] [1990] 2 AC 273, 289.
[24] *R v Secretary of State for Transport ex p Factortame* [1990] 3 CMLR 1 [20].

> jurisdiction to apply such law the power to do everything necessary at the moment of its application to set aside national legislative provisions which might prevent, even temporarily, Community rules from having full force and effect are incompatible with those requirements, which are the very essence of Community law (judgment of 9 March 1978 in *Simmenthal*, cited above, paragraphs 22 and 23).

The point is also supported by the decision of the ECJ in *Silhouette International v Hartlauer*[25] concerning the Trade Marks Directive. The question was whether the Austrian doctrine of international exhaustion was compatible with Article 7(1) of the Directive. The ECJ held as follows:

1. The Directive provided for harmonisation in relation to substantive rules of central importance to the functioning of the internal market.
2. Articles 5–7 of the Directive must be construed as embodying a complete harmonisation of the rules relating to the rights conferred by a trade mark.
3. Accordingly, the Directive cannot be interpreted as leaving it open to Member States to provide in their domestic law for exhaustion of rights in respective of products put on the market in non-member countries.[26]

It was argued by L'Oreal that the same reasoning applied to those articles in issue in *Special Effects*. In particular, Articles 3(1) and 4(1) contain mandatory grounds pursuant to which a registered trade mark shall be liable to be declared invalid. Just as with Articles 5–7, Articles 3(1) and 4(1) must be construed as embodying a complete harmonisation of those grounds of invalidity. In particular, Recital 7 to the Directive provides, inter alia, as follows:

> Whereas attainment of the objectives at which this approximation of laws is aiming requires that the conditions for obtaining and continuing to hold a registered trade mark are, in general, identical in all Member States; ...

Accordingly, L'Oreal submitted that a trade mark owner cannot continue to hold a registered trade mark if one or more of the absolute grounds of invalidity set out in Articles 3(1) or 4(1) is satisfied. If *res judicata*, which is a doctrine of domestic law, was applied to prevent challenges to validity on these grounds, which would otherwise be successful, this would be contrary to the requirements of the Directive and its object of harmonisation. Accordingly, L'Oreal submitted that the common law doctrine of *res judicata* cannot be used to prevent a party from challenging the validity

[25] *Silhouette International v Hartlauer* [1999] Ch 77.
[26] [1999] Ch 77 [24]–[26].

of a registered trade mark by way of defence and counterclaim in infringement proceedings on the basis of an unsuccessful opposition.[27]

GENERAL PRINCIPLES OF LAW

The application of *res judicata* in *Special Effects* may also be seen as being inconsistent with the general principles of law relating to cause of action estoppel, issue estoppel and abuse of process.

Before considering each species of estoppel relied on, it is important to bear in mind the well-known cautionary notes concerning their application, sounded by courts at the highest level. In particular, in *Johnson v Gore Wood*[28] Lord Bingham stated that:

> Litigants are not without scrupulous examination of all the circumstances to be denied the right to bring a genuine subject of litigation before the court: *Yat Tung Investment Co Ltd v Dao Heng Bank Ltd* [1975] AC 581, 590 per Lord Kilbrandon, giving the advice of the Judicial Committee; *Brisbane City Council v Attorney General for Queensland* [1979] AC 411, 425 per Lord Wilberforce, giving the advice of the Judicial Committee.

As he went on to observe, this does not mean that the court must hear in full and rule on the merits of any claim or defence which a party to litigation may choose to put forward. However, great care must be taken to ensure that the requirements for the application of the doctrine are clearly satisfied. This is why strict limitations on the doctrines have been established. They are not mere technicalities; rather they are safeguards which reflect the overall policy referred to above.

Cause of Action Estoppel

Requirement of Identicality

In order for this species of *res judicata* to apply, the cause of action must be identical in both proceedings:

> It is appropriate to commence by noticing the distinction between cause of action estoppel and issue estoppel. Cause of action estoppel arises where the cause of action in the later proceedings is *identical* to that in the earlier proceedings, the latter having been between the same parties or their privies and having involved the same subject matter. In such a case the bar is absolute in relation to all points

[27] This argument has its limitations. A party who unsuccessfully challenged the validity of a granted trade mark in the High Court would not be permitted to commence identical proceedings on a second occasion.

[28] *Johnson v Gore Wood* [2002] 2 AC 1, 22.

> decided unless fraud or collusion is alleged, such as to justify setting aside the earlier judgment.[29]

A primary requirement of cause of action estoppel is to identify with clarity the cause of action in the first proceeding and the cause of action in the second proceeding and show that they are identical. In *Special Effects* the claimant identified the relevant causes of action as 'the validity or otherwise of the Claimant's registered trade mark under the provisions of the Trade Marks Act 1994.'

However, the opposition proceedings did not raise or decide the validity of the SPECIAL EFFECTS registration. The registration did not exist at that time. The issue in the opposition proceedings was whether the application should be allowed to proceed to registration. The cause of action for validity of a registered trade mark (which is a granted right of property) could not subsist prior to the registration being completed.

The point may be emphasised further by reference to the decision of the Court of Appeal in *Buehler v Chronos Richardson*.[30] In an action in the Patents County Court for infringement of a patent which the defendant had unsuccessfully opposed in the European Patent Office, the claimant applied to strike out the defendant's allegations of invalidity as *res judicata*, having been decided by the Opposition Division. The issue was whether the defendant could rely on allegations of invalidity as grounds of defence and counterclaim in infringement proceedings when the same allegations had been dealt with by the EPO. The claimant submitted that the subject of the estoppel was the invalidity of the patent, and that both cause of action estoppel and issue estoppel applied.

The Court of Appeal rejected these contentions. Aldous LJ referred to the fact that cause of action estoppel can only apply where the cause of action in the earlier proceedings is identical to that in the later proceedings. He then considered the causes of action in the two sets of proceedings and concluded as follows:

1. The causes of action in the High Court proceedings could be ascertained from the defence and counterclaim. Invalidity was pleaded as a defence to an allegation of infringement. Thus the cause of action is infringement.
2. Before the Opposition Division of the European Patent Office, the cause of action, if it be a cause of action, was whether the patent should be maintained or revoked pursuant to the jurisdiction given to the Opposition Division by Articles 100 to 102.
3. The European Patent Office did not have before it and did not decide infringement. It followed that any submission that the respondents were

[29] Per Lord Keith: *Arnold v. National Westminster Bank Plc* [1991] 2 AC 93, 104.
[30] *Buehler v Chronos Richardson* [1998] RPC 609.

estopped from challenging the validity of the patent as part of their defence in the action could not be right.

Requirement of Finality

The decision of the hearing officer in the opposition in *Special Effects* was a final decision, since it could not be revised by that tribunal.[31] However, it was not a final decision on the validity of a registered trade mark.

A similar point again arose in *Buehler*. The decision of the Opposition Division was not a final decision as to the validity of the patent, since such decisions are reserved to the courts of the member states. Accordingly, although it concluded the opposition and was in that sense final, it could not found a cause of action estoppel.[32]

The same point can be raised in relation to the Trade Marks Act 1994, which provides for challenges to validity pre- and post-grant. Therefore, the pre-grant decision is not final. This argument did not arise in *Hormel*, since in that case, the claimant made two challenges to the validity of the granted trade mark, both under section 47 of the Act.

Issue Estoppel

Difference between Issue Estoppel and Cause of Action Estoppel

There is an important distinction between cause of action estoppel and issue estoppel. If cause of action estoppel is established, it cannot be avoided in the absence of collusion or fraud. By contrast, issue estoppel is applied with the overriding consideration that it should work justice and not injustice. Therefore special circumstances may avoid its application, even if its technical requirements are otherwise fulfilled.

In particular, in *Carl Zeiss Stiftung v Rayner & Keeler Ltd (No 2)*,[33] Lord Upjohn stated:

> All estoppels are not odious but must be applied so as to work justice and not injustice and I think the principle of issue estoppel must be applied to the circumstances of the subsequent case with this overriding consideration in mind.

In the same case, Lord Reid stated at page 917:

> The difficulty which I see about issue estoppel is a practical one. Suppose the first case is one of trifling importance but it involves for one party proof of facts which would be expensive and troublesome; and that party can see the possibility

[31] Spencer Bower, *The Doctrine of Res Judicata* (n 8) § 167.
[32] *Buehler* (n 30) 616 [1.20]–619 [1.22].
[33] *Carl Zeiss Stiftung v Rayner & Keeler Ltd (No 2)* [1967] 1 AC 853, 947.

> that the same point may arise if his opponent later raises a much more important claim. What is he to do? The second case may never be brought. Must he go to great trouble and expense to forestall a possible plea of issue estoppel if the second case is never brought? This does not arise in cause of action estoppel: if the cause of action is important, he will incur the expense: if it is not, he will take the chance of winning on some other point. It seems to me that there is room for a good deal more thought before we settle the limits of issue estoppel.[34]

These considerations are applicable to proceedings under the Trade Marks Act. Opposition proceedings are frequently not of great importance, since they do not determine the rights of any party to continue to use any mark. They are generally conducted by all parties on the basis of brief evidence, proportionate to what is in issue. It may therefore be unjust to hold that an unsuccessful opponent should be estopped from advancing any part of its defence to an infringement claim, on the basis that it should have gone to greater trouble and expense in the opposition.

Abuse of Process

The speech of Lord Bingham in the case of *Johnson v Gore Wood*[35] explains that there is much in common between abuse of process, cause of action estoppel and issue estoppel. They all rest on the same underlying public interest, and involve some abuse or misuse of the process of the court by a party seeking to raise a claim or defence which was or should have been raised in earlier proceedings.

Johnson v Gore Wood concerned a case of *Henderson v Henderson* abuse of process. However in *SGI v Deakin*[36] the Court of Appeal drew attention to the applicability of those comments to other forms of *res judicata,* ie cause of action estoppel and issue estoppel. At paragraph 10, Aldous LJ stated as follows:

> The principles upon which cause of action and issue estoppel are based are as stated by Lord Bingham: there must be finality in litigation and a litigant should not be twice vexed on the same matter. No doubt the phrases cause of action estoppel and issue estoppel are well known to lawyers, but they would not be recognised by educated members of the public as being an indication of those principles. It is therefore appropriate to use more recognisable names such as cause of action finality and issue finality. They are, as Lord Bingham pointed out, forms of abuse of process. That is misuse of the court's procedure in a way which would be manifestly unfair or otherwise bring the administration of justice into disrepute amongst right thinking people (see Lord Diplock in *Hunter v*

34 [1967] 1 AC 853, 917.
35 *Johnson v Gore Wood* [2002] 2 AC 1, 30–31.
36 *SGI v Deakin* [2001] EWCA Civ 777.

Chief Constable of the West Midlands [1982] AC 529 at page 536). However it is important to bear in mind that the application of those principles involves the denial of the right of access to the courts conferred by common law and is a right protected by the European Convention for the Protection of Human Rights. Thus such principles should only be applied where the circumstances are such that their application is necessary to prevent misuse of the court's procedure amounting to an abuse of process.

The Court of Appeal Judgment in *Special Effects*

The Court of Appeal overturned the judgment at first instance, and held that *res judicata* did not apply. In summary, Lloyd LJ, giving the judgment of the Court, held as follows:

1. It was easy enough to identify the cause of action in the High Court proceedings, namely a claim for infringement and a defence and counterclaim of invalidity. The same was not the case in relation to the opposition proceedings. It was doubtful whether there was a cause of action in opposition proceedings, and to describe the application as having a cause of action for registration would be an inappropriate and artificial use of language. Accordingly, cause of action estoppel could not apply.
2. The co-existence of the provisions for opposition and for a declaration of invalidity in the statute has the result that opposition proceedings are inherently not final. The terms of the legislation are such that, even though the Act has created a specific jurisdiction for the determination of registrability, which establishes the existence of a legal right leading to the registration of the trade mark, the principle of *res judicata* does not apply to give finality to that determination because the provisions as to a declaration of invalidity show an intention to exclude that principle.
3. The consequence of a failure of an opponent in opposition proceedings was that the mark would proceed to registration, although subject to the possibility of a later declaration of invalidity, either by the opponent or a third party. In such proceedings, there was no question of financial liability or an injunction. Accordingly, a potential opponent could reasonably take the view that more limited resources should be deployed in opposition proceedings that in court proceedings for infringement. It would be unusual to hold that a party who took advantage of the second opportunity to challenge validity provided by the legislation was abusing the process of the court.

In relation to finality, the Court of Appeal considered that recent decisions of the Federal Court of Australia under the Australian Trade Marks legislation provided a helpful analogy. In particular, in *Lomas v Winton Shire Council*,[37] the full Court stated at paragraph 18:

> An unsuccessful opponent would always have the opportunity to bring an expungement proceeding if the opposition proceeding fails. In an expungement proceeding, the validity of the trade mark can be fully explored.

Similarly, in *Health World Ltd v Shin-Sun Australia Pty Ltd*,[38] where there had been a previous unsuccessful opposition and an unsuccessful appeal, Jacobson J rejected an argument that the same points could not be raised because of estoppel. He said at paragraph 48:

> However, the effect of what was said in Lomas is that under the statutory scheme which relates to opposition proceedings, the decision cannot be said to be final. Because of the nature of opposition proceedings, a decision in an appeal under section 56 of the Act cannot, as a matter of law, finally determine the rights of the parties.

Was *Hormel* Correct?

The Court of Appeal in *Special Effects* did not need to decide this question, as they accepted the submission that the case was distinguishable. However, there are good reasons for considering that *Hormel* was merely a classic application of the principles of *res judicata*. It was a case where the validity of a granted registration had already been challenged in the Registry, and was sought to be challenged again in the High Court. If one considers the case of two successive High Court challenges by the same party to a granted trade mark, it seems clear that this would be an abuse. This, in substance, is what happened in *Hormel*.

THE *UNILIN* CASE

It may be regarded as surprising that the same process of reasoning that prevailed in *Special Effects* did not also preclude a finding of *res judicata* in *Unilin*. This may be seen from a consideration of the scheme of the Patents Act 1977 and the European Patents Convention. It is of course well known that the advantage of applying for a European Patent is that rights can be obtained in designated Convention countries by a single application. However, that advantage carries with it a disadvantage—revocation or limitation by the EPO means that all of the rights in each designated country are revoked or limited *ab initio*.

[37] *Lomas v Winton Shire Council* [2002] FCAFC 413.
[38] *Health World Ltd v Shin-Sun Australia Pty Ltd* [2006] FCA 647.

The Patents Act 1977

The Patents Act 1977 was enacted to give effect to the European Patent Convention. That is achieved, inter alia, by section 77. Section 77(1) treats a European Patent (UK) for the purposes of Parts I and III of the Act *as if it were* a patent under the Act granted in pursuance of an application made under the Act. Accordingly, the proprietor of a European Patent (UK) has the same rights and remedies as respects the UK, subject to the same conditions, as the proprietor of a patent under the Act, and references in Parts I and III are to be construed accordingly.

There are, however, important exceptions to section 77(1), which do not apply to domestic patents. These are contained in sections 77(2), (4) and (4A). In particular, section 77(2) provides as follows:

> Subsection (1) above shall not affect the operation in relation to a European patent (UK) of any provisions of the European Patent Convention relating to the amendment or revocation of such a patent in proceedings before the European Patent Office.

Subsections (4) and (4A) provide that where a European Patent UK is amended or revoked in accordance with the European Patent Convention, the patent shall be treated for the purposes of Parts I and III of the Act as having been amended or revoked under the Act.

The following provisions contained in Part I of the Act are therefore all to be read as subject to EPO opposition proceedings which may result in revocation or amendment. Sections 60–61 and 69—infringement and entitlement to injunctive relief, damages or an account of profits; section 72—power to revoke invalid patents; section 76—proceedings in which validity of a patent may be put in issue; sections 27, 75 and 76—amendment.

European Patent Convention

Section 77(1) and the exceptions thereto are necessary in order to give effect to the provisions of the EPC. In particular, Article 2(2) EPC provides that:

> The European patent shall, in each of the Contracting States for which it is granted, have the effect of and be subject to the same conditions as a national patent granted by that State unless otherwise provided in this Convention.

The power of national courts to grant relief for infringement of European Patents stems from Article 64(1) and (3), which provide as follows:

> (1) A European patent shall ... confer on its proprietor from the date of publication of the mention of its grant, in each Contracting State in which it is granted, the same rights as would be conferred by a national patent granted in that State ...
>
> (3) Any infringement of a European patent shall be dealt with by national law.

Article 67 deals with rights conferred by a European patent application after publication (see Patents Act 1977, section 69). The power to treat European patents as national patents, and to order relief in respect of European patents (UK), therefore stems from Articles 2, 64 and 67.

Article 68[39] deals with the effect of revocation of a European patent in the following terms:

> The European patent application and the resulting European patent shall be deemed not to have had, from the outset, the effects specified in Articles 64 and 67, to the extent that the patent has been revoked or limited in opposition, limitation or revocation proceedings.

So Articles 64 and 67 are deemed never to have applied if the patent is revoked in the EPO. In particular, the provision that infringement of a European patent should be dealt with by national law (Article 64(3)) is deemed never to have applied. In those circumstances the UK court has no power to grant any relief for infringement. It follows that if an opposition is successful, and the patent revoked in Munich, there is no power to order injunctive relief, damages or an account of profits for infringement, or to proceed with enquiries which will result in an order for such relief.

Conclusions in Relation to the Statutory Scheme

The 1977 Act, and the EPC, expressly contemplate two routes by which validity may be challenged by, amongst others, a defendant to infringement proceedings of a European Patent UK; first, by a defence and counterclaim for invalidity in the UK proceedings; and secondly, by an opposition in the EPO to the granted patent. The routes are not mutually exclusive—they may both be pursued at the same time. Furthermore, exactly the same grounds of invalidity may be (and frequently are) advanced both before the UK court and the EPO.

Even if a defendant fails to revoke or limit the patent pursuant to section 72 of the Act in the UK proceedings, he may still achieve those results in the EPO. That is expressly provided for by sections 77(2), (4) and (4A). If the patent is revoked or amended in EPO proceedings, then it is to be treated as having been revoked or amended under the Act for the purposes of Part I of the Act. This applies to the infringement section, and to the court's powers to grant injunctive relief, damages or an account.

European patents are created by the European Patent Convention. They are not domestic patents. They are only treated as if they were—see section 77(1). Section 77(1) implements Article 2(2) of the EPC. The legislature has not ignored the limitations imposed by Article 68. On the contrary, they have

[39] As amended by the EPC 2000, which came into force on December 13, 2007.

been incorporated by section 77(2). If a European patent is revoked by the EPO, Article 68 deems that from the outset there has been no power for the national courts to grant relief for infringement. Accordingly, if this patent is revoked (or amended, so that no question of infringement arises) in the EPO, then the provisions of the EPC require that no relief be granted. Since section 77(2) provides that section 77(1) shall not affect the operation of any of the provisions of the EPC relating to amendment or revocation of a European Patent (UK), the UK court cannot contravene those provisions (including Article 68) by proceeding to grant such relief.

The *ITP* Case

A situation analogous to the *Unilin* case arose in *ITP SA v Coflexip Stena Offshore*,[40] where the pursuers sued the defenders in Scotland for infringement of a European Patent (UK). At the trial the patent was held valid and infringed, and an account of profits was ordered. The defenders appealed by reclaiming motion. After the appeal was lodged, the Board of Appeal at the EPO revoked the patent on the grounds that it was obvious. The defenders then lodged an additional ground of appeal, that as a consequence of its revocation by the EPO, the patent fell to be regarded as void *ab initio* and that accordingly they could not have infringed it. Prior to the hearing of the Appeal, they withdrew all other grounds of appeal, ie all criticisms of the judgment at first instance.[41]

The appeal was heard by the Inner House (Court of Session) by a powerful court, comprising the Lord President, Lord MacFayden and Sir David Edward QC. The pursuers claimed that the decision of the EPO Board of Appeal contravened (amongst other things) their rights under Articles 6(1) and 13 of the ECHR. Unsurprisingly, this argument was rejected. The Court referred to the decision of the Court of Appeal in *Lensing AG's European Patent (UK)*[42] and in particular the judgment of Jacob LJ to the effect that, in relation to European Patents, the Board of Appeal was 'the final arbiter of revocation' and 'the agreed EPO equivalent of the House of Lords, Cour de Cassation or Bundesgerichtshof.'. Accordingly a national court could not query its doings, whether in a direct or collateral attack (*ITP* judgment, paragraphs 20–25).

At paragraphs 9–12 the Court of Inner Session considered the provisions of the Patents Act 1977 and the EPC. They noted that section 77(1) was enacted in accordance with Article 2 EPC, and that the rights granted by Article 64 are subject to the limitations set out in Article 68, which is given

[40] *ITP SA v Coflexip Stena Offshore* [2005] SC 116.
[41] [2005] SC 116 [1]–[5].
[42] *Lensing AG's European Patent (UK)* [1997] RPC 245.

effect pursuant to section 77(4A). Against this background, they considered and rejected an alternative submission on behalf of the pursuers at paragraph 27, that:

> the court could, on the one hand, accept the effect of revocation within the United Kingdom and other designated states, but on the other hand, preserve as between the pursuers and the defenders the liability which the Lord Ordinary had been found to be established.

This, of course is the effect of cause of action/issue estoppel: liability has been preserved as between the parties.

The Court held as follows at paragraph 27:

> A patent such as a European Patent is a right of property, and in suing the defenders the pursuers were seeking remedies based on their right of property. That right of property was created by the European Patent Convention. The effect of revocation under that Convention was that from the outset the pursuers had no substantive right to the patent. The United Kingdom was bound to give effect to that in legislation. There is nothing in the Patents Act which could justify preserving, as between the Patentee and another party, some residual effect of a revoked European Patent.

This reasoning was elaborated further by the decision of the Inner Session to award the costs of the trial, as well as the reclaiming motion, to the defenders. The pursuers argued that the process in the EPO was entirely separate from the Scottish proceedings, and that before the Lord Ordinary at first instance the pursuers had been successful on every point. The reclaiming motion from the merits of that decision had been withdrawn. Why, therefore, should the defenders be entitled to their costs of the trial in Scotland? The pursuers' submission was rejected on the basis that the defenders had ultimately been successful. The Court held as follows at paragraph 5:

> The pursuers chose to raise the action against the defenders—mainly, it seems with a view to recovering an account of profits—at a time when they knew that the defenders were insisting on challenging the validity of the patent. There is no question of their having been misled by the defenders into raising the action. They took the risk that the action might come to grief if the proceedings in the European Patent Office went against them …

This summarises the basic effect of the legislation. If a patentee chooses to pursue domestic proceedings whilst the European patent is under opposition, he assumes the risk of losing on validity by either route, both of which would result in a complete victory for the defendant. It also gives rise to the same point that prevailed in *Special Effects*. Since the legislation provides for two routes for challenging validity, validity cannot be said to have been finally determined until both routes have been exhausted.

The Court of Appeal Decision in *Unilin*

At first instance, HHJ Fysh applied the *ITP* case and held that *res judicata* could not apply since the validity of the patent was still being challenged in the EPO. The Court of Appeal overturned this decision. Their reasoning may be summarised as follows:

1. The Court of Appeal decisions in *Coflexip v Stolt*[43] and *Poulton v Adjustable Cover and Boiler Block Co*[44] established that a defendant who had lost a patent action was estopped from denying validity on a damages enquiry, even where the patent had subsequently been invalidated. That was the case even though revocation had retrospective effect.
2. Article 68 EPC had no equivalent in the 1977 Act, and was merely part of an international convention. In any event, infringement under Article 64(3) was not an 'effect' of the European Patent within the meaning of Article 68.
3. The *travaux* to the EPC indicated an intention not to interfere with the civil procedures of contracting states.

This reasoning requires a very narrow reading of sections 74–77 of the Act, and of Article 68 of the Convention. The primary 'effect' of a patent monopoly is the ability to enforce it by way of an action for infringement. The decision may be thought to ignore the fundamental purpose of those provisions of the EPC and of section 77 of the UK statute, which is to ensure that no effect is given to European patents which are revoked by the EPO, and are deemed never to have existed.

As to *travaux*, it is important to bear in mind the observations of Lord Steyn that when construing an international treaty by reference to the *travaux* in order to find a definite legal intention, 'only a bull's-eye counts'.[45] The *travaux* in relation to Article 68 cut both ways, as is frequently the case. In particular, the explanatory remarks to the amendments to Article 68 contained in EPC 2000 record the following:

> Article 68 EPC thus uniformly establishes the retroactive effect of limiting or revoking a European patent in opposition, limitation and (national) revocation proceedings. The inclusion of national revocation proceedings reflects the fact that the revocation of European patents now has an ex tunc effect on all contracting states, and it formalised the harmonisation achieved in that respect.

This shows that Article 68 is unquestionably intended to have retroactive effect. It is intended to achieve uniformity and harmonisation in relation to

43 [2004] FSR 34.
44 [1908] 2 Ch 430.
45 *Effort Shipping v Linden Management* [1988] AC 605, 625.

the effects of revocation or limitation in all contracting states. There is no suggestion that any residual effect of a revoked patent may be preserved. Further, it is undoubtedly intended to affect national revocation proceedings, notwithstanding procedural rules, because it says so expressly.

The Court of Appeal's Reliance in *Unilin* on *Coflexip* and *Poulton*

Are the Cases Distinguishable?

It is important to record what happened in the *Coflexip* case. In 1996 the claimant sued the defendant for infringement of a European patent (UK). There were no pending EPO opposition proceedings. In 2000 the Court of Appeal confirmed that the patent was valid and infringed. An enquiry as to damages was proceeding when a third party brought revocation proceedings in the UK, relying on prior art, which had not been relied on by the defendant. Those proceedings were successful, and the patent was revoked subject to a stay pending appeal.

In *Coflexip* the defendant sought a stay of the enquiry as to damages. It claimed that since revocation dated back to the grant of the patent, the defence on the enquiry would be that no damage had been suffered. The patentee claimed that cause of action estoppel applied. It relied on the fact that the defendant had had the opportunity to challenge the validity of the patent and had failed to find the relevant piece of prior art, which could have been discovered by the defendant had it searched more diligently before the trial.

The majority of the Court of Appeal, Neuberger LJ dissenting, held that cause of action estoppel applied (save in respect of unpleaded infringements, where issue estoppel applied). They were bound by the Court of Appeal's decision in *Poulton*, so that a defendant who had lost a patent action could not raise invalidity as a defence on the damages enquiry. The majority held that the policy considerations underlying *res judicata* did not tell in the defendant's favour. In particular, the aim of finality in litigation was not achieved by allowing a final decision on the validity of a patent and its infringement to be reopened if a third party invalidated the patent. The claimant would be vexed twice in the same matter, as a result of the defendant's failure to find and adduce the relevant prior art at the trial.

It may be suggested that *Coflexip* (and *Poulton,* which was decided many decades before the EPC) is distinguishable from *Unilin*. In particular:

1. No opposition proceedings were pending and the finding of invalidity was by a UK court. Accordingly none of the considerations set out above, concerning section 77 of the Patents Act, Article 68 of the EPC and the supremacy of EPO decisions, arose for consideration at all.

2. The Court of Appeal in *Coflexip* held that they were bound by *Poulton* to find that cause of action estoppel applied to prevent validity being raised as a defence in the enquiry. *Poulton* concerned re-litigation of the validity of a UK patent by the same defendant. It is not a binding authority in relation to European Patents (UK). None of the same considerations arise.
3. The defendant in *Coflexip* had exhausted all of its routes for contesting validity. As between the parties, the issue had been finally determined. In *Unilin* this issue had not been finally determined since it was still being contested in the EPO.
4. The defendant in *Coflexip* had failed to find the relevant prior art, which it could have relied on a trial with due diligence. This point did not arise in *Unilin*.
5. The defendant in *Coflexip* was seeking to benefit from the actions of an unconnected third party, whereas in *Unilin*, a Berry group company was pursuing the opposition.

Were Poulton *and* Coflexip Rightly *Decided?*

The parties to the *Unilin* case settled before the Court of Appeal judgment was handed down. Therefore, there was no question of an appeal to the House of Lords. It is likely that the issue will arise again, particularly in the context of applications to stay UK proceedings pending a final decision of the EPO. In those circumstances there may be good reason for a leapfrog appeal to the Supreme Court, where it will be possible to contend that *Poulton* and/or *Coflexip* were wrongly decided.

Powerful arguments against *Poulton* and the majority decision in *Coflexip* are set out in the dissenting judgment of Neuberger LJ (as he then was). These may be summarised as follows:

1. Where a patent is revoked, this is a decision *in rem* ie a conclusion against all the world as to status. It is retrospective in effect and therefore the patent is to be treated as non-existent when the acts of infringement occurred.
2. In *Poulton*, it was held that a defendant could rely on the subsequent revocation of a patent to put an end to an injunction, but could not rely on revocation as a defence in the damages enquiry. Since the effect of revocation was retrospective, this distinction was not persuasive.
3. Accordingly, there were grounds for concluding that *Poulton* (which held that subsequent invalidity of the patent could not be relied on as a defence in a damages enquiry) was wrongly decided.
4. In relation to issue estoppel the law had developed significantly since *Poulton* was decided in 1908. It was now to be applied with the overriding consideration of 'working justice and not injustice'.

5. Since in *Coflexip* the patent had been invalidated on the basis of prior art not cited by the defendants in that action, it was not a case of strict cause of action estoppel, which should be given a narrow compass. Therefore, even if *Poulton* was rightly decided, it was still open to the court to hold that the defendant could rely on revocation of the patent as a defence to damages, which would result in damages being assessed at nil.
6. It was unfair, and contrary to the public interest, for Coflexip to receive, and for Stolt to have to pay, substantial damages for infringement of a patent, which as a result of its revocation, had always been ineffective.

If *Poulton* and/or *Coflexip* were wrongly decided, then there are powerful grounds for concluding that the same conclusion would be reached in relation to *Unilin*. Indeed, for the reasons set out above, *Unilin* goes further than either of those decisions, in applying *res judicata* where an opposition was still pending in the EPO.

Consideration of the *ITP* Case in *Unilin*

The Court of Appeal in *Unilin* considered that the *ITP* case was distinguishable because an appeal was still pending when the Technical Board of Appeal revoked the patent[46]. However, the reasoning of the Inner House was not dependent on the timing of the appeal. Rather, it was based on an analysis of the legislation and Convention which is fundamentally inconsistent with the application of *res judicata*.

Consideration of the *Special Effects* Case in *Unilin*

The Court of Appeal in *Unilin* distinguished *Special Effects* on the basis that it was a decision limited to the consequences of trade mark oppositions, and did not establish any general principle that if a party has two routes of attack on the existence of a right, a final decision by one route is not to be regarded as final.[47] But fundamental to the reasoning in *Special Effects* was the proposition that *res judicata* cannot be applied to prevent a party from taking advantage of the scheme provided for by the legislation. This highlights what may be seen as a *lacuna* in the *Unilin* decision. Even if it is correct that Article 68 forms no part of UK law, based on an analysis of the Patents Act 1977 alone, validity could not be said to be finally decided until both of the permitted challenges had been concluded. In the absence of a final decision, *res judicata* cannot apply.

[46] [2007] FSR 25 [77]–[80].
[47] Ibid [83]–[85].

Further, it would appear that the public interest in finality in litigation, and the principle that a litigant should not be vexed twice in the same matter, cannot apply to the situation where a defendant in a patent action successfully revokes or amends the patent in EPO proceedings. This is because the legislation expressly contemplates that this very route may be taken, in addition to and at the same time as a challenge to validity in UK proceedings. It also contemplates that revocation or limitation in the EPO takes effect as if made under the Act. This is so whether or not the defendant has succeeded before the UK courts in his challenge to validity. Therefore, it cannot be a misuse of the court's procedure amounting to an abuse of process for a defendant to take the two routes open to him under the legislation, and to rely on success achieved by either route.

CONCLUSION

A central theme of this chapter is that the principles of *res judicata* have become unnecessarily complex. This complexity is increased in their application to intellectual property cases, where the relevant rights are the creation of statutes, intended to implement international conventions and EU Directives. This is illustrated by the cases discussed above: *Coflexip,* with its powerful dissenting judgment, and *Special Effects* and *Unilin,* where the judgments at first instance reached opposite conclusions to each other, and yet were both overturned on appeal. Over-complexity causes unpredictability of outcome, and a lack of consistency with other jurisdictions where the same rights exist.

The solution, it is suggested, is to go back to first principles. It is clear that fairness to a successful party, as well as the public interest in the efficient administration of justice, may well prevent re-litigation of an issue that has or ought to have been raised and decided in previous proceedings. However, this is most unlikely to apply where a statutory scheme allows a defendant more than one chance to challenge validity. Furthermore, fairness does not dictate that damages should be awarded in respect of an intellectual property right which has been revoked, and is therefore deemed never to have existed. Yet further, it cannot be said that validity has finally been determined whilst the parties continue to contest that very issue, in a manner permitted by the relevant legislation.

If the UK Court of Appeal had taken the same approach to patents as it has taken to trade marks, it would have decided that there was no final decision on validity until the EPO opposition proceedings had been completed. This result, it is submitted, would reflect the requirements of the EPC and give rise to more consistency with the approach taken in other member states, where national validity proceedings are frequently stayed pending the conclusion of EPO opposition proceedings. Furthermore, having regard to the decisions of the Australian Federal Court in relation to trade marks and *res judicata*, the *Unilin* approach in relation to patents seems anomalous. This issue is likely to arise again in the UK, for example where a defendant seeks a stay of UK patent infringement proceedings pending determination of EPO opposition proceedings. It may well be that the Supreme Court will have occasion to consider the *Poulton, Coflexip* and *Unilin* line of authorities in the future.

5

The Conduct of a Patent Trial from the Perspective of Practice in the US, UK and Canada

MARSHALL ROTHSTEIN, JAMES F HOLDERMAN, CHRISTOPHER FLOYD and KATHRYN PICKARD

INTRODUCTION

THE PATENT LAWS of the United States, the United Kingdom and Canada each seek the same goals, namely to incentivise investment in research and promote the disclosure of inventions to the public. Each jurisdiction seeks to protect an inventor's intellectual property rights by providing legal procedures that help him to enforce the limited monopoly that he receives from his respective government, namely the right to exclude all others, for a period of time, from making, using or selling his invention.

In order to ensure the effectiveness of patent protection, those legal procedures must meet three goals. The first and most important of these is that those procedures are just. Both parties to a dispute must be given fair opportunity to put their case. Secondly those procedures must not be unduly expensive. An excessively costly procedure may prevent patentees from litigating their patents at all, rendering the protection afforded by them nugatory. Similarly an expensive procedure will prevent interested persons from challenging the validity of patents that may stand in the way of effective competition. Thirdly there is a need for legal procedures to provide for speedy resolution of disputes. No party to patent proceedings ought to find itself caught up indefinitely in long, drawn-out litigation.

In this chapter we look at the way in which patent litigation has developed in the US, UK and Canada. We explore the different approaches that have been taken in each jurisdiction and consider why, given the shared goal of resolving patent litigation as speedily, cheaply and justly as possible, there are divergences in approach. We focus on the case management procedures introduced in the UK and Canada, the US *Markman* hearing, the processes governing disclosure, expert evidence and trial and the Canadian provisions used to resolve pharmaceutical disputes.

COMMON THEMES

There are a number of common themes uniting the US, UK and Canadian jurisdictions which make them ripe for comparative study.

Firstly, the substantive law of patents in all three jurisdictions is broadly similar. It is rooted in statute and developed by common law. Consequently the issues that typically arise in patent litigation are common to all three jurisdictions, namely the correct construction to be given to the claims of a patent, validity over the prior art, and infringement.

Secondly, common remedies are available in each jurisdiction. So, although the details differ, a successful patentee may expect to obtain an injunction, damages and costs following litigation. In addition, interim (also known as interlocutory) injunctions are, in principle, available in each jurisdiction at an early stage in proceedings.

Thirdly, the key stages in patent proceedings are the same. They comprise (a) the filing of the claim; (b) the exchange of written pleadings setting out the position of each party; (c) discovery; (d) trial preparation and (e) trial. Expert evidence on relevant technological points is admissible in all three jurisdictions.

The fundamental difference between patent litigation in the US compared with in the UK and Canada is the use of jury trials in the US. In the UK and Canada, patent trials are heard by a judge sitting alone. As we will see in this chapter, this difference leads to differences in pre-trial procedure as well as during trial.

In the UK, specialist patent courts are used for patent litigation. This is not the case in the US or Canada.

The US

In the US, the United States District Courts are the general federal trial courts of the United States and have exclusive original jurisdiction to hear and resolve patent cases at trial level. When a patent infringement case is filed in any district of the United States it, in common with any other federal civil case, is assigned to a United States district judge appointed by the President of the United States to serve in that district. The United States district judge to whom the patent case is assigned may or may not have patent law experience or expertise; United States district judges do not typically specialise in particular areas of the law.[1]

[1] See JF Holderman, 'Judicial Patent Specialization: A View from the Trial Bench' (2002) *University of Illinois Journal of Law, Technology & Poly* 425; JF Holderman, in collaboration with H Guren, 'The Patent Litigation Predicament in the United States' (2007) U Ill JL Tech & Poly 1.

Canada

In Canada, patent actions may be instituted in the Federal Court of Canada or in the Provincial Superior Courts. The Federal Court is an itinerant court with offices in all major Canadian cities and judges sit at all major centres throughout the country. Therefore, there is no geographical impediment to bringing an action in the Federal Court. The advantage of bringing a case in the Federal Court is that the decision will apply throughout Canada. Although an order of a Superior Court in one of the provinces may be practically conclusive of the issue between the parties, technically the decision will be enforceable only in that province. For this reason, most parties claiming patent infringement will commence their actions in the Federal Court. Canada does not have specialised patent courts, although at least one judge has expressed frustration with a field that 'cries out for reform'.[2]

The UK

The UK court system in fact comprises three different systems—the courts of England and Wales, Scotland and Northern Ireland. As the bulk of patent litigation in the UK takes place in England and Wales, it will be that system that is considered in this chapter. In England and Wales there are two specialist patent courts: the Patents Court, which is a specialist court in the Chancery Division of the High Court of Justice, and the Patents County Court. Judges with experience of patent law sit in both courts. The Patents County Court was established to hear smaller and less complex claims and, unlike in the Patents Court, patent agents can appear on behalf of their clients. Appeals in both cases lie to the Court of Appeal.

CASE MANAGEMENT

In an attempt to reduce the time and costs spent on litigation, the courts of both Canada and the UK have introduced formal systems of 'case management' in recent years. The US does not have a formal system of case management, although its rules of procedure may be adapted to improve the efficiency of pre-trial procedures.

[2] D Leduc-Campbell et al, 'Federal Trial Judge Calls for Reform of Patent Litigation', (1993) 7 WIPR 122—23 (quoting the 9 February 1993 opinion from Justice Francis C Muldoon in *Unilever PLC v Procter & Gamble* [1993] 2 FC null).

Canada

Until about 15 years ago, the prevailing view in many Canadian courts was that litigation belonged to the litigators. The courts were passive bystanders, with judges reacting to motions initiated by one party or the other. This approach applied to all civil litigation, including patent cases.

Commencing in the 1990s, it was recognised that the courts' passive role in the management of cases resulted in serious inefficiencies for parties and the courts. For example, cases that were scheduled and then adjourned at the last moment at the request of counsel resulted in downtime for the judge involved. Other cases could not be scheduled to fill the time he now had available on such short notice. This exacerbated the backlog of cases in the courts and resulted in further delays.

The result was the introduction of the new Federal Court Rules 1998, SOR/98–106 (the title was later changed to the Federal Courts Rules by the Rules Amending the Federal Court Rules 1998, SOR/2004–283) to provide specifically for case management and dispute resolution. The Federal Court Rules (which govern practice and procedure in both the Federal [trial] Court and the Federal Court of Appeal) now provide that all cases are subject to status review if appropriate further steps are not taken within the time specified in the Rules. In a status review, the plaintiff is required to show cause why the proceeding should not be dismissed for delay or, in the case of the defendant, why default judgment should not be entered. While in serious cases status reviews will be unlikely as the parties will be taking steps in a timely way, the time limits provide a residual discipline to ensure that cases do not languish.[3]

Alternatively, patent cases may be brought under special case management. Because of the length and complexity of these cases, special case management is often the course that is followed. Special case management involves the Chief Justice of the Federal Court appointing a judge or a prothonotary (a procedural judge) to deal with matters that arise prior to trial. This will include fixing the times for completion of all pre-trial steps, conducting pre-trial conferences and dealing with all pre-trial motions, including the setting of a trial date.[4]

The case management judge has a number of options for proceeding. He may order that the action be referred to a dispute resolution conference. At this conference, the judge or prothonotary may conduct a mediation where he meets with the parties together or separately to encourage a mutually acceptable resolution of the dispute. The judge may conduct an early neutral evaluation of the proceeding. This is to evaluate the relative strengths and weaknesses of the positions advanced by the parties and

[3] rr 380–82.
[4] rr 383–85.

render a non-binding opinion as to the probable outcome of the proceeding. Finally, he may conduct a mini-trial, presiding over presentations by counsel for the parties of their best case, and rendering a non-binding opinion as to the probable outcome of the proceeding.[5]

Dispute resolution conferences may result in settlement of the action, although in many patent disputes this is unlikely. However, dispute resolution may at least result in the resolution of a number of issues. This means that the length of the trial may be shortened.

In order that the case management judge may use all the tools available to settle the case, or at least reduce and clarify the issues, the judge who ultimately conducts the trial will not have been involved in the dispute resolution proceedings.

The UK

In the UK, formal case management procedures were introduced across the civil court system in 1999 following an extensive review of civil procedure carried out by Lord Woolf.[6] These procedures are contained in the Civil Procedure Rules (CPR). The over-arching principle of the CPR, the 'overriding objective', is that of dealing with cases justly. Dealing with cases justly requires ensuring that the parties are on an equal footing; saving expense; dealing with cases in a proportionate manner; ensuring expeditious and fair resolution of disputes, and allotting appropriate court resources to each case.[7] Both the court and the parties are under an obligation to comply with the overriding objective.

Part 63 of the CPR deals specifically with intellectual property claims, including patent proceedings. Many of the specific provisions relating to patent proceedings were already in place in the Patents Court before the introduction of the CPR, such procedures having been introduced following a notorious trial in the 1970s concerning a polymeric surgical suture which took over 100 days of court time.[8] As a consequence of those procedures[9] an equivalent case today (involving one patent and no unusual features) would typically take less than 10 days.

As in the Canadian system of case management, the UK system provides for the court to take an active role in managing the progress of cases. The court makes orders concerning the timetable to trial, and may penalise parties who do not comply with the timetable (the ultimate sanction being an order that a party's case be struck out).

[5] rr 386–91.

[6] *Access to Justice, Interim Report* (1995) and *Access to Justice, Final Report* (1996).

[7] CPR r 1.1.

[8] *American Cyanamid v Ethicon* [1979] RPC 215.

[9] Such procedures include provision for pre-reading, reduced disclosure, product and process descriptions and written evidence and are discussed further on in this chapter.

Unlike in Canada, the Patents Court does not designate one particular judge to deal with a case throughout, although in certain circumstances parties may request that issues relating to a case be reserved to a particular judge where such course may save time and costs. In particularly heavy litigation, the parties may apply for an order that a judge be nominated to hear the case and deal with all case management applications.[10]

Resolution of disputes by alternative dispute resolution (ADR) is encouraged in the UK, although the judges of the Patents Court and Patents County Court do not become involved in this. If the parties embark on ADR the court proceedings will be stayed pending resolution of the ADR. The most common form of ADR is mediation, in which an independent mediator is appointed by the parties. Mediations take place 'without prejudice', and, as a consequence, nothing that is said in mediation can be subsequently used in the litigation. There is no provision for the courts to give non-binding opinions on the merits.

The US

Once a case is filed in a United States District Court, the Federal Rules of Civil Procedure, which have nationwide application, and the Local Rules of that United States District Court, which apply only in that court, will be used in connection with the adjudication of that case. However United States district judges are usually open to counsels' agreed suggestions to modify the standard procedures set out in the Federal Rules of Civil Procedure to accommodate and efficiently resolve issues unique to patent cases, such as the scheduling and conducting of *Markman* hearings (a mini-trial used by the parties and the judge to define particular or ambiguous claim terms).[11]

Further, some United States District Courts have enacted certain of their local rules specifically for patent cases. The Northern District of California's Patent Local Rules, for instance, were upheld by the Federal Circuit in two cases in which summary judgment was granted for non-infringement and in which the Federal Circuit was not persuaded that the sanctions resulting from failure to comply with the Patent Local Rules were too harsh.[12]

[10] Chancery Guide 3.2.

[11] The Federal Rules of Civil Procedure are available online at www.law.cornell.edu/rules/frcp.

[12] See, *02 Micro International Limited v Monolithic Power Systems, Inc* 467 F3d 1355 (Fed Cir November 15, 2006); and *Safeclick, LLC v Visa International Service Association* 2006 WL 3017347 (Fed Cir October 23, 2006). Bass and Fisher, 'Federal Circuit Affirms: Local Patent Rules Have Strong Bite', ipFrontline, 19 December 2006, available at www.ipfrontline.com/depts/article.asp?id=13694&deptid=4.

DISCOVERY

The process of discovery (or disclosure, as it is known in the UK) has the potential to be extremely time-consuming and costly. In the US, where pre-trial discovery includes obtaining the facts available to witnesses (via the deposition process) as well as obtaining documentary materials from other parties in the case, it is the most time-consuming phase of a patent infringement lawsuit. The UK does not have a deposition procedure. Nevertheless, left unchecked, the process of disclosure can still be a time-consuming and thereby expensive one. Disclosure is the area that has been most radically attacked by the UK courts in order to decrease the time and cost of patent disputes. In Canada there is both documentary discovery and oral discovery through deposition.

In all three jurisdictions, discovery obligations now cover electronic, as well as hard copy, documents. The requirement to give electronic discovery (E-discovery) has imposed additional burdens upon parties to patent litigation.

The US

The scope of discovery in the US can be broad. The rules provide that discovery extends to any non-privileged matter that is relevant to any party's claim or defence, including the existence, description, nature, custody, condition and location of any documents or other tangible things and the identity and location of persons who know of any discoverable matter.[13] As a consequence, any discovery sought by a party that is reasonable calculated to lead to the discovery of admissible evidence may be relevant.

Some United States District Courts have a standard schedule in their local rules for certain pre-trial aspects of patent infringement cases, but most courts desire counsel to confer and recommend a schedule that more precisely fits their particular case. No matter how the pre-trial discovery schedule is set, it is the United States district judge presiding in the case, with input from counsel via a submitted discovery plan, who supervises the pre-trial discovery in the case through scheduling orders and protective orders that are entered after conferences with counsel.

A recent survey of the Fellows of the American College of Trial Lawyers revealed that every major discovery tool available under the Federal Rules, such as depositions, requests for admissions, and interrogatories were important, but not cost-effective.[14] Seventy-one per cent believed that discovery is an effective tool to force or encourage settlement.

[13] US, r 26(b)(1).

[14] Advancement of the American Legal System and the American College of Trial Lawyers Task Force on Discovery, Interim Report 2008, *Litigation Survey of Fellows of the American College of Trial Lawyers*, (9 September 2008) A-4.

The UK

The UK Patents Court has adopted a firm line towards disclosure in order to make significant time and cost savings. The scope of disclosure has been radically reduced, which has not only shortened the disclosure process but ultimately the trial process as well: it is the general experience that the more documents there are in a case, the longer the case will take to try. Every document is a potential source of a series of questions in cross-examination, as well as much pre-trial expenditure. Disclosure has been cut down in a number of ways.

Firstly, disclosure relating to any ground on which the validity of the patent is challenged is limited to documents in a four-year window, two years on either side of the priority date of the patent.[15] The rule is not rigid, in that specific disclosure can be sought outside the window if grounds are shown for ordering it.

Secondly, disclosure relating to any pleaded issue of commercial success of the invention is accomplished by the provision of schedules.[16] as opposed to original documents. Historical disclosure of documents going either to the way in which the invention was made or the way in which the defendant arrived at the alleged infringement was frequently sought to be deployed in relation to issues of obviousness or insufficiency. Evidence of an uphill technical struggle by the patentee, or an unsuccessful one by the defendant can be of some secondary relevance to inventive step, but there is usually some reason why the real life story is not strictly comparable with the question required to be answered under the statute. So, for example, if the relevant cited prior art was unknown to the patentee, his failure to come up with the invention in ignorance of it is unlikely to assist.

In *Nichia v Argos*[17] the late and much missed Pumfrey J (as he was then) refused to order disclosure going to the issue of obviousness at all.[18] The majority of the Court of Appeal (Jacob LJ dissenting) disagreed. But even the decision of the majority in that case has opened the way to a much more case-sensitive approach to disclosure of this kind. As Pill LJ said at paragraph 82:

> The decision making judge should consider, with the help of the parties, the features of the particular case with a view to making an order tailored to achieving a just outcome, which includes limiting, as far as possible, the costs incurred.

[15] CPR 63 PD 5.2.

[16] CPR 63 PD 5.3 and 4.

[17] *Nichia v Argos* [2007] EWCA Civ 741; [2007] FSR 38.

[18] The learned judge's remark, on making the order, that 'I have waited nine years actually to do this', revealed a commonly felt frustration with disclosure of inventors' notebooks: always voluminous, seldom informative and practically never determinative.

A third area in which disclosure may be dispensed with relates to documents concerning the allegedly infringing product or process. A defendant can avoid giving disclosure, at least initially, of documents going to the issue of infringement if the defendant provides a description giving '(a) full particulars of the product or process alleged to infringe; and (b) drawings and other illustrations, if necessary'.[19]

There is no doubt that there is a great advantage, from the point of view of trying the case, if all the relevant technical information about the alleged infringement is presented conveniently in a single document. The duties of parties in relation to the provision of such a document are the same as those in relation to disclosure.[20] A description of the product in general or tendentious terms is not acceptable.[21] There should therefore be no loss to the integrity of the trial process.

In general the provisions concerning product and process descriptions have bedded in well. Difficulties have, however, arisen when the parties do not direct their minds adequately to the degree of detail required. A defendant will naturally not wish to go into detail which is unnecessary for resolving the issue of infringement. The claimant, on the other hand, may have it in mind to argue for a narrower construction of the claim than that which the defendant expects. The narrower construction may require more detail in the product or process description to enable the infringement point to be decided on the narrower construction. Difficulties such as these need to be ironed out well in advance of trial, if the product or process description is to serve its purpose,[22] and to avoid the need for costly adjournment of the trial.

Canada

In Canada, which like the US has documentary discovery and depositions, the 'special case management' provisions may be used to manage the process.

Electronic Discovery

A recent—and drastic—change in US discovery rules is the opportunity for each party to now request, in addition to 'traditional' documentation, access to any or all of the other side's electronically stored information (ESI), or 'E-Discovery'. The scope of what is available to the other side is

19 CPR 63 PD 5.1.
20 *Alfred Taylor v Ishida (Europe) Ltd* [2000] FSR 224.
21 *Consafe Engineering (UK) Ltd v Emtunga UK Ltd* [1999] RPC 154.
22 *RIM v Visto Corporation* [2008] EWHC 335 [170].

breathtaking: if asked to do so, a party will have to produce 'electronically stored information' wherever it resides, such as in e-mail messages or e-mail attachments, Blackberries, PDAs, laptops, instant messenger, archives, and even from home computers that an employee might use now and then to catch up on work over the weekend. The sheer volume of discoverable electronic information is staggering and leads to problems such as distinguishing private communications from business correspondence and the potential waiver of privilege between a client and her patent attorney during e-mail interactions.

Unsurprisingly, 87 per cent of the lawyers surveyed by the American College of Trial Lawyers indicated that such E-Discovery increases the costs of litigation, and nearly 77 per cent believed that US courts do not understand the difficulties in complying with E-Discovery.

An equivalent discovery option is available in the UK, 'e-Disclosure', but a key difference in that jurisdiction is the scope of the e-Disclosure rules. The UK courts 'demand a narrow approach to e-Disclosure, requiring production only of documents which advance or damage the case of the giver or another party. That already narrow band may be further refined by wide discretionary powers'.[23] The CPR[24] provide that the parties should co-operate as to the manner in which e-disclosure should be undertaken and the exercise is, in any event, subject to conditions of reasonableness. In practice, it is common for parties to identify key words which they will use to automatically search identified electronic files.

Canada is dealing with similar issues and concerns. Last year, the Honorable Mr Justice Sharlow in Canada's Federal Court of Appeals, in *eBay Canada Limited v Canada (National Revenue)*,[25] required the appellants to provide to the Minister the 'required information [including] the names of the PowerSellers, their contact information, and the amount of their gross annual eBay sales'. That information could readily 'be found in electronic form in servers located in the United States'. Undoubtedly, each party and their counsel must make sure to devote substantial time to consider these E-Discovery issues in the US, UK, and Canada.

EXPERT EVIDENCE

Expert evidence is almost always necessary in patent cases so that the court can be brought up to speed with the relevant technology and equipped with the knowledge of the skilled person for the purposes of construing the

[23] C Dale, 'UK judge flies e-Disclosure flag in New York, the e-Disclosure Information Project', http://chrisdale.wordpress.com/2008/03/06/uk-judge-flies-e-disclosure-flag-in-new-york/.
[24] CPR 31 PD 2A.
[25] *eBay Canada Limited v Canada (National Revenue)* 2008 FCA 141 (CanLII).

patent. However expert evidence can be expensive and has the potential to add undue complexity to proceedings. It is therefore necessary to implement procedures to ensure that this useful tool does not take on a life of its own.

All three jurisdictions allow for relevant expert evidence to be admitted and, in each jurisdiction, experts are instructed and paid for by each of the parties to the litigation.[26] In the US, once written expert reports have been exchanged, the parties may choose to depose the expert witness of the other side. Any testimony of the expert at the deposition that is inconsistent with the expert's trial testimony may be used to impeach the expert witness. In Canada there is no right to pre-trial examinations of experts save with the leave of the court, and in the UK there are no expert depositions.

In both the UK and Canada, the role of experts has been subject to review. In the UK the use of experts was criticised by Lord Woolf[27] as leading to delay, excessive expense and unnecessary complexity. As a consequence of his concerns a section of the CPR[28] was devoted to expert evidence and the 'Protocol for the Instruction of Experts to give evidence in civil claims' was drawn up. The CPR make clear that it is the duty of an expert to help the court on matters within his own expertise and to give independent, objective and unbiased opinions notwithstanding the arguments being advanced by the party paying him. The rules prescribe the matters that must be included in the expert report including his qualifications, the details of any literature or materials relied upon by him in making his report, a statement of the facts and instructions given to him for the purposes of making his report and the reasons for the opinions he expresses in his report. The requirements set out by the US District Court rules for expert reports are similar to the UK requirements.[29]

A review of the role of expert witnesses has more recently been carried out in Canada where, in the spring of 2008, a sub-committee of the Federal Courts Rules Committee issued a report.[30] Among the concerns identified by the sub-committee, two are noteworthy. The first relates to experts taking on an adversarial role on behalf of the party that retained them, thereby diminishing the reliability of their evidence. The second is the impact expert evidence is having on the length of trials and the commensurate increase in the cost of litigation to parties.

To address the first problem, the sub-committee has proposed that a Code of Conduct be included in its Rules. That Code of Conduct would

[26] Although the UK procedural rules provide for the joint instruction of an expert, it is usual for each party to instruct their own expert.

[27] See *Access to Justice* Reports (Interim Report Chapter 23 and Final Report Chapter 13).

[28] CPR 35.

[29] r 26(a)(2) United States District Court Rules.

[30] That report has been circulated to the profession for comment and, after comments are received, the sub-committee will report to the Rules Committee with their recommendations.

impose an overriding duty on an expert to assist the court impartially on matters relevant to his area of expertise: that duty would override any duty to a party to the proceedings.

In order to reduce costs, it has been proposed that at the time the expert report is delivered,[31] the expert's proposed area of expertise be identified and the expert's CV be delivered with the report. Any objections to the expert testifying in the identified areas and the basis for those objections can then be dealt with at a pre-trial conference. Such proposal is an improvement on the current practice, which allows for parties to challenge the expertise of an expert at trial, a practice which takes up court time and places the judge in the position of potentially having to disqualify the expert at trial.

A further proposed improvement, in order to avoid the difficulties incurred where expert reports do not clearly set out the facts or assumptions on which the expert opinion is based or where competing expert reports fail to address the same issues, is that the Code of Conduct should list the information required to be in the expert report. This information would be similar to that required in both the UK and US, and include a statement of the issues addressed in the report, the qualifications of the expert, the facts and assumptions upon which the opinions were based, and the reasons for the opinions expressed.

A number of other proposals have been made. One is that the court may direct the expert witnesses to confer without the jurisdiction of counsel and the parties either before a judge (who would not preside at the trial) or prothonotary. The sub-committee recognised the controversial nature of this proposal:

> Whether the absence of counsel would foster the independent exercise of judgment by an expert is not entirely clear. This possibility would need to be weighed against a potential for the relative force of the experts' personalities to skew the outcome in a face to face meeting. Over time, this could in turn lead to a change in the approach taken to selecting experts. It remains to be resolved therefore whether specific provisions for experts' conferences held in the absence of counsel are necessary or whether it is sufficient simply to admonish experts in the Code of Conduct to maintain their independence when conferring with one another as directed by the Court.[32]

There is also provision in the UK rules for experts to have face-to-face meetings in the absence of each party's legal team in order to narrow the issues between them; that course is not routinely adopted in patent litigation.[33]

Another proposal of the Canadian sub-committee was the introduction of a procedure, colloquially referred to as 'hot tubbing', which has been implemented by the Canadian Competition Tribunal. The experts for both sides would appear as a panel and in addition to counsel examining, cross-examining and re-examining the experts, the experts could question

[31] At least 60 days before trial, or 30 days in the case of rebuttal evidence.
[32] Sub-committee Report, 6.
[33] Although it is common in other civil disputes, eg medical negligence actions.

each other and comment on the views of the other expert. The judge could question the experts on a point on which there was disagreement, to ensure he had a complete and clear understanding of the positions of the experts. The purpose of 'hot tubbing' is to ensure that the issues between the experts are properly joined, to enable the judge to understand as clearly as possible the areas of agreement and disagreement between the experts and to better test the strengths and weaknesses in the reports of each expert.

The question of the best way to deal with expert evidence is an important one for courts wishing to reduce the costs of patent proceedings, and is an area that should be kept under regular review.

THE US *MARKMAN* HEARING

The *Markman* hearing is a pre-trial hearing at which issues concerning construction of the patent are determined. In both the UK and Canada, issues of construction are dealt with at trial. The reason for the difference in approach between the US and the UK/Canada is that in the US, parties have a constitutional right to a jury trial. In the UK and Canada the case is heard by a judge sitting alone. Because the issue of construction is primarily one of law, it is appropriate for it to be determined pre-trial in the US. Typically the *Markman* hearing takes place before trial, although it can be done at any time during proceedings. The jury is usually provided with the trial judge's *Markman* construction at the end of closing arguments with the jury instructions.

The importance of claim construction in all three jurisdictions cannot be underestimated. Since it is only the claims of a patent that can be infringed, the scope of a patent's claims are almost invariably at issue in any patent litigation. This is a critical, but sometimes forgotten, aspect of all patent litigation. The comparison is not between the patented *device* and the accused infringing *device,* but between the words of the claim and the elements of the accused infringing device. It is because the words of the claim define the scope of the patentee's exclusive rights that construction of the meaning of those words is critical to any patent litigation. The definitions of the claims are almost always crucial to and frequently dispositive of a determination regarding patent infringement or patent validity.

Markman Hearings in the US

In *Markman v Westview Instruments*,[34] the case from which the term '*Markman* hearing' stemmed, the United States Supreme Court determined that it was United States judges, and not juries, that should decide the

34 *Markman v Westview Instruments* 415 US 370 (1996).

meaning of patent claim language. The Court emphasised that judges are better equipped than juries to construe the meaning of patent claim terms, given district judges' training and experience interpreting written instruments, such as contracts and statutes. The Supreme Court made it clear that by holding that United States district judges should be making patent claim construction determinations would better promote uniformity and certainty in patent claim construction. The Supreme Court also specifically noted that treating claim construction as a 'purely legal' issue would serve *stare decisis* principles, as courts are better situated to give due weight to decisions of other courts that have previously ruled on the same issues. Thus, in a *Markman* Hearing, the accused infringer's goal is to define a key term narrowly so that his or her activities or product falls outside their definition of the claim element. Conversely, the patent holder wants to proffer a broad definition so that the accused product falls squarely in their definition and therefore infringes the patent claim.

To carry out the Supreme Court's directive in *Markman*, most United States District Courts in patent cases order an initial disclosure by the patent litigants of their respective contentions on the issues of infringement and validity. Next, courts require the parties to identify the claim terms that require interpretation by the court and propose their respective interpretations of those patent claim terms. Courts then typically try to narrow the number of claim terms to be construed, and proceed to the *Markman* claim construction process by applying the key claim construction principles enunciated by the United States Court of Appeals for the Federal Circuit. Those key claim construction principles include:

1. The court starts with the ordinary meaning of a particular claim term, as an objective baseline and, if necessary, then determines the meaning by first evaluating the evidence intrinsic to the patent. This intrinsic evidence encompasses the claim language, the specification and figures of the application, and statements made during examination, which are affixed into the application file wrapper. Thus the Federal Circuit in *Phillps v AWH Corp*[35] emphasised the judge should first look at these forms of intrinsic evidence to define or understand a term or element in a patent claim, before looking to outside, or 'extrinsic', sources, such as to dictionaries, treatises, or expert or inventor testimony. Consequently, a consistent understandable usage of a claim term in both the patent and prosecution history provides a good basis for construction of that term. The construction that stays true to the claim language and most naturally aligns with the patent's description will, in the end, be the correct construction.

[35] *Phillps v AWH Corp* 376 F.3d 1382.

2. A term used in the claim is to be interpreted from the perspective of a person of ordinary skill in the art at the time the patent application was filed. However, any such evidence extrinsic to the patent or the patenting process that is considered by the court cannot contradict the intrinsic evidence.
3. A term cannot have a meaning that the patentee has clearly and unmistakably surrendered or disavowed during the patent's prosecution in the PTO.
4. Any limiting distinction over the prior art is to be considered to narrow the scope of the term's meaning.
5. When a patentee expressly defines a claim term in a specific way, then *that* meaning, not the claim term's ordinary meaning, is to be used.
6. The meaning of a patent claim term is generally not limited to the preferred embodiment. When the patent contains more than one claim, as most United States patents do, each patent claim is to be considered to have a different scope and the terms therein should be construed accordingly.

The *Markman* hearing may often proceed by way of legal argument only, without the need for any evidentiary hearing.

The advantage of the *Markman* hearing is that the parties receive an early determination on the issue of claim construction. That allows for the parties to reflect upon the merits of their respective cases and may, in turn, provide for early resolution of the dispute, either by way of settlement or by way of summary judgment.

Claim Construction in Canada

In Canada, claims are construed by looking at their plain language through the lens of 'the notional person skilled in the art'.[36] Courts may also look to the remainder of the patent specification to put the claims in context and attempt to ascertain the intention of the patentee.[37] However, statements made by the applicant in the prosecution of a patent application are not admissible for purposes of constructing the claims in the granted patent.[38] In other words, 'the court's analysis is restricted to the four corners of the patent'.[39]

[36] CJ Furman, 'Canadian Intellectual Property Awareness in Cross-Border Transactions: Patents', SN051 ALI-ABA 73, 80 (18–19 October 2007).

[37] Ibid. 80–81.

[38] Ibid 81–82.

[39] WH Richardson and A Sawchuk, 'Effectively Managing a Global Patent Litigation Strategy', www.mccarthy.ca/article_detail.aspx?id=3454 (2007).

The Canadian procedural rules governing patent infringement do allow for determination of preliminary issues before trial. Claim construction is a matter of law and is, in principle, suitable for pre-trial determination. However, the Canadian courts have resisted introducing a *Markman*-style hearing into patent proceedings. Indeed a 2004 decision of the Federal Court of Appeal poured cold water on the procedure in Canada (*Realsearch Inc v Valon kone Brunette Ltd*[40]). In *Realsearch*, the Federal Court of Appeal allowed an appeal from a decision of the Federal Court that had permitted a *Markman*-type hearing for the purposes of claim construction before trial on the question of patent infringement. In finding against the holding of a *Markman* hearing on a claim construction, the Court expressed the following concerns about these types of hearing:

1. There was a risk of 'delay, anxiety and expense' because there was no agreement as to the relevant facts.
2. It was not apparent whether the plaintiffs would suffer injustice from a preliminary construction of the patent claims. The plaintiffs could, for instance, lose the advantage of having the whole of the action tried by the same judge. Issues of claim construction and infringement are closely interwoven, even though the Court acknowledged that it would be wrong to construe the claims with an eye on the alleged infringing product.
3. There was no evidence as to how long pre-trial examinations or the trial were anticipated to take and how much time would be saved by granting a *Markman* hearing.
4. Unlike US practice in which no appeal may be taken from a *Markman* hearing decision prior to completion of the trial on infringement, in the Federal Court of Canada there could be an appeal of the *Markman* decision at the same time as the trial on infringement was taking place, possibly resulting in unnecessary duplication, cost and inconvenience. Alternatively, the trial on infringement would be delayed pending a decision from the Appeal Court on claim construction.
5. In Canada, patent trials are conducted by a judge alone without a jury. Considerations involving juries in the United States are not applicable in Canada.

The Court of Appeal allowed the appeal. In its view, it was preferable that the adoption of *Markman*-type proceedings which may have fundamental and far-reaching consequences should be by way of amendment to the Federal Court Rules after consultation and debate in the intellectual property bar.

[40] *Realsearch Inc v Valon kone Brunette Ltd* [2004] 2 FCR 514 (FCA).

Claim Construction in the UK

In the UK, the issues of infringement and validity are tried together, and are almost always linked by the issue of claim construction. The classic illustration of this is the so-called *Gillette* defence.[41] The defendant alleges that his product, the alleged infringement, is fully described in a prior publication to the patent. His defence is that, if he establishes that fact, then the patent is either invalid or he does not infringe, because no patent can validly cover what is old. Usually the dilemma for the patentee will not be so stark. Nevertheless, he will be aware that the wider he tries to stretch the language of his claim, the closer he will come to the prior art. The phenomenon has been described like this:

> Professor Mario Franzosi likens a patentee to an Angora cat. When validity is challenged, the patentee says his patent is very small: the cat with its fur smoothed down, cuddly and sleepy. But when the patentee goes on the attack, the fur bristles, the cat is twice the size with teeth bared and eyes ablaze.[42]

That case was unusual, in that the patentee had sought to bring its claim for infringement in the Court of First Instance. But the views it expresses are general ones. For instance, English courts have recently been asked to exercise their general declaratory jurisdiction to adjudicate on whether patents are 'essential' or 'inessential' to the operation of telecommunications standards.[43] 'Essentiality', like infringement, is extremely sensitive to the scope of claim. A wide claim may make it impossible to operate the standard, something a patentee may want to urge on the court: but the wide construction may work to his disadvantage and be more open to attacks on its validity. A narrower claim may be valid, but may open the way to operation of the standard by other means.[44] The phenomenon allows alleged infringers to run so-called 'squeeze arguments', namely that 'If my product infringes your patent then, as my product is simply a workshop variant on the prior art, your patent must be invalid'.

Others have pointed out the crucial importance of the issue of construction, some arguing that the proper approach to construction is too important a matter to be left to the courts at all, involving, as it does questions of industrial and economic policy. Thus, Vaver argues (about the system in Canada):

> The very scope of a patent is left uncertain. The Patent Act has left courts to develop a doctrine of 'substantial infringement' to catch activity that, at first

[41] *Gilette v Anglo-American* (1913) 30 RPC 465.

[42] *European Central Bank v Document Security Systems Inc* [2008] EWCA Civ 192.

[43] See eg *Nokia v InterDigital* [2007] EWHC 3077 (Pat) (Pumfrey J); [2006] EWCA Civ 1618 (CA).

[44] Normally the interests of justice would be served by trying validity and infringement together. But where, as in recent cases, a party wants declarations in relation to 20 or 30 patents, it may only be practicable to deal with essentiality, leaving validity to be determined in relation to those patents deemed essential: see *Nokia v InterDigital* (n 43) [6] (Pumfrey J).

> sight, does not fall within the patent's claims. With no jury to explain matters to, courts have produced a complicated analysis that promises certainty but fails to deliver. Parliament is, however, more to blame than the courts. The legislature should decide how wide a monopoly a Canadian patent should have ... The question of 'law' is really a question of economic and social policy.[45]

The English courts have recently foresworn complicated analysis in favour of a more unitary approach.[46] As Lord Hoffmann said in *Kirin Amgen*[47] the question is now determined by asking 'what the person skilled in the art would have understood the patentee to be using the language of the claim to mean'.

This brings in context and purpose, still allowing, probably, the court to hold that a lintel with a member 8 degrees from true vertical still could fall within a claim to be a vertical member, but perhaps forbidding the description of a certain tower in Italy as the Vertical Tower of Pisa.[48]

Despite the importance of the issue of claim construction to the ultimate outcome of the litigation on both infringement and validity, the English courts have not adopted the *Markman* hearing. Indeed, rather than putting construction arguments at the fore of litigation, it used to be said that the ultimate test of the skill of the advocate for the claimant in a patent trial in England was to avoid placing any construction on the claims of the patent until his speech in reply.[49] By that time, of course, there would be no opportunity for his opponent to expose the flaws in his interpretation.

The closest an English court would be likely to get to a US-style *Markman* hearing would be a preliminary issue on infringement. These are rare, however, as the defendant forgoes the squeeze arguments, discussed above, which an attack on validity usually brings.[50]

The written pleadings in patent cases follow a minimalist approach and are unlikely to illuminate what issues might require decision on construction of the claims. The traditional approach is that a party will not be ordered to give further particulars of its case if the request is formulated in such a way as to require him to construe the claims of the patent. In a case

[45] D Vaver, *Intellectual Property Law* (Chicago, Irwin Law, 1997) 278.

[46] cp *Catnic Components v Hill & Smith* [1982] RPC 183, 243 and *Improver Corporation v Remington* [1990] FSR 181, 189 with *Kirin Amgen v Hoechst Marion Roussel* [2004] UKHL 46; [2005] RPC 169 [52].

[47] [2005] RPC 169 [34].

[48] See D Vaver, 'Intellectual Property: State of the Art' [2000] LQR 621, 626, suggesting in a wry footnote that the House of Lords' decision in *Catnic*, buried in the specialist reports, 'deserves to be better known amongst those who insure builders, architects, engineers and surveyors against negligence'.

[49] A spoof 'Practice Direction' which used to circulate in chambers at 11 South Square, Gray's Inn, largely drafted by the inimitable GD Everington QC, included this as a requirement, along with the rule that whenever the judge asks whether the case is on target to finish on time, counsel shall reply: 'I am in your Lordship's hands.'

[50] A fairly recent example of such a preliminary issue on infringement was *Rohm & Haas v Collag* [2001] FSR 28 (Neuberger J); [2002] FSR 28 (CA).

decided before the advent of the civil procedure reforms,[51] such a request was refused, as the issues would emerge adequately in the exchange of written reports and witness statements.

A rigid application of the minimalist/traditional approach can give rise to difficulties. The evidence which a party wishes to call may depend on the construction placed on the claim by his opponent.[52] It is not necessarily enough to await the exchange of witness statements, because it is not necessary for a party to lay out his case on construction there either, provided that he proves, to the extent not admitted, every fact on which he intends to rely. Indeed, the principle that it is not appropriate for an expert to opine on the meaning of ordinary English words (as opposed to terms having a special technical meaning) could be argued to make such evidence inadmissible. A practice now adopted in expert reports is for the section of the report dealing with the claims to pay lip service to this rule,[53] whilst making clear what the party's position on construction is likely to be.

The court does have a salutary power to order a statement of case on any issue, and statements of case on infringement have been ordered in a number of cases. Such an order can require the patentee to identify where in the accused device or process each feature of the claim is to be found. Whilst this is far short of a memorandum on the construction of the claim, it does operate to focus and identify the issues of construction.

The measures required sufficiently to expose issues of construction will vary from case to case. It is possible that, consistently with the Civil Procedure Rules, English practice may develop a more flexible approach to the way in which these issues are exposed, falling short of a pre-trial hearing to determine them.

TRIAL

The Seventh Amendment to the United States Constitution gives parties in the US the right to a jury trial. The parties may, if they wish, waive the right to a jury trial, but in the most part, patent trials in the US are determined by juries. This immediately introduces an additional stage to patent proceedings in the US, namely jury selection, which is often referred to as the 'voir dire'.

[51] *Lux v Staffordshire* [1991] RPC 73, relying on earlier cases such as *Wenham v Champion as Lamp Co* (1891) 8 RPC 22.

[52] For a recent case where this was so, see *Novartis AG v Johnson & Johnson* [2008] EWHC 293 (Pat).

[53] 'I have been instructed that the meaning of the claims (apart from terms having a special technical meaning) is a matter for the Court alone. However I believe it would be helpful if I set out what I believe a person skilled in the art would understand from a reading of the claims …'

Once the jury is selected and seated, a typical patent infringement trial proceeds in the following way:

1. Opening statements: the lawyers are entitled to give the jury opening statements as to what they believe the evidence will show.
2. Presentation of the evidence: the next phase is the presentation of the evidence. The party with the burden of proof, usually the plaintiff, calls witnesses first and conducts direct examination of each called witness, who testifies under oath. The process by which the relevant factual and/or expert evidence is extracted from the witness is known as 'examination-in-chief'. Before each witness leaves the witness stand, opposing counsel has a right to conduct cross-examination of that witness. During this evidentiary phase, exhibits in the form of documents and other physical evidence that are determined to be admissible are received in evidence for the jury's examination.
3. Closing arguments: once all the evidence is received and the parties rest their respective cases, the lawyers make their closing arguments to the jury.
4. Instructions to the jury: the judge then reads the jury instructions on law. Those jury instructions will include any patent claim construction determinations.
5. Verdict: after the jury instructions are presented to the jury, the jury retires, deliberates, reaches a verdict and returns that verdict by announcing it in open court. The court then enters a judgment on the verdict.

The jury's reasoning in reaching a particular verdict in a patent case is seldom revealed, unless special interrogatories are presented to the jury by the court to be answered and returned by the jury when the jury returns its verdict. Special interrogatories can be very helpful, but US patent counsel tend to be reluctant to submit them for fear that the jury's answers may be inconsistent and may result in even more inexplicable ambiguity about the jury's thinking in reaching a particular result.

In contrast to the position in the US, in both the UK and Canada, patent trials are heard by a judge sitting alone. The trial progresses in a similar manner to a jury trial, with opening statements, presentation of the evidence and closing arguments. Following closing arguments the judge retires to consider his verdict, which is normally handed down in written form at a later date. The written judgment sets out fully the judge's reasoning.

The obvious advantage of a judge-only trial is that the time taken at trial can be significantly reduced. Not only is there no need to spend time on jury selection but, more importantly, the judge can be taken much more quickly through the evidence and legal arguments. The process can be further accelerated if evidence and argument is submitted in writing and the judge asked to read it out of court. This is an approach that has been adopted by the

UK courts where there is provision for pre-reading, written evidence and written submissions:

1. Pre-reading: no time in court is now taken up with putting the judge in possession of the basic documents—the patent specification, the prior art, details of the alleged infringement and the parties' opening arguments on the principal issues.[54] The relevant documents will all be pre-read by the judge and there is seldom any need for lengthy opening speeches. Before this reform it was common for the party opening the case to read the documents aloud to the judge in court.[55] There can be no doubt of the benefit of this reform: there is no justification for the parties, their advisers and others being required to be present whilst the judge acquires the basic framework of the case.
2. Written evidence: no court time is now taken up with examination-in-chief. All (or almost all) evidence is now exchanged in writing well in advance of the trial in the form of witness statements and expert reports which the witness merely confirms after taking the oath in court.[56] The judge will have pre-read this material as well. This reform was not wholeheartedly welcomed by judges, who, with justification, regarded the process of giving evidence-in-chief as an important part of the assessment of the reliability of the evidence. Moreover, despite strong ethical safeguards which are in place as to the manner in which witness statements and expert reports are to be prepared, concerns about witness statements remain. Witnesses who, under cross-examination, have to withdraw statements in their written evidence, look unreliable. But the fault may lie with the manner in which the legal representative assisted in the preparation of the statement, rather than with the witness himself. Plainly it is careless to confirm on oath an elaborate statement which contains some inaccuracy. But to do so does not make the witness a liar or an unreliable expert in respect of all their evidence. If the witness has given the evidence himself in chief, there is nobody else to blame.
   The use of witness statements and reports is therefore a compromise reached in the interests of keeping the trial short. Witness statements are, no doubt, popular with lawyers, as they reduce the risk element involved when the witness fails, in his or her oral evidence, to give the evidence confidently relayed to the lawyer in private before the trial.[57] They undoubtedly cut many days out of the trial timetable.

[54] CPR 63 PD 7.

[55] This practice was deprecated by the House of Lords in *Home Office v Harman* [1983] 1 AC 280, 305H–306B (Lord Diplock), 324F–G (Lord Roskill). The reading of large amounts of written material by the judge was characterised as part of his duty to the parties and other litigants.

[56] For witness statements see CPR 32.4; 32.5; for expert reports see CPR 35.10.

[57] Seasoned filmgoers will remember John Cleese as Archie Leach QC in the 1988 comedy *A Fish Called Wanda*, calling his lover (played by Jamie Lee Curtis) as an alibi witness who

The extent to which such written materials have reduced, overall, the cost of patent litigation is more open to debate. Such statements go through many drafts in the course of preparation for trial, far more than the rough (and privileged) proofs of evidence that counsel would have for the purposes of oral examination in chief. Many lawyer-days can be spent on the perfection of witness statements and reports, made necessary by the fact that they are to be disclosed in advance to the opposite side.

3. Final submissions in writing: a large part of the parties' final submissions will now be reduced to writing. This again reduces the time spent in court. The case is usually adjourned after the evidence is complete for the parties to summarise the evidence and their submissions in writing. The procedure allows the final speech to be both better organised and shorter.[58]

As a consequence of such measures the time taken for trial of a patent infringement action can be significantly reduced.

THE CANADIAN PATENTED MEDICINES (NOTICE OF COMPLIANCE) REGULATIONS

A large proportion of patent disputes, in all three jurisdictions, relate to pharmaceuticals. In Canada a very high proportion of pharmaceutical patent disputes are dealt with by way of a special procedure pursuant to the Patented Medicines (Notice of Compliance) Regulations.[59]

In 1993, the Parliament of Canada enacted amendments to the 1985 Patent Act,[60] and the Governor-in-Council brought into force the Patented Medicines (Notice of Compliance) Regulations. In some respects, the changes to the Patent Act and the Regulations bear a similarity to the US Drug Price Competition and Patent Term Restriction (Hatch-Waxman) Act of 1984.[61]

In brief, the amendments to the Patent Act provide for an 'early working exception' to patent infringement. Section 55.2(1) provides that:

> It is not an infringement of a patent for any person to make, construct, use or sell the patented invention solely for uses reasonably related to the development and submission of information required under any law of Canada, a province or

confirms the accused's whereabouts—but only until she saw him leaving the apartment on the day of the robbery with a sawn-off shotgun.

[58] As Mark Twain said: 'I did not have time to write a short letter, so I wrote a long one instead'.

[59] SOR/93-133.

[60] RSC 1985, c P-4.

[61] Pub L No 98-417, 98 STAT 1585.

a country other than Canada that regulates the manufacture, construction, use or sale of any product.

While the provision is not expressly related to pharmaceutical products, it is probably fair to say that it is most often relied upon by competitors of holders of pharmaceutical patents (generally generic producers) to enable them to enter the market as soon as the patent expires. Without this exception, the generic producers would be prohibited from taking steps for regulatory approval of their product until their competitor's patent had expired, resulting in delay in reaching the market.

Under the Notice of Compliance Regulations, a patent-holding drug company may file a patent list with the Canadian Minister of Health that contains a patent for a medicine or for its use (section 4(2)). A generic drug company is permitted to compare the product that it intends to market with the product of the patent-holder in order to establish its safety and efficacy and secure marketing approval from the government. This process saves the generic competitor time and resources. However, the Minister of Health will not issue a Notice of Compliance for safety and efficacy purposes, without which the generic cannot market its product, unless the patent on the product the generic producer is comparing with has expired, or the generic producer's product will not otherwise infringe the patent. Thus, the Regulations create a connection between government approval to market a drug product and the issue of patent infringement.

The Regulations provide that the generic producer must, in seeking a Notice of Compliance from the government, serve on the patent-holder whose patent is the subject of the comparison, a Notice of Allegation. The Notice of Allegation must allege, amongst other things, that the patent has expired, is invalid or will otherwise not be infringed (section 5(1)(b)). The patent-holder may then, within 45 days, apply for a writ of prohibition from the court prohibiting the Minister from issuing a Notice of Compliance to the generic producer, without which the generic product cannot be marketed (section 6(1)).

Until the court deals with the prohibition application, the proceedings act as a stay for up to 24 months, precluding the Minister from issuing a Notice of Compliance, pending the determination of the prohibition application by the court. Should the court grant the prohibition application, the generic producer will not be able to obtain a Notice of Compliance from the Minister until expiry of the patent. Should the prohibition application be dismissed, the Minister will be free to issue a Notice of Compliance to the generic producer, provided the generic product otherwise complies with government regulations. Should the court make no decision before the 24 month stay expires, the stay will be vacated and the Minister will be free to issue a Notice of Compliance to the generic (section 7(1)).

The prohibition proceedings will result in a decision by the court as to whether the allegation by the generic producer that the patent is expired, invalid or infringed, is or is not justified. Such a finding is not considered to constitute *res judicata* on the issue of patent infringement. A patent-holder may still bring an action for infringement and have the issues of validity or infringement dealt with on the basis of new evidence and argument.[62]

The process under the Regulations is treated as a judicial review and not an action. Evidence is by way of affidavit. Unlike in the case of patent trials, in which there is no pre-trial examination of experts' reports, under the Regulations there is usually extensive cross-examination on the experts' affidavits. Because of the amounts involved, the cross-examinations may consume many days and hundreds, if not thousands of pages of transcript. It is the experts' reports and the cross-examinations that will be the vast bulk of the evidence that will form the record before the judge.

In *Pfizer Canada Inc v Canada (Minister of Health)*,[63] Hughes J. summarised the jurisprudence to the effect that when a patent-holder applies for a writ of prohibition, the regulatory scheme places the burden on the patent-holder to disprove the generic producer's non-infringement allegations. If neither party were to introduce evidence on the issue of invalidity, the presumption of validity afforded by the Patent Act would likely satisfy the burden. However, in the normal case, both parties adduce evidence and the court will weigh all the evidence and determine the question on the balance of probabilities.

There has been an enormous amount of litigation involving these Regulations since they came into force in 1993. There have been at least four rounds of amendments to the Regulations to address deficiencies as seen by the courts and to reverse the effect of a court decision where government policy is inconsistent with that decision.

While much of the litigation under the Regulations deals with the merits of the allegations made by the generic producer, there is also considerable litigation involving the procedures under the Regulations. It is the latter type of litigation that has resulted in the successive amendments to the Regulations.

For example, because the application for prohibition is an application and not an action, a generic producer could not bring a motion to strike the prohibition application on the grounds that it did not disclose a reasonable cause of action.[64]

The Regulations are an important component of Canadian patent law. Much jurisprudence is generated under them, especially procedural jurisprudence. Parties in pharmaceutical cases are litigious because of the enormous stakes involved. As a consequence, although proceedings under the

[62] *David Bull Laboratories (Canada) Inc v Pharmacia Inc* [1995] 1 FC 588 (FCA) 598–600.
[63] *Pfizer Canada Inc v Canada (Minister of Health)* 2008 FC 11 [28]–[32].
[64] See *David Bull* (n 62) 598–600.

Regulations are conducted on written evidence (in contrast to other patent trials), the commercial importance of the outcome of these proceedings to the parties means that the costs incurred are often greater than in other patent trials.

CONCLUSIONS

Although united by common themes, there are significant differences between the way in which patent trials are conducted in the US, UK and Canada. The most obvious difference is the use of jury trials in the US, which necessitates early determination of issues of patent construction at the *Markman* hearing. Case management provisions have been introduced in Canada and the UK, and the courts' active management of disputes in both of these jurisdictions has improved the efficiency with which litigation is resolved. The use of judge-only trials in Canada and the UK allows for the possibility of shorter trials. However, whilst the use of written evidence and argument may reduce the amount of time spent in court, it does not necessarily reduce costs. As the Canadian experience under the Regulations illustrates, where the outcome of litigation is of huge commercial significance to the parties, those parties will spend commensurate amounts protecting their position, and there is little that the courts can do to prevent this.

Nevertheless, in each jurisdiction the courts have taken steps to make patent litigation more cost-effective and time-efficient. It is to be hoped that in the future the courts continue to review their own procedures to see where improvements can be made: whilst the big players, such as pharmaceutical companies, have the ability to draw on large resources, the courts must be astute to recognise the position of smaller parties and ensure that they are not unfairly shut out of patent litigation.

6

Emergent Diversity in the Common Law Relating to Intellectual Property

How Domestic Court Practice Informs Local Evolution of Law

ROGER T HUGHES

'ALL POLITICS IS local'—a quote attributed to Thomas 'Tip' O'Neill, the long-time Speaker of the House in the United States Congress.[1] It might equally be said that 'all law is local', when it comes to our common law traditions. We are quick to recognise the contributions of the Supreme and Appellate Courts, as well as those of reputable academics such as Professor David Vaver,[2] in defining and reshaping the course of the common law. However, one must not lose sight of our 'friends in low places',[3] where it all begins. Cases brought in the courts are shaped by the practice and procedures in those courts and the remedies there afforded. The day-to-day determination of disputes goes unnoticed, leaving academia to ponder the rarer cases brought and defended by the richer and more determined of our litigants.

IN THE BEGINNING

Asking how litigation begins is rather like asking how persons fall in love. The answer is that there are all sorts of ways, good, bad and indifferent. In the area of intellectual property, there are three typical scenarios. The first is the local, rather personal dispute: a local restaurant finds that another

[1] See T O'Neill et al, *All Politics is Local*, (Halbrook, MA, Random House, 1994).
[2] A listing of judicial citations in Canada of David Vaver's works appears as Appendix A to this chapter.
[3] Blackwell and Lee, 'Friends in Low Places', as sung by Garth Brooks.

newly opened establishment has much the same name; a musician finds that a local radio station is using a song composed by him or her, in an unauthorised way. The second is somewhat broader, a regional or even national organisation discovers that another organisation is using a similar name or get-up, has made what looks like a copy of its instructional manuals, or may even be copying a patented item. The third is where multinational organisations are clashing in many jurisdictions including, in our case, Canada. In this third scenario, while trade marks or copyright are sometimes involved, most often patents are the issue. Currently pharmaceutical patents are among the most commonly contested IP issue disputed by such multinationals.

In the first scenario, the local dispute is generally between modestly funded parties. These cases are usually brought in the local small claims court, where remedies are limited to damages and whatever vindication the winning party can derive from the victory. Self-represented parties are not unusual. Often such cases provide a training ground for new lawyers, or a bit of diversion for more seasoned litigators. If a judge or magistrate hearing the matter decides to write reasons, they often provide for interesting reading, touching on the human aspects so often lost in larger matters.[4] Rarely do such cases go further; nor are the decisions considered of great jurisprudential value.

The second scenario is the bread and butter of the local lawyer and even the national firms on occasion. Brought in the local superior courts by lawyers who know the system and the judges, the cases generally pass quickly to a decision. Trade marks, passing off, copyright, trade secrets and contract or quasi-contractual issues dominate this area. The decisions do not usually make new law.[5] Again, appeals are unusual.

The third category is the one that gathers most of the jurisprudential attention and is the focus of this chapter—the clash of the titans, played in the smaller arena of Canada. Dupont will clash with Allied Signal,[6] IBM will clash with Xerox,[7] and, Monsanto will clash with a very determined farmer.[8] Pharmaceutical cases proliferate, with brand companies such as Eli Lilly, Bayer, GlaxoSmithKline and AstraZeneca taking on generics including Apotex, Novopharm, Genpharm and others.[9] It is these cases that engage the international legal community, and there are many layers to the legal

[4] See eg *Rostad v Drynan* (1994) 59 CPR (3d) 8 (Ont Sm Cl Ct).

[5] See eg *Emma Foods Ltd v Mr Submarine* (1976) 34 CPR (2d) 177 (Ont HC); *MacKnight v MacCallum Building Supplies Ltd* (1990), 31 CPR (3d) 526 (NBQBTD).

[6] *AlliedSignal Inc. v Du Pont Canada Inc* (1993) 50 CPR (3d) 1 (FC), rev'd 61 CPR (3d) 417 (CA).

[7] *Xerox of Canada Ltd v IBM Canada Ltd* (1977) 33 CPR (2d) 24 (FCTD).

[8] *Monsanto Canada Inc v Schmeiser* (2001) 12 CPR (4th) 204 (FC), aff'd [2003] 2 FC 165 (CA), var'd [2004] 1 SCR 902.

[9] Too numerous to mention.

teams of each party. Canadian lawyers from notable firms represent them, while in the background in-house counsel from the international headquarters often involve their favourite lawyers from their home countries.

In these large cases, the Canadian lawyer is often asked to compare Canadian practice to that of the client's home country and to conduct the Canadian case in a manner as close as possible to the practice with which the client and the client's favourite lawyers are most comfortable. Often the client must manage cases going on simultaneously in several jurisdictions. It is trite to say that what goes on or is revealed in one jurisdiction may well influence what happens or becomes known in another. Everyone—the Canadian lawyers, the client, and the foreign lawyers—is constantly walking on tightropes, determined not to slip up and inadvertently giving away an issue vital to a proceeding elsewhere.

COMMENCING THE PROCEEDING

In Canadian courts an action is commenced by a plaintiff who files and serves a statement of claim. A defending party, the defendant, files a statement of defence, often coupled with a counterclaim in which the defendant seeks relief against the plaintiff. With a few changes in terminology, such as complaint instead of statement of claim, and claimant instead of plaintiff, the practice is more or less the same across the common law world. What sets Canada apart is the detail required in these pleadings. Canada requires a great deal of detail: the plaintiff is required to set out precisely what rights it asserts, why it asserts that the defendant is infringing upon those rights, what relief it seeks and why.

In the United States, most jurisdictions simply require what are called 'notice'-type pleadings in which the parties are identified, the right asserted identified (eg the identity of a patent or a trade mark), and a very brief description of the alleged infringement is provided. The defence and counterclaim, if any, are equally brief. However, such notice pleadings are quickly followed by a series of interrogatories put by one side to the other, which are intended to amplify the pleadings. The result is that at the end of the interrogatory process, information has been exchanged and positions taken that often exceed that established by Canadian pleadings.

From a Canadian perspective, the commencement of pleadings takes the form of shadow boxing. Much is said but little is revealed. A plaintiff in a patent action, for instance, may simply recite every claim of the patent in detail, alleging that the defendant's product or process has taken every element of the claims. The courts have been inconsistent in approving[10]

[10] *Tyhy v Schulte Industries Ltd* 2004 FC 1421.

or disapproving[11] such pleadings. A defendant, who may be caught by surprise in having an action commenced against it, may simply produce a laundry list of defences and counterclaims, hoping to buy time and be allowed to sort it out later.[12] In the end, pleadings tend to contain a lot of chaff as well as wheat on both sides of the issue. Much of this chaff remains, even until trial, simply because no party wants to appear to blink before the other.

Fortunately, this form of 'shadow boxing' pleadings in Canadian actions is largely confined to patent litigation. In trade mark and copyright proceedings, pleadings are usually directed to concrete matters that a party believes it can establish.

A different type of proceeding is that of an application. Certain trade mark and copyright proceedings, namely trade mark registration expungement[13] and copyright infringement,[14] may be commenced by a Notice of Application. A Notice of Application can be very brief indeed, indicating only the parties and the trade mark or copyright at issue. While a practice has evolved whereby the Notice contains much more by way of particulars, the responding party need do no more than file a notice that it intends to appear and identify the solicitors who will be representing it. This abbreviated process is largely due to the fact that the party instituting the proceeding must prove its case by way of affidavits filed within a few weeks after the proceedings are commenced, and that a respondent must do the same. Thus, in a relatively short time, each party must provide all of its evidence to the other, and pleadings are largely irrelevant.

As a bizarre twist to the application process there are proceedings under the Patented Medicines (Notice of Compliance) Regulations,[15] often called NOCs. These proceedings involve patents directed to drugs. Where a generic drug company seeks approval to sell a drug in Canada which has been designated by the drug's innovator, often called the brand, as being covered by claims of one or more patents, the generic must send the brand a document called a Notice of Allegation. In the Notice of Allegation the generic must allege that the patent-at-issue is invalid or not infringed or licensed, providing a 'legal and factual basis' for those allegations. This notice is something provided for in the NOC Regulations, not by the Federal Courts Rules of practice, and jurisprudence has developed such that the Notice, once served, cannot be amended.[16]

[11] *Litebook Co. v Apollo Light Systems Inc* (2006), 50 CPR (4th) 445 (FC).

[12] *Bauer Nike Hockey Inc v Easton Sports Canada Inc* (2002) 22 CPR (4th) 382 (FC) (Proth).

[13] Trade-Marks Act, RSC 1985, c C-13, s 58.

[14] Copyright Act, RSC 1985, c C-42, ss 34(4) & (5).

[15] SOR/93-133, as amended.

[16] *Pfizer Canada Inc v Canada (Minister of Health)* (2005), 46 CPR (4th) 25 (FC).

Court proceedings only begin when the brand files a Notice of Application with the Court. The Notice of Application is, in effect, a response to the Notice of Allegation in which some or all of the allegations may be contested. After that, the parties file and serve their affidavits and the matter proceeds to the cross-examination of the important affiants.

The result is awkward. The generic usually puts everything it can think of in the Notice of Allegation, since it cannot be amended. The brand is forced to engage issues that, as the evidence is filed, might never be substantiated. The result is that the proceedings are massive, occupying far too much judicial time in procedural matters and hearings. In addition, the final decision only determines if the allegations are 'justified'[17]—the determination does not constitute *res judicata* if any party chooses to institute a usual action as to infringement or validity of the patents at issue.[18] In instituting such proceedings, the brand gets an automatic 24 months' stay on any approval to sell that might otherwise be given by the government to the generic.[19]

From a jurisprudential standpoint, proceedings taken under the NOC Regulations are generating a mass of decisions relating to all kinds of patent law aspects: sufficiency, selection from a class, utility, obviousness and anticipation, just to name a few. This jurisprudence undoubtedly has some value, but the Federal Court has to decide the matters without the benefit of live witnesses and against the awkward standard of whether an allegation as to validity, infringement or license is 'justified'. Nevertheless, very recently the Supreme Court of Canada has decided one of these cases and written substantive law as to obviousness, anticipation, double-patenting and selection patents on the basis that the standards as to validity are the same as those in an ordinary action as to patent validity.[20]

DISCOVERY

Once pleadings have been exchanged, the parties in an action move to the next phase, discovery. In an application, the parties exchange affidavits and conduct cross-examination. That is, they proceed directly to the evidence, which is ultimately placed before a judge determining the matter in written form only.

On discovery a party is supposed to reveal its case. In terms of documents, a party is required to provide a list of all documents that it intends to rely upon to prove its case and to rebut the other party's case.[21] There is a

[17] NOC Regulations (n 15), s. 6(2).
[18] *Pharmascience In. v Sanofi-Aventis Canada Inc* (2006) 53 CPR (4th) 453 (FCA).
[19] NOC Regulations (n 15), s 7(1).
[20] *Apotex Inc v Sanofi-Synthelabo Canada Inc* 2008 SCC 61[16]–[17].
[21] Federal Courts Rules, SOR/98-106, rr 227 et seq.

continuing obligation to furnish documents that may be newly discovered.[22] Thus the process is one of self-selection by a party—what it intends to use at trial and what it considers relevant. An opposing party has an opportunity to come to the court asking for other documents to be provided. However, it has the burden of demonstrating that the documents probably exist and are relevant.[23]

In most trade mark and copyright actions of normal proportions, disclosure is forthcoming. Juxtaposed to this, in proceedings with international counterparts the strategy is often different. The United States has quite a different disclosure practice. While initial disclosure may be limited, it is almost inevitable that a party will be required to make available to the opposing side masses of documents that may have only a remote connection to a matter. The producing party need not list the documents or assert their relevance. Quite often a room full of documents is simply opened to lawyers for the opposite party, who then scan all the documents and mark by a 'Bates' number any document that they believe may have some relevance in the matter. Thus the 'self-selection' process is in the hands of the opposite party.

During this process it is not unusual for documents to come to light that have not been produced in the Canadian process. Often the parties in a Canadian action simply agree to produce all documents provided elsewhere, without any assertion as to relevance. Sometimes the Canadian court will be asked for an order for production. The effect is to import into Canada a broader concept of relevance than may have been intended, including production of documents that may only be relevant on the basis of some foreign concept unknown to Canadian law.

One notable example of foreign influences on the issue of relevance is the concept of file wrapper estoppel, a concept prevalent in the United States but expressly not part of the law in Canada.[24] Canadian Courts have rationalised file wrapper estoppel by analogy to contract law, where negotiations during the drafting of a contract should not be relevant to the interpretation of the final signed document.[25] Yet, a Canadian Court may require such documents to be produced on discovery, on the basis that somehow they may be relevant.[26]

Shortly after documents have been produced the parties embark upon oral discovery in a process that is uniquely Canadian. In Australia, no discovery beyond the production of documents is normally permitted. In the

[22] Ibid, r 226.
[23] Ibid, r 225.
[24] *Lovell Manufacturing Co. v Beatty Bros Ltd* (1992) 41 CPR 18 [38]–[39] (Ex Ch).
[25] *Free World Trust v Electro Sante Ltd* (2000) 2 SCR 1024 [62]–[67].
[26] *Foseco Trading AG v Canadian Ferro Hot Metal Specialties Ltd* (1991) 36 CPR (3d) 35 (FCTD).

United Kingdom, discovery of documents and written interrogatories is the normal practice. In the United States, written interrogatories and production of documents, as discussed previously, is followed by depositions of people likely to appear as witnesses at trial and those who may be thought to have relevant information. A party's representative may also be examined, but this is usually rather perfunctory, the deposition of witnesses being the more extensive and time-consuming process.

In Canada, interrogatories, although they may be ordered, are rare. In oral discovery a party provides one representative to answer questions. If that person cannot provide an answer to a relevant question, they are required to become informed and provide a suitable answer. In effect, it is like an extensive interrogatory process done orally, usually with at least two or three attendances required as the person receives information from others.

Again, with the United States process being more extensive, Canadian parties may be confronted with deposition transcripts from the United States proceedings and asked to confirm or deny what is said in the transcripts. Often this is done by agreement and, if no agreement is reached, the same questions are put to a Canadian person examined on discovery who is then obliged to become informed as to the answer. Just as with documents, this process results in the intrusion into Canadian law of legal principles established elsewhere.

Canadian discovery in complex intellectual property matters can be a never-ending process[27] and may continue even as the trial is going on.[28] The practical result is that the issues for trial are not really settled until the close of final argument. It is no wonder that the resulting judgment must deal with a great many issues, some with only limited evidentiary basis.[29]

EXPERTS

Experts in intellectual property cases come in many forms: the 'touch/sniff' expert who looks at an object, a chemical, a process and reports to say what it is and what properties it has; the survey expert who purports to put questions to certain segments of the population, collates the answers and draws conclusions from those answers; the economic expert who speaks to market conditions, what financial gains would have been made 'but for' the activity in question; and, most commonly, the opinion expert who purports to tell

[27] A matter criticised by the court on several occasions eg *Terra Nova Shoes Ltd v Nike Inc* (2003), 28 CPR (4th) 270 (FC).
[28] As was the case in *Merck & Co. v Apotex Inc.* (2006), 53 CPR (4th) 1 (FC).
[29] Eg *Merck* (n 28).

a court what the climate of those working in the field several years ago was and, most dangerously, what a patent and its claims mean.

There is a constant struggle between the court and the litigants, counsel and experts, as to just how much 'assistance' an expert can provide. Well-funded litigants can scour the world to find attractive, articulate 'experts' willing to offer the court interpretations of patents and prior art and the like favourable to their interests. Where both sides are well funded, counsel frequently turns a issue such as claim construction into a battle of experts. Time and again the court has to remind the litigants and their counsel that construction of a patent and the claims is the function of the court. The role of an expert, if any, is confined to providing assistance as to the meaning of terms and phrases not commonly understood, and, if needed, the background against which a patent should be read.[30]

The court is in danger of being overrun with experts in patent matters. Recently the Federal Court determined that no more than five experts per side should appear without special leave of the court.[31] Previously it was not uncommon for each side to present at least 15 experts, often giving repetitive evidence. This often resulted in a total of 30 or more experts, each providing opinions presumably to assist the court but on many occasions, moving perilously close to advocacy.

Survey experts occupy a field of their own. Surveys are used most often in the context of trade mark disputes, and are expensive to conduct. The court is careful to scrutinise how a survey is conducted,[32] how well the survey reflects actual conditions in the marketplace,[33] and how the questions are framed.[34] Even then the court will consider the result as assisting in a determination and not in making the determination itself.[35]

The expert flood is a problem common to many jurisdictions, not just Canada. Canada has not yet institutionalised guidelines regarding expert

[30] Eg *Eli Lilly Canada Inc v Novopharm Ltd* (2007) 58 CPR (4th) 214 [104], appeal dismissed for mootness 2007 FCA 359.

[31] *Eli Lilly and Co. v Apotex Inc* 2007 FC 1041.

[32] *Sun Life Assurance Co of Canada v Sunlife Juice Ltd* [1998] OJ No 114, 22 CPR (3d) 244 (HC); *Cartier Inc v Cartier Optical Ltd* [1998] FCJ No 266, 20 CPR (3d) 68 (TD). See *Labatt Brewing Co v Molson Breweries* [1996] BCJ No 2191, 73 CPR (3d) 544 (SC); *Altinor Inc v Nutravite Pharmaceuticals Inc* [2004] FCJ No 268, 31 CPR (4th) 12 [75]–[83], aff'd without discussion as to this point [2005] FCJ No 1333, 42 CPR (4th) 107 (CA).

[33] *Joseph E Seagram & Sons Ltd v Canada (Registrar of Trade-marks)* [1990] FCJ No 909, 38 FTR 96 at 107; *London Life Insurance Co v Manufacturers Life Insurance Co* [1999] FCJ No 395, 87 CPR (3d) 299 [36] and [24] (TD).

[34] *Bojangles' International LLC v Bojangles Café Ltd* [2006] FCJ No 843, 48 CPR (4th) 427 [58]–[62].

[35] *Choice Hotels International Inc v Hotel Confortel Inc* [1996] FCJ No 330, 67 CPR (3d) 340, 348 (TD), aff'd [2000] FCJ No 2015, 12 CPR (4th) 101 (CA); *Kirkbi AG v Ritvik Holdings Inc* [2002] FCJ No 793, 20 CPR (4th) 224 [81]–[137] (T.D.), aff'd without discussion on this point [2003] FCJ No 1112, 26 CPR (4th) 1 (CA), aff'd without reference to this point [2005] SCJ No 66 [2005] 3 SCR 302.

witness testimony, but some Canadian cases have adopted the United Kingdom guidelines in *The Ikarian Reefer*.[36] Australia has implemented guidelines respecting experts[37] which may become a model for Canada.

In its *Daubert*[38] decision the United States Supreme Court has endeavoured to come to grips with the problem of weeding out 'junk science' and to establish a set of criteria for measuring the reliability of expert evidence. The Supreme Court of Canada in *Mohan*[39] has adopted similar measures, rejecting any general test for applicability of evidence and requiring a case-by-case analysis as to the reliability of the expert evidence tendered. The fact that courts at the highest level have stepped in to deal with problematic expert evidence demonstrates the dangers that courts face in receiving such evidence and abdicating the adjudicative role to experts.

PRE-TRIAL MANAGEMENT—NARROWING THE ISSUES

Pleading and discovery do little to narrow the issues. Much shadow boxing and bluffing occurs. Only at the pre-trial management stage, when the judge who is to hear the case steps in, do the parties come to grips with the fact that the matter is going to trial and that they should know the case to be presented.

Canadian counsel are not always to be blamed for this last-minute formulation of the case. Major intellectual property litigation is conducted in several countries more or less at the same time. Indeed, some 'rocket docket' United States jurisdictions such as Virginia and Northern California may have already determined the matter, or part of it. If it is a jury determination, the reasons for the decision are not known, only the verdict and answers to any particular questions of fact put to the jury. If the matter is under appeal, the final determination is still in doubt. Decisions of a European forum are often cryptic and dependent on specialised laws such that little of any decision can be useful in Canada.

In addition, the Canadian marketplace may make Canadian litigation unimportant. There have been cases where a Canadian proceeding has gone to trial, and while the matter is under reserve, the matter is settled in another jurisdiction and a Canadian determination deemed to not be required. While a judge may be relieved not to have to release a decision, usually it has been partially written and the time wasted in preparing and hearing the case could have been well spent elsewhere. Given that there is

[36] *The Ikarian Reefer* [1993] 2 Lloyd's Rep 68–81.
[37] *Guidelines for Expert Witnesses*, Australia Federal Court, Version 6, 5 May 2008.
[38] *Daubert v Merrell Dow Pharmaceuticals* 509 US 579 (1993).
[39] *R v Mohan* [1994] 2 SCR 9.

no decision released there is nothing of public record to reflect this waste of resources—but I assure the reader that there have been several occurrences in this regard.

A pre-trial conference or series of conferences is, therefore, directed to determining whether the parties genuinely want a trial, settling the issues, arriving at an agreement as to certain evidence and dealing with such other issues as may ensure the just, most expeditious and least expensive determination of the proceeding on its merits.[40] This process puts the parties and their counsel squarely before the trial judge, the person who will decide upon the merits of the case, for the first time.

The United States courts assign a judge to a case early in the process but insert magistrates or deputy judges to deal with procedural matters. The United Kingdom, with its long history of senior barristers, seems to be much less in need of such a process. However only recently the English Court of Appeal[41] has been very critical of counsel taking proceedings in the Patent Court and raising innumerable issues on appeal.

TRIAL

Canada, like Australia, the United Kingdom and most other common law jurisdictions, conducts intellectual property trials before a judge without a jury. In the United States, where it is common to have jury trials, these are preceded by summary judgment motions and *Markman*[42] hearings before a judge alone. In effect, the United States is endeavouring to dispose of legal issues and complex matters by a judge without a jury.

Canadian Courts do not require the extensive pre-trial or post-trial briefings as submitted in United States proceedings. In Canada, a brief is submitted during argument, set out in short paragraph form with cryptic references to the case law and evidence. In the United States, counsel are likely to submit long narratives reciting in detail the facts and law pertaining to the case. Often parts of these narratives are copied wholesale into the reasons given by the court. When writing their reasons, Canadian courts are unlikely to adopt great portions of the argument as submitted by one or other of the parties because of their cryptic, non-narrative nature.

Canadian judges in the Federal Court each have one law clerk assigned to them. That clerk will assist in legal research and in proof-reading a judgment. While some judges and clerks have a technical background and intellectual property experience, cases are assigned to a broad range of judges.

[40] Federal Courts Rules, r 6.

[41] *Corus UK Ltd v Qual-Chem Ltd* (2008) EWCA Civ 1177 [2].

[42] *Markman v Westmere Investments Inc* 52 F2d 967 (Fed Cir 1995), aff'd 517 US 370 (1996).

Great efforts are made by the National Judicial Council and others to educate judges in this area and a bench book covering many relevant areas of the law is provided. However, opinions do vary.

APPEALS

Every final decision of a trial court in Canada can be appealed, as of right, to the appropriate provincial or federal Court of Appeal. After that, appeals to the Supreme Court of Canada are heard only with leave. The Canadian Supreme Court has, in recent years, heard a surprising number of intellectual property cases, averaging one or more per year. Intellectual property is an area where legislative reform is slow, often because even modest reforms become controversial. In copyright, for instance, where the Canadian statute is based on legislation passed in the United Kingdom in 1911, and thus approaching its centenary, the Supreme Court of Canada has stepped in to make what amounts to policy decisions.[43] Similarly in patent matters, the Supreme Court in the 'Harvard mouse' case has entered the policy-making realm in determining whether living things such as mice can properly constitute patentable subject matter.[44]

As a case passes through the appellate system, legal issues can change. For example, a case which, at the trial, turned on whether a farmer deliberately and knowingly planted patented seed,[45] at the Supreme Court became a case where the issue was whether such seed could properly be the subject of a patent.[46] This case followed on the heels of the 'Harvard mouse' case.

Other examples can be given of policy-making by the Supreme Court of Canada in intellectual property matters,[47] the point being that at the highest level, the Supreme Court will make policy.

REMEDIES

A party who 'wins' a lawsuit is awarded certain remedies by the court. The classic intellectual property litigation remedies available to a party are an injunction, damages or profits, delivery up or destruction of offending goods, and costs. It is usual to have a trial limited to issues of validity and infringement separated, that is, bifurcated, from a subsequent trial as to

[43] Eg *CCH Canadian Ltd v Law Society of Upper Canada*, [2004] 1 SCR 339; *Kraft Canada Inc. v Euro Excellence Inc* (2007), CPR (4th) 353.

[44] *Harvard College v Canada (Commission of Patents)* [2002] 2 SCR 45.

[45] *Monsanto Canada Inc v Schmeiser* (n 8).

[46] *Monsanto Canada In. v Schmeiser* [2004] 1 SCR 902.

[47] In trade marks, *Ritvik Holdings Inc v Kirby AG* (n 35), whether functional objects can be trade marks.

quantum of damages or profits if then required. Usually quantum issues, if infringement is found, are settled before the second part of the bifurcated trial begins.[48]

Getting back to the low places, some intellectual property litigation is conducted on an Anton Piller, John Doe basis, which rarely reaches a full-scale trial. In dealing with counterfeit goods it is common that trade mark and copyright features are copied by some offshore manufacturer on goods which are imported into Canada and sold through flea-markets, street vendors and the like. A practice has developed whereby the court will issue an order naming 'John Doe' and others as defendants. Such persons are identified as those selling counterfeit goods bearing the trade marks and copyrights (identified by registration number) of the plaintiff. They are required to turn over to a person who is said to be a neutral solicitor, offending goods in their possession, cease to sell such goods on an interim basis, and, if so advised make a motion to the court within 10 days to review or set aside the order.[49]

The result is that such proceedings are quickly settled and rarely go to court. It is a form of civil search and seizure warrant exercisable against anyone seeming to offend its terms. The court is still waiting for a full-scale contested proceeding by motivated parties to determine the propriety and limits of such an order.

Remedies such as punitive or exemplary damages or full indemnity as to costs are given rarely, and only where the conduct of the litigation, not the nature of the offending infringement, requires the court to express its indignation.[50]

Criminal remedies are afforded for some types of dealings in copyright and trade mark matters. Rarely do such matters reach the courts, possibly because of the difficulties in getting interest from law enforcement officers to prosecute such cases.[51]

Statutory damages, like those provided for in United States legislation, have been added to the Canadian Copyright Act.[52] There has been limited experience with these provisions.[53] Amendments to the Criminal Code have made it illegal to copy a motion picture while in a theatre, which amendments have provided for a few charges being laid.

[48] But not always, eg *DuPont Canada Inc v Allied Signal Inc* (1998) 78 CPR (3d) 129 (FC); aff'd (1999), 86 CPR (3d) 324 (FCA).

[49] Eg *Ragdoll Productions (UK) Ltd v Doe* [2003] 2 FC 120.

[50] Eg *2703203 Manitoba Inc v Parks* (2006) CPR (4th) 276 (NS).

[51] They do occur on occasion, for instance *R v Laurier Office Mart Inc* (1994), 58 CPR (3d) 403 (Provincial Court), aff'd (1995) 63 CPR (3d) 229 (Ont Court Gen Div) involving a photocopying service.

[52] RSC 1985, c C-42, s. 38.1.

[53] Most such cases are undefended eg *Wing v Van Velthuizen* (2000), 9 CPR (4th) 449.

COSTS

In Canadian courts, costs are awarded on what American lawyers call the 'English Rule': the winning party gets an award of costs on the partial indemnity basis, that is, about half of their lawyer's fees and most disbursements. In a situation where, in the conduct of the litigation and not the commission of the wrongful activity, the losing party has behaved badly, full indemnity recovery may be awarded.

In major litigation, costs are not a factor that motivates most decision-making. Costs are trivial compared to all the non-recoverable expenses involved in litigation. In situations where the defendant is unlikely to be found or, if found, unlikely to have any means to pay, costs are not a factor. They have been a factor in settlement where a party agrees to an injunction and costs have been awarded in a modest amount, which amount usually goes directly to the lawyer who enforces the order.

Costs can be a reason why smaller and sometimes potentially legally interesting cases never get judicially determined, or are determined only by a first instance court. In modest and mid-sized litigation, such as two restaurants in the same community quarrelling over a name, costs can be a factor. The losing litigant must pay its own expenses including its own lawyer and a good portion of the other party's expenses and legal fees. This is a strong incentive toward settlement. It also discourages a losing party from appealling a decision, for fear of losing the appeal and incurring a further costs order as well as having to pay their own lawyers yet more money. Academics cannot count on a free jurisprudential ride at the expense of a litigant.

WHERE DOES THIS LEAVE US?

From a jurisprudential point of view, the cases from the third scenarios, those with litigation being undertaken in many different jurisdictions simultaneously, seem to provide the majority of grist for the mill of authors and academics.

In terms of reasoned decisions involving substantive points of law, about 20 to 30 decisions a year are a normal number for the trial courts. Five to 10 decisions a year for the appellate levels and one or two at most from the Supreme Court can be expected. Of the cases that do go to appeal or the Supreme Court, the issues may change or, as they may put it, become refined. At that level, the grassroots controversies disappear and the textbook issues blossom.

The low places and local decisions are the bread and butter of the legal profession—most litigants want a resolution of their problems and care not at all about jurisprudence. Only a few major cases involving determined or well funded litigants become the bread and butter of the academics.

APPENDIX OF INTELLECTUAL PROPERTY
CASES THAT CITE PROFESSOR DAVID VAVER

Supreme Court of Canada

Euro-Excellence Inc v Kraft Canada Inc [2007] 3 SCR 20 [26]
Mattel Inc v 3894207 Canada Inc [2006] 1 SCR 772 [22]
Kirkbi AG v Ritvik Holdings Inc [2005] 3 SCR 302 [39]
Society of Composers, Authors and Music Publishers of Canada v Canadian Assn of Internet Providers [2004] 2 SCR 427 [56]
Monsanto Canada Inc v Schmeiser [2004] 1 SCR 902 [36], [41], [43], [53], [79], [145], [169]
CCH Canadian Ltd v Law Society of Upper Canada [2004] 1 SCR 339 [41], [48], [56]
Harvard College v Canada (Commissioner of Patents) [2002] 4 SCR 45 [61]
Théberge v Galerie d'Art du Petit Champlain inc [2002] 2 SCR 336 [30]
Whirlpool Corp v Camco Inc [2000] 2 SCR 1067 [53]

Federal Court of Appeal

CCH Canadian Ltd v Law Society of Upper Canada 2002 FCA 187 [59], [95], [126], [128]–[30], [148]–[49], [154] (CA)
General Motors du Canada v Décarie Motors Inc [2001] 1 FC 665 n 13 (CA)
Harvard College v Canada (Commissioner of Patents) [2000] 4 FC 528 [129], [173], nn 78, 83 (CA)
Édutile Inc v Automobile Protection Assn [2000] 4 FC 195 n 7 (CA)
Levi Strauss & Co v Roadrunner Apparel Inc (1997) 76 CPR (3d) 129 n 2 (FCA)
Boutiques Progolf Inc v Canada (Registrar of Trade Marks) (1993) 54 CPR (3d) 451, 458 (FCA)
Canada (Registrar of Trade Marks) v Harris Knitting Mills Ltd (1985) 4 CPR (3d) 488 n 5 (FCA)

Federal Court

Shire Biochem Inc v Canada (Minister of Health) 2008 FC 538 [64]
Pfizer Canada Inc v Canada (Minister of Health) 2007 FC 898 [78]
Pfizer Canada Inc v Canada (Minister of Health) 2005 FC 1725 [43]
Pfizer Canada Inc v Novopharm Ltd 2004 FC 1633 [48]–[49]
CCH Canadian Ltd v Law Society of Upper Canada [2000] 2 FC 451 [125], [127] n 13 (TD)
Hager v ECW Press Ltd [1999] 2 FC 287 [15] n 11 (TD)
Renaud Cointreau & Cie v Cordon Bleu International Ltd (1992) 45 CPR (3d) 374, 379 (FCTD)

Provincial Appellate Courts

Robertson v The Thomson Corporation (2004) 72 OR (3d) 481 [99] (CA)
Turgeon c Michaud [2003] JQ no 7722 [57] (CA)
Lapierre Desmarais c Edimag inc [2003] JQ no 3067 [40] (CA)
Lac d'amiante du Québec ltée c 2858-0702 Québec inc [1999] JQ no 1043 n 7 (CA)
Apotex Fermentation Inc v Novopharm Ltd [1998] MJ No 297 [111], [169] (CA)

PROVINCIAL COURT JUDGMENTS—FIRST INSTANCE

Fénollar c PRB Média [2006] JQ no 3348 [38] (CS)
Les Constructeurs I et S Inc c Camiré [2001] JQ no 2697 [58] n 28 (CS)
B & S Publications Inc v Max-Contacts Inc [2001] AJ No 143 [20] (QB)
Tobin v De Lanauze [2000] QJ No 3137 [62] (SC)
Polansky Electronics Ltd v AGT Ltd [1999] AJ No 1230 [35] (QB)
Wrebbit inc c Benoit [1998] JQ no 3242 [273]–[74], [277], [280], [283] (CS)
Mulroney c Canada (Procureur général) [1996] JQ no 518 n 15 (CS)
Apotex Fermentation Inc v Novopharm Ltd [1995] MJ No 339 [284] (QB)
REF-COM Commercial Inc v Holcomb [1991] QJ No 1267 (SC)
LEL Marketing Ltée v Otis [1989] QJ No 1229 (SC)
Montour ltée v Jolicoeur [1988] QJ No 702 (SC)
British Columbia Automobile Assn v Office and Professional Employees' International Union Local 378 [2001] BCJ No 151 [150] (SC)
Cadbury Schweppes Inc v FBI Foods Ltd [1994] BCJ No 1191 [6] (SC)
ICL Engineering Ltd v Associated Corrosion Contractors Inc [1985] BCJ No 527 [6] (SC)
HZPC Americas Corp v True North Seed Potato Co [2007] PEIJ No 29 [16]–[17] (SCTD)
Robertson v Thomson Corp [2001] OJ No 3868 [24] (Sup Ct Jus)
Techform Products Ltd v Wolda [2000] OJ No 5676 [16] (Sup Ct Jus)
Patsalas v National Ballet of Canada 13 CPR (3D) 522 AT 528
Dolmage v Erskine [2003] OJ No 161 [26], [43], [106], [109], [171–[73] (Sup Ct Jus Sm Cl Ct)

Patents

7

A Common Law Prescription for a Medical Malaise

TINA PIPER

INTRODUCTION

THE MEDICAL METHODS exception (MME) has always seemed remarkable. It presently excludes technologies applied on or in the body from patentability, claiming to protect medical practitioners treating patients from liability for patent infringement.[1] The exception's existence seems to argue that the medical profession's work is significant enough to society to warrant special rules in patent law. In so doing, the MME contradicts the technology-neutral, morally agnostic stance of patent law which leaves the regulation of polycentric disputes to other fora. More remarkable, however, is how the MME became an integral part of patent law doctrine and now the European Patent Convention (EPC), and what that process tells us about the common law. Its evolution demonstrates that the common law is not monolithic and self-contained, but relies on mixed legal and professional communities of reception to shape its content. These communities may transcend national boundaries. As a result, informal common law principles may reveal themselves to be better rooted than the seemingly clearer and more certain statutory sources of law, which thus become secondary. This chapter considers the origins of the common law rule followed by the nature and international dimensions of the legal and medical community that received and practised the rule, in particular of Commonwealth courts and Canadian physicians. I will illustrate through the history of the MME the hybrid nature of the common law as part rule and part custom, inaccurately modelled by either legal positivism or as merely the reception of customary norms.[2]

[1] Patents Act 1977 (UK) c 37. S 4A holds: '(1) A patent shall not be granted for the invention of—(a) a method of treatment of the human or animal body by surgery or therapy, or (b) a method of diagnosis practised on the human or animal body.'

[2] AWB Simpson, 'The Common Law and Legal Theory', in A Renteln and A Dundes (eds) *Folk Law: Essays in the Theory and Practice of* Lex Non Scripta: *Volume I* (Madison, U Wisconsin Press, 1994).

THE ORIGINS OF THE COMMON LAW RULE

The MME was recognised as a common law rule by the 1914 decision *Re C&W's Application*,[3] a decision that hardly justifies a principle of patent law that has existed for almost a century. *C&W* involved an application for a method that used electricity to extract lead from victims of lead poisoning, and was heard by the Solicitor General, Sir Stanley O Buckmaster, on appeal from a decision of the Supervising Examiner not to grant a patent. The invention acted on matter inside the human body and claimed a method rather than an apparatus, in contrast to the medical devices that were commonly patented at the time. *C&W* went on to be cited as foundational by all British cases (and most Commonwealth cases) that addressed the MME, although its pertinence as precedent began to be questioned in the 1960s and 70s.

The MME, for the better part of the twentieth century, was a common law rule, although its status as such cannot be understood merely by legal positivism. Legal positivism holds that common law rules are created by the law-making act of the judicial decision. To deal with the noted weaknesses of traditional legal positivist accounts,[4] the theory has been modified to posit the common law as a set of rules whose validity is prescribed by other rules such as the status or reputation of the judge or court deciding the case, and the decision's consistency with prior authority. Yet the authority of *C&W* is barely explained according to a legal positivist account. In *C&W*, Buckmaster briefly concluded in a one and a half page judgment, without relying on any prior common law authority and with limited reasons, that the invention was not patentable subject-matter.[5] He held that the impugned process did not create a vendible product, and that '[s]o far as human beings are concerned, it cannot be suggested that the extraction of lead from their bodies is a process employed in any form of manufacture or of trade.'[6] The basis for Buckmaster's decision remains unclear and has been the subject of debate throughout the Commonwealth.[7] As merely a law officer of the Crown, rather than a judge in a court under High Court jurisdiction, Buckmaster may not have even had the institutional authority to create binding precedent.[8]

[3] *Re C&W's Application* (1914) 31 RPC 235 (S-G) (*C&W*). No records remain of the Patent Examiner's file or of the documents submitted in this case at the PO, British Library, or the Public Records Office.

[4] Legal positivism suffers from the weakness that not all judicial decisions produce authoritative judgments, not all common law rules derive from judicial decision.

[5] *C&W* (n 3) 236.

[6] *C&W* (n 3) 236.

[7] Eg Barwick CJ in *Joos v Comr of Patents* (1972) 126 CLR 611 (HCA) (*Joos*).

[8] A White, 'The Grant of Patents for Discoveries of New Uses of Known Medicinal Products' (unpublished paper circa 1985, on file with the author) 3.

After it was introduced in *C&W*, the principle of a medical exception existed as an unchallenged common law rule enforced by the Patent Office, sufficiently robust to be accepted by courts in other Commonwealth countries until it was re-considered in the 1960s.[9] Its authority transcended its humble origins. British cases that subsequently uphold the non-patentability of medical methods all cite *C&W* as authority.[10] While the rule in the terms articulated by Buckmaster could not be said to have been a customary practice of the medical profession, it was, as he stated, 'well known that the medical profession do all in their power to discourage members of their body from obtaining protection for any discovery that has for its object the alleviation of human suffering'.[11] *C&W*, as I describe next, was the legal articulation of what the medical profession aspired to achieve. The authority of the common law MME is best understood by the circumstances of its continued reception, rather than the conditions of its origin.

THE NATURE OF CUSTOMARY PRACTICES AND THE COMMUNITY OF RECEPTION

The common law MME was received, validated and observed by a community of litigants, innovators, physicians, lawyers and judges. Since the rule affected in practice only the patent applications of innovators with medical credentials, the medical community, which particularly sought to distance itself from the market and the patent system as it professionalised in the era of patent medicines, was both the most affected and influential constituency.[12] From the early to mid-nineteenth century, UK physicians had been professionalising, which most importantly involved distancing the practice of medicine from the prevailing market morality. It also required addressing the conflicts of interests that arose when physicians profited from products marketed to patients against the backdrop of the patent medicines 'crisis'. Patent medicines accounted for an estimated one-fifth of patents granted in the UK from the late 1700s to the mid-1800s.[13]

[9] *Re US Rubber Co's Application* [1964] RPC 104 (PO) is the first reported subsequent case.

[10] Eg *Rantzen's Application* (1947) 64 RPC 63 (Pat App Trib); *Re US Rubber Co's Application* [1964] RPC 104 (PO) (referring to *NRDC v Comr of Patents* [1960] NZLR 775 (SC) (*NRDC*) and *Maeder v Busch* (1938) 59 CLR 684 (HCA)); *Neva Corporation's Application* [1968] RPC 481 (Pat App Trib) (considering but not applying obiter in *Maeder v Busch*, and considering *Swift & Co v Comr of Patents* [1960] NZLR 775 (SC)).

[11] He goes on to state that those 'question[s] of humanity' were put entirely out of his mind in adjudicating whether the patent was valid or not.

[12] Available sources suggest the nature of the discourse about medical patents, however the precise nature of the processes mentioned here remains opaque due to the passage of time and availability of archival sources.

[13] Equivalent statistics were unavailable for the late 1800s that is the principal focus of this study.

As MacLeod states, '[n]o other industry ever dominated the [patent] system to such an extent'.[14] Patents were used as a tool by 'medicine' manufacturers to attest to the quality and legitimacy of the products they sold by suggesting some sort of governmental approval of a product with secret ingredients in an otherwise unregulated market. They reached a receptive audience; besides suffering from genuine illnesses, Victorians were notorious hypochondriacs and by 1890 UK citizens were consuming an estimated 2,060 million pills per year, more than one pill per week for each citizen.[15] Patent medicines, however, proved often to be dangerous and sometimes fatal, and their secretiveness and association with medical practitioners damaged the general credibility of physicians.[16] Limiting the spread of dangerous patent medicines was difficult, however, as they were an important source of revenue for both government (through stamp duty) and early publishing empires (through advertising).[17] Eliminating patent medicines was one of the newly formed British Medical Association's first and most successful campaigns.[18] The real or perceived links between 'patent medicines' and the patent system were reinforced by their homonymy.

The medical profession was thus eager to discourage its members from patenting medical products, despite the fact that patenting the invention might disclose it to the public. Specifications for proprietary medicines were notoriously obscure, 'made imperfect with a view to concealing the manufacturing process'.[19] As a matter of practice, the UK medical profession had, since 1903, enjoined the patenting of medical technologies by medical investigators in a BMA resolution, which held '[t]hat it is ethically undesirable for a medical man who has invented a device intended for medical purposes to take out a patent for the purpose of deriving from such patent the financial results of a monopoly.'[20] This norm was enforced as an ethical, rather than disciplinary, standard that applied only to those medically trained (who were practising or researching), over a range of possible technologies that did not include instrumentation.[21] It was elaborated to members of the BMA through the pages of the *British Medical Journal.*

[14] C MacLeod, *Inventing the Industrial Revolution: the English Patent System, 1660–1800* (Cambridge, CUP, 1988) 154.

[15] TAB Corley, 'UK Government Regulation of Medicinal Drugs, 1890-2000' (2005) 47(3) *Business History* 337, 338.

[16] L Loeb, 'Doctors and Patent Medicines in Modern Britain: Professionalism and Consumerism' (Autumn 2001) 33(3) *Albion: A Quarterly Journal Concerned with British Studies* 404.

[17] P Vaughan, *Doctors' Commons* (Guildford, Billings and Sons, 1959) 92.

[18] Ibid 91.

[19] MacLeod (n 14) 50.

[20] Note that this is the modified version of the resolution from the 1920s: BMA Central Ethical Committee (CEC) Minutes 1931-32, index 16, Conference on Medical Patents 20 April 1932 'Professional Opinion and Practice in Relation to Medical Research and the Patent Law' 2.

[21] Ibid 2.

My research suggests that no formal sanction for violating the norm existed, although members of the medical profession felt themselves to be bound by its terms. It is certain that not all followed its directions. The BMA remained active before World War I in entreating its members not to use patents to peddle products to patients, though it moderated the resolution in 1920 to specify it did not intend to thwart more 'adequate recognition and recompense by the Government for medical workers in the field of science'.[22] The BMA successfully discouraged its members from patenting because its group structure was able to provide many key features of intellectual property rights such as disclosure, reward and peer recognition.

THE COMMON LAW EVOLVED WITH PRACTICES

The authority of the MME as a rule relied on its reception by its communities of practice: the lawyers and physicians directly implicated by the rule.[23] As the practices and values of the community of reception changed, so did the legal rule. After WWI and until the 1970s, the medical community and others started to accept the merits of patenting in some circumstances. The justification of the rule in case law simultaneously evolved from the reliability of the vendible product to public health and access reasons.

The transformation of the MME began after WWI when it became apparent that the BMA's ethical injunction against patenting would have to evolve as the conditions of scientific medical research and the self-identity of the profession changed after the war.[24] Three considerations prevailed. First, many members of the medical profession were now working in research, and felt blocked from commercial scientific research and inter-disciplinary collaboration in laboratories between medical and non-medical researchers, as some could patent and others could not.[25] Second, the profession's ethical prohibition was perceived to embody an anachronistic discomfort with doctors participating in the market that no longer represented the general practice of the professionalised medical corps. Third, scientific medicine had led to enormously significant discoveries including vaccines and antipyretics. Particularly after WWI's potent demonstration of the power of

[22] Ibid 2.

[23] It is interesting that at the early stages of this rule (pre-WWI) there is no other evidence of other significant 'stakeholder' involvement in the reception of the rule, possibly suggesting an early affiliation between the professions of medicine and law that could be further explored.

[24] BMA CEC Minutes (n 20) 3.

[25] BMA CEC Minutes, index 7, 1 October 1929, Research and Inventions Subcommittee Meeting, Conference of Representatives of Association of British Chemical Manufacturers (ABCM); Central Ethical and Science Committee Minutes 1930-31, index 22, Research and Invention Subcommittee, 24 February 1931; BMA CEC, index 5, Research and Inventions Subcommittee Meeting, 1 October 1929, 'An article by Professor Hans Zinsser, Harvard University Medical School 1927—Journal of Bacteriology, vol. 13, page 147'.

science and the industrial state, the role of patents was shifting from that of the pawn of dangerous medicine peddlers to a tool useful for mobilising the manufacture and commercialisation of beneficial medical products. The medical profession's aspirations adapted to these changed conditions.

The medical profession (represented by the BMA and Medical Research Council[26]) canvassed their options, from 'abolishing' medical patents altogether,[27] to installing a physician-examiner at the Patent Office, to creating a scheme that would compulsorily dedicate medical patents to the public interest.[28] Over the course of the inter-war period the profession became more concerned about ensuring physicians' access to valuable medical products than with conflicts of interest.[29] Government and industry evidently felt little inclination to support the profession's ethical objection to patenting with little or no evidence that it would benefit the 'public interest' in industrial development and innovation.[30] Hence the BMA's 1920 resolution was abolished in the 1950s[31] after many of the profession's concerns about access and a regular income were addressed by the creation of the National Research Development Corporation[32] and the National Health Service respectively.[33] Legal reform in the area of medical patents moved from a consultative, multi-stakeholder process that involved the medical profession, to a largely technocratic process of reconciling the laws of different European nations, particularly during the negotiation of the European Patent Convention.[34]

The common law rule adapted in tandem with changes in the views of the medical profession, industry and government toward medical patenting. While the mechanisms of this process are too subtle to delineate precisely, and the small number of cases make it difficult to draw definite conclusions, there is a notable concurrence between the common law and the community's reception of the norm. As the rule diminished in importance

[26] MRC.

[27] Eg BMA CEC, index 5 (n 25); FD 1/2145 MRC Submissions to BOT (1929) 5–6.

[28] BMA CEC Minutes 1929–1930, index 39, Subcommittee re the Ethics of Remuneration and Reward for Research and Inventions, 2 June 1930, Memorandum by Dr Myers Coplans, Report of Council; BMA CEC Minutes 1930–31, index 28, Research and Invention Subcommittee, 27 March 1931; Central Ethical and Science Committee Minutes 1930–31, index 22, Research and Invention Subcommittee, 24 February 1931.

[29] Eg BMA CEC Minutes 1931–32, index 16, Conference on Medical Patents, 20 April 1932 'Professional Opinion and Practice in Relation to Medical Research and the Patent Law' 3.

[30] Eg BMA Patents Committee Minutes 1943–44, index 1.

[31] —— 'Medical Patents' [1950] (suppl June 10) *British Medical Journal* 276.

[32] Which provided for dedication of innovation to the public interest.

[33] The NRDC was created by the Development of Inventions Act 1948 (UK) 11 & 12 Geo 6 c 60 to acquire, hold and license patents and secure the development or exploitation of valuable inventions resulting from public research or otherwise.

[34] J Pila, 'Article 52(2) of the Convention on the Grant of European Patents: What Did the Framers Intend? A Study of the Travaux Preparatoires' (2005) 36 *International Review of Iintellectual and Competition Law* 173.

to physicians, it became more difficult to justify legally. After *C&W*, the common law was silent on this issue until the late 1960s, when UK judges rejected patents for medical methods on the basis that medical methods did not result in a vendible product.[35] The non-patentability of methods of medical treatment was confirmed in 1971 in *Re Schering AG's Application*, though it did not apply in that case because the technology at issue (a method of contraception without the suppression of ovulation) produced a useful and desirable result in the human body that did not treat diseases and for which people were prepared to pay.[36] Whitford J cast doubt on the soundness of the common law MME, referring to obiter dicta in the Australian cases *Maeder v Busch*[37] and *National Research Development Corp v Comr of Patents* (*NRDC*),[38] especially the holding in the latter that medical treatment related to 'treating diseases of the human body'.[39] In *Bio-Digital Sciences Inc's Application* (1973), an application for a patent over a method of separating cells and measuring how much of a radioactive compound they absorbed was allowed. The Patents Appeal Tribunal held that a diagnostic test was not encompassed within the scope of methods of medical treatment, relying on reasoning in the Australian decisions *Joos v Commissioner of Patents* and *NRDC*.[40] Medical methods were directed to the cure or prevention of disease, whereas diagnostic testing was a preliminary step that could eventually lead to medical treatment.[41] Had the MME not been legislated in 1977 as a product of a European compromise, it is quite possible it would have eventually disappeared from UK patent law; The judicial trend indicated such a direction. The practices and groundswell of support from lawyers and physicians upon which the MME had been based had disappeared; systematic access to new medical technologies was no longer primarily an issue of patents, but more one of capacity, training and funding to be dealt with by the administrative state as part of the provision of socialised healthcare.

[35] Eg *Neva* (n 10); *Re Calmic Engineering Co's Application* [1973] RPC 684 (Comptroller General); *Re Dow Corning Corporation (Bennett's) Applications* [1974] RPC 235 (Pat App Trib).

[36] *Re Schering AG's Application* [1971] 3 All ER 177 (Pat App Trib). *Schering* was followed in *Upjohn Co (Robert's) Application* [1977] RPC 94 (CA) where the Court of Appeal found that a method to prevent excessive gastric secretion by the systematic administration of certain compounds was not patentable. The Patents Appeal Tribunal refused to resile from *Schering* in *Eli Lilly & Co's Application* [1975] RPC 438.

[37] *Maeder v Busch* (1938) 59 CLR 684 (HCA).

[38] *National Research Development Corp v Comr of Patents* (1959) 102 CLR 252 (HCA).

[39] *Schering* (n 36) 180.

[40] *Bio-Digital Sciences Inc's Application* [1973] RPC 668 (Pat App Trib). The application was for a method of separating cells and measuring their absorption of a radioactive compound; *Joos* (n 7); *NRDC* (n 10).

[41] *Bio-Digital* (n 40) 674.

A COMMUNITY OF RECEPTION BOUNDED BY INTEREST

The MME's community of reception was both legal and medical; as will be seen in the following section, the UK rule was shaped in part by the legal decisions of other countries. This section highlights that Canadian physicians and researchers also shaped the MME and documents the reception of the common law rule by an international community of practice. The activities of Canadian medical researchers played a major role during the period between WWI and World War II in transforming the UK medical profession's norm against patenting medical technologies. Canada mirrored, but on a smaller scale, medical research and professionalisation in the UK and US. The Canadian medical profession was quicker to professionalise than that of the UK, and did so more smoothly due to the small number of physicians and the strength of government medical institutions and standards.[42] However, Canada lagged behind the US and UK in medical research at universities and industrial laboratories.[43] The patent medicines problem in Canada was minor, as were the profits generated, although sufficient to warrant remedial legislation. The Canadian medical corps, in professionalising, drew from UK (and US) sources. The Canadian Medical Association (CMA) enjoined its members from patenting in order to restrict their association with dubious patent medicines, consistent with UK and US approaches. '[The] member of our profession who has made a discovery fraught ... with benefit to his fellows, should freely communicate that discovery ... with the intent that all should be able to utilise it for the good ... of humanity at large,' editorialised the *Canadian Medical Association Journal* in 1913.[44] The CMA's 1928 Code of Ethics stated in section 4 that '[e]qually reprehensible is it for a physician to receive remuneration from a patient for any surgical instrument or medicine, or to dispense a secret nostrum, whether it be the composition or exclusive property of himself, or others.'[45] This provision evolved in the CMA's Code of Ethics until 1977, to state: '[n]o advance or discovery in any branch of medical science made by a physician should ever be capitalised or marketed by him in any way for his personal gain, or kept secret for his private advantage. Such advance or discovery should be made common for the advantage of the whole profession, and for the progress of science'.[46] The ties between the countries were close: Canadian physicians on occasion even asked the BMA for advice on

[42] D Coburn et al, 'Medical Dominance in Canada in Historical Perspective: the Rise and Fall of Medicine' (1983) 13(3) *International Journal of Health Services* 407, 415.

[43] Ibid.

[44] Editorial, 'The Position of the Laboratory Worker' (1913) 3 *Canadian Medical Association Journal* 396, 396.

[45] Library and Archives Canada, Box MG28 I343 v5.

[46] Ibid; the Code of Ethics also cites directly the BMA's Decisions as its policy on 'Patent Preparations'.

resolving ethical dilemmas about patenting new technologies.[47] Canadian medical researchers who discovered insulin in this policy context helped shape the UK evolution of the medical exception.

The discovery of insulin by a team of researchers including the physician Frederick Banting at the University of Toronto in 1921 challenged the UK medical profession's norm against patenting at the same time as questions were being raised in the UK about the possible beneficial role of patents in manufacturing valuable medical substances. The discoverers of insulin contributed to the shift in perception amongst medical advocates in the inter-war period, particularly at the MRC, that patents could *serve* the public interest and not merely undermine it. The Toronto insulin researchers initially signed an agreement promising not to patent insulin on their own.[48] The team was reluctant to apply for a patent as it was 'contrary to the traditional principles of the medical profession to restrict the production or supply of a substance that may be used for the alleviation of human suffering'.[49] In addition to this pragmatic concern it also ran against the profession's 'ethical code for any physician to derive financial benefit from the sale of the substance'.[50] Soon after agreeing not to individually patent, however, the team concluded that they would collectively patent the discovery in the US and Canada as it became clear that the mass production of insulin would be highly complicated. 'It was believed that if these details [about insulin purification and production] were published without protection some manufacturing chemist might modify the process sufficiently so as to obtain a patent which would practically give him the exclusive right to manufacture for sale.'[51] Patenting the original process would ensure that the discovery was properly commercialised and would encourage a reputable pharmaceutical firm, Eli Lilly, to help bring insulin to patients as quickly as possible.[52] The patent became the tool that would ensure product standardisation, pharmaceutical collaboration, and public protection against medical quacks.

[47] BMA CEC Minutes 1929–1930, index 45B, Research and Inventions Subcommittee Meeting, 18 September 1929.

[48] Memorandum in reference to the cooperation of the Connaught Anti-Toxin laboratories, 25 January 1922, MS COLL 76 (Banting) Scrapbook 2, box 1, p 40, online: The Discovery and Early Development of Insulin, link.library.utoronto.ca/insulin/.

[49] Statement to the Insulin Committee regarding patents and royalties, JJR Macleod, 28 April 1924, University of Toronto Archives, A1982-0001, box 6, folder 1, online: The Discovery and Early Development of Insulin, link.library.utoronto.ca/insulin/ (Statement).

[50] Ibid.

[51] Statement (n 49).

[52] 'Insulin was the most important drug in the history of Eli Lilly and Company, doing more than any other to make the firm one of the major pharmaceutical manufacturers in the world.': JH Madison, 'Manufacturing Pharmaceuticals: Eli Lilly and Company, 1876–1948' (1989) 18 *Business and Economic History* 72, 76.

Banting's reputation, as the only member of the medical profession on the team, was the most jeopardised by the patent. In a melodramatic letter, he expressed the urgency of the matter:

> The act of taking out a patent for what we hope will prove to be a remedial agent of considerable value has awakened a great deal of criticism ... This criticism I feel I will have to meet for a long time and may indeed never live down.[53]

What he hoped might clear his name, and ultimately it appears did,[54] was that he and his co-patentees assigned their rights to the University of Toronto's Board of Governors.[55] The Board administered the patents in Canada and the United States in the public interest through the Insulin Committee. Its control of the insulin patent earned its members great respect from the medical community, and its manufacture and distribution was of such high quality and so widespread that it transformed diabetes from a death sentence to a manageable condition.[56] In order to finance the administration of its manufacture, an initial levy of 5 per cent was imposed as a royalty on the sale of insulin and the patent-holders agreed to direct all profits towards their future research.[57] The MRC played a similar role to the Insulin Committee in England, governing insulin's manufacture and standardisation in the UK.

As the MRC, with the BMA, had long advocated patent abolition in the medical field, its decision to manage the UK insulin patent seemed contradictory and inconsistent.[58] Because the MRC managed drug quality for the government under the National Health Insurance Act 1911,[59] the MRC was the obvious body for the Insulin Committee to approach when it was considering the UK distribution and manufacture of insulin.[60] The MRC accepted the British insulin patent rights in 1922, it claimed, in order to supervise its manufacture and distribution in Britain; documents suggest it also accepted the rights to strengthen its bureaucratic dominance in monitoring

[53] Letter, F Banting to Sir R Falconer, 27 January 1923, University of Toronto Archives, A1982-0001, box 6, folder 1, online: The Discovery and Early Development of Insulin, link.library.utoronto.ca/insulin/.

[54] Eg M Fishbein, 'Are Patents on Medicinal Discoveries and on Foods in the Public Interest—Medical Patents' (1937) 29 *Industrial & Engineering Chemistry* 1315, 1317.

[55] The Board had the power to handle patents since 1906. A Palmer, 'University Patent Policies' (1934) 16 *Journal of the Patent Office Society* 96, 100.

[56] Statement (n 49).

[57] JJR Macleod, 'Insulin and the Steps Taken to Secure an Effective Preparation' (1922) 12 *CMAJ* 899.

[58] J Liebenau, 'The MRC and the Pharmaceutical Industry: The Model of Insulin' in J Austoker and L Bryder (eds), *Historical Perspectives on the Role of the MRC* (Oxford, OUP, 1989).

[59] D Cantor, 'The MRC's Support for Experimental Radiology in the Inter-War Years' in Austoker and Bryder (n 58).

[60] C Sinding, 'Making the Unit of Insulin: Standards, Clinical Work, and Industry, 1920–1925' (2002) 76 *Bulletin of the History of Medicine* 231, 242.

drug quality in the UK.[61] The MRC then licensed British manufacturers on a royalty-free non-exclusive basis, tested batches and protected industry from imported insulin.[62] In 1923 it patented an improvement to insulin invented by MRC staff members and granted the North American rights to the University of Toronto.[63] Thus when the time came in the inter-war period for the MRC to articulate to government its position on the necessity of a legislative exception for medical treatment, the MRC was compromised, or 'embarrassed' in the language of the time.[64] The MRC was not even able to persuade its own members that an anti-patent position was tenable, given its experience with insulin and other drugs.[65] In this way, a Canadian physician's experiment with a patent to commercialise insulin played a role in limiting the UK medical profession's aspirations to avoid patenting medical discoveries. The MME's community of reception was bounded not merely by geography, but also by interest and by the historical circumstances of colonialism. The colonies' formal processes of receiving laws were mirrored by social processes based on shared experiences and approaches between professional groups in the colony and 'mother' country.

COMMON LAW COURTS IN OTHER JURISDICTIONS PLAYED A SIGNIFICANT ROLE

The community of interest that received and practised the common law rule enjoining medical patents by medical practitioners was international. Similarly the common law rule, introduced in *C&W*, evolved through an international dialogue between UK courts and other Commonwealth courts, particularly Australia, New Zealand and Canada. The community that received and validated the common law MME included an international community of jurists whose authority to determine patentable subject-matter rested largely on the shared section 6 of the Statute of Monopolies (SOM).

Australia

Australia adopted the common law MME and maintained a legal position consistent with the UK's until the legislation of a medical exception by the

[61] Liebenau in Austoker and Bryder (n 58).
[62] Liebenau in Austoker and Bryder (n 58).
[63] FD 1/2145 Memorandum on Medical Patents E.4920.
[64] FD 1/2145 'MRC Private and Confidential Research in Chemotherapy: Relations with Industry and Use of the Patent Law' 24 May 1938, 3.
[65] FD1/2147 Confidential Memo, 10 March 1948, 'Draft Memorandum on Application of the Patent Law to the Results of Medical Research'.

UK in 1977.[66] Australia is now unique among the common law countries considered in this chapter in that it has no common law or legislated MME, although a possible exception was believed to exist (as a consequence of the obiter dicta in *Maeder*) for much of the twentieth century.[67] When Australia first considered the patentability of medical methods in *Maeder* it relied on the authority of the holding in *C&W*.[68] While ultimately *Maeder* stands for the proposition that a method of permanently waving hair was not patentable due to prior public use of the claimed invention, two of the four judges argued in obiter dicta that a method applied to the human body (ie human hair) could not produce a vendible product.[69] *NRDC* subsequently dispensed with the requirement for a vendible product, effectively overruling *Maeder*, although it could be distinguished as it was not a case about medical methods.[70] In *Joos*, decided in 1972, the High Court of Australia held that a process for strengthening hair and nails was patentable, as it was a cosmetic process.[71] In coming to his decision, Chief Justice Barwick disregarded the earlier obiter dicta in *Maeder* and argued that the UK Patent Office's *Manual of Practice*, which excluded 'processes for the treatment of human beings' from patentability,[72] was 'radically wider than the expression used by Lord Buckmaster which, to [his] mind, went no further than to exclude from monopoly processes for medical treatment of diseases of the human body.'[73] Barwick CJ either felt drawn to adopt UK common law decisions that had narrowed the scope of the MME or found it convenient to do so in this case, evidencing a community of practice. He stated in fact that:

> [w]hilst the decisions of the Tribunal of the United Kingdom are not binding on this Tribunal, there is no reason to think that the law with respect to the grant of letters patent for inventions should be any less liberal in Australia than that

66 The vast majority of Australian intellectual property law was inherited from the UK. Section 6 of the Statute of Monopolies (SOM), enacted in 1623, was the first statutory declaration in the UK of what constitutes a patentable invention. That definition was incorporated into the UK's first modern patent statute, the Patent Designs and Trade Marks Act 1883(46 & 47 Vict c 57), where an invention under the 1883 Act was 'any manner of new manufacture … within section six of the Statute of Monopolies [including] an alleged invention'. Prior to federation each Australian colony had patent legislation modelled on the 1883 Act, which stayed in force until the Patents Act 1903 (Cth) was enacted. The 1903 Act and all subsequent legislation up to Sch 1 of the Patent Act 1990 (Cth) have preserved a definition of invention that means 'any manner of new manufacture the subject of letters patent and grant of privilege within section 6 of the Statute of Monopolies': MJ Davison, AL Monotti and L Wiseman, *Australian Intellectual Property Law* (NY, CUP, 2008).

67 *Bristol-Myers Squibb Co v F H Faulding & Co Ltd* (2000) 97 FCR 524.

68 Maeder (n 37).

69 Ibid 706–707.

70 NRDC (n 10).

71 *Joos* (n 7).

72 Ibid 620.

73 Ibid 620.

> which obtains in the United Kingdom; and, although there is no imperative that it should be, the desirability of such law being the same in both countries is readily acceptable.[74]

He also noted, in order to bolster his reliance on *NRDC*, that it has 'since been adopted in the United Kingdom'.[75]

In 1994, however, the possibility of an Australian medical exception from patentability was further reduced. While the court in *Anaesthetic Supplies Pty Ltd v Rescare Ltd* decided that a method of treating obstructive sleep apnoea was not patentable as it was insufficiently described, the majority of the three-judge full Federal Court went on to state that if that ground had not been invalid, the mere fact that it was a method of medical treatment would not have barred its patentability. In coming to this conclusion the majority considered *C&W, Joos, NRDC* and *Maeder*, but also referred to decisions in the United States, Germany and Israel, as well as the more predictable UK, Canada and New Zealand.[76] Justice Lockhart, writing for himself and Wilcox J, noted that these broader authorities 'go some distance towards recognising the patentability of methods of treatment of human beings.'[77] The 'conservative' UK approach was attributed to its adoption of a legislated MME in the Patents Act 1977, and distinguished; *C&W* was held to be overruled in Australia by *NRDC*.[78] Dissenting, Sheppard J referred to the 'substantial body of international thinking … that it is undesirable for patents to be granted for inventions relating to methods of treatment of disease'.[79] Sheppard J argued that it is the practice of medical practitioners to share information and knowledge about their field openly through conferences, publications, travel and training; it is through this process of constant learning that their techniques improve; and presumably the common law should reflect this reality.[80] Nevertheless, Justices Lockhart and Wilcox's obiter dicta were adopted by the majority of the Federal Court of Australia in *Bristol Myers Squibb v Faulding*.[81] The majority also noted that it was significant that the Australian legislature had not chosen to clarify the non-patentability of medical methods in 1990 when it had both the opportunity to do so, and knowledge of the Australian Patent Office's practice of accepting patents over medical methods of treatment.[82] Australian case law suggests that the codification of an MME in the UK disrupted Australia's evolving dialogue with the UK

74 Ibid 622.
75 Ibid 617.
76 *Anaesthetic Supplies Pty Ltd v Rescare Ltd* (1994) 50 FCR 1 (NSW Gen Div) 8.
77 *Rescare* (n 76) 16.
78 Ibid 17; 44.
79 Ibid 38.
80 Ibid 41.
81 *BMS* (n 67).
82 Ibid [16].

around the patentability of medical methods, thus limiting the possibility of a common (law) approach to their patentability.

New Zealand

New Zealand,[83] in contrast to Australia, has continued to follow *C&W*. New Zealand jurisprudence excludes medical methods from patentability[84] and appears to extend the same treatment to diagnostic methods,[85] although diagnostic testing that does not require surgery may still be patentable.[86] The non-patentability of medical methods of treatment in New Zealand rests on the notion that they are not a 'manner of manufacture' or are 'generally inconvenient' under section 6 of the SOM.[87] The exclusion of medical methods from patentability was supported in *Maeder v Ronda,* which held in 1943 that a treatment on the human body cannot create a vendible article, or one that could directly or indirectly be used in commerce, but that holding was cast into doubt when the Supreme Court later applied *NRDC* in *Swift* (a method of tenderising meat products, not a medical treatment).[88] Then in *Wellcome*, the NZ Court of Appeal rejected efforts to undermine the authority of *C&W* and reversed the High Court's decision under appeal that medical methods were patentable.[89] The court noted that it was torn between its traditional respect for English authority, a plea to maintain consistency in commercial law between New Zealand and Australia,[90] and patriotic loyalty to the lower court decision of a judge of a national court.[91] Justice Somers held, however, that *C&W* 'amounts to no more than a case in which the first articulation of a proposition can be seen. Its timing may have been fortuitous or may simply have reflected the growth of scientific knowledge', suggesting, perhaps, that *C&W* is best seen as the expression of a deeper, shared, underlying principle. Somers J concluded that efforts to undermine the authority of *C&W* as a legal

[83] Patent law in New Zealand is governed by the terms of the Patents Act 1953, and as with earlier versions of patent legislation, is a substantial re-enactment of an English statute (in this case the Patents Act 1949 (UK)). It adopts the SOM definition of "invention", holding in s 2(1) that an invention 'means any manner of manufacture the subject of letters patent and grant of privilege within s 6 of the Statute of Monopolies': A Brown and A Grant, *The Law of Intellectual Property in New Zealand* (Wellington, Butterworths, 1989).

[84] *Wellcome Foundation Ltd v Comr of Patents* [1983] NZLR 385 (CA).

[85] *Pfizer Inc v Commissioner of Patents* (2004) 60 IPR 624 (NZ CA) [95].

[86] *Pharmaceutical Management Agency Ltd v Comr of Patents* [1999] NZCA 330, 24.

[87] *Wellcome* (n 84); *Pfizer* (n 85).

[88] *Maeder v 'Ronda' Ladies' Hairdressing Salon* [1943] NZLR 122 (SC), criticised in *Wellcome* by Cooke J; *Swift* (n 10).

[89] *Wellcome* (n 84).

[90] *Pfizer* (n 85) 74.

[91] *Wellcome* (n 84).

decision can consequently have little effect.[92] A Patent Bill, motivated by a range of influences, is now before the legislature; it codifies an exception for 'methods of medical treatment of human beings'.[93]

Canada

Canada diverged early from the UK-inspired common law on medical methods, possibly because its patent law is influenced by both the UK and the US. Unlike the UK, Australia and New Zealand, Canadian patent legislation borrowed from US law to define 'invention' as any 'art, process, machine, manufacture or composition of matter'[94] rather than adopt section 6 of the SOM which specified only 'any manner of new manufactures'.[95] The Patent Act has no statutory MME[96] but medical methods other than diagnostic methods are excluded from patentability by effect of the common law.[97] Medical methods are not regarded as 'inventions' under the Patent Act, since they are 'essentially non-economic and unrelated to trade, industry or commerce'. The leading decision in 1974, *Tennessee Eastman,* addressed the patentability of a surgical method of bonding living animal tissue by applying a known adhesive. The Supreme Court of Canada (SCC) held that medical methods of treatment are not included in the definition of 'invention'. Pigeon J, speaking for the court, preferred UK case law that supported the exclusion of medical methods of treatment from patentability (citing *Schering* but not mentioning *C&W*) and rejected decisions that cast doubt on requiring a vendible product for patentability, such as *Swift* and *NRDC*.[98] In doing so, Justice Pigeon doubted that decisions under 'the UK Act'[99] were entitled in Canada to the weight that doctrinal commentators argued they deserved.[100] As a basis for disregarding the New Zealand and Australian decisions, he cited Justice Estey in *Commissioner of Patents v Winthrop* on the proposition that 'the Canadian Act is not modeled on the British Act', rather than the UK decision (*Schering*) cited in support of

92 *Wellcome* (n 84).

93 Patents Bill 235-1 (2008) www.legislation.govt.nz/bill/government/2008/0235-1/latest/whole.html?search=ts_bill_patents#DLM1419001.

94 Patent Act RS 1985 (Canada) c P-4 s 2.

95 D Vaver, *Intellectual Property Law: Copyright, Patents, Trade-Marks* (Toronto, Irwin, 1997).

96 RS 1985 c P-4: a suggestion to amend the Act to exclude medical treatment procedures from patentability was never implemented: *Working Paper on Patent Law Revision, Department of Consumer and Corporate Affairs* (Minister of Supply and Services Ottawa 1976) 119.

97 *Tennessee Eastman v Comr of Patents* [1974] SCR 111.

98 *Tennessee Eastman* (n 97) [16].

99 Presumably the Statute of Monopolies.

100 *Tennessee Eastman* (n 97) [18].

his conclusion.[101] Pigeon J also considered US case law, whose persuasive authority he found to be limited.[102] He was likely aware of the 1970 case *Lawson v Commissioner of Patents,* which held that 'professional skills are not the subject-matter of a patent',[103] as they are not a manual or productive art that produce a 'vendible product'.[104] As Vaver has commented, '[w]ere it otherwise, the professions would be hindered in exercising, sharing, and disclosing their skills in the best interests of their clients or patients.'[105]

The SCCs decision in *Tennessee Eastman* was subsequently followed by the Federal Court of Appeal in *Imperial Chemical Industries*, which found that the exclusion of medical methods from patentability was a general principle of Canadian patent law, independent of any specific provisions of the Patent Act.[106] The FCA held that the MME does not extend to diagnostic methods, although this expansion of patentability was not decided based on UK common law authority like *Bio-Digital* but rather by parsing existing Canadian decisions[107] and distancing diagnosis from medical treatment.[108] This patentability of diagnostic methods diverges from the current UK position; the Canadian common law position on medical methods is similar to the pre-1977 UK Patent Act.[109] Canadian judges have referred to the judge-made law of the UK, Australia, New Zealand and the US to inform the Canadian MME.

Thus the UK common law rule evolved in dialogue with judges and courts from Australia and New Zealand, encouraged by the common statutory base of 'general inconvenience'. The legislation of a MME in 1977, however, ended the UK's conversation with other common law jurisdictions; Australia conclusively held no MME, New Zealand now proposes to legislate a MME and Canadian law evolved, relying on UK and other sources, to a position that resembles the pre-1977 UK common law (ie diagnostic methods are not patentable). In all four jurisdictions (including the UK), judges adverted to the notion that whether or not *C&W* is good law, the exception expresses the norm that medical professionals openly share information as a means of enhancing their practice. The Commonwealth courts also served as a shared legal community of reception (through precedent),

[101] Ibid [18].
[102] Ibid [21].
[103] *Lawson v Commissioner of Patents* [1970] 62 CPR 101 [37] (Exchequer Court).
[104] Manual of Patent Office Practice, available at www.cipo.ic.gc.ca/epic/site/cipointernet-internetopic.nsf/en/h_wr00720e.html, p 12-3; reiterated in *Shell Oil Co v Canada (Patent Commissioner)* 142 DLR (3d) 117, [1982] 2 SCR 536 and *Tennessee Eastman* (n 97).
[105] Vaver, *Intellectual Property Law* (n 95).
[106] *Imperial Chemical Industries Ltd v Canada (Patent Comr)* [1986] 3 FC 40 (Fed CA). See also *Re Senentek* (1997) 77 CPR (3d) 321.
[107] *Tennessee Eastman* (n 97); *Imperial Chemical* (n 106).
[108] *Re Goldenberg* (1988) 22 CPR (3d) 159.
[109] Ibid.

validation (through following *C&W*) and, in some cases, rejection of the common law rule.

In narrowing the scope of the medical exception, by the 1970s the common law had been functioning at its best in the UK, reflecting the rule's reception by the relevant community. In contrast, the exception legislated in the 1977 EPC reflected a (past) social consensus in the UK that had been resuscitated to forge compromise between members of a new community, the nations negotiating the EPC. These nations embraced a diversity of approaches. Some countries, for example Italy and France, wanted to exclude not only medical methods of treatment but also therapeutic substances (eg pharmaceuticals). Others, such as the UK and Sweden, advocated broad patentability.[110] The British delegation to the EPC argued initially that exceptions from patentability should not be included in the Convention to allow flexibility in the development of what can and cannot be patented.[111] The compromise of excluding medical methods of treatment seemed safe, since the consensus held that no European country allowed patents carte-blanche in that area. It has, however, meant an uneasy tension between the common law and the interpretation of the legislative exception whose scope and purpose remain unclear to commentators and adjudicators alike.[112] Legislative codification unmoored the exception's legal development from the common law and local practices, creating an empty provision and trouble for adjudicators who have been attempting to articulate the purpose and scope of the provision since its codification.[113]

CONCLUSION

Contrary to a traditional narrative of the common law, the MME derived its authority more from its reception and validation by a community of practice than from the fact that it was created by a judge. The common law rule expressed the aspirations of a professionalising medical corps, and as those aspirations changed, so did the common law. The UK common law rule influenced and was transformed by a legal community of reception that included Commonwealth courts. It also integrated the experiences of Canadian physicians, suggesting that formal processes of reception of

[110] T Terrell, *Terrell on the Law of Patents*, 14th edn (London, Sweet & Maxwell, 1994) 2.14.

[111] UNEPA and UNICE requested that specific exceptions from patentability should be eliminated and that this should be left to develop flexibly in the jurisprudence: Proceedings BR/169e/72lor/KM/gc 6.

[112] For a more detailed treatment see: ST Piper 'The Emergence of a Medical Exception from Patentability in the 20th Century' (DPhil, Oxford 2008).

[113] For eg *Bristol-Myers Squibb Co v Baker Norton Pharmaceuticals Inc* [1999] RPC 253 (Pat Ct) [51], aff'd in part [2001] RPC 1 (CA); most recently *R v Cygnus* [2002] EPOR 26 (Tech Bd App); *Opinion of the Enlarged Board of Appeal* [2006] OJEPO 334.

laws by the colonies were mirrored by more informal ones. The common law rule was further sustained by a community of reception constituted by national and international legal practitioners and policy bureaucrats. Formally codifying the legal rule in legislation has not made it more certain, even though the content of the rule (the legislative text) and its source of authority (the legislator) are clearer than they ever were at common law. The history of the MME demonstrates that the processes by which a common law norm is created, justified and transformed are a complicated mix of the legal, practical and international, suggesting that the common law is reassuringly responsive to the state of play.

8

Claiming a Life: are Organisms Inherently Unpatentable?

GRAHAM DUTFIELD*

INTRODUCTION

HISTORICALLY, LIVING ORGANISMS have only rarely been patented. This situation persisted until the 1980s. Before the biotechnology era there was little interest in patenting life forms anyway. But it also reflects the fact that most legal jurisdictions encountered quite serious difficulties in incorporating chemicals, drugs and biological matter into their patent systems. Many continental European countries dealt with them by the simple means of excluding them statutorily. But common law ones have tended not to name or list those things to be kept outside the patent system other than discoveries, ideas and laws of nature.[1] Consequently, common law jurisdictions have the most experience in determining where lines should be drawn between unpatentable discoveries and patentable inventions in the fields of biology and biochemistry.[2]

Of course, this is not to say that common law jurisdictions will always arrive at the same results. In *Diamondv Chakrabarty*,[3] the United States Supreme Court found Chakrabarty's oil-eating bacterium to be patentable, after an earlier rejection by the Patent and Trademark Office. Twenty-one years later, in 2001, the Court confirmed the patentability of plants, relying in part on the precedent it had set those two decades earlier.[4] In the United Kingdom, a patent application on Chakrabarty's invention was granted by

* The author gratefully acknowledges comments made on an earlier draft by Uma Suthersanen.

[1] Admittedly, the 1919 UK Act to amend the Patents and Designs Acts denied product protection in the case of inventions relating to substances prepared or produced by chemical processes or intended for food and medicine. This provision remained in force for 30 years.

[2] This is a fair generalisation. Nonetheless, some European continental jurisdictions allowed plants to be patented during the 20th century. Moreover, in 1975 the German Federal Supreme Court declared that micro-organisms are patentable.

[3] *Diamond v Chakrabarty* 447 U.S. 303 (1980).

[4] *JEM Ag Supply v Pioneer Hi-Bred Int'l Inc* 122 S Ct 593 (2001).

the Patent Office without resort to the courts.[5] In the 2002 *Oncomouse* case,[6] the Canadian Supreme Court, in the face of very similar statutory language to that of the US, diverged from the latter country in finding that while lower life forms are acceptable subject matter, it did not follow that higher life forms could also be classed as inventions.

Subject matter judgments of these kinds are not particularly new. Since as far back as the early 1900s, patent-granting offices and courts have been called upon to determine whether a product sourced from nature is by definition a gift of nature whose discoverer is masquerading as an inventor, or whether human perspiration or inspiration can transform such a product into a human artefact that may be patented. Uncertainties and inconsistencies notwithstanding, they have accommodated biological substances within the patent system. They have done so even when those substances have been little known or understood. Thus adrenaline (epinephrine) and insulin were patented in the early twentieth century despite their being hormones produced by mammals, including humans, and notwithstanding the difficulties their inventors had in describing them correctly if at all. Allowing such substances to be patented is now completely normal and causes little controversy.

However, while a reasonable case can be made for analogising purified hormones, antibiotics, proteins and genes to chemicals synthesised or recombined in the laboratory, living organisms are another matter. With patents on life forms being filed on a more regular basis from the 1980s, uncertainty and divergence crept back into some of the common law regimes. Admittedly, from that decade micro-organisms soon became patentable throughout the common law world, as well as in continental Europe, which by then had almost fully accepted the patentability of chemicals and drugs. However, with the Canadian Supreme Court's *Oncomouse* decision, the common law consensus concerning the patentability of whole organisms has broken down again. Canada's most senior judges, faced presumably with the best scientific knowledge of the time at their disposal, were unable to accept that a higher life form could be classed as a human invention, despite this going against the policies and views of granting offices and courts in the United States, where the statutory language was virtually identical, the UK and in the rest of Europe.

Which of the two supreme courts came to the right decisions? Or were they both wrong? How sound was the reasoning applied in each case? This essay seeks answers to such questions on the basis, in part, of lessons drawn from some ongoing and very wide-ranging discussions about life involving scientists and philosophers. These discussions focus specifically

[5] UK Patent no 1,436,573, published on 19 June 1976.

[6] *Harvard College v Canada (Commissioner of Patents)* 2002 SCC 76.

on questions of agency, autonomy, organisation and functional complexity in life. Three specific queries are as follows:

1. Is life *inherently* complex and organised in ways that non-living systems and human artefacts cannot be?
2. How far have we progressed in our understanding of this complexity and organisation?
3. What causes them, and what drives life to keep achieving further and more varied complexity and organisation?

This essay also poses and seeks to answer a fourth question that has mostly *not* been considered so far:

4. In light of the above questions, to what extent can humans become agents of organised functional complexity and therefore the authors of the life forms in which that complexity is embedded?

THE ARGUMENT

This essay argues that irrespective of any consequentialist justifications for concluding that the public benefits from patenting life forms—and these may well be very compelling—fundamental difficulties exist in applying patenting to such subject matter that are of sufficient weight as to give patent regulators pause. These difficulties are made evident in scientific and philosophical discussion concerning apparent design in life and the special qualities all life forms share that differentiate them from non-living 'compositions of matter'. Such discussion goes back 200 years but seems to have intensified of late. Since the early 1800s, if not earlier, learned people have sought to explain the mystery of complexity and design in biology. Understanding organised functional complexity in living things was no easy task then. Now that the intricacy and sophistication of all life, from the simplest unicellular organisms to human beings, are more apparent than they have ever been, it is no less controversial today. This is so despite—arguably because of—the vast improvements in our biological knowledge.

Together, the ongoing discussion among these and other scholars and thinkers should provoke jurists and others interested in biotechnology patenting to consider a rather vital question: in light of the immense and barely understood complexity, sophistication and creativity of living cells, are the intrusions of genetic engineers sufficient for claims to have invented a new organism to be scientifically tenable? I argue in the negative. Whether we have God or natural processes alone to thank, much of the difficult work has already been done—in many cases, millions of years ago. Putting it in its bluntest terms, genetic engineers are really just free-riders who tinker half-knowingly with what they have got, and actually create nothing that was not there before.

That sounds dreadfully harsh, if not ungrateful. But I hope to demonstrate that there is much more than a grain of truth in this. The present author feels reluctant to take the argument too far and deny any patent claims in molecular biology, especially to processes and perhaps to products-by-process too. Furthermore, the argument does not apply fully to modifications and improvements of the structural and functional *components* of living organisms. Complex and little understood as they may be, I am not denying the patentability of such things, at least not according to this particular line of argument. What I am saying is this: in light of what we know and do not know about life, claims to *whole* life forms do appear very hard to justify scientifically.

On the basis of the foregoing discussion, which brings together the latest (and most controversial) scientific and philosophical thinking on the matter, I argue as follows: living things, including bacteria, are far more complex and organised than any human artefact (so far) and any known non-living systems. However, to date, our progress in understanding the highly complex, systematic and creative properties and workings of life is quite limited. Natural forces, including evolution, over which humans only have limited control, are responsible for the intense functional complexity and the dynamic and diverse nature of living systems.

Following this, I put forward the following three-part argument: (i) molecular biology and biotechnology are suitable fields for the patent system no more or less than other fields of science and technology, but (ii) at the present time claims to whole organisms, including micro-organisms, plants and animals, are premature, and (iii) the fact that such claims are allowed marks a radical departure from, rather than a logical and scientifically sound extension of, traditional patent practice which we ought to reconsider.

PATENTING HORMONES

One could be forgiven for regarding the patenting of antibiotics as *the* pivotal development in the stretching of the patent system into nature, because of the fact that the post-Second World War antibiotics revolution involved so much patenting activity. However, it is hormones that really made the difference.[7] Once hormones were shown to be patentable, there was no reason to deny protection to other chemicals found in living things

[7] Hormones are chemical messengers that perform a range of regulatory functions relating to growth, development, metabolism, and general well-being, including immunity. Hormones include adrenaline (epinephrine), insulin, erythropoietin (EPO) and steroids. For a detailed discussion on the history of hormone discovery and patenting, see G Dutfield, *Intellectual Property Rights and the Life Science Industries: Past, Present and Future* (Singapore, World Scientific Publishing, 2009).

as long as they were purified or at least isolated in a way that made them available to the public for the first time. And from such natural products, it was not such a big analogical and practical leap to micro-organisms, whether or not such an extension makes scientific sense. Perhaps the most important hormones in the context of this essay are adrenaline and insulin. Space allows us to discuss only the former, the first of the two to be discovered.

The first commercial hormones, particularly adrenaline, presented particular challenges for the United States patent system, and the way these challenges were met has had long term repercussions in terms of drawing the line between the patentable and the unpatentable in biotechnology in the United States and elsewhere. The US product of nature doctrine, which was formulated by the courts in the previous century, set certain limits on the extent to which natural substances and life forms could be protected. Nevertheless, as the pharmaceutical industry increased its ability to develop new products, the Patent Office was often quite flexible in its application of the doctrine to the extent of allowing purified or isolated natural products to be protected. In addition, the courts sometimes interpreted the law in ways that favoured owners in cases where the patentability boundaries relating to new kinds of product were unclear and needed to be demarcated.

Around the turn of the twentieth century, John Jacob Abel at Johns Hopkins University produced a relatively pure form of the active principle of part of the adrenal gland called the adrenal medulla, which he called epinephrin. A few years later, Jokichi Takamine came up with an extract of sufficient purity to display some of the effects of the hormone as it functioned in the body—not that the function of adrenaline was understood at the time, except to a rudimentary degree. He filed two patents in 1903 and 1904 for a glandular extractive product claiming purified forms of adrenaline, as it was also called,[8] and for this compound in a solution with salt and a preservative.[9] Takamine licensed the patents to Parke Davis. Around this time, a number of adrenaline-based products were sold in the US and Germany, but Parke Davis's trademarked Adrenalin products became market leaders on account of their relative purity, safety and efficacy.

Takamine's two adrenaline patents were the subject of a 1911 court case in which Parke Davis successfully sued HK Mulford & Co for infringement.[10] The influence of the judgment, delivered by the famous Learned Hand, has proved far more long-lasting than the sales of the adrenaline products concerned. It appears to be the first time that a court was called upon to consider the patentability of a purified form of a natural product

[8] US Patent no 730,176 ('Glandular extractive product'), issued on 2 June 1903.

[9] US Patent no 753,177 ('Glandular extractive compound'), issued on 23 February 1904.

[10] *Parke Davis and Co. v H.K. Mulford and Co*, 189 Fed 95 (SDNY 1911) aff'd, 196 Fed 496 (2nd Cir 1912).

extracted from a living organism. The court established that the novelty of such extracts was not necessarily destroyed by the prior existence of less pure extracts or by the fact that the essence of the product claimed was a naturally occurring substance, as long as the active principle itself was not claimed.[11] This opened the door for other kinds of natural product decades later to be patented, from antibiotics to DNA sequences and ultimately to microbes and mice.

Judge Hand accepted that the active principle itself could not be patented. On the other hand, he denied that there was any rule to prevent the patentability even of natural products merely extracted from living things, if to do this made it 'available' for the first time. He went on to argue to the effect that even had Takamine's purification of the active principle been insufficient for the award of the patent, his product was still 'for every practical purpose a new thing commercially and therapeutically', which to him was 'a good ground for a patent'. As he expressed it, 'the line between different substances and degrees of the same substance is to be drawn rather from the common usages of man than from nice considerations of dialectic.' Accordingly, regarding the first of the two patents, Hand held that:

> Takamine was the first to make it available for any use by removing it from the other gland-tissue in which it was found, and, while it is of course possible logically to call this a purification of the principle, it became for every practical purpose a new thing commercially and therapeutically.[12]

FROM MICROBES TO ANIMALS

Living things are of course another matter entirely. Or are they? Organisms are chemical substances, albeit of a highly complex kind. In 2002, researchers at State University of New York announced in 2002 they had synthesised *in vitro* the polio virus out of bits of DNA acquired by mail order.[13] Admittedly, viruses are normally considered not to be living things per se, comprising little more than short stretches of DNA or RNA wrapped in a protein coat and being incapable of reproducing independently. But they are about as close to life as non-life can get. In the article announcing their

[11] Takamine had originally claimed the natural substance itself, but this was refused by the examiner.

[12] *Parke Davis and Co v HK Mulford and Co* 189 Fed. 95 (SDNY 1911) aff'd, 196 Fed 496 (2nd Cir 1912).

[13] J Cello, AV Paul and E Wimmer, 'Chemical synthesis of poliovirus cDNA: generation of infectious virus in the absence of natural template' (2002) 297 *Science* 1016; J Couzin, 'Active poliovirus baked from scratch' (2002) 297 *Science* 174. Impressive as this is, to be more precise they had synthesised 'a nucleic acid that allows the virus to be produced once it has been inserted into a cell' (M Morange, *Life Explained* (New Haven, Yale University Press, 2008), 9).

breakthrough, the polio-makers commented as follows: 'if the ability to replicate is an attribute of life, then poliovirus is a chemical $[C_{332,652}H_{492,388}N_{98,245}O_{131,196}\text{-} P_{7501}S_{2340}]$ with a life cycle.'[14]

But here is where the consensus started to break down. Whereas the United Kingdom, Canada and Australia had little difficulty in finding micro-organisms to be patentable, it was a different story in the United States where there happened to be most commercial interest in acquiring such patents. The product of nature doctrine had since the 1880s apparently precluded the patenting of any further life forms. At least that was the view of the United States Patent and Trademark Office (USPTO) when it rejected claims in Chakrabarty's application that were directed to the micro-organism itself.

In 1980, the USPTO's appeal at the Supreme Court not to allow such claims was rejected by five to four. In making this decision, the Court treated the micro-organism as a natural compound that had been structurally modified and thus transformed into a new 'article of manufacture' or 'composition of matter' that was no longer natural. By treating the micro-organism as a natural chemical substance into which a useful new characteristic had been introduced and thereby rendered unnatural, the court found that it was patentable in accordance with long-established practice with respect to chemical products.

In 1987, the Commissioner of Patents and Trademarks publicly announced that the Patent and Trademark Office would examine 'claims directed to multicellular living organisms, including animals'.[15] Nonetheless, the announcement was insufficient in itself to settle the question of whether or not plants and animals are patentable. In December 2001, the Supreme Court, recalling *Chakrabarty* in its decision, finally confirmed the legality of patents on plants.[16]

Following the Court's logic, no distinction needed to be made between microbes and more complex life. This was a reflection of reality since things had obviously moved on since *Chakrabarty*. In 1988, the first-ever animal patent was granted in the United States, the aforementioned Oncomouse.[17] The patent specification describes a mouse into which a gene has been introduced which induces increased susceptibility to cancer. The US patent was extremely (and unjustifiably) broad, claiming 'a transgenic nonhuman mammal' containing an activated oncogene sequence. Patents on the same invention were filed elsewhere including Canada and at the European Patent

[14] Cello et al (2002) op cit, 1018 (citations deleted from quote).

[15] DJ Quigg, 'Animals—patentability' (1987) 69 *Journal of the Patent and Trademark Office Society* 328.

[16] *JEM Ag Supply v Pioneer Hi-Bred Int'l Inc* 122 S Ct 593 (2001).

[17] US Patent no 4,736,866 ('Transgenic non-human mammals'), issued on 12 April 1988.

Office. In the United States, the product and process claims were allowed without any major modification, and this was never challenged legally.

In Canada, though, the product claims of the equivalent patent were rejected by the Supreme Court on the basis that higher life forms cannot be classed as inventions in the way that machines, chemicals and microbes can be. As the Court explained:

> Patentable micro-organisms are formed in such large numbers that any measurable quantity will possess uniform properties and characteristics. The same cannot be said for plants and animals. It is far easier to analogize a micro-organism to a chemical compound or another inanimate object than it is to analogize an animal to an inanimate object. Moreover, several important features possessed by animals distinguish them from both micro-organisms and plants and remove them even further from being considered a 'composition of matter' or a 'manufacture'.

Nonetheless, claims to the method of producing oncomice were accepted.[18] Appeals to consistency with practice elsewhere were not accepted by the majority.

COMPLEXITY AND 'DESIGN'

Life, even in its most primitive state, is complex almost beyond our imaginations. We know surprisingly little about it. What goes on within the walls and membranes of cells, and between them and their surroundings including neighbouring cells, is still for the most part a mystery. So how can we make sense of life? Recent scientific and philosophical discussions seeking to advance our understanding have achieved a high level of sophistication. While much remains unexplained, discussion and debate have been productive. Scientists and philosophers offer explanations that are either naturalistic and materialist, or supernatural and immaterial. I have managed to identify three currents of thinking, all of which have an interest in describing and emphasising biological complexity in order to show that their explanation best fits the facts, and which have something to say about agency, which is not just a scientific issue but a philosophical one, and a matter crucially important for our purposes.

First, we have the Darwinists, who hold that natural selection working on minor intergenerational modifications is sufficient to explain most if not all functional complexity in living things, from microbes to humans. There is no design as such; and neither is there any grand purpose. As Richard Dawkins puts it, 'biology is the study of complicated things that give the

[18] *Harvard College v Canada (Commissioner of Patents)* 2002 SCC 76.

appearance of having been designed for a purpose'.[19] At the other extreme from the Darwinists are the 'Intelligent Designers'. While adherents tend to be hostile to Darwinism, some are willing to concede a role for evolution, if not of the Darwinian stripe. But they believe this role, at best, to be limited in its explanatory power. The same, they claim, goes for any other naturalistic theory that one could conceive. Divine intervention of some kind is necessary for life to exist and to be as it is.

Darwinists and Intelligent Designers are currently locked in a heated debate. Interestingly, Darwinian and other opponents of supernatural explanations have been inspired by their proponents, just as supporters of Darwinian evolution have provoked creationists to seek scientifically credible alternatives to which Darwinists, in turn, have found themselves having to react. Thus, William Paley, the architect of the so-called argument from design, according to which the intricate functional order of life can only have been designed by a deity, has been an inspiration to prominent scientists past and present, especially Charles Darwin and Richard Dawkins, both of whom have seen him as a worthy apologist for 'natural theology', the title of his classic 1802 book.[20] Similarly, Michael Behe's concept of 'irreducible complexity', the unsolvable problem locked inside what he calls 'Darwin's black box', is supposed to prove the fatal inadequacies of Darwinism and materialist science more generally.[21] Behe defines an irreducibly complex system as one that 'is necessarily composed of several well-matched, interacting parts that contribute to the basic function, and where the removal of any one of the parts causes the system to effectively cease functioning'.[22] The usual analogy is an arch built of bricks, which will become unstable and eventually collapse if any one of the bricks is taken out. Each brick alone is useless, but together they *are* the arch. He claims that even the most primitive cells comprise irreducibly complex systems. As the argument goes, Darwinism cannot possibly explain how the parts could evolve one by one when they could serve no useful purpose until *every* part of the system had come into being. Examples range from the bacterial flagellum to the Krebs cycle, the human eye and the blood-clotting cascade. Darwin's defenders have of course been forced to accept the challenge and explain away a concept that seems on its face to be entirely plausible. They have done so by showing how ID's 'argument from incredulity', that highly complex living systems are just too complicated to explain scientifically, hence the resort to God, is scientifically and intellectually impoverished.

19 R Dawkins, *The Blind Watchmaker* (London, Penguin Books, 1986), 1 (emphasis added).

20 W Paley, *Natural Theology* (Oxford, Oxford University Press, 2006 [1802]).

21 M Behe, *Darwin's Black Box: The Biochemical Challenge to Evolution* (New York, Free Press, 1996).

22 Ibid.

Numerous plausible hypotheses have been put forward to show that each component of a given complex system[23] can come into existence or persist by providing some selective advantage or other.[24]

But present discussion on organised functional complexity and agency is not just between Darwinists and Intelligent Designers. Helpful as it undoubtedly is, one does not need to go through participants in the Darwinism-intelligent design (ID) debate like Dawkins, Behe, Michael Ruse[25] and William Dembski[26] to arrive at an appreciation of the amazing complexity, sophistication and creativity displayed within all living organisms. Other leading scientists have done much to explain what life is about at all scales, from the molecular to the cellular to the multicellular, in all of its extraordinary complexity, and how at least some of it works.[27] This takes us to the third current of thinking, which comprises those who believe that reductionism, the idea that the whole can only be comprehended by breaking it up into its smallest parts and treating those as the focus of investigation, is inadequate for explaining the complexity of living systems. Non-reductionists, who for want of any better label I will call 'Systematists', are a mixed group, but all treat complexity as the focus of investigation.[28] One important sub-group holds that once complexity emerges, systems have an innate tendency to become more complex and ordered, and to evolve this way

[23] Mitchell offers two definitions of 'complex system': (i) 'a system in which large networks of components with no central control and simple rules of operation give rise to complex collective behaviour, sophisticated information processing, and adaptation via learning or evolution'; and (ii) 'a system that exhibits nontrivial emergent and self-organizing behaviours'. M Mitchell, *Complexity: A Guided Tour* (New York, Oxford University Press 2009), 13.

[24] Biological complexity is not by definition elegant, though it certainly can be stunningly so. Like Heath Robinson's hilarious imaginary contraptions, functional systems in living things may be built from parts 'that just happen to be lying around', originally serving quite different purposes from the one for which the system is intended. While inelegant systems can still provide considerable evolutionary advantages, from an optimal design perspective they may be seriously flawed. But they are good enough to do the job. See also N Shubin, *Your Inner Fish: A Journey into the 3.5-Billion Year History of the Human Body* (London, Penguin, 2008).

[25] M Ruse, *Darwinism and its Discontents* (Cambridge, Cambridge University Press, 2006).

[26] W Dembski, *The Design Inference: Eliminating Chance through Small Probabilities* (Cambridge, Cambridge University Press, 1998).

[27] Such as Steven Rose, Denis Noble, Paul Davies and Lynn Margulis. See S Rose, *Lifelines: Life Beyond the Gene* (London, Vintage, 2005); D Noble, *The Music of Life* (Oxford, Oxford University Press, 2006); P Davies, *The Origin of Life* (London, Penguin, 2003); L Margulis and D Sagan, *Microcosmos* (London, Allan & Unwin, 1987).

[28] 'Whereas the early molecular biologists supposed that order was to be found in the construction and arrangement of the organism's molecular components, scientists now look instead to the self-organisation and integrated functioning of these components. Accordingly, the task facing the new post-genomic technologies is to describe organic complexity'. For Morange, complexity and emergence (which sees life as undergoing constant change and novelty) have become key concepts according to this new paradigm, which is also seeing a devaluation of 'the informational model that previously dominated research in the life sciences'. Morange, *Life Explained* (n 13) 21–22.

completely spontaneously.[29] These 'Self-Organisers' are just as materialistic as the Darwinists, finding no place either for supernatural explanations. They tend to respect Darwinism and acknowledge much of its explanatory power, but consider that descent with minor modification as per Darwinism cannot be the only driver of life's complexity. As Stuart Kauffman puts it, in addition to order arising from descent with modification, nature provides what he calls 'order for free'.[30] Another important sub-group are the Systems Biologists, who strive to integrate biological knowledge at all levels from the molecular to the whole organism.[31]

One can argue, as many no doubt do, that the materialists seem easily to have the upper hand over the adherents to natural theology, with intelligent design being unconvincing even to scientifically trained theologians.[32] However, the need for Darwinists and other evolutionists to respond to the view that living things are too complex, ordered and well-designed to have emerged without a supernatural tinkerer has been fruitful.

First, it has forced evolutionists to give serious thought to the apparent existence of design and teleology in biology, and the results can be illuminating. Even Dawkins, with his jaundiced views about religion, natural theology and intelligent design, has written some of his most thought-provoking work, and most colourful metaphors, in reaction to the so-called 'argument from design'. Just consider *The Blind Watchmaker* and *River Out of Eden*, to name just two of his book titles.

Second, these meaning-of-life discussions are attracting and provoking scientists and thinkers from a growing number of disciplines, and not just biochemistry and genetics. Conventional thinking and ways of doing science increasingly seem unviable, misleading and unable to answer or even pose the right questions. Biochemists and geneticists are increasingly thinking outside the 'boxes' of their own scientific and academic fields, resulting in some truly insightful work. This is as it should be. Life is still mysteriously complex and increasingly seems to require micro-ecological and interdisciplinary approaches for us to understand what it is and what it does.

[29] The leading light is Stuart Kauffman. See S Kauffman, 'Prolegomenon to a general biology' in WA Dembski and M Ruse (eds), *Debating Design: From Darwin to DNA* (New York, Cambridge University Press, 2004).

[30] SA Kauffmann, *At Home in the Universe* (New York, Oxford University Press, 1995).

[31] 'Systems Biology is defined as the quantitative analysis of the dynamic interactions between several components of a biological system and aims to understand the behaviour of the system as a whole, as opposed to the behaviour of its individual constituents. It applies the concepts of systems engineering to the study of complex biological systems through iteration between computational and/or mathematical modelling and experimentation.' Academy of Medical Science and the Royal Academy of Engineering, *Systems Biology: A Vision for Engineering and Medicine* (London, AMS and RAE, 2007) 9–10.

[32] For example, see J Polkinghorne, 'The inbuilt potentiality of creation', in WA Dembski and M Ruse, *Debating Design: From Darwin to DNA* (New York, Cambridge University Press, 2004) 246–60.

One of the consequences of this trend is an increasing questioning of long-established metaphors and analogies. The issue may not be that of whether these are wrong or misleading in themselves, but whether they are sufficient. More fundamentally, it is now evident that reliance on any one discipline, whether biochemistry, molecular biology, computer science or physics, cannot generate all of the right questions, or answers, that we need to explain life. It may well be true, as the physicist Alan Sokal points out, that 'Newtonian physics is perfectly capable of describing complex interactive systems'.[33] But Steven Rose explains convincingly that all life forms must have the ability 'to *be* and to *become*',[34] which in turn requires a biology that encompasses 'epistemological pluralism'.[35] He also makes the fascinating point that because biology 'developed in the shadow of physics', a consequence is 'the power of technological metaphor in biology, whereby living systems become analogised to machines ... thus reversing a much older tradition in cultures in which the physical world too was regarded as if it were alive'.[36] To Rose, these metaphors are problematic. For patent attorneys and biotechnologists they can be rather convenient, since organisms can thus be cast, in US patent law parlance, as 'articles of manufacture'.

WHY LIFE IS TOO COMPLEX AND LITTLE UNDERSTOOD TO INVENT—BUT ONE DAY WILL NOT BE

The view, accepted under current patent law and practice, that living things can be claimed as inventions, is *not* supported by what we know so far, what we know we don't know, and what we know how to do. As we have seen, scientists and philosophers are making some fascinating attempts to understand the hows and whys of living systems, and there is some real progress here—despite some wrong directions such as ID. But there is no overall consensus, and we have a long way to go. Ignorant of so much, our control over life is far more rudimentary than we often tend to believe. But at least we are becoming aware of the extent of this ignorance, not that this humility has yet reached the patent community. Patent laws, practices and jurisprudence still assume, when it comes to claims over whole organisms, that 'inventors' can do more to turn living things into human artefacts than they are really able. Even the simplest life forms are too complex and little understood for such claims to be objectively plausible. Scientists cannot make or invent life as they can make or invent complex devices like computers,

[33] A Sokal, *Beyond the Hoax: Science, Philosophy and Culture* (Oxford, Oxford University Press, 2008).
[34] S Rose, *Lifelines: Life Beyond the Gene* (London, Vintage, 2005) 142.
[35] Ibid 14.
[36] Ibid 19.

robots or space rockets, which are unlikely to be subjects of single patents anyway. There are three reasons for this, which *taken together* make an overwhelming case for this argument.

First, as is increasingly evident, *all* living things seem to be far more complicated and creative than any genuinely human artefact.[37] For instance, the extent of the metabolic activity going on during every second of the life of every single cell in an organism is mind-boggling.[38] Paul Davies describes beautifully the mysterious, wonderfully complex and chaotic yet orderly hustle and bustle of life at the cellular level:

> As a simple-minded physicist, when I think about life at the molecular level, the question I keep asking is: How do all these mindless atoms know what to do? The complexity of the living cell is immense, resembling a city in the degree of its elaborate activity. Each molecule has a specified function and a designated place in the overall scheme so that the correct objects get manufactured. There is so much commuting going on. Molecules have to travel across the cell to meet others at the right place and the right time in order to carry out their jobs properly. This all happens without a boss to order the molecules around and steer them to their appropriate locations. No overseer supervises their activities. Molecules simply do what molecules have to do: bang around blindly, knock into each other, rebound, embrace. At the level of individual atoms life is anarchy—blundering, purposeless chaos. Yet somehow, collectively, these unthinking atoms get it together, and perform the dance of life with exquisite precision.'

Second, the ways that biochemical elements of cells interact to make metabolism and replication possible are still poorly understood. Neither are we close yet to understanding how, with respect to higher life forms, organisms develop from the initial clusters of undifferentiated cells that form just after fertilisation. So we have mind-boggling complexity and incomplete understanding. Admittedly, one could just about make a case that patentability is not completely precluded on either or even both of these grounds.

But the third argument is, in my view, the clincher. Unlike machines, living things can do without our help in carrying out most functions throughout their whole lifespans. They are autonomous and self-creating ('autopoietic')[39] in terms of how they make, renew and remake themselves, *and* in their independence from us—unlike machines which are assembled and directed to specific tasks by human operators. Multicellular organisms perform the astounding and so far inexplicable 'trick' of periodically replacing all of their parts while remaining the same. The operational life of each cell in the human body, for example, is considerably shorter than our

[37] Indeed, it is likely that biological systems can achieve feats of complexity that no non-living systems can emulate, including those fashioned by homo sapiens. The human brain is often referred to as the most complex known system in the universe.

[38] P Davies, *The Origin of Life* (London, Penguin, 2003).

[39] HR Maturana and FJ Varela, *Autopoiesis and Cognition: The Realization of the Living* (Boston, Reidal, 1980).

average lifespan. Of course, bacteria do not have to perform such amazing feats. And yet, bacteria are also highly evolved and able to survive, adapt, mass-replicate and thrive virtually anywhere on the surface of the planet, all without our help and in some cases despite our best efforts to exterminate them.

So what are we now to make of the US and Canadian Supreme Courts' decisions in *Diamond v Chakrabarty* and *Harvard College v Canada*? First, Chakrabarty's bug was, with all due respect to him, nature's handiwork and not man's.[40] A living microbe cannot avoid being that. Second, the legal line drawn in the latter case between lower and higher life forms is a dubious one. No legal distinction is scientifically trustworthy. If higher life forms are unpatentable, the same should probably go for lower ones.

I must stress that none of this is to deny the immense ingenuity of many life scientists. Scientists are able to achieve extraordinary feats with respect to the manipulation of living cells, including both unicellular and multicellular life. Scientists can now create enormous numbers of different proteins that have no natural counterparts. And of course we've been *consciously* modifying plants and animals for a long time. At some level, domesticated plants and animals *are* human artefacts. But in my view this is not enough to say they can be inventions.

But this is all eventually going to change. Systems biology confronts and seeks to understand life's complexity. Practical applications are yet to be fully explored. Synthetic biology aims at creating simplified artificial cells and life forms *functionally* indistinguishable from naturally occurring ones and interoperable with them. Synthetic biology, which like systems biology is at its early stages, can only work with simplified models and thus deliberately avoids complexity. Unsurprisingly, systems biology and synthetic biology operate mainly in parallel universes. But once the two come together and converge, immense possibilities will emerge. As mentioned, an artificial virus has already been constructed, and it seems only a matter of time before somebody produces the first rudimentary life forms able to do many things that 'natural' life forms can do. But most probably this is going to require a great convergence of systems biology with synthetic biology and nanotechnology. Of course, we cannot be sure when that union will occur; but it definitely will.

At present, synthetic biology lends itself to commercial applications far more than does systems biology. Consequently, we can expect a great deal of patenting activity, despite the hacker mentality of many of its practitioners. Indeed, it is possible that synthetic biology will provide the language for biotech patenting in the future. Synthetic biology is regarded by many

[40] Of course, such distinctions as we all make are grossly anthropocentric. Everything in existence is natural; nothing is synthetic or artificial, since we are just as much a part of nature as chimpanzees, carnations and cyano-bacteria, as is everything we produce.

of its practitioners as an engineering discipline, a biological counterpart to chemical and mechanical engineering. Engineering is of course a very long established patent 'language' for which the system is well accustomed.

To conclude, molecular biology and biotechnology are suitable fields for the patent system. However, at the present time, claims to whole organisms are premature. Moreover, the fact that such claims are allowed marks a radical departure from, rather than a logical and scientifically sound extension of, traditional patent practice which we ought to reconsider. Humans are not yet able to be agents of organised functional complexity to the extent of becoming authors of the life-forms in which that complexity is embedded.

It is quite possible, then, that the recent re-emergence of jurisprudential divergence in the common law world may be a temporary phenomenon. Whether or not this turns out to be the case, the decidedly un-monolithic common law of intellectual property is in for some interesting times in this field as in others.

9

Divergent Approaches in Defining the Appropriate Level of Inventiveness in Patent Law

ANN MONOTTI

INTRODUCTION

ALTHOUGH IT IS clear that the nature of the invention will directly influence what constitutes an inventive step,[1] the determination of an appropriate level for this step along with its assessment is not necessarily consistent among jurisdictions. This essay considers the reasons for the divergence in defining that level in two jurisdictions which share a history of close legal and political ties: the United Kingdom and Australia.

This history of close legal ties can be traced to the eighteenth century when the British settled in the Australian colonies. They brought with them the common law of England so far as it was locally applicable,[2] and each colonial legislature became active in developing a body of statutory law that was based usually upon British legislation. One area was patent law. For example, within three years of its separation from New South Wales in July 1851, and prior to the proclamation in 1855 of its first Constitution Act, the Colony of Victoria enacted on 31 March 1854 An 'Act to Regulate Grants for Patents for Inventions in the Colony of Victoria'.[3] This Act was modelled upon the Patents Act 1852,[4] whose origins came from the common law[5] rights of the Crown preserved in section 6 of the Statute of Monopolies 1623. Under the 1854 Act, the patentee was to be entitled to

[1] *Biogen Inc v Medeva plc* [1997] RPC 1 (HL) 34.

[2] Australian Courts Act 1828 (Imp).

[3] 17 Vict No 15.

[4] 15 & 16 Vict c 83.

[5] T Terrell, C Terrell and DH Corsellis, *The Law and Practice Relating to Letters Patent for Inventions*, 7th edn (London, Sweet & Maxwell, 1927) 1; *Darcy v Allin* (1602) Noy 182, 1 WPC 1; see also: J Pila, 'The Common Law Invention in its Original Form' [2001] *Intellectual Property Quarterly* 209.

the same privileges in Victoria as a patentee of a patent granted under the Great Seal of England enjoyed in England.[6]

Following a volatile period of reform proposals,[7] the UK Parliament enacted the Patents, Designs and Trade Marks Act 1883[8] (1883 Act) which introduced a structure for the registration of patents on which we base our modern patent system. Until the UK altered its patent law in 1977 to comply with the European Patent Convention (EPC), Australia continued to use UK patent law as its model. This, together with the requirement that the Australian High Court and all other courts must follow decisions of the Privy Council,[9] resulted in many common approaches to patent law issues.[10] Despite the later severance of all formal legal and constitutional ties with the Privy Council,[11] UK decisions under the Patents Act 1949 (UK) (1949 Act) continued to influence Australian patent law.[12]

The enactment of the Patents Act 1977 (UK) (1977 Act) to comply with the EPC marked a defining time for divergence and introduced some radical differences with the Australian Patents Act 1952 (Cth) (1952 Act). Both the 1977 Act and the increasing influence of other trading partners' patent laws diluted the significance of UK patent law in Australia. Differences continue under the Patents Act 1990 (Cth) (1990 Act). Although both share the same philosophy regarding the starting point from which to assess inventive step,[13] they do not necessarily arrive at the same point, for various reasons that are discussed in this chapter.

DIVERGENCE IN RAISING THE THRESHOLD OF INVENTIVENESS: A STATUTORY OVERVIEW

Both jurisdictions have gradually raised the threshold of inventiveness through rebalancing 'policy considerations in patent law of encouraging and rewarding inventors without impeding advances and improvements

[6] An Act to regulate Grants for Patents for Inventions in the Colony of Victoria (17 Vict No 15), s 1.

[7] F Machlup and E Penrose, 'The Patent Controversy in the Nineteenth Century' (1950) X *Journal of Economic History* 1, 5; K Boehm, *The British Patent System 1: Administration* (Cambridge, CUP, 1967) 27–29.

[8] 46 and 47 Vict c 57.

[9] *Viro v R* (1978) 141 CLR 88 (HC) 118 (Gibbs J); *Skelton v Collins* (1966) 115 CLR 94(HC) 104.

[10] eg *Regina v Patents Appeal Tribunal. Ex parte Swift & Co* [1962] 2 QB 647 (DC) 663–64.

[11] Privy Council (Limitation of Appeals) Act 1968 (Cth); Privy Council (Appeals from the High Court) Act 1975 (Cth); Australia Acts 1986 (Cth) and Australia Acts 1986 (UK).

[12] M Kirby, 'Precedent law, practice and trends in Australia' (2007) 28 *Australian Bar Review* 243, 244, n 5.

[13] *Aktiebolaget Hassel v Alphapharm Pty Ltd* (2002) 212 CLR 411 (HC) 427; *Société Technique de Pulverisation Step v Emson Europe Ltd* [1993] RPC 513 (CA) 519.

by skilled, non-inventive persons'.[14] That rebalancing has taken different paths.

United Kingdom

The weight of authority supports the view that no requirement for an inventive step emanates from section 6 of the Statute of Monopolies. Prior to the 1883 Act, scrutiny of patent applications in the UK was largely one of mere formalities, unless a patent was challenged. Law officers were charged with determining whether the patent would be legal under the Statute of Monopolies, and were not required to consider inventive step prior to grant. They were concerned only with the economic and social effects of the invention described in the final words of section 6. The applicant would take the patent at his own risk,[15] with questions of novelty, utility or inventiveness arising in proceedings brought by *scire facias* to repeal a patent.[16]

Hence, the law on inventive step developed in the late nineteenth and early twentieth centuries through the common law arising from these proceedings.[17] Edmunds explained its emergence 'as a brake upon the too rapid progress of patents for analogous uses' which was added to patent law by 'modern judges' as a 'counterpoise ... to the admission of 'analogous use' on the subject matter of a patent'.[18] Beier believed it was 'primarily a reaction of the courts to the all too liberal patenting of unimportant improvements which differed only insignificantly from known apparatus or processes'.[19] However, even if section 6 itself provided no express requirement for an inventive step, its later development was justified in the words appearing in section 6, namely 'mischievous by hurt of trade by raising the price of commodities or generally inconvenient'.[20]

The 1883 Act significantly reformed the patent system in a variety of ways. It abolished repeal of a patent by way of *scire facias* proceedings and

[14] *Lockwood Security Products Pty Ltd v Doric Products Pty Ltd (No 2)* (2007) 235 ALR 202 (HC) 216.

[15] J Roberts, *The grant and validity of British patents for inventions* (London, J Murray, 1903) 18.

[16] C MacLeod, *Inventing the Industrial Revolution: The English patent system, 1660—1800* (Cambridge, CUP, 1988) 41–42; JW Gordon, *Monopolies by patents and the statutable remedies available to the public* (London, Stevens and Sons, 1897) 38.

[17] HG Fox, *Monopolies and Patents: A Study of the History and Future of the Patent Monopoly* (Toronto, University of Toronto Press, 1947) 227; Gordon, *Monopolies by patents* (n 16) 38.

[18] L Edmunds and TM Stevens, *The Law and Practice of Letters Patent for Inventions*, 2nd edn (London, Stevens and Sons, 1897) 84, 95–96.

[19] FK Beier, 'The Inventive Step in Its Historical Development' (1986) 17 *International Review of Industrial Property and Copyright Law* 301, 312.

[20] *Elias v Grovesend* (1890) 7 RPC 455 (CA) 467.

permitted all grounds formerly available under that action to be used as a defence to an action for infringement and as a ground of revocation.[21] One of the grounds was that 'the invention is not an invention of such a nature as may be made the subject of a patent privilege'—referred to as 'want of subject matter' or 'want of sufficient inventive ingenuity',[22] the forerunner of obviousness. Although the judiciary referred to the term 'subject matter' in two senses,[23] our interest is with its equivalence with 'the exercise of inventive faculty'[24] to enable the eradication of inventions that 'are so simple as to interfere with existing trades'.[25] Lack of 'subject matter' became interchangeable with obviousness, or lack of inventive step.[26]

An Act to Amend the Patents and Designs Acts, 1907 to 1928[27] (1932 Act) introduced lack of inventive step as an express ground for revocation following the recommendations of the Sargant Committee.[28] The ground, that 'the invention is obvious and does not involve any inventive step having regard to what was known or used prior to the date of the patent',[29] was modelled on the common law.[30] Upon the recommendation of the Sargant Committee to reject the introduction of obviousness as a ground for opposition, its availability was limited to grounds for revocation. Although this restriction would affect the level of inventiveness of granted patents, the risk of an increase in the number of oppositions, hardship to inventors and cost[31] apparently outweighed that disadvantage. After some years it became evident that obviousness should be considered pre-grant to prevent the register being 'cluttered up with patents which would be certain to be revoked by the court in a revocation action',[32] and to achieve cheaper and quicker post-acceptance and post-grant proceedings.[33]

[21] Patents, Designs and Trade Marks Act 1883, s 26(3).

[22] WM Hindmarch, *A treatise on the law relating to patent privileges for the sole use of inventions microform: and the practice of obtaining letters patents for inventions* (London, V & R Stevens & GS Norton, & W Benning & Co, 1846) 266.

[23] Terrell, *Patent for Inventions* (n 5) 47.

[24] Ibid 57.

[25] Roberts, *The grant and validity of British patents* (n 15) 20 n 2.

[26] K E Shelley, *Terrell and Shelley on the Law of Patents*, 9th edn (London, Sweet & Maxwell, 1951) 115. *Final Report of the Departmental Committee on Patents and Designs Acts (Patents and Designs Acts)* (Swan Committee), Cmd 7206 (1946–47) [126].

[27] 22 & 23 Geo 5 c 32.

[28] *Report of the Departmental Committee on the Patents and Designs Acts and Practice of the Patent Office* (Sargant Committee), Cmnd 3829 (1931).

[29] Patents and Designs Act 1932 22 & 23 Geo 5 s 3 inserted a new s 25(2) into Patents and Designs Act 1907 Edw 7.

[30] Patents and Designs Bill 1932, 2nd reading speech 7 June 1932, 1891 (Mr Hore-Belisha); note *Ajinomoto Co Inc v NutraSweet Australia Pty Ltd* (2008) 166 FCR 530 (FFC) 543.

[31] Sargant Committee (n 28) [71].

[32] *General Electric Co's Applications* [1964] RPC 413 (CA) 452.

[33] *The British Patent System: Report of the Committee to Examine the Patent System and Patent Law* (Banks Committee), Cmnd 4407 (1970) [138]ff.

The 1949 Act, which was enacted following the recommendation of the Swan Committee Final Report,[34] introduced obviousness as a ground for opposition and altered the language of the ground generally to include an express territorial limitation to the UK. This limitation may have lowered the inventiveness threshold, but only if earlier decisions had considered what was known or used extra-territorially. The Committee was unable to recommend how to define the precise 'degree of ingenuity or the character of the inventive step that is requisite to endow an invention with patentable subject matter'.[35] Instead, it considered that the common law continued to provide the best definition.

The enactment of the 1977 Act again raised levels by providing a universal prior art base in s 2(2) for the assessment of both inventive step and novelty. In addition, inventive step could now be considered at all stages of the patent process.[36]

Australia

Significant parallels exist in the development of the Australian inventive step requirement, although reform in the UK was slow to filter into Australian legislation. It gained statutory force only when it became a ground for both opposition and revocation under the 1952 Act.

A brief review of the pre-1952 common law position demonstrates both the close connections between Australian and UK patent law at this time and the relative independence that the young colonies and then the Commonwealth exercised. Both followed the English and later British and UK law as much as possible, but only after independent examination of other options. For example, before the Colony of Victoria adopted the provisions of the 1883 Act as the basis for its Patents Law Consolidation and Amendment Bill 1889, it considered both the English and the US systems. In his second reading speech in the Legislative Assembly, Mr Wrixon explained that one benefit of adopting the existing English patents system was that '... Victoria would, in all matters affecting the patents law, have the decisions given on the subject from time to time in the English courts to go upon'.[37] Another benefit was to achieve consistency with the systems already adopted in New South Wales, Queensland and South Australia so as to 'pave the way to ... one uniform patents law for the whole of the colonies'.[38]

[34] *Final Report of the Departmental Committee on Patents and Designs Acts (Patents and Designs Acts)* (Swan Committee), Cmd 7206 (1946–47).

[35] Swan Committee (n 34) [127].

[36] Banks Committee recommendation (n 33) [138]ff.

[37] Victoria Parliamentary Debates, Session 1889, Legislative Assembly, 2117.

[38] Ibid 2119.

Uniform Australian patent law was accomplished following Federation in 1901 with the enactment of the Patents Act 1903 (Cth), largely based upon the 1883 Act, following recommendations in a report of a conference of states' patent officers that had met in Melbourne in April 1901. Echoing the above comments of Mr Wrixon, Sir Edmund Barton, Minister for External Affairs, noted that 'by following the lines of legislation passed in England [*sic*] we shall have the advantage of a long series of decisions which have been given upon patents law to guide us in the application of our own measures'.[39]

Among the similarities were the grounds for revocation being defined in section 86(3) with reference to those on which a patent might at common law be repealed by *scire facias*, which therefore included obviousness.

No further significant patent reform occurred until 1952 when a report of the Dean Committee included a Patent Bill which had as close correspondence with the British Act as possible. In adopting this approach, the Committee noted the importance of the close historical ties between Australia and Britain, the influence these had upon the development of Australian patent law and the extensive examination and report by committees which had preceded patent reform in Britain. Further, there were other practical reasons to follow British patent law: '... it is desirable that British inventors and their advisers should not be troubled about differing laws, and that Australian inventors and their advisers should be similarly assisted by uniformity. We have accordingly recommended the adoption of very many of the provisions of the existing British Act'.[40]

The 1952 Act therefore bore close correlation with the 1949 Act. It introduced enumerated grounds for revocation and opposition. The ground relating to novelty was inexplicably modelled on the 1932 Act, which contained different language from its later equivalent in the 1949 Act. This difference in the statutory grounds for novelty, as opposed to inventive step, had a significant impact on later divergence in levels of inventiveness in the two jurisdictions.[41] The prior art base for inventive step differed only in its territorial limitation to 'what was known or used *in Australia* on or before the priority date of that claim'.[42] (emphasis added) Nevertheless, this difference alone meant that levels of inventiveness were likely to differ.

Major reform finally occurred in Australia with the enactment of the 1990 Act. In stark contrast to the need for the 1903 Act and the 1952 Act

[39] Commonwealth of Australia, Parliamentary Debates, House of Representatives, 17 September, 1903, 2nd Reading, 5216. (Sir Edmund Barton).

[40] *Report of the Committee Appointed by the Attorney-General of the Commonwealth to Consider What Alterations are Desirable in the Patent Law of the Commonwealth* (1952) [5].

[41] See s 3.2.

[42] Patents Act 1952 (Cth) s 100(1)(e).

to conform as much as possible with British patent law, the debate on the Patents Bill 1989 (Cth) that subsequently formed the basis for the 1990 Act, emphasised the wider international context which influenced its drafting: the then on-going negotiations regarding TRIPS, the WIPO proposal for harmonisation of patent law, the revision of patent laws by some of its neighbours in the rapidly expanding economies in East and South East Asia and the need for closer economic ties with New Zealand. The aim was to 'place Australia in a sounder position in relation to the negotiations in both GATT and WIPO'.[43] British influence was now diminished, but nevertheless, strong connections with pre-1977 UK patent law remained because many of its provisions were drawn in substance from the 1952 Act.

The 1990 Act adjusted the standard of inventiveness for standard patents to 'bring the requirement into line with similar requirements in most of Australia's trading partner countries'.[44] It did this in two ways. First, as in the UK, obviousness was now available as a ground to reject a patent application. Secondly, it expanded the obviousness prior art base, but to a level below that of its UK counterpart. The Patents Amendment Act 2001 (Cth) further strengthened the inventive step requirements of the 1990 Act 'to more closely align [this test] with international standards' and in particular to 'align our practices with those of Europe and the United States'.[45] Again, despite the expansion, the Australian prior art base remained narrower than in the UK.

FACTORS THAT HAVE AN IMPACT ON LEVELS OF INVENTIVENESS

Variations in the legislation, along with different statutory and judicial solutions for assessment of inventive step have affected the levels of inventiveness. The specific factors, discussed below, are the structural approaches to assessment of inventive step, the different prior art bases that apply in each jurisdiction, the level of advance over the prior art base and the relevance of secondary factors, but more specifically, the 'obvious to try test'.

Structural Approaches

Courts have attempted to resolve the question of obviousness with uniformity and consistency, seeking objectivity through the perception of the notional skilled person in the relevant art. For many years, UK (and Australian) cases determined obviousness by applying the 'Cripps question',[46] or a modified

[43] Patents Bill 1989 House of Representatives 2nd Reading (Mr Jones).
[44] Ibid.
[45] Patents Amendment Bill 2001 House of Representatives 2nd Reading (Mr Entsch).
[46] *Sharp & Dohme v Boots* (1928) 45 RPC 153 (CA) 173.

form thereof if it was inappropriate for the relevant subject matter.[47] Even when inventive step became a statutory ground for revocation and a defence to infringement, courts found the question remained useful. Change occurred in the UK in 1984 when Oliver LJ replaced the 'Cripps question' with a structured procedural strategy that he developed in *Windsurfing International Inc v Tabur Marine (Great Britain) Ltd*.[48] The fact-finding tribunal now had a uniform approach to 'equip itself with the tools to answer the statutory question'.[49] Although the *Windsurfing* formula was a useful, but not essential, tool[50] it was used almost universally. Reproduction of the formula helps us appreciate better the impact of recent development of the structured test upon relative levels of inventiveness.

> There are, we think, four steps which require to be taken in answering the jury question. The first is to identify the inventive concept embodied in the patent in suit. Thereafter, the court has to assume the mantle of the normally skilled but unimaginative addressee in the art at the priority date and to impute to him what was, at that date, common general knowledge in the art in question. The third step is to identify what, if any, differences exist between the matter cited as being 'known or used' and the alleged invention. Finally, the court has to ask itself whether, viewed without any knowledge of the alleged invention, those differences constitute steps which would have been obvious to the skilled man or whether they require any degree of invention.[51]

It is now clear that this test presents some problems. The identification of the inventive concept was no simple matter, as the statute does not require a specification to state the inventive 'concept' involved in the claimed invention. If this 'inventive concept' is the same thing as the 'inventive step',[52] it should differ according to the claim that is being construed. However, this test suggests that there might be one inventive concept 'embodied in the patent in suit' that is relevant to all claims. An additional complication in the application of these steps arose when Lord Hoffmann stated in *Biogen Inc v Medeva plc* that: 'A proper statement of inventive concept needs to include some express or implied reference to the problem which it required invention to overcome'.[53] This appeared to refer to the problem and solution approach which the EPO imposes to

[47] TA Blanco White, *Patents for Inventions and the Protection of Industrial Designs*, 4th edn (London, Stevens & Sons, 1974) 127.

[48] *Windsurfing International Inc v Tabur Marine (Great Britain) Ltd* [1985] RPC 59 (CA).

[49] *Zipher Ltd v Markem Systems Ltd* [2008] EWHC 1379; [2009] FSR 1 (Pat) [284]; *Research in Motion UK Ltd v Visto Corporation* [2008] EWHC 335 (Pat) [72].

[50] *David J Instance Ltd v Denny Bros Printing Ltd* [2002] RPC 14 (CA); *Nichia Corporation v Argos Ltd* [2007] EWCA Civ 741, [2007] FSR 38 (CA) [22].

[51] *Windsurfing International v Tabur Marine* (n 48) 73–74.

[52] *Generics (UK) Limited v H Lundbeck A/S* [2009] UKHL 12 [101] (Lord Neuberger).

[53] *Biogen v Medeva* (n 1) 45; *Lockwood v Doric* (n 14) 220.

achieve consistency among its examiners.[54] Not only did this approach risk diverting attention from the actual language of the claim, but it caused the Australian High Court in *Lockwood Security Products Pty Ltd v Doric Products Pty Ltd (No 2)* to observe that the 'structured approach' under the *Windsurfing* principles had raised the threshold of inventiveness in the UK because it required courts to isolate the 'inventive concept' in terms of 'problem and solution'.[55]

Recent decisions in the UK show some withdrawal from these more problematic aspects of the *Windsurfing* steps. They display less attraction for the 'inventive concept' framed with reference to the problem and clarify that the inventive concept is something that relates to each individual claim. The first decision was that of the Court of Appeal in *Pozzoli v BDMO SA*, which restated and elaborated the *Windsurfing* steps, in part to reflect the different structure of the 1977 Act as follows:

1. Identify the notional 'person skilled in the art'; and identify the relevant common general knowledge of that person.
2. Identify the inventive concept of the claim in question *or, if that cannot readily be done, construe it.*
3. Identify what, if any, differences exist between the matter cited as forming part of the 'state of the art' and the inventive concept of the claim *or the claim as construed.*
4. Ask: viewed without any knowledge of the alleged invention *as claimed*, do those differences constitute steps which would have been obvious to the person skilled in the art or do they require any degree of invention?[56] (Emphasis added.)

The reformulation of steps (ii) and (iii) redirects the attention on some generalised concept gained from the specification to the language of each respective claim. Jacob LJ clarified the reason for the restatement: 'Different claims can, and generally will, have different inventive concepts. ... One is trying to identify the essence of the claim in this exercise'.[57] What matters is the difference between what is claimed and the prior art. If the parties cannot agree on the inventive concept, then 'the sensible way to proceed is to forget it and simply work on the features of the claim'.[58] Notably, Jacob LJ

[54] PG Cole, 'Inventive step: meaning of the EPO problem and solution approach and implications for the United Kingdom: Part 1' (1998) 20 *European Intellectual Property Review* 214; Part 2 (1998) 20 *EIPR* 267; GSA Szabo, 'The problem and solution approach in the European Patent Office' (1995) 26(4) *International Review of Industrial Property and Copyright Law* 457.

[55] *Lockwood v Doric* (n 14) 220–21. S Crennan, 'Obviousness - Different paths through Scylla and Charybdis' (2007) 71 *Intellectual Property Forum* 12, 15.

[56] *Pozzoli v BDMO SA* [2007] EWCA Civ 588, FSR 38 (CA) [23].

[57] Ibid [17].

[58] Ibid [19].

ignores the problem and solution approach to the process for identification of an inventive concept.

The second significant decision is that of the House of Lords in *Conor Medsystems Inc v Angiotech Pharmaceutical Inc*.[59] The critical issue was how you identify the 'inventive concept' embodied in the invention which may constitute the 'inventive step' for the purposes of Article 56 of the EPC and section 1(1)(b) of Patents Act 1977. Framed in this way, 'inventive concept' becomes a paraphrase for 'inventive step' and moves attention to the statutory language. Lord Hoffmann stated: 'It is the claimed invention which has to involve an inventive step. The invention means prima facie that specified in the claim'.[60] And further: 'In my opinion ... the patentee is entitled to have the question of obviousness determined by reference to his claim and not to some vague paraphrase based upon the extent of his disclosure in the description'.[61]

Neither Lord Hoffmann nor the Court of Appeal referred to the *Pozzoli* steps. Lord Hoffmann focused on answering the statutory question by construing the relevant claim to identify the invention and the alleged inventiveness. [62] Furthermore, Lord Hoffmann made no reference to his statement in *Biogen Inc v Medeva plc* regarding the need to frame the inventive concept with reference to the problem to be solved. Hence, its relevance is now one of many 'tools' to assist courts in answering the statutory question. As Jacob LJ had earlier noted in *Nichia Corporation v Argos Ltd:* 'attempts to force all questions of obviousness into a "problem-solution" approach can lead to trouble, though often the test can be a helpful guide'.[63] This is consistent with Australian law, which only views the test as helpful in particular cases to overcome the difficulties of hindsight.[64] If isolation of the inventive concept in terms of 'problem and solution' does raise the threshold of inventiveness, as claimed by the High Court in *Lockwood*, the removal of this requirement is likely to lower that threshold. It also probably renders redundant the court's earlier comments regarding the impact of *Windsurfing* upon comparative thresholds of inventiveness.

How does this position in the UK compare with that in Australia? Prior to the 1990 Act, Australian courts followed an approach that is discussed in the next section which resulted in considerable divergence in levels of inventiveness. The *Windsurfing* steps bear some similarities with that approach

[59] *Conor Medsystems Inc v Angiotech Pharmaceutical Inc* [2008] UKHL 49, [2008] 4 All ER 621 (HL).

[60] Ibid [17].

[61] Ibid [19].

[62] For later cases, see eg *Zipher Ltd v Markem Systems* (n 49) [284]–[285]; *Re Eli Lilly and Co v Human Genome Sciences Inc* [2008] EWHC 1903 (Pat).

[63] *Nichia v Argos* (n 50) [22]; Australian comparisons: *Lockwood v Doric* (n 14) 221; *Polwood Pty Ltd v Foxworth Pty Ltd* (2008) 165 FCR 527, 537 (FFC).

[64] *Alphapharm* (n 13); *Lockwood v Doric* (n 14) 221.

but were never applied by our courts either before or after the enactment of the 1990 Act.

The 1990 Act incorporates a structured approach within section 7(2) and (3) and Schedule 1. Since the reformulation of *Windsurfing* in the *Pozzoli* steps, we see some convergence between these approaches. This is evident when *Pozzoli* is compared with a structured form of the 1990 Act provisions that was recently articulated by the full Federal Court in *Insta Image Pty Ltd v KD Kanopy Australasia Pty Ltd.*[65]

The inventive step threshold may well be higher in the UK, but it no longer appears that the structured approach under *Pozzoli* will bear much responsibility for any differences. The sources are more likely to be found elsewhere. The most obvious are the different prior art bases, which incorporate within them the concept of common general knowledge.

Different Prior Art Bases

Revocation on the ground of obviousness appeared in similar language in the 1932 Act, the 1949 Act and the 1952 Act. All provided that obviousness was to be tested 'having regard to what was known or used' before the priority date of the relevant claim. Both the 1949 Act and 1952 Act contained an express territorial limitation. UK courts settled on the view that this inquiry was through the eyes of the notional person skilled in the art who is attributed with a 'very good background technical knowledge—the so-called common general knowledge'.[66] The meaning of 'known or used' was something which is in addition to that common general knowledge: 'what was or ought to have been known to a diligent searcher'.[67]

One might have anticipated that Australian courts would apply this UK jurisprudence as to the meaning of the phrase 'what was known or used' in the equivalent section in the 1952 Act. This is especially so given that consistency in practice was an express aim of the government when it modelled its 1952 legislation so closely upon the UK legislation. Early decisions under the 1952 Act[68] followed UK decisions, but in 1980 the High Court

[65] *Insta Image Pty Ltd v KD Kanopy Australasia Pty Ltd* (2008) 78 IPR 20 (FFC) [80]. The outlined structured approach applies equally to the current s 7(2) and (3). A table appears as an appendix to this chapter.

[66] *Nichia v Argos* (n 50) [10]; *Technograph Printed Circuits Ltd v Mills and Rockley* [1972] RPC 346 (HL) 355 (Lord Reid) and *Technip France SA's Patent* [2004] RPC 46 (CA) [7].

[67] *Technograph v Mills and Rockley* (n 66) 355; *General Tire & Rubber Co Ltd v Firestone Tyre & Rubber Co Ltd* [1972] RPC 457 (CA) 497; *Lockwood v Doric* (n 14) 219. See: S Gratwick, 'Having regard to what was known or used' [1972] 88 *Law Quarterly Review* 841.

[68] *HPM Industries Pty Ltd v Gerard Industries Ltd* (1957) 98 CLR 424 (HC) 437; *Sunbeam Corporation v Morphy-Richards (Aust) Pty Ltd* (1961) 180 CLR 98 (HC).

in *Minnesota Mining and Manufacturing Co v Beiersdorf (Australia) Ltd*[69] rejected the relevance of those UK authorities[70] on the basis that they had dealt with the 1949 Act which contained a novelty ground that differed in form from that in both the 1932 Act and the 1952 Act. They relied upon this difference in language to construe the identical words in the obviousness ground in section 100(1)(e) to mean the common general knowledge of the skilled person 'without regard to documents in existence but not part of such common general knowledge'.[71] Hence, any prior disclosures which were publicly available information, but not part of Australian common general knowledge, were excluded from consideration.[72] This decision was pivotal in creating greater divergence in levels of inventiveness. Its effect remains in the current 1990 Act with the express territorial limitation of common general knowledge in Australia.

The enactment of the 1977 Act again raised levels of inventiveness in the UK by expanding its prior art base. Consistently with the EPC, it now required assessment through the eyes of the person skilled in the art, having regard to the 'state of the art', which is broadly defined in section 2(2) to:

> comprise all matter (whether a product, a process, information about either, or anything else) which has at any time before the priority date of that invention been made available to the public (whether in the United Kingdom or elsewhere) by written or oral description, by use or in any other way.

This is the same conception that operates in assessing novelty (with the exception of the prior specifications subsequently published). The skilled person will be assumed to have common general knowledge in his art at the priority date and 'will be assumed to have looked at and read publicly available documents and to know of public uses in the prior art'.[73] Hence, any cited prior art will be assumed to have been read with interest and understood.[74] Significantly, for purposes of comparison with Australia, this test does not 'depend on the standard of a skilled person's opinion of the relevance of the information',[75] or upon the ability to find and understand any information. However, the law does not require the skilled person to assume that every piece of prior art is relevant to the problem he is

[69] *Minnesota Mining and Manufacturing Co v Beiersdorf (Australia) Ltd* (1980) 144 CLR 253 (HC) (*3M v Beiersdorf*).

[70] *Allmanna Svenska Elektriska Aktiebolaget v Burntisland Shipbuilding Company Ltd* (1952) 69 RPC 63 (CA); *Martin & Biro Swan Ltd v Millwood Ltd* [1956] 73 RPC 125 (CA).

[71] *Wellcome Foundation Ltd v VR Laboratories (Aust) Pty Ltd* (1981) 148 CLR 262 (HC) 270; *3M v Beiersdorf* (n 69) 293–95; *Alphapharm* (n 13).

[72] *Lockwood v Doric* (n 14) 218.

[73] *Nichia v Argos* (n 50) [11]; *Pfizer Ltd's Patent* [2001] FSR 16 (Pat) [62].

[74] *Cairnstores Ltd v Aktiebolaget Hässle* [2002] EWHC 309 (Ch) [94].

[75] *Lockwood v Doric* (n 14) 239.

addressing. 'Having considered it, he may conclude that it is simply not a worthwhile starting point and so put it to one side'.[76]

Therefore, at this time, the Australian standards remained 'less rigorous or "lower"'.[77] The position changed with the enactment of the 1990 Act. One of its objectives was to raise the threshold of inventiveness for a standard patent. The government rejected a recommendation of the Industrial Property Advisory Committee (IPAC) in its 1984 report to raise the threshold in line with international standards[78] and adopted a less ambitious option, which nevertheless raised the threshold compared with the 1952 Act. The statutory tests in section 7(2) and (3) and Schedule 1 of the 1990 Act directed the skilled person to evaluate the invention with reference to the common general knowledge in Australia alone or in combination with specific kinds of information. Initially these were confined to single acts in Australia or documents anywhere in the world or combinations of related documents or of related acts where the skilled person would treat them as a single source.[79] The acts or documents were limited further to those which the skilled person could, before the priority date of the relevant claim, be reasonably expected to have ascertained, understood and regarded them as relevant to work in the relevant art in the patent area. In *Lockwood,* the High Court construed section 7(3) as being directed to 'publicly available information (not part of common general knowledge) which a person skilled in the relevant art could be expected to have regarded as relevant *to solving a particular problem* or meeting a long-felt want or need as the patentee claims to have done'. In other words, the skilled person would be led only to those elements of prior art designed to solve the same problem.

A further limitation was that the prior art had to be relevant to 'work in the relevant art in Australia'. The full Federal Court in *Ajinomoto Co Inc v Nutrasweet Australia Pty Ltd*[80] construed the word 'work' to mean 'real work', as opposed to hypothetical work. Hence, prior art which might be otherwise relevant to the problem to be solved could be excluded because there was no work actually carried out in Australia in the area of the invention. The Court was mindful that this restriction would limit the breadth of the prior art base and could result in Australia becoming a 'resting ground for bad patents'.[81]

This decision makes it abundantly clear that the government's decision to reject the broader recommendation of IPAC when it framed its 1990 Act was responsible for continuing lower levels of inventiveness in Australia. Policy-makers became mindful of this problem and, upon the recommendation of

[76] *Eli Lilly v Human Genome Sciences* (n 62) [295].
[77] Industrial Property Advisory Committee, *Patents, Innovation and Competition in Australia* (1984) [7.1].
[78] A neat summary is found in *Ajinomoto v NutraSweet Australia* (n 30) 546.
[79] Patents Act 1990 (Cth) s 7(2) & (3).
[80] *Ajinomoto v NutraSweet Australia* (n 30).
[81] Ibid 553.

the Intellectual Property and Competition Review Committee (IPCRC)[82] in 2000, the prior art base was again expanded under the Patents Amendment Act 2001 (Cth). It removed the territorial restriction for acts and permitted consideration of any combinations of prior art information (both acts and documents) with the common general knowledge in Australia, provided that it would be reasonable to do this. However, it still fell short of both the IPAC and IPCRC recommendations to remove the territorial restrictions on common general knowledge. The limitation to prior art information that the skilled person could be reasonably expected to have ascertained, understood and regarded as relevant remained, but it was no longer necessary that they be relevant 'to work in the relevant art in the patent area'. The court in *Nutrasweet* impliedly confirmed that this restriction would not apply in future: 'at least after 2001 Australia would approach the question of obviousness in a manner more cognizant of the fact that scientific developments are now appreciated on a global basis'.[83] It is unclear whether the court's observation in *Lockwood* that the skilled person would be led only to those elements of prior art designed to solve the same problem survives the 2001 amendment to section 7(3). Its survival would perpetuate one cause for divergence in the inventive thresholds because the UK does not impose this restriction.[84]

In summary, different prior art bases continue to produce differences in the levels of inventiveness for two principal reasons. First, only information that the skilled person could be 'reasonably expected to have ascertained, understood and regarded as relevant' is considered with the common general knowledge in Australia. In contrast, the skilled person in the UK knows of and is assumed to have read all relevant published material. Secondly, common general knowledge has a territorial restriction to Australia. In some fields, this may equate with a universal 'real world' standard which applies in the UK. In others, it may be more limited; a smaller pool of prior art information may be available because the level of knowledge possessed by the skilled person will influence what prior art would be ascertained, understood and regarded as relevant.

Level of Advance over the Prior Art Base

The preceding discussion shows that the level of the step that will justify the grant of a patent is dependent upon the scope of the prior base. There is another sense in which to discuss the level of inventiveness—namely, the level of advance over that defined prior at base. In the past, UK and

[82] Intellectual Property and Competition Review Committee (IPCRC), *Review of intellectual property legislation under the Competition Principles Agreement* (2000) 16.
[83] *Ajinomoto v NutraSweet Australia* (n 30) 552–53.
[84] See the US approach: *KSR International Co v Teleflex Inc* 550 US 398 (2007).

Australia adopted the same approach to the question 'Is it obvious?'—a question that had proved problematic. As Tomlin J said in *Samuel Parkes & Co Ltd v Cocker Brothers Ltd*[85] in 1929:

> Nobody, however, has told me, and I do not suppose anybody ever will tell me, what is the precise characteristic or quality the presence of which distinguishes invention from a workshop improvement. Day is day, and night is night, but who shall tell where day ends and night begins?[86]

The result was that little was demanded of the inventor, and the courts adopted a 'modest' approach: the advance only required a 'scintilla of invention' to support a patent.[87]

The Australian High Court in *Lockwood* has confirmed that both a qualitative and quantitative approach continue to apply in Australia, with a 'scintilla of invention' being sufficient.[88] In contrast, UK courts regard these old expressions of a quantitative level as unhelpful.[89] They treat the assessment of inventive step as wholly objective, being a comparison between the state of the art and what the patentee claims to have invented.[90]

Sometimes 'quantitative' language continues to appear in the context of the attributes of the notional skilled person who is 'incapable of a scintilla of invention'[91] and has reappeared recently in the context of the level of inventiveness that is sufficient to support a patent.[92] Nevertheless, the judicial statements in such cases as *Mölnlycke AB v Procter & Gamble Ltd* are clear that the level of the advance is irrelevant.[93]

There is clearly divergence in the rhetoric that courts in each jurisdiction adopt, but it is not clear whether this amounts to a difference in fact. In one sense it is of marginal interest if differences in the prior art base result in assessment with reference to a different starting point.

Answering the Statutory Question: Is it Obvious?

The approach taken to answering the statutory question provides a further cause for divergence. The development of the UK common law included

[85] *Samuel Parkes & Co Ltd v Cocker Brothers Ltd* (1929) 46 RPC 241 (CA).
[86] Ibid 248.
[87] Ibid. *Chiron Corporation v Organon Teknika Ltd (No 3)* [1994] FSR 202 (Pat C) 221; *Woolworths Ltd v W B Davis and Son Ltd Inc* (1942) 16 ALJ 57 (HC) 59.
[88] *Lockwood v Doric* (n 14) 217.
[89] *Mölnlycke AB v Procter & Gamble Ltd* [1994] RPC 49 (CA) 112.
[90] UKIPO: Inventive step consultation document (www.ipo.gov.uk/p-law-inventive.htm): Annex A A1.
[91] *Nichia v Argos* (n 50) [10]; *Technip France SA's Patent Application* [2004] RPC 46 (CA); *Technograph v Mills and Rockley* (n 66) 355.
[92] *Generics (UK) v H Lundbeck* [2007] EWHC 1040, [2007] RPC 32 (Pat) [237].
[93] *Nichia v Argos* (n 50) [31].

various strategies to maintain some consistency in approach in assessing whether an invention was obvious.

One strategy was to express the statutory language in other terms that were better understood. Such expressions included: 'workshop improvement', 'mere workshop adjustment', 'workshop alteration',[94] and many others. Australian courts readily followed the UK precedents to assist them in their task. However, the dangers with this approach are now evident, particularly if the phrase is not readily synonymous with 'obvious'.[95] At some point 'a statute becomes encumbered in such a way as to obscure its operation and obfuscate the meaning of the simple words used (such as here, "obvious" and "inventive step"). At this point, it is time to return to basics.'[96]

It seems that the UK judiciary is returning to basics, with its emphasis upon the language of the statute and rejection of overly rigid rules and paraphrases for 'obvious'.[97] As Jacob LJ noted recently in the Court of Appeal in *Nichia*: 'The statutory question is the statutory question and no other'.[98]

This approach contrasts with that of the majority in *Aktiebolaget Hassel v Alphapharm Pty Ltd*,[99] which has been accused of replacing the statute with complex verbal formulae and for inappropriately giving authoritative value to judicial statements as to the meaning of obviousness. In its assessment of obviousness under section 100(1)(e) of the 1952 Act, the majority considered itself bound by the following paraphrased statement of that section in *The Wellcome Foundation Ltd v V R Laboratories (Aust) Pty Ltd*:

> The test is whether the hypothetical addressee faced with the same problem would have taken as a matter of routine whatever steps might have led from the prior art to the invention, whether they be the steps of the inventor or not.[100]

As the parties disagreed on the meaning of the words 'matter of routine', the court construed them in a manner which was consistent with the reformulation of the 'Cripps question' by Graham J in *Olin Mathieson Chemical Corp v Biorex Laboratories Ltd*:[101]

> Would the notional research group at the relevant date, in all the circumstances, which include a knowledge of all the relevant prior art and of the facts of the nature and success of ... directly be led as a matter of course to try ... in the

[94] Blanco White, *Patents for Inventions* (n 47) 128.
[95] *Alphapharm* (n 13) 427.
[96] Ibid 460 (Kirby J).
[97] *Nichia v Argos* (n 50) [22]; *Conor Medsystems v Angiotech* (n 59).
[98] *Nichia v Argos* (n 50) [22].
[99] *Alphapharm* (n 13).
[100] *The Wellcome Foundation Ltd v V R Laboratories (Aust) Pty Ltd* (1981) 148 CLR 262 (HC) 286.
[101] *Olin Mathieson Chemical Corp v Biorex Laboratories Ltd* [1970] RPC 157 (Ch D).

> expectation that it might well produce a useful alternative to or better drug than ... or a body useful for any other purpose?[102]

This mode of analysis drew strong dissent from both McHugh and Kirby JJ. McHugh J disagreed that the *Wellcome* statement was binding on the court. This and other judicial statements: 'do not lay down any legal principles and they have no precedent value. They are not binding upon judges hearing future cases'.[103] Kirby J pointed to the fact that some judicial expositions of this test had elevated it to almost statutory status, although it was no more than a 'synonym to convey an attribute of obviousness existing in some cases'.[104] He pointed to the problem that judges face when 'having entangled themselves in a web of horrible verbal formulae, [they] must do their best to explain their conclusions where, in the past, juries simply announced their verdicts'.[105]

The decision also attracted criticism from the UK. In the Court of Appeal decision in *Angiotech Pharmaceuticals Inc v Conor Medsystems Inc*,[106] Jacob LJ described the approach of the majority in *Alphapharm* as 'over elaborated' and 'coupled with a massive citation of authority' so that it becomes 'metaphysical or endowed with unwritten and unwarranted doctrines, sub-doctrines or even sub-sub-doctrines'. More recently, Pumfrey J soundly rejected the *Alphapharm* test when it was argued before him in *Cipla Ltd v Glaxo Group Ltd*.[107] He considered that this reformulation contains an implicit definition of the word 'obvious' in 'directly be led as a matter of course to try' and is inappropriate to UK law, which places the emphasis upon the statutory language itself. He emphasised that:

> Each case depends upon the invention and the surrounding facts. No formula should be substituted for the words of the statute. In every case the Court has to weigh up the evidence and decide whether the invention was obvious. This is the statutory task.[108]

The principles applied in *Alphapharm* to the question of inventive step under the 1952 Act remain relevant under the 1990 Act. Although section 2.5.1.5 of the *Australian Patent Manual of Practice and Procedure* merely includes this as one of a number of tests that can assist its examiners, the treatment of the above passage as binding suggests otherwise. These differences are likely to affect the comparative levels of inventiveness, although it

102 Ibid 187–88.
103 *Alphapharm* (n 13) 445.
104 Ibid 463.
105 Ibid 448.
106 *Angiotech Pharmaceuticals Inc v Conor Medsystems Inc* [2007] RPC 20 (CA); see also *Cipla Ltd v Glaxo Group Ltd* [2004] EWHC 477 (Pat) [37].
107 *Cipla Ltd v Glaxo Group Ltd* (n 106).
108 Ibid [42]. See also *Nichia v Argos* (n 50) [22].

is difficult to gauge the size of that impact in isolation from any particular invention.

Role of Secondary Factors: 'Obvious to Try'

Irrespective of whether a quantitative approach is articulated, the reality is that there is a difference between 'obviousness' and 'inventiveness' which has always proved difficult to identify in practice. Prior to the 1977 Act, the courts developed strategies that involved the resort to secondary evidence that might suggest the invention was not obvious, such as satisfying a long-felt want or need, commercial success, copying by others or their attempts and failure to find a solution to the problem. Australian courts readily adopted these approaches, and courts in both jurisdictions continue to see them as having a role to play that varies from case to case.[109]

However, use of the test commonly labelled as 'obvious to try' or 'worth trying' has proved to be contentious. In the UK, the 'obvious to try' expression entered the law of obviousness by virtue of *Johns-Manville Corporation's Patent*[110] in the context of a simple invention: there was a known process using flocculating agents to aid filtration. The patent was for the old process using a new flocculating agent which was disclosed in prior art. This was effectively the type of fact situation that was often described as a new use of a known product for a purpose for which it was known to be suited. The respondent's case was that the skilled person would read the prior art and realise 'that here was a flocculating agent which was well worth trying out in the filtration process used in his own industry in order to see whether it would have beneficial results'.[111] Lord Justice Diplock, as he then was, agreed that if this had been established, the respondents would have made out their case of obviousness and said: 'It is enough that the person versed in the art would assess the likelihood of success as sufficient to warrant actual trial'. Actual trial would have been a simple procedure that would produce the result. Significantly, Diplock LJ doubted that any verbal formula is appropriate to all classes of claims and refused to coin a definition of obviousness which counsel could cite in future cases relating to different types of claims.

As Jacob LJ interpolated in *Angiotech*, 'he failed there!' The test which was originally formulated in the context of this simple invention 'took on a life of its own'[112] when it was later applied to high-tech research, especially

[109] *Mölnlycke AB v Proctor & Gamble Ltd (No 5)* [1994] RPC 49 (CA) 112; *Nichia v Argos* (n 50) [32]. *Lockwood v Doric* (n 14) 233.
[110] *Johns-Manville Corporation's Patent* [1967] FSR 327 (CA).
[111] Ibid 332.
[112] *Conor Medsystems v Angiotech* (n 59) [47] (Lord Walker).

in the fields of pharmaceuticals and biotechnology which involve lengthy research comprising many steps. Not surprisingly, application of the test in these contexts invited criticism.[113] In 2002, the Australian High Court majority referred to UK authorities and claimed that its use in chemical and biotechnological patents under the 1977 Act—ie 'worth a try' and 'well worth trying out'—had marked a divergence from the treatment of obviousness in the decisions of the High Court. Whether or not that was an accurate reflection,[114] the consequence was its preference for the reasoning in various US authorities which rejected a notion of 'obvious to try' as a criterion for obviousness.[115] Its conclusion was to reject its application altogether, stating: 'the adoption of a criterion of validity expressed in terms of 'worth a try' or 'obvious to try' and the like begs the question presented by the statute'.[116]

The tide has turned also in the UK, but only to reduce the scope of the 'obvious to try' test. Recently in *Conor Medsystems*, Lord Hoffmann reined in the past expansive approach to this test but approved its continuing utility in limited circumstances set out by Jacob LJ in the Court of Appeal:

> He correctly summarised the authorities, starting with the judgment of Diplock LJ in *Johns-Manville Corporation's Patent* ..., by saying that the notion of something being obvious to try was useful only in a case in which there was a fair expectation of success. How much of an expectation would be needed depended upon the particular facts of the case.[117]

Lord Hoffmann then approved the following statement of principle by Kitchen J at first instance in *Generics (UK) Ltd v H Lundbeck A/S*:

> The question of obviousness must be considered on the facts of each case. The court must consider the weight to be attached to any particular factor in the light of all the relevant circumstances. These may include such matters as the motive to find a solution to the problem the patent addresses, the number and extent of the possible avenues of research, the effort involved in pursuing them and the expectation of success.[118]

Although this chapter only compares UK and Australian law, the influence of the US law on the decision in *Alphapharm* makes it important to refer to recent changes in attitude of both the US and Canadian Supreme Courts. They may influence the High Court to review its approach to 'obvious to try', which in retrospect may have 'thrown out the baby with the

113 H Laddie, 'Patents—what's invention got to do with it?' in D Vaver and L Bently (eds), *Intellectual Property in the New Millennium: Essays in Honour of William R Cornish* (Cambridge, CUP, 2004) 91.
114 *Generics (UK) v H Lundbeck* [2007] EWHC 1040, [2007] RPC 32 (Pat) [43].
115 *Alphapharm* (n 13) 441; *Re O'Farrell* 853 F 2d 894, 903 (1988).
116 *Alphapharm* (n 13) 443.
117 *Conor Medsystems v Angiotech* (n 59) [42].
118 *Generics (UK) v H Lundbeck* [2007] EWHC 1040, [2007] RPC 32 (Pat) [72] which was also endorsed in *H Lundbeck A/S v Generics (UK) Ltd* & Ors [2008] EWCA Civ 311 (CA) [24]–[25].

bathwater'. First, in 2007, the US Supreme Court in *KSR International Co v Teleflex Inc*[119] rejected the former restrictive approach at the Federal Court of Appeals level and has made it clear that the 'obvious to try' test could be relevant to an obviousness inquiry. More recently, the Supreme Court of Canada in *Sanofi-Synthelabo Canada Inc v Apotex Inc*,[120] has also re-examined the formerly restrictive approach to its test in *Beloit Canada Ltd v Valmet Oy*[121] (*Beloit* test) in light of developments in both the US and the UK. The *Beloit* test, which bears a strong resemblance to the test applied in *Alphapharm*, is:

> The question to be asked is whether this mythical creature ... would, in the light of the state of the art and of common general knowledge as at the claimed date of invention, *have come directly and without difficulty to the solution taught by the patent*. It is a very difficult test to satisfy.[122]

The lower court in *Sanofi-Synthelabo* stated that the *Beloit* test would 'not accommodate a "worth a try" test by the skilled person'. After noting the convergence of the UK and US law on the 'obvious to try' test, the Supreme Court rejected that restrictive approach and has accepted that the 'obvious to try' test may be used, but will only work 'where it is very plain or, to use the words of Jacob LJ, more or less self-evident that what is being tested ought to work'.[123]

The application of this limited test may or may not affect the threshold of inventiveness because it is not useful where nothing is predictable and where there is simply no likelihood of success.[124] It is eminently suitable to dispose of a simple invention, especially one that involves a mere new use of a known product for a use for which it is known to be suitable.[125] The important issue is that Australia stands alone among its trading partners in its apparent rejection of the 'obvious to try' test, unless *Lockwood* is later interpreted as merely rejecting a more expansive application of that test.

CONCLUDING COMMENTS

More than a century after the recognition of the need for an inventive step, different legal solutions continue to define the difference between obviousness and inventiveness in Australia and the UK. While the early common

[119] *KSR International Co v Teleflex* 550 US 398 (2007).
[120] *Sanofi-Synthelabo Canada Inc v Apotex Inc* 2008 SCC 61.
[121] *Beloit Canada Ltd v Valmet Oy* (1986) 64 NR 287, 8 CPR (3d) 289 (Fed CA).
[122] Ibid [17].
[123] Ibid [65].
[124] *Saint-Gobain PAM SA v Fusion Provida Ltd, Electrosteel Castings Ltd* [2005] EWCA Civ 177 (CA) [25]–[28].
[125] Examples: *Pharmacia Corp v Merck & Co Inc* [2002] RPC 41 (CA) [123]; *Instituto Gentili SpA, Merck & Co Inc v Teva Pharmaceutical Industries Ltd* [2003] EWCA Civ (CA) 1545.

law shared many common standards, levels of inventiveness diverged with the imposition of territorial limitations on the prior art base in each country. Why have different legal solutions been devised to address this fundamental aspect of patent law? The above discussion vests responsibility for the divergence in the once 'monolithic' common law in this area on a number of factors, the principal ones being a reduction in the influence of UK patent law in Australia and the impact in this area of international standards. We have seen that the importance to Australia of maintaining consistency with UK patent law has been replaced with both the parliament and the judiciary seeking guidance from the laws of its main trading partners, including the US, Europe, Canada, South East Asia and New Zealand. This focus upon greater international consistency is gradually closing the gaps that exist in levels of inventiveness in Australia and the UK.

Nevertheless, the above discussion demonstrates that divergence remains conspicuous. This may not necessarily be a problem for either jurisdiction, but the evidence demonstrates to the contrary. It seems that there will be no change in the immediate future in the UK. A report of the UKIPO into inventive step concluded that there was no need for any change to the basic law in the UK as it relates to inventive step.[126] In contrast, the report *Venturous Australia: Building Strength in Innovation*,[127] released in 2008 commented that 'arguably the current threshold of inventiveness for existing patents is ... too low'. It recommended that: 'Patent law should be reviewed to ensure that the inventive steps required to qualify for patents are considerable, and that the resulting patents are well defined, so as to minimise litigation and maximise the scope for subsequent innovators'.[128]

It is not clear what the authors mean by 'considerable', but a good starting point would be to have a common approach to the meaning of common general knowledge and to remove the requirement in section 7(3) that only prior art which the skilled person could be reasonably expected to have ascertained and understood can be considered. This would not mark a return to the once 'monolithic' common law in this area, but would clearly improve certainty for patentees who seek patents in both jurisdictions.

[126] Public consultation on level of the inventive step required for obtaining patents—the government's response www.ipo.gov.uk/response-inventive.pdf.

[127] Cutler & Company Pty Ltd, *Venturous Australia—building strength in innovation* (2008): www.ipo.gov.uk/response-inventive.pdf.

[128] Ibid, Recommendation 7.2. IP Australia commenced this process of revision in 2009 (after the completion of this chapter) with the issue of a number of consultation papers. One of these concerns inter alia discussion of the appropriate level of inventiveness for an Australian patent. *Getting the Balance Right: Toward a Stronger and More Efficient IP Rights System* (March 2009). The relevant recommendations for discussion include removal of the Australian limitation on common general knowledge (para 4.1), and an amendment to the relevant prior art in s 7(3) (para 4.2). A controversial proposal is to revise the inventive step test to a test where the claimed invention is obvious if it was 'obvious for the skilled person to try a suggested approach, alternative or method with a reasonable expectation of success' (para 4.3).

APPENDIX: *POZZOLI* TEST COMPARED WITH THE 1990 ACT PROVISIONS

United Kingdom—Pozzoli test	Australian 1990 Act
1. Identify the notional 'person skilled in the art'; and identify the relevant common general knowledge of that person.	1. Identify the 'person skilled in the relevant art'. 2. Identify the common general knowledge as it existed in Australia before the priority date.
2. Identify the inventive concept of the claim in question or, if that cannot readily be done, construe it.	3. Identify the invention 'so far as claimed in any claim'.
3. Identify what, if any, differences exist between the matter cited as forming part of the 'state of the art' and the inventive concept of the claim or the claim as construed.	
4. Ask: viewed without any knowledge of the alleged invention as claimed, do those differences constitute steps which would have been obvious to the person skilled in the art or do they require any degree of invention?	4. Inquire under section 7(2) whether the invention ... would have been obvious to the person referred to in (1) above in light of the knowledge referred to in (2) above. 5. Inquire whether that invention would have been obvious to that person in the light of that knowledge when that knowledge is considered together with either kinds of information mentioned in section 7(3) (additional prior art information).

Note: Although *Pozzoli* step 3 is missing from the 1990 Act, Australian courts apply it in practice.

10

Sufficiency of Disclosure in the Common Law

Complexity, Divergence and Confusion

SIVARAMJANI THAMBISETTY

THE REQUIREMENT THAT a patent should include a specification that contains a description of the invention, allowing a person skilled in the art to practise, use or work the invention, is a basic tenet of modern patent law in a number of jurisdictions. Several legal histories have thrown light on this requirement, which was at one time a new concept in the common law. Recent work has corrected Hulme's earlier contention that Mansfield's decision in *Liardet v Johnson* (1778)[1] was a departure from previous English practice. Adams and Averley, and Walterscheid among others, note that the specification developed some time at the beginning of the eighteenth century when law officers began to require a written specification as a condition of the patent grant and thereafter to make it a routine requirement.[2]

There is also a subtle point of disagreement on whether *Liardet* amounted to the mere formalisation of the gradual change in the law from what the inventor brings by way of personal effort and capital to the disclosure in the patent specification, or in fact spelt the beginning of the end of this process.[3] Some time before Lord Mansfield's observations in this case, the principal aim of the patent grant shifted. Indeed 'neither specification nor written disclosure was required in the vast majority of Elizabethan

[1] *Liardet v Johnson* (1778) 1 WPC 53 (reproduced in *Hayward's Patent Cases*, vol 1, 196–201).

[2] JN Adams and G Averley, 'The Patent Specification: The Role of *Liardet v Johnson*' (1986) 7 *Journal of Legal History* 156–77 and EC Walterscheid, *To Promote the Progress of Useful Arts: American Patent Law and Administration, 1798–1836* (Rothman and Co, Colorado, 1998) 399–420.

[3] Adams and Averly, 'The Patent Specification' (n 2).

grants'[4]—a feature that follows from the original consideration offered for monopoly privileges—to work the industry and train English apprentices.[5]

However there seems to be general agreement that Lord Mansfield's third instruction to the jury in *Liardet* formalised the point at which the law began to accept written descriptions as a condition and requirement of the patent grant:

> The third point is whether the specification is such as instructs others to make it. For the condition of giving encouragement is this: that you must specify upon record your invention in such a way as to teach an artist, when the term is out, to make it—and to make it as well by your directions: for then at the end of the term, the public shall have benefit of it.

The disclosure in the patent specification has since then been restated in terms of a 'contract', a quid pro quo with the state in return for the grant of a patent. MacLeod for example writes that with the above words, 'for the first time, the recognised quid pro quo for the award of a patent was the disclosure of the invention'.[6] Mossoff in particular suggests that the restatement of the substantive principle behind the requirement of the specifications was in effect predicated on a natural rights approach to patents, specifically Locke's social contract theory.[7]

Over-use of this imprecise 'quid pro quo' metaphor can lead to confusion particularly as the interpretation of the 'contract' is entrusted to two different tribunals. Others have noted that the so-called contract theory or bargain is useful not as a justification but as an explanation in law of the mechanics of the evaluation and granting of patents.[8] The origin of the patent specification appears historically to be rooted in an instrumental view of what the patent system could achieve and what was administratively most feasible[9]—an approach that endures within some contexts of modern disclosure requirements (such as 'subjective' best mode disclosures in the US and timing of amendments in Australian law). In modern patent statutes, an expedient approach to disclosure requirements is perhaps best reflected in the lack of detail in many provisions describing sufficiency. This lack of detail

[4] RA Klitzke, 'Historical Background of the English Patent Law' (1959) 41 *Journal of the Patent Office Society* 615, 641–42.

[5] See C MacLeod, *Inventing the Industrial Revolution: The English Patent System, 1660–1800* (Cambridge, CUP, 2002) 48–49.

[6] Ibid 49. Also see Walterscheid, *To Promote the Progress of Useful Arts* (n 2) 404.

[7] A Mossoff, 'Rethinking the Development of Patents: An Intellectual History, 1550–1800' (2001) 52 *Hastings Law Journal* 1255.

[8] Robinson, *The Law of Patents for Useful Inventions* (Boston, Little Brown, 1890) 59.

[9] MacLeod believes the rise of the specification in the early to mid-eighteenth century shifted responsibility from the law officers to the courts thus allowing the system to be self-policing and the law officers to be spared much tedious investigation. MacLeod, *Inventing the Industrial Revolution* (n 5) 51, 53.

has facilitated diverse legal doctrines and outcomes in different jurisdictions, even in association with apparently simple requirements.

Professor Vaver refers to the contract or bargain metaphor as nothing more than a rhetorical flourish whose sustained use is damaging to certainty in intellectual property law.[10] At the very least, the idea glosses over the prosaic institutional and administrative beginnings of the requirement to provide a specification; at worst, the metaphor is a source of error and confusion. The discussion in this chapter attempts to demonstrate that although the bargain metaphor is a useful indicator of the common history of patents, the idea may be used to justify so many variations on what amounts to sufficient disclosure that it is of little analytical value. This chapter focuses on two aspects of contemporary common law: the divergence in sufficiency requirements and the overlap between sufficiency and other criteria of invalidity. Both aspects expose distortions of the bargain metaphor, leading to potential for confusion and error.

ARE PATENT DISCLOSURES USEFUL SOURCES OF TECHNICAL INFORMATION?

It is useful first to consider briefly the continued relevance in a modern context of the aim of disclosure stated so clearly in *Liardet,* principally whether 'the specification is such as instructs others to make it'. What is the true value of patent disclosures—are patent specifications useful sources of technical information? Machlup and Penrose point out that although the diffusion of technology through patent disclosures is an old argument, economists have been sceptical of it at least since the 1950s.[11] Not all patentable inventions are patented, and concealable inventions remain concealed,[12] therefore the argument goes that patents reveal little that would not otherwise be revealed.[13] Economic literature is peppered with explicit findings that patent disclosures appear to have no measurable impact on information flows from other firms and therefore no measurable impact on R & D productivity.[14]

[10] D Vaver, *Intellectual Property Law: Copyright, Patents, Trademarks* (Toronto, Irwin Law, 1997) 12–13, suggesting that the metaphor or analogy was perhaps more useful in the eighteenth century when intellectual property laws were cryptic and each patent was self-contained and spelt out the conditions of its grant.

[11] Machlup and Penrose, 'The Patent Controversy in the Nineteenth Century' (1950) 10(1) *The Journal of Economic History* 1–29.

[12] However, see Bessen, 'Patents and The Diffusion of Technology', www.researchoninnovation.org/disclose.pdf.

[13] See Roin, 'Disclosure function of the Patent System (or lack thereof)' (2005) 118(6) *Harvard Law Review* 2007, debunking several assumptions about whether patents disseminate technical information.

[14] Arora et al, 'R&D and the Patent Premium' NBER Working Paper No 9431, 2003. available at www.nber.org/papers/w9431. Also see Cohen et al, 'R&D Spillovers, Patents

However case law in a number of jurisdictions weave a different narrative, and observations such as those made in *Paulik v Rizkalla* remain exceptional but valuable indicators of the significance of technical disclosures in patents:

> The obligation to disclose is not the principal reason for a patent system; indeed, it is a rare invention that cannot be deciphered more readily from its commercial embodiment than from the printed patent.[15]

Clarisa Long mirrors this concern when she emphasises that patents often tell observers more about the patentee (for example about the financial prospects of the firm) than the invention itself.[16]

An interesting insight into the disparity between legal reasoning and economic accounts is provided by recent empirical surveys that highlight the increasing complexity and voluminosity of patent applications. [17] Does this development indicate a more thorough disclosure of inventions, or does it merely represent disruptive strategies, such as creating uncertainty by 'polluting the technological field or circumventing disclosure requirements by hiding major inventions'?[18]

Zeebroeck's study points out several results that shed light on the effect of varied disclosure requirements in the law.[19] For example, emerging sectors (biotech, computer science, audio, video and medial technologies) with less established vocabulary and practices can lead to larger patent applications than more traditional areas.[20] Drafting styles also account for important differences between civil and common law countries, with the latter having much longer patents on average. This difference would not be a problem for the common law in itself but for the increasing success of

and the Incentives to Innovate in Japan and the United States' (2002) 31(8–9) *Research Policy*, 1349–67 and Hall et al, 'Barriers to the Use of Patent Information in UK Small and Medium-Sized Enterprises: Part 2(1): Results of In-depth Interviews' (2000) 26(2) *Journal of Information Science* 87–99, 94.

[15] *Paulik v Rizkalla* 760 F 2d 1270, 1276 (Fed Cir 1985).

[16] C Long, 'Patent Signals' (2002) 69 *University of Chicago Law Review* 625–79. Also see Oppenheim, 'How SMEs Use the Patent Literature' Summary Report for the UK Economic and Social Research Council (1998).

[17] Based on the number of pages and number of claims. The study also considers other parameters of size with respect to other recent surveys. Archontopoulous et al, 'When Small is Beautiful: Measuring the Evolution and Consequences of the Voluminosity of Patent Applications at the EPO', CEB Working Paper 06/019 (2006). Also see Dudas, 'The Patent System Today and Tomorrow', Statement Before the Subcommittee on The Judiciary, United States Senate (2005).

[18] Archontopoulous, 'When Small is Beautiful' (n 17).

[19] Zeebroeck et al, 'Claiming More: The Increased Voluminosity of Patent Applications and its Determinants', Working Paper CEB 06-018 RS (2006).

[20] This resonates with 'intrinsic uncertainty' in emerging technologies. Thambisetty, 'Patents as Credence Goods' (2007) 27 *Oxford Journal of Legal Studies* 707–40.

the PCT route, resulting in the harmonisation of drafting styles worldwide towards the US model.[21]

However, it is often substantive legal requirements that lead to voluminous disclosures. These include the doctrine of equivalents in the US that effectively encourages applicants to embed within their drafts detailed fall-back options that can be used in case of litigation, to salvage as much of the scope of the patent as possible. The mandatory best mode requirement in US applications often results in patentees detailing several utilisation modes to hide the 'best' one, possibly leading to longer descriptions.

Additionally, although it is in the public interest to have all prior art considered by the patent office, only US law takes a stringent view on the disclosure of prior art. The patent applicant is obliged to disclose all prior art of which he is aware, failing which the patent may be unenforceable, possibly triggering treble damages in infringement actions. This approach can lead to an 'if in doubt, disclose' rule, resulting in long lists of marginal relevance, making examination more difficult and adding to the expense of litigation.[22] On the other hand, the UK and Australia do not require specific disclosure of relevant art, except for citations made in parallel applications prosecuted in other countries.[23] Changes to New Zealand's Patents Act 1953, expected to come into effect this year, will require similar disclosure of the results of prior art searches made on corresponding overseas applications relating to the same invention.[24] Despite these differences if the application is filed through the PCT route and claims US priority then it is likely to adopt the disclosure requirements of the US patent system by default.

DISCLOSURE AND ENABLEMENT: TIMING, ANTICIPATION AND BEST MODE

The centrality of disclosure remains an agreed principle in common law jurisdictions[25] while insufficiency of disclosure is a ground for attacking the validity of a patent.[26] The various twists and turns of this central principle in different jurisdictions begs the question of the quid pro quo. The following

[21] Zeebroeck, 'Claiming More' (n 19).

[22] T Roberts, 'Sufficiency of Disclosure (Enabling Disclosure, Disclosure of Prior Art, Best Mode' (2006), www.wipo.int/meetings/en/2006/scp_of_ge_06/presentations/scp_of_ge_06_roberts.pdf.

[23] Ibid, but see r 26, EPO Guidelines.

[24] Patents Bill 235-1 (2008) cl 9.

[25] ss 14(3) and 14(5)(c), The UK Patents Act (linking concepts drawn from Arts 83 and 84 of the EPC, s 40 of the Australian Patents Act 1990, s 27 of the Canadian Patents Act 1985, 35 USC § 112 (1986) and s 10 of the New Zealand Patents Act 1953).

[26] In the UK s 72(1) (which does not as such include non-compliance with s 14(5)(c)), s 138(3) in Australia which cites the list of grounds for revocation, 35 USC § 282 (2000), s 41(h), (i) New Zealand Patents Act 1953, s 53 Canadian Patents Act 1985.

is a discussion of three features based on a common denominator that the specification must be sufficient to disclose the invention clearly enough and completely enough for it to be performed by a person skilled in the art without undue burden. Generally, 'the key word is "undue", not "experimentation".'[27]

First, the date of the assessment is pivotal because it indicates, inter alia, the content of the common general knowledge that may supplement the disclosure in the specification. In most jurisdictions including in the UK and US, the law requires that the invention be fully described at the date of filing of the application. However, in Australia, while section 40(2)(a) requires a 'complete specification to describe the invention fully including the best method known to the applicant of performing the invention', there is no further direction as to the date at which adequate disclosure is to be assessed. Case law has veered between the filing date and the date of patent grant.[28] In *Pfizer Overseas Pharmaceuticals v Eli Lilly and Company*[29] the requirement of disclosing the best method known to the applicant was held satisfied by the full Federal Court even though the relevant method was introduced into the specification some three years after the filing.

The operative limitations on the power of amendment are the same in UK and Australian law. The test of added subject matter is whether a skilled man would, upon looking at the amended specification, learn anything about the invention that he could not learn from the unamended specification,[30] including what is disclosed implicitly and explicitly. However, putting together the requirement of 'complete specification' with the scope of allowable amendments under section 102, the Australian Federal Court concluded that it is the specification as amended that must be construed for compliance with section 40(2)(a). On this basis the date for assessing complete disclosure was not earlier than the grant and could be as late as the date of commencement of proceedings.

While a key restraint on this aspect of disclosure continues to be the date at which common general knowledge is assessed,[31] the possibility that new

[27] *Re Angstadt* 537 F 2d 498, 504 (Cust and Pat App 1976). 'Undue burden' is sensitive to the nature of the invention, to the abilities of the skilled person, and the art in which the invention has been made. *Wobben v Vestas-Celtic Wind Technology Ltd* [2007] EWHC 2636 (Pats) [197].

[28] In *Rescare Ltd v Anaesthetic Supplies Pty Ltd* (1992) 111 ALR 205, an obiter comment by Gummow J noted that adequacy of disclosure must be judged with reference to the filing date. However, in *Kimberly-Clark Australia Pty Ltd v Arico Trading International Pty Ltd* (2001) 207 CLR 1 (Gleeson CJ, McHugh, Gummow, Hayne and Callinan JJ) the HC took an opposite view, stating that the relevant time was when the patent was granted.

[29] *Pfizer Overseas Pharmaceuticals v Eli Lilly and Company* [2005] FCAFC 224.

[30] *Richardson-Vicks Patent* [1995] RPC 568, 576. Also see *Corus UK Ltd v Qual-Chem Ltd* [2008] EWCA Civ 1177.

[31] *Pfizer v Eli Lilly* (n 29) [327]–[328], [385]–[391]. The court stopped short of deciding whether there is a latest date by which an amendment may never be allowed in order to

matter can be introduced into a specification as late as the date of grant of a patent is a serious divergence from other common law jurisdictions[32] and is in effect a distortion of the 'bargain' metaphor; it potentially allows the applicant to withhold until grant the full nature of the invention and the means for performing it, leading to considerable uncertainty for the public and competitors.

Secondly, central to the law of sufficiency is 'enablement'—a concept that owes much to judicial exegesis.[33] Under US law, §112 is interpreted in such a way that three distinct requirements, including the enablement requirement (the other two being the written description and best mode requirement), are said to spring from it.[34] In the UK enablement has been found to exist in a number of contexts in patent law,[35] and the principle 'explained in *Beloit* and *General Tire* has been accepted in Canada without reservation.'[36]

In the context of sufficiency of disclosure there may be enablement even if the skilled man needed to correct obvious errors or depart in obvious ways from the teaching in the patent application—a concession that extends to the requirement for anticipatory enablement under novelty in the UK.[37] Following on from *Synthon,* the Canadian Supreme Court accepted a two-part test whereby prior disclosure and enablement would need to be considered separately and proven for anticipation. Noting Lord Hoffmann's alignment of enablement in anticipation and sufficiency, the SC declined to consider whether the law in Canada is identical to the UK position.[38]

While recognising the value of the phrase 'enabling disclosure' with respect to the disclosure required for anticipation of a process or method claim, the law in Australia finds little, if any, relevance of this phrase to the anticipation of a product claim or a claim for a chemical compound by formula. The novelty of a product claim lies in the product, and not the means of producing it[39]—this limited but significant divergence in the law of novelty destroying disclosures is compounded in another way.

overcome a specification's failure to state the best method as required by s 40(2) (a). Also see discussion in [366]–[378].

32 'Getting the Balance Right: Toward a Stronger and More Efficient IP Rights System', IP Australia Consultation Paper (March 2009) [3.2].

33 *Synthon BV v Smithkline Beecham Plc* [2005] UKHL 59 [26]–[27].

34 Merges, Menell and Lemley, *Intellectual Property in the New Technological Age*, 3rd edn (Aspen Publishers, 2003) 201.

35 *Asahi Kasei Kogyo KK's Application* [1991] RPC 485.

36 *Apotex Inc v Sanofi-Synthelabo Canada Inc* 2008 SCC 61 [22] citing *Free World Trust v Lectro Sant Inc* 2000 SCC 66.

37 *Synthon v Smithkline Beecham* (n 33). A proposition previously rejected by the CA in *BASF v Smithkline Beecham plc* [2003] RPC 49.

38 *Apotex v Sanofi-Synthelabo* (n 36) [26].

39 *Apotex Pty Ltd (formerly GenRx Pty Ltd) v Sanofi-Aventis* [2008] FCA 1194 [49].

Australian law requires that anticipatory disclosures be of appropriate quality to form the basis for revoking patents for want of novelty. The reverse infringement test is still a necessary condition for anticipation in UK law but it is no longer sufficient—a position that is shared historically in Australian law.[40] But in an approach that is much narrower than 'enabling disclosure', laid out so elegantly by Lord Hoffmann in *Synthon*, Australian law requires anticipatory disclosures to teach (direct, recommend or suggest) the claimed invention with sufficient clarity[41] and there will be no anticipation if the person skilled in the art was forced to 'rummage through the flag locker' to find a flag which the prior patentee possessed and could have raised.[42]

Thirdly, during the course of the eighteenth and nineteenth centuries, practice and common law had come to distinguish between the part of the specification in which the patentee discharged his duty to disclose the best way of performing the invention and the part that delimited the scope of the monopoly that he claimed.[43] Historically a statement of the best method of performance of the invention as an integral aspect of the quid pro quo, was required even before statutes expressly required it.[44] The duty of the patent applicant to disclose the best method of performing his invention continued in the UK until the changes brought about by the 1977 Act.[45] It remains the law in the US where the specification must inter alia 'set forth the best mode contemplated by the inventor of carrying out his invention'.[46]

How broadly the requirement sweeps has been a matter of considerable confusion and dispute.[47] In the US ambiguity rises chiefly from the language in 35 USC § 112, as 'mode' and 'carrying out the invention' are terms that are not definable with precision.[48] The requirement here, as in

[40] *Meyers Taylor Pty Ltd v Vicar Industries Ltd* (1977) 137 CLR 228, 235.

[41] *Bristol-Myers Squibb Co v FH Faulding and Co Ltd* (2000) 97 FCR 524. Also see *Nicaro Holdings v Martin Engineering* (1990) 91 ALR 513 (the terms of the prior art must enable the skilled person to 'perceive and understand and be able practically to apply the discovery without the necessity of further experiments').

[42] *ICI Chemicals and Polymers Ltd v The Lubrizol Corp Inc* [2000] FCA 1349 [51].

[43] *Kirin Amgen v Hoechst Marion Roussel* [2005] All ER 667, 677, Lord Hoffmann citing Fletcher-Moulton LJ in *British United Shoe Machinery v A Fussell and Sons* (1908) 25 RPC 631, 650.

[44] *Liardet v Johnson* (n 1) 198.

[45] ss 32(1)(h) and 4(3)(b), 1949 Act.

[46] 35 USC § 102(b).

[47] Marchese, 'Confusion, Uncertainty and the Best Mode Requirement' (1992) 2 *Federal Circuit Bar Journal* 1.

[48] *Wahl Instruments Inc v Acvious Inc* 950 F 2d 1575, 1579 (CAFC 1991). Also see Marchese, 'Promoting the Progress of the Useful Arts by Narrowing Best Mode Disclosure Requirements in Patent Law' (1993) 54 *University of Pittsburgh Law Review* 589 and Allison and Lemley, 'Empirical Evidence on the Validity of Litigated Patents' (1998) 26 *American Intellectual Property Law Association Quarterly Journal* 185 (estimating that this 'subjective element of US patent law has been the cause of at least 10 per cent of all patent invalidations in

Australia[49] and New Zealand,[50] is designed to prevent a patentee from 'holding back' information, in effect maintaining part of the invention as a trade secret while protecting the whole under patent law.[51] However, neither US nor Australian law[52] require the best mode to be identified, increasing the possibility of voluminous applications where a number of modes of performing the invention may be safely buried.

Further, under Australian law section 40(2)(a) requires a complete specification to 'describe the invention fully including the best method known to the applicant of performing the invention.' This is generally regarded as the requirement of sufficiency of description,[53] for purposes of assessing which it is not necessary to disclose all alternative means.[54] Given that the 'best method' requirement is an inclusion in the sufficiency requirement, it is subject to the same date of assessment, namely the date of grant (the date by which a complete specification, with amendments if any, is filed).[55] In contrast, the time for determining compliance with the 'best mode' in US law is the date of filing; this cannot be rectified subsequently by amendments. The divergence in timing is a challenge to the bargain metaphor as Australian law appears to allow the patentee to monopolise a greater field than has been disclosed to the public.

The 'best mode' requirement is emerging as a stormy issue in international harmonisation negotiations—the US, Brazil, India and Mexico are in favour of providing best mode disclosure, although most countries are against it.[56] Given that Article 29(1) of the TRIPS Agreement states that members 'may' require the applicant to indicate the best mode for carrying out the invention known to the inventor at the filing date, or where priority is claimed, at the priority date of the invention; substantive harmonisation on best mode requirements seems unlikely to take place. However, as noted above, due to international filing strategies via PCT applications, it is likely to become the norm, at least in those applications that claim US priority.

the 1990s'. In *Northern Telecom Inc v Datapoint Corp* 908 F 2d 931, 946 (Fed Cir) Newman J observes that the best mode 'challenge is easy'.

[49] s 40(2)(a).

[50] s 10(3)(b).

[51] 'The sole purpose of the best mode requirement is to restrain inventors from applying for patents while at the same time concealing from the public preferred embodiments of their inventions which they have in fact conceived.' *Re Gay* 309 F 2d 769, 772 (CCPA 1962).

[52] *Pfizer* (n 29) [374].

[53] Ibid [328].

[54] *Lockwood Security Products Pty Ltd v Doric Products Pty Ltd* [2004] HCA 58 [60].

[55] *Pfizer* (n 29) [347]—a position that is in keeping with English case law under the 1949 Act. *C Van Der Lely NV v Ruston Engineering Co Ltd* [1993] RPC 45 (56).

[56] Correa, 'The Politics & Practicalities of a Disclosure of Origin Obligation' (2005) 7/98 *South Bulletin*, February.

FAIR BASIS AND BROAD CLAIMS

One of the most exciting recent developments in common law jurisdictions has been the reconsideration of *Biogen v Medeva*[57] by the House of Lords, in *Generics (UK) Ltd v H Lundbeck A/S*.[58] While the review of insufficiency is interesting in itself, it highlights the overlaps between insufficiency and other grounds of invalidity, and is of broad relevance to the assessment of the quid pro quo. The specific question framed as a matter of divergence between the UK and Australian law is this: how does the fair basing principle as a ground of invalidity differ between the UK and Australia, and what do these differences mean for the ability to prevent broad claims that are unsupported by adequate disclosure?

Modern insufficiency in the UK links two concepts drawn from EPC Articles 83 and 84 which are echoed in section 14(3) (requiring clear and complete disclosure) and section 14(5)(c) (requiring claims to be supported by the description) of the1977 UK Patents Act. Although only the former is a basis for revocation under section 72, since *Asahi*, the requirements of section 14(3) have been read to necessarily include the latter.[59] Thus the substantive effect of section 14(5)(c), namely that the description should, together with the rest of the specification, constitute an enabling disclosure, is given effect by section 72(1)(c).[60]

In Australian law there is a not dissimilar split, in that section 40(2)(a) of the Patents Act 1990 requires a complete specification to describe the invention fully (including the best method), and section 40(3) provides that the claim or claims be clear and succinct and fairly based on the matter disclosed in the specification. Unlike the fusion seen above in UK law, non-compliance of each is a distinct ground of revocation, as a result of which considerable judicial time has been spent on analysing what the 'fair basis' ground might involve that can invalidate a patent, over and beyond the requirement of a complete specification.[61]

In the UK, under the Patents Act 1949, an inventor was bound to disclose information about the invention in good faith and honesty,[62] in addition to which section 32(1)(i) required that the claim be 'fairly based on the matter disclosed in the specification'. Both of these provisions are at the heart of the quid pro quo of patents, such as it exists. Before the introduction of this

[57] *Biogen v Medeva* [1997] RPC 1 (HL).

[58] *Generics (UK) Ltd v H Lundbeck A/S* [2009] UKHL 12.

[59] *Asahi Kasei Kogyo KK's Application* [1991] RPC 485, 535–36.

[60] *Biogen* (n 57) 47.

[61] In particular see *Lockwood v Doric* (n 54).

[62] The Patents Act 1949 s 32(1)(h) required the description to be fair and to disclose the best method known to the patentee. See Cornish and Llewelyn, *Intellectual Property: Patents, Copyright, Trade Marks and Allied Rights* (London, Sweet & Maxwell, 2003) 164, 229–30.

statutory fair basis objection in 1949, the House of Lords had formulated the substance of the provision in the following terms:

> It is the consideration which the patentee gives to the public by disclosing his inventive idea which entitles him in return to protection for an article which embodies his idea, but not for an article which is described in terms which cover things quite unrelated to his idea and which do not embody it at all.[63]

The disappearance of these provisions, and the compulsion to follow related EPO authorities, led Lord Hoffmann to state in *Biogen* that the general principle of 'lack of fair basis' exists in substance so that where the breadth of the claims exceeds the invention disclosed, the court may apply a broader approach to 'enabled disclosure'.

In Australian law as elsewhere, *Biogen* was interpreted as authority for the proposition that the breadth of a claim will exceed the 'technical contribution' to the art if it claims every way of achieving a result but only enables one such way.[64] This decision created unease in Australia in a pre-*Generics* era and in the context of the lack of an explicit fair basis provision in the UK. Due to the fair basis provision in section 40(3), the decision was relegated in relevance, as being a better fit for the question of sufficiency in section 40(2). Thus the High Court in *Lockwood Security Products* took the position that it was 'Lord Hoffmann's view ... that it was a requirement of English law that there be an enabling disclosure across the whole width of the claim. That is not and never has been the law in Australia.'[65] Whether this really makes Australian law 'mechanistic and impoverished' in the sense in which Lord Hoffmann applied the words in *Biogen* to the general rule that an invention was sufficiently disclosed if the skilled man could make a single embodiment, is debatable. On fair basing however, it was enough for the Australian High Court to declare that current UK law is no guide to Australian law.[66]

There is another persuasive reason for the High Court to move away from the UK's approach to fairness, and this is the confusion evident in *Biogen* and addressed explicitly in *Generics* regarding the so-called 'consistory',[67]

[63] *Mullard Radio Valve Co Ltd v Philco Radio and Television Corporation of Great Britain* (1936) 53 RPC 323, 347.

[64] *Lockwood v Doric* (n 54) [63]–[67].

[65] Per Bannon in *Kimberly-Clark Australia Pty Ltd v Arico Trading International Pty Ltd* (2001) 207 CLR 1.

[66] *Lockwood v Doric* (n 54) [67].

[67] 'A general description of what the invention is said to consist of' normally followed by parts of the specification that describe features that 'generally' or 'preferably' exist, and illustrative, rather than exhaustive of how the invention might be put into effect. This kind of clause is identified by the courts as originating from a time before the 1883 Patents, Trademarks and Designs Act which made it compulsory for the first time to list the claims separately: *Lockwood v Doric* (n 54) [10], [91]–[92].

'covetous' claim[68] or broad claim of a general principle or application. The proposition in *Fuel Oils/EXXON*[69] that is the genesis of the approach to insufficiency in *Biogen* is this: 'that the extent of the monopoly as defined by the claims should correspond to the "technical contribution" to the art in order for it to be supported or justified.' In evaluating its application in *Biogen*, Lord Hoffmann uses 'inventive concept' interchangeably with 'technical contribution to the art'.[70]

In contrast, the House of Lords in *Generics* is at pains to distinguish between the two concepts—a difficult task in abstraction. Thus:

> inventive concept is concerned with the identification of the core of the invention—the idea or principle, of more or less general application which entitles the inventor's achievement to be called inventive. The invention's technical contribution to the art is concerned with the evaluation of its inventive concept—how far forward has it carried the state of the art?

It is crucial to note that the distance and difference between the two concepts is not firmly established as the decision tries to define the extra-statutory 'technical contribution to the art' regularly adopted by the TBA of the EPO. In fact Lord Neuberger notes that the insufficiency reasoning apart from the *Biogen* reasoning given by Kitchin J in the lower court was similar to arguments considered on obviousness by the Board in a number of cases.[71] Further it is the focus on inventive step for product claims that can lead to error; where the claim is for a process or includes a process, the issue of how the alleged invention was achieved, in other words, the inventive step, may be more to the point.[72] *Generics* clearly limits the applicability of the *Biogen* insufficiency principle to rare cases where the claim is to a product identified in part by how it was made and in part by what it did.

Thus although *Generics* has reconsidered *Biogen* insufficiency, it also highlights the difficulty in keeping 'inventive step' separate from 'technical contribution to the art' in the context of insufficiency. This problem is unlikely to go away for at least two reasons. First the fair basis objection that endures and can be traced to *Fuel Oils/EXXON* historically overlaps in the common law with other grounds of invalidity, including obviousness.[73] The second reason is the willingness of the TBA of the EPO to conflate inventive step and inadequacy of disclosure in a line of authority

[68] A 'central claim that travels beyond the matter disclosed in the specification': ibid [58] citing *Mullard v Philco* (n 63) 21.

[69] *Fuel Oils/EXXON* [1994] OJEPO 653.

[70] *Generics v Lundbeck* (n 58) [45].

[71] Ibid [89] referring to reasons given by Kitchin J in [2007] RPC 32 [264]–[265].

[72] Ibid [101].

[73] TA Blanco White, *Patents for Inventions and the Protection of Industrial Designs*, 5th edn (London, Stevens and Sons, 1983) [4-801]. However, White did not cite any authorities to support this view, only illustrations based on 'overlapping' provisions. Also see *Lockwood Security Products Pty Ltd* (n 55) [47].

where claims to broad classes of chemical compounds alleged to have some common technical effect have been rejected for obviousness when there is nothing to show that they would all have that technical effect.[74]

Lockwood's rejection of *Biogen* is suffused with the need to avoid a similar conflation between issues of obviousness and fair basing, which perhaps provides a kinder justification of the divergence than Lord Mance's amusement in *Generics* would seem to indicate.[75] More to the point, the kind of fair basing apparently achieved in *Biogen* and which persists in EPO jurisprudence is not the same as the words 'fairly based' in section 40(3), where they refer to a relationship between what is claimed and what is described in the body of the specification. They do not refer to 'abstract fairness'.

SPECULATIVE INVENTIONS AND SUFFICIENCY

The idea of the patent bargain seems almost lyrical and the divergence in interpretations shows the limited value it has as a unifying analytical concept. An emerging theme apparent from the discussion of sufficiency and fair basing, is the manner in which disclosure requirements may overlap with other validity criteria. Such overlap is directly related to the assessment and disclosure of the consideration given in exchange for a patent. This potential source of confusion and error may be further explored in the context of specifications that contain no more than speculative information about the usefulness or industrial application of an invention.

Increasingly, 'utility' under US patent law is being adopted as the terminology of choice to describe the 'usefulness' of an invention over and above 'industrial application', despite several reasons why this conflation may be substantively inaccurate.[76] Nonetheless, utility elaborated as 'specific, substantial and credible' has been used by the EPO, UKIPO, the UK High Court,[77] is a part of the new Patents Bill in NZ,[78] is included in the

[74] *AGREVO/Triazoles* T 0939/92 [1996] OJEPO 309. See for example the obviousness analysis in evaluating insufficiency in *Scinopharm Taiwan Ltd v Eli Lily and Company* [2009] EWHC 631 (Pat) [140]–[142].

[75] *Generics v Lundbeck* (n 58) [56].

[76] Some of these include the association of 'industrial' with 'technical' ('utility' does not suffer a similar link), and the public policy concerns associated with 'industrial' that is not matched under 'utility'. For a detailed analysis of these and other differences, see Thambisetty, 'Legal Transplants in Patent Law: Why "Utility" is the new "Industrial Applicability"' (2009) 49 *Jurimetrics* 155–201.

[77] *Eli Lilly and Company v Human Genome Sciences Inc* [2008] EWHC 1903 (Pat) [187] applied by *Laboratorios Almirall SA v Boehringer Ingelheim International GmbH* [2009] EWHC 102 (Pat).

[78] See n 24. The explanatory notes say that for an invention to be useful, the Bill requires that inventions demonstrate specific, substantial, and credible utility.

Australia-United States Free Trade Agreement,[79] and figures prominently in international negotiations.[80]

That the correspondence between 'utility' as it is applied in US law and 'industrial application' in the UK is superficial, can be gathered from the differences in the relationship between each of these criteria (as conventionally understood) to disclosure and enablement requirements. In US law subsequent to *Brenner v Manson*[81] it was established that the enablement requirement, or the 'how to use' prong of § 112 incorporates the requirement of 35 USC § 101 that the specification disclose as a matter of fact a practical utility for the invention. If the application fails as a matter of fact to satisfy § 101 then the application also fails as a matter of law to enable one of ordinary skill in the art to use the invention.[82] From here utility in US law has developed as the bridge between speculation and specificity based on actual experimental evidence disclosed or 'well-established' conventions in a technological field. It is this context that brings a threat of confusion between the functional roles of utility and the written description and enablement requirements—a matter of concern for those jurisdictions that have adopted the 'specific, substantial and credible' standard of utility.

In the context of 'speculative inventions', a line of cases have developed in the US where the examiners require further substantiating evidence of utility, unless one with ordinary skill in the art would accept the allegation as obviously correct. *Amgen Inc v Chugai Pharmaceutical Co*[83] illustrates this approach. The CAFC invalidated Amgen's broad claims supported by an insufficient number of examples of use. Due to the lack of predictability in the art of isolating and using purified DNA sequences encoding for human erythropoietin the court held that 'for DNA sequences, [an applicant must disclose] how to make and use enough sequences to justify the grant of the claims sought'.[84] This suggests that if the applicant is able to fully enable his invention the court may have been less stringent in applying utility as a ground for invalidity; correspondingly if the enablement is weak, the court may well demand a complete and specific indication of utility.

[79] Arts 17.1 and 17.9. Currently in Australian law usefulness is only a ground for opposition and revocation through courts, and is not assessed during examination. Several bodies, including the Australian Law Review Commission and IPAustralia recommend the inclusion of usefulness during examination which would only be satisfied if the specification discloses a specific, substantial and credible use for the invention. 'Getting the Balance Right' (n 32) [5.1].

[80] For example, see WIPO Standing Committee on The Law of Patents, SCP 7/8 (2002) [167], [171].

[81] *Brenner v Manson* 383 US 519 (1966).

[82] *Re Zeigler* 26 USPQ 1600, 992 F 2d 1197 (Fed Cir 1993) 1200–201.

[83] *Amgen Inc v Chugai Pharmaceutical Co* 927 F.2d 1200, (Fed Cir 1991) 1212–14.

[84] Ibid 1215.

The conflation between utility and enablement in US law is often accompanied by sector-specific rules of disclosure that do not apply to other areas—such as in the case of gene sequences[85] and human gene therapy where the USPTO appears to have set up a presumption that the field itself is unpredictable.[86] The USPTO Utility Guidelines suggest that the methods to treat unspecified diseases do not meet the substantial utility prong of the specific, substantial and credible test of utility.[87] Hence claims specifying a pharmaceutical composition without a disease target (a likely scenario, given the state of the art in gene therapy) or specifying a method for introducing genes without a gene therapy target may fail the substantial utility test, as a result of which an enablement rejection follows.[88]

In contrast to the above, industrial application has historically passed through a period of doctrinal confusion between sufficiency and utility and emerged in its present modern form where it is associated with insufficiency of disclosure only in rare cases of extraordinary inventions such as perpetual motion machines.[89] (While such machines do not have industrial application, an alternate objection may be that the specification is not complete enough to allow the invention to be performed.)

The conceptual link between industrial application and insufficiency in the UK in the period between 1932 and 1977 throws some light on present developments in US law. The overlap and relationship is explained in *Valensi v British Radio Corporation Ltd*:

> The objections of inutility and insufficiency overlap. To prove inutility it is, in our view, necessary to show that the invention so far as claimed, will not work as described or with any modification which the addressee can properly be expected to make. If any proposed modification is one which he cannot be expected to make then the specification is insufficient.[90]

In Blanco White's words, 'insufficiency is when you cannot make the thing, inutility is when you can but it doesn't work when you have'.[91]

[85] For a general discussion of industry specific practice related to written description see Burk and Lemley, 'Policy Levers in Patent Law' (2003) 89 *Virginia Law Review* 1575.

[86] USPTO, Training Materials for Examining Patent Applications With Respect to 35 USC § 112, First Paragraph—Enablement Chemical/Biotechnological Applications (1996), Example G. This is guided in part by an NIH report cited specifically by the USPTO as evidence of the state of the art. Orkin and Motulsky 'Report and Recommendation of the Panel to assess the NIH Investment in Research on Gene Therapy, NIH (1995), www.nih.gov.news/panelrep.html.

[87] USPTO, Revised Interim Utility Guidelines Training Materials (1999).

[88] See Pascal, 'The Heightened Enablement Requirement for Gene Therapy Patents: Is Undue Experimentation the Undoing of Gene Therapy? (2005) 24 *Biotechnology Law Reports* 257.

[89] See *Eastman Kodak Co v. American Photo Booths Inc* BL/O/457/02 and Manual of UK Patent Practice [4.05].

[90] *Valensi v British Radio Corporation Ltd* [1972] FSR (CA (Civ Div)) 273, 312.

[91] Blanco White (n 73) [4–404].

In order to remove the considerable uncertainty that existed previously in the common law, the UK Patents Act 1932 introduced for the first time, the requirement of 'utility' as a separate ground on which a patent could be revoked in addition to the requirement that the complete specification should sufficiently and fairly describe the nature of the invention and manner in which the invention is to be performed.[92] From 1932 to 1977 the link between 'utility' and sufficiency was interpreted to mean that every claim in the invention must be useful,[93] and if a claim covered a mechanism or a process that did not produce the result, or one of the results claimed expressly or impliedly in the specification, the entire patent was deemed invalid.[94]

This was regarded as a harsh position by the Banks Committee which recommended in 1970 that the lack of utility should be a ground for revocation only if the 'invention claimed covers no useful embodiments';[95] if part of the subject matter of the application was useful the patent should be granted. Crucially, in order to address the danger of wide and speculative claims being filed the Committee identified the different functional possibilities of sufficiency of disclosure and inutility; it recommended that only the former be used to tackle broad claims. A statutory requirement was therefore proposed to deal with claims that were unduly wide, having regard to the disclosure in the complete specification.[96] 'Utility' as 'workability' was therefore deemed redundant under the 1977 Act. [97] Thus:

> It is important to remember that the old law which provided for revocation if the claims were not fairly based on the description or lacked utility was swept away by the 1977 Act. The law is now that set out in the 1977 Act. Section 4(1) states that inventions shall be taken to be capable of industrial application 'if it can be made … in any kind of industry'.[98]

This observation formalises the different functional roles played by 'industrial application' and 'sufficiency of disclosure' in modern UK law in contrast

[92] s 25(2)(e) and s 25(2)(f).

[93] Ng-Loy Wee Loon, 'Patenting of Genes—A Closer Look at the Concepts of Utility and Industrial Applicability' (2002) 33 *International Review of Industrial Property and Copyright Law* 393, 403.

[94] See *Norton and Gregory Ltd v Jacobs* (1937) 54 RPC 271. This position, according to Ng-Loy Wee Loon, mirrors the literal construction of claims – an approach that was subsequently softened by the 'purposive' approach to claim construction. Loon, 'Patenting of Genes' (n 93) 403–404.

[95] Committee on the Patent System and Patent Law, *British Patent System: Report of the Committee to Examine the Patent System and Patent Law (1970–71)* chaired by Maurice Banks, Cmnd 4407 [376].

[96] Ibid [533]. This view coincided with a more 'modern' and favourable view of patents. UK Patents Act 1977 s 14(3).

[97] See Ford J's observations on why 'utility' was dropped in favour of the requirement of sufficiency in *Roussel Uclaf v Imperial Chemical Industries plc (No 3)* [1991] RPC 51, 67.

[98] *Chiron Corporation v Murex Diagnostics Ltd* [1996] FSR 153 at 177 (Morritt LJ).

to the confusion between utility and disclosure and enablement in US law. While it could be argued that given the common legal history convergence in meaning between 'utility' and 'industrial application' is to be expected, reading the former as fulfilling the latter, at the very least, opens up the possibility of an unwelcome throwback to the confusion that existed between 1932 and 1977 in the common law. Additionally 'utility' as it is championed by the US (via bilateral trade agreements and in WIPO negotiations) does not carry the same weight as usefulness applied under the rubric of 'industrial'.[99] Convergence in substantive meaning between utility and industrial application in common law jurisdictions calls for thorough judicial scrutiny. So far acceptance of the 'specific, substantial and credible' language in the UK has been piloted not so much by higher courts but by patent office practice—first by the EPO and then the UKIPO.[100]

Further, the specific, substantial and credible standard of utility, as it is developing in the US, appears explicitly linked to the state of the art evaluations, in order to ascertain what the patentee has disclosed in relation to what already exists in the field—an enquiry that is better made under the obviousness criterion. In *Re Fisher*[101] judge Rader notes the conceptual closeness between specific, substantial and credible and the 'inventive step' standard, to conclude that policy concerns with inventions such as ESTs are better addressed through non-obviousness—a doctrine considerably hamstrung in US law by the *Re Deuel*[102] decision.

It is fruitful here to consider the law in Canada that also uses the 'new and useful' terminology.[103] The doctrine of 'sound prediction' reaffirmed by the Canadian Supreme Court in *Apotex v Wellcome Foundation Ltd*[104] is based on the public interest in the disclosure of new and useful inventions even before their utility has been verified by tests, while avoiding the cluttering of the public domain with useless patents and monopoly rights in exchange for misinformation.[105] The Supreme Court noted that the key was to avoid 'speculation'. The utility requirement is met at the priority date only if either it is demonstrated or there is sound prediction based on the information and expertise then available. First, there must be a factual basis for the prediction. Secondly, the inventor must have on the date of the patent application, an articulable and sound line of reasoning from which

[99] Thambisetty (n 76) 160–70.

[100] *ICOS Corp/Novel V 28 seven transmembrane receptor* 6 OJEPO 293 (2002), *Aeomica Inc* BL O/286//05.

[101] *Re Fisher* 421 F 3d 1367 (Fed Cir 2005), 1381–82.

[102] *Re Deuel* 51 F 3d 1552 (Fed Cir 1995).

[103] s 2 defines an invention as 'any new and useful art, process, machine, manufacture or composition of matter, or any new and useful improvement in any process, machine, manufacture or composition of matter.'

[104] *Apotex v Wellcome Foundation Ltd* [2002] SCC 77.

[105] Ibid [66].

the desired result can be inferred on the factual basis. Thirdly, there must be adequate disclosure of the logic or reasoning used to achieve the prediction.[106] 'Sound prediction' does not mean 'certainty', and is a more nuanced bridge between the requirement of 'utility', the cognitive ability to foresee technological innovations and improvements, and the information function of the patent system that requires in various measures sufficient disclosure, enablement, enabling disclosure, or written description.

CONCLUSION

A major factor in the evolution of sufficiency of disclosure appears to be the increasing 'Europeanisation' of UK law that has, for example, made pre-1977 UK case law more relevant to Australia than post-1977 law. The UK is working ever closer with the EPO both in terms of procedure[107] and substantive law,[108] and this can either exacerbate or mitigate the differences with other common law jurisdictions. It has led for example in the case of fair basing, to divergence with Australian law, and in the case of the utility standard to convergence with many other major jurisdictions.

Sufficiency of disclosure is often referred to as an 'internal' requirement of patentability in an attempt to signify that sufficiency is normally assessed after the other substantive criteria have been evaluated, or that it is not quite on par with other grounds of invalidity. However the picture emerging from the above discussion is one of a complex criterion, laced with the 'rhetorical flourish' of the patent bargain, and that in most common law jurisdictions appears to borrow elements from other substantive patentability requirements. Thus in the UK sufficiency has developed a 'fair basing' requirement that assesses 'technological contribution to the art' and in particular contexts, 'non-obviousness'; in the US 'usefulness' and 'enablement' are conflated.

The content of sufficiency thus appears to draw on the approach to other grounds of invalidity determined by how strictly separate they can be or are kept during patentability evaluations that include consideration of more then one ground. Australia appears to have allowed pragmatism to trump complicated explorations of policy and purpose behind sufficiency provisions, and keeping grounds of invalidity separate appears to be a major preoccupation. Other jurisdictions do not seem to be as careful with the juxtaposition of the utility standard and sufficiency. Although the legal history of insufficiency shows overlaps between other grounds of invalidity,

106 Ibid [70].

107 *Eli Lilly and Co v Human Genome Sciences* [2009] EWCA Civ 168 (CA).

108 See for example observations on the need to align UK law with EPO decisions in *Actavis UK Ltd v Merck and Co Inc* [2008] EWCA Civ 444 (CA) and in *Generics* (n 58).

the quid pro quo in *Liardet* refers to the disclosure of the invention, not disclosure of the other substantive requirements such as inventive step or utility of the invention. It is only the common history that ensures in the face of significant diversity in patent disclosure requirements, and potential for confusion and error, that the quid pro quo of the patent bargain endures in spirit in the common law but it is an eviscerated spirit best put to rest.

Copyright

11

Common Law Approaches to the Requirement of Originality

SAM RICKETSON

INTRODUCTION

COPYRIGHT LAW IN common law countries has always swayed uneasily between two poles: the need to preserve a thriving public domain of ideas and information,[1] and the desire to prevent egregious free-riding on the backs of others' efforts.[2] These competing notions come immediately to the fore in any consideration of the qualitative threshold standard, namely originality, which is to be applied in the protection of literary and artistic works. The purpose of the present chapter is to examine this issue, both conceptually and by reference to history, and to consider whether there is a common approach to be found in countries, such as Australia and Canada, that have a shared legal past with the United Kingdom.

STARTING POINTS

Let us begin with some general observations or caveats about originality.

1. In common law countries, which are former British self-governing dominions such as Australia and Canada, originality stands as the dividing line between the works of 'authors' and the productions of 'non-authors' or 'makers'—rights that in civil law jurisdictions would be described as 'neighbouring rights'. There is a common statutory thread that links these countries to the United Kingdom, namely the Copyright Act 1911

[1] A view expressed long ago by Lord Mansfield CJ in *Sayre and Others v Moore* (1785) 1 East 316 n 5; 102 ER 139, 140.

[2] A sentiment admirably summarised in Peterson J's famous aphorism in *University of London Press Ltd v University Tutorial Press Ltd* [1916] 2 Ch 601, 609–10: 'after all, there remains the rough practical test that what is worth copying is prima facie worth protecting.'

(UK),[3] which first brought together the terms 'author' and 'original … works' and incorporates an older legal heritage that goes back to the earlier British Copyright Acts and cases (see further below). This is obviously not so in that other great common law system, the United States, but the protection of 'Authors' and their 'respective Writings' has had a constitutional status in that country from its very foundation,[4] and the requirement of originality for copyright subsistence has long been acknowledged by the US courts.[5] This suggests an immediate connection between the person of the author and the requirement of originality, with the first supplying the second, but actually tells us very little else of what originality means. At the same time, it is the critical hurdle that would-be claimants for protection must clear, after otherwise establishing the requisite points of attachment (nationality, residence, etc) and material form, and before they can claim the more elevated exclusive rights available to authors of works.[6] This threshold requirement for protection can be contrasted with the more complex requirements for other intellectual property rights, such as a patent (novelty, inventiveness, utility, etc), a design (newness and distinctiveness) and a trade mark (distinctiveness).

2. As a number of contemporary discussions, both by courts and commentators, reveal,[7] these common historical connections remain relevant today, although reference to British decisions preceding the Copyright Act 1911 may be a little out of place. A plethora of different findings is to be seen here, on subject matter as diverse as calendars of court officials and East India Company personnel,[8] road directories,[9] directories

[3] s 25(1) of the Copyright Act 1911 provided for these dominions to apply the Act within their territories, and this was done by Australia (with some modifications) in the Copyright Act 1912 (Cth) and by Canada in the Copyright Act 1921 (Cth). Other self-governing dominions of that period that applied the 1911 Act in the same way were Newfoundland, the Irish Free State, New Zealand and India. The 1911 Act, however, was applied directly to all other British colonies and Protectorates.

[4] See Art I § 8 cl 8 of the US Constitution, which authorises Congress to 'secur[e] for limited Times to Authors … the exclusive Right to their respective Writings.'

[5] Most recently, and authoritatively, in *Feist Publications Inc v Rural Telephone Service Co Inc* [1991] 499 US 340; 113 L Ed 2d 358.

[6] In the Australian Copyright Act 1968, compare the list of exclusive rights for works granted under s 31(1) with the more limited list of rights accorded to other subject matter, such as sound recordings (s 85), cinematographic films (s 86), broadcasts (s 87) and published editions of works (s 88).

[7] See, for example, the extensive discussion of nineteenth century precedents by the Australian full Federal Court in *Desktop Marketing Systems Pty Ltd v Telstra Corp* (2002) 55 IPR 1; and two recent and very thorough scholarly discussions by D Lindsay, 'Copyright protection of broadcast program schedules: IceTV before the High Court' (2008) 19 *Australian Intellectual Property Journal* 195 and J Pila, 'Compilation copyright: A matter calling for a "certain sobriety"' (2008) 19 AIPJ 231.

[8] *Matthewson v Stockdale* (1806) 12 Ves Jun 270; 33 ER 103.

[9] *Kelly v Morris* (1866) LR 1 Eq 697.

of traders,[10] abridgments of railway timetables,[11] compilations of public documents[12] and journalists' reports of the speeches of a retired Liberal imperialist prime minister.[13] Interesting themes and approaches are to be found in these cases, but too much may be made of them by twenty-first century courts and scholars looking for guidance. Times and circumstances change, and precedents of this antiquity may provide fragile support for a particular desired legal and policy outcome today.[14]

3. More assistance, however, may be gained from noting certain matters that have a continuous history throughout this period and into the present, particularly as these matters are common throughout the British common law jurisdictions that are the subject of this essay. Most notable here are the notions of 'authors' and 'authorship'. Thus, 'authors' made their first appearance in the preamble to the Act of Anne in 1710, even if this might have been perceived as a ruse by publishers to secure their own interests as 'purchasers' of authors' copies.[15] The same expression was repeated in the Dramatic Copyright Act 1833, the Lectures Copyright Act 1835, and, then, most notably, in the Copyright Act 1842. Although the last-mentioned did not define the expression,[16] the 'author' was clearly the source of the rights conferred by the Act and one of the reference points for determining the term of protection.[17] Moreover, authors were at the centre of the famous debates in the House of Commons over the 1842 Act, where names such as Johnson and Wordsworth were bandied about in support of competing views, rather than other possible recipients of protection such as the writers of trade catalogues or the

[10] *Morris v Ashbee* (1866) LR 7 Eq 34.

[11] *Leslie v Young & Sons* [1894] AC 335.

[12] *Trade Auxiliary Co v Middlesbrough & District Tradesmen's Association* (1889) 40 Ch D 425.

[13] *Walter v Lane* [1900] AC 539.

[14] See further ch 3 in this volume by K Bowrey, 'On clarifying the role of originality and fair use in nineteenth century UK jurisprudence'.

[15] See further M Rose, *Authors and Owners: The Invention of Copyright* (Cambridge, MA, Harvard University Press, 1993) 36. For detailed treatments of the background to the passing of the Act, see also J Feather, 'The Book Trade in Politics: The Making of the Copyright Act of 1710' (1980) 8 *Publishing History* 19–44; LR Patterson, *Copyright in Historical Perspective*, (Nashville, TN, Vanderbilt University Press, 1968) 138–42; H Ransom, *The First Copyright Statute* (Austin, TX, University of Texas Press, 1956) 89–92; but compare the more nuanced reading of the origins and effect of the statute by Deazley, who refers to provisions that were against the interests of the booksellers and genuinely in favour of the promotion of authorship, the production of useful books and the 'free market of ideas': R Deazley 'Commentary on the Statute of Anne 1710', in L Bently and M Kretschmer (eds), *Primary Sources on Copyright (1450–1900)* (www.copyrighthistory.org, 2008).

[16] It is noteworthy that s 2 otherwise was the repository of a number of definitions, such as 'book', 'dramatic piece', 'copyright', 'personal representative', 'assigns' and so on.

[17] The life of the author plus seven years, or 42 years, whichever was the longer: Copyright Act 1842 (5&6 Vict c 45) s 3.

compilers of tide tables.[18] Thus, even if its content was uncertain, it was a familiar and well-worn term by the time it found its modern home in the first modern UK copyright legislation in 1911.[19]

4. While these early British Acts concerned with literary-type productions may have said nothing explicit about the qualities required for 'authorship', it is interesting to note that, during the same period, there were other persons, sometimes also referred to as 'authors', whose productions had received copyright-style protection.[20] In some instances, this had also been done with a clearer indication of the standard required. For example, the first Engraving Copyright Act 1734 gave protection to 'every person who shall invent and design, engrave, etch or work ...',[21] the Sculpture Copyright Act 1814 to 'every person ... who shall make or cause to be made any new and original sculpture or model ....',[22] and the Fine Arts Copyright Act 1862 to the 'author ... of every original painting, drawing and photograph ...'.[23] When the Copyright Act 1911 was enacted, it swept up all these persons under the general rubric of authors of 'original literary, dramatic musical and artistic work[s]'.[24]
5. It has been suggested that the Copyright Act 1911 was primarily a codification and consolidation of the previous piecemeal enactments of the previous two centuries, with a view to ensuring uniformity throughout the then British Empire.[25] Certainly, this had been the recommendation of the Copyright Commissioners in 1878,[26] but it is also clear that the 1911 Act had a more far-reaching objective: to ensure consistency between UK law and the extensive changes that had been introduced into the Berne Convention in its latest revision at Berlin in 1908. The UK Government reacted with unusual speed in appointing a Board of

[18] See, for example, the speech of TB Macaulay, *House of Commons Debates*, 5 February 1841, 350 ff. See further C Seville, *Literary Copyright reform in Early Victorian England,* (Cambridge, CUP, 1999) and R Deazley, 'Commentary on Copyright Amendment Act 1842', in *Primary Sources on Copyright* (n 15).

[19] Copyright Act 1911 (UK) (1&2 Geo 5 c 46) ss 1(1) and 5.

[20] The texts of these statutes can now be readily accessed at www.copyrighthistory.org.

[21] 8 Geo II c 13 s 1; to similar effect, see also the Engraving Copyright Act 1766 (7 Geo III c 38) s 1.

[22] 54 Geo III c 56 s 1.

[23] 25&26 Vict c 68 s 1. In one of the cases arising under this Act, the Court of Appeal found the concept of 'authorship' an unusual one to use in the case of paintings and drawings where the term 'artist' was more commonly used, and had even more difficulty in applying had difficulty in understanding how this might apply in the case of photographs: see *Nottage v Jackson* (1883) 11 QBD 627, 630–31 (Brett MR referring here to the 'strangeness of the phraseology') and 634 (Cotton LJ).

[24] Copyright Act 1911 (1&2 Geo 5 c 46) s 1(1).

[25] K Bowrey, 'On clarifying the role of originality and fair use in nineteenth century UK jurisprudence', ch 3 in this volume. This is a reference to the essay by K Bowrey which I understand is to appear in the Festschrift volume—my chapter reference may be wrong.

[26] Royal Commission on Copyright, C-2086 (1878) xiii [13]. See further R Deazley, (2008) 'Commentary on the Royal Commission's Report on Copyright (1878), in *Primary Sources on Copyright* (n 15).

Trade Committee under Lord Gorell, and the report of the Committee is notable for its careful examination and comparison of the different texts of the Convention (Berne 1886 and Berlin 1908) and the need for changes to UK law to accommodate accession to the Berlin text.[27] Significant changes included the protection of cinematographic and choreographic works,[28] the removal of formalities[29] and the adoption of the life of the author plus 50 years term of protection.[30] Equally significant was the adoption of new terminology which can only have had its provenance in the Berne text, most notably the expression 'literary and artistic works', which was elaborated upon in the new Act as 'literary, dramatic, musical and artistic works'. This was language that was generally unfamiliar to common lawyers, whose previous statutory descriptors had been more concrete and descriptive: 'books', 'dramatic pieces', 'lectures', 'engravings', 'sculptures' and so on.[31] The Berlin text also provided a definition of 'literary and artistic works' which, while open-ended and inclusive, nonetheless suggested the need for there to be boundaries around what was to be protected:

> (1) The expression 'literary and artistic works' shall include every production in the literary, scientific and artistic domain, whatever may be the mode or form of its expression, such as books, pamphlets and other writings; dramatic or dramatico-musical works, choreographic works and entertainments in dumb show, the acting form of which is fixed in writing or otherwise; musical compositions with or without words; works of drawing, painting, architecture, sculpture, engraving and lithography; illustrations, geographical charts; plans, sketches and plastic works relative to geography, topography, architecture or science.

The boundaries propounded here were with respect to 'productions in the literary, scientific and artistic domain'. While the adjective 'scientific' is somewhat mysterious, it seems that it was not intended to

[27] *Report of the Committee on the Law of Copyright*, Cd 4976 (HMSO, 1909).

[28] Berlin Act 1908 Arts 2(1) and 14(1) and (2).

[29] Ibid Art 4(2).

[30] Ibid Art 7(1). This, however, was not a mandatory obligation until the Brussels Revision of 1948.

[31] Thus, the word 'works' unqualified by the adjectives 'literary' and 'artistic' was first used in the International Copyright Act 1844 (7 & 8 Vict c 12), s 2 of which provided for the extension of the British Acts by Order in Council to 'all or any particular Class or Classes of the following Works, (namely,) Books, Prints, articles of Sculpture, and other Works of Art to be defined in such Order…' In the same way, the International Copyright Act 1852 (15 & 16 Vict c 12), giving effect to the Anglo-French Convention of 1851 and the protection of translation rights for foreign works, referred in its preamble to 'Works of Literature and the Fine Arts', but thereafter to 'Books' and 'Dramatic Pieces'. There was reference to 'Works of Art' in the final part of the Copyright Consolidation Bill 1879, which followed the work of the Copyright Commission of 1878 and, in Australia, a distinction between 'books' and 'works of art' was drawn in the Copyright Act 1905 (Cth). These, however, seem to be incidental or passing uses.

extend to such things as inventions and discoveries, but rather as a description to capture works relating to scientific matters or of a scientific character (as in the listed examples of 'illustrations, geographical charts; plans, sketches and plastic works relative to geography, topography, architecture or science').[32] Indeed, the long list of examples that follows the general definition suggests that the term 'literary and artistic' was to be interpreted broadly, and that the longer expression 'literary, dramatic, musical and artistic' in the 1911 Act simply represented a desire by the UK drafters to be more accurate as to what fell within its bounds. The term 'production' in Article 2(1) was undefined, but it seems only to have been intended to indicate that the work must have come into existence before protection could be claimed[33]—a reference, perhaps, to the need for a work to have assumed some definite 'form', rather than being no more than a simple idea or thought in the author's head. No direct reference was made in Article 2(1) of the Berlin text to the need for 'productions in the literary, scientific or artistic domain' to be 'original', but indirectly an indication that this was to be so could be derived from Article 2(2), which was concerned with derivative works such as 'translations, adaptations, arrangements and other reproductions in altered form of a literary or artistic work': these were to be protected 'as original works, without prejudice to the rights of the author of the original work'. It could be argued that the adjective 'original' was used in two senses here: first, to refer to the quality that other works protected under the Convention in Article 2(1) must have, ie that they should be 'original', and, secondly, to indicate the work that was first in time, ie the work on which the derivative work was based. An alternative reading is that the first 'original' simply embodied a non-discrimination requirement, namely that the adaptation was to be treated no differently from the first or 'original' work from which it was derived. The records of the Berlin revision conference provide little further assistance on this point, although it is noteworthy that the rapporteur (Louis Renault) referred to translations as being 'un travail intellectuelle, souvent difficile'.[34] A more explicitly substantive threshold requirement, however, was to be seen in Article 14(2), which provided that cinematographic productions were to be protected as literary or artistic works 'if, by the arrangement of the acting form or the combination of the incidents represented, the author had given the work

[32] See further Ricketson and Ginsburg, *International Copyright and Neighbouring Rights: the Berne Convention and Beyond* (Oxford, OUP, 2006) [8.06].

[33] Ibid 403.

[34] *Actes de la Conference reunie a Berlin du 14 octobre au 14 novembre* 1908, 232–33. For an English translation made by WIPO in 1986, see www.oup.com/uk/booksites/content/9780196259466/15550026, p 184: 'The translator has accomplished intellectual and often difficult work.'

a *personal and original* character' (emphasis supplied). Furthermore, Article 14(3) provided that the reproduction by cinematography of a literary, scientific or artistic work was to be protected as an '*original* work' (emphasis supplied) and, in his report, Renault referred to cinematographic adaptations and reproductions alike as serving to 'give form to a creation'.[35] It therefore seems reasonable to conclude, from these provisions, that the drafters of the Berlin text assumed that 'originality' was a requirement for literary and artistic works generally. No further assistance as to the meaning and content of this term, however, was provided in the Convention, meaning that this was essentially a matter for national laws to interpret for themselves.

5. The 1911 Act itself provided no further statutory guidance as to the meaning of 'original', but its inclusion in that Act indicates that it did not come out of thin air and clearly had reference to the Berlin text of Berne. Prior to this, it may be noted that, in the celebrated case of *Walter v Lane*, the Court of Appeal[36] had been the first British court to interpolate the requirement of 'originality' explicitly as a gloss to explain the scope of the term 'author' under the 1842 Act—an initiative subsequently overruled by the House of Lords.[37] However, there were suggestions of such a standard to be found in several of the other copyright statutes then in force (see above) as well as some of the case law.[38] Furthermore, when the 1911 Copyright Bill was in committee, the Solicitor General (Sir John Simon) refused a proposed amendment to delete the word 'original'. While stating that this did not mean novelty of subject matter, he went on to stress that some element of intellectual effort was required, meaning that before a person could claim copyright protection, the work:

> should really be his in the sense that his is the brain that has first of all applied itself to the subject matter and produced the composition, or, at any rate, that his is the brain which, though it has not produced the composition, has expressed it in a new form.[39]

[35] See www.oup.com/uk/booksites/content/9780196259466/15550026, p 213.

[36] *Walter v Lane* [1899] 2 Ch 749.

[37] [1900] AC 539.

[38] See, for example, *Dick v Yates* (1881) 18 Ch D 76 (CA); *Chilton v Progress Printing & Publishing Co* [1895] 3 Ch 29 ('no literary composition' in a single word constituting the opinion of the plaintiff as to the likely winner of a horse race); see further, *Primrose Press Agency Co v Knowles* (1886) 2 TLR 404 (Ch D) and *Broad v Meyer* (1912) 57 Sol Jo 145 (Ch D); *Broemel v Meyer* (1912) 29 TLR 148 (Ch D). In relation to the *Fine Arts Act* 1862, note also the interesting view of Deazley that the word 'original' was inserted as a means of ensuring that artists who had lost their copyright through the transfer of a painting to a purchaser without any reservation should not thereafter be able to turn around and create another closely similar work without infringing copyright: see Deazley, R. (2008) 'Commentary on the *Fine Art Copyright Act* 1862', in *Primary Sources on Copyright* (n 15).

[39] Hansard HC col 1911–14 (28 July 1911).

6. Underlying the developments described above are two further assumptions that bear repeating, however trite they may appear.
   a. While it is unusual to find in common law jurisdictions general statements of the kind now to be found in Article 9(2) of the WIPO Copyright Treaty:

      > Copyright protection shall extend to expressions and not to ideas, procedures, methods of operation or mathematical concepts as such.

      it is clear that this was a basic concept that was understood by the courts in interpreting the rights granted under the pre-1911 Acts. Thus, in *Chilton v Progress Printing & Publishing Co*,[40] the Court of Appeal refused protection to what was, in effect, an opinion rather than the plaintiff's literary expression of that opinion. The same point has been made, time and again, both pre- and post-1911 with respect to ideas and concepts, methods and schemes, as well as facts and data.[41] In a limited way, the Berne Convention itself reflected the same assumption with respect to 'news of the day or to miscellaneous facts having the character of mere items of press information'.[42]
   b. Linked to the above is the notion that subject matter is only protected when in some kind of material or tangible form. Under the 1842 legislation, this directed attention to the need for some kind of printing, as in a book or letter-press;[43] post-1911, it was clear that other forms would suffice,[44] but it was equally clear that unfixed forms of expressions would not.[45]

[40] *Chilton v Progress Printing & Publishing Co* [1895] 2 Ch 29.

[41] See, for example, *Jeffreys (C) v Boosey (T)* (1854) 4 HLC 815; *Donoghue v Allied Newspapers Ltd* (1948) Ch 106, 109; *Gleeson v HR Denne Ltd* [1975] RPC 471; *Catnic Components Ltd v Hill & Smith Ltd* [1975] FSR 405; *LB (Plastics) Ltd v Swish Products Ltd* [1979] RPC 551; *Plix Products Ltd v Frank M Winstone (Merchants) Ltd* (1984) 3 IPR 390 (HC, NZ), 5 IPR 156 (CA, NZ); *Green v Broadcasting Corp of New Zealand* [1989] RPC 700; *Designers Guild Ltd v Russell Williams (Textiles) Ltd* [2001] FSR 11; *Elwood Clothing Pty Ltd v Cotton On Clothing Pty Ltd* [2008] FCAFC 197. Recall also the words of Augustine Birrell in his celebrated lectures on copyright at the end of the nineteenth century: 'Ideas, it has been admitted, … are as free as air'; A Birrell, *The Law and History of Copyright in Books*(London, Cassell and Co, 1899) 167. A similar point was made by L Renault in his report at the Berlin Revision Conference in 1908 in relation to cinematographic adaptations when he emphasised that this was not a 'question of monopolising an idea or a subject but of protecting the form given the idea or the development of the subject': see www.oup.com/uk/booksites/content/9780196259466/15550026, p 213.

[42] Berlin Act 1908 Art 9(3).

[43] Copyright Act 1842 s 1.

[44] Copyright Act 1911 s 1(1)(b) requiring the work to be 'made'.

[45] It is only since the Stockholm/Paris Act of 1967–1971 that it has been clear, for the purposes of the Convention, that fixation in a material form is a matter for national laws: see Art 2(2).

THE MEANING OF ORIGINALITY

So much for historical antecedents, but what does it all mean? Perhaps the best starting point here is a consideration of the concept of 'author'—the one statutory term that has remained constant throughout. And one can hardly do this without asking, 'author of what?' Earlier Acts spoke of 'books',[46] but, as noted above, the 1911 Act extended this to 'literary, dramatic, musical and artistic works'—and 'original literary, dramatic, musical and artistic works', at that. In *Sands & MacDougall v Robinson*,[47] Isaacs J of the High Court of Australia, drawing upon the pre-1911 law as well as the provisions of the recently drafted Berlin text of the Berne Convention, pulled these terms together in the following way:

> ... in copyright law the two expressions 'author' and 'original work' have always been correlative; the one connotes the other, and there is no indication in the Act that the Legislature intended to depart from the accepted signification of the words as applied to the subject matter. Indeed, the circumstance of reciprocal connotation is the key to the meaning of the enactment. We find in the *Oxford Dictionary*, vol. *i.*, p. 571, col. 1, 'author' defined as 'the person who originates or gives existence to anything.'[48]

If authorship and originality were correlatives, certain other matters were also clear. Invention and/or novelty were not required, notwithstanding hints of this in several nineteenth century decisions (see above). These are qualities that are more apposite to the ideas and concepts embodied in a work, rather than the form in which those ideas are expressed. Thus, authorship for the purposes of the legislation was concerned with the fact that the expression of a work emanated from the author and was not copied.[49] There might therefore be as many different renditions of a particular literary or dramatic subject or theme as there were 'authors', so long as each did so in his or her own words. This concept was also readily applicable to renditions of externally observable phenomena in the real world (or 'facts'), such as reports of events or representations of a person or animal, a street- or landscape. In crude terms, we might then add 'facts' or data to ideas and concepts (as mental constructs) to the dichotomy we now draw with the form or manner in which such matters are expressed.

[46] Note here the comments of Brett MR in *Nottage v Jackson* (1883) 11 QBD 627, 630, that, while he could understand the usage of 'author' in relation to books, it was a strange terms to use in relation to paintings and drawings (let alone photographs), and not a term used by anyone else other than '[p]ersons who draw Acts of Parliament'.

[47] *Sands & MacDougall v Robinson* (1917) 23 CLR 49.

[48] Ibid 55–56.

[49] See, for example, *University of London Press Ltd v University Tutorial Press Ltd* [1916] 2 Ch 601; *Sands & McDougall* (1917) 23 CLR 49; *Walter v Lane* [1900] AC 539.

Having said this, was there nonetheless some qualitative standard that had to be satisfied before the authorship-originality criterion was met? This is a question that, in turn, invites an inquiry into what acts will suffice for the purposes of authorship. It is only if these can be adequately identified, that the qualitative issue can be more properly considered.

Acts of Authorship

If authorship is concerned with giving a material expression to something (a 'production', to use the language of Article 2(1) of the Berne Convention), then clearly the most common understanding of this term will provide our starting point: an author will be the person who does so in the form of words, notation, lines and shapes, in other words, the person who gives material shape or expression to the work. This much is beyond dispute, and may be thought not to require, and indeed does not receive, express statutory definition. For example, the Australian Copyright Act 1968 contains only one provision concerning authorship, providing that, in the case of a photograph, an author is the person who took the photograph, ie the person responsible for the image being recorded by the camera.[50] Section 9(1) of the UK Copyright, Designs and Patents Act 1988 is more embracing (and perhaps more question-begging): 'author', in relation to a 'work' means the 'person who creates it'.

But it was also clear, both before and after 1911, that other kinds of acts would suffice for the purposes of literary authorship: translation (changing the form of expression from one language into another);[51] adaptations and other alterations (reworking or transforming the expression of a work);[52] abridgement (bringing a larger work within a smaller compass);[53] editing and annotation (providing a more coherent form of a pre-existing work, with additions);[54] recording, transcribing, and correcting;[55] anthologies

[50] Copyright Act 1968 s 10(1).

[51] *Byrne v Statist Co* [1914] 1 KB 622; *Pollock v JC Williamson Ltd* [1923] VLR 225. For cases recognising the existence of copyright in translations prior to the Copyright Act 1911 (UK), see *Burnett v Chetwood* (1720) 2 Mer 441, 35 ER 1008, 1009; *Murray v Bogue* (1852) 1 Drewry 353, 61 ER 487; *Parry v Moring & Gollancz* [1901–04] MacG Cop Cas 49 (Ch D); *Evans v Tout* [1905–10] MacG Cop Cas 213 (Ch D).

[52] See, for example, *Tree v Bowkett* (1896) 74 LT 77.

[53] Some of the earliest cases under the Statute of Anne concerned abridgements see, for example, *Curia Cancellaria* (1773) Lofft 775; 98 ER 913 (Apsley LC). See also *Dodsley v Kinnersley* (1761) Amb 403, 27 ER 270; *Bell v Walker & Debrett* (1785) 1 Bro CC 451, 28 ER 1235; *Gyles v Wilcox* (1749) 2 Ack 141, 26 ER 489. For the position post-1911, see *MacMillan v Cooper* (1924) 93 LJ PC 113, 116.

[54] See, for example, *Tree v Bowkett* (1896) 74 LT 77; *Blackie & Sons Ltd v Lothian Book Publishing Co* (1921) 29 CLR 396 (Starke J); *Moffat & Paige v Gill* (1901) 84 LT 452 (Ch D); *Warwick Film Productions Ltd v Eisinger* [1967] Ch 367.

[55] *Walter v Lane* [1900] AC 539; *Express Newspapers plc v News (UK) Ltd* [1990] 1 WLR 1320 (Ch D); *Sawkins v Hyperion Records Ltd* [2005] 1 WLR 3281.

(selecting literary or artistic materials already in existence, but presenting them in a particular order or thematic arrangement);[56] and, most controversially perhaps, compilations of factual information (timetables, trade catalogues, directories).[57] The other kinds of authorial activities encompassed by the post-1911 laws could be described in the same way with reference to the particular kind of work involved:

1. In the case of artistic works, the lines, shapes, colours, shading, etc adopted by the visual artist to depict an object or concept.
2. In the case of a musical work, the sounds and their ordering or presentation.
3. In the case of a dramatic work, its 'representational' or 'performance' aspects, although there will obviously be an overlap with 'literary works' inasmuch as such works can also be appreciated in much the same way by passive reading and comprehension.

The Qualitative Standard Required

If inventiveness or novelty per se are not required (apart from a general requirement that there should be no copying), neither is any particular aesthetic standard or level of execution: the novels of the late Barbara Cartland have parity with the more inaccessible works of a Nobel Prize winner, such as Orhan Pamuk or Patrick White. This also appears to have been clearly understood in the context of the Berne Convention where, at the time of the Berlin revision conference of 1908, an amendment to provide that the merit or purpose of a work were to be disregarded was rejected on the basis that it might provide uncertainty as to what the previous position had been, ie that the amendment was necessary to change a previous conventional requirement in this regard.[58]

Nonetheless, cases in British common law jurisdictions are replete with references to variously described minimum requirements for the purposes of original authorship, including such terms as 'skill', 'judgment', 'taste', 'time', 'labour' and 'expenditure/money/resources'. The statements vary

[56] *Macmillan v Suresh Chunder Der* (1890) 17 ILR (Calc Series) 951; *Cambridge University Press v University Tutorial Press* (1928) 75 RPC 335 (Ch D);

[57] See, for example, *Hotten v Arthur* (1863) 11 WR 934 (Ch D); *Grace v Newman* (1875) 19 LR Eq Cas 623; *Cable v Marks* (1882) 52 LJ Ch 107; *Maple & Co v Junior Army & Navy Stores* (1882) 21 Ch D 368 (CA). See also *Comyns v Hyde* (1894) 72 LT 250 (Ch D); *Davies v Benjamin* [1906] 2 Ch 491; *Lawrence v Bushnell* (1908) 35 Ind LR Calc 463 (Ind); *Collins v Cater, Stofel & Fortt* (1898) 78 LT 613 (Ch D); *Harpers Ltd v Barry, Henry & Co Ltd* (1892) 20 Sess Cas (4th Ser) 133 (Sc); *Masson Seeley & Co Ltd v Embosotype Manufacturing Co* (1924) 41 RPC 160 (Ch D); *Purefoy Engineering Co Ltd v Sykes, Boxall & Co Ltd* (1955) 72 RPC 89 (CA); *A-One Accessory Imports Pty Ltd v Off Road Imports Pty Ltd [No 2]* (1996) 34 IPR 306 (Fed Ct of Aust).

[58] Ricketson and Ginsburg, *International Copyright* (n 32) 403–404.

from case to case,[59] but a rough division can be made between those terms which imply some kind of intellectual or mental component, such as 'skill', 'judgment' and 'taste', and those terms with a physical or non-mental connotation to them, such as 'time', 'labour' and 'expenditure'. It is also never entirely clear from the cases whether these qualities are referred to conjunctively or disjunctively, ie whether skill and judgment alone would be enough, or whether these needed to be combined with, or supported by, the application of time, labour and expenditure, or even whether time, labour and expenditure on their own might suffice. At the analytical level, however, the following also seems correct: the application of skill and judgment (including any element of 'taste' or 'ingenuity') will always imply the presence of some kind of mental or intellectual activity,[60] whereas it is possible that time, labour and expenditure may have none of this, other than simple mechanical and repetitive application ('sweat of the brow') or the deployment of money and resources (including provision of infrastructure).

The relative mix of these components will usually not be an issue: in the great bulk of instances there will be sufficient of the skill and judgment component present in the expression of a work for it to be unnecessary to inquire closely into how much, if any, of the time, labour and expenditure component is also represented. For example, decisions as to what words or visual elements to use, and likewise the selection and ordering of material, will always entail some kind of intellectual activity—the application of skill and judgment, even if of a fairly hackneyed kind. Time, labour and effort will almost always be involved as well, although to sharply differing

[59] Some random examples: 'skill and expenditure' (Lord Halsbury LC in *Walter v Lane* [1900] AC 539, 547); 'skill and expenditure' (Lord Brampton in *Walter v Lane* [1900] AC 539, 556); 'labour and therefore ... expense' (Joyce J in *H Blacklock & Co v A Arthur Pearson Ltd* [1915] 2 Ch 376, 380); 'considerable time, skill, labour and expense' (Astbury J in *British Broadcasting Corporation v Wireless League Publishing Co* [1926] Ch 433, 442); 'What is the precise amount of the *knowledge, labour, judgment or literary skill or taste* which the author of any book or other compilation must bestow upon its composition in order to acquire copyright in it within the meaning of the Copyright Act of 1911 cannot be defined in precise terms. In every case it must depend largely on the special facts of that case, and must in each case be very much a question of degree.' (Lord Atkinson in *Macmillan & Co Ltd v K & J Cooper* LR 51 Ind App 109, 125; 93 LJ (PC) 113, 121); 'judgment or skill' (*GA Cramp & Sons Ltd v Frank Smythson Ltd* [1944] AC 329, 336, and 'labour and judgment', per Lord Macmillan in the same case at 338); '... some labour, skill, judgment or ingenuity has been brought to bear upon the compilation' (Upjohn J in *Football League Ltd v Littlewoods Pools Ltd* [1959] Ch 637, 650); 'skill, judgment and labour' (Lord Reid in *Ladbroke (Football) Ltd v William Hill (Football) Ltd* [1964] 1 WLR 273, 278, Lord Evershed to the same effect at 281, 'skill and labour' per Lord Hodson at 287, 'time, skill and experience' and 'substantial degree of skill, industry or experience employed by him [the author]' per Lord Devlin at 289, and 'labour or skill or ingenuity or expense' per Lord Pearce at 292); 'effort, skill and time' (Mummery LJ in *Sawkins v Hyperion* [2005] 1WLR 3280, 3285 [15].

[60] See further *CCH Canadian Ltd v Law Society of Upper Canada* [2004] SCC 13, (2004) 236 DLR (4th) 395 [16] (MacLachlin CJ for the Supreme Court of Canada on the meaning of 'skill' and 'judgment').

degrees—even at the level of ordinary written expression, there are those who can write relatively quickly and effectively, for example, journalists and publicists, and those who struggle to write a line or two a day of what may become immortal prose. As with the concepts of inherent and acquired distinctiveness in trade mark law, it may be that different kinds of expressions will comprise differing mixtures of these elements, but the overall result will be a work of original authorship. At the same time, the absence of novelty or inventiveness in the ideas or subject of the work should be irrelevant in determining the originality of what is expressed and the form of this expression. But, as with most areas of human life, there are always problems that arise at the margin. In the present context, these occur most sharply in the cases of fact-based or informational works and it is to these we must now turn.

INFORMATIONAL OR FACT-BASED WORKS

The preceding discussion has put facts or data into the same general category as ideas and subjects/objects, but this grouping requires further investigation. Informational or fact-based works have long received explicit statutory protection in common law countries. Thus, the definition of 'literary work' in s 35(1) of the Copyright Act 1911 provided that this term included 'maps, charts, plans, tables and compilations', the last-mentioned term being inserted during the course of passage of the 1911 Act and being intended to ensure that nothing previously protected should be excluded from the coverage of the new Act.[61]

What do we mean, however, by the term 'facts'? These are more directly analogous to the subject of an artistic work—just as the object or scene depicted is 'out there' for the purposes of recording or representing, so too is the objectively ascertainable 'fact', such as the result of a horse race, the name of a street and the identity of the persons living at a particular address, the time at which the tides rise and fall in a particular place, the postage rates for particular kinds of letters and parcels, and so on. These may be recorded in the compiler's own written language, but the overlap between fact and expression may be almost complete—a case of merger, as suggested in *Kenrick & Co v Lawrence & Co*[62] where anything but the most literal protection would enable the compiler to claim the effective right alone to reproduce and disseminate those facts. Thus, in *Victoria Park*

[61] See the discussion of the parliamentary debates accompanying this amendment (moved by Lord Gorell himself) in *Desktop v Telstra* (n 7) 24 (Lindgren J) and 88–89 (Sackville J). Lord Gorell gave Bradshaw, the railway timetable guide, as an instance of a compilation that would now be included under the Act: Hansard HL vol 10 col 211 (15 November 1911).

[62] *Kenrick & Co v Lawrence & Co* (1890) LR 25 QBD 99.

Racing v Taylor[63] Latham CJ said, in relation to postings of race results on boards at a race track:

> The law of copyright does not operate to give any person an exclusive right to state or to describe particular facts. A person cannot by first announcing that a man fell off a bus or that a particular horse won a race prevent other people from stating those facts.[64]

In relative terms, the skill and judgment involved in the identification and collection of this kind of data may also be slight,[65] when compared, say, to the work of a historical researcher who must make careful judgments as to what to include in his or her final book or article; on the other hand, the time, labour and resources required for this collection activity may be considerable (for example, the funds needed to employ canvassers to collect names and street addresses or to record and tabulate race results). There may be persuasive arguments of policy in favour of protecting such 'industrious collections of facts', but these are not necessarily based on the presence of authorship and originality in any meaningful sense but rather on inchoate notions of unfairness and the desire to prevent reaping without sowing.[66] Whether such efforts should be regarded as sufficient for the purposes of authorship and originality is altogether another question, but, before we go on to consider this more fully, there is another contrasting category of facts that should be noted.

These are facts that are not 'out there', in the sense of awaiting identification and collection, but facts which originate from the compiler him or herself, such as the decision of a trader to include particular items of merchandise in a catalogue at a particular price or the selection made by a television or radio station to broadcast a particular programme at a particular time on a particular day.[67] 'Facts' of this kind are in no way discoverable by third parties until the compiler has actually disclosed them—there is simply no other source. They may well be described as novel or inventive, in that they were both unknown and unknowable prior to this time, and the level of intellectual skill and judgment involved in their development may be of a high order. On the other hand, their form of expression, once arrived at, may be as bald and unadorned as the list of race results in *Victoria Park*. Protection, if it is to be granted, will therefore go beyond matters of expression and, if characterised as 'authorial', will be closer to protection of invention or first creation rather than expression.

[63] *Victoria Park Racing v Taylor* (1937) 58 CLR 439.

[64] Ibid 498.

[65] All that may be required is '... a certain sobriety': see Eve J in *Greyhound Racing Association Ltd v Shallis* [1923–28] MacG Cop Cas 370, 373.

[66] As exemplified in the closing paragraph of Lord Devlin's speech in *Ladbroke v Wm Hill* [1964] 1 WLR 273, 291.

[67] As in *IceTV Pty Ltd & Anor v Nine Network Australia Pty Ltd* [2009] HCA 14; see also *British Broadcasting Corporation v Wireless League* (n 59) 442.

There is yet a further category of facts that should be included in our discussion, namely facts that are contributed by third parties and then received and aggregated by the compiler. These are not facts that are already in existence, in the sense of being 'out there' and available for discovery and collection by the compiler, and, by definition, they do not originate from the mind of the compiler as the result of an exercise of the latter's own skill and judgment. A striking example is provided by the directories of names, addresses and numbers of telephone subscribers that have recently been in issue in Australia and elsewhere.[68] These facts are provided by the subscribers themselves, with the contribution of the collector being simply the verification, aggregation and alphabetical ordering of these details, together with the allocation of a telephone number (a process that can take place in an automated manner).

What does the above analysis suggest so far as the requirements of originality and authorship in the jurisdictions under consideration are concerned? The following propositions seem defensible and find solid, although by no means unanimous, support in the many and diverse authorities dealing with these issues. As will be seen, however, we begin to enter tiger territory in relation to propositions 6 and 7.

1. The collection and bare statement or reporting of facts that are 'out there' is in itself not an act of authorship; something more is required at this stage by way of expression or shaping or presentation of the data collected.
2. In the same way, self-generated facts, however new or inventive, will not be protected, as the focus of such protection would otherwise be the facts themselves, rather than their form of expression: something more again is required here.
3. Likewise, third-party generated facts should be incapable of receiving protection in the hands of their recipients: something more likewise is required here.
4. The 'something more' that will justify protection in each instance will be where the putative author then provides some order or coherence to the facts so collected or generated, through such acts as arrangement, ordering and presentation. It is in this context that references to skill and judgment—the notion of some form of intellectual contribution—begin to make sense. The collected facts lose their individuality and form part of a greater whole that is the result of the expressive contribution of the compiler. This, indeed, is really the basis for the vast majority of cases dealing with trade catalogues and directories, almanacs, timetables, betting

[68] This was the case in *Desktop v Telstra* (n 7), and likewise in *Feist Publications v Rural Telephone Service Co* (n 5) and *Tele-Direct (Publications) Inc v American Business Information Inc* (1997) 154 DLR (4th) 328.

coupons and other kind of factual compilations: the collected facts form a protectable expression by virtue of their collocation and relationship to each other. While it is clear that the requisite level of compilatory skill has generally been set at a low level by common law courts, some must nonetheless be present. For example, simple chronological and alphabetical ordering may be insufficient, on the basis that it is so commonplace and 'predictable'.[69]

5. Perhaps the most striking instances where common law courts have emphasised the need for a minimal application of skill and judgment has been where selection has been the sole contribution of the compiler—and no other arrangement or presentation of the data or material is involved. The case of anthologies is an obvious one which finds direct recognition in the Berne Convention,[70] but the House of Lords' decision in *Cramp v Smythson*[71] stands as a landmark here, where the 'commonplace selection of gobbets of information' (the choice of standard tables to go in the front of an annual diary) was insufficient to confer originality.
6. So far, so good, but the above analysis excludes from consideration what might be called preliminary or preparatory work done at the 'pre-expression' stage. This is a matter requiring some closer investigation. As noted above, such work may be of two broad kinds: collection (including receipt from third parties) and self-generation of data. Both involve differing kinds of inputs. Thus, collection alone may require substantial investments of time, labour and resources, but involve no real element of skill and judgment apart from mechanical repetition, and no 'expression' apart from simple aggregation, particularly where it is directed at being comprehensive or 'whole of universe' within its given sphere. On the view adopted above, any protection given at this stage will therefore be against unfair takings by third parties who have not gone through the same arduous steps of collection and is not linked in any meaningful sense to the concepts of authorship and originality outlined above. Self-generation of data, on the other hand, may suffer from the opposite vice, as this will often involve high levels of skill and judgment, even ingenuity, but if protection is to be allowed in such cases, it will go beyond what we have thus far described as matters of expression, and will involve the protection of facts or ideas alone. Protection in either of these categories

[69] Instances, old and new, are to be found in *Leslie v Young & Sons* [1894] AC 335 (mere collection and publication of railway timetables obtained from publicly accessible sources); *Greyhound Racing Association Ltd v Shallis* [1923–28] MacG Cop Cas 370, 373 (list of greyhounds in a race, requiring no literary skill or ability to collect other than a 'certain degree of sobriety', per Eve J); and *Data Access Corporation v Powerflex Services Pty Ltd* (1999) 202 CLR 1, 45 IPR 353 [93]–[95] (list of reserved words for use as commands in a computer system).

[70] Berne Convention (Paris Act) Art 2(5).

[71] *Cramp v Smythson* [1944] AC 329.

of case, if granted, will therefore will be on a different basis than that usually accorded to original literary and artistic works, something that might better be described as unfair competition or the unfair copying of facts and ideas.

7. It cannot be denied that protection of the kind described in the preceding paragraph has been given in several common law jurisdictions, notably in the UK and Australia, but this has usually occurred in an indirect fashion, with courts saying that it is not possible to partition off such preliminary work so long as it is ultimately directed towards the production of a final literary or artistic work.[72] Such preliminary work, whether purely mechanical and 'sweat of the brow' or highly intellectual and creative, can then bolster the expressive contributions by way of original authorship that are otherwise present, ie in relation to such matters as selection and arrangement. Such arguments, however, become a mere rhetorical fig leaf in the case of whole of universe compilations lacking even minimal levels of arrangement, selection or ordering. Of this, more below when we come to consider recent Australian case law.

DIFFERING APPROACHES—ADJUSTING THEORY TO REALITY

Conceptual consistency is not always to the fore in common law jurisdictions, where courts will more readily adopt more pragmatic and inductive responses to problem-solving. While the above classification of authorial and non-authorial contributions appears both coherent and capable of justification by reference both to principle and previous statute and case law, there are nonetheless divergences to be seen between different common law jurisdictions, particularly in the case of factual compilations.[73]

At one end of the spectrum is the US approach, exemplified in *Feist v Rural Telephone Service Co*,[74] where the Supreme Court found originality to be a constitutional requirement, which, in the case of a factual compilation required a sharp distinction to be drawn between the facts contained

[72] The leading example here is the chronological list of football fixtures in *Football League v Littlewoods Pools* [1969] Ch 637, prepared by one Sutcliffe for the League after 'prolonged and skilled cogitations': see further Upjohn J at 655–56. This approach was approved by the House of Lords in *Ladbroke v Wm Hill* [1964] 1 WLR 273, with the caveat of Lord Devlin that a different result might follow where there had been no intention of producing a list or coupon following the initial preparatory work.

[73] As Bently and Sherman remark, the protection of such productions has only become of legal importance with the advent of electronic databases, as '[i]n the past, the distinction between labour and skill was less momentous (and, indeed, the line drawn between labour and skill was less obvious).': L Bently and B Sherman, *Intellectual Property Law,* 3rd edn (Oxford, OUP, 2009) 95.

[74] *Feist Publications v Rural Telephone Service Co* (n 5).

therein and the presentation of those facts. Original authorship in such a case could only be founded upon acts of expression: selection, arrangement and/or some individualised description of those facts would suffice, so long as this involved a 'minimal degree of creativity'.[75] In the view of the Court, this was not an onerous requirement: it was, indeed, 'extremely low', need not be novel or inventive, and would be readily satisfied in the case of most works, so long as 'some creative spark' was present. Notwithstanding this last caveat, the court's equation of 'originality' with a 'minimum degree of creativity' appears to have brought US law more closely into alignment with the standards applied in civil law countries.[76] In particular, the Court made it clear that the 'sweat of the brow', time and resources expended in the processes of preparation and collection were not to be protected as original works of authorship (overruling here earlier decisions of US courts to this effect), in the absence of some creative contribution to the form of expression of the final work.

By contrast, other common law countries, such as Australia and Canada, have fallen short of enunciating a *Feist*-like standard of minimum creativity, while the UK now appears to have differing standards of originality that may apply as between different categories of works. Furthermore, in each of these countries, just as in the USA pre-*Feist*, courts have at times equated the requirement of originality with sweat of the brow or industrious collection alone. These developments are sketched briefly in the following sections, with most emphasis being given to the tortuous journey that has recently been taken by the Australian courts.

Australia

Up to the end of the last millennium, Australian decisions on originality had generally been in line with those of UK courts, particularly with respect to the relevance of preliminary or pre-expressive work in the case of factual compilations.[77] The issue of 'whole of universe' compilations (White and

[75] Ibid [11], [16].

[76] For example, France where protection is given to 'original works of the mind' reflecting the 'imprint of the author's personality' and the author's 'exercise of creative choice': see A Lucas and P Kamina, R Plaisant, 'France' in P Geller and M Nimmer, *International Copyright Law and Practice*, Vol 1, *(London, LexisNexis) para* 2[1][b][ii]; and Germany, where only works that are 'personal intellectual creations' are protected: A Dietz, 'Germany' in Geller and Nimmer, op cit, Vol 2, para 2[1][b] (German Copyright Act 1965 s 2(2)).

[77] See, for example, *Kalamazoo (Australia) Pty Ltd v Compact Business Systems Pty Ltd* (1985) 5 IPR 213 (Supreme Court, Queensland); *A-One Accessory Imports v Off Road Imports* (n 57); *Autocaps (Australia) Pty Ltd v Pro-Kit Pty Ltd* (1999) 46 IPR 339 (Federal Court). Note, however, a more generous view that the act of tracing would supply the necessary skill for the purposes of originality in the case of drawings was taken in *Interlego AG v Croner Trading Pty Ltd* (1992) 25 IPR 65, 97–98 (Gummow J), as compared with the Privy Council decision in *Interlego AG v Tyco Industries Inc* [1989] AC 217.

Yellow Pages telephone directories and headings books), however, was not directly raised until the *Telstra v Desktop* litigation in 2000.[78] For reasons hard to identify, following a Full Federal Court decision affirming the findings of Finkelstein J at first instance, special leave to appeal to the High Court was refused,[79] leading to the conclusion that Australia had fully endorsed a sweat of the brow, industrious collection approach to the questions of authorship and originality. This decision, however, must now be treated with considerable caution, following the recent High Court decision in *IceTV v Nine Network*, [80] although the kind of compilation involved in that case (a weekly TV programme) was of a qualitatively different kind to the directories in issue in the earlier litigation and subsistence was not directly in contention.

Telstra v Desktop

At the outset, it should be said that the judgments of the full Court (and Finkelstein J at first instance) are notable for their exhaustive and painstaking examination of previous UK and Commonwealth case and statutory law. Their conclusion was that nothing in these prior authorities excluded such compilations from protection as original literary works, even if their principal characteristic was that of collection and authentication of all the names, addresses and telephone numbers of subscribers within a given locality. This was on the basis of (a) the intense application of labour and expense in compiling this information, and (b) the value to subscribers of being in possession of a comprehensive and up to date collection of such data. Critical to this was the view that antecedent work was not to be excluded, although it may be doubted that the kind of antecedent work involved in the creation of the White and Yellow Pages directories had quite the same degree (if any) of intellectual skill and judgment as, say, the working out of wagers and what bets to offer in *Ladbroke v Wm Hill* or the selection of teams for football fixtures in *Football League v Littlewoods Pools*.[81] Furthermore, given their comprehensive character, the element of selection was essentially lacking, while the element of arrangement (alphabetical ordering) was clearly insufficient on its own. Nonetheless, their Honours felt compelled by authority (mostly nineteenth century British, but some more contemporary) to conclude that labour and effort on their own

[78] *Telstra Corporation Ltd v Desktop Marketing Systems Pty Ltd* (2001) 51 IPR 257 (Finkelstein J); (2002) 55 IPR 1 (full Court on appeal).

[79] 20 June 2003: see http://www.austlii.edu.au/au/other/hca/transcripts/2002/M85/1.html.

[80] *IceTV Pty Ltd & Anor v Nine Network Australia Pty Ltd* (2009) 80 IPR 451, [2009] HCA 14. For the decision of the full Federal Court in this case, see *Nine Network Australia Pty Ltd v IceTV Pty Ltd & Anor* (2008) 76 IPR 31.

[81] Or, indeed, in the skilful programming decisions made by the Channel Nine employees in the *IceTV* litigation.

could suffice for the purposes of originality. This was nicely crystallised by Lindgren J as follows:

> Decisively for the present case, there is no principle that the labour and expense of collecting, verifying, recording and assembling (albeit routinely) data to be compiled are irrelevant to, or are incapable of themselves establishing, origination, and therefore originality; on the contrary, the authorities strongly suggest that labour of that kind may do so ...[82]

Detailed analysis of the cases cited by Lindgren J (as well as by Sackville J in his lengthy concurring judgment) might lead to the conclusion that each nonetheless entailed some minute element of intellectual skill and judgment in relation to selection and ordering not present in the case of Telstra's directories,[83] but it seems clear that this would not have been an impediment to their Honours' judgments in any event: neither recoiled from the proposition that the labour, time and infrastructure involved in receipt and collection alone were acts of 'origination' that would suffice for the purposes of protection. Black CJ, in a brief concurring judgment, took a similar view, saying that such cases turned, in general, upon 'a reluctance of the Courts to allow unfair advantage to be taken of the outlays of another in originating a work.'[84] In other words, there was an unfair competition rationale for the decision that gave the terms 'originality' and 'author' an extended meaning in Australian copyright law. However justifiable such an approach might be as a matter of general policy, this could well be seen as an indirect way of achieving an end (protection against unfair competition) that the High Court has blocked in other contexts on several occasions.[85] Indeed, for all their thoroughness, there is an element of ahistoricity about the judgments of the full Court in *Desktop*. The earlier decisions chiefly relied upon were English, pre-1911 and generally of lower courts:[86] it is possible, however, to see a more nuanced and careful approach in appellate decisions of the same period,[87] even including that of the House of Lords

[82] (2002) 55 IPR 1, 43. To similar effect, see the propositions of Sackville J at (2002) 55 IPR 1, 102–103.

[83] This was certainly so in the interesting case cited by both Lindgren and Sackville JJ concerning a collection of accounting forms in *Kalamazoo (Australia) Pty Ltd v Compact Business Systems Ltd* (1985) 5 IPR 213.

[84] Ibid, 7.

[85] See *Victoria Park Racing v Taylor* (n 63) and, in particular, Dixon J at 509; *Moorgate Tobacco Co Ltd v Phillip Morris Ltd (No 2)* (1984) 156 CLR 414, 440–46 (Deane J).

[86] See, for example, *Kelly v Morris* (1866) LR 1 Eq 697; *Morris v Ashbee* (1866) LR 7 Eq 34; *Cate v Devon & Exeter Constitutional Newspaper Co* (1889) 40 Ch D 500; *Walter v Lane* [1899] 2 Ch 7349 (the first instance decision of North J). See also the interesting decision of Malins VC in *Cox v Land & Water Journal Co* (1869) LR 9 Eq 324, which was concerned with lists of masters, huntsmen and whips.

[87] See, for example, *Chilton v Progress Printing & Publishing Co* [1895] 3 Ch 29 (CA; *Leslie v Young & Sons* [1894] AC 335 (HL).

in *Walter v Lane*[88] where several of their Lordships[89] laid considerable emphasis upon the skill and judgment of the *Times* reporters. These earlier lower courts, as one commentator has recently suggested,[90] may even have been invoking a form of protection outside the Copyright Acts, providing injunctive protection against the commission of a kind of 'equitable wrong' of unfair copying of the 'results of the labours undergone by others'.[91] Such cases, therefore, have a tenuous relevance to the interpretation of a statutory originality standard in the twenty-first century. On the other hand, it should not be thought that the full Court proceeded in ignorance of developments that had occurred in other jurisdictions, notably in the USA (with *Feist*), Canada or in Europe (with the Database Directive). Such matters, in fact, were strongly relied upon by the respondent, both at first instance and on appeal, but their relevance was rejected by both courts on the basis of different circumstances and constitutional arrangements in those other jurisdictions, leading to the conclusion that the weight of prior Anglo-Australian authority favoured protection of 'sweat of the brow' compilations and any change here would therefore need to be made by either the legislature or the High Court (as the peak court in the Australian court hierarchy).[92] Given this, it was surprising that the High Court refused special leave to appeal.

Other significant issues were left hanging by the *Desktop* decision, notably the question of who were the actual authors of the Telstra directories. This was not a matter that was before the court at first instance, although it was clearly something that concerned Finkelstein J, the trial judge. There were literally hundreds of Telstra employees who had contributed towards the production of the directories: were these to be treated as authors, or joint authors, for the purposes of copyright subsistence? As Finkelstein J said:

> These are difficult questions for which there are no ready answers. These matters will not be elucidated by this judgment. Although I raised these issues during argument, the case was contested on the apparent assumption that it was either unnecessary for Telstra to establish that a telephone directory has an author, or that those involved in its preparation are joint authors. I will proceed as if these assumptions are correct. But they may not be.[93]

Identification of putative authors is obviously a critical issue to be addressed before the question of the sufficiency of their contributions, individual or joint, for the purposes of originality can be considered. For example, could

[88] *Walter v Lane* [1900] AC 539.

[89] Notably Lord James of Hereford at [1900] AC 554–55 and Lord Brampton at 559.

[90] J Pila, 'Compilation copyright: A matter calling for a "certain sobriety"' (2008) 19 AIPJ 231, 238–39.

[91] See, for example, *Cox v Land & Water Journal Company* (1869) LR 9 Eq 324, 332 (Sir W Malins VC) (although no interlocutory injunction was granted in that case).

[92] (2002) 55 IPR 1 [181]–[217], (Lindgren J, in particular at [217]) and [410]–[430] (Sackville J, in particular at [429]).

[93] (2001) 51 IPR 257 [4].

the concept of joint authorship, although in principle available under Australian law, have had a meaningful application in the case of a telephone directory where the putative authors were numerous, ever-changing and often anonymous and/or unidentifiable? What implications would this have had for the duration of protection in the directories which were produced? And, in the event that a directory changed only by small degrees from year to year, would the process of updating and verifying have constituted a fresh act of joint authorship for each annual directory? Finally, what, indeed, is 'authored' in the case of a directory such as these where the aim is comprehensiveness and no particular acts of selection or arrangement are involved? None of these questions could be addressed by the full Court in *Telstra*, although it is possible that the relevance of industrious collection and aggregation by so many nameless individuals might have assumed a different perspective had this been so.

IceTV v Nine—in general

The decision of the High Court in this case, while significant in many respects, does not take matters much further in formal terms. As noted above, this was a different kind of compilation than the Telstra directories, involving a compilation (of weekly TV programming details) where the preliminary work of 'collection' was of a far higher order and considerable skill and judgment was required to determine which programmes to offer at which times and on which days.[94] The real question before the Court, however, was not one of subsistence, that is, whether the weekly schedule of programmes was an original literary work (this seems to have been accepted), but one of infringement—whether the taking of individual 'slivers' of time and programme information by the respondent who had otherwise built up its programme guides 'independently'[95] constituted a 'substantial part' of the copyright work for the purposes of establishing infringement.[96] Under Australian law (and this is undoubtedly true for other common law jurisdictions), substantiality is to be determined on a qualitative as much as a quantitative basis. 'Quality' here has been interpreted by the Australian courts as a reference to the originality of what has been taken.[97] Accordingly, the principal issue in *IceTV* was

[94] For an excellent analysis and discussion of this case, both at first instance and before the full Court, see D Lindsay, 'Copyright protection of broadcast program schedules: *IceTV* before the High Court' (2008) 19 AIPJ 195.

[95] This was done by one of the respondent's employees sitting in a hotel room watching the applicant's broadcasts for several weeks (a process described as 'torture') and compiling a 'template' of the applicant's programming schedule from his own notes of what had been broadcast and at what times: see (2008) 76 IPR 31, 43.

[96] Copyright Act 1968 (Aust) s 14(1).

[97] *Autodesk Inc v Dyason (No 2)* (1993) 176 CLR 300 [9]–[11] (per Mason CJ), approved in *Data Access Corporation v Powerflex Services Pty Ltd* (1999) 202 CLR 1, [83]–[84] (Gleeson CJ, McHugh, Gummow and Hayne JJ).

whether the undoubted skill and judgment of the programmers involved at the initial stage in devising individual items of program information was relevant in determining whether the items taken directly by the respondent could amount to a substantial part. At first instance, Bennett J held that they did not, taking the view that this was skill and judgment too remote from the production of the ultimate weekly programme as a compilation.[98] On appeal, the full Federal Court[99] held that these 'slivers'[100] of information were relevantly significant, as they gave the real value to the applicant's compilation, namely its currency and accuracy, and the respondent's competing compilation would have been of limited utility without these updates. These 'slivers' were undoubtedly facts of the 'invented kind', unavailable to third parties until such time as they had germinated and grown to maturity in the minds of the skilled TV programmers who then compiled them into a weekly schedule. But was this preliminary work of discovery and identification really relevant to the question of authorship of the ultimate protected compilation? Bennett J saw them as being too anterior and, in their individualised form, too slight for the purpose, even when aggregated, of forming a substantial part of the weekly programme schedule. The full Court, however, saw all this preliminary skill and judgment as being inseparable from the ultimate compilation, finding, in effect, that it infused the whole and gave it its true value, namely currency and accuracy. The respondent, in taking these individual items, while at the same time being able to confirm the accuracy overall of its other entries, was taking a substantial part of this 'true value' and therefore infringing copyright. Once again, this appears to be extending the concepts of authorship and originality by reference to an unfair competition rationale, but, as distinct from *Telstra*, doing this in relation to invented data, rather than to data already 'out there' and ripe for collection. When special leave to appeal to the High Court was granted, the members hearing the special leave application took a different view than their predecessors in the *Telstra* special leave application, indicating their interest in revisiting the whole concept of originality, 'starting at the bottom',[101] and these concerns were further ventilated by the full Court in vigorous interchanges with counsel when the case was heard in October 2008.[102] Unfortunately, the final decision of the Court, delivered on 22 April 2009, does not fulfil this wider promise, for the simple reason that subsistence

[98] (2007) 73 IPR 99, 143–144.

[99] Comprised of the same judges who made up the full Court in *Desktop v Telstra* (n 7): Black CJ, Lindgren and Sackville JJ.

[100] The expression used by Bennett J at first instance: (2007) 73 IPR 99 [190].

[101] http://www.austlii.edu.au/au/other/HCATrans/2008/358.html (26 August 2008). The judges who heard the application were Gummow, Kirby and Kiefel JJ. It should be noted that special leave applications in civil law matters often do not succeed before the Court. The criteria for special leave are set out in s 35A of the Judiciary Act 1903 (Cth), which essentially emphasises the public importance of the question of law involved and whether or not the law is presently unsettled and in need of final appellate determination.

[102] http://www.austlii.edu.au/au/other/HCATrans/2008/358.html (16 and 17 October 2008).

was not in issue. Nonetheless, there is sufficient in the judgments of the court to indicate that the Australian standard of originality should henceforth be higher, and most probably will no longer embrace White and Yellow Pages directories of the *Telstra* kind.[103] There are two joint judgments, each with three judges apiece. The first judgment, delivered by French CJ, Crennan and Kiefel JJ, is perhaps the easier to follow. The second judgment, given by Gummow, Hayne and Heydon JJ, is lengthier, more complex and wider-ranging. Both judgments, however, are to the same effect, namely that IceTV's activities had not infringed the copyright in the weekly programmes.

IceTV—First Judgment

While repeating the mantra that originality for the purposes of subsistence requires that the literary work in question originated with the author and was not merely copied from another work,[104] their Honours found that originality was lacking so far as the question of infringement was concerned. While the programme as a whole might be protected as 'an original collocation of both information and creative material [summaries of the programmes to be offered]',[105] in the case of the individual items of data (the time and title information), the fact that each originated from the authors of the programme (the compilers) did not mean that it was 'necessarily a substantial part of the whole work'.[106] It is clear here that their Honours were focusing on the form of expression of the data items, rather than their underlying value or commercial significance. But the originality of what was taken was quite a different thing, and the expression of the time and title information, in respect of each programme, was not a 'form of expression which requires particular mental effort or exertion', there being 'little, if any, choice in the particular form of expression adopted, as that expression was essentially dictated by the nature of that information.'[107] The same was true of an argument that there had been a taking of the chronological arrangement of the time and title information for various programmes. While selection or arrangement might confer originality in appropriate cases, that was not the case here, where such an arrangement of times was 'obvious and prosaic, and plainly lack[ing] the requisite originality.'[108]

[103] Significantly, in one case involving White and Yellow Pages directories that was then pending before the Federal Court in the Victorian registry, the trial judge (Gordon J) felt impelled to adjourn the proceedings until these questions were resolved by the High Court decision, as the parties in the case had been proceeding on the basis of the correctness of *Telstra v Desktop*: *Telstra Corporation Ltd v Phone Directories Company Pty Ltd*, No VID 276 of 2007, 25 November 2008.

[104] *IceTV Pty Ltd v Nine Network Australia Pty Ltd* (2009) 80 IPR 451, [2009] HCA 14 [33] (French CJ, Crennan and Kiefel JJ).

[105] Ibid [41].

[106] Ibid [38] (French CJ, Crennan and Kiefel JJ).

[107] Ibid [42].

[108] Ibid [43].

The first judgment also considered the relevance of 'skill and labour', albeit by way of obiter dicta in relation to subsistence, noting that rather than being 'antinomies in some sort of mutually exclusive relationship in the mental processes of authors or joint authors', the elements of 'industrious collection' or 'sweat of the brow', on the one hand, and 'creativity', on the other, were 'kindred spirits of a mental process which produces an object, a literary work, a particular form of expression which copyright protects.' Ultimately, however, their Honours felt it unnecessary to say more about this, apart from noting that it may be that 'too much has been made, in the context of subsistence, of the kind of skill and labour which must be expended by an author for a work to be an "original" work.' In this regard, they noted that the requirement of the Act was only that the work 'originates with an author or joint authors from some independent intellectual effort.' [109] Nonetheless, the issue of skill and labour was still relevant in the context of infringement, in determining the originality of what had been taken, and here the first judgment reiterated that the question here was always to be focussed on the nature of the skill and labour taken in relation to the originality of the particular form of expression. In particular, this meant that preparatory work, however skilful or valuable: was to be disregarded:

> Rewarding skill and labour in respect of compilations without any real consideration of the productive effort directed to coming up with a particular form of expression can lead to error. The error is of a kind which might enable copyright law to be employed to achieve anti-competitive behaviour of a sort not contemplated by the balance struck in the Act between the rights of the public and the entitlements of the reading public.[110]

In this regard, the first judgment carefully distinguished prior UK authorities, such as *Littlewoods* and *Ladbroke*, noting that in the first there was a taking not only of essentially the whole of the information but also its arrangement while, in the second, the reproduction was more extensive than in *IceTV* and included aspects of arrangement.

IceTV—Second Judgment

This is to much the same effect, although containing a more detailed analysis of the facts and excursus into the development of Australian copyright law generally. In particular, their Honours emphasised

> … the dangers when applying the Act of adopting the rhetoric of 'appropriation' of 'skill and labour.' A finding that one party has 'appropriated' skill and labour, of itself, is not determinative of the issue of infringement of a copyright work.

[109] Ibid [48].
[110] Ibid [52] (footnotes omitted).

> The Act does not provide for any general doctrine of 'misappropriation' and does not afford protection to skill and labour alone.[111]

This, in turn, drew attention to the question of authorship and what the authors of a work had contributed to the form of expression of that work, rather than the underlying information and skill and labour applied in arriving at that information. In this regard, their Honours noted that identification of the alleged authors of any work was always a critical first inquiry, referring here to the need to treat the decision in *Desktop v Telstra* with 'particular care' as this issue had not been considered in that case.[112] In particular, they cautioned against the errors that could arise when the question of what was a substantial part was assessed by reference to the 'interest protected by the copyright', rather than inquiring whether the part taken was a substantial part of the expression of the work.[113] In focussing on the value of the preparatory work undertaken by the Nine programmers (the 'interest protected by the copyright'), the full Federal Court had therefore 'tipped the balance too far against the interests of digital free to air television in the dissemination by means of new technology of programme listings.'[114] On proper analysis, however, the authorial contributions of the Nine programmers were the 'extremely modest skill and labour' in setting down the programmes already selected at the preparatory stage. Furthermore, so far as the individual items of time and title information were concerned, a real problem of merger between facts and expression arose:

> ... baldly stated matters of fact or intention are inseparable from and co-extensive with their expression. It is difficult to discern the expression of thought in statements of which programmes will be broadcast and when this will occur.[115]

The Australian Position Post-IceTV

What is the status of *Desktop v Telstra* after the decision in *IceTV*? As noted above, the latter was concerned only with originality in the context of infringement, not subsistence, and *Desktop* therefore remains in place until the High Court comes to consider the subsistence issue directly. Nonetheless, both judgments clearly cast doubt on the authority of *Desktop*,[116] as well

[111] Ibid [131].
[112] Ibid [134].
[113] Ibid [155]–[160].
[114] Ibid [161].
[115] Ibid [170].
[116] See, in particular, the remarks of Gummow, Hayne and Heydon JJ at ibid [188] ('It may be that the reasoning in *Desktop Marketing* with respect to compilations is out of line with the understanding of copyright over many years.'). In this regard, it should be noted that the issue of copyright subsistence in White and Yellow Pages directories has now received extended judicial consideration at first instance as a preliminary issue in the Federal Court proceeding referred to in n 103 above: see *Telstra Corporation Ltd v Phone Directories Co Pty Ltd*

as containing some significant pointers as to the kinds of issues that will be relevant to such a case in the future:

1. Preliminary work and effort, however skilled, is to be disregarded if it is not directly concerned with the making of the material expression of the work. Copyright law is not concerned with misappropriation of the commercial value or 'interest' underlying the work.
2. Bare statements of information or fact should not receive protection if their form of expression is dictated by the nature of those facts.
3. Some independent intellectual effort will be required for a compilation of facts to be regarded as 'original', ie some degree of skill and judgment in relation to such matters as selection, ordering and arrangement.
4. The level of skill and judgment required at this stage is a matter of degree: while it must be more than simple alphabetical or numerical ordering, there is nothing in the judgments to suggest that this must display any particular creativity of the kind that appears to be implicit in other national laws or even the 'minimum creativity' required by *Feist*.
5. It will always be critical to identify the author(s) of a work, and, in particular, the extent of their original contribution to the expression of the work. It can be predicted that this will impose an almost insuperable barrier to future claims for protection of such whole of universe databases as the White and Yellow Pages directories, where the work is principally that of collection and verification and is conducted by large teams of employees.

Canada

Canada, unlike Australia, has been subject to other influences in the development of its originality standard. In part, this appears to have been because of the North American Free Trade Agreement and a greater readiness on the part of Canadian courts to consider US case law, but in doctrinal terms it has also been based on a more nuanced and discerning application of the older UK authorities referred to above. Notably, in *Tele-Direct (Publications) Inc v American Business Information, Inc (CA)*,[117] a case that also involved a whole of universe directory, the Canadian Federal Court of Appeal read references in these earlier cases to 'skill, labour and/or

(2010) 263 ALR 617 (8 February 2010). In this decision, Gordon J found, on the authority of *IceTV*, that no copyright subsisted in the directories, referring in particular to the difficulty in identifying any relevant authors of the directories. This decision is presently on appeal to the Full Federal Court and is to be heard in August 2010, but, regardless of the findings of that court, a further appeal to the High Court of Australia must be considered likely.

[117] *Tele-Direct (Publications) Inc v American Business Information, Inc* (1997) 154 DLR (4th) 328.

judgment' conjunctively rather than disjunctively,[118] decisively rejecting a 'sweat of the brow' standard of originality and even suggesting that:

> The use of the word 'copyright' in the English version of the Act has obscured the fact that what the Act fundamentally seeks to protect is '*le droit d'auteur*'. While not defined in the Act, the word 'author' conveys a sense of creativity and ingenuity.[119]

The reference here to '*le droit d'auteur*' may serve as a subtle reminder of the civilian influence underlying the Berne Convention revision of 1908 that led ultimately to the passing of the Copyright Act 1911 (the common legislative source for the UK, Canada and Australia), but the suggestion that a 'sense of creativity and ingenuity' is required for the purposes of originality may have gone too far, and, in any event, now appears to have been superseded by the later decision of the Supreme Court of Canada in *CCH Canadian Ltd v Law Society of Upper Canada*.[120] In this case, the Court opted for a standard of originality falling somewhere between that of 'sweat of the brow' and a higher level that would require some element of creativity of the *Feist* kind. The key requirement for the Court (per McLachlin CJ) was whether the work was the result of the application of skill and judgment by the author, not whether it was 'creative':

> ... an 'original' work under the *Copyright Act* is one that originates from an author and is not copied from another work. That alone, however, is not sufficient to find that something is original. In addition, an original work must be the product of an author's exercise of skill and judgment. The exercise of skill and judgment required to produce the work must not be so trivial that it could be characterized as a purely mechanical exercise. While creative works will by definition be 'original' and covered by copyright, creativity is not required to make a work 'original'.[121]

McLachlin CJ also supplied the following useful descriptions of the terms 'skill' and 'judgment':

> By skill, I mean the use of one's knowledge, developed aptitude or practised ability in producing the work. By judgment, I mean the use of one's capacity for discernment or ability to form an opinion or evaluation by comparing different possible options in producing the work.[122]

In the instant case, this led to the conclusion that the headnote, case summary, topical index and compilation of reported judicial decisions were all original works, but that there was insufficient skill and judgment present in the 'trivial' changes and additions made in the publisher's edited version of a judgment for this to warrant protection.[123]

[118] For earlier 'sweat of the brow' cases in Canada, see the cases cited in n 21 of T Scassa, '"Original Facts" Skill, Judgment, and the Public Domain' (2006) 51 *McGill Law Journal* 3, 9.

[119] (1997) 154 DLR (4th) 328 (Décary J).

[120] *CCH Canadian Ltd v Law Society of Upper Canada* [2004] 1 SCR 339, 2004 SCC 13.

[121] Ibid [25].

[122] Ibid [16].

[123] Ibid [35].

Hence, it seems that Canadian courts have been able to enunciate a clear originality standard, albeit not one without its critics.[124] Several questions remain unsettled here:

1. If 'sweat of the brow' or mere mechanical operations are to be filtered out from matters of skill and judgment, where exactly is this dividing line to be drawn? What qualitative standard is to be applied here: is it, in substance, any different from the *Feist* minimum creativity criterion?
2. Did the Court actually recognise two levels of authorship for the purposes of originality in Canadian law: informational works, on the one hand, and 'creative works' on the other, with creativity, however defined, being equated to 'skill and judgment' for the purposes of protection, but with no other indication as to what more, if anything (or less), that 'creativity' requires?[125]

United Kingdom

While the UK Copyright Act 1911 and the previous UK law may have provided a common starting point for both Australia and Canada, UK models no longer provide unambiguous guidance on the issue of originality. This is because UK law has now become enmeshed with European Community law, notably through the various copyright harmonisation directives. It is therefore now possible to discern several different standards of originality in the UK: 'traditional' British originality, and European originality. In the words of two distinguished commentators, the first of these can be described, in terms familiar to both Australian and Canadian courts, as 'labour, skill and judgment',[126] although there are diverging decisions as to whether these requirements are cumulative or disjunctive, with some suggesting that industrious collection alone may suffice, [127] that pre-expressive contributions of skill and judgment are to be included,[128] and even that the standard of originality may differ according to the kind of work in question.[129]

On the other hand, 'European' originality is now embodied directly in UK law in the case of databases, which are only to be protected as original literary works 'if, and only if, by reason of the selection or arrangement

[124] See, for example, T Scassa, 'Recalibrating Copyright Law?: A Comment on the Supreme Court of Canada's Decision in *CCH Canadian Ltd et al v Law Society of Upper Canada*' *Canadian Journal of Law and Technology* 89; T Scassa, 'Original Facts' (n 118) 3; WL Hayhurst, 'The Canadian Supreme Court of Copyright: *CCH Canadian Ltd v Law Society of Upper Canada*' (2004) *Canadian Business Law Journal* 134.

[125] See further T Scassa, 'Original Facts' (n 118) 3.

[126] Bently and Sherman, *Intellectual Property Law* (n 73) 97.

[127] See, for example, *Waterlow Publishers Ltd v Rose* (1989) 17 IPR 493. To similar effect, see K Garnett, G Davies and G Harbottle, *Copinger and Skone James on Copyright*, 15th edn (London, Sweet & Maxwell, 2005) 132.

[128] As in *Ladbroke v Wm Hill* [1964] 1 WLR 273.

[129] *Interlego v Tyco Industries* (n 77) 262–63 (Lord Oliver).

of the contents of the database the database constitutes the author's own intellectual creation.'[130] The reference here to selection or arrangement—authorial acts directed specifically to the shaping and forming of a factual work such as a database—indicate that pre-expressive contributions, such as collection, aggregation and verification are not relevant in the assessment of originality for databases, although they might well continue to be so in the case of literary works that are not databases, such as tables or compilations (these are now listed separately within the definition of 'literary work').[131] However, the reference here to the author's 'own intellectual creation', while clearly resonant of European standards of originality, has a curious ambiguity in relation to non-database works under UK law. Thus, 'intellectual creation' was specified as a criterion for subsistence of copyright in computer programs in the EC Computer Software Directive of 1991,[132] but no change to reflect this was made in UK law when the Directive was implemented, presumably on the basis that such a requirement applied under UK law in any event.[133] The inference from this might be that 'intellectual creation' was already synonymous with originality of the traditional kind under UK law, but this would then arguably include preparatory efforts which would be inconsistent with the higher standard that 'intellectual creation' under the Software Directive might have been thought to embody and which are specifically excluded under the Database Directive.[134] Further complications arise in the case of photographs under the Duration Directive[135] where there is a distinction drawn between 'original' and 'non-original' photographs, but this does not seem to be reflected in current UK law.[136]

It will therefore be seen that UK law now provides only uncertain guidance to other common law countries such as Australia and Canada on issues of originality, although clearly older UK decisions will continue to be regarded as relevant by the courts of those countries. At the same time, it should be remembered that the UK, in consequence of the Database Directive also accords a limited *sui generis* protection for non-original databases, where the object of the protection is the 'substantial investment in either the obtaining, verification or presentation of the contents' of the

[130] Copyright, Designs and Patents Act 1988 (UK) s 3A(2). This reflects the language of the EC Directive on Databases: Directive 96/9/EC. See further M Davison, *The Legal Protection of Databases* (Cambridge, CUP, Intellectual Property Series, 2003).

[131] Copyright, Designs and Patents Act 1988 (UK), s 3(1). See further *Copinger and Skone James* (n 127) 133.

[132] 91/250/EEC.

[133] *Copinger and Skone James* (n 127) 133.

[134] See further E Derclaye, 'Do sections 3 and 3A of the CPDA violate the Database Directive?' [2002] *European Intellectual Property Review* 466.

[135] Directive 2006/116/EC (12 December 2006).

[136] See further the discussion in Bently and Sherman, *Intellectual Property Law* (n 73) 109–11.

database.[137] Rightly or wrongly, this is a response to the claims of those database producers, whose claims under copyright law have been rejected by the highest US and Canadian courts, and who will probably face the same fate now in Australia, following the *IceTV* case.

The international conventions

As noted above, the Berne Convention embodies, albeit indirectly, an originality standard, and this clearly had a terminological influence on the drafting of the 1911 Act. On the other hand, the Berlin Act of Berne wisely left the interpretation of this requirement to national laws. Does this continue to be the case, in the light of a specific provision dealing with compilations that was inserted into the Brussels Act of Berne in 1948?[138] This now appears in Article 2(5) of the Paris Act, which provides that 'collections of literary or artistic works, such as encyclopaedias and anthologies which, by reason of the selection and arrangement of their contents, constitute intellectual creations shall be protected as such …'.

While the words 'as such' may suggest that this is a category of subject matter to be protected separately from the broader genus of literary and artistic works that are protected under the other provisions of Article 2, there is nothing in the Convention records to support such an interpretation.[139] Accordingly, the better reading of Article 2(5) is that such collections are to be protected as literary and artistic works on the basis that all such productions will share the common characteristic of being 'intellectual creations,' but that it was only 'thought necessary to make this explicit in the case of collections, because the authorship inherent in the collection, as opposed to that in the works collected, may not be as readily discernible.'[140] The same interpretation was suggested above with respect to the use of the term 'original work' in Article 2(2) in the case of derivative works such as translations and other adaptations. In other words, both 'originality' and 'intellectual creation' are correlatives under the Convention, with one connoting the other, and are likewise implicit requirements for all literary and

[137] See the Copyright and Rights in Databases Regulations 1997 (1997/3032) reg 13(1). See also Database Directive Art 1(1) and see further Bently and Sherman, *Intellectual Property Law* (n 73) 310ff; *Copinger and Skone James* (n 127) ch 18; Laddie, Prescott and Vitoria, *The Modern Law of Copyright*, 3rd edn (London, Butterworths, 2000) ch 30.

[138] It was Art 2(3) in this text. Prior to this, 'collections of different works' were included as a category of derivative works under Art 2(2) of the Berlin Act.

[139] See further the report of Marcel Plaisant at the Brussels Revision Conference: *Records of the Conference, convened in Brussels June 5 to 26, 1948*, 257–58: English version available at www.oup.com/uk/booksites/content/9780/98259446/1555028.

[140] Ricketson and Ginsburg, *International Copyright* (n 32) 488.

artistic productions that are to be protected under Article 2(1).[141] While no direct reference is made in the Berne text to the idea/expression dichotomy, the implication from Article 2(1) must be that it is only the form of expression of a work that is to be protected, namely 'every production in the literary, scientific and artistic domain, whatever may be the mode or form of its expression …'. This is also reflected in the 'news of the day' and 'mere items of press information' exception in Article 2(8).[142]

Having said all this, the term 'intellectual creation' is just as open-ended and non-prescriptive as the term 'original work', particularly when viewed in the particular context of Article 2(5) which relates this specifically to the acts of selection and arrangement. No particular standard or level of intellectual creation is indicated here, which leaves it open to member states to opt for a 'minimum spark of creativity' (as in the USA) or for a more prosaic requirement of intellectual skill and judgment (as in Canada and the UK and now, presumably, Australia). Both standards can be readily accommodated within the Berne framework, although this would not extend to the industrious work of collection and aggregation embodied in the *Telstra* directories or the extensive and skilful preparatory work of the compilers in *IceTV.*[143] On the other hand, nothing in Berne prohibits countries extending protection to these kinds of contributions if they so desire, although this may raise definitional issues as to the scope of their obligation to accord national treatment under Article 5(1).[144]

CONCLUSIONS

The present chapter has examined the shifting interpretations of 'authorship' and 'originality' that have been adopted by various common law jurisdictions over the past century or so. A shared starting point for each, other than the USA, has been the Copyright Act 1911 and the pre-1911 UK law, and it has been argued that there is a constant, but not always consistent, thread of authority to be seen here that has favoured the confinement of originality to expressive acts of authorship that comprise some element of skill and judgment, although the need for creativity in the sense of invention or aesthetic or artistic achievement has usually been denied. It has been suggested that,

[141] It will be noted that Art 5 of the WCT extends this protection beyond just collections of literary and artistic works to 'compilations of data or other material, in any form …'.

[142] Note, however, that the dichotomy is now expressly contained in Art 9(2) of the TRIPs Agreement and in Art 2 of the WCT.

[143] For an argument that something more by way of intellectual contribution is still required by Berne, see D Gervais, 'The compatibility of the skill and labour originality standard with the Berne Convention and the TRIPs Agreement' [2004] 26(2) EIPR 75–80.

[144] See further D Vaver, 'The National Treatment Requirements of the Berne and Universal Copyright Conventions: Part One' (1986) 17 *International Review of Industrial Property and Copyright Law* 577; 'Part Two' (1986) 17 IIC 715.

conceptually, this has the advantages both of logic and coherence. It also provides a workable way of achieving a balance between the competing objectives of copyright protection referred to at the start of the chapter.

It has been seen, however, that this balance has been threatened in some instances where courts, such as those in Australia until recently, have extended the concepts of originality and authorship by taking account of preliminary contributions, whether simply those of industrious collection and aggregation (as in *Telstra)* or highly skilled selection and judgment (as in the intermediate appellate decision in *IceTV*), and treating these as primary determinants of original authorship. In doing so, these courts, in effect, have transmuted the requirement of original authorship into a form of protection against unfair copying. However, it now seems that this position has been wound back following the High Court's decision in *IceTV*, with the consequence that the position in Australia and Canada now appears to be broadly similar, with the UK remaining somewhat less clear.

While none of these national standards is inconsistent with the international framework provided by the Berne Convention, a final question for consideration is whether there is any real utility nowadays in asking whether there is a 'common law' standard of originality, by contrast with any other, and presumably higher, standard, that is adopted in other legal systems, for example, as in civil law countries? At one time, given the shared legislative starting point for Australia, Canada and the UK, such an inquiry may well have been fruitful: the Copyright Act 1911, for a period, applied across a large part of the globe and a uniform approach to its application would clearly have been desirable, particularly with the benefit of a common appellate tribunal provided by the Privy Council. But times and circumstances have changed dramatically since 1911, and there is no need now for an Australian court (or any other Commonwealth court) to have regard, in terms of precedential authority, to what has happened, or is happening, in the UK (or Canada or the USA, for that matter) or to do so to the exclusion of any guidance that might be provided by other non-common law systems. Given the centrality of the concepts of authorship and originality in all national copyright laws, as well as under the Berne Convention, the question now is simply how these requirements are to be interpreted and applied in light of the objects of sound copyright policy. No primacy attaches any longer to the laws of any one country or any one kind of legal system or tradition, and the inquiries to be made in each remain the same, namely what are the relevant acts of authorship that give rise to a particular form of protected expression, and what qualitative standard is to be applied? If, following these inquiries, gaps in protection arise, *sui generis* forms of protection, as in the EC, may provide an answer; a more general right of action outside copyright in respect of unfair copying may be another. Protection of all forms of preliminary skill and effort as original works of authorship, however, goes too far.

12

Finding Originality in Recreative Copyright works

BURTON ONG

INTRODUCTION

COPYRIGHT REGIMES IN all common law jurisdictions demonstrate two striking features. Firstly, copyright protects a remarkably diverse range of subject matter. The realm of copyrightable subject matter has expanded over the years in tandem with advances in technology and the new forms of human enterprise that have emerged from such developments. Thus copyright has extended its reach beyond the realm of 'authorial' works (literary, dramatic, musical and artistic works) to encompass the products of 'entrepreneurial' investment as well, including sound recordings, cinematographic films, broadcasts and published editions of printed materials. Even within the realm of 'authorial' works, the various categories of copyright works have had to accommodate new types of subject matter that have emerged over the years—'literary' works, for example, now include computer software and data compilations, while avant-garde performances and art forms might qualify as 'dramatic', 'musical' or 'artistic works'. Secondly, despite the sheer variety of the types of works that have found their way into the copyright system, there is just a single qualifying criterion for copyright subsistence in these works: they must meet the legal standard of 'originality'.[1]

The 'originality' requirement, as the legal criterion for copyrightability, is not a difficult threshold to meet where most works are concerned. Originality simply requires 'that the work must *not be copied* from another

[1] s 1(1)(a) of the UK Copyright, Designs and Patents Act 1988 ('Copyright is a property right which subsists in ... original literary, dramatic, musical or artistic works'); 17 USC § 102 ('Copyright protection subsists, in accordance with this title, in original works of authorship'); s 32 of the Australian Copyright Act 1968 ('copyright subsists in an original literary, dramatic, musical of artistic work').

work—that it should *originate* from the author.'[2] Greater challenges may arise when the concept is applied to derivative works, which necessarily involve acts of copying from antecedent raw materials, but not where the copying is limited to ideas or information.[3] There is, however, one category of works where the co-existence between 'originality' and 'copying' has created some difficulty for the courts, with different common law jurisdictions having developed different approaches towards evaluating the copyrightability of such works. These are cases where the author is essentially a very sophisticated copyist who has set out to replicate, as perfectly as possible, the entire expressive content of an antecedent work. Can such an extreme form of 'copying' give rise to an 'original' copyright-protected work?

The discussion below will outline various examples of recreative works that attract these difficulties with the concept of originality. This will be followed by an overview of how the originality requirement has been interpreted and applied in the context of such cases by the common law copyright regimes on both sides of the Atlantic. The thesis offered here is that differences between the approaches adopted by jurisdictions towards the originality criterion can be reconciled if the following propositions are fully factored into the analysis: (i) that the perfectly executed recreative work that is identical to the antecedent work it was copied from should always be clearly distinguished from the antecedent work over which no rights have been asserted; and that (ii) when evaluating the originality of such works, the focus should always lie in the *process* by which they were made, rather than by the final *output* that is produced by such recreative endeavours.

DERIVATIVE WORKS WHICH RECREATE ANTECEDENT LITERARY, MUSICAL AND ARTISTIC WORKS

The Reconstructed Dead Sea Scrolls

The 'MMT'[4] was a unique document written in an unusual form of ancient Hebrew which contained 150 lines of text about a particular Jewish sect and its religious laws. It was one of the many ancient religious manuscripts that comprised the 'Dead Sea Scrolls' which were discovered in the caves of

[2] *University of London Press v University Tutorial Press* [1916] 2 Ch 601, 608–09, per Peterson J (emphasis added). The same sentiments were expressedby the English Court of Appeal in *Sawkins v Hyperion Records* [2005] EWCA Civ 565 [31] (Mummery LJ), where it was noted that '[a] work need only be "original" in the limited sense that the author originated it by his efforts rather than slavishly copying it from the work produced by the efforts of another person'.

[3] Even infringing works that copied from antecedent works might, in the right circumstances, qualify as 'original' works. See *Warwick Film Productions v Eisinger* [1969] 1 Ch 508, 524–25.

[4] The 'Miqsat Ma'ase Ha-Torah', which translates into 'Some Precepts of the Torah'.

the Khirbet Qumran region in the West Bank of the Dead Sea. When these scrolls were first discovered in the late 1940s and early 1950s, a complete copy of the MMT was unavailable. In 1954, countless fragments from six different manuscripts containing the MMT were identified, transcribed and recombined to reconstruct 120 lines of its text by Professors John Strugnell and Elisha Qimron.

Reconstructing the text of the MMT required the professors to arrange hundreds of parchment fragments in a way which they thought would have most accurately represented the complete text when it was first written on these scrolls. Even after the fragments had been assembled, more than half the scroll was missing and the professors had to engage in extensive research into philology and Jewish legal history in order to fill in the missing parts of the text. The professors had to make a number of critical decisions connected to how the scroll fragments ought to be assembled, such as whether they should be assembled lengthwise or widthwise, as well as speculating on what Hebrew letters ought to be read into those parts of the scroll that were missing. These decisions were highly significant to deciphering the meaning of the paragraphs that made up the MMT text. For example, after his extensive research into Jewish religious laws, Professor Qimron arrived at the conclusion that the missing letter in one of the words of the text was the Hebrew letter *ayin*, so that the word in question referred to 'animal hides', rather than the letter *aleph*, as Professor Strugnell had suggested, which would have produced a reconstructed word that meant 'lights'.[5]

The ancient religious scholars who wrote the Hebrew text onto the Dead Sea Scrolls were most certainly authors of original literary works. Could the professors who reconstructed the MMT text claim copyright in the fruits of their labour as 'original' literary works?

The Photo-Reproduction of Public Domain Images from Paintings onto Transparencies

Bridgeman Art Library Ltd made high-quality reproductions of well-known paintings by capturing photographic images of these artworks, many of

[5] For more facts about, and a detailed analysis of, the case (*Elisha Qimron v Hershel Shanks and others* (1993) 69(iii) PM 10 [District Court of Jerusalem], and *Eisenman v Qimron* CA 2790/93, 2811/93, 54(3) PD 817 [Supreme Court of Israel, sitting as the Court of Appeals for Civil Matters], neither of which is available in an official English translation), see David Nimmer, 'Copyright in the Dead Sea Scrolls: Authorship and Originality' 38 *Houston Law Review* 1 where the author systematically challenges the correctness of the decision to recognise Qimron's copyright in the MMT text, arguing (at p 81) 'that sound copyright doctrine should always doom the claim of any scholar to copyright over the reconstruction of an antecedent manuscript'. Nimmer's analysis of the case, using US copyright law principles, is premised on fact that the trial judge (but not the Supreme Court) had decided the case on the basis that US copyright law was the applicable governing law in that case.

which were already a part of the public domain, on transparencies. Making photo-reproductions of these paintings required the exercise of specialist skills and technical judgment in selecting and configuring the right equipment, as well as managing various other technical aspects of the photographic process. The steps in this process include the photographer setting up appropriate lighting for the artwork, computing the exposure, selecting the best film and shutter speed, determining what filters to use, as well as developing the captured image.

These photo-reproductions were maintained in a library of large format colour transparencies and digital files. Bridgeman attached colour correction strips to each transparency 'to ensure that the image captured was a genuine reflection of the original work as it existed in the circumstances in which it was photographed.'[6] Bridgeman sought to produce photographic images which recreated the artistic works found in the antecedent public domain artworks as perfectly as possible. Bridgeman distributed these images as transparencies and digital files on CD-ROMs, making its high-resolution transparencies available to clients who entered into licensing arrangements with it. These clients could then commercially exploit these images by printing them onto posters, postcards, apparel and all manner of museum-gift-shop paraphernalia.

Could Bridgeman assert copyright in these photo-reproduced images to prevent their unauthorised reproduction by third parties on the basis that they were 'original' artistic works?

The Restoration of the Sistine Chapel Fresco Paintings

Michaelangelo painted the walls and ceilings of the Sistine Chapel in the sixteenth century with biblical images widely recognised as some of the most important artworks of the Italian Renaissance. These fresco paintings were damaged by the ravages of time, water, smoke and various chemicals applied by artisans in the course of their restoration efforts during in the seventeenth and eighteenth centuries. Between 1980 and 1999, a total restoration of these frescoes was undertaken with the financial backing of the Nippon Television Network, which provided US$4.2 million in exchange for exclusive reproduction and filming rights over the restored images.

The restoration process sought to alter the darkened and faded appearance of these frescoes, through a series of technically complex restoration procedures, so that they would bear as close a resemblance as possible to what Michaelangelo had created when his paintings were first

[6] *Bridgeman Art Library v Corel Corporation* 25 F Supp 2d 421 (1998) 423–24 *('Bridgeman Art 1')*.The case was subsequently reheard in *Bridgeman Art Library v Corel Corporation* 36 F Supp 2d 191 (1999) *('Bridgeman Art 2')*.

completed. The restoration process involved various acts of removing layers of impurities that had accumulated over time to obscure the underlying painted images, as well as various acts of adding plaster and paint to the walls and ceilings to recreate the full palette of colours and textures which were present before these paintings degraded over time. Cracks, flaking and other structural defects in the walls and ceilings were repaired and, where the physical deterioration resulted in the elimination of parts of the frescoes, fresh paint was applied to match the pigments used by Michaelangelo in those parts of the painting that had remained intact. The skilled efforts of the many professional artisans and craftsmen who participated in this project resulted in paintings that were significantly brighter, with much sharper images and richer colours, compared to the appearance of the frescoes before the restoration process commenced.

Michaelangelo was the indisputable author of an original artistic work in the fresco paintings he created 500 years ago. The copyright question it poses is whether the *restored* fresco paintings or, more precisely, the visual images produced as a result of the restoration efforts funded by NTN, are also 'original' artistic works?

The performing editions of French baroque musical compositions

Michel-Richard de Lalande composed a number of seventeenth- and eighteenth-century *grand motets*—sacred music written during the reign of the French monarchs. Few of Lalande's original manuscripts have survived.

Dr Lionel Sawkins was a musicological scholar and a world authority on Lalande's musical works. In 2001, after spending hundreds of hours making changes and corrections to the existing records of the musical notations of Lalande's works (for a total of 3000 editorial interventions), Dr Sawkins completed modern performing editions of three of Lalande's musical compositions in the form of musical scores containing information in conventional modern musical notation, with indications and directions for performers which affected the sounds they produced while playing their instruments, as well as the combination of sounds heard by listeners hearing the performance. Dr Sawkins had sought 'to reproduce faithfully Lalande's music in the form of an accurate edition close to the composer's original intentions'.[7] This process involved researching into and consulting many different manuscripts and printed source materials of Lalande's music found in various libraries across Europe, selecting the best versions to edit, transcribing the music from the original scores into modern notation and

[7] *Sawkins v Hyperion Records* (n 2) [22] (Mummery LJ). His Lordship went on to find that Dr Sawkins' performing editions were 'original' copyright works, despite the fact that 'Dr Sawkins made his editions of that music with the intention that they should be as close as possible to the Lalande originals' at [32].

interpreting the musical 'shorthands' used by Lalande which were meant to contain instructions for performers of these works.

Various necessary corrections and additions were made to the original scores of Lalande's music in the course of Dr Sawkins' transcription process, including the addition of 'advisory' or courtesy indications such as tempo and ornamentation, the construction of a figured bass line in one work, the insertion of a viola part in the missing passages of another work, and the correction of wrongly recorded notes found in all three works. Dr Sawkins' corrections and additions to the musical notations of Lalande's compositions were meant to improve the playability of these works by enhancing the performers' comprehension of the chords.

Could Dr Sawkins assert copyright in these performance editions as 'original' musical works to prevent third parties from making unauthorised sound recordings of an orchestral performance which used these performance editions Lalande's music?

ORIGINALITY AS THE LEGAL CRITERION FOR COPYRIGHTABILITY

First Principles: Origination and Independent Creation

Originality requires the author of the work in question to establish that the work *originated* from him.[8] More precisely, he must show that the authorial expression found in the work, rather than just the ideas or facts expressed therein, originates from him. It would, however, be a mistake to simply equate the originality criterion with a requirement that the work is 'not copied' from elsewhere. Doing so would misleadingly reduce 'originality' into an unworkable negative criterion that could not sensibly be applied to a wide range of cases in which some form or degree of copying was involved in the production of a copyright work. For example, portrait painters and courtroom sketch artists who produce true-to-life artistic works which replicate the facial features of their subjects must be said to have produced 'original' copyright works, notwithstanding that they were made by copying the physical attributes and appearance of these subjects. The same conclusion should be reached when someone minutes a meeting by making a written record of the verbal exchanges between his colleagues, when a landscape photographer takes a high-resolution panoramic photograph of

[8] See n 2 above and accompanying text. A similar emphasis on 'independent creation' as a threshold requirement for 'originality' can be found in US copyright law. See *L Batlin & Son v Snyder* 536 F 2d 486 (1976) 490 ('Originality is, however, distinguished from novelty; there must be independent creation, but it need not be invention in the sense of striking uniqueness, ingeniousness, or novelty ... Originality means that the work owes its creation to the author and this in turn means that the work must not consist of actual copying.') and *Durham Industries v Tomy Corp* 630 F 2d 905 (1980), 910.

a scenic location, and when a birdwatcher with perfect-pitch accurately transcribes the bird song that he has heard into musical notes. The literary, artistic and musical works which result from the intellectual enterprises of these individuals should not be viewed as unoriginal simply because acts of copying were integral to their production.

Originality in the common law copyright universe requires neither novelty, inventiveness nor distinctiveness in the expressive contents of a copyright work. The substantive merits of the final output produced by the author are generally irrelevant to the originality determination. A literary or artistic work which is original meets this threshold regardless of its literary or artistic *merit*. Similarly, the amount of time or effort spent in the creation of the work should not, as a matter of general principle, have any direct bearing on the originality of a work for the purposes of copyright protection. What matters is that the work in question is the product of an author's independent intellectual efforts—it must be produced, in the parlance of copyright lawyers, with the requisite 'authorial intent'.

The US courts require a 'minimal' level of creativity to be established, such that simply showing that there has been 'sweat of the brow' expended by the author is not enough.[9] UK copyright law, in contrast, has consciously avoided the language of 'creativity' in its formulations of the originality criterion, perhaps to steer clear of any sort of inquiry into the qualitative facets of the work in question. The UK courts have preferred instead to frame the originality requirement in terms of the 'skill, judgment and labour'[10] exercised by the author in the course of producing the work, while recognising that quantum of effort necessary to cross the 'originality' threshold is ultimately a question of degree that will depend on the facts of each case.[11]

The elasticity of the concept of originality in copyright law is compounded by the fact that the courts have tried to distinguish between different *types* of skill, judgment or labour expended by the author in the process of creating his work—singling out for vilification, in particular, the exercise of skill, judgment and labour in the process of *copying*. While the UK Law Lords have refused to draw sharp distinctions between the preparatory efforts of the author in coming up with the ideas underlying his work, and his efforts in ultimately expressing those ideas in the finished work itself,

[9] In *Batlin v Snyder* (n 8) 490, the court described the 'test of originality [as a] concededly low one' where 'the quatum of originality that is required may be modest indeed'. The US Supreme Court raised the bar for originality slightly, albeit significantly, when Justice O'Connor took the view that originality required not only that the work was 'independently created by the author (as opposed to copied from other works)', but that it possessed 'some minimal degree of creativity' or 'some creative spark'. See *Feist Publications v Rural Telephone Service Company* 111 S.Ct 1282 (1991), 1287 and 1294.

[10] *Ladbroke v William Hill* [1964] 1 WLR 273, 282.

[11] Ibid 279 (Lord Reid), 282 (Lord Evershed) and 285 (Lord Hodson).

when evaluating the originality of literary compilations,[12] doubts have been expressed about whether originality can be found in a case where an artistic work has been produced as a result of copying:

> Take the simplest case of artistic copyright, a painting or photograph. It takes great skill, judgment and labour to produce a good copy by painting or to produce an enlarged photograph from a positive print, but no one would reasonably contend that the copy painting or enlargement was an 'original' artistic work in which the copier is entitled to claim copyright. *Skill, labour or judgment merely in the process of copying cannot confer originality.*[13]

At first glance, one might interpret this judicial statement as indicative of a generally hostile attitude taken by UK copyright law towards any attempt to establish the originality of works that have been copied from antecedent works.[14] However, it should be noted that this statement, from the Privy Council's decision in *Interlego v Tyco*, was made in a very narrow context. The Court's refusal to recognise copyright in the plaintiff's engineering drawings of its interlocking toy bricks, which had been redrawn from earlier design drawings with a number of minor alterations, was premised on a very specific policy concern—that copyright law should not be used as a vehicle to create fresh intellectual property rights over commercial products after the expiry of patent and design rights which had previously subsisted in the same subject matter.[15]

These remarks by the Privy Council should not be taken literally because of the more nuanced positions that have been taken by other UK courts in cases decided both before and after it, involving works that were produced by acts of 'copying'. Two categories of cases of works produced by copying from antecedent works are discernible. In the first category, part or all of

[12] Ibid 287 (Lord Hodson: 'I cannot accept that preparatory work must be excluded in this case so as to draw a line between the effort involved in developing ideas and that minimal effort required in setting those ideas down on paper.') Similar views were shared by Lords Devlin (290) and Pearce (293).

[13] *Interlego v Tyco* [1988] RPC 343 (PC) 371(Lord Oliver, who rejected the proposition that 'that which is an exact and literal reproduction in two dimensional form of an existing two dimensional work becomes an original work simply because the process of copying ... involves the application of skill and labour. There must in addition be some element of *material alteration or embellishment* which suffices to make the totality of the work an original work ... even a relatively small alteration or addition qualitatively may, if material, suffice or convert that which was substantially copied from an earlier work into an original work ... But copying, per se, however much skill or labour may be devoted to the process, cannot make an original work.')(Emphasis added.)

[14] Indeed, such statements were relied upon heavily by Judge Kaplan in the US District Court in the *Bridgeman Art Library* case, where he purported to apply UK copyright law to reach the conclusion that transparencies containing photo-reproductions of paintings were not 'original' artistic works that enjoyed copyright protection. See *Bridgeman Art (1)*, 426 and *Bridgeman Art (2)* 198–99, both above at note 6.

[15] *Interlego v Tyco* (n 13) 365–66. ('By attributing new periods of copyright protection to every minor alteration in the form of a brick which is recorded in such a drawing they seek to obtain, effectively, a perpetual monopoly.').

the antecedent work is copied and incorporated into the derivative work, with the author of the derivative work making whatever adjustments or additions that are necessary for his or her own purposes. In the second category, the author of the derivative work seeks to replicate the antecedent work in its entirety and his acts of copying are carried out with the underlying objective of recreating, as perfectly and accurately as possible, the antecedent work. It is this second category of recreative derivative works that this chapter takes a particular interest in. Given the unique characteristics of the derivative works which fall into this second category, the discussion below will seek to explain why greater care must be exercised when applying the originality criterion to assess the copyrightability of such works. While matters such as the qualitative merits of a work and the nature of the process behind its creation are generally irrelevant where most other copyright works are concerned, these are highly relevant factors that ought to be considered carefully when determining the originality, and hence copyrightability, of recreative derivative works.

Originality from Acts of Copying: Conventional Derivative Works

Derivative works necessarily involve copying from antecedent works, though typically do not involve making wholesale reproductions of the latter. In assessing the originality of derivative works, UK copyright law has traditionally focused on analysing the differences between them. It is not enough to show that the derivative work was made by, or *originated from*, an author. In *Interlego v Tyco*, for example, the Privy Council suggested that a derivative artistic work must contain 'some element of material alteration or embellishment which suffices to make the totality of the work an original work'.[16] This means that the more striking the differences between the derivative work and the antecedent work it has copied from, the more likely the derivative work will satisfy the originality requirement for copyright protection. Almost identical sentiments were expressed by the US courts in *Batlin v Snyder*, a case in which a plastic version of a pre-existing metal coin bank was held to lack the requisite originality for copyright to subsist, because 'to support a copyright there must be some substantial variation, not merely a trivial variation such as might occur in a translation to a different medium'.[17]

[16] See n 13 above.

[17] *L Batlin & Sons v Snyder* (n 8) 491. (The plastic version of the classic 'Uncle Sam' metal coin banks, which were already in the public domain, reduced the proportions of the classic coin bank from a height of 11 inches to approximately 9 inches, with a number of differences in 'minute details' which were 'not perceptible to the casual observer').

A product of independent creation will, generally speaking, satisfy the originality criterion even if its contents are, at the end of the day, identical to those found in another work. Why are derivative works that have been made by copying from antecedent works held to a different, ostensibly higher, standard of originality? At least two distinct, if unarticulated, theoretical perspectives may underlie the stance taken by the courts when they insist upon the presence of a 'material alteration or embellishment' or a 'substantial variation' in the derivative work, as compared to the antecedent work from which copying has taken place. Firstly, from a utilitarian perspective of copyright law such as the one embraced in the United States—where the constitutional mandate for copyright law prescribes that of advancing the public interest by promoting progress in the arts[18]—there would be a stronger justification for recognising the subsistence of a fresh copyright in a derivative work if it was something sufficiently different from pre-existing works already available to the public. Conversely, allowing the originality requirement for derivative works to be satisfied too easily where an earlier derivative work is very similar to the antecedent work might impede subsequent makers of derivative works against whom allegations of copyright infringement may be made even though these subsequent derivative works may not have copied from the earlier derivative work but were, in fact, copied from the original antecedent work itself.[19] In this context, the originality criterion moves closer towards the 'novelty' standard used in patent law, where the author of the derivative work has to show that he has added something that was *not already found* in prior art. Secondly, adopting a desert-based theoretical framework of copyright law, the author of a derivative work only *deserves* to be rewarded with copyright protection if he can show that he has done enough to change the antecedent work he has copied from, such that the derivative work can be properly described as something that is his own.[20]

However, neither of these theoretical justifications for interpreting the originality requirement in this way is entirely satisfactory. It is difficult to see why copyright law should only seek to incentivise the creation of works which are materially different from pre-existing works—there might well be situations where it would clearly be in the public interest for authors to make identical replicas of antecedent works which were, for example,

[18] Art 1, s 8, cl 8 of the Constitution of the United States of America empowers the legislature to 'To promote the Progress of Science and useful Arts, by securing for limited Times to Authors and Inventors the exclusive Right to their respective Writings and Discoveries'.

[19] See *Gracen v Bradford Exchange* 698 F 2d 300, 304–05 ('The requirement of originality is significant chiefly with derivative works, where if interpreted too liberally it would paradoxically inhibit rather than promote the creation of such works by giving the first creator a considerable power to interfere with the creation of subsequent derivative works from the same underlying work').

[20] *Alfred Bell & Co v Catalda Fine Arts Inc* 191 F 2d 99 (1951) 103 ('All that is needed ... is that the "author" contributed something more than a "merely trivial" variation, something recognizably "his own"').

of major cultural significance or extremely inaccessible, or both. Similarly, there might well be cases where the author of a derivative work deserves to be rewarded with copyright by virtue of the enormous intellectual skill, labour and effort he has expended—even if the end result is just not that different from the antecedent work he has copied from.

The US courts have been prepared to permit a deviation from the general proposition that the originality of a derivative work requires the presence of more than just acts of actual copying. US copyright cases have been prepared to acknowledge the originality, for the purposes of copyright subsistence, of a highly accurate replica of an artistic work made by 'an extremely skilled sculptor' who produces a scale reduction of an intricate sculpture with a high degree of 'complexity and exactitude'.[21] In *Alva Studios Inc v Winninger*, also commonly referred to as the 'Hand of God' case involving a scaled-down replica of a sculpture by Rodin, a US court held that a scaled-down but otherwise exact artistic reproduction of a complex sculptural work by Rodin was an original work because it required 'great skill' and 'many hours working directly in front of the original' to create.[22] This exception was considered by Judge Oakes in the US Court of Appeal decision of *Batlin v Snyder* where he concluded that the plastic copy of the classic metal coin bank lacked the requisite originality for copyright subsistence because the 'physical skill' or 'special training' involved in the production of the derivative work was *insufficient* on the facts of the case before him:

> A considerably higher degree of skill is required, *true artistic skill*, to make the reproduction copyrightable ... If there be a point in the copyright law pertaining to reproductions at which *sheer artistic skill and effort* can act as a *substitute* for the *requirement of substantial variation*, it was not reached here ... [the] appellant's plastic bank is neither in the category of exactitude required by *Alva Studios* nor in the category of substantial originality; it falls within what has been suggested by the amicus curiae is a copyright no-man's land.[23]

Recreative Derivative Works

Given that many recreative derivative works are the products of an author's substantial intellectual skill, labour and effort, it is submitted that there is no sound basis on which they should be denied copyright protection. The 'identicality' between the recreative derivative work and the antecedent

[21] *Batlin v Snyder* (n 8) 490–92.

[22] *Alva Studios, Inc v Winninger* 177 F Supp 265 (1959) 267 ('Its copyrighted work embodies and resulted from its skill and originality in producing an accurate scale reproduction of the original. In a work of sculpture, this reduction requires far more than an abridgement of a written classic; great skill and originality is called for when one seeks to produce a scale reduction of a great work with exactitude.')

[23] *Batlin v Snyder* (n 8) 491–92 (emphasis added).

work from which it was copied renders the test for originality discussed above—where the originality criterion depends on the presence of material *differences* between these works—practically unworkable within this category of cases.

Take the example of a carefully photographed image of an artistic work which reproduces all the expressive elements of the photographed subject matter. More than a century ago, in *Graves' Case*, it was held that three photographs of engravings were copyrightable artistic works on the basis that '[a]ll photographs are copies of some object, such as a painting or statue ... that a photograph taken from a picture is an original photograph, in so far that to copy it is an infringement of this statute'.[24] As leading copyright commentators have pointed out, the decision probably remains sound insofar as it is consistent with the position that an original copyright work is produced through the exercise of substantial independent skill, labour, judgment—since 'there may have been special skill or labour in setting up the equipment to get a good photograph, especially with the rather primitive materials available in those days'.[25]

A similar approach was applied in the context of a literary work in *Walter v Lane*, where the House of Lords held that a reporter's published report of a public speech by Lord Rosebery—where the reporter who heard the speech made shorthand notes, transcribed them, corrected, revised and punctuated them to produce a verbatim record of the speech—was an original copyrightable work even though it was made with the intention to faithfully reproduce the 'words and ideas of somebody else'.[26] Lord James emphasised that the reporter was more than 'a mere scribe' and that 'a reporter's art represents more than mere transcribing or writing from dictation ... requiring considerable training, and does not come within the knowledge of ordinary persons'.[27] Other public policy considerations in favour of making copyright protection available to this work included the desirability of preventing the defendants from misappropriating something of value from the plaintiffs,[28] and to encourage and reward those who make such reports of speeches available to the public when they would have otherwise been confined to a limited audience.[29]

These principles were more recently adopted and applied by the UK courts in the context of musical works in *Sawkins v Hyperion Records*, where it was held that the modern-day performance editions of seventeenth and

[24] *Graves' Case* (1869) LR 4 QB 715, 722.

[25] Laddie, Prescott and Vitoria, *The Modern Law of Copyright and Designs,* 3rd edn, (London, Butterworths, 2000) 229–30.

[26] *Walter v Lane* [1900] AC 539, 547 (Halsbury LC).

[27] Ibid 554.

[28] Ibid 552 (Lord Davey).

[29] Ibid 555 (Lord James of Hereford, who observed that 'it may also be that the report has been obtained under circumstances of particular difficulty').

eighteenth century French orchestral compositions could qualify as 'original' copyright works, notwithstanding the fact that they were created with the objective of reproducing, as accurately as possible, a record of the musical notes and sounds which the original composer had intended his audience to hear.[30] Two specific copyright principles were emphasised by the court.

Firstly, the performance editions in which copyright was asserted were viewed as musical works that were legally distinct from the earlier musical works composed by the French composer Lalande, even though the contents of the latter were comprehensively copied in the process of producing the former. [31] By prising the derivative work apart from the antecedent work, whose expressive contents are identical when a perfect copy of the latter has been produced by the creator of the former, the presence or absence of the requisite degree of originality in each, for the purposes of determining copyrightability, may be assessed separately.[32]

Secondly, evaluating the originality of this category of derivative works—faithful reproductions of antecedent works—requires close scrutiny of *how* the copying took place. The maker of the derivative work who has exercised sufficient intellectual skill, labour or judgment should be distinguished from the 'mere copyist', with originality attaching to the work of the former but not those made by the latter:

> I think the true position is that one has to consider the extent to which the 'copyist' is a mere copyist—merely performing an easy mechanical function. ... In the end the *question is one of degree*—how much skill, labour and judgment in the making of the copy is that of the creator of that copy? Both individual *creative input* and *sweat of the brow* may be involved and will be factors in the overall evaluation ... [O]ne is bound to consider whether what Dr Sawkins did involved enough to confer originality—*did it go beyond mere servile copying*? [The trial judge] held that it did ... mere photocopying or merely changing the key would not be enough. But a high degree of skill and labour was involved ... This was *not mere servile copying*. It had the practical value (unchallenged) of making the work playable. He re-created Lalande's work using a considerable amount of personal judgment. His *re-creative work* was such as to create something really new using his own original (not merely copied) work.[33]

[30] See n 7 above; *Sawkins v Hyperion Records* (n 2) [22].

[31] A parallel was drawn with the facts of *Walter v Lane*, where the report made by a newspaper reporter of a speech was distinguished from the speech delivered by Lord Rosebery himself. Ibid [33] (Mummery LJ).

[32] This was the approach taken by Lord Davey in *Walter v Lane* (n 26) 551. ('In my opinion the reporter is the author of his own report. He it was who brought into existence in the form of a writing the piece of letterpress which the respondent has copied ... he and he alone composed his report. The materials for his composition were his notes, which were his own property, aided to some extent by his memory and trained judgment.')

[33] *Sawkins v Hyperion Records* (n 2) [82] and [84]–[85] (Jacob LJ, who noted that the generality of the statements made in *Interlego v Tyco* had to be interpreted narrowly in order to achieve consistency with the approach taken in *Walter v Lane*). Emphasis added.

Derivative works which fall into this category of 're-creative' works cross the threshold for the originality requirement even if their contents are identical to the antecedent works they have copied from. When copyright law refers to protectable subject matter as 'original works', the originality inquiry should not focus myopically on the *contents* of the work—the final *output* produced—with the insistence that such contents must not have been entirely reproduced from elsewhere. The 'work' that attracts copyright protection extends beyond the actual end product to include the *process* through which it was made.[34] UK copyright law thus appears to provide a more sophisticated analytical framework, compared to US copyright law, for evaluating the originality of recreative derivative works.

OBJECTIONS AND COUNTER-ARGUMENTS

We now turn to four specific arguments that have been raised, in judicial proceedings on both sides of the Atlantic, against recognising recreative works as 'original' derivative works in which copyright might subsist. The first two objections are closely intertwined and invoke the closely allied concept of authorship, while the third and fourth objections are premised on specific public policy concerns.

Authorship Required for Originality Absent

Recreating all of the expressive contents of an antecedent work, it may be argued, involves the maker of the derivative work engaging in activities which fall short of that which is required to establish authorship. The close proximity between the legal concepts of authorship and originality was recognised by the US courts in the *Bridgeman Art* decisions, where Judge Kaplan noted that 'a very modest expression of personality will constitute sufficient originality'[35] and that, conversely, there could be no originality and hence no copyright 'where a photograph or other printed matter is made that amounts to nothing more than slavish copying'.[36] The photographer who makes an exact photo-reproduction of a two-dimensional artistic

[34] That is why UK copyright law has been unwilling to ignore all the preparatory efforts involved in the production of literary compilations when assessing the originality of such works. Seen 12 above and accompanying text. Jacob LJ reaffirmed this approach in *Sawkins v Hyperion Records* (n 2) (see text accompanying n 33 above) when he made reference to the relevance of both 'creative input' and 'sweat of the brow' as relevant factors in the evaluation of the originality of a work.

[35] *Bridgeman Art 2* (n 6) 196, citing MB Nimmer and D Nimmer, *Nimmer on Copyright* (Matthew Bender, 1998) §2.08[E][1].

[36] Ibid, citing the same treatise at §2.08[E][2].

work cannot, it was argued, qualify as an author because he has simply reproduced all the authorial choices made by the author of the antecedent artistic work.

There are at least three variants of the argument against regarding such a photographer as an author for copyright law purposes:

1. In making an identical reproduction of an antecedent work, the photographer has simply reproduced an image that was *authored* by someone else.
2. In making recreative works, however difficult the process, the maker of such works cannot be said to have exerted any relevant *authorial* skill, labour or judgment.
3. The maker of such recreative works cannot be said to have acted with the requisite authorial *intention* that was necessary for him to qualify as an author.

The first argument focuses on the identicality between the recreative work and the antecedent work that was copied, from which it is extrapolated that the *only* true author of the expressive contents found in these works is author of the antecedent work:

> '[T]here has been no independent creation, no distinguishable variation from preexisting works, nothing recognizably the author's own contribution' that sets Bridgeman's reproductions apart from the famous works it copied.[37]

Two responses can be made to this argument. The identicality between the works should not, on its own, preclude the maker of the derivative work—the copy of the antecedent work—from qualifying as an 'author' of an original work. In a case where a photo-reproduction is made of an underlying artistic work, there are always two distinct works involved—the antecedent work and the copy of that work, each of which was capable of having their own authors. The author of the copy does not in any way claim authorship of the expressive content found in the antecedent work that he has copied from. He is simply the author of the copy—the recreative work—that he has made. His authorial expression lies not in the appearance of the final product that constitutes the recreative work, which was intended to be identical to the antecedent work, but in the ingenuity of the choices that *he* made and the steps that *he* took to produce that copy.

Turning to the second variant of the authorship-based argument against recognising the originality of such works, it has been argued that the replicative efforts of the maker of the recreative work cannot be regarded as *authorial* in character, however much effort or resources have been expended. In *Bridgeman Art Library v Corel Corporation*, the plaintiffs

[37] *Bridgeman Art 1* (n 6) 427, citing *Durham Industries Inc v Tomy Corp* 630 F 2d 905 (1980) 910.

who made high-resolution photo-reproductions of paintings were described as 'photocopiers'[38] and could not claim originality in these works even though 'allegedly greater skill [was] required to make an exact photographic, as opposed to Xerographic or comparable, copy' because '[s]kill, labour or judgment merely in the process of copying [could not] confer originality'.[39]

Equating photography with photocopying oversimplifies the skill, labour and judgment that would have been exercised in the process of producing such works. While it is true that the maker of a recreative work lacks the same freedom of authorial expression as the author of the underlying antecedent work he is seeking to recreate—simply because his intention is to reproduce the literary, musical or artistic expression of the earlier author to the best of his ability—it would not be accurate to dismiss all of his intellectual efforts as devoid of any authorial character whatsoever. Makers of recreative derivative works do have some degree of choice in how they go about executing their plans and may well have to exercise independent judgment in choosing what equipment to use, which techniques to employ and what alterations and adjustments to make along the way. In contrast, photocopiers often do nothing more than push a button or two, as do others who engage in wholly mechanical methods of copying.[40] One who creates an accurate replica of an antecedent work should not automatically be placed in the same category as someone who takes dictation from another, such as an amanuensis or a stenographer, just as the reporter in *Walter v Lane* was not a 'mere scribe' because what he did required the exercise of mental efforts that could only be acquired through specialised training.[41] This is not to say that all the exertions of the maker of a recreative work can be considered authorial in character, as some clearly are not,[42] but that authorship can and should be found in many of the carefully considered decisions that were taken by him throughout the recreative *process*. Such an inclusive approach towards what counts as relevant authorial skill for the purposes of satisfying the originality criterion would be consonant with the

38 *Bridgeman Art 1* (n 6) 427.

39 *Bridgeman Art 2*(n 6) 198, where Judge Kaplan relied upon dicta from *Interlego v Tyco* (n 13).

40 See, for example, *Reject Shop plc v Manners* [1995] FSR 870 (copyright held not to subsist in enlarged photocopies of drawings). Query whether the result would have been different if the photocopier had employed some of the more 'advanced' features of his photocopying machine to alter the proportions, tonality and qualities of the image that was reproduced.

41 See text accompanying n 27 above, as well as the House of Lords' decision at [1900] AC 539, 551 (Lord Davey: 'memory and trained judgment') and 557 (Lord Brampton: 'mental effort of memory').

42 *Sawkins v Hyperion Records* (n 2) [43] where Mummery LJ, while rejecting a narrow approach towards what counts as relevant authorial skill, noted that some aspects of Dr Sawkins' exertions—such as 'time and labour spent on the discovery or retrieval of the original scores and in their layout on the page'—were irrelevant for the purposes of determining copyright subsistence.

UK copyright law tradition of not completely disregarding the relevance of the preparatory efforts that go into making a compilation when assessing the originality of these literary works.[43]

The third variant of the authorship-based argument against the legal recognition of originality in recreative derivative works asserts the lack of *authorial intention* on the part of the person who has copied the entirety of the antecedent work. The maker of a recreative work is said to lack this intention because he does not intend to express any ideas of his own, but seeks to recreate the expression of someone else's ideas instead. Thus, in the context of the scholar (Qimron) who recreated an ancient text from incomplete fragments of the Dead Sea scrolls, David Nimmer has argued that:

> ... at the end of the day, Qimron lacked the intent to author original expression ... Qimron's efforts were backwards-oriented ... Qimron aimed to reconstruct a text that had already been composed in the past, instead of imbuing some of his own subjectivity onto the new creation of a literary text with an open-ended future... Qimron did not string together words with the intent to author them. He therefore lacked 'intent to author' even at the most simple level. By definition, the act of decipherment eschews 'original intent'—the intention to create a work of original ('new') expression—rather it seeks recover of the (old) creativity previously exhibited by another.'[44]

However, having an intention to copy something to the best of one's ability should not automatically preclude the presence of authorial intent. After all, portrait photographers and painters often seek to realistically capture their subjects on film or on canvas and no one could deny that the artistic works resulting from their efforts were produced with genuine authorial intention. Why should it make a difference if the image they were seeking to recreate was not the appearance of a human being, but an antecedent artistic work instead?

In the context of literary works, the UK courts have had no difficulty distinguishing between a speech and a verbatim report of that speech as distinct copyright works,[45] implicitly recognising that these two works were produced as a result of the distinct authorial intentions of the respective parties responsible for making them. While the cultural significance of Lord Rosebery's speech may not have come anywhere close to that the

[43] See nn 12 and 34 above and accompanying text.

[44] Nimmer, 'Copyright in the Dead Sea Scrolls' (n 5) 211–12 (footnote citations omitted). Nimmer argues, at 126, that the recreative scholar 'was not acting as the author of a literary text. Instead, he was acting akin to the psychiatrist who could unravel his patient's thought processes ... to the extent that he succeeded, Qimron simply recaptured words that [the author of the scrolls] had written millennia ago'. By the same token, at 34, he argues that artisans who restore a painting to its former glory do not demonstrate the authorial intention required for copyright law to recognise that they have produced an original artistic work because 'the restorers are trying to duplicate as exactly as possible the artistic genius of their predecessor'.

[45] See *Walter v Lane* (n 26) 551. See also nn 31–32 above and accompanying text.

importance attached to the reconstructed text from the Dead Sea scrolls, that alone should not be enough to explain why UK copyright law was prepared to treat an accurate transcription of the former as an original literary work while US copyright law, on Nimmer's analysis, reaches the opposite conclusion with respect to a recreated version of the latter. The substantive or qualitative value of the contents of a work should have no bearing on the analysis except to the extent that it may shed light on the difficulties encountered by the individual engaged in the recreative process.

No Creativity or Subjectivity Demonstrated

In replicating *all* of the expressive elements of the antecedent work, the work produced by the recreative author is said to be unoriginal because it is devoid of creativity or subjectivity. The maker of a recreative work denies himself the opportunity to make his own subjective contribution to the expressive content of the literary, musical or artistic work he recreates.[46] Given these particular constraints, the recreative derivative work cannot be properly described as an 'original' work since its expressive content is dictated by literary, musical or artistic expression originating entirely from somewhere and someone else. Originality, it is argued, requires some degree of authorial independence and subjective freedom which the recreative author does not possess.[47]

Underlying this argument are two premises. Firstly, that the authorial 'creativity' required for originality must be, and can only be, reflected in the perceptible features of the final output that is produced at the end of the recreative process. If there is no distinguishable variation between the antecedent work and the recreative derivative work, then there is no evidence of 'creativity' that merits a finding of originality.[48] Secondly, that the authorial 'creativity' which is relevant to the originality inquiry can only be found in the literary, musical and artistic contributions made by an author to the

[46] Since his goal is to achieve absolute fidelity in the recreative process, it may be argued that there is no room for any authorial subjectivity on his part—a point pithily captured in *Matthew Bender & Co v West Publishing Co* 158 F 3d 674, 688 (1998) ('the creative is the enemy of the true').

[47] In the context of craftsmen who restore a fresco to its former glory, Nimmer has argued ('Copyright in the Dead Sea Scrolls', n 5, 209) that there is no originality '... when the subjective expression is wholly subordinated to a higher intent to conform to external factors, protection may be denied ... [such as where a work is made with] the intent to match a prior artifact, rather than out of the desire to imbue new subject insights onto the fresco'.

[48] *Bridgeman Art 1* (n 6) 427 (at fn 41). The identicality between the recreative work and an antecedent work is only a contentious issue where an exact replica is made of a currently existing work, such as a painting, and does not create as many difficulties when the antecedent work being recreated has been damaged, has some of its parts missing, or where the recreated work is the only complete and available record of the antecedent work in recent history.

expressive contents of his work.[49] A distinction is thus drawn between these 'expressive' efforts, on the one hand, and other instances of intellectual skill, effort and labour which relate to 'physical' or 'technical' aspects of the production of a work and are to be disregarded for the purposes of the originality inquiry. Thus, in the *Bridgeman Art* case, Judge Kaplan viewed the photo-reproductions as unoriginal works that involved nothing more than 'sweat of the brow':

> Elements of originality ... may include posing the subjects, lighting, angle, selection of film and camera, evoking the desired expression, and almost any other variant involved ... But 'slavish copying', although doubtless requiring *technical skill and effort*, does not qualify ... As the Supreme Court indicated in *Feist*, 'sweat of the brow' alone is not the 'creative spark' which is the *sine qua non* of originality ... In this case, plaintiff by his own admission has labored to create 'slavish copies' of public domain works of art. While it may be assumed that this required both skill and effort, there was no spark of originality—indeed, the point of the exercise was to reproduce the underlying works with absolute fidelity. Copyright is not available in these circumstances.[50]

Both of these premises are problematic. Why should authorial creativity be limited to just the expressive content and perceptible features of the final output produced by the recreative author? The recreative author's creativity could lie in the methods and techniques he selected and successfully executed in the course of the recreative process, the manner in which he overcame the obstacles he encountered along the way, and the way in which he has utilised his understanding and interpretation of the antecedent work to recreate its missing or damaged parts. It is submitted that, when searching for evidence of authorial creativity, one ought not confine oneself to looking just at the *results* of the recreative process but should also scrutinise the recreative *process* itself.

Furthermore, choosing to regard all the highly specialised skills performed in the course of copying the antecedent work as irrelevant to the originality inquiry, simply on the basis that they relate to 'technical' or 'physical'

[49] For example, in arguing against the copyrightability of the reconstructed text from the Dead Sea Scrolls made by a scholar (Qimron), Nimmer ('Copyright in the Dead Sea Scrolls', n 5, 117) takes the view that the skills and effort put into deciphering the ancient text are of such a vastly different character from the literary skills exercised by a poet—the paradigm author—that they cannot result in copyrightable works. ('Consider that one inspired to compose a stream of consciousness ode based on glimpsing the scrolls undeniably obtains copyright protection for her work product. The farther that Qimron stands from the poet—the closer his painstaking research and analysis bring him to reconstructing [the original scroll-writer's] words—the less his protection').

[50] *Bridgeman Art 2* (n 6) 196–97 (emphasis added, citations omitted). One wonders if the court was less impressed by the photography skills of the transparency maker when he made photo-reproductions of the paintings, as compared to the sculpting skills of the craftsmen in *Alva Studios* where their scaled-down replicas of a Rodin sculpture were held to be original artistic works because they were the products of 'true artistic skill'. See nn 22 and 23 above and accompanying text.

skill, rather than 'artistic' or 'expressive' skill, grossly undervalues and discriminates against the intellectual energies which have been expended by the recreative author. Those who use cameras and sophisticated technology should not be automatically prejudiced compared to those who use simpler tools and basic implements. The focus should always be on *how* the equipment deployed by the recreative author is used. Mechanically-driven recreative processes should not result in the production of original copyright works, whereas recreative processes which involve significant degrees of human input should.

In addition, authorial creativity should be considered from the perspective of the reading, viewing or listening audience. The recreative author is ultimately responsible for what the audience perceives and took deliberate steps towards achieving his goal: he wants them to experience exactly the same literary, artistic or musical expression as that found in the antecedent work. However, how he presents the recreative work to the public will depend on how he perceives and understands the expressive content of the antecedent work and the authorial intentions of its maker.[51] In cases where there is no complete record of the antecedent work in tact at the time the recreative work was produced, different parties engaged in the recreating the same antecedent work may produce very different versions of what each of them believes to be an accurate reconstruction of the earlier work.

Misappropriation of Subject Matter that Belongs in the Public Domain

This argument against recognising the originality of recreative works proceeds on the basis that it would be contrary to public policy to permit a recreative author to secure for himself a copyright monopoly over subject matter that was copied from an antecedent work found in the public domain:

> To extend copyrightability to miniscule variations would simply put a weapon for harassment in the hands of mischievous copiers intent on *appropriating* and *monopolising public domain work*.[52]

There are at least two specific underlying policy concerns here. Firstly, that works already in the public domain should remain freely available to everyone, and that recognising the recreative work as an original work which attracts a copyright monopoly of its own might put this in jeopardy.

[51] For example, in *Sawkins v Hyperion records* (n 2) [49] (Mummery LJ), it was acknowledged that the professional views held by the musicologist played a significant role in how he constructed his performance edition of the antecedent musical work ('... the fact [is] that the totality of the sounds produced by the musicians are affected, or potentially affected, by the information inserted in the performing editions produced by Dr Sawkins').

[52] *Batlin v Snyder* (n 8) 492 (Oakes J) (emphasis added).

Secondly, that granting the recreative author a copyright monopoly over his work is unjustified when all that he has done is to make a copy of a pre-existing work from the public domain.

In response to the first policy concern, the recognition of a copyright monopoly over a recreative work does not, as a matter of law, impinge upon the freedom of the public to continue using and copying from any antecedent work that is part of the public domain.[53] Copyright would give the recreative author an exclusive right to reproduce the recreative work, which translates into a right to stop unauthorised copying *from the recreative work only*.[54] If the antecedent work that was copied to make the recreative work was already a part of the public domain, its status remains unchanged. Therefore, regarding the recreative work as 'original' and eligible for copyright protection would not deprive the public of access to the antecedent work—assuming, of course, that the antecedent work was accessible to the public in the first place.

With the second policy concern, one might adopt a labour-desert based theory of intellectual property protection and take the view that the recreative author does not *deserve* a copyright monopoly for his efforts because the recreative process is substantially wrapped around comprehensive acts of copying.[55] However, automatically rejecting *all* forms of copying as incapable of giving rise to original copyrightable works on this basis would not be fair because of the great disparity, in terms of the intellectual energies expended by the copyist, between the various different types and forms of copying that might have been employed. The UK courts have, for instance, distinguished between the copyist who makes a mechanical copy of an antecedent work and the recreative author whose replicative efforts involve a significantly higher order of skill and sophistication. Even if one considers the efforts of the recreative author to be not as deserving as those expended by an author who has not copied from someone or somewhere else, any copyright enjoyed by the former is always a very 'thin' legal monopoly because the copyright owner is *only* entitled to enjoin infringing acts committed in respect of *his* recreative copy of the antecedent work.

[53] Though this freedom may be qualified by the practical obstacles relating to the accessibility of the antecedent work, a point discussed further below. See nn 54 and 56 and accompanying text.

[54] In *Batlin v Snyder* (n 8) 493–94, the three judges who were in the dissenting minority were prepared to recognise Snyder's derivative work as 'original' and entitled to copyright protection because '[g]ranting Snyder a copyright ... would ensure only that no one could copy his particular version of the bank now in the public domain'.

[55] See nn 38 and 39 above and accompanying text, for example, where the court in the *Bridgeman Art Library* case analogised the conduct of plaintiffs to photocopying when they made transparencies containing photo-reproductions of paintings.

Diminished Accessibility to Important Works of Cultural Significance

The remaining arguments against the copyrightability of recreative works share common consequentialist concerns: allowing individuals to claim copyright in these works would have an adverse impact on the accessibility and availability of the culturally significant antecedent works that have been recreated. Firstly, the availability of copyright protection over recreative works may inconvenience members of the public seeking to access and make use of the underlying antecedent works. Secondly, giving copyright protection to recreative works might stifle competition between rival producers of such works, such as competitors in the market for high quality artwork reproductions, thereby limiting the overall supply and availability of these reproductions to consumers. Thirdly, allowing a fresh copyright to subsist in a recreative work might unduly extend the scope of intellectual property protection over works that ought to remain freely available in the public domain, potentially creating additional legal obstacles for members of the public who believe that they are free to make use of the recreative work because it is identical to a non-copyright antecedent work.

The first argument is strongest where the antecedent work that has been copied is locked away and highly inaccessible to the public and where there is an exclusive arrangement between the party who has control over the vessels which record the antecedent work and the recreative author. While the availability of copyright protection in respect of the recreative work would not, as a matter of law, preclude the public from making use of or copying from the antecedent work, this freedom could not be realistically exercised if there were severe restrictions on public access to the artifacts or paintings containing the antecedent work. Furthermore, the recreative author who obtains exclusive rights of access to the artifacts or other unique raw materials necessary to produce the recreative copyright work could exercise complete control over who may study the work, should he decide to keep it unpublished.[56]

The second argument relates to the evidential burdens that are placed on a hypothetical defendant who has been accused of infringing the plaintiff's copyright in a recreative work such as a photo-reproduction of an antecedent painting. Copyright owners alleging copyright infringement typically have to show that: (1) there is substantial similarity between the copyright work and the defendant's image, and (2) the defendant had access to the copyright work. Establishing these two elements allows the court to draw

[56] This was the scenario in the Dead Sea Scrolls case, where access to the scroll fragments containing the many parts of the ancient literary text was tightly controlled by the Israel Antiquities Authority. Nimmer ('Copyright in the Dead Sea Scrolls', n 5, 89) argues that the scholar who asserted copyright in the reconstructed text to prevent others from making copies of it wanted to 'stifle discussion' of the text.

an inference that copying has taken place, and the evidential burden then shifts onto the defendant who must prove that his image was not copied from the plaintiff's copyright work.[57] The defendant would have to show that his image was copied from an alternative source such as the antecedent painting, and this would be an onerous burden, given the near-identicality between the plaintiff's recreative work, the defendant's image and the antecedent painting. Avoiding this difficulty is one of the main reasons given by the US courts for insisting upon a higher standard of originality when evaluating the copyrightability of derivative works.[58]

The third argument is concerned with the public interest in ensuring the continued availability of non-copyright works, including ancient works and works in which copyright protection has expired, to the public at large. Parties who recreate these public domain works and are able to assert copyright over their recreative works might be able to create 'perpetual monopolies' over subject matter that should be freely available for the public to use and enjoy.[59] These recreative works are intended to be identical to the non-copyright antecedent works which they purport to replicate and if the public is entitled to have free access to the latter, it may be incongruous for copyright law to require them to pay for a licence before they can make use of the former.

If there is a genuine concern about copyright-holders restricting public access to antecedent works after making recreative copies of them, then the real issue which the law needs to address is the exclusive character of the personal property rights enjoyed by private parties over the physical objects which embody the antecedent work. Whether or not the recreative work is viewed as 'original' for the purposes of copyright law, and hence entitled to copyright protection, should not be coloured by concerns relating to the accessibility of the underlying antecedent work used to make that work, or how the author of the work may choose to exploit the recreative work. As for the fear that allowing copyright to subsist in a recreative work might have a chilling effect on competition between the copyright owner and his rivals, the more sensible way to address this concern is for courts to recalibrate the evidential burdens placed on the parties in these types of cases, so as to lessen their prejudicial effect on potential defendants.

[57] *LB (Plastics) v Swish Products Ltd* [1979] RPC 611, 621; *Designers Guild Ltd v Russell Williams (Textiles) Ltd* [2000] 1 WLR 2416, 2425.

[58] See *Gracen v Bradford Exchange* (n 19) 304 ('[where A and B have made reproductions of the *Mona Lisa* painting] if the difference between the original and A's reproduction is slight, the difference between A's and B's reproductions will also be slight, so that if B had access to A's reproductions, the trier of fact would be hard pressed to decide whether B was copying A or copying the *Mona Lisa* itself').

[59] This was one of the public policy concerns considered by the English Court of Appeal in *Sawkins v Hyperion Records* (n 2) [40].

In any case, these public policy concerns are probably outweighed by the public policy arguments in favour of allowing certain recreative endeavours to qualify as original literary, musical or artistic works which enjoy copyright protection. Where the antecedent work is something of great cultural significance and yet not easily accessible to the public at large, one could argue that copyright law ought to *incentivise* the making of high-quality accurate reproductions of the antecedent work by ensuring that those who engage in such activities are able to secure copyright protection for their recreative works:

> The solution here accords with a reasonable view of public policy—that the sort of work done by Dr Sawkins should be encouraged. It saves others the time and trouble of re-creation of near-lost works, but in no sense creates monopoly in them. If someone wants to use Dr Sawkins' short-cut, they need his permission.[60]

MAKING ROOM FOR 'ORIGINAL' RECREATIVE WORKS WITHIN THE COMMON LAW COPYRIGHT REGIMES

The discussion above has illustrated some divergence in the judicial approaches that have been taken by the courts on both sides of the Atlantic towards evaluating the originality of recreative derivative works. The US courts have demonstrated greater caution in this area, insisting on a marginally higher standard of originality in most cases where the work in question is the product of copying. Mass-producers of 'knock-off' products seeking copyright protection for their wares before the US courts have not had as much success as makers of 'fine art' reproductions, with federal court vigorously defending the borders of the public domain from unmeritorious copyright claims. The UK courts, on the other hand, have demonstrated a greater willingness to acknowledge the originality of certain recreative derivative works in the right circumstances by employing a more sophisticated analytical framework which clearly distinguishes the copy from the antecedent work. However, lurking just beneath the jurisprudential surface in these two copyright regimes lies a common framework of principles and policies concerned with the legal character of the recreative enterprise, the authorial status of the parties engaged in the production of such works, as well as the impact upon the public interest if copyright should subsist in such works. At the end of the day, both copyright regimes share a common interest in, respectively, developing a coherent concept of 'originality' that produces just and fair outcomes when it is used as a legal criterion to assess the copyrightability of recreative derivative works.

[60] *Sawkins v Hyperion Records* (n 2) [86] (Jacob LJ).

Professor David Vaver once wrote that '[a] fair intellectual property system ... would ensure that intellectual property deserves its 'intellectual' epithet and is not a cover for protecting the trivial, the ephemeral and the opportunistic'.[61] Those who replicate antecedent literary, musical or artistic works will often demonstrate such a high level of skill, labour and judgment that make the 'intellectual' character of their recreative endeavours fairly obvious, especially when the task is made more challenging by the absence of a complete contemporary record of the antecedent work. Such recreative works deserve copyright protection because they are the products of genuine, uncommon and substantial intellectual energies expended by their makers—scholars, artisans and craftsmen—even if 'copying' technologies have been employed in the recreative process. A fair copyright regime should thus be prepared to recognise that such recreative derivative works can, in the appropriate factual circumstances, qualify as 'original' copyright works even though they are highly similar, or perhaps identical, copies of antecedent works.

[61] D Vaver, 'Recreating a Fair Intellectual Property System for the 21st Century' (2001) 15 *Intellectual Property Journal* 123, 141.

13

The Emancipation of Fair Use in Israel

LIOR ZEMER*

INTRODUCTION

THE ENACTMENT OF the new Copyright Act 2007 is a special event in Israel's legal environment.[1] The Act ended the hegemony of the British Copyright Act 1911 and the 1924 Copyright Ordinance Israel inherited from the British Mandate.[2] The many changes introduced by the Act created a new copyright reality for rightholders, users, the industry and the general public.

One of the main goals of the Act was to accommodate the tension between the allocation of property rights in authorial and artistic endeavours and the social goals that copyright systems strive to secure. The fair use doctrine is one of the primary copyright principles crafted by both courts and legislatures in order to settle this tension. The new version of the fair use doctrine embedded in the new Copyright Act in Israel is the latest attempt by a legislature to meet this challenge. The Act departed from the old fair dealing doctrine and embraced the fair use doctrine from the American copyright jurisprudence.[3] Although the doctrine has been challenged and modified by the case law of the Israeli Supreme Court, this legislative change, this chapter argues, completely emancipated Israeli

* I would like to thank Leslie Kim Treiger-Bar-Am, Guy Pessach, Tony Greenman, Irena Zolotova and the editors of this collected edition for their comments on earlier drafts. For excellent research assistance I thank Ortal Tzarfati and Aviv Gaon. This chapter is also in appreciation of the continuous support I receive from Vered Zemer-Shkalim, without which it would not have reached fruition.

1 The 2007 Copyright Act entered into force on 25 May 2008 (hereinafter referred to as 'the new Act').

2 The 1911 Copyright Act was applied to mandatory Palestine via the King's Order in Council on the Copyright Act 1911 (Extension to Palestine), 1924 LP Vol C (H) 2661, (E) 2499 (hereinafter referred to as 'the 1911 Act'). In 1924 the Copyright Ordinance was enacted in order to amend the 1911 Act. LP Vol A (H) 364, (E) 389 (hereinafter referred to as 'Copyright Ordinance').

3 See the new Act, Chapter D: 'Permitted Uses'.

copyright law from the narrow definition of fairness associated with the fair dealing doctrine found in other common law jurisdictions.

This chapter is divided into six parts. Following the introductory part, it discusses the pre-2007 Act fair dealing regime and the role of the Israeli Supreme Court in redefining its scope. The heart of the present chapter comparatively examines the new fair use doctrine and its four factors, analysing its fundamental effect on the copyright reality in Israel. Prior to the concluding part, there is an analysis of the interaction between judicial ideology and copyright which argues that legislative changes are insufficient: the role of courts in the design of fair use principles is fundamental to the success of the objectives underlying contemporary copyright systems.

THE IDEOLOGICAL KERNEL OF FAIR USE DOCTRINES

Fair use doctrines strive to maintain a strong civic culture that benefits from a reasonably balanced social and institutional system of copyright. Fair use is a doctrine that affects the free flow of ideas and knowledge, social and cultural exposure and democratic dialogue,[4] and balances between harmful and harmless uses.[5] In order to accommodate the social and economic goals of copyright, fair use has been defined as a zero-price compulsory licence on copyrighted works for particular uses identified by the law, ensuring that certain acts do not infringe copyright even in the absence of the author's permission. Calls to redesign the doctrine are abundant.[6] Although, as Paul Goldstein put it, the fair use doctrine 'endlessly fascinates us',[7] there is no uniform definition of the legitimate boundaries of fair use.[8] Nevertheless, the actual goal of the doctrine is well-established. In the words of Wendy Gordon, fair use 'seeks to accommodate the author's need to remuneration and control while recognising that in specific instances that author's rights must give way before a social need for access and use.'[9] Unfortunately, the general nature of this definition, coupled with jurisdictional differences

[4] In his tour de force justifying 'democratic copyright', Neil Netanel shows the fundamental contribution of fair use doctrines to a stronger public domain, richer democratic dialogue, and to a freer communicative sphere. NW Netanel 'Market Hierarchy and Copyright in Our System of Free Speech' (2000) 53 *Vanderbilt Law Review* 1879, 1926. See also by the same author 'Copyright and a Democratic Civil Society' (1996) 106 *Yale Law Journal* 283, and *Copyright's Paradox* (Oxford, OUP, 2008).

[5] See WJ Gordon, 'Harmless Use: Gleaning from Fields of Copyrighted Works' (2009) 77 *Fordham Law Review* 2411.

[6] See eg, the recent Symposium held in Columbia Law School entitled 'Fair Use: Incredibly Shrinking or Extraordinarily Expanding', published in (2008) 31 *Columbia Journal of Law & the Arts*.

[7] P Goldstein, 'Fair Use in Context' (2008) 31 *Columbia Journal of Law & Arts* 433.

[8] Arguably, there is no single definition of fair use under international copyright that states accept and follow. See, WTO, *United States—Section 110(5) of the US Copyright Act*, WT/DS160/R (June 2000).

[9] WJ Gordon, 'Fair Use as Market Failure: A Structural and Economic Analysis of the *Betamax* Case and its Predecessors' (1982) 82 *Columbia Law Review* 1600, 1602.

and competing approaches to fair use, makes it impossible to harmonise a workable toolkit for fair use incidents. This is a consequence of many different factors of which one reign supreme: classical notions of property still play a decisive role in the definition of the ownership spectrum in copyright. This tendency has led James Boyle to coin the slogan: 'Authors tend to win'.[10]

I agree that a property right is the legitimate Blackstonian wish of every individual or group of individuals.[11] But, given the social impact of copyrighted materials to the development of society and its members, alongside the contribution that the latter makes to the creative process,[12] systems allocating exclusive rights of use and exploitation in cultural properties must remain attentive to the social consequences of this preference. Treating cultural properties as assets that can be subject to exclusive ownership essentially means that our culture and social reality can be owned, with the perquisites of buying, selling, destroying, abandoning, transferring and excluding. The fair use doctrine is one example of the legal mechanisms designed in order to overcome such consequences.

Israeli copyright law has developed a preference for Benthamite-style utilitarianism as the best option for the system's ideological basis.[13] As such, the enactment of the fair use doctrine in the new Act is expected, using the words of former President of the Supreme Court, Meir Shamgar, to 'encourage the diversity of expressions and knowledge and to enrich the pool of expressions.'[14] However, maintaining a copyright legal culture that successfully secures these objectives is not an easy task. If the general case for copyright is an uneasy one,[15] then the case for fair use is no different. It is, after all, 'the most troublesome in the whole law of copyright.'[16]

[10] J Boyle, *Shamans, Software and Spleens: Law and the Construction of the Information Society* (Cambridge Mass, Harvard University Press, 1996) 116.

[11] W Blackstone, *Commentaries on the Laws of England*, 16th edn (London, Butterworth and son, 1825) bk 2, 1.

[12] I further explore this argument in (2006) 43 'The Copyright Moment' *San Diego Law Review* 99.

[13] J Bentham, A *Manual of Political Economy* (New York, GP Putnam, 1839).

[14] *Interlego A/S v Exin-Line Bros SA* 48(4) PD 133, 161 (1994). Subsequent cases followed suit. See eg, *City of Holon v NMC Music* CA 326/00, 57(3) PD 658 (2003). See also, CA (Dist TA) *The Football Association Premier League Ltd v Amoat'za Lehesder Ha'himurim Basport* Tak-District 08(3) 938 (2008). It should be noted, however, that after *Interlego*, natural right justifications did not completely disappear. See eg, Justice Dorner's remarks in PLA 6141/02 *ACUM Ltd v Galey Zahal Radio Station* 57(2) PD 625 (2003). See generally, G Pessach, 'Copyright in the Supreme Court: Trends, Considerations and a Look towards the 'Information Age' (2002) *Aley Mishpat* 347 (in Hebrew).

Legislative applications of the utilitarian theory can be traced back to the first modern copyright law, the Statute of Anne, 1709. The wording of the US Constitution also shows a preference for utilitarianism: Congress is empowered '[T]o promote the Progress of Science and useful Arts, by securing for limited Times to Authors and Inventors the exclusive Right to their respective Writings and Discoveries'. US Constitution Art 1 s 8 cl 8. See eg, *Mazer v Stein* (1954) 347 US 201, 209.

[15] S Breyer, 'The Uneasy Case for Copyright: A Study of Copyright in Books, Photocopies, and Computer Programs' (1970) 84 *Harvard Law Review* 281.

[16] *Universal City Studios Inc v Sony Corp of Am* 659 F2d 963, 969 (9th Cir 1981).

In this chapter I attempt to show how the Israeli legislature approached this troublesome area by recently embracing in the new Act a doctrine already invited into Israeli copyright law by the courts. Israel's new Copyright Act is the most recent legislative attempt in the world confirming that fair use is not 'incredibly shrinking.'[17] The departure from the old legal chains of the British 1911 Copyright Act and following the US fair use system in the new Act, amounts to a complete social and legal emancipation from the old narrow and dogmatic fair dealing regime.

THE OLD FAIR DEALING DOCTRINE

Legislative History

The new Act marks a historical departure from one of the long-lived laws Israel inherited from the British Mandate.[18] The 1911 Copyright Act was imported into Israel in 1924 during the British Mandate and remained the governing statute until the entry into force of the new Act, negotiated over the course of three decades, was adopted by the Knesset.[19] The old law was enacted in an era when the movie industry was taking its early steps, the television was not yet invented, video, DVD, multimedia, file-sharing, thumbnail photos or Wikies were not even conceived. The enactment of the new Act in Israel was crucial in order to meet the needs of the creative, legal and user communities, technological changes[20] as well as obligations under international copyright laws and other bilateral agreements.[21]

[17] 'Fair Use: Incredibly Shrinking or Extraordinarily Expanding' (n 6).

[18] On the evolution of Israeli public law, see I Zamir and A Zysblat (eds), *Public Law in Israel* (Oxford, OUP, 1997); S Navot, *Constitutional Law of Israel* (Wolters Kluwer, 2007).

[19] Other legislative instruments affecting the development of copyright norms include: the Unjust Enrichment Act 1979, s 200A of the Customs Ordinance [New Version] (detention of infringing goods), and s 38 of the Israel Broadcasting Authority Act 1965. For a complete list see T Greenman, 'Copyright Throughout the World: Israel' in S von Lewinski (ed), *Copyright Throughout the World (Copyworld)* (London, Thomson Reuters/West, 2009) ch 20:2 entitled 'The Current Legislative Acts Governing Copyright and Its Enforcement.'

[20] On the challenges to copyright exceptions by technological changes see generally, R Burrell and A Coleman, *Copyright Exceptions: The Digital Impact* (Cambridge, CUP, 2005).

[21] Israel is a member of the majority of international treaties and conventions in intellectual property. Within the area of copyright, Israel is a member of the following conventions: Berne Convention for the Protection of Literary and Artistic Works (Paris Act entered into force in 2004), the Agreement on Trade Related Aspects of Intellectual Property (TRIPs) (member of the WTO since 1995), the Universal Copyright Convention (UCC) (ratified, 1955), the Rome Convention for the Protection of Performers, Producers and Phonograms and Broadcasting Organizations (entered into force in 2002), the Geneva Convention for the Protection of Producers of Phonograms against Unauthorised Duplication of their Phonograms (entered into force, 1978). Israel signed WIPO's Copyright Treaty (WCT) and Performances and Phonograms Treaty (WPPT), but has yet to ratify these. Interestingly, the 2007 Act incorporates principles from these treaties. See also, Israel-US bilateral copyright treaty from 1950, and the Association Agreement between Israel and the EU (1995).

The 1911 Act was ill-defined and unclear and had been unable to provide coherent legal mechanisms. The original version of the Act was subtle and ambiguous and included references to colonies and the rights of universities and colleges that are mentioned in the British Copyright Act 1775. In the Hebrew-translated version there were several omissions that created a legal reality lacking in core principles necessary for the copyright community. For example, the requirement of originality was omitted from section 1 of the translated version.[22] Since the inception of the State of Israel, several changes were made to the Act. Nevertheless, until 2008, one had to resort to the British version in order to understand some of the principles in the translated version.

In 1924, the British Mandate enacted a Copyright Ordinance in order to amend the 1911 Act. Until the entry into force of the 2007 Act, changes and amendments to copyright were made via the 1924 Ordinance. For example, moral rights did not exist under the 1911 Act, but were added to the Ordinance,[23] and, while the duration of copyrighted works in the 1911 Act was life plus 50 years, the Ordinance imposed life plus 70, following the European Directive[24] and the US CTEA.[25] Thus, in order to get a complete vision of the state of copyright law in Israel, the 1911 Act and the 1924 Ordinance had to be read in tandem.[26] After the enactment of the new Act, copyright law in Israel, more than before, as Tony Greenman remarks, 'no longer mirrors British copyright law and has some distinctively American, Continental European and local flavours.'[27]

Fair Dealing under the 1911 Act

Section 2(1) of the 1911 Act prescribed a closed and exhaustive list of non-infringing incidents,[28] such as making a photograph of a work that is

[22] The Supreme Court did not remain silent with its criticism of the Act. See eg, CA 360/83 *Strosky Ltd v Glidat Vitman Ltd* 40(3) PD 340 (1985).

[23] Copyright Ordinance 1924 s 4(a); Copyright Act 2007 c7 ss 45–46. See also, CA 2790, 2811/93 *Eisenman v Qimron* 54(3) PD 817 (2000). (the 'Dead Sea Scrolls Case'). On the economic and moral rights of authors in Israel, see Greenman (n 19) ch 20:19–20:20 entitled 'Contents of Protection' and T Greenman, *Copyright*, 2nd edn (Eesh Yarok, 2008) vol 1, chs 5 and 14 (in Hebrew).

[24] Council Directive 93/98/EEC harmonising the term of protection of copyright and certain related rights, Art 1(1), 1993 OJ L290.

[25] See, Sonny Bono Copyright Term Extension Act of 1998, Pub L No 105–298, 112 Stat 2827 (1998) (codified as amended at 17 USC §§ 108, 203(a)(2), 301(c), 302, 303–04 (2000)). See eg, *Eldred v Ashcroft* 537 US 183 (2003). *Cf*, Copyright Act 1911 s 3 and Copyright Ordinance 1924 s 5(4). See also Copyright Act 2007 c 6 ss 38–44.

[26] See Copyright Ordinance 1924 s 8.

[27] Greenman (n 19) ch 20:1. Jewish law sources do sometimes take part in the courts' attempts to develop copyright principles. See eg, N Rakover, *Copyright in Jewish Literary Sources* (Jerusalem, 1991) (in Hebrew).

[28] s 2(1) of the 1911 Act provides:

Infringement of Copyright

2.-(1) Copyright in a work shall be deemed to be infringed by any person who, without the consent of the owner of the copyright, does anything the sole right to do which is by this Act

permanently in a public place, or publication in a newspaper of a report of a lecture delivered in public. In these incidents a user will not be liable for infringement in cases of use of the rightholder's work without consent or requested to pay any royalties. In addition to these exceptions the legislature enacted a specific provision in 1996 regulating private use.[29]

In addition to the prescribed list of permitted uses, section 2(1)(i) contained a more general norm: 'any fair dealing with any work for the purpose of private study, research, criticism, review or newspaper summary.' This provision is an earlier version of the classic fair dealing doctrine found in other common law countries such as the UK,[30] Australia, Canada, India, New Zealand, South Africa and Singapore.[31] However, the narrow nature of this provision made it difficult for courts to adequately respond to contemporary copyright challenges and to balance between the many competing interests while preserving a robust public domain.

Fair Use as a Judicial Legal Transplant

Fair use doctrines are judicially created. The first legislative appearance of any such doctrine in a common law jurisdiction was in the British 1911 Copyright Act. Until 1911, UK fair dealing was closer to a quasi-US fair use doctrine, since the UK courts were expected to determine fairness on grounds not specified in legislation.[32] Eventually, fair dealings with which courts had to deal made their way to the 1911 Act. In the US, section 107 of the Copyright Act 1976 is based on and follows Justice Story's analysis of fair use in *Folsom v Marsh*,[33] where he examined the factors to be considered before a fair use claim is approved. Over a century later, the Canadian Supreme Court had taken a similar role to redefine the scope of

conferred on the owner of the copyright: Provided that the following acts shall not constitute the infringement of a copyright …

[29] See,Copyright Ordinance 1924 s 3C.

[30] See, Copyright, Designs and Patents Act 1988 (hereinafter referred to as 'CDPA 1988') c III: 'Acts Permitted in Relation to Copyright Works'. Chapter III complies with the list of exceptions and limitations provided under Art 5 of Directive 2001/29/EC of the European Parliament and of the Council on the Harmonisation of Certain Aspects of Copyright and Related Rights in the Information Society (22 May 2001) (hereinafter referred to as 'InfoSoc Directive'). See generally, K Garnett, G Davies and G Harbottle, *Copinger and Skone James on Copyright*, 15 edn (London, Sweet & Maxwell, 2005) ch 9.

As Bently and Sherman put it: under UK fair dealing doctrine the dealing must be fair for the purposes enumerated in the closed list and 'it is irrelevant that the use might be fair for a purpose not specified in the Act, or that it is fair in general.' L Bently and B Sherman, *Intellectual Property Law*, 2nd edn (Oxford, OUP, 2004) 193.

[31] See respectively, Part III, Division 3, Australian Copyright Act 1968; s 29, Canadian Copyright Act 1921; c XI, Indian Copyright Act 1957; ss 42–43 New Zealand's Copyright Act 1994; s 12, South African Copyright Act 1978; s 35, Singapore Copyright Act 1987.

[32] See eg, *Wilkins v Aikin* (1810) 17 Vesey 422; *Smith v Chato* (1874) 31 LT 77.

[33] *Folsom v Marsh* 9 F Cas 342 (CCD Mass 1841).

fair dealing. In *CCH Canadian Ltd v Law Society of Upper Canada* the[34] the Court unanimously held that the Law Society of Upper Canada did not infringe copyright because its Great Library reproduction services were permitted under the fair dealing list of exceptions. Here the Court endorsed the following six factors to determine the fairness of the dealing: the purpose (and the commercial nature) of the dealing, the character of the dealing, the amount taken, alternatives to the dealin, the nature of the work, and the effect of the dealing on the work.[35]

Similarly, the presence of an outdated copyright law in Israel and the lack of a bright-line fair dealing standard[36] required guidance from the courts. The Supreme Court responded to this need in *Geva v Walt Disney Company*.[37] This case concerns a dispute between Walt Disney, the owner of the Donald Duck character, and one of the famous cartoonists in Israel, the late Dudu Geva. The latter used Donald Duck's image in his story 'Mobi Duck' published in his book entitled 'The Duck's Book'. The court examined whether Geva's use of the character constituted a fair dealing and, for the first time, imported the fair use four-factor test from section 107 of the US Copyright Act 1976. This resulted in the creation of a two-prong cumulative test for fair use that was based on both the British 1911 fair dealing and the US test. Indeed, Justice Maltz remarked in *Geva*, that in every case of fair dealing the court will have to separately examine the purpose of the use and its fairness. The resulting situation, Niva Elkin Koren remarked, was more difficult because now litigants had to show that the use was included in the list of fair dealings and that it was fair on the basis of the four factors. The new test for fairness, she argued, suffered from too many problems: 'a lack of flexibility resulted from the nature of the closed list of exceptions in the fair dealing doctrine and the lack of legal certainty associated with the four conditions.'[38]

Subsequent cases applied the two-prong test. In *Mifal Hapais v The Roy Export Establishment Company*, a case concerning the use of Charlie Chaplin's character in a commercial for the Israeli lottery, the court rejected

[34] *CCH Canadian Ltd v Law Society of Upper Canada* 2004 SCC 13 1 SCR 339, 236 DLR (4th) 395.

[35] For a comparative analysis of the six factors see generally, Giuseppina D'Agostino, 'Healing Fair Dealing? A Comparative Copyright Analysis of Canada's Fair Dealing to UK Fair Dealing and US Fair Use' (2008) 53 *McGill Law Journal* 309.

[36] In their attempt to eliminate uncertainty in fair use, Parchomovsky and Goldman recommended bright-line, quantitative safe harbours for certain types of appropriation. For example, they argue that 'for any literary work consisting of at least one hundred words, the lesser of fifteen percent or three hundred words may be copied without the permission of the copyright holder.' G Parchomovsky and KA Goldman, 'Fair Use Harbors' (2007) 93 *Virginia Law Review* 1483, 1511.

[37] *Geva v Walt Disney Company* PLA 2687/92 48 (1) PD 251 (1993).

[38] N Elkin-Koren, 'Users' Rights under Copyright' in M Birnhack and G Pessach (eds), *Authoring Rights: Readings in Copyright Law* (Nevo, 2009) 327, 353 (in Hebrew).

the argument that the use was fair because a fictional character does not deserve copyright protection and that the use was for non-profit purposes and for matters of criticism. Justice Tirkel found that the first part of *Geva*'s test, the purpose of the use, is less important, while the second part, the fairness of the use, is crucial. Justice Tirkel held that the use of Sir Charles Spencer's character 'Charlie Chaplin' was for commercial purposes and therefore is not fair dealing.[39]

In the later case of *Eisenman v Qimron*,[40] the court reapplied *Geva*'s test and held that the reconstruction and decipherment of over 800 Dead Sea Scrolls entitled its author for copyright. The Scrolls, claimed to be the single most important archaeological find of the twentieth century,[41] provide fresh evidence of the period in which Judaism was consolidated and Christianity was born. Scholars reconstructed the text of the ancient Scrolls and, although they were not the authors of the Scrolls, argued for copyright in their version, because of the many educated guesses that the fallible process of reconstruction necessitated. The court supported their claim for copyright. Here again, Justice Tirkel emphasised the role of the two-prong test and in just a couple of paragraphs dismissed the fair dealing defence because the appellants used the deciphered text in its entirety and without any attribution to Qimron.[42]

THE NEW FAIR USE FORMULA

Definition

The fair use formula is grounded in Chapter D of the new Copyright Act, entitled 'permitted acts'. Chapter D prescribes 12 permitted uses and an open-textured norm directing courts to review fair use according to four factors of fairness. This formula was influenced by fair use systems from other jurisdictions[43] including, the Australian Act, by the

[39] *Mifal Hapais v The Roy Export Establishment Company* CA 8393/96 54(1), PD 577, 587 (2000) (hereinafter referred to as '*Charlie Chaplin*').

[40] *Eisenman v Qimron* (n 23).

[41] See generally, H MacQueen, 'Copyright and the Dead Sea Scrolls: a British perspective' in H MacQueen, TH Lim, CM Carmichael (eds) *On Scrolls, Artefacts and Intellectual Property* (Sheffield, Sheffield Academic Press, 2001) 99–115; See also, D Nimmer, 'Copyright in the Dead Sea Scrolls: Authorship and Originality' (2001) 38 *Houston Law Review* 1.

[42] *Eisenman v Qimron* (n 23) [19]–[20].

[43] On comparative aspects of fair use see, P Goldstein, *International Copyright: Principles, Law and Practice* (Oxford, OUP, 2001) § 5.5. See also S Ricketson and J Ginsburg, *International Copyright and Neighbouring Rights: The Berne Convention and Beyond*, 2nd edn (Oxford, OUP, 2006) ch 13. For a general comparative reading of the new Act see Y Weisman, 'Comparative Reading: the Copyright Act 2007, Continental Law and Common Law' in Birnhack and Pessach, *Authoring Rights* (n 38) 69.

European closed list of exceptions and limitations[44] and by the British CDPA 1988. Still, the present fair use in the new Act is almost identical to its US counterpart.[45]

Section 107 of the US 1976 Copyright Act provides:

> Notwithstanding the provisions of sections 106 and 106A, the fair use of a copyrighted work, including such use by reproduction in copies or phonorecords or by any other means specified by that section, for purposes such as criticism, comment, news reporting, teaching (including multiple copies for classroom use), scholarship, or research, is not an infringement of copyright. In determining whether the use made of a work in any particular case is a fair use the factors to be considered shall include—
>
> (1) the purpose and character of the use, including whether such use is of a commercial nature or is for nonprofit educational purposes;
> (2) the nature of the copyrighted work;
> (3) the amount and substantiality of the portion used in relation to the copyrighted work as a whole; and
> (4) the effect of the use upon the potential market for or value of the copyrighted work.The fact that a work is unpublished shall not itself bar a finding of fair use if such finding is made upon consideration of all the above factors.

Six core changes were introduced in Chapter D: replacing 'fair dealing' with 'fair use', opening the closed list of exceptions and limitations, replacing 'newspaper summary' with 'journalistic reporting', adding new uses such as 'quotations' and 'instruction and examination by an educational institution', legislating *Geva*'s cumulative test, and providing the Minister of Justice a role in determining further conditions for fair uses.

The remainder of this chapter presents and comparatively examines Chapter D. It explores its normative and practical implications, the challenges to courts, and analyses Chapter D's general impact on Israel's copyright environment.

[44] See Art 5, InfoSoc Directive. For example, the main items in s 24 dealing with exceptions in the field of computer programs were borrowed from EC Directive 91/250/EEC on the Legal Protection of Computer Programs OJ L122/42, but not only: s 24(c)(2) is based on s 47F of the Australian Copyright Act 1968.

[45] Despite the similarities between the US fair use doctrine in s 107 and Chapter D, the doctrines are not fully identical. For example: (1) US courts do not pay much attention to the purpose of the use and emphasise the four factors of fairness, while in Israel, courts are expected to apply both parts of the *Geva*'s test; (2) the first factor in s 19(b) refers to 'the purpose and character of the use' while s 107 of the US Act mentions 'the purpose and character of the use, including whether such is of a commercial nature or is for nonprofit educational purposes'; (3) under s 19(c), '[t]he Minister may make regulations prescribing conditions under which a use shall be deemed a fair use.' This ministerial prerogative does not exist in the US doctrine. I further explore these differences in the analysis below. See, NW Netanel, 'Israeli Fair Use from an American Perspective', in Birnhack and Pessach, *Authoring Rights* (n 38) 377.

Open-Textured Norm

A fair use doctrine is expected to create 'a checklist of things to be considered rather than a formula for decision.'[46] Section 19 of the new Act follows this logic:

(a) Fair use of a work is permitted for purposes *such as*: private study, research, criticism, review, journalistic reporting, quotation, or instruction and examination by an educational institution.
(b) In determining whether a use made of a work is fair within the meaning of this section the factors to be considered shall include, inter alia, all of the following:

    (1) The purpose and character of the use;
    (2) The character of the work used;
    (3) The scope of the use, quantitatively and qualitatively, in relation to the work as a whole;
    (4) The impact of the use on the value of the work and its potential market.

(c) The Minister may make regulations prescribing conditions under which a use shall be deemed a fair use. [47]

Chapter D cured many of the deficiencies in the old law by expanding the scope of fair use, adding new uses and opening the interpretive boundaries of the doctrine. The addition of the term 'such as' in section 19(a) opened up the list of exceptions that would allow courts a flexible interpretation of fair use.[48] Before the enactment of Chapter D, courts struggled to use copyright laws to solve problems relating to developments in copyright law and policy and reached absurd decisions in clear cases of fair dealing. For example, section 2(1) of the 1911 Act does not refer to education purposes or instruction and examination. In *Ronen Bergman v The State of Israel*, the court refused the grant of fair dealing defence in a case brought against the Ministry of Education by a journalist and author. The former used one of the latter's essays for its matriculation exam. Although the court found the use to be worthy and for an educational cause, it ruled that the conditions for fair dealing were not satisfied because an exam is not covered by section 2(1).[49]

The old law also did not include quotation as a fair dealing. Courts expanded the exceptions of criticism and interpreted it generously. In the

[46] See *Ty, Inc v Publ'ns Int'l Ltd* 292 F3d 512, 522 (7th Cir 2002).

[47] For a brief account on s 19 see O Fischman-Afori, 'An Open Standard "Fair Use" Doctrine: A Welcome Israeli Initiative' [2008] *European Intellectual Property Review* 85 [Opinion].

[48] The original version of s 19(a) referred to 'inter alia' instead of 'such as'. The legislature adopted the latter since it considered the former too wide in scope. It is questionable whether 'such as' and 'inter alia' are distinct to the degree that Courts will apply them differently.

[49] *Ronen Bergman v The State of Israel*, CC (Mag Haifa) 12595/98 (unpublished, 2 Jan 2001).

Geva saga, parody was recognised as a form of legitimate criticism.[50] In the later *Charlie Chaplin* case, the court broadened the scope of 'criticism' and included satire—as opposed to the US approach.[51] This generous interpretation, however, was mainly theoretical since in both cases the court rejected the fair use claim. In only one case a court allowed a fair use claim in parody. In *Mosinzon v Haephrati*, Judge Zaft of the Tel Aviv-Yaffo District Court held that a 'modern sequel' parodying a famous children's series of stories came under the fair dealing exception. Here, the author of the sequel imagined the heroes of the children's stories at their maturity and ridiculed them as adults.[52] Although criticism and review are now part of section 19(a), the open character of the section will allow courts to further widen the boundaries of the doctrine and invite new uses into its scope.

Individual Exceptions and Limitations

Chapter D provides a list of 12 incidents where users can access copyrighted materials absent agreement of the copyright owner and without paying any royalties for the use.[53] These incidents include: use of works in judicial or administrative procedures;[54] reproduction of a work deposited for public inspections;[55] incidental use;[56] broadcasting or copying of a work in a public place;[57] reproduction or making of a derivative work of a computer program by a possessor of an authorised copy of the program, in instance of, for example, back-up copies, maintenance and service and error corrections;[58] ephemeral recordings;[59] temporary copies when the copy 'is an

[50] *Geva v Walt Disney* (n 37).

[51] See *Dr Seuss Enterprises v Penguin Books USA* 109 F3d 1394 (9th Cir 1997).

[52] *Mosinzon v Haephrati*, CC (Dist TA) 1437/02, 03(2) Tak-District 30775 (2003).

[53] Section 18 provides:

Notwithstanding the provisions of section 11 [copyright subject matter and what copyright means], the doing of the actions specified in sections 19 to 30 is permitted subject to the conditions specified respectively in the aforesaid sections and for the purpose of carrying out the objectives specified therein, without the consent of the right holder or payment, however with respect to the activities specified in section 32—upon payment and in accordance with the provisions of that section.

Section 32 of the Act creates a compulsory license to reproduce musical works in sound recordings against payment of royalties. *Cf* CDPA 1988 s 303(2); 17 USC § 115.

[54] The new Act, s 20. *Cf* CDPA s 45 and InfoSoc Directive Art 5.3(e).

[55] Ibid s 21. *Cf* CDPA ss 47 and 49.

[56] Ibid s 22. *Cf* CDPA s 31. S 22 also provides that: '... the deliberate inclusion of a musical work, including its accompanying lyrics, or of a sound recording embodying such musical work, in another work, shall not be deemed to be an incidental use.' See CDPA s 31(3).

[57] Ibid s 23. *Cf Leicester v Warner Bros* 232 F 3d 1212 (9th Cir 2000).

[58] Ibid s 24.

[59] Ibid s 25. See InfoSoc Directive Art 5(2)(d); 17 USC § 112.

integral part of a technological process';[60] additional artistic works made by an artist;[61] copying for preservation, renovation and reconstruction of buildings;[62] public performance in educational institutions;[63] uses by libraries and archives.[64] Chapter D also provides that the Minister may designate, by way of regulations confirmed by the Knesset's Economic Committee, other types of educational institutions, libraries or archives which may make preservation of copies. In doing so the Minister must take into consideration 'the character of their respective activities'.[65]

Two additional comments should be made in order to provide a more complete picture of fair use as grounded in the new Act. First, private copying is still governed by the 1924 Copyright Ordinance that provides that recording and reproduction of a recording of a copyrighted work for non-commercial, private and domestic use is allowed.[66] These exceptions refer to recording on a recording device such as a tape-recorder on which a visual or audio recording can be made. However, the 1924 provisions do not apply to devices 'designed for use in a computer'.[67]

Second, although the new version of fair use in the Act seems more receptive for societal needs, it is unfortunate to find that uses by the disabled were not explicitly included in the Act. Interestingly, in their attempt to design copyright 'Eurotopia',[68] the framers of the proposal for the EC Information Society Directive included a special exception for people with disabilities. However, the original exception was limited to only visually impaired or hearing-impaired persons, and excluded all other disabled people from the exception. It excluded those with, for example, learning difficulties or mental or other physical disabilities. This was changed in the

[60] This exception is mainly to use of works on a computer program and in a communication network. ibid s 26. This provision is almost identical to Art 5(1) of the InfoSoc Directive.

[61] Ibid s 27.

[62] Ibid s 28. See Art 5(3)(e), InfoSoc Directive.

[63] Ibid s 29. See CDPA 1988 s 34. At the time of writing, a draft regulation designating a list of educational institutions is awaiting the Minister's approval.

[64] Ibid s 30. For similar arrangements see Art 5(2)(c) of the InfoSoc Directive; CDPA 1988 ss 37–42; 17 USC § 108. See also *City of Holon v NMC* (n 14).

[65] Ibid s 31. Other laws complement the exception in the new Act. For example, s 6 of the Communications (Telecommunications and Broadcasts) Act 1982, requires that licensed cable and satellite operators in Israel carry broadcasts confirmed under the Second Television and Radio Authority Act and by the Israel Broadcasting Authority (IBA). Licensees are exempted for paying royalties to the owners of copyright or performers' rights in these broadcasts; the pending Electronic Commerce Bill provides exemption for ISPs from liability for copyright infringement in certain situations. Interestingly, the Tel Aviv-Yafo Magistrate Court has recently exempted an ISP from liability for hosting infringing copies of works by applying the fair dealing doctrine. See, CC (Mag TA) 64045/04 *'Al-Hashulchan' Gastronomic Centre Ltd., v Ort Israel* 07(14) Pad'or 486 (2007).

[66] Copyright Ordinance 1924 s 3C.

[67] Ibid s 3B. Also, these provisions, the Supreme Court held, apply to devices such as CD-R, DVD-R or other similar devices. See *City of Holon v NMC* (n 14).

[68] D Vaver, 'Copyright in Europe: the Good, the Bad, and the Harmonized' (1999) 10 *Australian Intellectual Property Journal* 186.

final version of the Directive's Article 5(3)(b) that now covers all persons 'with a disability'. Still, the updated version—with its restrictive language that the exception only applies 'directly' to the disability, and that it should be of 'non-commercial nature'—raises similar concerns to those raised with regards the original version. It is hoped that application of fair use for the disabled will attract the optimal interpretive flexibility.

Changing Tendencies

Conceptual Tendencies: From Defences to Rights

The many changes introduced by Chapter D raise the inevitable question as to whether the new fair use doctrine is composed of mere privileges of use,[69] a prescription of defences against infringement,[70] a list of users' rights[71] in the strict sense of the word or a combination of these.[72]

Fair use in the new Act is grounded in three different ways: first, in the 'old way', that is, defining permitted uses as non-infringing acts. For that matter, section 47 provides that:

> [a] person who does in relation to a work, any of the acts specified in section 11, or who authorizes another person to perform any such act, without the consent of the copyright owner, infringes the copyright, unless such act is permitted pursuant to the provisions of Chapter D.

Second, section 18 that opens Chapter D, states that the chapter creates a list of uses that every user can make without the consent of the rightholder or payment of any royalties.[73] Third, section 19 created an open-ended list of exceptions and limitations and a four-factor test to determine the fairness of a given use. The later is also of an open character, given that section 19(b) provides that 'the factors to be considered shall include, *inter alia*' those specified in the section.

Despite the fact that the explanatory memorandum to the new Act refers to 'interests' and not to 'rights', the language used in Chapter D and the stipulation of sections 18, 19 and 47 unveil the legislature's implicit intention to elevate the status of the previous list of fair dealings to that of users' rights. This assumption is supported by the Supreme Court's frequent remark that fair use should not be strictly interpreted.[74]

[69] See eg, *Rosemont Enterprises Inc, v Random House Inc* 366 F2d 303, 306 (2nd Cir 1966). See also, *Bill Graham Archives v Dorling Kindersley Ltd* 448 F3d 605, 608 (2nd Cir 2006).

[70] See eg, *Fisher v Dees* 749 F2d 432, 435 (9th Cir 1986); *Perfect 10 Inc v Amazon.com Inc* 508 F3d 1146, 1163 (9th Cir 2007).

[71] *CCH v Law Society* (n 34).

[72] *Harper & Row v Nation Enterprises* 471 US 539, 550 (1985).

[73] The new Act, s 18.

[74] See eg, *Charlie Chaplin* (n 39) 596.

Users' rights in the new Act are independent rights. Using Hohfeldian terminology, the 2007 Act created rights for users, and not mere privileges or defences in cases of infringement. Correlative to the right of a user is the owner's duty not to bar the former from accessing the said copyrighted work because 'even those who use the word [right] and the conception "right" [or claim] in the broadest possible way are accustomed to thinking of "duty" as the invariable correlative.'[75] In this chapter I argue that the new Act narrowed the scope of authors' rights, mainly the right of 'exclusive use and enjoyment of that which is exclusively his',[76] and compelled us to think of the *duty* on the rightholder to allow use and access to his works.[77] Using the parlance of rights and duties in the context of fair use is a welcoming development. It creates a user-centric normative reality and supports a more flexible problem-solving approach to copyright's inherent conflicts.

In *CCH*—a pro-user judgment—the court treated users' rights as part of copyright law, stating that fair dealings 'should not be given restrictive interpretation.'[78] The Canadian Supreme Court 'sought to align itself ... with the more flexible US approach',[79] something the Israeli Supreme Court had already done in the *Geva* decision. In *CCH* the Court adopted David Vaver's argument that '[u]ser rights are not just loopholes. Both owner rights and user rights should therefore be given the fair and balanced reading that befits remedial legislation.'[80] The Court held:

> Reviewing the scope of the fair dealing exception under the *Copyright Act*, it is important to clarify some general considerations about exceptions to copyright infringement. Procedurally, a defendant is required to prove that his or her dealing with a work has been fair; however, the fair dealing exception is perhaps more properly understood as an integral part of the *Copyright Act* than simply a defence. Any act falling within the fair dealing exception will not be an infringement of copyright. The fair dealing exception, like other exceptions in the *Copyright Act*, is a user's right. In order to maintain the proper balance between the rights of a copyright owner and users' interests, it must not be interpreted restrictively.[81]

Since the new Israeli Copyright Act entered into force, the user-centric reality has been made part of Israel's copyright legislative reality. In fact,

[75] WN Hohfeld, *Fundamental Legal Conceptions* (New Haven, Yale University Press, 1919) 31. See also Hohfeld's earlier article, 'Fundamental Legal Conceptions as Applied in Judicial Reasoning' (1913) 23 *Yale Law Journal* 16.

[76] Lord Cottenham LC in *Prince Albert v Strange* (1849) 1 Mac & G 25.

[77] In the words of Waldron: 'It is always tempting to take the perspective of the right-bearer ... The virtue of the Hohfeldian analysis is that it compels us to concentrate on the other side of the coin: the correlative duty.' J Waldron, 'From Authors to Copiers: Individual Rights and Social Values in Intellectual Property' (1992–1993) 68 *Chicago-Kent Law Review* 841, 844.

[78] *CCH v Law Society* (n 34) [54].

[79] D'Agostino, 'Healing Fair Dealing?' (n 35) 325.

[80] D Vaver, *Copyright Law* (Toronto, Irwin Law, 2002) 171.

[81] *CCH v Law Society* (n 34) [48].

in one of the pioneering and controversial decisions based on the new Act, Judge Michal Agmon-Gonen of the the Tel Aviv-Yaffo County Court, held that the status of users' rights in the new Act has been seriously strengthened. Labelling fair uses as rights rather then defences or privileges, it was held, is fundamental to the achievement of the democratic goals of contemporary copyright systems.[82]

Chapter D's list is a newcomer in the landscape of copyright law and policy in Israel. It has transformed the status of the fair dealing doctrine from a provider of defences against liability for infringement to that of a storehouse of users' rights. It transformed the fluid and unbalanced relationship between public and authors to that of a relationship between right-holders and duty-holders: it created a list of duties on owners of copyrighted materials to permit members of the public, by virtue of their status as rightholders, legitimate access and use of protected copyrighted materials. It is one possible way to remind authors and artists that they work in a social context and to prohibit appropriation of, as Wendy Gordon once wrote, the 'gift all artists receive, namely, a tradition and world they have not made.'[83]

Additional User-Centric Tendencies

Chapter D indicates that the Israeli legislature aimed at changing existing social tendencies in copyright, to upgrade the general public interest, secure free speech and democratic dialogue, and allow better access to knowledge while maintaining free competition in the marketplace of ideas. Apart from the above-mentioned changes, additional provisions in the new Act reflect these tendencies. For example, section 22 allows incidental use of a work 'by way of including it in a photographic work, in a cinematographic work or in a sound recording, as well as the use of a such work in which the work was thus incidentally contained, is permitted …'; section 23 provides that '[b]roadcasting, or copying by way of photography, drawing, sketch or similar visual description, of an architectural work, a work of sculpture or work of applied art, are permitted where the aforesaid work is permanently situated in a public place'; and section 26, following the European Directive,[84] permits 'transient copying, including incidental copying, of a work … if such is an integral part of a technological process …'

[82] CC (Dist TA) 11646/08 *The Football Association Premier League Ltd v Ploni* (unpublished judgment from 2 September 2009). See also, Greenman, *Copyright* (n 23) vol I, 330–35 (in Hebrew); N Elkin-Koren, 'Users' Rights under Copyright' (n 38).

[83] WJ Gordon, 'Render Copyright unto Caesar: On Taking Incentives Seriously' (2004) 71(1) *The University of Chicago Law Review* 75, 77.

[84] See InfoSoc Directive, Art 5(1).

Other provisions that also reflect and satisfy the public-oriented goal of the new fair use doctrine include provisions extending permitted uses by educational institutions and archives,[85] uses of a computer program for purposes of back-up copies, maintenance, correction of errors or making a derivative work in order to obtain information which is needed to adapt to a different and independently developed computer system or program,[86] and uses of architectural works and the drawings and plans for matters of renovation or reconstruction of buildings.[87]

THE FOUR FACTORS

The Purpose and Character of the Use

The new Act gave legislative status to the *Geva* two-prong test. The second part of the test is composed of the four factors specified in section 19(b).[88] When applying the first factor, the important question to ask—as held in the US landmark case, *Campbell v Acuff-Rose Music Inc*—is whether the use is transformative.[89] Transformative use recasts the original work and creates a new work by virtue of the added value created, altering the original source with new expression, meaning, or message. That is, '[t]he more transformative the new work, the less will be the significance of other factors, like commercialism, that may weigh against a finding of fair use.'[90] Pierre Leval viewed the extent of transformative nature as critical to whether a use 'fulfill[ed] the objective of copyright law to stimulate creativity'[91] Proponents of this argument hold that the transformative nature of use supports fair uses without the consent of the rightholder in exchange of introducing some social value.[92]

[85] The new Act ss 29–30.

[86] Ibid s 24.

[87] Ibid s 27. It should be noted that the legislature narrowed the scope of several exceptions in order to limit illegitimate uses. For example, ss 20 and 21 permit the use 'to the extent that is justified taking into consideration the purpose of the aforesaid use.' Versions of this condition exist in most provisions. Furthermore, some provisions contain no explanation for the limits they impose. For example, s 22 does not include incidental use of a musical work: '... the deliberate inclusion of a musical work, including its accompanying lyrics, or of a sound recording embodying such musical work, in another work, shall be deemed to be an incidental use.'

[88] For a hierarchical organisation of the factors, see D'Agostino, 'Healing Fair Dealing?' (n 35) 356–58.

[89] *Campbell v Acuff-Rose Music Inc* 510 US 114 S Ct 1164, 1171 (1994).

[90] Ibid 579.

[91] PN Leval, 'Toward a Fair Use Standard' (1990) 103 *Harvard Law Review* 1105, 1111.

[92] Laura Heymann even argues that 'everything is transformative'. LA Heymann, 'Everything is Transformative: Fair Use and Reader Response' (2008) 31 *Columbia Journal of Law & Arts* 445. On the theoretical basis of transformative use, see K Treiger-Bar-Am, 'Kant on Copyright: Rights of Transformative Authorship' (2008) 25 *Cardozo Arts & Entertainment Law Journal* 1059.

There is a fundamental difference between the stipulation of the first factor in section 107(1) of the US Act and section 19(b) in the new Act. While the former—following the rationale that 'fair use is not a license for corporate theft, empowering a court to ignore a copyright ...'[93]—provides that the examination of the purpose and character of the use should include 'whether such use is of a commercial nature or is for nonprofit educational purposes', the latter does not refer to the commercial nature of the use and does not make an explicit distinction between commercial uses and non-profit uses. This omission is a signal from the Israeli legislature to courts to put less emphasis on the commercial nature of the use. This message to courts is similar to the interpretation of the first factor in the *CCH* case holding that this factor 'should not be given a restrictive interpretation or this could result in the undue restriction of users' rights.'[94]

At the same time, however, commercially-oriented uses are expected to display other qualities and advantages that will justify the use.[95] For example, in *Kelly v Arriba Soft Corp*,[96] the Ninth Circuit held that the defendant's search engine's copying lower-resolution thumbnail constituted fair use. The court held that the new version of the images used served a novel function from the original images; therefore, they were sufficiently transformative and hence fair. Similarly, in *Perfect 10 v Google* the same court concluded that the transformative nature of Google's use overrides any commercial aspects of Google's search engine and website.[97]

Parodies are a good example here. Most parodies are distributed to the public and the financial gains to the parodists can sometimes be significant. However, if they are sufficiently transformative, advance other social values, cultural criticism and creativity, and if they are not solely for profit-making motivations,[98] they may enjoy exemption under fair use doctrines. Israeli copyright experience prior to the new Act, made fair use exemptions unavailable for parodies and satires where the social aspect of the use was

[93] *Iowa State Univ Research Found Inc v American Broadcasting Co* 621 F2d 57, 61 (2nd Cir 1980).

[94] *CCH v Law Society* (n 34) 54.

[95] See eg, *Loew's Inc v Columbia Broadcasting System* 131 F Supp 165 (SD Cal 1955).

[96] *Kelly v Arriba Soft Corp* 336 F 3d 811, 815 (9th Cir 2003).

[97] *Perfect 10 v Amazon* (n 70). Paul Goldstein warns us of the danger in decisions like Perfect 10: '[A] slogan or catch phrase will be mistaken for a fair use category. "Transformative use" is a current, notable example. This concept, that the Court employed in *Campbell v. Acuff-Rose* to measure the claims of a particular parody, has become, in cases like ... *Perfect 10 v. Amazon* ... a triumph of mindless sound bite over principled analysis. Parody is a fair use category; the mere transport of a work intact from one medium to another—without abridgment or other modification—is not.' Goldstein, 'Fair Use in Context' (n 7) 442. See also, J Litman, 'Lawful Personal Use (2007) 85 *Texas Law Review* 1871, 1898; and R Tushnet, 'Copy this Essay: How Fair Use Doctrine Harms Free Speech and How Copyright Serves it' (2004) 114 *Yale Law Journal* 535.

[98] See *Rogers v Koons* 960 F 2d 301 (2nd Cir 1992). See also, *Basic Books v Kinko's Graphics Corp* 758 F Supp 1522 (SDNY 1991).

secondary to the commercial aspect.[99] In light of the wording of the first factor in section 19(b) that does not require a mandatory examination of the commercial nature of the use, balancing between the commercial nature of a use and its social impact is likely to be less complicated in the future.

The Character of the Work Used

While the first factor relates to the later work, the second factor relates to the original work. Here a court will have to examine whether the work merits protection, namely whether it is creative and not a mere idea, whether it is published or unpublished, and hence 'closer to the core of intended copyright protection than are more fact-based works.'[100] For example, some works are more fact-based and hold great historical significance, such as the photos of the assassination of President Kennedy[101] or Prime Minister Rabin. It would be essential to copy them in their entirety. Also, the *CCH* case held that: 'for the purpose of research or private study, it may be essential to copy an entire academic article or an entire judicial decision.'[102]

Published works are more likely to qualify as fair use. When unpublished works are at stake, a defendant will find it difficult to justify fair use. In *Harper & Row Publishers v Nation Enterprises* the US Supreme Court created a presumption against fair use of unpublished works.[103] Here, a magazine, *The Nation*, published the previously unpublished manuscript of former President Gerald Ford's autobiography. Despite the newsworthiness of the subject matter, the court rejected the magazine's claim for fair use because, inter alia, authors enjoy the right to control the first publication of their work, which includes the choice of where and how to publish it. In a similar way, the Israeli Supreme Court held in the *Dead Sea Scrolls* case that the fair use defence was not available because the defendants violated the author's right of first publication.[104] The question remains, what if the unpublished work is of a great public interest? In *CCH* it was held that 'if a work is unpublished, the dealing may be more fair in that its reproduction with acknowledgement could lead to a wider public dissemination of the work.'[105]

[99] See *Geva v Walt Disney* (n 37); *Charlie Chaplin* (n 39). *Cf Leibowitz v Paramount Pictures Corporation* 137 F 3d 109 (2nd Cir 1998).

[100] *Kelly v Ariba* (n 96) 820.

[101] *Time Inc v Bernard Geis* 293 F Supp 130 (SDNY 1968).

[102] *CCH v Law Society* (n 34) 56.

[103] *Harper & Row* (n 72). See also *Salinger v Random House Inc* 650 F Supp 413 (SDNY 1986), rev'd, 811 F 2d 90 (2nd Cir 1987); *Wright v Warner Books Inc* 953 F 2d 731 (2nd Cir 1991). For the UK see, *Hyde Park Residence Ltd v Yelland* [2000] EWCA 37, [2000] 3 WLR 215.

[104] *Eisenman v Qimron* (n 23).

[105] *CCH v Law Society* (n 34) 58.

The Scope of the Use, Quantitatively and Qualitatively, in Relation to the Work as a Whole

This factor, typically considered the least important, concerns the question of whether the amount and substantiality of the part used in relation to the copyrighted work as a whole is qualitatively and quantitatively reasonable in relation to the purpose of the copying. If a defendant has taken an excessive amount that is not commensurate with the purpose of the use, the use will not be fair. This third factor 'operates on a sliding scale: the more a dealing goes beyond *de minimis* use, the more likely it goes against fair use.'[106] In most instances, copying the entire work or verbatim copying of a substantial part is unfair. In the *Dead Sea Scrolls* case it was held that there was an infringement of copyright since the entire work was copied and published. In *Haper & Row* only 300 words verbatim were taken from a 200,000 word manuscript.[107] This was considered excessive taking, because these words constituted the heart of the manuscript. However, in *Campbell*, the use by 2 Live Crew of the line 'Pretty woman, walking down the street'—the heart of the work—was fair use, because they produced distinctive lyrics, making the parody they produced sufficiently transformative.[108]

In other situations, copying the entire work will be the only possibility. In *Perfect 10* the court dealt with Google's search engine that displayed thumbnail versions of Perfect 10 photographs and provided 'in-line' links to third party websites, which provided full-size versions of the photographs.[109] The court found that Google's use of the photographs was a highly transformative use, although they minimised in full the original photographs. In such situations the third factor will not play a decisive role and the courts will have to emphasise the other three factors.

The Impact of the Use on the Value of the Work and Its Potential Market

The fourth factor requires evaluation of the actual and potential market harm to the original work caused by the use. The tendency in US courts to treat

[106] D'Agostino, 'Healing Fair Dealing?' (n 35) 347.

[107] *Harper & Row* (n 72).

[108] The court held: 'If 2 Live Crew had copied a significantly less memorable part of the original, it is difficult to see how its parodic character would have come through.' *Campbell v Acuff-Rose* (n 89) 1176. For similar reasons it was held that Randell's book was fair use of 'Gone with the Wind'. See *SunTrust Bank v Houghton Mifflin Co*, 268 F 3d 1257 (11th Cir 2001).

[109] See *Perfect 10 v Amazon* (n 70); *Kelly v Arriba* (n 96). See also the Canadian case of *Allen v Toronto Star Newspapers Ltd* (1995) 26 OR (3d) 308, 129 DLR (4th) 171.

this factor as the most important one[110] was changed in *Campbell*, where it was held that the importance of each factor should be examined on a case-by-case basis. Israeli courts, unlike the Canadian approach in *CCH*,[111] still treat this factor as an important one. The reason for emphasising this factor in this way is due to the fact that avoiding disproportionate market harm may severely limit the incentives necessary for creativity. Section 19(b) of the new Act refers to harm to market value and the potential market of the work. Indubitably, disproportionate harm will be caused where a use is directed to a market similar to that of the original work or where the new work acts as a substitute for the original. The art of evaluating potential harm is a difficult task because of the unpredictability of the fair use doctrine. In order to avoid unbalanced interpretations of the fourth factor, courts will have to remain steadfast to the social objectives underlying copyright law.

Other Factors

Section 19(b) provides that '[i]n determining whether a use made of a work is fair within the meaning of this section the factors to be considered shall include, *inter alia*, all of the following …' This allows courts ample space to take into account additional considerations, not specified in the new Act, before a use is labelled fair. In practice, courts involve in this process other principles of justice and equity. For example, normally, a fair use claim will be dismissed if the moral right of the author is infringed. In the *Dead Sea Scrolls* case the paternity right was infringed, since the defendant did not credit the decipherer of the Scrolls in the publication.[112] In another case, a court held that the use of a part of a film in a documentary programme produced by the Israeli Broadcasting Authority, infringed the author's moral right because the use was made in a context that mutilated the creative idea behind the original film.[113]

The frequency of the use might also affect the legitimacy of the use. That is, newspapers are eligible to use news and reports as long as these are informational. However, such use may sometimes exceed the legitimate boundaries of fair use and will not be permitted.

[110] See eg, *Harper & Row* (n 72) 451.

[111] *CCH v Law Society* (n 34). This factor is in line with the Berne three-step test requirement that fair uses must not disproportionably prejudice the legitimate interests of rightholders or unreasonably affect the normal exploitation of the work. See Berne Convention (n 21) Art 9(2).

[112] *Eisenman v Qimron* (n 23) 838. One commentator suggested to add the provision of credit and attribution as a fifth factor to the fair use test. See G Lastowka, 'Digital Attribution: Copyright and the Right to Credit' (2007) 87 *Boston University Law Review* 41, 85. The CDPA 1988 recognises the requirement for 'sufficient acknowledgement' for the fair dealing defence to apply in certain circumstances. See CDPA 1988 ss 29(1) and (1B), 30(1), 30(2), 30(3), and 178. See also *Pro Sieben Media v Carlton Television* [1999] FSR 610, 625.

[113] CC (Mag TA) 2228/95 *Peled v IBA Dinim Shalom* 15 (1999) 675.

Furthermore, one must remember the ambiguous nature of principles like 'fairness'. Even if courts can find common patterns in fair use cases, as Pamela Samuelson recently argued,[114] one cannot avoid the interpretive problems that general legal principles create. David Nimmer once wrote that the four factors are so unclear that 'had Congress legislated a dartboard rather than the particular four fair use factors ... it appears that the upshot would be the same.'[115] In order to overcome definitional deficiencies in copyright law, Israeli courts frequently apply the principles of unjust enrichment[116] and good faith. Another possibility is, like in *CCH*, to examine possible alternatives for the use in cases where use of the copyrighted work was not 'reasonably necessary to achieve the ultimate purpose.'[117]

COPYRIGHT EMANCIPATION AND JUDICIAL IDEOLOGY

The above examination of fair use doctrines show the ample space they provide courts for interpretation of the appropriate balance between rights and duties in copyright.[118] One of the reasons for this is, I argue, the ambiguity of legal principles such as 'fair use' and 'fair dealing'. Congress itself recognised that even for the courts that developed the four factor test, the factors were 'in no case definitive or determinative', but rather 'provided some gauge for balancing the equities'.[119]

Although the role of the courts in the design of fair use ideologies is unquestionable,[120] jurisdictions differ in the way they perceive this role. The fair use doctrine, the court reminded us in *Campbell*, is fundamental for the attainment of the social objectives of the institution of copyright. Quoting *Emerson v Davies*, the court wrote that fair use 'permits courts to avoid rigid application of the copyright statute when on occasion, it would stifle the very creativity which that law is designed to foster.'[121]

[114] P Samuelson, 'Unbundling Fair Uses (2009) 77 *Fordham Law Review* 2537, 2541.

[115] D Nimmer, '"Fairest of Them All" and Other Fairy Tales of Fair Use' (2003) 66 *Law & Contemporary Problems* 263, 280.

[116] See eg, CA 5768/94 *Ashir Import Production and Distribution v Forum Avisarim and Consumption Products* 52(4) PD 289.

[117] *CCH v Law Society* (n 34) 57.

[118] See generally, WF Patry, *The Fair Use Privilege in Copyright Law* (Bna Books, 1995).

[119] HR Rep No 1476 94th Cong 2d Sess 65 (1976). The lack of a clear definition of fair use is compensated in Israel, to some degree, by s 19(c) of the new Act authorising the Minister to 'make regulations prescribing conditions under which a use shall be deemed a fair use.'

[120] On the role of ideology in judicial reasoning see eg, RA Posner, 'Foreword: A Political Court' (2005) 19 *Harvard Law Review* 315; AD Martin et al, 'The Median Justice on the United States Supreme Court' (2005) 83 *North Carolina Law Review* 1275; A Barak, 'Foreword: A Judge on Judging: The Role of a Supreme Court in a Democracy' (2002) 116 *Harvard Law Review* 16; GC Sisk et al, 'Charting the Influences on the Judicial Mind: A Empirical Study of Judicial Reasoning' (1998) 73 *New York University Law Review* 1377.

[121] *Campbell v Acuff-Rose* (n 89) 1170, quoting *Emerson v Davies* 8 F Sas 615, 619 (CCD Mass 1845) and *Stewart v Abend* 495 US 207, 236 (1990).

In *Geva*, the court redefined the basic idea behind the existing fair dealing doctrine. It has imported the fair use doctrine into Israeli copyright law. And, in the Canadian *CCH* case a six-factor test was invented. These three decisions, using the words of David Vaver, continue a tradition, dating from nineteenth century US and British practice:

> … of letting judges set and monitor a reasonable balance of rights between copyright holders and users as different technologies and usages arise and develop. On this theory, while specific targeted exceptions serve a purpose, legislatures can neither anticipate new developments nor respond to them effectively and quickly; so courts are assigned the role of creating appropriate boundaries between private rights and the public domain in the course of deciding concrete disputes.[122]

As opposed to the US, Canada and Israel, UK courts remain steadfast to the fair dealing doctrine and its definitional boundaries. Courts will examine the fairness of the use using parameters that have emerged from UK case law:[123] is the work unpublished?, how the work was obtained,[124] the amount taken,[125] use made of the work,[126] motives for the dealing,[127] consequence of the dealing,[128] and could the purpose of the use have been achieved by different means?[129] However, regardless of the ambiguous nature of these parameters, Ungoed-Thomas J remarked that fair dealing is a 'dealing which is fair for the approved purposes and not dealing which might be fair for some other purpose or fair in general.'[130] In *Pro Sieben Media v Carlton Television,* Laddie J held that the fair dealing provisions 'are not to be regarded as mere examples of a general wide discretion vested in the courts to refuse to enforce copyright where they believe such refusal to be unfair and reasonable.'[131]

Cornish and Llewelyn provide one explanation to why the UK should not adopt the fair use standard: '[j]udges … are not to be furnished with any general tool for criticizing the scope of the legislation. Their role is confined to interpretation of its meaning.'[132] At the same time, however, UK courts do not remain aloof towards social needs and have encouraged a liberal

[122] See D Vaver, 'Canada's Intellectual Property Framework: A Comparative Overview' (2004) 17 *Intellectual Property Journal* 125, 150.

[123] See Bently and Sherman, *Intellectual Property Law* (n 30) 194–96.

[124] *Beloff v Pressdram* [1973] 1 All ER 241.

[125] *Hubbard v Vosper* [1972] 1 All ER 1023.

[126] *Newspaper Licensing Agency v Marks & Spencer plc* [2000] 4 All ER 239 (CA).

[127] *Hyde Park v Yelland* (n 103) 379.

[128] *Hubbard v Vosper* (n 125).

[129] *Hyde Park v Yelland* (n 103).

[130] *Bellof v Pressdram* (n 124) 262.

[131] *Pro Sieben AG v Carlton UK Television Ltd* [1998] FSR 43, 49 (rev'd Court of Appeal, [1999] 1 WLR 605, [1999] FSR 610). See generally, J Griffiths, 'Preserving Judicial Freedom of Movement—Interpreting Fair Dealing in Copyright Law' [2000] *Intellectual Property Quarterly* 164.

[132] B Cornish and D Llewelyn, *Intellectual Property: Patents, Copyrights, Trade Marks and Allied Rights,* 5th edn (London, Sweet & Maxwell, 2003) para 11–38.

approach to what constitutes fair dealing[133] because, as Lord Denning once remarked, '[i]t is impossible to define what is "fair dealing".'[134] In addition, one must remember that the fair dealing doctrine in the UK is complemented by an escape clause when public policy matters override proprietary interests of copyright owners,[135] and by the Human Rights Act 1998 requiring courts to invite public interest considerations more often.[136]

Consequently, calls to adopt a fair use formula in the UK were rejected.[137] Indeed, the recent Gowers Review of Intellectual Property recommends no serious change to be made to the present state of fair dealing under the CDPA apart of updating the closed list via the introduction of new exceptions such as format shifting,[138] caricature and parody,[139] and a wider exception for libraries and archives.[140]

The unclear nature of principles such as 'fairness', 'dealing', and the four-factor test affect the achievement of legal certainty. However, does this mean that courts' interpretive authority should be limited? Arguably, the copyright community needs best practices in fair use. However, before any such set of rules is developed and receives international recognition—especially given arguments that jurisdictional differences are not abundant[141]—courts should be expected to use the interpretive authority fair use doctrines given to them in order to guide owners and users of copyrighted materials on when a use is fair.[142] This interpretive authority is crucial for the attainment of the social goals and economic objectives of contemporary copyright regimes. The former President of the Israeli Supreme Court, Aharon Barak, most poignantly put it: every Supreme Court has two primary concerns: 'bridging

[133] See *Newspaper Licensing v Marks & Spencer* (n 126) 257; *Pro Sieben Media* (n 131) 620; and *Ashdown v Telegraph Group Ltd* [2002] Ch 149, 172.

[134] *Hubbard v Vosper* (n 125) 1027.

[135] See CDPA 1988 s 171(3). See eg, *Glyn v Weston Features Film* [1916] 1 Ch 261. *Cf*, *Stephens v Avery* [1988] FSR 510.

[136] See Human Rights Act 1998 s 12.

[137] The Whitford Committee's recommendation to adopt a similar formula of US fair use in the UK was rejected by the Government. Report of the Committee to Consider the Law of Copyright and Designs, Cmnd 6732, paras 672–77.

[138] HM Treasury, *Gowers Review of Intellectual Property* (London, HMSO, 2006) recommendation 8.

[139] Ibid recommendation 10a.

[140] Ibid recommendation 12. Similar to the Gowers Review, attempts to adhere to a US fair use formula in Australia were rejected but for several amendments similar to these recommended by the Gowers Review. See Australian Copyright Amendment Act 2006.

[141] As D'Agostino remarks: 'While Canada and the United Kingdom appear to have a rigid "fair dealing" framework, and the United States appears to have a more flexible structure in fair use, the legal outcomes in the three jurisdictions have been for the most part similar ...' ('Healing Fair Dealing?' (n 35) 356).

[142] Michael Madison argued for a pattern-oriented approach to fair use and suggested amending §107 in order to give courts greater freedom to identify the social practices that should inform fair use analysis. See MJ Madison, 'Rewriting Fair Use and the Future of Copyright Reform' (2005) 23 *Cardozo Arts & Entertainment Law Journal* 391.

the gap between law and society and protecting democracy.'[143] Copyright laws were designed to reward authors and artists but at the same time to balance their rights with societal values such as democratic dialogue and the free flow of knowledge. The lack of clarity associated with fair use doctrines create ample situations in which courts are the only appropriate forum that can bridge between the law and the democratic ambitions of society.

In a recent study, Barton Beebe reaches the conclusion that, as opposed to other legal disciplines, courts do not involve ideology in fair use cases.[144] This perhaps explains why, to date, only 32 cases in Israeli courts have dealt with fair use and why the defence was allowed in only a handful of these cases.[145] These findings raise serious concerns regarding the future development of the fair use doctrine and the clarity needed in its application by both creators and users. Courts are expected to develop norms and principles, based on existing legislation, that will be as precise as possible in order to guide copyright behaviour.[146] After all, reality tells us that fair use is 'so case-specific that it offers precious little guidance about its scope to artists, educators, journalists, Internet users, and others who require use of another's copyrighted expression in order to communicate effectively.'[147]

CONCLUSIONS

Fair use law in Israel is now completely emancipated. The departure from the British Copyright Act and the enactment of a law that combines lessons and principles from other legal jurisdictions have created in Israel a fair use legal reality that will be able to better address the many challenges that technology and social developments expect copyright systems to address. However, the success of this new fair use legal reality is dependent on the dialogue and interaction between owners and users and the willingness of courts to fully explore their interpretive authority under the new Act. Israeli courts have already proved their responsibility to develop coherent copyright norms. The enactment of the new fair use doctrine did not change the need for judicial involvement in the development of copyright norms and principles and it is anticipated that Israeli case law will continue to produce new norms commensurate with the challenges of contemporary copyright.

[143] Barak, 'Foreword' (n 120) 28. On the role and responsibility of judges to interpret laws and develop clear legal principles, see generally A Barak, *Purposive Interpretation in Law* (Nevo Publishing, 2003) (in Hebrew).

[144] B Beebe, 'Does Judicial Ideology Affect Copyright Fair Use Outcomes?: Evidence from the Fair Use Case Law' (2008) 31 *Columbia Journal of Law & Arts* 517, 522.

[145] Elkin-Koren, 'Users' Rights under Copyright' (n 38) 354.

[146] See MJ Madison, 'A Pattern-Oriented Approach to Fair Use' (2004) 45 *William and Mary Law Review* 1525.

[147] MW Carroll, 'Fixing Fair Use' (2007) 85 *North Carolina Law Review* 1087, 1090.

Trade Marks and Unfair Competition

14

Unfair Competition by Misappropriation: the Reception of International News in the Common Law World

CHRISTOPHER WADLOW

THE *INTERNATIONAL NEWS* DECISION

The Case and its Importance

IF THERE WERE any field of intellectual property law in which one might have expected to find substantial agreement across the whole common law world, it would be probably be the law of unfair competition. Not only is the law of the United Kingdom almost completely untouched by European harmonisation, but the laws of the various states of the common law tradition are still relatively unaffected by statute. To this day, it is still possible to treat the law of passing-off, at least, as essentially uniform across the United Kingdom and the former Dominions, and little different in the United States. However, despite the common heritage between the United States and the rest of the common law world, there are significant differences where doctrines outside the narrow scope of passing-off are concerned. One such is the doctrine of misappropriation of what are compendiously called valuable intangibles, or trade values, which differs from classic passing-off in that no element of misrepresentation is concerned. Although there is considerable diversity of opinion as to how far doctrines of misappropriation are recognised in the various component jurisdictions of the United States, there is a very clear divide indeed between the United States and the rest of the common law world.

The case with which this chapter is principally concerned is the decision of the United States Supreme Court in *International News Service v Associated*

Press,[1] which was almost single-handedly responsible for launching the common law misappropriation doctrine into the world. Both parties were American news agencies, AP, the older and larger, being organised as a co-operative with restricted membership, and INS, the relative newcomer, being an ordinary commercial company owned by the media magnate William Randolph Hearst. Hearst's outspoken opposition to American involvement in the First World War earned him a reputation as a German sympathiser in the eyes of the British government, and in the autumn of 1916, while America was still neutral, his agency was effectively barred from Europe. With Hearst and his papers cut off from the most important source of foreign news, INS resorted to various subterfuges to replace the missing bulletins, some of them ethically questionable, and some undoubtedly illegal.[2]

Melville Stone, the General Manager of Associated Press, was passionately committed to the idea that news was property, and that like any other kind of property it should be protected by law. In January 1917 AP sued INS in the Federal Court for the Southern District of New York, and applied for various interlocutory injunctions.[3] The first was to restrain use of news leaked by an individual telegraph operator in Cleveland, Ohio. The second was to restrain INS from using unpublished AP bulletins provided by a Hearst paper which was a member of AP, in clear beach of its terms of membership. Finally, it was alleged in very general terms that INS had made a practice of copying AP news items from the public bulletin boards and early morning editions of subscribing East Coast papers, and telegraphing the contents to their mid-Western and West Coast subscribers in time for publication in their own early editions.

At first instance, Judge Augustus Hand granted interim injunctions against the first two practices. However, he was unwilling to enjoin INS in respect of the third, on an interlocutory application, when to do so would have made new law. The Court of Appeal for the Second Circuit added the third injunction to the two previously granted.[4] INS appealed to the Supreme Court.

[1] *International News Service v Associated Press* 248 US 215, 39 S Ct 68, 63 L Ed 211 (1918). The continuing relevance of the doctrine in the United States is shown by the recent decision in *Associated Press v All Headline News Corp* 608 F Supp 2d 454 (SDNY, 2009), refusing to dismiss common law claims against an internet site for misappropriation of AP's 'hot news'.

[2] For the factual background to *INS*, see DG Baird, 'The Story of *INS v AP*: Property, Natural Monopoly, and the Uneasy Legacy of a Concocted Controversy' in JC Ginsburg and RC Dreyfuss (eds), *Intellectual Property Stories* (New York, Foundation Press, 2006).

[3] *Associated Press v International News Service* 240 F 983 (District Court, New York, 1917); Baird 'Story of *INS*' (n 2) 23–28.

[4] *Associated Press v International News Service* 245 F 244 (Circuit Court of Appeals, Second Circuit, 1917).

The Supreme Court

The Supreme Court was divided, but upheld all the injunctions. Speaking for the majority, Justice Pitney said:[5]

> The fault in the reasoning [that the plaintiffs' rights were lost upon publication] lies in applying as a test the right of the complainant as against the public, instead of considering the rights of complainant and defendant, competitors in business, as between themselves. The right of the purchaser of a single newspaper to spread knowledge of its contents gratuitously, for any legitimate purpose not unreasonably interfering with complainant's right to make merchandise of it, may be admitted; but to transmit that news for commercial use, in competition with complainant—which is what defendant has done and seeks to justify—is a very different matter. In doing this defendant, by its very act, admits that it is taking material that has been acquired by complainant as the result of organization and the expenditure of labor, skill, and money, and which is salable by complainant for money, and that defendant in appropriating it and selling it as its own is endeavoring to reap where it has not sown, and by disposing of it to newspapers that are competitors of complainant's members is appropriating to itself the harvest of those who have sown. Stripped of all disguises, the process amounts to an unauthorized interference with the normal operation of complainant's legitimate business precisely at the point where the profit is to be reaped, in order to divert a material portion of the profit from those who have earned it to those who have not; with special advantage to defendant in the competition because of the fact that it is not burdened with any part of the expense of gathering the news. The transaction speaks for itself and a court of equity ought not to hesitate long in characterizing it as unfair competition in business.

Of the rest of the Supreme Court, Justice Holmes (with whom Justice McKenna concurred) would have found for AP on much more limited grounds, but the majority entirely concurred with Justice Pitney. Justice Brandeis dissented.[6]

The Judicial Reception of *INS*

Taken to the full extent of its possible implications, the majority judgment in *INS* would surely have created something approximating to an all-embracing shadow system of common law intellectual property rights, extending far beyond the familiar regimes of copyright, patents, designs and trade marks, and all without any Constitutional mandate, or any legislative or administrative supervision. With just such concerns in mind

[5] *International News Service v Associated Press* 248 US 215 (1918) 239.
[6] Ibid 248.

the Second Circuit soon reversed direction and ruled, in *Cheney Bros v Doris Silk Corporation*,[7] that notwithstanding *INS*, there was no liability in unfair competition for copying fashionable fabric designs. *INS* was further undermined in 1938 with the decision of the Supreme Court in *Erie v Tompkins*,[8] which denied that any separate system of general federal common law existed in diversity cases such as *INS*,[9] and referred all such claims to state law. Also in 1938, the Supreme Court decided the 'Shredded Wheat' case, *Kellogg v National Biscuit*,[10] which would have given it an ideal opportunity to reinstate the former's underlying philosophy and much of its reasoning, had it wanted to do so. Instead, Justice Brandeis, the solitary dissenter before, delivered the opinion of the Court, in which he pointedly ignored *INS* altogether.

The next historical phase in the history of *INS* lasted until the twin Supreme Court decisions in *Sears Roebuck v Stifel*[11] and *Compco v Day-Brite*,[12] and during this phase the doctrine was the property of the state courts alone. *Sears/Compco* decided that the application of the misappropriation doctrine was subject to federal pre-emption when it intruded on areas already occupied by the federal patent and copyright laws; but perhaps surprisingly this caused no more than a temporary setback, and the doctrine continued to thrive in at least some state courts, and at least some factual contexts, though never with all the generality inherent in *INS* itself. The immediate post-*Sears* period ended with the Supreme Court decision in *Goldstein v California*,[13] which endorsed much of this state-level adventurousness, disapproved the excessive caution of *Sears/Compco*, and seemed to usher in a golden age for the misappropriation doctrine. The latter proved short-lived, however, because the new codification of copyright law in 1976[14] redefined the boundaries between (federal) copyright law and (state) unfair competition law, very much to the disadvantage of the latter.[15]

[7] *Cheney Bros v Doris Silk Corporation* 35 F2d 279 (CA, Second Circuit, 1929).

[8] *Erie Railroad Co v Tompkins* 304 US 64, 58 S Ct 817, 82 L Ed 1188 (1938); reversing *Swift v Tyson* 41 US 1, 10 L Ed 865 (1842).

[9] Ie cases in which the jurisdiction of the federal courts arose from the fact that the parties were citizens of different states, and not from the fact that federal law was in issue.

[10] *Kellogg Co v National Biscuit Co* 305 US 111, 59 S Ct 109, 83 L Ed 73 (1938). The Court decided that there was no liability for copying the appearance of 'Shredded Wheat' biscuits, effectively confining liability in such cases to situations demonstrating secondary meaning and confusion.

[11] *Sears Roebuck & Co v Stiffel Co* 376 US 225, 84 S Ct 784, 11 L Ed 2d 661 (1964).

[12] *Compco Corp v Day-Brite Lighting Inc* 376 US 234, 84 S Ct 779, 11 L Ed 2d 669 (1964).

[13] *Goldstein v California* 412 US 546, 37 L Ed 2d 163, 93 S Ct 2003 (1993).

[14] Copyright Act 1976. The Act came into effect on 1 January 1978. Pre-emption was addressed by §301(a) and (b).

[15] See (inter alia) HB Abrams, 'Copyright, Misappropriation and Preemption: Constitutional and Statutory Limits of State Law Protection' (1983) 11 *Supreme Court Review* 509–81.

Which *INS*?

In so far as 'hot news' as such is concerned, the present state of the doctrine in American law is probably best taken from *NBS v Motorola*.[16] The claim was in respect of a hand-held pager which displayed near real-time information on the scores and progress of professional basketball matches. The Second Circuit held that the 'hot news' doctrine of *INS* survived federal pre-emption by the Copyright Act only in very narrow circumstances. Specifically, the court held, dismissing the misappropriation claim:[17]

> [T]he surviving 'hot-news' *INS*-like claim is limited to cases where: (i) a plaintiff generates or gathers information at a cost; (ii) the information is time-sensitive; (iii) a defendant's use of the information constitutes free-riding on the plaintiff's efforts; (iv) the defendant is in direct competition with a product or service offered by the plaintiff; and (v) the ability of other parties to free-ride on the efforts of the plaintiff or others would so reduce the incentive to produce the product or service in question that its existence or quality would be substantially threatened.

However, at the opposite end of the scale to *NBA v Motorola* there stands *Board of Trade of the City of Chicago v Dow Jones & Co*,[18] in which the doctrine was held to apply to prevent the Chicago Board of Trade introducing a futures contract based on the *Dow Jones Index*. So at one end of the scale we have an action which is crucially dependent not only on actual competition, but on the imminent prospect of destruction of the very product or service copied; whereas at the other (*Dow Jones*) end there is neither competition nor damage, and we seem to be dealing with unjust enrichment pure and simple.

THE RECEPTION OF *INTERNATIONAL NEWS* OUTSIDE AMERICA

The Common Law, and the Constitutional Background

Well before *International News Service v Associated Press* there was fairly generous copyright protection for factual information in English law,[19] both before and after publication, and for information of all kinds under the law of confidence.[20] With the wisdom of hindsight, it is clear that the latter kind of protection was irretrievably lost on publication, but both sets of cases could be mined for dicta to support the idea of property

[16] *National Basketball Association v Motorola Inc* 105 F3d 841 (CA, Second Circuit, 1997).

[17] Ibid 845.

[18] *Board of Trade of the City of Chicago v Dow Jones & Co* 456 NE 2d 84 (Ill SC, 1983)

[19] Such as the 'directory cases', some of which were cited by Justice Pitney.

[20] The 'telegraph cases', likewise.

in the information as such, based either on the effort with which it was compiled, or on its commercial value and vulnerability to piracy. On the other hand, in favour of the defendants, there was the decision in the *Our Dogs* case,[21] as well as the fact that the English copyright cases could not simply be replicated in the United States because of a different and less favourable statutory framework.

Although Australia and Canada have federal constitutions in which copyright is a federal matter, and unfair competition is at least to some degree a matter for the several states or provinces, this seems to have contributed little or not at all to their reception (or not) of *INS*, nor to the spontaneous creation of any similar doctrine. In respect of the constitutional division of powers in Canada, David Vaver noted:[22]

> [T]he Trade-Marks Act does not, any more than the common law, set out to 'prevent unfair competition and the misappropriation of intellectual property.' The one explicit provision in the *Act* that did so was ruled unconstitutional by the Supreme Court in 1976.

In the case of the United Kingdom, of course, the tension between federal and state law has no counterpart, unless it be between Scots and English law, which show no perceptible divergence in this respect.

Judicial Citation of *INS*

In the English law reports, *INS* appears to have been invoked only two or three times. The first of these cases[23] cited it only for the dissenting judgment of Justice Holmes, and the support the latter gives for the relatively uncontroversial and incremental concept of reverse (or inverse) passing-off, which unlike the misappropriation doctrine favoured by the *INS* majority, involves no major breaks with traditional common law thinking. The second was the decision of the Privy Council in the *Pub Squash* case,[24] which really belongs to the history of Australian, rather than English, law. In the third, counsel attempted to argue (inevitably without success) that *Pub Squash* had somehow endorsed the misappropriation doctrine of *INS*.[25]

[21] *Sports and General Press Agency Ltd v 'Our Dogs' Publishing Co Ltd* [1916] 2 KB 880 (Horridge J), aff'd [1917] 2 KB 125, CA.

[22] D Vaver, *Intellectual Property Law* (Concord, Ont, Irwin Law, 1997) 175. See text at n 52.

[23] *Bristol Conservatories v Conservatories Custom Built* [1989] RPC 455, CA.

[24] *Cadbury-Schweppes Pty Ltd v The Pub Squash Co Ltd* [1981] 1 WLR 193, [1981] RPC 429, PC.

[25] *Harrods Ltd v Schwartz-Sackin & Co Ltd* [1986] FSR 490, rev'd (without reference to this point) (1987) [1991] FSR 209, CA.

This is not to say that the doctrine of *INS* was or is unknown to English practitioners, or to academics.[26] It has certainly been cited often enough in the literature, if only as a footnote, whether in support of the perennial argument for better legal protection against unfair competition in general, or for the deserving causes of the moment. At first sight, *INS* should have been the special favourite of those interest groups and lobbyists who have difficulty in stating what legitimate interest their members or clients have in combating 'misappropriations' of various kinds which involve no misrepresentation, and typically cause no damage.

On the contrary, what is most noticeable is that reliance on *INS* in court actually seems to have been avoided, even in cases to which its broad formula of misappropriation would appear to be directly applicable, and in which a modest venture into comparative law would have been entirely possible. A particularly obvious case in point is *L'Oreal v Bellure*,[27] the case of the replica designer perfumes. Bellure copied, crudely but recognisably, the principal olfactory characteristics of a range of expensive fine fragrance brands developed and marketed by L'Oreal,[28] and sold them through retailers in various down-market locations at less than a twentieth of the price of the original. The names and packaging selected by Bellure might be said to have contained some kind of allusion to the corresponding brand names and get-up of L'Oreal, but there was far too little resemblance for there to be classic passing-off either by name or get-up, even before taking into account the different sales channels, the very low prices, and the very different target markets. No one who bought 'Nice Flower' (from Bellure's *Création Lamis* range) would have expected to get L'Oreal's 'Anaïs-Anaïs', although they would (rightly) have expected to get something smelling vaguely similar.

To that extent L'Oreal's claim can only have been for some hitherto unknown common law tort of 'unfair copying', and it duly failed.[29] However, *INS* was never cited, even in argument, and rightly so, since the concern of L'Oreal's lawyers was to win their case for their clients, not to impress with their academic credentials. Their reason might have been that *INS* simply has too many possible interpretations. But the more fundamental explanation is that in English forensic usage, *INS* has long since gone the same way as the term 'unfair competition'[30] itself. Both now serve the sole function of alerting

[26] *International News* has had a paragraph or so to itself in all editions of the classic textbook by William Cornish, first published in 1981. For the present edition, see W Cornish and D Llewellyn, *Intellectual Property*, 6th edn (Cambridge, CUP, 2007) at §1–15.

[27] *L'Oreal SA v Bellure NV* [2007] EWCA Civ 968, [2008] ETMR 1.

[28] TRESOR, MIRACLE, ANAIS ANAIS and NOA.

[29] Issues of registered trade mark infringement are not dealt with here.

[30] 'To draw a line between fair and unfair competition ... passes the power of the Courts.' Per Fry LJ in *Mogul Steamship Co Ltd v McGregor Gow & Co* (1889) LR 23 QBD 598 (CA) 625; aff'd [1892] AC 25 (HL).

the court to the approach of an unarguable and unwinnable point of law, and both are consciously eschewed by well-advised claimants as a result.

Before leaving *L'Oreal v Bellure*, it is actually a very good example of the uncertainty as to just what *INS* is supposed to stand for. If *INS* were concerned solely with unjust enrichment in the sense of commercial parasitism, or 'free riding', or *concurrence parasitaire*; in short if 'reaping without sowing' were the sole determinative criterion, then L'Oreal would have been home and dry. Here, after all, was a particularly blatant appropriation of 'valuable intangibles' of two distinct kinds: the scent itself, considered as a desirable sensory experience, which was almost certainly the work of a master *parfumier*, exercising the skill and judgment of a lifetime; and the goodwill or prestige attaching to the product per se (as opposed to the distinctive name) which was partly due to the quality of the product and its presentation, and partly the result of expensive advertising and careful nurturing of its luxury image. Yet there is an equally prevalent interpretation of *INS* which crucially depends on there being actual competition between the parties, and actual damage to the claimant, even to the extent of liability depending on the real prospect of parasitic competition imminently destroying a particular line of business.[31] On this latter interpretation of *INS*, L'Oreal's case was hopeless.

Perhaps, in other circumstances, *INS* or some of its American progeny might have gained a foothold of acceptance in specific factual situations such as the piracy of 'hot' news, or other kinds of valuable information.[32] What we tend to find instead is that the common law typically had no need of *INS*, not least because 'neighbouring rights', as well as copyrights in various kinds of entrepreneurial productions, were much more readily available than in the United States, as was copyright in purely factual 'sweat of the brow' materials.[33] The common law is typically incremental, and like the proverbial journey, needs to begin with a first step. Since there seemed to be little or no need to take even the first step on the road marked 'unfair competition by misappropriation', when other roads such as that marked 'copyright' were so much more convenient, that first step was never taken, and so the road was never travelled at all.

Victoria Park: the Facts and the Judgment

The obvious candidate for a case which in which that crucial first step might have been taken, but was not, is the decision of the High Court of Australia in *Victoria Park Racing v Taylor*.[34] The defendant, Taylor, owned land

[31] *National Basketball Association v Motorola* (n 16).
[32] For some paradigm situations see below, after n 75.
[33] See also below, after n 92.
[34] *Victoria Park Racing v Taylor* (1937) 58 CLR 479 (High Court of Australia, Full Court).

overlooking the plaintiffs' race course and he allowed the second defendants, a radio station, to erect a tower from which they broadcast live commentaries on the races, with the not surprising result that attendance at the race meetings declined and off-course betting flourished. The High Court dismissed the action by a majority of three to two. In the judgment, which has been most influential in later times, Dixon J fully endorsed the dissenting judgment of Justice Brandeis in *INS* as accurately stating the common law:[35]

> The fact is that the substance of the plaintiff's complaint goes to interference, not with its enjoyment of the land, but with the profitable conduct of its business. If English law had followed the course of development that has recently taken place in the United States, the 'broadcasting rights' in respect of the races might have been protected as part of the quasi-property created by the enterprise, organisation and labour of the plaintiff in establishing and equipping a racecourse and doing all that is necessary to conduct race meetings. But courts of equity have not in British jurisdiction thrown the protection of an injunction around all intangible elements of value, that is, value in exchange, which may flow from the exercise by an individual of his powers or resources whether in the organisation of a business or the use of ingenuity, knowledge, skill or labour. This is sufficiently evidenced by the history of the law of copyright and by the fact that the exclusive right to invention, trade marks, designs, trade name and reputation are dealt within English law as special heads of protected interests and not under a wide generalisation.
>
> In dissenting from a judgment of the Supreme Court of the United States by which the organised collection of news by a news service was held to give it in equity a quasi-property protected against appropriation by rival news agencies, Brandeis J. gave reasons which substantially represent the English law and he supported his opinion by a citation of much English authority (*International News v Associated Press*). His judgment appears to me to contain an adequate answer both upon principle and authority to the suggestion that the defendants are misappropriating or abstracting something which the plaintiff has created and alone is entitled to turn to value. Briefly, the answer is that it is not because the individual has by his efforts put himself in a position to obtain value for what he can give that his right to give it becomes protected by law and so assumed the exclusiveness of property, but because the intangible or incorporeal right he claims falls within a recognised category to which legal or equitable protection attaches.

From *Victoria Park* to *Moorgate v Phillip Morris*

Between about 1960, with *Henderson v Radio Corporation*[36] and the decision of the Privy Council in the *Pub Squash* case in 1980,[37] a number

[35] Ibid 508–10.
[36] *Henderson v Radio Corporation* [1960] NSWLR 279, [1969] RPC 218 (Full Court).
[37] *Cadbury-Schweppes v Pub Squash* [1981] 1 WLR 193, [1981] RPC 429 (PC).

of Australian judgments flirted with variations on the misappropriation doctrine in the context of personality rights, programme format rights, and unfair competition generally. These are mostly outside the scope of the present chapter, however, and there was generally no explicit reliance on *INS* as opposed to the general principle it stood for. In *Pub Squash*, *INS* was indeed cited at trial and on appeal, but the Privy Council dismissed the appeal with no more than a non-committal reference to it.[38] A final attempt (at least for the present) to establish a misappropriation-based tort of unfair competition in Australia failed in *Moorgate v Philip Morris*.[39] Deane J, delivering the judgment of the full Court, took the opportunity to reopen the scar tissue on the wounds left by Dixon J after *Victoria Park*, and pour in some acid comments of his own. Noting the strong dissent of Justice Brandeis and the disagreement of Justice Holmes, Deane J went on to cite *Kellogg v National Biscuit* as evidence that *INS* had fallen from favour even in the Supreme Court, and concluded (from the partial example of the Second Circuit) that the subsequent trend even in lower courts had been to confine it to its facts.

Academic Opinion in the Commonwealth

A new approach to unfair competition law in general was becoming apparent—not least in Australia—from about 1970 onwards, but this development was short-lived and became something of a spent force with the relatively conservative decisions of the House of Lords in *Advocaat* in 1979,[40] the Privy Council in *Pub Squash* in 1980,[41] and the High Court of Australia in *Moorgate* in 1984.[42] However, there was at least one precursor to this phenomenon, in the person of Professor WL Morison. In 1951,[43] and more definitively in 1956,[44] he had dealt quite extensively with *INS*, and had concluded (without obvious regret) that passing-off was likely for

[38] 'Their Lordships prefer to express no opinion on [*INS*] in a case such as the present where the facts do not require that it be considered.'

[39] *Moorgate Tobacco Co v Philip Morris Ltd (No 2)* (1984) 156 CLR 414, (1984) 3 IPR 545.

[40] *Erven Warnink BV v J Townend & Sons (Hull) Ltd* [1979] AC 731, [1980] RPC 31 (HL). Early responses to *Advocaat* sometimes treated is as foreshadowing acceptance of the principle of *INS*, but this was not to happen. For examples see J Lahore 'Intellectual Property Rights and Unfair Copying: Old Concepts, New Ideas' (1992) 14 *European Intellectual Property Review* 428; G Dworkin, 'Unfair Competition: Is the Common Law Developing a new Tort?' (1979) 1 *European Intellectual Property Review* 241.

[41] *Cadbury-Schweppes v Pub Squash* (n 24).

[42] *Moorgate v Philip Morris* (n 39).

[43] WL Morison, 'Unfair Competition at Common Law' (1951) 2 *University of Western Australia Law Review* 34.

[44] WL Morrison, 'Unfair Competition and Passing-off: the Flexibility of a Formula' (1956) 2 *Sydney Law Review* 50.

the foreseeable future to remain a tort of misrepresentation rather than becoming one of misappropriation.

In his wide-ranging article of 1972 William Cornish cited the *INS* decision only once, and in a minor footnote reference at that.[45] A year later, in *Economic Torts*,[46] Professor JD Heydon gave a short but perceptive account of the place of the *INS* misappropriation doctrine in relation to passing-off and the nominate economic torts. According to him, to base *INS* in property was circular, since it was the law which determined what constituted property in the first place, and it was equally unsatisfactory to base it on a moral criterion as vague as that of reaping without sowing. A better justification was that appropriation of the fruits of another's expenditure, ideas or work would be enjoined if the public interest demanded it, but only then. This might justify specific applications of the principle, but in many cases innovation would occur without the need for any such doctrine; and the public interest in favour of protection always had to be set against several countervailing factors: in particular those of legal certainty, freedom of competition, and freedom to copy from the public domain.

On the other side of the argument, one need only read the title of Sam Ricketson's 1984 article '"Reaping without sowing": Unfair Competition and Intellectual Property Rights in Anglo-Australian Law' to guess that *INS* would be favourably received, as indeed it was;[47] and by 1988 *INS* may be said to have dominated Andrew Terry's 'Unfair Competition and the Misappropriation of a Competitor's Trade Values'.[48] While several of these analyses had emphasised the proprietary aspects of *INS*, an unequivocally restitutionary interpretation of the *INS* decision was advanced by Brian Fitzgerald and Leif Gamertsfelder as a justification for the protection of 'informational products' in general.[49] It may be noted that despite a mix of English and Australian publications, and despite the negativity of the *Victoria Park* case, all these authors were Australians.[50] In New Zealand, Susy Frankel has endorsed the rejection of a general tort of 'unfair competition'

[45] W Cornish, 'Unfair Competition? A Progress Report' (1972) *Journal of the Society of Public Teachers of Law* 126.

[46] JD Heydon, *Economic Torts* (Modern Legal Studies) (London, Sweet & Maxwell, 1973).

[47] S Ricketson, '"Reaping without sowing": Unfair Competition and Intellectual Property Rights in Anglo-Australian Law' (1984) 7 *University of New South Wales Law Journal* 1 (Special Issue).

[48] A Terry, 'Unfair Competition and the Misappropriation of a Competitor's Trade Values' [1988] *Modern Law Review* 296.

[49] BF Fitzgerald and L Gamertsfelder, 'Protecting informational products (including databases) through unjust enrichment law: an Australian perspective' (1998) 20 *European Intellectual Property Review* 244.

[50] Some further contributions by Australian nationals in England are considered below, at n 62 *et seq*.

against attempts to anchor it in doctrines of 'misappropriation' or 'unjust enrichment'.[51]

As compared to Australia, New Zealand, or the United Kingdom, Canada was perhaps rather more susceptible to the influence of *INS* for reasons of geographical proximity to the United States, but the possibility of this happening at the federal level was cut short by the Supreme Court of Canada in *MacDonald v Vapor Canada*,[52] in which the Court struck down as unconstitutional section 7(e) of the Trade Marks Act RSC c T-10.[53] This was a trade secret case, but it was argued that the facts of *INS* would have fallen under section 7(e). *INS* does not seem to have found favour in the provincial courts, and the academic literature is not plentiful. At the theoretical and jurisprudential level, *INS* influenced Stephen Waddams in his *Dimensions of Private Law*,[54] and some examples of *INS* being invoked in argument are given below.[55]

Canada is, of course, a bi-jural jurisdiction, though there does not appear to be any separate body of law based on *INS* in the civil law of Quebec,[56] and the same may be said for the mixed jurisdiction of Scotland. In South Africa, however, *INS* seems to have struck a chord with its local Roman-Dutch tradition, as evidenced by Loubster[57] and Neethling.[58] Whether this is an aspect of Aquillian liability, or is due to the greater prominence of unjust enrichment in the civil law, is for the Romanists.

International News in English Academic Literature

INS is nowhere like as prominent in English academic literature as in the former Dominions. Authors on passing-off as such tend to agree with

[51] S Frankel, 'Unfair Competition Law—"Over Protection Stifles the very Creative Force it is Supposed to Nurture"' in CEF Rickett and GW Austin (eds), *International Intellectual Property in the Common Law World* (Oxford, Hart Publishing, 2000).

[52] *MacDonald v Vapor Canada* [1977] 2 SCR 134.

[53] 'No person shall ... do any other act or adopt any other business practice contrary to honest industrial or commercial usage in Canada'.

[54] S Waddams, *Dimensions of Private Law* (Cambridge: CUP, 2003) 173–75.

[55] At nn 82 and 87.

[56] Though *INS* contributed to the decision of Jean-Louis Péloquin J in *Vidéotron Ltée c Industrie Microlec Produits Électroniques Inc* [1988] RJQ 546 (Quebec *Cour Superieur*), holding that the supply of signal decoders was actionable as *concurrence déloyale* at the suit of the television cable companies under Art 1053 of the Civil Code of Lower Canada (as noted by D Vaver, 'Intellectual Property Today: Of Myths and Paradoxes' [1990] *Canadian Bar Review* 98, 101, n 7).

[57] MM Loubster, 'Principles and Policy in Unlawful Competition: An Aquilian Mask' [2000] *Acta Juridica* 168.

[58] J Neethling, 'Passing off and Misappropriation of the Advertising Value of Trade Marks, Trade Names, and Service Marks' [1993] *South African Mercantile Law Journal* 306; J Neethling, 'Misappropriation or Copying of a Rival's Performance as a Form of Unlawful Competition (Prestasieaanlampling)' [1993] *South African Law Journal* 711.

Morrison,[59] that the narrow justification of *INS* in terms of 'inverse' passing-off is compatible with the common law in its present state of development, but that any wider doctrine of unfair competition by 'misappropriation' of 'valuable intangibles' is not.[60]

That leaves *INS* to three camps of commentators: it provides one alternative paradigm for those who would radically overhaul the entire common law of unfair competition in favour of liability on a much wider basis, possibly by analogy also with Continental European law. Andrew Terry[61] is an obvious example of this approach, as is Anselm Kamperman Sanders.[62] Both are heavily influenced by Rudolf Callmann,[63] who so to speak provides the missing link between the common law and civil law doctrines.[64] It is sometimes hard to draw the line between these commentators and a more numerous, but less ambitious camp, who would retain passing-off much as it is, but would use *INS* to graft on a concurrent source of liability for 'misappropriation', to balance the latter's fixation with misrepresentation.[65] Finally there are those who have an axe to grind in support of some specific cause or interest group.[66] These may be rather less concerned with the wider implications of *INS*, which they may indeed disclaim so as not

[59] Morrison, 'Unfair Competition' (n 44).

[60] C Wadlow, *The Law of Passing-off: Unfair Competition by Misrepresentation*, 3rd edn (London, Sweet & Maxwell, 2004); H Carty, 'Inverse Passing off: a Suitable Addition to Passing off?' (1993) 15 *European Intellectual Property Review* 370; H Carty, *An Analysis of the Economic Torts* (Oxford, OUP, 2000).

[61] Terry, 'Unfair Competition' (n 48): an Australian, but writing in an English journal, as is true for several more of the authors who follow.

[62] A Kamperman Sanders, *Unfair Competition Law: The Protection of Intellectual and Industrial Creativity* (Oxford, Clarendon Press, 1997). Compare PJ Kaufmann, *Passing off and Misappropriation: An Economic and Legal Analysis of the Law of Unfair Competition in the United States and Continental Europe* (Weinheim, VCH, 1986).

[63] Rudolf Callmann (1892–1976) was a prominent German unfair competition lawyer, who was forced to emigrate to the United States in 1936. He was highly supportive of the *INS* doctrine in his numerous works on American unfair competition law, most notably the monumental treatise (first published in 1945) which is now continued as L Altman and M Pollock (eds) *Callmann on Unfair Competition, Trademarks, and Monopolies*, 4th edn (St Paul, Minn, Thomson-West, loose-leaf).

[64] The present author has in preparation an article on Callmann and *INS*, provisionally entitled 'Rudolf Callmann and the Misappropriation Doctrine in the Common Law of Unfair Competition'.

[65] Examples from one or other of these camps include P Burns, 'Unfair Competition: A Compelling Need Unmet' (1981) 3 *European Intellectual Property Review* 311; JN Adams, 'Unfair Competition: why a Need is Unmet' (1992) 14 *European Intellectual Property Review* 259; D Harms, 'Hark! There goes a tort' (1995) 17 *European Intellectual Property Review* 453; A Horton and A Robertson, 'Does the United Kingdom or the European Community need an unfair competition law?' (1995) 17 *European Intellectual Property Review* 568. On the other hand, it is quite possible to call for reform of passing-off without invoking either *INS* or misappropriation: eg A Booy, 'A half-way house for unfair competition in the United Kingdom—a practitioner's plea' (1991) 13 *European Intellectual Property Review* 439.

[66] Examples include JN Adams, 'Is There a Tort of Unfair Competition? The Legal Protection of Advertising Campaigns and Merchandising' [1985] *Journal of Business Law* 26; and H Beverley-Smith *The Commercial Appropriation of Personality* (Cambridge, CUP, 2002).

to arouse unnecessary opposition. For them, *INS* is primarily valuable in so far as it evidences high judicial approval of what is essentially a moral precept against 'reaping where one has not sown.' It is not unfair to say of all these camps, that the more experienced their authors are in the ways of English law, the less reliance they are likely to place on *INS*. To the experienced, *INS* is damaged goods.

Finally, *INS* may be addressed—or more probably dismissed—by authors whose attitude to it is hostile, sceptical or critical,[67] such as Peter Kaufmann,[68] Hazel Carty,[69] William Cornish,[70] Gerald Dworkin,[71] Michael Spence,[72] and myself.[73] For David Vaver the majority opinion in *INS* embodied much that is wrong with the modern intellectual property system itself, with its all too ready assumptions that more protection is always better, that imitation is inexcusable, and that no degree of effort is too low to be worth protecting:[74]

> [T]he prejudice that often masquerades today as policy analysis—'what is worth copying is prima facie worth protecting'—was trotted out in 1916 by a U.K. court to extend IPRs to the commonplace .... The opposite stance—'what is worth copying is prima facie worth letting be copied' [essentially the position taken, although not in those precise words, by Brandeis J. in *International News Service v Associated Press*, albeit, significantly, in dissent] would at least have focused greater attention on when, why and how far IPRs should be granted?

THREE PARADIGM SITUATIONS

News, Geography and Culture

Several of the differences between the United States and the common law countries considered here may be illustrated by three paradigm situations: 'hot' news, broadcasts of sports events, and the recording of live performances for commercial purposes (or 'bootlegging').

[67] A number of non-English authors are included in this list because of their closer connection with England (especially at the relevant times of publication), or simply for want of a better home.

[68] Kaufmann, *Passing-off and Misappropriation* (n 62).

[69] H Carty, 'Passing Off and the Concept of Goodwill' [1995] *Journal of Business Law* 139; Carty, *Economic Torts* (n 60); H Carty, 'The Common Law and the Quest for the IP Effect' [2007] *Intellectual Property Quarterly* 237.

[70] W Cornish, 'Genevan Bootstraps' (1997) 19 *European Intellectual Property Review* 336.

[71] G Dworkin, 'Unfair Competition: Is it Time for European Harmonisation?' in D Vaver and L Bently (eds) *Intellectual Property in the New Millennium: Essays in Honour of William R Cornish* (Cambridge, CUP, 2004).

[72] M Spence, 'Passing off and the Misappropriation of Valuable Intangibles' (1996) 112 *Law Quarterly Review* 472–98.

[73] Wadlow, *Passing-off* (n 60).

[74] D Vaver 'Taking Stock' (1999) 21 *European Intellectual Property Review* 339. A footnote has been incorporated into the text for the sake of clarity, where it is indicated by square brackets.

So far as news is concerned, one must take account of important factual and cultural differences, as well as purely legal ones. The *INS* case only happened in the first place—or at least, it only caught the imagination—because Hearst could exploit the time lag between the East and West coasts. Compare the United Kingdom, where there is a single time zone and the time difference between East and West coasts is a matter of minutes, and where the London press is effectively the national press. Even so, copying has occurred, and there was English authority prior to *INS* which was considerably more favourable to claimants. In *Walter v Steinkopff*[75] the defendant, the publisher and proprietor of the *St James' Gazette*, was restrained from copying news items and features taken from that day's edition of *The Times*. Admittedly, the copying was wholesale and extensive, and the judgment acknowledged that it was not the news itself, but the form of expression which was protected by copyright; but even so the difference in result was striking, and the barriers to success considerably lower than in *INS*.

In Canada and Australia two of the factors of *INS* were reproduced, namely the geography of a vast country divided into several time zones, and the absence of a national press, but the markets were smaller and even more concentrated in single time zones, and the all-important element of competition between rival news agencies seems to have been absent, or at least muted. At any rate, neither country gave rise to any decision comparable to *INS*.[76]

Sports Events

Turning to the broadcasting of sports events, as in *Victoria Park* itself, the remaining jurisdictions to consider are Canada and the United States.[77] In the latter, and in a decision coincidentally issued within a year of *Victoria Park*, virtually identical behaviour was enjoined under the *INS* misappropriation doctrine in a case in which the defendant radio station rented an apartment overlooking the field of play of the 'Pittsburgh Pirates' baseball team, and used it to broadcast live commentaries.[78] With new developments in

[75] *Walter v Steinkopff* [1892] 3 Ch 489 (North J). The original sources were acknowledged.

[76] One must also take into account the unfavourable legal environment, with *Our Dogs* from 1917, and *Victoria Park* from 1937.

[77] *Victoria Park* being determinative in Australia, and *Our Dogs* in the UK. *Victoria Park*, especially, would also have been strongly persuasive elsewhere. See J-P Blais, 'The Protection of Exclusive Television Rights to Sporting Events held in Public Venues: An Overview of the Law in Australia and Canada' (1992) 18 *Melbourne University Law Review* 503–39. However, *Victoria Park* was effectively reversed on its facts in 1956, when the Broadcasting and Television Act 1942 (Commonwealth) was amended, initially to protect the organisers of the 1956 Melbourne Olympic Games, though the new s 115 was in perfectly general terms. See Blais, op cit n 36.

[78] *Pittsburgh Athletic Co v KQV Broadcasting Co* 24 F Supp 490 (D Pa 1938).

technology a further problem arose: that of one broadcaster retransmitting a broadcast originally made with the consent of the owner of the ground or the promoter of the event. In the United States, rebroadcasting of sporting events was enjoined under the *INS* doctrine at the suit of the authorised broadcaster in *Mutual Broadcasting System, Inc v Muzak Corp*;[79] and at the suit of the home team (the New York Giants) in *National Exhibition Co v Fass*.[80]

In Canada, the same problem arose in *Canadian Admiral Corp Ltd v Rediffusion Inc*,[81] in which the defendants intercepted authorised broadcasts of games of the Montreal *Alouettes* football team (for which the plaintiffs, as sponsors, had exclusive broadcasting rights) and distributed them by cable to subscribers. However *Canadian Admiral* was argued and decided (against the plaintiffs) solely on the basis of copyright law, and it was left to commentators to speculate on how it might have been decided under unfair competition law and the *INS* doctrine.[82]

Bootlegging

The final scenario is 'bootlegging',[83] and its close equivalents. The United States never acceded to the Rome Convention,[84] and until very recently there was no federal protection for performers in their capacity as such. There was, however, considerable activity at state level to provide a degree of performers' protection either by statute, or in the courts under the rubric of unfair competition law,[85] and in due course this development was legitimated by the Supreme Court in *Goldstein*.

In the United Kingdom, the Performers' Protection Acts 1958–72 gave effect to the provisions of the Rome Convention, which the UK ratified in 1964.[86] These Acts gave rise to criminal liability only, and considerable ingenuity was expended in trying to create a civil law cause of action to

[79] *Mutual Broadcasting System, Inc v Muzak Corp* 177 Misc 489, 30 NYS2d 419 (1941). (Commentaries on World Series baseball games retransmitted on leased telephone lines).

[80] *National Exhibition Co v Fass* 133 NYS2d 379 (NY Sup Ct 1954); *National Exhibition Co v Fass* 143 NYS2d 767 (NY Sup Ct 1955).

[81] *Canadian Admiral Corp Ltd v Rediffusion Inc* (1954) *Canadian Patent Reporter* 75 (Exchequer Court of Canada).

[82] W Filipuk, 'The *Canadian Admiral* case—Canada's Law of Unfair Competition' (1958) 16 *Faculty Law Review* 109; Anon, (note) (1955) *Harvard Law Review* 712.

[83] Bootlegging in the narrow sense involves recording a live performance, at the event itself.

[84] The International Convention for the Protection of Performers, Producers of Phonograms and Broadcasting Organizations (Rome, 1961).

[85] Notable examples being *Waring v WDAS Broadcasting Station* 327 Pa 433, 194 Atl 631 (1937); *Metropolitan Opera Ass'n v Wagner-Nichols Recorder Corp* 199 Misc 786, 101 NYS2d 483 (1950), aff'd, 279 AD 632, 107 NYS2d 795 (1951).

[86] Performers' protection in the UK dated back much further, to the Dramatic and Musical Performers' Protection Act 1925.

correspond.[87] In so far as this was a step in the direction of a general law of 'unfair competition', however, the emphasis was firmly on the illegality of the defendants' conduct, and the consequent damage to the rights or interests of the claimants (whether the artists themselves, or their record companies); rather than on moral condemnation of 'reaping without sowing', and the defendants' unjustified enrichment of themselves. There was no reference in any of these cases to *INS* itself, nor to any genus of protected 'valuable intangibles', and next to none to 'misappropriation' as a legal concept. The arguments were based on entirely different and indigenous legal traditions: the tort of unlawful interference with property, contract, or business in general; the equitable jurisdiction to grant injunctions; and the circumstances in which breach of a statutory duty gave rise to legal liability.

Like the United States, Canada was relatively late to adopt statutory protection for neighbouring rights,[88] and there were some doubts about the constitutional validity of federal legislation in this field. The possibility of protecting performers by way of an *INS*-inspired extended action for unfair competition under provincial common law was raised by commentators,[89] but seems not to have resulted in any reported cases.

In Australia, a bootlegging case involving a performance by Michael Jackson[90] was unsuccessfully argued by reference to classic passing-off, the Trades Practices Act 1974 and the supposed right of publicity, but not *INS*. In the United States this kind of case would have been a prime candidate for the misappropriation doctrine.

THE TWO DESTINIES OF *INS* COMPARED

Copyright and the Constitutional Separation of Powers

How was it then that the misappropriation doctrine of *International News v Associated Press* originated in the United States, and has it really fared

[87] *Ex p Island Records Ltd* [1978] Ch 122, [1978] FSR 505 (CA); disapproved by *Lonrho Ltd v Shell Petroleum Co Ltd (No 2)* [1982] AC 173 (HL); not followed in *RCA Corporation v Pollard* [1983] Ch 135, [1983] FSR 9 (CA).

[88] Despite the recommendations of a Parliamentary committee in 1985, Canada did not amend its copyright law to provide for performers' protection until 1997, when obliged to so by TRIPs, Art 14. See D Vaver, *Copyright Law* (Toronto, Irwin Law, 2000) 57 *et seq*; JS McKeown (ed), *Fox's Canadian Law of Copyright and Industrial Designs* (Scarborough, Carswell, 2000) 266–67.

[89] B Green, 'Protection of Musical Performers' Rights in their Performances' (1980) 48 CPR (2d) 113 (specifically referring to *INS*, and to the American *Waring* and *Metropolitan Opera* cases); RW Judge, 'Protecting Performers' Performances in Light of the Canadian Charter of Rights for Creators' (1987) 13 CPR (3d) 1.

[90] *Sony Music Australia v Tansing* (1993) 27 IPR 649 (Federal Court).

so differently there, compared to the rest of the common law world? Is it a mere coincidence that we are observing, or are there lessons to be learned? I tentatively offer the following thoughts in partial explanation.

First, there are the peculiarities of the American copyright system and its place under the Constitution. To a reader in the early twenty-first century, accustomed to American copyright policy as manifested in the likes of TRIPs[91] and the DMCA,[92] it may seem surprising that in the two centuries after independence American copyright law was actually destined to remain very much in the state in which the founding fathers had left it. Partly, this was due to what were perceived at the time as inherent constitutional limitations; partly, to a restrictive statutory model which afforded little or no practical protection to news and suchlike ephemera; partly, to Congressional indifference or hostility to copyright reform; and finally, to the United States' lack of engagement with the major international intellectual property treaties,[93] which may be compared with the respective positions in the United Kingdom,[94] Australia,[95] and Canada.[96]

As the law stood in 1918,[97] statutory (federal) copyright attached only to published works, and two preconditions for copyright protection were that the work should be registered with the Register of Copyrights prior to publication, and that every authorised copy of the work issued to the public should bear a copyright notice with the copyright owner's name and the year of publication. So far as newspapers were concerned this was not necessarily a problem for individual features and commissioned pieces, especially if they were not time-crucial and could wait a day or two for publication, but it was out of the question for breaking news items, arriving every day at AP by the thousand, and all of them needing to be rushed into print hours before the Register was open for business. Registration and notice were entrenched parts of the copyright system, and were not abolished until 1976. Copyright in unpublished works was governed by state common law, and existed without formalities, but of course common law copyright was lost on publication.

[91] The WTO Agreement on Trade-Related Aspects of Intellectual Property Rights (Marrakesh, 1994).

[92] The Digital Millennium Copyright Act 1998.

[93] Most notably the Berne Convention for the Protection of Literary and Artistic Works (Paris, 1971), to which the United States only acceded in 1989. More relevantly, for present purposes, the United States is still not a party to the International Convention for the Protection of Performers, Producers of Phonograms and Broadcasting Organizations (Rome, 1961). With effect from 1974, the United States has been a member of the much less ambitious 'Geneva Phonograms Convention': the Convention for the Protection of Producers of Phonograms against Unauthorized Duplication of their Phonograms (Geneva, 1971).

[94] UK: Berne: 1887; Rome: 1964; Phonograms: 1973.

[95] Australia: Berne: 1928; Rome: 1992; Phonograms: 1974.

[96] Canada: Berne: 1928; Rome: 1998; Phonograms: pending.

[97] The relevant statute was the Copyright Act 1909.

New Laws for New Technologies

Where the purely legal differences between the United States and the rest of the world became important was with new technologies developed or popularised after each of the two World Wars. These created new opportunities for copying old materials, as well as new kinds of material to copy, or protect. The United States was quick to adopt the technologies themselves, but it was slow to update its copyright laws, and claimants understandably looked to unfair competition law to see if they could fill the gaps. But one should again be careful not to treat one aspect of the situation in isolation. For the new technology of radio, for instance, there was all the difference in the world between the monolithic, monopolistic, and publicly owned BBC, unsullied by thought or fear of competition of any kind; and the situation in the United States, where privately owned commercial radio stations proliferated, as diverse in their ethical and professional standards as the three- or four-letter call-signs that denoted them.

The United States Constitution had made provision for patents and copyrights, but not for the other intellectual property rights with which we are increasingly familiar. Consequently these were subject only to state law, except to the extent that federal legislation existed and could be justified either under the patents and copyright clause, or under the separate powers conferred by the commerce clause. Constitutional doctrine declared that in a field where Congress had validly legislated, state law was pre-empted. State law was free to regulate unfair competition pure and simple, but whenever unfair competition law bordered on patents, or copyright, or trademarks, or affected interstate trade, it had to yield to the relevant federal legislation.

This balance between state and federal law was maintained by the Supreme Court, but the Court had little or no jurisdiction over the content of state law—except to review it for consistency with the Constitution—and we have already seen that in *Erie* the Supreme Court had renounced its previous mission of formulating a general 'federal common law' in opposition to state law. After *Erie*, unfair competition law was wholly under the control of the states, except to the extent that it exposed itself to the danger of federal pre-emption. This division of judicial powers between the centre and the states accounts for several crucial features in the development of the *INS* doctrine from *Erie* to the present day.

First, *Erie* minimised the precedential value *INS* would otherwise have had as a decision of the Supreme Court. Before *Erie*, *INS* seemed to say that as a matter of federal common law there existed a doctrine, of equal Constitutional status with statutory federal copyright law, which protected hot news (and arguably much else besides) against misappropriation by competitors. After *Erie*, there was no substantive 'federal common law' to which the *INS* doctrine could be attached, and all that could be deduced for certain from *INS* itself was that if the actual result was to stand, then federal copyright law (as of 1918) had not pre-empted protection of published news items under whatever state laws of unfair competition had been applicable.

Secondly, *INS* could only be interpreted, in retrospect, as an application of substantive state common law[98]—but even the Supreme Court had to take state common law from the relevant state courts, and the federal judges had no jurisdiction to foist their own innovations or inhibitions on the state courts under the pretext of applying or interpreting the law which the latter alone administered. Their only weapon was the blunt one of federal pre-emption. Finally, a vicious circle of isolationism was encouraged. State competence over unfair competition removed responsibility for the content of the substantive law away from Washington, and therefore even further from the influence of international norms such as those embodied in the Berne and Rome conventions; and if the states lacked the power to adhere to any of these treaties, then the federal government lacked the will. Foreign observers tended (as always) to take the case law of the Second Circuit as representative of the whole country, when in fact the former was abnormally hostile to *INS*.

Understanding the Development of *INS* at Home

After *Erie,* almost all innovation in the field of unfair competition occurred at state level, whether by the passage of state legislation, or by new doctrines being recognised judicially in the case law, or by a mixture of the two, as existing state unfair competition statutes were given more expansive interpretations. The federal court system in general, and the Supreme Court in particular, had only a very limited role to play in all these developments. The federal courts had the power to restrain the expansion of the misappropriation doctrine in so far as the doctrine of federal pre-emption required or permitted them to do so, but their influence could only be negative, since their whole power was confined to exercising a veto over state initiatives. Federal courts might adjudicate questions of state unfair competition law in cases of diversity jurisdiction, or in so far as its constitutional validity was questioned, but they were bound to take the content and policy of the law as read. They could sometimes roll it back, as the Supreme Court attempted to do in *Sears/Compco*, or they could approve from the sidelines, as it did in *Goldstein*, but they could not drive it forwards.

[98] See, for example, *Associated Press v All Headline News Corp* (n 1), deciding inter alia that the *INS*-type cause of action arose under New York, rather than Florida, state law.

The second factor mentioned above accounts both for the significance of *Sears* and *Compco*, and for how they were so easily circumvented. But for *Erie*, the Court which decided *Sears* and *Compco*, or *Shredded Wheat* before them, might simply have disowned Justice Pitney and reversed *INS*: by no means an uncommon fate even for Supreme Court decisions. But in *Erie* the Supreme Court had, whether intentionally or not, washed its hands of all responsibility for the doctrine. Besides, even *Sears* and *Compco* were pleaded and argued not as applications of the misappropriation doctrine, but as legally orthodox (if factually unusual) examples of acquired secondary meaning. What the Supreme Court could do, and did in *Sears* and *Compco*, was to oppose the inroads made by the state courts with an obstructive exercise of the doctrine of federal pre-emption, which was unequivocally under its own control. But though this blocked the *INS* doctrine on that occasion, it left it unchallenged whenever federal pre-emption was not engaged, and with suitable ingenuity at state level, and a change in mood in the Supreme Court with *Goldstein*, the doctrine of *INS*, such as it was, survived *Sears* and *Compco* remarkably well.

But the doctrine which survived was a far cry from that apparently enunciated by Justice Pitney. It is typically to the senior federal courts that one looks for grand theories, if at all, and especially to the Supreme Court. But in this case the Court had ruled itself out of any such role in *Erie*, and the state courts, had they been so minded as to take its place, were kept in order by federal pre-emption. What remained was not a Grand Doctrine of the sort which had terrified the Second Circuit in *Cheney*, but a rather modest and disparate collection of incremental innovations, as was almost inevitable given their origins in state courts and legislatures. Many of these were obviously fair and useful, and of the rest most were unobjectionable enough.

International News and the Professors

Another particular factor relevant to the level of interest in *INS* in its homeland may be the significance of the case in American legal education. Not the least of the insights offered by Professor Douglas Baird[99] is that *INS* is featured prominently in Henry Hart and Albert Sacks' widely used *Legal Process* materials.[100] *INS* is also prominent in Kitch and Perlman's student casebook *Regulation of the Competitive Process*,[101] though this is

[99] Baird, 'Story of INS' (n 2) 9.

[100] HM Hart et al, *The Legal Process: Basic Problems in the Making and Application of Law* (Westbury, NY, Foundation Press, 1994) (first published 1957).

[101] EW Kitch and HS Perlman, *Legal Regulation of the Competitive Process: Case Materials, and Notes on Unfair Business Practices, Trademarks, Copyrights, and Patents*, 4th edn (Mineola, NY, Foundation Press, 1991).

hardly due to the editors holding any very exalted opinion of the decision's fundamental rightness.[102] Outside the United States, casebooks are less prevalent. *INS* is cited by some English and Australian intellectual property textbooks, though by no means all. So far as Canada is concerned, *INS* is not cited by name in David Vaver's *Intellectual Property Law*,[103] though his attitude to it is clear enough from his tongue-in-cheek definition of 'unfair competition' as 'an abusive, legally insignificant term an enterprise may use to describe any practice by which another manages to undersell it.'[104]

The Role and Scope of Unfair Competition Law

One feature which the United States does share with the rest of the common law world is the lowly status of unfair competition law in comparison to intellectual property properly so called. On its face, *INS* is an application of unfair competition law pure and simple. In particular, Justice Pitney made it perfectly clear that no property rights existed even in 'hot' news, and that INS's liability for misappropriation crucially arose from the fact that they were in competition with AP.

America was always rather more receptive to the language of 'unfair competition' than the United Kingdom or the Dominions. In the first place, the mere phrase 'unfair competition' did not automatically evoke the celebrated reaction of Fry LJ in *Mogul*.[105] As against that, 'unfair competition' in actual legal usage was no term of art. It was used either as a near-synonym for passing-off, or it evoked the antitrust acts, or it was merely pejorative. In America too, the intellectual dominance of the domesticated version of Locke's labour theory of property meant that the rhetoric of *INS* seemed to lead inexorably to the apotheosis of full property rights in news, or whatever kind of 'valuable intangible' was under consideration, with protection under the law of unfair competition being seen merely as a half-way house dictated by a mix of caution and Constitutional propriety. Conversely, American law (notwithstanding Professor Rawls[106]) has always been distinctly averse to basing legal liability on anything resembling distributive justice, with which the 'fairness' criterion of *INS* is easily confused.

Outside the United States, one indirect effect of *Victoria Park*, but a lasting one, was to define the Anglo-Australian perception of what *INS* effectively

[102] RC Denicola and HS Perlman 'A Foreword to the Symposium on the Restatement of Unfair Competition' (1996) 47 *South Carolina Law Review* 1.

[103] Vaver, *Intellectual Property Law* (n 22).

[104] See the entry for 'unfair competition' in the glossary (298), where this is usage number (3) of three.

[105] n 30.

[106] J Rawls, *Justice as Fairness: A Restatement* (Cambridge Mass, Harvard University Press, 2000).

stood for, and with that the terms of argument as to how (if at all) the law should develop. Dixon J saw clearly enough that *INS* was ultimately about the recognition or creation of new property rights, though on its face *INS* dealt only with unfair competition, and not with property at all. This distinction never fitted very well even into American patterns of thought—dominated as they were by invocations of Locke and Madison—but was necessitated by the thought that recognition of a true proprietary interest in news would have been tantamount to the creation of a common law copyright in published information, in flagrant contradiction to the statutory scheme of copyright protection and the doctrine of federal pre-emption.[107]

SOME PROVISIONAL CONCLUSIONS

I hope I have given some explanations for why *INS* developed the way it did in its homeland, and at least by implication why it never made much of an impression elsewhere. The factors which held it back, such as the innate conservatism of the common law, its preference for case-by-case analogy over grand theory and far-reaching principle, and the willingness of judges to defer to the legislature on matters of social and economic policy, were present to an equal or greater extent in the rest of the common law world. Not the least of these factors outside the United States was the calibre of the opposition to *INS* which could be marshalled after the decisions in *Cheney* and *Victoria Park*: Justices Holmes and Brandeis; Judge Learned Hand and Sir Owen Dixon were among the great jurists of the twentieth century, any one of whom far outshone the lacklustre Justice Pitney *et al.* As for the factors that drove the doctrine of *INS* forward in its homeland, such as the respect afforded to the Supreme Court, its perennial fascination for commentators, its inclusion in students' programmes of study, the scope it afforded for legal innovation at state level, and the complete absence (or comparative belatedness) of adequate copyright or *sui generis* protection for (and against) new technologies: these were not generally reproduced elsewhere, or to nowhere like the same extent.

But the apparent pro-*INS*, anti-*INS* division between the United States and the rest of the common law world as a whole has always been mirrored within the United States itself. Though *INS* was an invention of the Second Circuit in 1917, the latter spent most of the next eight decades—from *Cheney* to the present day—in trying to put the genie it had released back

[107] For a view of *INS* in a wider historical perspective see RJR Peritz, *Competition Policy in America: History, Rhetoric, Law* (New York, OUP, 1996) 69–72, locating *INS* in relation to traditional ideas of property as tangible 'things' with use-value, Lockean ideas of property as the fruit of labour, the economists' concept of property as something having value in exchange, and Holmes' and Brandeis' positivism, under which 'property' was the creation of the law.

into the bottle, as can be seen in *NBS v Motorola*. Yet the Second Circuit, for all its prestige, did not speak for the whole judicial system. In fact, the state courts of New York have always been rather pro-*INS*, as were many state and federal courts elsewhere.[108] Attitudes in (and within) the Supreme Court itself have varied: compare the majority judgment of Justice Pitney in *INS* itself with the dissents of Justices Holmes and Brandeis; or *Sears/ Compco* with *Goldstein*. It is also as well to remember that legislatures may be more receptive to the charms of *INS* than the courts, whether within the United States or abroad.[109]

So just as the common law world was divided over *INS*, so was its home country. *INS* was conceived in discord, and disagreement over its merits has not decreased with time.

[108] See *McCarthy on Trademarks and Unfair Competition*, 4th edn (New York, Clark Boardman Callaghan), §§10.53–58.

[109] For example, the (Australian) Broadcasting and Television Act 1942 s115, above n 77, effectively reversing *Victoria Park* on its own facts, and in its home country.

15

The Common Law and Trade Marks in an Age of Statutes

GRAEME B DINWOODIE

TRADE MARKS ARE a creature of the common law.[1] So spoke the United States Supreme Court in 1879 in *The Trade-Mark Cases*.[2] Thus, although the Court struck down as unconstitutional the then-extant federal trade mark statute, under which registration of marks was secured, the common law continued to recognise and offer protection to marks absent statutory provision. Likewise, the English courts (of both Law and Equity) had long recognised causes of action that effectively protected marks, prior to the enactment of statutes delineating the scope of trade mark protection, though these causes of action were not consistently denominated as 'trade mark infringement' until Parliament legislated on the matter of trade marks.[3] During times of absent legislative stewardship, courts on both sides of the Atlantic were well able to develop protection for trade marks under the common law.

The characterisation of trade mark law as a field of common law may now seem an essentially historical statement. Indeed, David Vaver has suggested

1 The term 'common law' has a number of different (though somewhat related) meanings. The term can be used to denote a body of law developed by judges. See, eg, RA Posner, *How Judges Think* (Cambridge, Harvard University Press, 2008) 5 (arguing that because contract law is 'part of the common law ... it is ... created by [judges]'). This is the sense in which I am primarily using the term in this chapter.

2 *The Trade-Mark Cases* 100 US 82 (1879).

3 See L Bently, 'The Making of Modern Trade Marks Law: The Construction of the Legal Concept of Trade Mark (1860–80)', in Bently, Davis and Ginsburg (eds), *Trade Marks and Brands: An Interdisciplinary Critique* (Cambridge, Cambridge University Press, 2008) (arguing that 'British trade marks law did not really take anything like its modern shape until the middle of the nineteenth century'); L Bently, 'From Communication to Thing: Historical Aspects of the Conceptualization of Trademarks as Property', in Dinwoodie and Janis (eds), *Trademark Law and Theory: A Handbook of Contemporary Research* (Edward Elgar, Cheltenham, 2008) 3, 4–5 ('At mid-[nineteenth]-century, there were many laws, some general and some specific, which regulated the uses of signs in trade, but the most important was the general protection provided by the Common Law and the supplementary protection of the Chancery courts against misrepresentation in trade').

that 'aside from the occasional hiccup and exception such as trade secrets and passing-off, there has been no common law of IP since the end of the eighteenth century. IP rights depend on legislation.'[4] Although Professor Vaver offered these observations primarily with respect to UK law, the landscape has also changed in the United States. There, Professor Vaver's conclusion may hold true most easily insofar as copyrights and patents are concerned. But the picture is more complicated with trade mark law.[5]

In the United States, the early twentieth century saw the adoption of a series of federal trade mark registration statutes, and in 1946 Congress enacted even more comprehensive trade mark legislation, namely the Lanham Act.[6] That statute not only liberalised the federal registration scheme (the details of which Congress set out in provisions taking up most of the statute) but also facilitated uniform national enforcement of marks by creating federal jurisdiction over claims for unfair competition.[7] Since then, Congress, has episodically—but with increasing frequency—revised the trade mark statute. Sometimes Congress has acted to resolve ambiguities revealed by conflicting court decisions (or to overrule singular problematic judicial developments) or to tweak the statute to ensure US compliance with international obligations.[8] But on occasion these interventions have been more fundamental,[9] whether to liberalise the registration scheme to permit intent-to-use or Madrid Union-based applications, or to create new causes of action such as dilution or cybersquatting.[10]

[4] See D Vaver, 'Reforming Intellectual Property Law: An Obvious and Not-So-Obvious Agenda: The Stephen Stewart Lecture for 2008' (2009) *Intellectual Property Quarterly* 143, 154.

[5] See GB Dinwoodie and MD Janis, 'Lessons From the Trademark Use Debate' (2007) 92 *Iowa Law Review* 1703, 1710–1711 (contrasting copyright and trade mark law).

[6] See Trade-Mark Act of July 5, 1946, 60 Stat 428 (1946), codified at 15 USC §§ 1051 et seq.

[7] Ibid § 43(a), codified at 15 USC § 11125(a).

[8] See, eg, Trademark Law Treaty Implementation Act, Pub L No 105–330, § 201(a)(2) (1998) (resolving circuit split on burden of proving functionality); Trademark Clarification Act of 1984, Pub L No 98–620, § 102, 98 Stat 3335 (overruling *Anti-Monopoly Inc v General Mills Fun Group Inc* 684 F 2d 1316 (9th Cir 1982)); Uruguay Round Agreements Act § 521, Pub L No 103–465, 108 Stat 4809 (1994) (amending section 45 definition of 'abandoned' and changing the period of non-use that establishes a prima facie case of abandonment from two years to the present standard of three years, in order to comply with the TRIPS Agreement).

[9] Mere legislative activity does not *necessarily* signal a normative shift in trade mark law. Of course, it might well be argued that such a shift has occurred during the era of greater legislative intervention, and many scholars would argue that trade marks are now conceived as valuable property in and of themselves, to be freely traded and offered close-to-absolute protection. But it is by no means clear that any trend toward greater protection of trade mark rights can be traced merely to legislative action.

[10] See, eg, Trademark Law Revision Act of 1988, Pub L No 100-667, 102 Stat 3935 (introducing intent-to-use applications); Madrid Protocol Implementation Act, Pub L No 107–273, 116 Stat 1758 (2002) (implementing US accession to the Madrid system for registration of marks); Federal Trademark Dilution Protection Act 1995, Pub L No 104–98, 109 Stat 985 (codified at 15 USC § 1125(c) (1996)); Federal Trademark Dilution Revision Act 2006, Pub L No 109–312, 120 Stat 1730 (codified at 15 USC § 1125(c) (2006)); Anti-Cybersquatting Consumer Protection Act 1999, Pub L No 106–13, 113 Stat 1536, 1501A-545 to 1501A-552 (1999) (codified at 15 USC § 1125(d) (2008)).

However, in light of such increased statutorification of trade mark law, what is the role of the common law in developing appropriate protection for trade marks? Has the legislature wholly superseded the courts as the law-maker in this field? Are US courts to be reduced to mere interpreters of legislative text?[11] The US courts have had to grapple with the question generally, reconstructing a common law in an age of statutes, in the felicitous phrase of Guido Calabresi.[12] What is to be said of trade mark law in this regard? In this chapter, I suggest that, despite substantial legislative intervention, both Congress and the Supreme Court appear content that the development of trade mark and unfair competition law in the United States remain heavily dependent on common law law-making by the courts.

TRADE MARK LAW AS COMMON LAW

In 1879, the United States Supreme Court decided *The Trade-Mark Cases.*[13] Prosecutions had been brought for violation of an 1876 federal statute that criminalised the 'fraudulent use, sale, and counterfeiting of trade-marks registered' under the Trademark Act of 1870. The validity of the 1870 Act, the first federal trade mark legislation, was thus a predicate for the criminal prosecutions. The Supreme Court struck down the 1870 Act as unconstitutional, finding it beyond the (then-understood) scope of Congressional legislative authority.[14]

[11] The question is not unique to the United States. It can also be asked in other common law jurisdictions, most notably the United Kingdom. Starting in 1875, the UK Parliament enacted broad legislative schemes for the protection of trade marks. See C Wadlow, *The Law of Passing Off: Unfair Competition by Misrepresentation,* 3rd edn (Sweet & Maxwell, 2004) 28. The most recent legislative overhaul of UK trade mark law complicates the question further. The Trade Marks Act 1994 revised UK law to conform to the provisions of the EC Trade Mark Directive, a relatively comprehensive instrument that purported to harmonise the registered trade mark laws of the EC member states (but, unlike the Lanham Act, nominally left broader unfair competition regimes untouched). See Trade Marks Act 1994; First Council Directive 89/104/EEC of 21 December 1988 to Approximate the Laws of the Member States Relating to Trade Marks, 1990 OJ L40/1; see also Directive 2008/95/EC of the European Parliament and the Council of 22 October 2008 to Approximate the Laws of the Member States relating to Trade Marks (codified version). Formally, trade mark infringement claims require UK courts to interpret a UK statute, but how should the European provenance of the statute affect that task and what does it mean for English common law? This is a variation on the US question, but beyond the scope of this chapter.

[12] The title of this chapter draws consciously from Guido Calabresi's classic work *A Common Law For the Age of Statutes* (Cambridge, Harvard University Press, 1982).

[13] 100 US 82 (1879).

[14] Modern federal trade mark legislation does not suffer from the same infirmity in part because of an evolution in the Court's reading of the Commerce Clause and in part because the Lanham Act is expressly limited to activities that occur in commerce (as that term is constitutionally understood). See text accompanying nn 42–44 (discussing constitutional basis of the Lanham Act).

The 1870 legislation was not expressly limited to interstate commerce (which might have justified its enactment under the Commerce Clause) and it could not be sustained under the Copyright and Patent Clause of the Constitution (despite being included in a statute entitled 'An Act to revise, consolidate, and amend the statutes relating to patents and copyrights') because trade marks differed importantly in kind from copyrights and patents.[15] As the Court explained:

> The ordinary trade-mark has no necessary relation to invention or discovery. The trade-mark recognized by the common law is generally the growth of a considerable period of use, rather than a sudden invention... . If we should endeavor to classify it under the head of writings of authors, the objections are equally strong. In this, as in regard to inventions, originality is required ... . The trade-mark may be, and generally is, the adoption of something already in existence as the distinctive symbol of the party using it. At common law the exclusive right to it grows out of its use, and not its mere adoption.[16]

But the Court's stingy reading of federal legislative authority arguably reflected prevailing sentiments regarding federal authority rather than any particular disposition toward trade mark rights. The Court's affirmation of the venerable heritage of trade marks emphasised this point, and in so doing laid the foundation for the future relationship of substantive trade mark principles, on the one hand, and schemes for registration and enforcement, on the other:

> The right to adopt and use a symbol or a device to distinguish the goods or property made or sold by the person whose mark it is, to the exclusion of use by all other persons, has been long recognized by the common law and the chancery courts of England and of this country, and by the statutes of some of the States. It is a property right for the violation of which damages may be recovered in an action at law, and the continued violation of it will be enjoined by a court of equity, with compensation for past infringement. This exclusive right was not created by the act of Congress, and does not now depend upon it for its enforcement. The whole system of trade-mark property and the civil remedies for its protection existed long anterior to that act, and have remained in full force since its passage.[17]

Trade marks, and their protection, were thus not dependent upon legislative enactment. Despite the invalidation of the 1870 statute, the courts continued to offer marks protection under the rubric acknowledged by the Supreme Court.

[15] See *Trademark Cases* (n 2) 93–94 ('Any attempt, however, to identify the essential characteristics of a trade-mark with inventions and discoveries in the arts and sciences, or with the writings of authors, will show that the effort is surrounded with insurmountable difficulties').
[16] Ibid 94.
[17] Ibid 92.

Of course, a system of registration can offer important advantages to mark owners, including enhanced certainty and notice of potentially competing rights. And *federal* registration, to the extent that it enabled national enforcement, was particularly important to the development of a national economy. As the Court had intimated in *The Trade-Mark Cases*, 'such legislation [enabling federal registration] may be a judicious aid to the common law on the subject of trade-marks, and may be within the competency of legislatures whose general powers embrace that class of subjects.'[18] Thus, Congress remedied the deficiencies of its earlier work product, and throughout the first half of the twentieth century enacted successive registration statutes targeting marks used in interstate commerce.[19] But the theory of these statutes was that, consistent with the Supreme Court's suggestion in *The Trade-Mark Cases*, registration merely facilitated enforcement of rights that existed at common law, the contours of which would continue to be developed by the courts.[20] Congress essentially superimposed a federal notice and enforcement mechanism on top of the common law system.

In the years prior to the Lanham Act, when the federal statutes were clearly conceived in these terms, courts exercised their common law powers to develop substantive principles of trade mark (and unfair competition) law. Thus, during this time, courts began to expand the types of signifiers (eg, product shapes) that might warrant protection, and broadened the scope of trade mark rights beyond use on competing goods.[21] They also articulated important limits on the scope of trade mark rights, lest the trade mark system be used to restrain competition or circumvent limits imposed by patent law.[22]

And the courts continued to develop and refine the theoretical basis of US trade mark and unfair competition law, enabling the promulgation of doctrines that allowed the law to adapt to a growing national economy

[18] Ibid 86.

[19] Although Congress responded as soon as 1881, it was only with the 1905 statute that a comprehensive registration scheme was put in place. See JT McCarthy, *Trademarks and Unfair Competition* (BNA Press, 2009) § 5.3. However, that too was limited, permitting registration only of so-called 'technical trade marks', which we would now call 'inherently distinctive' marks. Although the 1920 statute sought to liberalise registration (for example, with respect to descriptive terms), it failed to do so effectively because of the lack of any useful presumption flowing from a 1920 Act registration. See ibid.

[20] See R Callman, *The Law of Unfair Competition and Trade-Marks* (Chicago, 1945) vol 2, 846 (writing, one year before the Lanham Act, that 'registration does not create a trade-mark and it confers no new or greater rights than those that existed at common law. Registration merely facilitates the remedy, confers jurisdiction upon courts and gives the registrant certain procedural advantages.'). See also ibid, 1671–73.

[21] See *Crescent Tool Co v Kilborn & Bishop Co* 247 F 299 (1917) (tracing protection of product design under the rubric of unfair competition or trade dress protection to 1904); *Aunt Jemima Mills Co v Rigney & Co* 247 F 407, 409–10 (2d Cir 1917) ('we think that the goods, though different, may be so related as to fall within the mischief which equity should prevent'); *Yale Electric Corp v Robertson* 26 F 2d 972 (2d Cir 1928).

[22] See *Singer Mfg Co v June Mfg Co* 163 US 169 (1896).

and new technologies. For example, in a pair of cases decided two years apart, the Supreme Court affirmed the fundamental principle of *The Trade-Mark Cases* that substantive trade mark rights 'grow out of use, not mere adoption.'[23] Relying heavily upon English authorities, the Court reasoned that, as a result, there was no 'such property right [in a trade mark] except as appurtenant to an established business or trade in connection with which the mark is used.'[24] Thus, a trader who used a mark on goods in one area of the United States could not restrain use by another trader who had in good faith adopted and used the same mark in another part of the country.[25]

As the Court expressly contemplated in the second of those decisions, in 1918,[26] a system of federal registration enacted in 'judicious aid' of common law rights later required some modification of this 'good faith remote junior user' doctrine.[27] And changing patterns of commerce might of themselves cause courts over time to modify further common law doctrines that are based upon local use.[28] But the core principles underlying these evolving doctrines continue to inform US trade mark law to this date.[29] And courts are in the vanguard of any revision efforts that social change might warrant.

This should not be a surprise. The Supreme Court clearly saw the development of trade mark law as something within the judicial remit (even as it contemplated appropriate legislative intervention). The same was true of unfair competition law more generally understood. Indeed, in its 1916 *Hanover Star Milling* opinion, the Court had emphasised that 'the common law of trademarks is but a part of the broader law of unfair competition'.[30]

[23] *Hanover Star Milling v Metcalf* 240 US 403, 415 (1916); *United Drug Co v Theodore Rectanus Co* 248 US 90 (1918).

[24] *Hanover Star Milling* (n 23) 414.

[25] See generally GB Dinwoodie, 'Trademarks and Territory: Detaching Trademark Law From the Nation-State' (2004) 41 *Houston Law Review* 885, 893–95.

[26] See *United Drug* (n 23) 98 ('[T]he adoption of a trade-mark does *not, at least in the absence of some valid legislation enacted for the purpose*, project the right of protection in advance of the extension of the trade, or operate as a claim of territorial rights over areas into which it thereafter may be deemed desirable to extend the trade') (emphasis supplied).

[27] See Dinwoodie, 'Trademarks and Territory' (n 25) 987–99. The Lanham Act sought to facilitate national enforcement by deeming registration of a mark on the Principal Register to be nationwide constructive notice of the registrant's claim to ownership. See 15 USC § 1072 (2009). Since 1988, the filing of an *application* for registration now constitutes 'constructive use of the mark, conferring a right of priority, nationwide in effect' (assuming a registration ultimately issues). See 15 USC § 1057(b). Under either regime, federal registration secures nationwide priority, notwithstanding the use of a mark in an area less than the entire United States. Dinwoodie, 'Trademarks and Territory' (n 25) 897.

[28] *Cf Circuit City Stores Inc v Carmax Inc* 165 F 3d 1047 (6th Cir 1999) (Jones J, concurring) (critiquing rule in *Dawn Donut Co v Hart's Food Stores Inc* 267 F 2d 358 (2d Cir 1959)); *Sterling Drug Inc v Bayer AG* 14 F 3d 733, 750 (2d Cir 1994) (suggesting a need to rethink prior approaches to extra-territorial enforcement in light of global trade).

[29] See Dinwoodie, 'Trademarks and Territory' (n 25) 913–32 (discussing judicial interpretation of the concept of 'use in commerce' and the well-known marks doctrine).

[30] *Hanover Star Milling* (n 23) 413.

And only two years later, the Court applied those broader principles to a then-new technological setting when it decided *International News Service v Associated Press*.[31] Associated Press (AP) published news reports in early editions of newspapers on the East Coast. International News Service, a competitor in the gathering and distribution of news, copied the AP reports and relayed them to its member newspapers on the West Coast. A majority of the Supreme Court recognised a claim of unfair competition based upon the defendant's misappropriation of the plaintiff's stories, noting that the defendant was 'endeavoring to reap where it [had] not sown.' The Court upheld a preliminary injunction prohibiting the defendant from distributing or publishing AP's reports for the short period of time necessary to avoid appropriation of the commercial value of the reports.[32] Thus, the Supreme Court had signalled an active role for the courts in the development of both trade mark and unfair competition law.

When the Supreme Court decided *The Trade-Mark Cases* in 1879, its narrow reading of federal authority served not only to elevate the residual role of courts over the recent intervention by Congress, but also to promote the role of state law. The 'common law' of which the Court then spoke was in large part *state* common law.[33] And thus the choice of common law development of the law (validated by the Court as a result of the intrinsic nature of trade marks, but influenced by prevailing notions of federal authority) necessarily involved allocation of substantial law-making authority to those charged with superintendence of state laws (whether courts or state legislatures).[34] However, the earlier decision of the Court in *Swift v Tyson*,[35] which authorised federal courts exercising diversity jurisdiction to develop and apply federal common law to supplement state statutes made federal courts—but not the federal legislature—partners with state institutions in the trade mark law-making project.[36]

[31] *International News Service v Associated Press* 248 US 215 (1918).

[32] See generally DG Baird, 'Property, Natural Monopoly, and the Uneasy Legacy of *INS v AP*', in JC Ginsburg and RC Dreyfuss (eds), *Intellectual Property Stories* (Foundation Press, 2005) 9.

[33] See *The Trade-Mark Cases* (n 2) 93 ('the property in trade-marks and the right to their exclusive use rest on the laws of the States.'). State law was not the only form of common law. At the time, federal common law remained of importance. See below, text accompanying nn 35–36.

[34] The conceptualisation of trade marks in England in the later nineteenth century can also been seen in light of jurisdictional battles, most notably between the courts of Law and Equity. See Bently (n 3). And the development of contemporary trade mark principles within the EU might ought to be informed by more general concerns about allocation of law-making authority (though this is not apparent on the face of ECJ judgments).

[35] *Swift v Tyson* 41 US (16 Pet) 1 (1842) (holding that a federal court exercising diversity jurisdiction should apply general federal common law).

[36] Federal courts have so-called diversity jurisdiction over disputes between citizens of different states above defined amounts. See 28 USC § 1332.

THE EVOLUTION OF THE LANHAM ACT

This was the institutional structure underlying US trade mark and unfair competition law when Congress first seriously considered the revision of the federal statute in the 1930s.[37] However, during that revision process, the power to develop US trade mark and unfair competition law was affected by broader changes in the allocation of law-making powers generally. First, the Supreme Court's 1938 decision in *Erie v Tompkins* substantially limited the capacity of federal courts to create federal common law under their diversity jurisdiction.[38] Thus, decisions such as *INS v Associated Press* were immediately rendered infirm, on constitutional, rather than substantive intellectual property, grounds. (To be sure, the Supreme Court decision that same year in *Kellogg v National Biscuit Co*[39] may independently and substantively have engineered the demise of the *INS* misappropriation doctrine in federal law.[40] But *Erie* probably would have achieved the same on its own.[41]) Second, in the face of extensive federal legislation as part of the New Deal, the Supreme Court's reading of Congress's Commerce Clause authority broadened substantially.[42] Thus, in 1946, Congress enacted the Lanham Act, free from constitutional infirmity by the simple expedient of restricting its legislation to matters affecting interstate commerce,[43] a limitation rendered essentially meaningless by the Court's intervening interpretation of the Commerce Clause.[44]

The Lanham Act did not dramatically alter the allocation of law-making authority made prior to its enactment. Early versions of the legislation had

[37] The roots of the revision effort go back even further. See S 2679, 68th Cong, 1st Sess (1924).

[38] See *Erie RR v Tompkins* 304 US 64 (1938) (holding that a federal court sitting in diversity jurisdiction must apply state law as determined by the state's highest court).

[39] 305 US 111 (1938).

[40] The 'hot news' misappropriation doctrine lives on in narrow form at the state law level. See *Associated Press v All Headline News Corp* 89 USPQ 2d (BNA) 2020 (SDNY 2009) (permitting a claim for misappropriation of 'hot news' to proceed under New York common law where the defendant's dissemination of reports of breaking news to its subscribers involved copying news reports prepared by the Associated Press, removing the identification of the Associated Press as author, and distributing the story under the defendant's banner); see also *National Basketball Ass'n v Motorola Inc* 105 F 3d 841 (2d Cir 1997).

[41] See GB Dinwoodie, 'The Story of *Kellogg Co. v. National Biscuit Co.*: Breakfast with Brandeis', in Ginsburg and RC Dreyfuss (eds), *Intellectual Property Stories* (n 32) 220, 255.

[42] See eg *Wickard v Filburn* 317 US 111, 120 (1942) (holding that Congress's Commerce Clause powers extended to any activities having 'actual effects' upon interstate commerce, and reading that notion broadly).

[43] By limiting the Lanham Act to activities that occur in commerce, Congress made statutory scope coterminous with constitutional authority. See 15 USC § 1127 (2009) (defining 'use in commerce' and 'commerce').

[44] See Rep No 79-1333 (1946) 4 ('There can be no doubt under the recent decisions of the Supreme Court of the constitutionality of a national act giving substantive as distinguished from merely procedural rights in trade-marks in commerce over which Congress has plenary power …') (remarks of Senator Pepper).

clearly adopted the theory of the early twentieth century statutes, treating the federal statute as a procedural device to assist enforcement of common law rights.[45] As deliberations proceeded, however, the proponents of the legislation became more ambitious. Several aspects of the existing regime were regarded as inadequate: the existence of multiple state trade mark statutes, uncertainties regarding the value of federal registration, difficulties with national enforcement of rights in a growing national economy, and dubious compliance with international obligations (among other things).[46] The newly recognised authority of the federal Congress to legislate broadly in the field of commerce presented an opportunity to remedy those deficiencies.[47]

Thus, the Lanham Act, as finally adopted, not only clarified existing law by consolidating trademark statutes in a single piece of legislation, but also implemented international obligations and 'modernized the trade mark statutes so that they would conform to legitimate present-day business practices.'[48] This modernisation included most significantly the liberalisation of the grounds for registration to include the possibility of registering a descriptive mark that had acquired secondary meaning (and receiving the full benefits of registration, including after five years the quiet title that flowed from the newly created status of 'incontestability').[49] However, a similarly dominant motivation for the legislation was the goal of facilitating national enforcement of rights in an economy

[45] See ES Rogers, 'The Lanham Act and the Social Function of Trade-Marks' (1949) 14 *Law & Contemporary Problems* 173, 179 (commenting that the theory of the 1931 Vestal Bill 'was that a federal trademark statute is procedural only, a kind of practice act assisting common-law protection by simplifying procedure. The theory of the [1937] committee draft was broader.').

[46] Despite concerns about divergent state laws, the Lanham Act did not expressly pre-empt state trade mark and unfair competition laws, unlike the position adopted by later federal copyright and patent statutes. Thus, until 1995, state law was the only source of protection (in a bare majority of states) against dilution. Even in some matters that might seem core questions of trade mark law, such as the protection of well-known marks within the meaning of Art 6*bis* of the Paris Convention, state law may offer protection arguably unavailable at the federal level. See *ITC Ltd v Punchgini Inc* 9 NY 3d 467 (2007) (casting such protection in terms of state unfair competition law). And some states recognise causes of action for unfair competition grounded in notions of misappropriation that have largely been rejected at the federal level. See ibid 476 (explaining that New York's common law of unfair competition has long recognised claims of misappropriation of property or commercial advantage). The continued role of state common law, and to a lesser extent state statutes, thus complicates the picture in the United States in a number of ways; it muddies analysis regarding the development of common law, federal common law having been substantially curtailed in 1938 by *Erie v Tompkins*, and it further clouds discussion of the relationship between trade mark law and unfair competition law. These problems warrant much lengthier and more sustained analysis than offered in this chapter.

[47] See Rogers, 'The Lanham Act' (n 45) 179–80.

[48] See S Rep No 79-1333 (1946) 3 (remarks of Senator Pepper).

[49] See K Stolte, 'A Response to Jerome Gilson's Call For an Overhaul of the Lanham Act' (2004) 94 *Trademark Reporter* 1335 ('Certain portions of the Lanham Act and its predecessor statutes introduced purely statutory procedures and rights that were not part of the common law, such as trademark registration procedures. Moreover, the Lanham Act also specifically expanded protections accorded to trademark owners beyond those protections that were available at common law, including, for example, incontestable rights.').

that was increasingly national in scope.[50] This was achieved not only by liberalising the grounds for federal registration, but also by conferring independent jurisdiction on federal courts (in section 43(a)) to hear cases of unfair competition.[51]

Obviously, 'liberalization of registration and enforcement inevitably did affect substantive principles of trademark law, and caused the enlargement of federal law.'[52] However, the statute was still seen largely as a codification of common law principles.[53] Congress's efforts to facilitate national enforcement did not seem explicitly to derogate from the theory of prior statutes, namely, that the statutes were designed to facilitate enforcement of rights determined to exist in accordance with existing judicial precedent. The statute was overwhelmingly focused on matters of registration rather than principles of substantive trade mark law. It did not at that time contain, for example, any guidance on the means by which courts should determine the distinctiveness of marks or what forms of confusion were actionable. Indeed, the provision authorising actions for infringement omitted the requirement from earlier statutes that the defendant had used the mark on goods of the 'same descriptive properties',[54] opting for a more general 'likely confusion' standard that the courts had already developed notwithstanding the prior statutory language.[55]

THE COURTS AND CONGRESS AFTER THE LANHAM ACT

The allocation of law-making authority underlying the Lanham Act continues to structure contemporary development of US trade mark law,

[50] See S Rep No 79-1333 (1946) 4.

[51] After *Erie*, unfair competition had become a matter for state law. See C Bunn, 'The National Law of Unfair Competition' (1949) 62 *Harvard Law Review* 987, 991 (discussing three Supreme Court decisions in the four years after *Erie* that declared unfair competition law to be a matter of state law).

[52] Dinwoodie, 'The Story of *Kellogg Co. v. National Biscuit Co*' (n 41) 256 n 121.

[53] See RC Denicola, 'Some Thoughts on the Dynamics of Federal Trademark Legislation and the Trademark Dilution Act of 1995' (1996) 59 Law & Contemp. Probs. 75, 79–80 ('Putting aside statutory innovations directly linked to the public notice provided by the Act's registration system, the Lanham Act codifie[d] the basic common law principles governing both the subject matter and scope of protection.'); *Inwood Lab Inc v Ives Lab Inc* 456 US 844, 861 n 2 (1982) (White, J, concurring) (noting that the purpose of the Lanham Act was 'to codify and unify the common law of unfair competition and trademark protection.'); *Chevron Chem Co v Voluntary Purchasing Groups Inc* 659 F 2d 695, 700–01 (5th Cir 1981); *cf* Callman, *The Law of Unfair Competition and Trade-Marks* (n 19) 1667 (suggesting that because of the effect given to registration by the then-pending Lanham Bill, 'it is undeniable that the Bill affects the substantive law of trade-marks ...'); *Qualitex Co v Jacobsen Prods Inc* 514 US 159 (1995) ('The Lanham Act significantly changed and liberalized the common law to "dispense with mere technical prohibitions," S Rep No 1333, 79th Cong, 2d Sess, 3 (1946), most notably, by permitting trademark registration of descriptive words ... where they had acquired "secondary meaning."')

[54] See Trademark Act of 1905, § 16.

[55] See 15 USC § 1114(a) (1946).

notwithstanding frequent statutory amendment in recent years. Certainly, the approach of courts since the Lanham Act has suggested no radical revision of the proposition that courts were to continue developing the substantive principles of trade mark and unfair competition law.[56] Thus, based upon the accumulated experience of decades of decisions, Judge Henry Friendly articulated the classic spectrum of distinctiveness still used by courts to determine the protectability of marks,[57] and formulated the multifactor likelihood of confusion test to determine the appropriate scope of rights afforded trade mark owners.[58] As courts expanded the subject matter amenable to trade mark protection, they simultaneously developed doctrines such as aesthetic functionality to cabin the scope of rights.[59] Many more examples abound. In short, however, the courts remained the primary law-makers in the field of trade mark and unfair competition law.

This is not to say that courts have not paid attention to the language of the Lanham Act. But the statutory language is often sufficiently open-ended to permit the courts to invoke the statute in support of the conclusions they would likely have reached according to common law principles of trade mark law. Indeed, even where interpreting statutory language that is precise, courts frequently still refer to the common law principles upon which the statutory provision appears to have been based.[60] When Congress has liberalised the language of the statute further, the courts have been particularly keen to buttress their own expansion of trade mark by reference to congressional action, as seen most notably in dealing with the extended

[56] On the latter question of unfair competition law, the curtailment of federal judicial power imposed by *Erie* (n 38) was mitigated (and in practice over time eradicated) by the grant of federal question jurisdiction in section 43(a). Indeed, *Erie* to some extent precipitated the Lanham Act because it further decentralised enforcement at the very time that a national economy was developing. See Dinwoodie, 'The Story of *Kellogg Co. v. National Biscuit Co*' (n 41) 256 n 121.

[57] See *Abercrombie & Fitch Co v Hunting World Inc* 537 F 2d 4 (2d Cir 1976) (noting that 'the cases, and in some instances the Lanham Act, identify four different categories of terms with respect to trademark protection').

[58] See *Polaroid Corp v Polarad Elects Corp* 287 F 2d 492 (2d Cir 1961); see also *Nabisco Inc v PF Brands Inc* 191 F 3d 208 (2d Cir 1999) ('When Judge Friendly made his famous list of factors pertinent to an infringement analysis in *Polaroid*, his opinion drew on generations of analysis of the laws of trademark infringement. And even then his list was non-exclusive; the opinion took pains to insist that in other cases other factors would no doubt emerge as relevant ...').

[59] See *Pagliero v Wallace China Co* 198 F 2d 339, 343 (9th Cir 1952) (articulating rule that a design that was 'an important ingredient in the commercial success' of a product was de jure functional and thus unprotected even if that feature was aesthetic). *Pagliero* has been overruled, but the doctrine lives on. See *TrafFix Devices Inc v Marketing Displays Inc* 532 US 23 (2001).

[60] See, eg, *KP Permanent Make-Up Inc v Lasting Impression I Inc* 543 US 111, 114 (2004).

forms of actionable confusion both pre-sale and post-sale.[61] By the same token, when Congress has intervened to correct mistaken judicial interpretations,[62] provide specific definitions[63] or resolve circuit splits on particular issues,[64] courts have dutifully followed legislative instruction. And on matters not found in the body of common law, such as the incontestability of registered marks or dilution protection for famous marks, courts have generally been assiduous in adhering to congressional language.[65]

Congress does not appear unhappy with this allocation of law-making functions. It has been willing to intervene when courts appear unable to reach a consensus on a particular issue or where courts have misconstrued congressional intent, detected statutory gaps, or rendered wholly unsatisfactory opinions.[66] Moreover, when courts have developed trade mark law in a direction favoured by Congress, Congress has been willing to codify such expansions in later amendments of the statute, often expressing confidence in the ability of courts to play a role in the development of trade mark law.[67]

[61] See *Ferrari SPA Esercizio v Roberts* 944 F 2d 1235 (6th Cir 1991) (post-sale confusion actionable, citing 1962 reforms); *Syntex Labs. Inc v Norwich Pharmacal Co* 437 F 2d 566 (2d Cir 1971) (non-competing goods); *Boston Professional Hockey Ass'n Inc v Dallas Cap & Emblem Mfg Inc* 510 F 2d 1004 (5th Cir 1975) (confusion as to endorsement, citing 1962 broadening of language); *Checkpoint Sys Inc v Check Point Software Technologies Inc* 269 F 3d 270, 295 (3d Cir 2001) (initial interest confusion, citing 1962 language changes). But see *Electronic Design & Sales Inc v Electronic Data Sys Corp* 954 F 2d 713 (Fed Cir 1992) (drawing narrower significance of language change).

[62] See, eg, Trademark Clarification Act of 1984, Pub L No 98-620, §102, 98 Stat 3335 (overruling *Anti-Monopoly Inc v General Mills Fun Group Inc* 684 F.2d 1316 (9th Cir 1982)).

[63] Ibid (providing definition for generic term).

[64] See Trademark Law Treaty Implementation Act, Pub L No 105-330, §201(a)(2) (1998) (allocating burden of proving functionality).

[65] See *Park 'N' Fly Inc v Dollar Park And Fly Inc* 469 US 189 (1985); *TCPIP Holdings Inc v Haar Comm Inc* 244 F 3d 88 (2d Cir 2001) (only inherently distinctive marks could qualify for protection against dilution under section 43(c), relying in part on the statute's reference to marks that were 'famous and distinctive'); *Moseley v V Secret Catalogue Inc* 537 US 418 (2003) (holding that the 1995 federal dilution statute required a showing of actual dilution, in part because Congress had not used the phrase 'likelihood of dilution', a formulation that had been used in a number of state statutes, and because Congress had used the phrase 'likelihood of confusion' in defining dilution). In some respects, the courts appear to regard such statutory innovations as derogations from the common law, requiring them to be narrowly but faithfully construed. Thus, ambiguities have allowed courts to insist on common law principles. See text accompanying nn 85–86.

[66] See Trademark Dilution Revision Act of 2006 (TDRA) (abrogating *V Secret* interpretation of dilution provisions); Trademark Law Treaty Implementation Act, Pub L No 105-330, § 201 (1998) (remedying failure to include functionality as a defence available in action for infringement of incontestable marks and thus overruling *Shakespeare Co v Silstar Corp. of America Inc* 9 F 3d 1091, 1099 (4th Cir 1993)).

[67] See 15 USC § 1125(a) (1988) (amended provision including expanded forms of confusion); *cf* 15 USC § 1125(c)(3)(A) (codifying nominative fair use defence in dilution actions); see also *Two Pesos v Taco Cabana Inc* 505 US 763, 783 n 18 (Stevens J) ('As the Senate Report [to the 1988 reforms] explained, revision of § 43(a) is designed 'to codify the interpretation it has been given by the courts. Because Section 43(a) of the Act fills an important gap in federal unfair competition law, the committee expects the courts to continue to interpret the section.').

Although this arrangement has consistent with developments throughout the world in systems with diverse legal cultures and political economies, tended to result in the expansion of trade mark rights, the US courts have not been reluctant to constrain trade mark rights when appropriate. For example, courts have developed a number of functionality doctrines,[68] the nominative fair use defence,[69] and free-speech based limits on rights.[70] And, on the whole, Congress has been willing to codify these defences just as much as expansions of rights.[71]

Likewise, the Supreme Court has accepted the active role of lower courts in developing trade mark law. For example, in *Two Pesos v Taco Cabana*, the court considered whether the décor of a restaurant could be protected as inherently distinctive trade dress under section 43(a) of the Lanham Act.[72] Justice White's opinion sustaining such a possibility rested ostensibly on the lack of any statutory barrier to inherently distinctive trade dress, noting that protection for non-verbal marks served the same purpose as protection for words and thus there was no reason to apply different tests to non-verbal marks. However, he acknowledged that 'it would be a different matter if there were textual basis in § 43(a) for treating inherently distinctive verbal or symbolic trademarks differently from inherently distinctive trade dress.'

Justice Stevens was even more candid:

> [T]he text of §43(a) of the Lanham Act, 'does not mention trademarks or trade dress.' Nevertheless, the Court interprets this section as having created a federal cause of action for infringement of an unregistered trademark or trade dress and concludes that such a mark or dress should receive essentially the same protection as those that are registered. Although I agree with the Court's conclusion, I think it is important to recognize that the meaning of the text has been transformed by the federal courts over the past few decades. I agree with this transformation, even though it marks a departure from the original text, because it is consistent with the purposes of the statute and has recently been endorsed by Congress.[73]

This justification for the holding reflects the notion of the courts and the Congress as partners in the project of trade mark law-making.[74] Just as Justice White was willing to accept the judicial expansion of protection

[68] See generally *TrafFix Devices v Marketing Displays* (n 59).

[69] See *New Kids on the Block v News America Publishing Inc* 971 F 2d 302, 306 (9th Cir 1992); *Century 21 Real Estate Corp v LendingTree Inc* 425 F 3d 211 (3d Cir 2005).

[70] See *Rogers v Grimaldi* 875 F 2d 994 (2d Cir 1989); *E.S.S. Entm't 2000 Inc v Rock Star Videos Inc* 547 F 3d 1095 (9th Cir 2008).

[71] See 15 USC § 1052(e)(5) (functionality); *cf* 15 USC § 1125(c)(3) (nominative fair use, in dilution actions).

[72] 505 US 763 (1992).

[73] Ibid 776 (citation omitted).

[74] The Court substantially undermined its ruling on the inherent distinctiveness point only eight years later. See *Wal-Mart Stores Inc v Samara Bros. Inc* 529 US 205 (2000). But, as explained below, the Court's reasoning in the later case does not contradict what the *Two Pesos* opinions suggest about the respective roles of courts and Congress.

where consistent with the purposes of the law absent no countervailing statutory language,[75] Justice Stevens placed great store in later Congressional endorsement and acquiescence:[76]

> Congress has revisited this statute from time to time, and has accepted the 'judicial legislation' that has created this federal cause of action. Recently, for example, ... Congress codified the judicial interpretation of §43(a), giving its *imprimatur* to a growing body of case law from the Circuits that had expanded the section beyond its original language.

Of course, this latter explanation fits well with simple canons of statutory interpretation, without accepting a more active law-making role for courts.[77] However, Justice Stevens was unconcerned that Congress had not addressed the particular question (inherent distinctiveness of trade dress) before the Court. A general indication of congressional satisfaction with the trend of judicial activity supported his conclusion.

Justice Thomas, perhaps unsurprisingly given his more general interpretive philosophy, was unwilling to endorse judicial development of the law beyond the language of the statute. However, he reached the same conclusion as the rest of the Court because section 43(a) codified common law torts and judges had, over time, concluded that 'a particular trade dress ... is now considered as fully capable as a particular trademark of serving as a "representation or designation" of source under §43(a).' In such circumstances, Justice Thomas concluded, protection of inherently distinctive trade dress was fully consistent with the statutory language.[78]

These separate opinions in *Two Pesos* reveal a Court comfortable with judicial development of trade mark and unfair competition law, whether by reference to canons of statutory construction, because of later congressional endorsement, or by implicit recognition that 'codification of the common law' in the Lanham Act was essentially a delegation of law-making powers to the courts. The idea of a law-making partnership between the courts and Congress does not appear problematic. Justice Breyer's opinion for the Court three years later in *Qualitex* is similarly relaxed about such

[75] Justice Stevens did not disagree with teleological interpretation as a justification. See *Two Pesos* (n 67) 781–82 ('even though the lower courts' expansion of the categories contained in §43(a) is unsupported by the text of the Act, ... it is consistent with the general purposes of the Act.').

[76] Justice Breyer adopted a similar approach when confronted with the question whether colour per se could be registered. See *Qualitex Co v Jacobsen Prod Inc* 514 US 159 (1995).

[77] See *Tiger v Western Investment Co* 221 US 286, 309 (1911) ('When several acts of Congress are passed touching the same subject-matter, subsequent legislation may be considered to assist in the interpretation of prior legislation upon the same subject.').

[78] Justice Scalia also noted the relevance of the common law derivation of section 43(a). See *Two Pesos* (n 67) 776 ('I write separately to note my complete agreement with Justice Thomas' explanation as to how the language of § 43(a) and its common-law derivation are broad enough to embrace inherently distinctive trade dress. Nevertheless, because I find that analysis to be complementary to (and not inconsistent with) the Court's opinion, I concur in the latter.'). This is especially noteworthy given Justice Scalia's opinion for the Court in *Dastar*.

a partnership, though perhaps more cautiously phrased. Justice Breyer found an unchecked trend in favour of a liberal approach to registration of colour per se, as reflected in Patent and Trademark office practice as well as lower court opinions, to signal congressional assent to registration of colour given statements of support in legislative history. 'At a minimum', he suggested, 'the Lanham Act's changes left the courts free to reevaluate the preexisting legal precedent which had absolutely forbidden the use of color alone as a trademark.'

These Supreme Court opinions were written by members of a Court noted for a textualist approach to statutory construction.[79] In some respects, therefore, they may seem surprising. And, certainly, to the extent that the Court has backtracked on *Two Pesos* in its *Wal-Mart* opinion, one might be loathe to rely simply on the Court's approach in *Two Pesos*. But even in cases such as *Wal*-Mart, in which the Court clearly reversed course on the substantive issue of trade mark law decided in *Two Pesos*, the Court's opinion is not inconsistent with the understanding of the role of the courts displayed in *Two Pesos*. In *Wal-Mart*, when presented with the question of whether product design (as opposed to restaurant décor) could be inherently distinctive, the Court started from the proposition that the 'the text of §43(a) provides little guidance as to the circumstances under which unregistered trade dress may be protected', and then filled that void with the type of reasoning that one would expect from a common law court. The Court drew distinctions between the functions of words and shapes, and highlighted analogies in the treatment of descriptive terms and colours in prior case law and the statute. Justice Scalia's opinion for the Court canvassed a number of policy concerns, some grounded in core trade mark principles (such as distinctiveness) and others in prudential values such as commercial certainty.[80]

A detailed analysis of all the influences in even more recent Supreme Court trade mark opinions is beyond the scope of this chapter.[81] And, to be sure, finding complete consistency in the Court's approach over the last 15 years is challenging.[82] However, those opinions suggest a continuing commitment to the role of courts in developing the contours of trade mark protection in a common law fashion. For example, in *TrafFix*, in which the Court endorsed a robust functionality exclusion from trade mark protection, the Court drew its primary test of functionality from dicta in a footnote in a prior Supreme Court opinion. And it supported a judicially

[79] See WN Eskridge, Jr, 'The New Textualism' (1990) 37 *UCLA Law Review* 621. Obviously, the writers of the opinions vary in their commitment to textualism.

[80] The *Wal-Mart* opinion is open to criticism on other grounds. See GB Dinwoodie, 'The Seventh Annual Helen Wilson Neis Lecture on Intellectual Property Law: The Trademark Jurisprudence of the *Rehnquist* Court' (2004) 8 *Marquette Intellectual Property Law Review* 187.

[81] For an effort, see ibid.

[82] See ibid.

developed inference of functionality from the existence of a prior utility patent by reference to the discrete purposes of patent and trade mark law, more general Supreme Court case law on the role of imitation and reverse engineering in a competitive economy, and the same prudential concerns raised in *Wal-Mart*. This is hardly a surprise. The entire body of functionality law was developed by the courts. Importantly, the Court simply took from the minimal statutory provision on the matter (assigning the burden of proving non-functionality to a plaintiff holding no registered rights) an endorsement of the judicially created rule that functional features are not protected by trade mark law.

KP Permanent and *Moseley* are interesting examples of how this law-making partnership might work in an era of more extensive legislative intervention.[83] *KP Permanent* dealt with the defences available in an action for infringement of an incontestable mark, a concept introduced by the Lanham Act; *Moseley* involved the interpretation of federal dilution protection, which existed only by virtue of statutory enactment in 1995. As such, these seem candidates ripe for substantial deference to the legislature. And, indeed, the Court started its opinion in both cases from an analysis of the statutory text, drawing on canons of interpretation.[84] But it did not end it there in either instance. In *KP Permanent*, the Court buttressed its conclusion that fair use could be found notwithstanding the existence of some confusion by reference to the parallel rule in the common law of unfair competition and the 'typical course of litigation in an infringement action'. These general principles informed and supported the interpretation that the Court offered of the Lanham Act. Moreover, the Court explicitly left it to lower courts to work out the different considerations that would infuse the amorphous terms 'fair' and 'good faith' with real content.

At first blush, *Moseley* is an avowedly textual decision, reflecting the subordination of courts to Congress. But in fact, it can be read quite differently. To be sure, the Court's primary grounds for decision are textual, grounded in typical canons of statutory interpretation: for example the word 'likelihood' appeared in both state dilution statutes and the federal confusion-based infringement provision but was absent from the federal dilution provision, and that distinction must matter. In truth (as is perhaps the case in almost all matters of textual interpretation), there was another plausible reading of the text based on the nature of the relief in dilution cases, the legislative history, and international standards. But that reading—quite clearly, to most observers, what was intended by the legislature—was rejected.

[83] See *KP Permanent Make-Up v Lasting Impression I* (n 60); *Moseley v V Secret* (n 65).

[84] See, e.g. *KP Permanent Make-Up v Lasting Impression I* (n 60) 118 ('[W]here Congress includes particular language in one section of a statute but omits it in another section of the same Act, it is generally presumed that Congress acts intentionally and purposely in the disparate inclusion or exclusion') (citation omitted).

Thus, under the rubric of textualism, the Court was in fact resisting legislative supremacy, even in an area of trade mark law created wholly by statute. Why? Because the grant of dilution protection, conferring protection where no consumers would be confused, was in fact a derogation from the general principles of common law. As the Court explained before even tackling the terms of the statute in detail, 'unlike traditional infringement law, the prohibitions against trademark dilution are not the product of common law development, and are not motivated by an interest in protecting consumers.' In such a context, the Court implies, any congressional derogation from common law principles—whether an expansion in protection or contraction—will be narrowly construed. The Court will not assume statutory abrogation of common law principles without clear instruction.[85] Congress eventually made its intent clear in 2006, and courts have accepted the more generous likelihood of dilution standard. But the judicial distaste for badly articulated legislative departures from common law principles will likely ensure a continued tendency among courts to assert the vitality of the background common law in interpreting the revised dilution statute.[86]

Dastar is the recent Supreme Court decision that might cause greatest doubt regarding the Court's acceptance of a law-making partnership with Congress in matters of trade mark and unfair competition.[87] In *Dastar*, the plaintiffs sued under section 43(a) of the Lanham Act, arguing that the defendant's failure to credit the artistic source of the public domain television series on which it based its derivative audio-visual work amounted to reverse passing off.[88] Section 43(a), the federal unfair competition provision, by its language prohibits 'false designations of origin'. The failure to include a reference to the television series was only a false designation of

[85] *Cf Wagamama Ltd v City Centre Restaurants PLC* [1995] FSR 713 (Ch D).

[86] See GB Dinwoodie and MD Janis, 'Dilution's (Still) Uncertain Future' (2006) 105 *Michigan Law Review* First Impressions 98, available at http://students.law.umich.edu/mlr/firstimpressions/vol105/ dinwoodie.pdf.

[87] *Dastar Corp v Twentieth Century Fox Film Corp* 539 US 23 (2003). There is a certain irony if the strictness of the statute was indeed most acutely felt in *Dastar*, because that was a case resting on principles of unfair competition rather than trade mark law proper. In most other countries, unfair competition tends to be more judge-made than trade mark law. Of course, the Court's decision that the plaintiff's claim was not encompassed by the Lanham Act would not of itself preclude a claim under state law principles of unfair competition (a dynamic seen also in the European Union), although the presence of copyright claims in the dispute might raise complicated questions of pre-emption.

[88] The plaintiff was the owner of a copyright in a television series based upon President Eisenhower's book, *Crusade in Europe*. After that television series fell into the public domain for failure to comply with copyright renewal formalities, the defendant Dastar purchased tapes of the series, edited them, and added additional material of it own and sold the revised video tapes. The packaging for the product made no reference to the original television series: it said 'Produced and Distributed by' a Dastar subsidiary.

'origin' if 'origin' meant the artistic origin of the product; the defendant *was* the origin of the tangible product sold.

Because Justice Scalia's opinion starts with an analysis of the dictionary definition of 'origin', it again appears at first blush to be a classic textualist exercise in interpretation, privileging the statute. Likewise, the Court's statement that 'because of its inherently limited wording, § 43(a) can never be a federal "codification" of the overall law of "unfair competition," but can apply only to certain unfair trade practices prohibited by its text,' suggests some disquiet with the broad expansion of Section 43(a) that had been effected by the courts. But, as I have argued elsewhere, 'given that the language of Section 43(a) is clearly susceptible to more than one interpretation, one might suspect that there is something else going on.'[89] Do the other considerations that informed Justice Scalia's opinion suggest distaste for judicial law-making in this field?

To be sure, the protection (effectively, of moral rights) that prior law had conferred on plaintiffs in similar circumstances had been judicially constructed. The Ninth Circuit had affirmed the judgment for the plaintiffs primarily based upon prior case law to the effect that the 'bodily appropriation' of a plaintiff's work without attribution was sufficient to support a Lanham Act claim. The Court effectively rejected this case law. In some parts of the opinion, however, Justice Scalia recognises the law-making partnership between courts and Congress in the field. Thus, for example, consistent with the view he expressed in *Two Pesos*, he notes without criticism that although a 'proper reading' of the original Section 43(a) would have limited origin 'to the geographic location in which the goods originated,' the federal courts had read the language expansively 'thereby creating a federal cause of action for traditional trademark infringement of unregistered marks.'[90]

Perhaps, the unwillingness of the Supreme Court to endorse the expansion that the Ninth Circuit had readily accepted may have had less to do with a general concern with judicial over-reaching than with a concern of how Congress should properly make its participation in the law-making partnership known. Congress *had* spoken on this issue: but while the

[89] See Dinwoodie, '*Rehnquist* Court' (n 80).

[90] This uncritical acceptance of the judicial role must be tempered by the fact that, as Justice Scalia noted, Congress had adopted the expansion in the Trademark Law Revision Act of 1988 and that its language was now 'amply inclusive … of reverse passing off.' It is not wholly clear what Justice Scalia would have thought of this judicial activity absent legislative endorsement in 1988. Justice Scalia might simply be reciting history no longer germane to the question before the Court, given statutory amendment. See *Dastar Corp v Twentieth Century Fox* (n 87) 32 n 5 ('This stretching of the concept "origin of goods" is seemingly no longer needed: The 1988 amendments to §43(a) now expressly prohibit the use of any "word, term, name, symbol, or device," or "false or misleading description of fact" that is likely to cause confusion as to "affiliation, connection, or association … with another person," or as to "sponsorship, or approval" of goods.'). The use of the verb 'stretch' might seem reproving.

Lanham Act might have been vague, the Copyright Act was not.[91] Congress had created a limited system of moral rights in 1990 in the Visual Artists Rights Act of 1990, but had imposed limits on that cause of action that made it unavailable to the plaintiff in *Dastar*.

The Court is thus able to support its result by reference to canons of statutory interpretation, suggesting a subservient judicial role: an expansive interpretation of section 43(a) would (purportedly)[92] render the Copyright statute superfluous.[93] But this strict reading of section 43(a) can also be explained in terms more supportive of the conceptual understanding of the Lanham Act suggested in this chapter. When Congress enacted a wholly statutory right (moral rights), it derogated from the common law rule in the United States that public domain works could be freely copied.[94] The Court would not simultaneously disregard the clear limits in that statute and long-standing common law principles of intellectual property, which the Court had announced in a number of earlier opinions. This suggestion is supported by a passage toward the end of the Court's opinion: 'Reading the phrase "origin of goods" in the Lanham Act in accordance with the Act's *common-law* foundations (which were not designed to protect originality or creativity), and in light of the copyright and patent laws (which were), we conclude that the phrase refers to the producer of the tangible goods that are offered for sale, and not to the author of any idea, concept, or communication embodied in those goods.'[95] Common law trade mark is about misrepresentation rather than misappropriation.[96]

[91] *Dastar Corp v Twentieth Century Fox* (n 87) 33 ('The problem with this argument according special treatment to communicative products is that it causes the Lanham Act to conflict with the law of copyright, which addresses that subject specifically). Moreover, Congress had also made clear that works published without copyright notice prior to 1989 fell into the public domain.

[92] See JC Ginsburg, 'The Right to Claim Authorship in US Copyright and Trade marks Law' (2004) 41 *Houston Law Review* 263.

[93] The Court described the plaintiff's argument as seeking to create a species of 'mutant copyright.' See *Dastar Corp v Twentieth Century Fox* (n 87) 34.

[94] The Court can be faulted for a narrow reading of the common law rule. The right to copy public domain works has, as a matter of common law, always been conditioned on minimising the possibility of confusion through misrepresentation. See Dinwoodie, 'The Story of *Kellogg Co. v. National Biscuit Co*' (n 41).

[95] See *Dastar Corp v Twentieth Century Fox* (n 87) 37 (emphasis added). Indeed, in certain other respects the Court's decision clearly represented an assertion of judicial power over congressional intent in that the Court also rejected the apparent endorsement in the legislative history to the 1988 Berne Convention Implementation Act of the type of claims advanced by the plaintiff.

[96] As discussed more fully elsewhere, the Court may have been influenced by any number of additional considerations, such as the practical difficulties of ascertaining the persons—authors, directors, actors, publishers, broadcasters—who would have to be identified. The Court appears concerned that competitors be able to make use of public domain works without the litigation chill of being sued no matter what attribution strategy it followed. See Dinwoodie, '*Rehnquist* Court' (n 80).

To some, the idea that Justice Scalia (of all members of the current Court) would support broad judicial authority in an area extensively dealt with by Congress might seem counterintuitive. However, in the context of antitrust law, the Supreme Court has long accepted that the Sherman Act essentially reflects a decision by Congress to permit the development of antitrust law by the courts. Justice Scalia has acquiesced in this position. The Sherman Act is what the Court has described as a 'common law statute.'[97] Such a statute is congressional recognition of the continuing common-law powers of courts to develop the law within a general framework established by Congress and subject to intervention by Congress where appropriate.[98] This characterisation of antitrust law reflects a theoretical conception of US trade mark and unfair competition law clearly in place prior to the Lanham Act.[99] However, as suggested by the history recounted above, this basic conception continues to inform both congressional action and judicial decision. As Judge Pierre Leval has suggested, 'the words of the [Lanham Act] simply will not provide the answers and were not intended by the legislature to do so. In passing delegating statutes, legislatures recognize that they function together with courts in a law-making partnership, each having its proper role.'[100]

Some scholars and courts have suggested that contemporary trade mark law may be less receptive to such a law-making partnership. For example, Professor Michael Grynberg detects a growing formalism in recent trade mark opinions, both of the Supreme Court and lower courts.[101] As part of this formalism, Professor Grynberg highlights what he sees as the courts' recent tendency to readily allow the text of the statute to constrain judicial

[97] See *Leegin Creative Leather Prods v PSKS Inc* 551 US 877, 887 (2007); see also Posner (n 1) 48.

[98] Thus, for example, Congress enacted the Foreign Trade Antitrust Improvements Act 1982 to modify judicial decisions regarding the extraterritorial scope of the antitrust law. Once congressional intent was clear, the courts have operated within their new remit.

[99] See text accompanying nn 19–35. In the late nineteenth century, substantive principles of UK trade mark law were a matter for the judiciary, with statutory intervention serving to facilitate the registration and enforcement of such judicially recognised rights. The 1875 registration statute was not dramatically different in conception from the US registration statutes of similar vintage. See Bently (n 3) 28 (noting that 'in contrast with later trade-marks acts, [the 1875 Act] did not report to establish a self-contained or exhaustive scheme. Rather, the 1875 act built upon the existing common-law system…'). The UK Act 'did not create a cause of action for infringement, assuming that one already existed at common law and in equity. Its purpose was to create procedural and evidential advantages for registered marks, and in order to encourage registration it provided that no one was to be entitled to institute proceedings to prevent infringement of any trade mark as defined in the Act unless and until it had been registered.' See Wadlow, *The Law of Passing Off* (n 11) 28. An express statutory infringement cause of action was eventually provided by the 1905 Act.

[100] See PN Leval, 'Trademark: Champion of Free Speech' (2004) 27 *Columbia Journal of Low & Arts* 187, 198.

[101] M Grynberg, 'Things Are Worse Than We Think: Trademark Defenses in a Formalist Age', 24 *Belk. Tech. L.J.* 897 (2009).

law-making. He traces the change neither to different levels of congressional intervention in trade mark law nor any normative reassessment of trade mark law, but rather to a broader change in judicial philosophy (to law, and not trade mark law alone).[102]

Although I disagree with Grynberg's assessment of the continued room for judicial law-making, his warning is no less relevant for its grounding in changes to judicial attitudes generally. History suggests that as we consider the appropriate allocation of law-making power in trade mark and unfair competition law, the question cannot be answered wholly apart from broader considerations of judicial and legislative authority.[103] The subordination of statutory provisions to common law principles in US trade mark law prior to the Lanham Act reflected no analysis of the institutional competence of legislators versus courts in matters of trade mark law or the theoretical relationship between trade mark law and unfair competition law (which is how we might now approach the question in an era of broad Commerce Clause authority).[104] Rather, it reflected the constitutional allocation of law-making powers between the federal and state governments, which substantially shifted over time. The constitutional jurisprudence of the early twentieth century (operating under *The Trade-Mark Cases* and *Swift v Tyson*) empowered federal courts but not Congress. The Supreme Court's revised understanding of the Commerce Clause, induced by the New Deal, and the decision in *Erie*, empowered Congress and constrained the federal courts' law-making powers (at least under diversity jurisdiction). These particular constitutional questions no longer constrain the development of U.S. trade mark law,[105] but their centrality to the development of trade mark law suggests we take Grynberg's warning seriously.[106]

[102] Some courts also appear to see the Lanham Act as more pre-emptive than I suggest. See *NuPulse Inc v Schlueter Co* 853 F 2d 545 (7th Cir 1988) ('When we view the Lanham Act in its totality, it is clear that Congress intended to create a self-contained statutory device to deal with all kinds of trademark infringement and unfair competition.').

[103] See text accompanying nn 33–44.

[104] This is not to say that there was no discussion in decisions at the time regarding the law-making competence of different institutions in the field of trade mark law. Thus, for example, in his dissent in *INS*, Justice Brandeis expressly noted that the courts were ill-equipped to determine the conditions for the grant of a new right of property. See *INS* (n 31) 267. When his alternative misrepresentation-based conception of unfair competition was ultimately validated in *Kellogg*, Justice Brandeis indicated no similar concerns with the ability of courts to pass on the appropriateness of measures designed to minimise consumer confusion about competing products of a similar shape.

[105] Parallel questions might be more relevant to the appropriate development of trade mark and unfair competition law in the European Union where legislative competence is not (yet) so centrally controlled, and questions of national state sovereignty (subsidiarity) may resonate politically in the way that the United States experienced in the twentieth century.

[106] Moreover, Grynberg finds evidence of these broader changes to judicial philosophy in trade mark opinions. See Grynberg, 'Things Are Worse Than We Think' (n 101). As suggested above, I believe there is plenty of support for a continued active judicial role.

Grynberg suggests that the formalism he detects is of particular concern because the open text of the provisions in the Lanham Act establishing liability hardly constrains courts regarding what might be actionable as trade mark infringement or unfair competition. In contrast, the narrow language of the statute with respect to defences precludes much further development of common law defences to those actions. Yet, the development of doctrines permitting unauthorised third party uses of marks may be extremely important in an era of expanding trade mark owners' rights.[107] As suggested above, without disagreeing about the relative precision in the infringement and defences provision of the statute, I read the Supreme Court's recent case law as broadly supportive of active judicial involvement in the development of most aspects of trade mark law. To be sure, acceptance of the role of courts in the development of trade mark law does not suggest that courts should have unfettered discretion about the direction in which to go. Both the legitimacy of congressional action and the different institutional competence of courts and Congress require proper respect for statutory provision. But the general philosophy described in this Chapter should enable traditional development of defences proper, albeit with deference to Congress in dealing with causes of action that are wholly statutory in nature (such as dilution) or with mechanisms that did not exist at common law (such as registration).[108]

CONCLUSION

Trade mark and unfair competition law, both in the United States and the United Kingdom, has deep common law roots. Despite the increasingly frequent intervention of Congress, US law remains a matter for active development by the courts in partnership with Congress. Of course, the balance of authority is not descriptively the same as it was in the early twentieth century; Congress is now a more regular contributor. But both Congress and the Supreme Court seem largely content with the notion of trade mark law as their joint work product, with their precise contributions reflecting the exigencies of cases that come before the courts and the urgency of matters brought before Congress. As a result, although the US scope of trade mark law has dramatically changed in the last 60 years, the institutional responsibility for its future development has not.

[107] See GB Dinwoodie, 'The Ninth Annual Distinguished IP Lecture: Developing Defenses in Trademark Law' (2009) 13 *Lewis & Clark Law Review* 99.

[108] Occasionally, this deference might still, as Professor Grynberg fears, limits the capacity of courts to develop common-law defences to trade mark infringement. See ibid 130. And, as noted above, this deference might also be accompanied by a requirement that Congress carefully delineate any derogation from the common law.

16

Protecting Extraterritorial Goodwill

Exploring the Impetus Behind a Common Law

A KELLY GILL*

A COMMON LAW exists only in so far as there are common societal goals and norms. A review of international jurisprudence concerning the protection of foreign trade marks through the common law of passing off where there is no use of that trade mark in the jurisdiction,[1] confirms this proposition. International jurisprudence concerning extraterritorial goodwill is, at worst, conflicting, and, at best, difficult to reconcile when examining the issue from purely legal principles. As one commentator has stated:

> The problem of the foreign claimant whose goods or business may be known in a particular jurisdiction although he has no business there is one of the most intractable in the law of passing-off. It is one of the very few topics where it is impossible to say that the underlying substantive law is essentially uniform throughout the common law world; and there are differences in national case law which are too great to dismiss as the inevitable result of different judges using different words in applying the law to differing factual situations.[2]

However, when one examines the jurisprudence from a broader socio-economic perspective, it seems clear that the jurisprudence consistently reflects the idiosyncratic attitudes of that country towards, most particularly, international trade. Although differing views may be held as to the impetus behind British jurisprudence on the topic, countries that depend on or promote international free trade are generally far more likely to protect extraterritorial goodwill than those that do not.

* I would like to extend my thanks to James Blonde for his extensive research assistance, and to Scott Jolliffe, James Tumbridge and Bruce Ewing for their comments on early drafts of this chapter.

[1] Hereinafter referred to as 'extraterritorial goodwill'.

[2] C Wadlow, *The Law of Passing-Off*, 3rd edn (London, Sweet & Maxwell, 2004) 154.

This chapter will explore the international jurisprudence concerning extraterritorial goodwill, not from a strict analysis of legal principles, but instead looking at some of the broader socio-economic trends at play in the countries at the various times of certain decisions. What emerges is that there can be no common law unless there are also common societal goals and norms.

THE UNITED STATES – NEW YORK STATE

New York State courts have recognised two theories of common law unfair competition that can be used to protect extraterritorial goodwill: palming-off[3] and misappropriation. Palming-off is meant to prevent the same form of wrongdoing that the common law of passing-off seeks to prevent, namely one trader misrepresenting his goods or services as coming from or being connected to the goods or services of another. In order to establish a claim of unfair competition by palming-off, a plaintiff must establish a likelihood of consumer confusion between its protectable trade mark and the defendant's trade mark, a protectable trade mark being a mark that is capable of or in fact does indicate a single source. Mala fides are unnecessary to found an action for palming-off and, similarly, good faith is no defence.[4]

Unfair competition also recognises a second type of tort, referred to as misappropriation. For there to be unfair competition by misappropriation, a plaintiff must prove that the defendant wilfully misappropriated the plaintiff's trade mark. The plaintiff does not need to prove a likelihood of consumer confusion. However, the plaintiff must prove bad faith or intentional wrongdoing on the part of the defendant.

Since at least 1936, New York courts have protected foreign plaintiffs whose trade marks were misappropriated, even when those plaintiffs had never operated within New York. In the two earliest and most notable decisions, relief was granted to owners of restaurants located in France as against restaurants established in New York that had misappropriated similar names in connection with similar types of establishments.[5] In both instances, French plaintiffs established protectable reputations within New York State whose existence was not dependent upon actual trade mark use, and which was misappropriated by the defendants.[6] These two cases were recently reaffirmed by the Second Circuit Court of Appeals in yet another

[3] See eg *Electrolux Corp v Val-Worth Inc* 161 NE 2d 197, 203.

[4] *Madison Square Garden Corp v Universal Pictures Co* 255 AD 459, 464, 7 NYS 2d 845, 850 (1st Dep't 1938).

[5] *Maison Prunier v Prunier's Rest & Cafe Inc* 159 Misc 551, 288 NYS 2d 529 (Sup Ct NY Co 1936) and *Vaudable v Montmartre Inc* 20 Misc 2d 757, 193 NYS 2d 332 (Sup Ct NY Co 1959).

[6] *Maison Prunier* (n 5) 553–54 and 535–36 and *Vaudable* (n 5) 334. See also *Lincoln Rest Corp v Wolfies Res Inc* 291 F 2d 302 (2d Cir 1961) and *Ambassador East Inc v Shelton Corners Inc* 120 F Supp 551 (SDNY 1954).

case involving a foreign restaurant, this time located in India.[7] In reviewing the jurisprudence, the Court of Appeals stated the following:

> What *Prunier* and *Vaudable* stand for, then, is the proposition that for certain kinds of businesses (particularly cachet goods/services with highly mobile clienteles), goodwill can, and does, cross state and national boundary lines ...we simply reaffirm that when a business, through renown in New York, possesses goodwill constituting property or a commercial advantage in this State, that goodwill is protected from misappropriation under New York unfair competition law. This is so whether the business is domestic or foreign.[8]

The Court of Appeals clarified that there can be protectable trade mark goodwill in New York State owned by a foreign entity even when there is no use of the mark in the state provided that, 'at a minimum, consumers of the good or service provided under a certain mark by a defendant in New York must primarily associate the mark with the foreign plaintiff'.[9]

The US unfair competition torts do not explicitly require proof of actual damage or a likelihood of damage as a required element. Instead, the torts implicitly recognise that a business can be damaged through a myriad of malpractices:

> The modern view as to the law of unfair competition does not rest solely on the ground of direct competitive injury, but on the broader principle that property rights of commercial value are to be and will be protected from any form of unfair invasion or infringement and from any form of commercial immorality, and a court of equity will penetrate and restrain every guise resorted to by the wrongdoer. The courts have thus recognized that in the complex pattern of modern business relationships, persons in theoretically non-competitive fields may, by unethical business practices, inflict as severe and reprehensible injuries upon others as can direct competitors.[10]

New York State is and has been one of the most important trading centres in the world. As the International Trademark Association stated in its brief for amicus curiae filed in support of neither party in *ITC Limited v Punchgini Inc*,

> New York is one of the world's foremost commercial centers and the focus of more national and international trading activity than perhaps any other U.S. jurisdiction. It is essential to the sound operation of U.S. trademark law that New York continue to maintain its longstanding, robust protections against unfair competition.[11]

7 *ITC Ltd v Punchgini Inc* Court of Appeals, Second Circuit Docket No 05-0933.

8 Ibid 13–14.

9 Ibid 14.

10 *Metropolitan Opera Ass'n Inc v Wagner-Nichols Recorder Corp* 199 Misc 786, 796, 101 NYS 2d 483, 492 (Sup Ct NY Co 1950), aff'd 279 AD 632, 107 NYS 2d 795 (1st Dep't 1951).

11 Brief for Amicus Curiae International Trademark Association in Support of Neither Party, filed October 2, 2007 in *ITC Limited v Punchgini Inc* Court of Appeals, Second Circuit Docket No 05-0933, 6.

Implicit from the INTA's submission is that the United States' protection of extraterritorial goodwill is necessary and fully understood in the context of that country's promotion of international trade; denying foreign plaintiffs protection for their extraterritorial goodwill will inevitably result in the denial of protection for American companies doing business abroad.[12]

ENGLAND

If the United States, exemplified by New York State, protects extraterritorial goodwill on the foundation of protecting free competition devoid of business malpractices, England might be considered the opposite. The English courts have historically been reluctant to protect marks where the plaintiff was a foreign entity that did not carry on business in England. The high water mark is represented by the 1967 decision of *Alain Bernardin et Compagnie v Pavilion Properties Ltd*[13] ('*Crazy Horse*'). The plaintiff owned the Crazy Horse Saloon, a well-known and popular Paris-based night spot famous for its nude cabaret show. The Paris Crazy Horse advertised and promoted itself in England and was frequented by British tourists in Paris.[14] The English defendant had chosen the identical name as the famous Parisian 'Crazy Horse Saloon', copied its decorations and advertisements, and had done this for 'the sole purpose of cashing in on the reputation … of the [Parisian] plaintiff'.[15] Despite these findings, the plaintiff's action failed because the court held that a trader cannot acquire goodwill in England without some sort of user in that country.[16]

Not all courts took the same approach as that in *Crazy Horse*. The 1977 decision of *Maxim's v Dye*[17] contained facts almost identical *to Crazy Horse,* but the court came to the opposite conclusion. Here the world-famous Paris-based restaurant Maxim's successfully sued a London-based restaurant of the same name for passing-off, notwithstanding that the Paris Maxim's had no place of business in the UK. In his judgment, Graham J declined to follow *Crazy Horse*, holding that 'I see no reason why the reality of the reputation in the United Kingdom should not be protected and I believe that our courts could properly be regarded as being out of touch with reality if they have not the power to protect such goodwill.'[18]

[12] Note however that the protection of extraterritorial goodwill is not uniform throughout the United States. See AG LaLonde, 'Don't I Know You From Somewhere? Protection in the United States of Foreign Trademarks that are Well Known But Not Used There' (2008) 98 *Trade Mark Reports* 1379.

[13] *Alain Bernardin et Compagnie v Pavilion Properties Ltd* (1967) 19 RPC 581 (Ch D).

[14] Ibid 584–85.

[15] Ibid 558.

[16] Ibid 584.

[17] *Maxim's Ltd v Dye* [1977] FSR 364 (Ch D).

[18] Ibid 367 and 371.

Crazy Horse and *Maxim's* appear to be directly at odds, and represent two distinct approaches that are quite impossible to reconcile under accepted principles of passing-off. The approach exemplified by *Crazy Horse* was preferred in the 1979 decision *Athlete's Foot*[19] and in the 1982 decision *Anheuser-Busch*.[20] The approach exemplified by *Maxim's v Dye* is represented in reported cases as early as the 1920 decision of *Poiret*,[21] and includes examples in the 1960s[22] and the late 1970s.[23]

In the 1990s, the courts struggled to reconcile all of these cases by holding that goodwill will only be protected when business is carried on in England, but that the presence of customers in England would be sufficient to constitute carrying on of business, whether or not the services are provided in England and whether or not there is otherwise a place of business in England and even when the number of proven customers in England might be limited.[24]

Various social, economic, and political currents may explain the waxing and waning of the English approach to foreign marks. As the Ontario Court of Appeal noted when reviewing the jurisprudence,[25] the English Channel and the Atlantic Ocean separate England from Europe and the Americas; this physical separation symbolises the sometimes enormous cultural differences between England and its nearest trading partners, particularly those in mainland Europe. Such cultural differences caused by geography have nevertheless been tempered by the enormous international reach that England historically held in the days of the British Empire and the influence it continues to exert in business and politics in many parts of the globe. The hard-line cases perhaps reflect England's physical and cultural isolation, while the softer-line cases reflect England's prominence in global affairs in which business and cultural influence will inevitably flow across its physical borders.

Several more specific background facts gleaned from the cases demonstrate the competing cultural and political forces with which English law has had to contend. England's relationship with France has been fraught since at least the Norman Conquest of 1066, and the countries are culturally very distinct, separated not only by language, but also by religion, legal and political systems, and numerous other cultural forces. However,

[19] *Athlete's Foot Marketing Association Inc v Cobra Sports Ltd* (1979) [1980] 12 RPC 343 (Ch D).

[20] *Anheuser-Busch Inc v Budejovicky Budvar NP* [1984] FSR 413 (CA and Ch D).

[21] *Poiret v Jules Poiret Ltd* [1920] RPC 177 (Ch D).

[22] *Sheraton Corpn of America v Sheraton Motels Ltd* (1964), 8 RPC 202 (Ch D).

[23] *Baskin-Robbins Ice Cream Co. v Gutman* [1976] FSR 545 (Ch D).

[24] *Pete Waterman Ltd v CBS United Kingdom Ltd* (1990) 20 IPR 185 (Ch D); *Jian Tools v Roderick Manhattan Group Ltd* [1995] FSR 924 (Ch D).

[25] *Orkin Exterminating Co Inc v Pestco Co of Canada Ltd* (1985) 5 CPR (3d) 433, 450 (Ont CA).

given France's close proximity, the countries share significant aspects of their history, and in modern times trade and tourism between France and England are important parts of each country's economy. It is no surprise, then, that *Crazy Horse*[26] and *Maxim's v Dye*,[27] the two cases that best represent the hard- and soft-line approaches to extraterritorial goodwill, both arose out of disputes between French and English companies. In *Crazy Horse*, Pennycuick J does not explicitly discuss the cultural gulf between France and England, but some of the facts in the case reveal these differences and may have influenced the decision. Although the English defendant had copied the décor and marketing of the French original, it is clear that the experience one would have at each establishment would have been very different: at the French Crazy Horse, patrons were treated to a 'nude spectacle ... whereas the [English Crazy Horse] provide[d] a dinner and dance'.[28] The fact that the English defendant was ready to copy the superficial aspect of the French defendant's business, but not its risqué substance, speaks volumes about the cultural differences between the nations, while simultaneously exemplifying each culture's awareness of the other. Elsewhere in the judgment, language differences are noted when the French Crazy Horse presented evidence that it took pains to provide advertising and programmes in English.[29] Almost 50 years earlier, in the *Poiret* decision, it was noted how incensed English dressmakers had been when the Prime Minister's wife exhibited the French plaintiff's gowns at 10 Downing Street,[30] underscoring a certain nationalistic sentiment to trade. Clearly these cases were decided against a backdrop of significant cultural differences tempered by the familiarity engendered by proximity.

By the time *Maxim's v Dye* was decided in 1977, England had finally acceded to the Treaty of Rome establishing the European Economic Community. That the courts moved from the hard approach exemplified by 1967's *Crazy Horse* to the soft approach in 1977—in cases that are factually almost identical—may therefore have been reflective of a social and political paradigm shift towards a less insular England, interested in establishing bonds with the rest of Europe. Indeed, a discussion of the Treaty of Rome forms part of the *Maxim's v Dye* decision, with the court holding that protecting the reputation of foreign marks well-known in England is consistent with the country's obligations under the Treaty.[31]

The English accession to the Treaty of Rome is a discreet example of the geopolitical shifts occurring in the second half of the twentieth century

[26] *Alain Bernardin et Compagnie v Pavilion Properties Ltd* (1967) 19 RPC 581 (Ch D).
[27] *Maxim's v Dye* (n 17).
[28] *Alain Bernardin v Pavilion Properties* (n 26) 583.
[29] Ibid 582.
[30] *Poiret v Jules Poiret* (n 21) 184.
[31] *Maxim's v Dye* (n 17) 371.

towards multi- and international political, legal and business frameworks. The court in *Pete Waterman Ltd v CBS United Kingdom Ltd* explicitly commented on these changes and how the law needed to respond to them:

> The changes in the second half of the twentieth century are far more fundamental than those in nineteenth century England. They have produced worldwide marks, worldwide goodwill and brought separate markets into competition one with the other. Radio and television with their attendant advertising cross national frontiers. Electronic communication via satellite produces virtually instant communication between all markets. In terms of travel time, New York by air is as close as Aberdeen by rail. This has led to the development of the international reputation in certain names, particularly in the services fields, for example Sheraton Hotels, Budget Rent A Car.
>
> In my view, the law will fail if it does not try to meet the challenge thrown up by trading patterns which cross national and jurisdictional boundaries due to a change in technical achievement.[32]

While the court in the later case of *Jian Tools v Roderick Manhattan Group Ltd* does not comment upon shifting trade patterns, the facts of the case demonstrate that the shift to worldwide markets was in the background of the decision. The American plaintiff sold its software product in the United States, and was searching for a partner to expand its market into England.[33] There was evidence of customers seeing reviews of the software product at issue in US magazines circulated in England, and of English residents purchasing the product while in the US or by importing it.[34] One can also speculate that the rise to prominence of American corporations in international trade influenced the courts' decisions in *Waterman* and *Jian Tools* in part because of the shared language, history and culture of these countries which facilitate the free flow of business, people, and cultural products, once communication technology developed to bridge the Atlantic ocean.[35]

IRELAND

In the frequently cited 1975 case of *C&A Modes v C&A (Waterford) Ltd*,[36] the English plaintiff operated a series of successful clothing shops in England and Northern Ireland, but it did not have an establishment in the Republic of Ireland. Despite not having a place of business in the Republic, the evidence showed extensive spill-over advertising from UK-based television and newspapers. In addition, the court noted that many citizens of

32 *Pete Waterman v CBS* (n 24) 203.
33 *Jian Tools v Roderick Manhattan Group* (n 24) 929.
34 Ibid 933–34.
35 Both decisions involved US trade mark owners, and both succeeded.
36 *C&A Modes v C&A (Waterford) Ltd* [1978] FSR 126 (SC of Ireland).

the Republic shopped at the plaintiff's establishment while in the UK (and particularly in Belfast, just across the border in Northern Ireland). Given the obvious fluidity of the border between the UK and Ireland, the Supreme Court of Ireland had no trouble holding that:

> The legal wrong known as passing off includes the incorporation in the Republic of Ireland of a company with a name likely to give the impression to the public that it is subsidiary or brand of or is associated or connected with another company which has a an established goodwill, whether the latter company is corporated in the Republic or outside it.
>
> ...
>
> The defendants urged that this principle should be limited to cases where the well-known company had acquired some of its goodwill in the Republic by user or trading in this country. I do not see any reason why this limitation on the general principle should be imposed to-day when extensive advertising can be carried out by television, radio and newspapers—all of which go into almost every home in this State.[37]

The court was clearly influenced by the obvious economic, cultural, and geographical connection to the UK. The court noted that UK television is regularly viewed in Ireland and that international trade in domestic goods has become extensive.[38] Elsewhere in the concurring judgment of Henchy J he notes that 'it would be remarkable, considering the movement of people between this State and the United Kingdom, if there were not a significant number of at least intermittent C&A customers in this State'.[39] The evidence showed that British newspapers and magazines, and Northern Ireland newspapers, were circulated in the Republic.[40] The court also noted that the plaintiff subcontracted with a Republic of Ireland-based factory to supply it goods.[41]

The factors at play in the background of *C&A Modes* are directly analogous to those in other similarly placed countries, such as Canada which is discussed next: two nations with strong economic, cultural and geographical ties.

CANADA

The Ontario Court of Appeal decision in *Orkin Exterminating Co Inc v Pestco Co of Canada Ltd*[42] is a landmark Canadian decision that firmly

[37] Ibid 140 (Kenny J).
[38] Ibid.
[39] Ibid 138 (Kenny J).
[40] Ibid 138 (Kenny J).
[41] Ibid 138 (Kenny J).
[42] *Orkin Exterminating Co Inc v Pestco Co of Canada Ltd et a.* (1985) 5 CPR (3d) 433 (Ont. CA), aff'g (1984) 80 CPR (2d) 153 (Ont HCJ).

established the principle that a foreign mark will be protected in Canada, even when the mark has not actually been used or registered in Canada, if that foreign mark has developed a reputation in Canada. The plaintiff, Orkin, was a very successful and well-known American pest-control company, but with no operations in Canada. The defendant was a Canadian pest-control company called Pestco which adopted and began using the Orkin name some 13 years before the action was commenced, first by listing their phone number next to the 'Orkin' entry in phone books and, a few years later, by presenting the Orkin marks on its invoices. Orkin successfully sued Pestco for passing-off, notwithstanding that they were never in direct competition with Pestco since they did not offer their services in Canada.

Orkin is an important and interesting decision because the Court of Appeal had to grapple with apparent inconsistencies between the British approach to international reputation marks and that of other countries, including Ireland and the United States. The decision strongly endorses the view that foreign marks that have earned an international reputation at home are entitled to protection abroad. On appeal, the Court focused its attention squarely on the issue of whether a plaintiff who does not carry on business in Ontario, but whose trade mark has a reputation in Ontario, nevertheless has goodwill in Ontario that can be damaged. The parties cited numerous decisions from other Canadian, British, Irish and American courts. In response, the Court of Appeal stated that:

> [un]doubtedly, there is ample room for debate on what the exact ratio of some of these judgments is. However, I do not think it is of any practical use to repeat these exercises of wide and narrow interpretation in these reasons because none of the authorities are binding on us and so the issues before us should turn on considerations of principle and policy.[43]

The Court of Appeal dealt first with the principle of damage and noted that passing-off does not require that the parties be in direct competition for there to be damage:

> If the plaintiff's trade name has a reputation in the defendant's jurisdiction, such that the public associates it with services provided by the plaintiff, then the defendant's use of it means that the plaintiff has lost control over the impact of its trade name in the defendant's jurisdiction. The practical consequence of this is that the plaintiff is then vulnerable to losing the Ontario customers it now has as well as prospective Ontario customers, with respect to services provide in the United States. Also, it can result in Orkin being prevented from using its trade name in Ontario when it expands its business into Ontario. [44]

[43] Ibid 443.
[44] Ibid 444.

The Court also addressed the defendant's related argument that goodwill cannot exist outside the area where it carries on business. In support, the defendant cited the then recent decision of the English Court of Appeal in *Anheuser-Busch Inc v Budejovicky Budvar NP*.[45] The Court of Appeal noted that the meaning ascribed to goodwill by the English Court of Appeal had been based upon a definition assigned to the word in a tax case. The Court stated that:

> Virtually no words have a single fixed meaning, particularly goodwill, and, with respect, I do not think that the meaning appropriate in the *Muller* [tax] case is necessarily appropriate in a passing-off case which involves issues of remote territorial use. In this kind of case I think that the main consideration should be the likelihood of confusion with consequential injury to the plaintiff. Generally, where there is such confusion there is goodwill deserving of protection.[46]

Orkin went to trial in the early 1980s and was decided in 1984, with the appeal decision released in 1985. A review of the background facts presented in the case provides a picture of some of the social, economic and political conditions that may have contributed to the finding in *Orkin*. First, the Court noted that, at the time, millions of Canadians travelled to the United States every year, particularly to the southern vacation states where Orkin's operations were extensive.[47] Also, Canadians at this time were exposed to a wide variety of American publications and could receive US television and radio advertisements from stations originating in the US but received in Canada.[48] It was common for Canadians to own or rent houses in the US, and many large American corporations had operations in Canada.[49] The Court also noted similarities in language, culture, and consumer attitudes between the US and Canada, and their geographical proximity, stating that, as a consequence, 'the flow of trans-border goodwill is almost inevitable in North America'.[50] In contrast, the Court noted that the English courts may be less inclined to protect international reputations, due to enormous cultural and geographic barriers between England and its neighbours.[51]

Clearly this was a time of enormous border fluidity between the US and Canada, with capital, people, and media moving easily between each nation. Historically, until approximately the end of World War II, the UK had been Canada's largest trading partner. But commencing in the late 1940s, the United States rapidly and dramatically became Canada's largest

[45] n 20.
[46] *Orkin Exterminating Co v Pestco* (n 42) 450.
[47] *Orkin Exterminating Co v Pestco* (n 42) 436.
[48] *Orkin Exterminating Co v Pestco* (n 42) 437, 450.
[49] Ibid.
[50] *Orkin Exterminating Co v Pestco* (n 42) 450.
[51] Ibid.

trading partner, to the point that by 1975 trade between Canada and the US was more than ten-fold that between Canada and the UK. Further reinforcing the Canada and US trade relationship, and just a year after the *Orkin* Court of Appeal decision, the two countries began discussions which would culminate in the 1988 signing of the Canada–United States Free Trade Agreement,[52] crystallising a social and economic partnership decades in the making. The Court in *Orkin* recognised this factual background by holding that the defendant's activities left Orkin vulnerable to losing Canadian customers with respect to services provided in the US and that the defendant's continued use of Orkin's marks might have prevented Orkin from using its trade name when it expanded into Canada.[53]

At the time of the decision, *Orkin* stood as a relatively high water mark for protecting extraterritorial goodwill: in order to obtain relief, it is not necessary for a foreign trader to have used the mark in Canada, or to have carried on business in Canada, or even to prove that the mark is well-known in Canada. All that is required is proof that a mark has a reputation amongst the relevant sector of the Canadian population, and that confusion and damage are likely. This judgment appears to reflect the fluidity of the US and Canadian border at a time when it was quite reasonable to conclude that a large number of Canadians would be exposed to US-only products, services, and media.

Later courts that have considered *Orkin* throughout the late twentieth century were all decided against a backdrop of significant Canadian exposure to American products, services, and media as a result of Canadians travelling to the US for business or pleasure, reading US magazines and newspapers, watching American television, listening to American radio, and purchasing or renting American properties. In *Borden*,[54] the court considered (and for the most part dismissed as hearsay) a great deal of evidence of Canadians travelling to the southern US, of Canadians receiving television and radio signals from US border cities such as Albany and Buffalo, and of Canadians reading US magazines circulated in Canada.[55] In *HQ Network*[56] the court noted the extent to which the US trade mark owner advertised to attract Canadian businessmen to use its office support services while in the US.[57] *United States Shoes*[58] included evidence of Canadians

[52] www.canadianeconomy.gc.ca/English/economy/1989economic.html.

[53] *Orkin Exterminating Co v Pestco* (n 42) 444.

[54] *Borden Inc v Hostess Food Products Ltd* (1989) 28 CPR (3d) 45 (FCTD).

[55] Ibid 60–61.

[56] *HQ Network Systems Inc v HQ Office Supplies Warehouse Inc* (1990), 30 CPR (3d) 558 (FCTD).

[57] Ibid 567–68, where the evidence showed advertisements placed in Canadian newspapers and in US magazines and newspapers with Canadian circulation.

[58] *United States Shoes Corp v Premiere Vision Inc* (1990), 33 CPR (3d) 353, 356–57 (TMOB).

from border towns travelling to the US to do their shopping. The plaintiff in *Nature Co*[59] established many of its nature-theme shops in cities described by the court as 'major vacation areas as well as [border cities] Buffalo, New York, and Seattle, with the result that many Canadians shop in such stores'. There was evidence that the Buffalo store had more Canadians than Americans patronising it on weekends. Also, by the time of this decision, the court was able to take judicial notice that many American publications had circulation in Canada. Finally, in the 1995 decision in *Disney*,[60] the Alberta Court of Appeal noted 'the great number of Canadians who visited the [US-based] Disney facilities annually'.

Orkin was decided at a time when the national border between the US and Canada was largely an illusion, with money, people, and media moving between the countries relatively unimpeded. With this backdrop, it is easy to see how Canadian courts could conclude that even a little-known American mark may have extraterritorial goodwill worthy of protection in Canada. The Court of Appeal itself had this to say on the subject:

> It might be nothing more than speculation to attempt to account for the differences between the English decisions, which appear to require some business activity by the foreign plaintiff in the jurisdiction of the court, and the Canadian and U.S. authorities [citations omitted] which do not. However, it may be that the various North American jurisdictions where the plaintiffs and defendants, in most of the cases, carry on business, have substantially more in common with respect to language and other cultural features, including consumer attitudes, than do the places from which the parties in the English cases come. Having regard to the travel patterns of the population and mass advertising through television, radio and various publications, the flow of trans-border goodwill is almost inevitable in North America. The English cases involve foreign plaintiffs who are separated from England by the Atlantic Ocean or the English Channel and it is possible that this is an underlying factor in the developments of the relatively 'hard line' [citations omitted] which has generally been followed in the English cases.[61]

AUSTRALIA

In 1947, the *Seven Up*[62] case made it clear that, in the absence of fraud, it was not unlawful for a trader to adopt a mark used by a foreigner, however extensively, if the foreign mark had not been used in Australia. By the late 1980s however, the decisions in *TV-am* and *Kelly* began to challenge

[59] *Nature Co. v Sci-Tech Educational Inc* (1991) 40 CPR (3d) 184, 186 and 191 (FCTD), rev'd on other grounds (1992) 41 CPR (3d) 359 (FCA).

[60] *Walt Disney Productions v Triple Five Corp* (1994) 53 CPR (3d) 129 (Alt CA), aff'g (1992), 43 CPR (3d) 321 (Alt QB).

[61] *Orkin Exterminating Co v Pestco* (n 42) 450.

[62] *The Seven Up Company v O.T. Ltd* (1947) 75 CLR 203 (HC of Aust).

this view, and in the early to mid-1990s, the decisions in *ConAgra*[63] and *Al Hayat*[64] held that, as the world had changed, so too should the law of international reputation; thus, in *ConAgra*, after an exhaustive review of international extraterritorial goodwill jurisprudence, Lockhart J was able to conclude:

> [I]t is not necessary in Australia that a plaintiff, in order to maintain a passing off action, must have a place of business or a business presence in Australia; nor is it necessary that his goods are sold here. It is sufficient if his goods have a reputations in this country among persons here, whether residents or otherwise, of a sufficient degree to establish that there is a likelihood of deception among consumers and potential consumers and of damage to his reputation.[65]

Between 1947 and 1992, the respective years *Seven Up* and *ConAgra* were decided, Australia's place in global politics, business, and culture shifted dramatically, and Australia's approach to the protection of extraterritorial goodwill shifted accordingly. As Shanahan and Freeman[66] have noted, as an island nation many thousands of miles away from its major trading partners, the protection of foreign marks made little sense. Justice Lockhart in *ConAgra* noted that the principle underlying the refusal to protect such marks was a reluctance to restrain someone in their own territory thereby stifling local competition and enterprise.[67] This principle made sense in the Australia of the 1940s. In Lockhart J.'s words:

> In earlier times when television and radio were in their infancy and when international trade in domestic goods was less extensive than it is today, it is understandable why the 'hard line' cases developed in England separated from foreign plaintiffs by the English Channel and the Atlantic Ocean. But in today's age of satellite television stations, massive improvements in all forms of global communications and frequent international travel, the maintenance of a 'hard line' is no longer defensible, at least in Australia.

The judgment in *ConAgra* was therefore clearly responding to the rise of communications technology and globalised business, two factors noted in the English case of *Pete Waterman*. Lockhart J neatly summarised why the old principle was no longer supportable:

> It is no longer valid, if it ever was, to speak of a business having goodwill or reputation only where business is carried on. Modern mass advertising through television (which reaches by satellite every corner of the globe instantaneously), radio, newspapers and magazines, reaches people in many countries in the world.

63 *Conagra Inc v McCain Foods (Aust) Pty Ltd* (1992), 23 IPR 193 (FC of Aust, Full Ct).
64 *Al Hayat Publishing Co Ltd v Ahmed Sokarno,* [1996] FCA 1354 (FC of Aust).
65 *Conagra v McCain* (n 63) 235. This view was also adopted in *Al Hayat Publishing Co Ltd v Ahmed Sokarno* [1996] FCA 1354 [46] (FC of Aust).
66 Shanahan and Freeman in FW Mostert, *Famous and Well-Known Marks* (New York, INTA, 2007) 4–29 (loose-leaf).
67 *Conagra v McCain* (n 63) 232.

> The international mobility of the world population increasingly brings human beings, and therefore potential consumers of goods and services, closer together and engenders an increasing and more instantaneous awareness of international commodities. This is an age of enormous commercial enterprises, some with budgets larger than sovereign states, who advertise their products by sophisticated means involving huge financial outlay. Goods and services are often preceded by their reputation abroad. They may not be physically present in the mark of a particular country, but are well known there because of the sophistication of communications which are increasingly less limited.[68]

Elsewhere in *ConAgra*, Lockhart J also discussed the Ontario Court of Appeal decision in *Orkin* and drew parallels between the US and Canadian relationship with that of Australia and New Zealand, holding that *Orkin* was decided in the context of two nations with 'large elements of commonality. Similar considerations apply in my view as between Australia and New Zealand'.[69] Thus, although the plaintiff and defendant in *ConAgra* were American and Australian, the court appeared to be alluding to the fact that, just as it would be preposterous to deny that reputations spill over from New Zealand to Australia due to their many commonalities, in the technologically sophisticated and globalised world of 1992 it would be preposterous to deny that reputations spill over from the US to Australia.

The evolution of communications technology, then, forms a substantial part of the basis for the decision in *ConAgra*. By contrast, in *Orkin* geographical proximity between the US and Canada was at the forefront. Proximity and communication technology are alike in that both facilitate the flow of commerce and culture. Also, Canada, Australia and the US share a language and have not totally dissimilar histories. It may be that the cultural overlaps between Canada and the US, and between Australia and the US, were important in leading both Canada and Australia to adopt a similar rule protecting the marks of US-based companies, once sufficient commercial ties became established, in Canada first, due to geography and in Australia second, due to improved communication.

NEW ZEALAND

While cases as early as 1977's *Pioneer v Hy-Line*[70] might be considered to state that extraterritorial goodwill could be protected in New Zealand,

[68] *Ibid*, 233.
[69] *Ibid*.
[70] *Pioneer Hi-Bred Corn Co v Hy-Line Chicks Pty Ltd* [1979] RPC 410, [1978] 2 NZLR 50 (CA of New Zealand).

the 1987 decisions in *Dominion*[71] and *Midas*[72] represent the earliest clear recognition that business reputations can cross borders and are entitled to protection.

In Dominion, Cooke P stated in obiter dicta that an international business may have one single international goodwill and that, as a business expands, its goodwill may correspondingly expand beyond national boundaries.[73] He then stated his opinion that:

> an Australian company's reputation and goodwill can extend to New Zealand (and vice versa) and, at least if there is a sufficient business connection with this country, will be entitled to protection here ... [I]t seems to me artificial to analyse such a state of affairs by saying that the company has one goodwill in Australia and another in New Zealand. Rather the goodwill transcends territorial boundaries.[74]

The decision is underpinned by the recognition of the fluid border between Australia and New Zealand, at least with regard to trade. Again, geographical proximity and a shared culture appear to have shaped the considerations taken into account in the obiter dicta of this case.

Another background fact that was explicitly considered in *Dominion* was the bilateral New Zealand-Australian Free Trade Agreement ('NAFTA'), and several other bilateral agreements of the day. With regard to this agreement, the court stated:

> I think that the courts of the two countries should be prepared, as far as reasonably possible, to recognize the progress that has been made towards a common market. From 1966 there was a very substantial increase in two-way trade under the [NAFTA] and this has been accelerated by the CER Heads of Agreement 1982 and the Australia-New Zealand Closer Economic Relations Trade Agreement (ANZ-CERTA) 1983.
>
> ...
>
> I am suggesting, not that these Agreements have any direct bearing on the present litigation, but that ... they are part of a background which should influence the development of the common law in Australasia.

The decision in *Dominion* was clearly influenced by developments in trade policy occurring in the years leading up to 1987.

A decade later, in *VB Distributors*, the High Court of New Zealand affirmed the *Dominion* obiter dicta and pointed out that it was appropriate, in certain cases,

[71] *Dominion Rent-A-Car v Budget Rent-A-Car System* [1987] 2 NZLR 395, 9 IPR 367 (CA of New Zealand).

[72] *Midas International Corp v Midas Auto Care Ltd* (27 November 1987), unreported decision discussed in *Conagra v McCain* (n 63) 233 at 223.

[73] *Dominion Rent-A-Car v Budget Rent-A-Car* (n 71) 379–80.

[74] *Dominion Rent-A-Car v Budget Rent-A-Car* (n 71) 380.

> ... to take in to account circumstances involving the use of a mark overseas.... This is particularly true of the distinct facts of the commercial relationship between New Zealand and Australia, and the frequency with which citizens of each country visit each other for business and pleasure. There are no passport or currency restrictions, and the overhead bins of aircraft on trans-Tasman flights are mute testimony to the way in which consumer goods are carried from one country to another. [75]

The *Midas* case, decided in the same year as *Dominion*, represented an even stronger statement that foreign marks with a reputation in New Zealand were entitled to protection. Although the court ultimately held that some degree of actual activity was necessary, even slight activity (such as negotiating to establish a franchise in New Zealand) could suffice, in the court's opinion it would not be long before there would be no requirement of any business activity.[76]

The court in *Midas* considered a great deal of evidence showing that the trade marks in question had become transnational. The evidence showed that the MIDAS mark in question could be seen in advertisements in international magazines that circulated in New Zealand, that citizens were exposed to the mark while traveling abroad, and that immigrants were aware of the trade mark by its use in their home countries.[77] The court noted the diminished importance of international boundaries in the face of the communications explosion, which was precisely the concern of the Australian court in *ConAgra*.[78] *Dominion*, *Midas,* and *VB Distributors* were decided in a political, economic, and cultural climate characterised by increased bilateral trade with Australia, increased international business transactions, and an increased flow of cultural products and people across the New Zealand border.

INDIA

Two landmark Indian cases established the principle that a mark with an international reputation may be protected in India even when it has not been used there: the 1989 decision in *Kamal Trading*[79] and the 1994 decision in *Whirlpool.*[80] *Kamal Trading* signalled a shift in judicial thinking

[75] *VB Distributors Ltd v Mitsushita Electrical Industrial Co Ltd* [1999] 53 IPR 466 [83], (1999) 9 TCLR 349 (High Court of NZ).
[76] *Midas International Corp v Midas Auto Care Ltd* (27 November 1987), unreported decision discussed in *Conagra v McCain* (n 63) 223.
[77] Ibid.
[78] Ibid.
[79] *Kamal Trading Co v Gillette UK Ltd* (1988) 1 PLR 135 (Division Bench, Bombay High Court).
[80] *WHIRLPOOL Trade Mark* (1996) [1997] FSR 905 (1994, HC of Delhi, aff'd 1996, SC of India, both judgments reported at this reference). This case is also reported as *NR Dongre v Whirlpool Corp.*

away from protecting local industry above all and towards protecting foreign marks with international reputations. In this case, the Bombay High Court held that Gillette had acquired worldwide goodwill in its 7 O'CLOCK brand, and therefore was able to prevent the Indian defendant from using its mark, despite the fact that Gillette carried on no business in the jurisdiction. The Court explicitly distinguished the English case of *Anheuser-Busch* and held that:

> ... goodwill is not limited to a particular country because in the present day, trade is spread all over the world and goods are transported from one country to another very rapidly and on an extensive scale. The goodwill acquired by a manufacturer is not necessarily limited to the country where the goods are freely available because the goods, though not available, are widely advertised in newspapers, periodicals, magazines and in other media. The result is that though the goods are not available in the country, the goods and the mark under which they are sold acquire reputation. Take for example, television and video cassette recorders manufactured by National, Sony or other well-known Japanese concerns. These televisions and VCRs are not imported in India and sold on the open market because of trade restrictions, but is it possible even to suggest that the word 'National' or 'Sony' has not acquired reputation in the country? In our judgment, the goodwill or reputation of goods or marks does not depend upon their availability in a particular country.[81]

By the time of the 1994 trial decision in *Whirlpool*, the High Court of Delhi was able to observe:

> Thus a product and its trade name transcend the physical boundaries of a geographical region and acquire a trans-border or overseas or extra-territorial reputation not only through import of goods but also by their advertisement. Knowledge and awareness of the goods of a foreign trader and of its trade mark can be available at a place where goods are not being marketed and consequently not being used. The manner in which or the source from which the knowledge has been acquired is immaterial.

Calvin Klein[82] was decided in the same year as the *Whirlpool* trial decision and supports the principle that reputation may be protected without use. *Yahoo Inc*[83] and *Milmet Oftho*[84] are more recent affirmations of the principle in *Whirlpool*.

These late twentieth century decisions reflect the drastic shift in the politics and economy of India during this time period. After obtaining independence from Britain in 1947, India struggled to shift its economy to benefit Indians, since its economy had previously operated in the service of British

[81] *Kamal Trading*, as quoted in *Whirlpool* (n 80) 916.

[82] *Calvin Klein Inc USA v International Apparel Syndicate*, [1995] FSR 515 (HC Calcutta).

[83] *Yahoo! Inc v Akash Arora* [1999] FSR 931 (HC Delhi).

[84] *Milmet Oftho Industries & Ors v Allergan Inc* [2004] INSC 390 (SC of India).

manufacturers.[85] India's leadership embraced the principle of economic autonomy, rather than open foreign trade, and therefore imposed strict controls on imports and exports (such as those noted on televisions and video recorders in *Kamal Trading*). India became isolated from the global market and it is not surprising that Indian courts had little reason to protect foreign marks in their jurisdiction.

In the 1970s and 80s, India's economy grew, but this growth was limited by the scarce resources of Indian investors. In the mid-eighties, the government turned to foreign aid to stimulate growth, which led to a severe deficit. India's economic woes at the time were compounded by political turbulence caused by the 1990 fall of the central government. In order to boost its economic viability, in 1991 India instituted the New Industrial Policy ('NIP') to liberalise its economy and encourage foreign investment. Thereafter, the US became India's largest foreign investor, and as one commentator has pointed out, with US money came criticism of India's enforcement of intellectual property.[86] India responded by becoming a signatory to TRIPS in 1994.

While *Kamal Trading* and *Whirlpool* both discuss the international nature of modern business, it is clear that these judgments reflect a political and economic policy shift from a closed, insular economy to one increasingly dependent on foreign dollars. This shift was almost certainly on the minds of the *Kamal Trading* and *Whirlpool* judges; it may be that, in contrast to the cases discussed in other sections above, India adopted the reputation-without-use principle in part response to criticism of lax enforcement of intellectual property rights and a desire to appease its largest foreign investor. In this sense, then, the reputation-without-use principle may be said to have been adopted as a condition of foreign investment.

HONG KONG

The concept that extraterritorial goodwill is entitled to protection appears to have solidified in Hong Kong law following the 1983 decision in *Hong Kong v Maxim's*[87] and the 1989 decision in *Tan-Ichi*.[88] In *Hong Kong v Maxim's*, another case involving the Paris restaurant, the court reviewed the conflicting English authorities on extraterritorial goodwill and rejected the 'hard-line' approach represented by *Crazy Horse*, holding that it could

[85] See generally N Jatana, 'Did *Whirlpool* Make Its Mark In India?: *NR Dongre v Whirlpool Corp*' (1997) 10 *Transnational Law* 331.

[86] Ibid.

[87] *Hong Kong Caterers Ltd v Maxim's Ltd* [1983] HKLR 287 (Hong Kong High Court).

[88] *Tan-Ichi Company Ltd v Jancar Ltd*, [1990] FSR 151 (SC of Hong Kong) The earlier case of *Weinerwald Holding AG v Kawn Wong Tan and Fong (A Firm)* [1979] FSR 381 (HC (HK)) also shows movement towards protecting extraterritorial goodwill in Hong Kong.

see no rational basis for the insistence on a domestic user, and that the only evidential effect of a domestic user was proof of local customers. On this point, the court held that '[t]his may have been apt in the travelling conditions of times past. But the law it could now be said should recognise that satellite TV transmissions enter the public's home direct without benefit of visa'.[89] Thus, like in many of the extraterritorial goodwill cases from other countries during this period, the court in *Hong Kong v Maxim's* recognised that modern communications technology could spread reputations far and wide.

Another interesting feature in the background of *Hong Kong v Maxim's* is section 23 of the then in-force Trade Marks Ordinance,[90] which the court held was 'a clear indication of legislative disapproval of the piracy of foreign marks'.[91] In the decades before this case was decided, Hong Kong was considered a haven for intellectual property infringement; it is possible, then, that the strong protection for extraterritorial goodwill established in the late 1970s and early 1980s may have been, in one commentator's words, 'due to a guilty conscience about the era when Hong Kong was one of the world's most famous pirates.'[92]

In *Tan Ichi*, the plaintiff owned a chain of Japanese restaurants and was negotiating to bring the restaurant to nearby Hong Kong. The defendant opened a restaurant in Hong Kong, deliberately copying the plaintiff's logo. The court granted an injunction against the defendants. Citing *Orkin* (Canada), *Dominion* (New Zealand) and *Hong Kong v Maxim's*, the court held:

> Will the Hong Kong courts protect a foreign trader whose name is being used, without his consent, by a competing business, when he himself has no active business here? This, in view of the proximity of Hong Kong to other such major international centres as Singapore, Tokyo, Bangkok and Kuala Lumpur raise a matter of some importance.
>
> It appears clear that this is an evolving field of law, and that a court must respond to the changes which have occurred in international communications. The large number of tourists crossing and re-crossing national boundaries; the speed and

89 *Hong Kong v Maxim's* (n 87) 294–95.

90 Trade Marks Ordinance (c 43), [1 January 1955] GNA 143 of 1954 Section 23 reads: 23 (1) Subject to subsection (3), the Registrar may refuse to register any trade mark relating to goods in respect of any goods or description of goods if it is proved to his satisfaction by the person opposing the application for registration that such mark is identical with or nearly resembles a trade mark which is already registered in respect of:
(a) the same goods;
(b) the same description of goods; or
(c) services or a description of services which are associated with those goods or goods of that description,
in a country or place from which such goods originate.

91 *Hong Kong v Maxim's* (n 87) 295.

92 M Pendleton, 'The Evolving law of Unfair Competition', Law Lecturers for Practitioners, (1982) *Hong Kong Law Journal* 76.

> efficiency of modern technology which cause business reputation to be more widely spread and recognized than in the past.
>
> ...
>
> I would respectfully adopt the same approach [as in *Orkin*, *Dominion*, and *Hong Kong v Maxim's*]. I must look at the evidence so far disclosed to discover whether the plaintiffs have established a prima facie case that they have an international goodwill which should be protected in Hong Kong.[93]

This passage is quite explicit in noting that geography—Hong Kong's proximity to other nations—and communications technology are important considerations in establishing whether a mark has an international reputation worthy of protection. Elsewhere in the judgment, the court reviewed evidence pointing to the large number of Japanese citizens residing in and touring Hong Kong, and the fact that Hong Kong is a major international centre with a 'cross-play' of trading and commerce with Japan.[94] As in many of the international reputation cases, this 'cross-play' of money and people forms the background of the Court's willingness to protect the extra-territorial goodwill of a Japanese-owned and used mark.[95]

SOUTH AFRICA

South Africa was considered by some to be more 'hard-line' with respect to the requirement of a local user to found an action for passing-off than perhaps any other country, including England.[96] Time and again the South African courts adopted the approach exemplified by *Crazy Horse* and required actual use of the mark within South Africa as an essential element of a passing-off action. However, much in the same way as we will see happened in Malaysia, Singapore and Mauritius, in 1995 legislative changes to South African trade mark legislation harkened a potential change in approach. In the 1997 case of *Joburgers*[97] the court considered the impact of the coming into force in 1995 of the new Trade-marks Act 194 of 1993, which (like the UK Trade Marks Act 1994) in section 35[98] gave explicit effect to Article 6*bis* of the Paris Convention and TRIPS section 16 requiring

[93] *Tan-Ichi v Jancar* (n 88) 154.

[94] Ibid 155

[95] See also *Kabushika Kaisha Yakult Honsha v Yakudo Group Holdings Ltd* (2004) HCA 2409/2002.

[96] C Wadlow, *The Law of Passing–Off*, 2nd edn (London, Sweet & Maxwell, 1995) 98–99.

[97] *McDonald's Corpn v Joburgers Drive-Inn Restaurant (Pty) Ltd* (1996) [1997] S African L Rep 1 (SC of South Africa, Appellate Division).

[98] s 35 read (at the time of this decision):

(1) References in this Act to a trade mark which is entitled to protection under the Paris Convention as a well-known trade mark, are to a mark which is well known in the Republic as being the mark of—

signatories to protect well-known marks in their jurisdiction, regardless of use or situate goodwill. The court began by referring to the historical fact that under English and South African common law, a trader was required to be doing business in the jurisdiction before they could protect their marks.[99] Interestingly, the court declined to comment on whether this principle was no longer appropriate, and instead founded its decision on the newly enacted section 35 of the Trade-marks Act 194 of 1993, holding that the section extends the protection of a passing-off action to extraterritorial goodwill:

> It seems to me that McDonald's contention must be sustained. The Legislature intended to extend the protection of a passing-off action to foreign businessmen who did not have a business or enjoy a goodwill inside the country, provided their marks were well known in the Republic. It seems logical to accept that the degree of knowledge of the marks that is required would be similar to that protected in the existing law of passing-off. The concept of a substantial number of person is well established. It provides a practical and flexible criterion which is consistent with the terms of the statute.[100]

Two years after *Joburgers*, the Supreme Court of Appeal in *Caterham*[101] settled the matter at common law, holding that the question to be asked in determining whether a trader has achieved a protectable extraterritorial goodwill is: has the plaintiff, in a practical and business sense, a sufficient reputation amongst a substantial number of persons who are either clients or potential clients of his business? The locality of the plaintiff's business is to be merely one of many facts that may be used to establish such a reputation.[102] The Court specifically considered the definition of 'goodwill' derived from the English *Muller*[103] tax case that had been used by both the English and South African courts to underpin their requirement that goodwill through use be present in the jurisdiction. As we have seen, earlier decisions by courts in Canada and Australia had held that that definition

(a) a person who is a national of a convention country; or
(b) a person who is domiciled in, or has a real and effective industrial or commercial establishment in, a convention country, whether or not such person carries on business, or has any goodwill, in the Republic.

(2) A reference in this Act to the proprietor of such a mark shall be construed accordingly.
(3) The proprietor of a trade mark which is entitled to protection under the Paris Convention as a well-known trade mark is entitled to restrain the use in the Republic of a trade mark which constitutes, or the essential part of which constitutes, a reproduction, imitation or translation of the well-known trade mark in relation to goods or services which are identical or similar to the goods or services in respect of which the trade mark is well known and where the use is likely to cause deception or confusion.

[99] *McDonald's v Joburgers* (n 97) 19.
[100] Ibid 21.
[101] *Caterham Car Sales v Birkin Cars (Pty) Ltd* [1998] 3 SA 938 (SCA).
[102] Ibid 950.
[103] *Inland Revenue Commissioners v Muller & Co's Magarine Ltd* [1901] AC 217 (HL).

of goodwill was inappropriate for use in passing-off actions. The Supreme Court of Appeal agreed specifically with the Australian jurisprudence and held that passing-off protects 'reputation' and that the

> ... decisions of our Courts to the opposite effect can no longer be considered to be good law. They are based upon a misunderstanding of Lord Macnaghten's *dictum* [in *Muller*], they are inconsistent with general principles and incompatible with the world we live in and modern foreign jurisprudential trends.[104]

When the Supreme Court of Appeal again dealt with the issue in 2005 it merely stated that passing-off 'protects the local reputation of a foreign undertaking, whether or not it trades locally.'[105]

The situation in South Africa is a stunning example of how there can be no common law without common societal goals and norms. Prior to the 1990s, South Africa was an ostracised nation saddled with economic and cultural trade sanctions meant to force the country to abandon its Apartheid regime. Extraterritorial reputation jurisprudence from this time period reflects a country that was culturally and economically exiled from the rest of the common law world. When Apartheid was dismantled during the early 1990s, and South Africa became a democracy that was welcomed back to the world order, it became a country eager to benefit from international trade. In terms of extraterritorial reputation, from Apartheid to post-Apartheid, South Africa completely reversed itself from an outright refusal to protect extraterritorial goodwill, to an explicit rejection of that hard-line common law when it became in that country's best economic interest. That South Africa quickly went from being the most extreme in not protecting extraterritorial goodwill, to following the jurisprudence of such countries as Canada in protecting extraterritorial goodwill, is not surprising if one ascribes to the view that the common law is nothing but a reflection of a nation's socio-economic realities.

MAURITIUS, SINGAPORE AND MALAYSIA

In 1999 the Privy Council in *Sprints Ltd v Comptroller of Customs (Mauritius)*[106] had the opportunity to consider extraterritorial goodwill in the context of an appeal of a trade mark registration opposition decision.

[104] *Caterham Car Sales v Birkin Cars (Pty) Ltd*, [1998] 3 SA 938 (SCA) at p 949.

[105] *AM Moolla Group Ltd v Gap Inc* [2005] ZASCA 72 In support the Court cited its decision in *Caterham Car Sales v Birkin Cars (Pty) Ltd*, n 101 above, but also noted that the same approach had been adopted in a number of other jurisdictions: New Zealand: *Dominion Rent–A–Car Ltd v Budget Rent–A–Car Systems* [1987] 2 NZLR 395; Canada: *Orkin Exterminating Co Inc v Pestco of Canada* 80 CPR (2d) 153, 11 DLR (4th) 8; India: *Calvin Klein International v Apparel Syndicate* [1995] RPC 515 (HC); Australia: *Conagra Inc v McCain Foods (Aust) Pty Ltd* n 63 above.

[106] *Sprints Ltd v Comptroller of Customs and Chipie Design and Signoles* [2000] FSR 814 (PC).

The appellant unsuccessfully sought registration of the mark CHIPIE in the face of an opposition by a foreign company who owned registrations for the same mark in numerous other countries but not Mauritius. The Privy Council dismissed the appeal on the basis that there was sufficient evidence of actual prior use of the mark by the foreign company in Mauritius. However, the Privy Council went on to consider the situation had there been no prior use of the mark in Mauritius by the foreign company. Here, the Privy Council stated that under the Trade Marks Act 1868 (as amended),[107] a registration could be successfully opposed by the owner of a confusing internationally established trade mark with a reputation in Mauritius even without any actual use in that country. The Privy Council noted that the growth of international commerce and communication made this ground of opposition now possible, perhaps foreshadowing that protection of extraterritorial goodwill in England through passing-off might soon be a possibility in light of changes to international trade and communication:

> In order to create the risk of confusion there must essentially be a knowledge on the part of the public of the mark with which the confusion may occur. In many cases user may well be the means of establishing the reputation of the mark in a particular country, and at a period when international travel and intercommunication was less intensive than it has now come to be, user in the locality would be the ordinary or even the only way of establishing the local reputation. But it is essentially the reputation of the mark which will give rise to possible confusion in light of the growth in international commerce and communication it may now be possible in the case of an internationally established trade mark to proceed upon evidence of its notoriety in a country even without any actual user of the mark there.[108]

However, the Privy Council specifically distinguished this ground of opposition under the applicable legislation from a common law passing-off action, the former of 'which is more readily established than what would be required for a case of passing-off.'[109] The Privy Council also declined to consider the English decision of *Crazy Horse* and the issue of extraterritorial goodwill passing-off.[110]

The Privy Council also took note of the 1999 Singapore Court of Appeal decision in *Tiffany & Co v Fabriques de Tabac Reunies SA*[111] which also concerned an opposition to registration. The Court of Appeal had there cited the New Zealand decision of *Pioneer v Hy-Line* and distinguished the

[107] Equivalent legislative provisions to those at play in this decision are based upon those found in England's legislation.

[108] *Sprints Ltd v Comptroller of Customs* (n 106) 822.

[109] Ibid.

[110] Ibid 824.

[111] *Tiffany & Co v Fabriques de Tabac Reunies SA* [1999] 3 SLR 147 (CA Singapore).

House of Lords' decision in *BALI Trade Mark*[112] in holding that use was not necessary to oppose a registration:

> [I]f true likelihood of confusion and deception can be shown, we are unable to see why 'use' of the opposing mark is required within the jurisdiction before this may be established. Even without the appellants' use of the mark 'Tiffany' in Singapore at the time of the respondents' application, there could be a real chance that a substantial number of members of the public would be confused into thinking that the respondents' goods were somehow connected to or originated from the appellants. Further, the *Bali* case was decided in 1969, during a time when tourism and the dissemination of information was not quite as widespread. Since then, modern technology and communication have improved at such a rapid rate that we in Singapore may be as familiar with famous international marks as someone in the country where the mark is actually in use.[113]

Interestingly, the Privy Council took pains to state that Lord Upjohn's Reasons in the *BALI* case should not be read as requiring use of the foreign trade mark in the national market to establish a likelihood of confusion sufficient to oppose a trade mark application, but that such 'does not necessarily entail all the ingredients necessary for the protection of a mark at common law.'[114]

The High Court in Malaysia similarly followed this approach in the 2003 case of *Thrifty*,[115] in the context of an opposition to registration. The court reviewed the strong tide of extraterritorial goodwill cases from other jurisdictions and held that 'the courts in Malaysia should adopt a more liberal, flexible approach in evaluating whether a foreign plaintiff has acquired goodwill or reputation, as is the trend in other Commonwealth jurisdictions in recent years',[116] seeming to suggest that extraterritorial goodwill should now be protected at common law. Interestingly, the court concluded with the following statement of policy:

> The court would and could not allow the first respondent to persist with such irresponsible and unconscionable conduct and in the process ensuring Malaysia does not become a haven for 'pirates' of well-known marks which would clearly hurt our economy and international reputation in the eyes of the world.[117]

Thus we see the Court of Appeal (Singapore) in *Tiffany*, the High Court of Malaya in *Thrifty Rent-A-Car*, and the Privy Council in *Sprints Ltd* echo a familiar refrain of improvements to communications technology, and greater international travel and trade as factors favouring the protection of extraterritorial goodwill, but only in so far as these were grounds to oppose

[112] *BALI Trade Mark* [1969] RPC 472.
[113] *Tiffany & Co v Fabriques de Tabac* (n 111) [36].
[114] *Sprints Ltd v Comptroller of Customs* (n 106) 822–24.
[115] *Thrifty Rent-A-Car System Inc v Thrifty Rent-A-Car Sdn Bhd* (2003), [2004] 2 AMR 57.
[116] Ibid [35].
[117] *Thrifty Rent-A-Car* (n 115) [52].

registrations under the applicable legislation. While the Privy Council's comments may suggest a time when extraterritorial goodwill could be protected at common law, the Court refused to delve into the issue in any detail, and an answer to that issue under English law will have to wait for another day.

SUMMARY

The single biggest factor in the development of the common law of extraterritorial goodwill has been a nation's approach to international trade. That certain countries may or may not protect extraterritorial goodwill, or may have explicitly changed their position, can be directly linked to international trade. The United States was one of the first countries to protect extraterritorial goodwill. It did so based upon the policy objective of supporting its international trade; if the US would not protect foreign marks with a reputation in the US, other countries would not protect US marks abroad, a situation that would not be conducive to the international expansion of its multinational corporations. The nations which first followed suit, Ireland, New Zealand, and Canada, are similar in that they each have very close economic and cultural ties to a larger nation of close geographic proximity. The actual and metaphorical fluidity of their borders, combined with shared cultural and economic histories, explains why these countries explicitly did not follow the common law of England regarding extraterritorial goodwill.

As the importance of international trade has grown, both informally and through multi- and international trade instruments such as *TRIPS* and regional free trade agreements, so too has the number of countries whose common law has changed to protect extraterritorial goodwill. Combined with significant advancements in communications technology that have bridged geographical barriers, protection of extraterritorial goodwill is really nothing more than a recognition that the world of business has changed and that a country's market is now global and not local. The situation in South Africa is a stunning example of how there can be no common law without common societal goals and norms: an ostracised nation saddled with international trade sanctions, to a post-Apartheid country eager to benefit from international trade, South Africa completely reversed itself from an outright refusal to protect extraterritorial goodwill, to an explicit rejection of that hard-line common law when it became in that country's best economic interest. That South Africa quickly went from being the most extreme in not protecting extraterritorial goodwill, to following the jurisprudence of such countries as Canada in protecting extraterritorial goodwill, is not surprising if one ascribes to the view that the common law is nothing but a reflection of a nation's socio-economic realities.

17

Death of a Trade Mark Doctrine? Dilution of Anti-Dilution

LOUIS TC HARMS

No part of trademark law that I have encountered in my forty years of teaching and practicing IP law has created so much doctrinal puzzlement and judicial incomprehension as the concept of 'dilution' as a form of intrusion on a trademark.[1]

INTRODUCTION

THE STATEMENT OF the Privy Council chosen by the editors as the subject of this *Festschrift*, that the common law is no longer monolithic, was made in the context of the law of evidence, more particularly, about evidential privilege in New Zealand.[2] It was an appropriate choice considering that the young(ish) David Vaver was first quoted—with approval, obviously—by the Appellate Division of the Supreme Court of South Africa[3] in a case dealing with the law of evidence and, above all, an aspect of the law of privilege.[4] At the time he was still in Auckland, New Zealand, but he must already have had his eye on Canada, because the article was published in a Canadian law review. David, by the way, is not the only one who was able to move seamlessly from the law of evidence to intellectual property law. Lord Hoffmann wrote the classic *The South African Law of Evidence*, first published in 1963, and moved on to become one of the main exponents of IP law in the House of Lords.[5]

[1] JT McCarthy, 'Dilution of a Trademark: European and United States Compared' (2005) 94 *The Trademark Reporter* 1163, 1163 quoted by J Bosland 'The Culture of Trade Marks: An Alternative Cultural Theory Perspective' (2005) 10(2) *Media & Arts Law Reports* 99 and many others.

[2] *B & Ors v Auckland District Law Society (New Zealand)* [2003] UKPC 38 [55].

[3] *Naidoo v Marine & Trade Insurance Co Ltd* 1978 (3) SA 666 (A).

[4] D Vaver, '"Without Prejudice" Communications—Their Admissibility and Effect' (1974) 9 *University of British Columbia Law Review* 85.

[5] LH Hoffmann, *South African Law of Evidence* (Durban, Butterworths).

This may prove the similarities of the law of evidence and IP law, because both lack a coherent theoretical basis or 'a conceptual map of issues, a rough working model of costs and benefits',[6] an issue David has often addressed.[7] The individual rules in both areas sprouted from a belief that logic required them, while many of them cannot be justified or explained. In addition, neither the law of evidence nor IP law is monolithic.

The dilution by courts of anti-dilution provisions, to use Judge Cooke's phrase[8] noted by Tony Martino in his excellent monograph *Trademark Dilution*,[9] is a common occurrence in common law jurisdictions. Simone A Rose complains that only a small minority of courts in the USA have accurately applied their dilution statutes and granted relief when appropriate; instead, she says, numerous courts have ignored the plain statutory meaning; while others have avoided any substantive dilution analysis and 'continue to fall victim to the enticing, but false, rhetoric of dilution "monopolyphobia".'[10] Graeme B Dinwoodie and Mark D Janis speak of 'an underlying hostility to dilution law'.[11] The problem is not limited to common law countries. Kenneth L Port states that trade mark dilution jurisprudence in Japan is in a state of confusion because, he thinks, courts are reticent to recognise the full scope of the dilution right because it is seen to be inconsistent with the purposes of trade mark protection.[12]

It is unsurprising that, although anti-dilution laws differ in origin and in detail, judges are commonly not enamoured of them, in spite of their many apologists.[13] Judges dislike applying laws that do not serve a material tangible interest. And they are uncomfortable with laws that purport to protect private interests that appear to be illusory and unreal. Since 'the theoretical basis of dilution liability is fraught with so much uncertainty and incomprehension',[14] judges may have a knee-jerk reaction when they have to deal with dilution cases. In this chapter I intend to explore this phenomenon.

[6] J Boyd, 'A Politics of Intellectual Property: Environmentalism For the Net?' [1997] *Duke Law Review* 87.

[7] D Vaver, 'Intellectual Property: The State of the Art' [2001] *VUWL Review* 2.

[8] *Allied Maintenance Corp v Allied Mechanical Trades Inc* 198 USPQ 418 (NY Ct App 1977) 423.

[9] T Martino, *Trademark Dilution* (Oxford, Clarendon Press, 1996).

[10] SA Rose, 'Will Atlas Shrug? Dilution Protection for Famous Trade-Marks: Anti-Competitive Monopoly or Earned Property Right?' (1995) 47 *Florida Law Review* 653, 567–658.

[11] GB Dinwoodie and MD Janis, 'Dilution's (Still) Uncertain Future' (2006) 105 *Michigan Law Review* First Impressions 98.

[12] KL Port, 'Trademark Dilution in Japan' (2005–2006) 4 *New Journal of Technology & Intellectual Property* 228.

[13] See lately E Kaseke, 'Trademark Dilution: A Comparative Analysis' (LLD thesis, University of South Africa, 2006) which is available on the Internet at etd.unisa.ac.za/ETD-db/theses/available/etd-10112006-121411/unrestricted/thesis.pdf.

[14] J Bosland, 'The Culture of Trade Marks: An Alternative Cultural Theory Perspective' (n 1).

Judges are not alone in being unimpressed by the xenophobic nature of anti-dilution laws. Many academics are of a like mind.[15] Even our celebrant is a dilution-sceptic. He sees anti-dilution provisions as an example of 'how brand owners came to wrap their power grab in a mantle of respectability', and he regards the sense of grievance of owners of well-known mark owners, which led to the adoption of anti-dilution laws, as unjustified.[16]

The reason, I guess, why I have been asked to deal with this subject is that beyond the borders of the USA, I wrote one of the few judgments that upheld a dilution claim in a (quasi-) common law country. It was the *Laugh It Off* case,[17] a judgment given in the Supreme Court of Appeal of South Africa. My fame was short-lived, because the judgment was overruled by our Constitutional Court.[18] David, I sense, agreed with the latter judgment[19] (at least with the result, maybe not with the reasoning), but tactfully refrained from saying too much about it in my presence. This may be the occasion to do some explaining.

THE STATUTORY SCENE

Anti-dilution legislation (state[20] and federal) in the USA is usually[21] ascribed to the advocacy of Frank I Schechter.[22] The Schechter virus spread and mutated. Canada adopted during 1953 a provision that proscribed the use of a registered trade mark 'in a manner that is likely to have the effect of depreciating the goodwill attaching thereto.'[23] It wormed its way into the EU Directive on Trade Marks (1989), the TRIPS agreement (albeit in a somewhat diluted form) and the English Trade Marks Act of 1994.[24]

[15] Eg DJ Franklyn, 'Debunking Dilution Doctrine: Toward a Coherent Theory of the Anti-Free-Rider Principle in the American Trademark Law' (2004–2005) 56 *Hastings Law Journal* 117. He lists some of the literature in n 2. J Litman, 'Breakfast with Batman: The Public Interest in the Advertising Age' (1998–1999) 108 *Yale Law Journal* 1717.

[16] D Vaver, 'Unconventional and Well-known Trade-Marks' [2005] *Singapore Journal of Legal Studies* 1, 13–14.

[17] *Laugh It Off Promotions CC v South African Breweries International* (242/2003) [2004] ZASCA 76 (16 September 2004).

[18] *Laugh It Off Promotions CC v South African Breweries International (Finance) BV t/a Sabmark International* (CCT42/04) [2005] ZACC 7 (27 May 2005).

[19] D Vaver, 'Chocolate, Copyright, Confusion: Intellectual Property and the Supreme Court of Canada' *Osgoode Hall Review of Law and Policy* (http://ohrlp.ca/).

[20] Not all states have such legislation.

[21] For a revision of history, see RG Bone, 'Schechter's Ideas in Historical Context and Dilution's Rocky Road (2008)' 24 *Santa Clara Computer and High Technology Law Journal*.

[22] FI Schechter 'The Rational Basis of Trademark Protection' (1927) 40 *Harvard Law Review* 813.

[23] Trade-marks Act s 22(1). See D Vaver, 'Canada's Intellectual Property Framework: A Comparative Overview' at 31 available at http://strategis.ic.gc.ca/epic/site/ippd-dppi.nsf/vwapj/01-EN%20Vaver.pdf/$file/01-EN%20Vaver.pdf.

[24] Trade Marks Act 1994 s 10(3).

Recent tinkering at federal level[25] sought to overrule the effect of the Supreme Court's judgment in the *Victoria's Secrets* case.[26]

South Africa followed Britain's legislative lead, not only because it felt comfortable with what its erstwhile colonial master did but also because some of the underlying Continental concepts fitted more comfortably with basic Roman-Dutch concepts (the South African 'common' law, which is in many respects similar to Scots law).[27]

Other common law countries followed suit, using similar language, but the scope of their legislation is not necessarily the same.[28] Michael Handler, for instance, argues that the anti-dilution provisions in the Australian legislation[29] are not truly anti-dilution provisions,[30] although this view appears to be in conflict with that of the Australian High Court.[31] This is, however, not the occasion to provide a synopsis or analysis of the different laws. It will be sufficient to use in general terms Advocate-General Jacobs's[32] summation of the EU Directive's anti-dilution provisions. They:

protect the proprietor of a mark with a reputation;
against use of an identical or similar sign;
where use of that sign:

takes unfair advantage of the mark's distinctive character,
takes unfair advantage of its repute,
is detrimental to the mark's distinctive character, or
is detrimental to its repute.

[25] Trademark Dilution Revision Act adopted on October 6, 2006. For further information see Barton Beebe, 'A Defense of the New Federal Anti-dilution Trademark Law' [16] *Fordham Intellectual Property Media & Entertainment Law Journal* 1143 and his 2008 'The Continuing Debacle of U.S. Antidilution Law: Evidence from the First Year of Trademark Dilution Revision Act Case Law', available at http://ssrn.comb/abstract=1147965.

[26] *Moseley v V Secret Catalogue, Inc* 537 US 418 (2003). See RG Bone 'A Skeptical View of the Trademark Dilution Revision Act' (2007) 11 *Intellectual Property Law Bulletin* 187.

[27] s 34(1)(c) of the Trade Marks Act 194 of 1993 provides that the rights acquired by registration of a trade mark are infringed by the unauthorised use in the course of trade in relation to any goods or services of a mark which is identical or similar to a trade mark registered, if such trade mark is well known in the Republic and the use of the said mark would be likely to take unfair advantage of, or be detrimental to, the distinctive character or the repute of the registered trade mark, notwithstanding the absence of confusion or deception. The proviso can be discounted for present purposes.

[28] Trade Marks Act 2002 s 89(1)(d) (New Zealand); Australian Trade Marks Act 1995 s 120(3).

[29] Trade Marks Act 1995 s 120(3).

[30] M Handler, 'Trade mark Dilution in Australia?' [2007] *EIPR* 307.

[31] *Campomar Sociedad Limited v Nike International Limited* [2000] HCA 12 (9 March 2000) para 42–43.

[32] *Adidas-Salomon v Fitness World* Case C-408/01 [2004] FSR 21. See now the opinion of AG Sharpston in *Intel Corporation Inc v CPM United Kingdom Limited* (Case C-252/07, June 26 2008) and the judgment of 27 November 2008 (ECJ).

These proscribed acts have been encapsulated into two words, namely 'blurring' and 'tarnishing', and for purposes of this generalised contribution I intend to use these shorthand tags.

REVISITING SCHECHTER:[33] BLURRING WITHOUT CONFUSION

Importantly, by statute and in theory, dilution does not require confusion. This, at first glance, is inimical to basic trade mark principles because, as our celebrant has pointed out, '[o]nce trade mark law moves away from the object of protecting consumers from confusion, it starts looking distinctly dodgy'.[34] Further, as I shall attempt to show, dilution by blurring without confusion is a theoretical possibility that has no factual foundation. Laws may state that black is white, but when it comes to a factual decision, black remains black. In other words, although statutes may state that blurring is possible without confusion, it is extremely doubtful whether that could be so in real life.

Schechter thought otherwise. His evidence before the US House of Representatives Committee on Patents needs quoting:[35]

> If you take Rolls Royce—for instance, if you allow Rolls Royce restaurants and Rolls Royce cafeterias, and Rolls Royce pants, and Rolls Royce candy, in ten years you will not have the Rolls Royce mark any more. *That is the point.* [Emphasis added.]

Before discussing whether it is really 'the point', I think it is necessary to turn to his article on dilution.[36] Schechter was not concerned with tarnishment, only with blurring.[37] He sought to expose what was in his eyes the myth that a trade mark is a badge of origin. For him the true function of a trade mark is 'to identify a product as satisfactory and thereby stimulate further purchases by the consuming public' (at 818) and 'the preservation of the uniqueness of a trademark should constitute the only rational basis for its protection' (at 831). This guarantee of quality function, he reasoned, can be damaged if the mark is used on dissimilar goods in spite of the lack of confusion. His thesis was not about marks with a reputation (ie, well-known marks); instead he

[33] Many have done this exercise in more detail, usually with a different emphasis. See esp S Stadler Nelson, 'The Wages of Ubiquity in Trademark Law' (2002–2003) 88 *Iowa Law Review* 731.

[34] D Vaver, 'Unconventional and Well-known Trade-Marks' (n 16) 16.

[35] Quoted by WJ Derenberg, 'The Problem of Trademark Dilution and the Antidilution Statutes' (1956) 44 *California Law Review* 436, 449.

[36] Schechter, 'The Rational Basis of Trademark Protection' (n 22) 813.

[37] There is another view, and that he was concerned with protecting a trade mark's uniqueness, and not with blurring: Beebe, 'A Defense' (n 25) 1145: I would have thought that one protects a trade mark's uniqueness by preventing blurring (in fact by preventing any act of infringement) but little turns on the point for present purposes.

sought broader protection for 'technical' trade marks, namely those that consist of 'arbitrary, coined or fanciful marks or symbols' (at 828). His examples included Rolls-Royce, Kodak and Mazda,[38] all arbitrary, coined and fanciful.[39]

Schechter did not have any empirical data for his assumption that the use of those marks on entirely dissimilar goods could destroy them. Instead, he used precedents but they did not support his thesis. I shall refer to three. The first, from the USA, was the then recent *Vogue* judgment.[40] Although trade mark infringement was a cause of action, the court chose to assume that 'relief could not be given under the law of technical trade-marks' because it did not wish to enter into a consideration of the question whether the infringing goods (in this case hats) had the 'same descriptive qualities' of the trade-marked goods (magazines). The court then turned to the question of unfair competition (an inappropriate name for passing off since passing off is a species of unfair competition), ie 'the doctrine that no one should be allowed to sell his goods as those of another.' Having found that the defendant's use of the trade mark created the impression that the hats had been manufactured by the plaintiff or 'were in some way vouched for or sponsored or approved by the plaintiff' it granted the relief sought.

The second, from the UK, was the *Kodak* case[41] (concerning the registration of Kodak for bicycles). It was a confusion case, the ratio of the decision to refuse the registration of Kodak for bicycles being that it was likely to deceive the public in believing that the bicycles originated from the photographic company.

Last, he used the *Odol* case. A German court had held that the trade mark Odol, having a reputation in relation to a mouthwash, could not be used in relation to steel products because the drawing power of Odol for mouth wash would be diluted ('verwässert', ie, watered down), since the mouthwash company's ability to compete in its own field would be impaired if the significance of the mark was lessened.

The *Vogue* and *Kodak* cases did not support him, although Schechter's response would have been that the courts in those and similar cases had resorted to 'an exceedingly laborious' exercise to find some or other kind of 'injury' to justify their conclusion.[42] The *Odol* case (its result,

[38] Nothing to do with Mazda cars. The use of the name may be objected to on cultural or religious grounds. Mazda is the name of the Zoroastrian god.

[39] My understanding is that trade mark infringement in the USA developed as the remedy designed to protect these so-called 'technical' trade marks as they were the only ones that could be registered, while unfair competition rules protected non-technical ones: *Allied Maintenance Corp v Allied Mechanical Trades* (n 8) 420.

[40] *Vogue Co v Thompson-Hudson Co et al* 300 F 509 (Circuit Court of Appeals, Sixth Circuit).

[41] *Eastman v Griffiths* (1898) 15 RPC 105, 111 lines 17–24.

[42] Schechter, 'The Rational Basis of Trademark Protection' (n 36), 825.

I believe, was artificial and merely gained acceptance as a precedent by way of repetition) did not deal with trade mark principles (as Schechter realised) but was based on general civil law delictual principles, namely that an act *contra bonos mores*, which injures another, creates liability in delict (tort). What this means is that conduct is wrongful if public policy considerations demand that in the circumstances the plaintiff has to be compensated for the loss caused by the negligent act or omission of the defendant. This depends on the legal convictions of society. The Dutch test, for instance is: 'in strijd .... met hetgeen volgens ongeschreven recht in het maatschappelijk verkeer betaamt' ('contrary to what is acceptable in social relations according to unwritten law'). South African law is to the same effect.[43]

There is another dimension arising from the *Vogue* judgment. The judgment mentioned that there is no fetish in the word 'competition', meaning that if there is (a) injury to the plaintiff and (b) fraud on the customer, nothing else is needed to create liability. This judgment gave rise to an anonymous note in the *Harvard Law Review*, which argued that it should not be necessary for purposes of unfair competition that the parties should have been in actual competition.[44] (It is now generally accepted that competition is not an element of passing-off.) This, perforce, means that whilst trade mark infringement is ordinarily considered to be a species of passing-off, it will not always be true in the case of dilution by blurring. Accordingly, while blurring, in the civil law tradition, can be considered to be a wrongful act even in a non-trade mark context, one runs into difficulty by attempting to categorise it within the common law's traditional reliance on passing-off. Put differently, Schechter's conjecture can apply where the mark is used otherwise than on unrelated goods or services. Like comparative advertising, blurring is in principle not a trade marks issue, although it can be.[45]

Although it is now generally accepted that a trade mark does more commercially than serve as badge of origin, trade mark laws and courts still deem it to be a badge of origin[46]—at least for purposes of primary infringement and, usually, for registration.[47] I have previously expressed the opinion that dicta in *Johnstone v R*[48] about trade mark use (ie, use as a badge of origin) are wide enough to require it in the context of dilution

[43] *Telematrix (Pty) Ltd v Advertising Standards Authority SA* (459/2004) [2005] ZASCA 73 (9 September 2005).

[44] 'Unfair Competition: Necessity for Actual Competition' (1925–1925) 38 *Harv LR* 170.

[45] P Reeskamp, 'Is Comparative Advertising a Trade Mark Issue?' [2008] *EIPR* 130. Compare *O2 Holdings Limited & O2 (UK) Limited v Hutchison 3G UK Limited* Case C-533/06 (ECJ).

[46] *National Fittings (M) Sdn Bhd v Oystertec Plc* [2006] FSR 40 (HC Singapore).

[47] *Mattel Inc v 3894207 Canada Inc* 2006 SCC 22 (CanLII).

[48] *Johnstone v R* [2003] UKHL 28 [UK].

cases, but that anti-dilution provisions are aimed at more than safeguarding a trade mark's 'source-denoting function' and rather protect the reputation, advertising value or selling power of a well known mark.[49] Ng-Loy Wee Loon considers the position under the EU Directive (and consequently in England) because of *Arsenal*[50] to be in this regard ambiguous.[51] She is probably correct, unless one interprets *Adam Opel*[52] or, for that matter, *Intel*[53] to hold that the trade mark use requirement does not apply in a case of dilution. However, since the legal rationale for trade mark protection remains guaranteeing origin, courts find it difficult to accord them some other, rather vague, function and to protect that function. And, as Robert G Bone said, Schechter never addressed the normative question: 'why the law *should* protect a mark's grip on consumers when that grip is due to factors other than information about the quality of the product (which is protected by confusion-based theories)?'[54]

David Vaver's affinity towards Lexus cars is well known. He was once involved in a serious accident and believes that the Lexus in which they were being driven saved his and Maxine's life. It is consequently fitting to test Schechter's theorem with reference to two cases involving the trade mark Lexus. The first, from the USA, concerned an attempt by Mead Data to prevent Toyota from using the name Lexus because it would dilute its Lexis mark for its computerised legal research services.[55] It is not necessary to analyse the judgments delivered. The claim was dismissed. And history has shown that the rejection was fully justified.[56] One query: since the court was impressed by the fact that the Lexus was intended to be a luxury vehicle, one may wonder what the result would have been if the car had been in the same class as the East German Trabant (lovingly or loathingly called Trabi), or would that then have been a case of tarnishment? Ten years later the Lexus brand had become a famous mark and now someone sought

[49] *Verimark (Pty) Ltd v Bayerische Motoren Werke AktienGesellschaft; Bayerische Motoren Werke AktienGesellschaft v Verimark (Pty) Ltd* (250/06) [2007] ZASCA 53; [2007] SCA 53 (RSA) (17 May 2007). Jeremy Philips in his IPKat blog was not happy with this aspect of the judgment. *Cf* for the USA SL Dogan and MA Lemley, 'The Trademark Use Requirement in Dilution Cases' (2007–2008) 24 *Santa Clara Computer & High Technology LJ* 541.

[50] *Arsenal Football Club plc v Matthew Reed* Case C-206/01 (ECJ).

[51] N-LW Loon, 'Time to Re-think the Ever Expanding Concept of Trade Marks? Recalibrating Singapore's Trade Mark Law after the Controversial US-Singapore FTA' [2008] *EIPR* 151, 157.

[52] *Adam Opel AG v Autec* Case C-48/05 (ECJ).

[53] *Intel Corporation Inc v CPM United Kingdom Ltd* (n 32).

[54] RG Bone, 'A Skeptical View of the Trademark Dilution Revision Act' (n 26).

[55] *Mead Data Central Inc v Toyota Motor Sales USA Inc* 10 USPQ 2d 1961 (1989 Court of Appeals Second Circuit).

[56] As far as my evidence may be admissible or relevant: I write for the local LexisNexis company and I drive a Lexus and it was only when I read this judgment that I became aware of the link.

to register the name for canned food and juices. (In his papers, David used the example of canned *dog* food being called Lexus.) Toyota opposed the application, in the event unsuccessfully.[57] The test that had to be applied was the likelihood of confusion. If Lexus for cars does not dilute Lexis for electronic legal services, how could Toyota believe that Lexus for canned food would dilute Lexus for cars?

Courts outside of the USA in general do not buy Schechter's Rolls-Royce example.[58] Lord Justice Robin Jacob said as much in *Intel*:[59]

> I do not see that trade mark law need be so oppressive and all powerful. I would hold that a 'link' requires more than such a tenuous association between the two marks. If a trade mark for particular goods or services is truly inherently and factually distinctive it will be robust enough to withstand a mere passing bringing to mind when it or a similar mark is used for dissimilar goods or services. The average consumer is a reasonably sensible individual. He is used to lots of trade marks in different fields—some of which may resemble trade marks for other fields. In this country for example, for a long time Jif lemon juice and Jif washing up liquid co-existed happily, not to mention Jiffy for padded bags and condoms. Sometimes, but perhaps not surprisingly, trade mark owners of big brands want more protection than they really need ...
>
> Consider Schechter's example of Rolls-Royce. If that trade mark were used for pants (the American word for trousers) I suppose these days some members of the public might speculate that there is some sort of licensing arrangement. ...
>
> However one must be careful with Schechter's example in any event. It subtly goes a bit too far. For however much Rolls-Royce were used for dissimilar goods, it would be wrong to say it would not exist for cars and jet engines. (Actually there are two Rolls-Royces now, with no harm to either caused by the existence of the other).[60]

Other courts have been equally sceptical about the assumption.[61] The Supreme Court of Canada for one dismissed a dilution claim in *Veuve Clicquot Ponsardin*, a case where the trade mark owner of the champagne

[57] *Toyota Jidosha Kabushiki Kaisha v Lexus Foods Inc (CA)* 2000 CanLII 16447 (FCA).

[58] J Bosland, 'The Culture of Trade Marks: An Alternative Cultural Theory Perspective' (n 1): 'some may argue that ROLLS ROYCE is expressively generic for indicating the "best" of a particular type of goods—"the Rolls Royce of its class", for example.' However, the German Federal Supreme Court held, as a question of law, that the use of a Rolls-Royce in an advertisement for Jim Bean whiskey could amount to unfair competition because such use could be considered to be *contra bonos mores*: *Rolls-Royce Motors Ltd v Gramm & Grey GmbH & Co KG* (9.12.1982 Case I ZR 133/80). However, in *Ferrari v Jägermeister* (03.11.2005 Case I ZR 29/03) the court found that offering a Ferrari car as a prize in a competition by the liqueur maker Jägermeister did not amount to trade mark infringement.

[59] *Intel Corporation Inc v CPM United Kingdom Ltd* [2007] EWCA Civ 431 (15 May 2007).

[60] He could have added that the car brand now belongs to the German BMW company, but maybe pride prevented him.

[61] For Scotland: *Pebble Beach Company v Lombard Brands* [2002] ScotCS 265 (24 September 2002). South Africa: *Verimark (Pty) Ltd v Bayerische Motoren Werke AktienGesellschaft; Bayerische Motoren Werke AktienGesellschaft v Verimark (Pty) Ltd* (n 49).

brand sough to prevent the use of the mark Cliquot (omitting the second 'c') in relation to women's wear shops. It rejected the idea that linkage with a famous mark follows as a matter of course (as some would have it) and that 'acceptance of the argument that depreciation *could* occur, is not acceptance of the assertion that on the facts of this case depreciation is *likely* to occur, still less that depreciation *did* occur'.[62] It is too soon to assess the impact of the ECJ's *Intel* judgment.[63] On the one hand it suggests that mere linkage is insufficient (para 32) and on the other that it is sufficient (para 60). If linking is tantamount to thinking about, what can 'mere linkage' consist of? Not thinking? Although the judgment denies that confusion is required it does not say what else would suffice unless anything would. I, for one, am thankful that I do not have to apply this judgment because it simply repeats the generalities of the ECJ's previous judgments. How easy it is to fall back on 'global appreciation' and 'consider all the facts', as if one is dealing with the exercise of some discretion. Things may now improve under the *L'Oreal* decision.[64]

Struggling to find a public interest element in trade mark law, US courts,[65] particularly Judge Posner, developed the theory that trade marks save consumers search time and costs:[66]

> [T]here is concern that consumer search costs will rise if a trademark becomes associated with a variety of unrelated products. Suppose an upscale restaurant calls itself 'Tiffany'. There is little danger that the consuming public will think it's dealing with a branch of the Tiffany jewelry store if it patronizes this restaurant. But when consumers next see the name Tiffany they may think about both the restaurant and the jewelry store, and if so the efficacy of the name as an identifier of the store will be diminished. Consumers will have to think harder—incur as it were a higher imagination cost—to recognize the name as the name of the store. So 'blurring' is one form of dilution.

Like so many judge-made theories (*cf* those relating to sentencing), this one has no factual basis. How much does it cost to think? I would suggest nothing. Is any risk involved? My answer would be no. Buying a car, how long does a consumer think about a Lexis legal electronic system? Or when buying Claeryn Dutch 'jenewer' (gin), does it cost even a Dutchman

[62] *Veuve Clicquot Ponsardin v Boutiques Cliquot Ltée* 2006 SCC 23 (CanLII) [67].

[63] *Intel Corporation Inc v CPM United Kingdom Limited* (n 32).

[64] See the postscript below.

[65] *WT Rogers Co v Keane* 778 F 2d 334 at 338 (7th Circuit 1985): 'The purpose [of trade mark protection] is to reduce the cost of information to consumers by making it easy for them to identify the products or producers with which they have had either good experiences, so that they want to keep buying the product (or buying from the producer), or bad experiences, so that they want to avoid the product or the producer in the future.'

[66] *Ty Inc v Perryman* 306 F 3d 509 (7th Circuit 2002). He had developed this theory in Landes and Posner, 'Trademark Law: An Economic Perspective' (1987) 30 *Journal of Law & Economics* 265.

anything if he instead thinks about a liquid detergent named Klarein?[67] (Some courts apparently have a very low opinion of the level of intelligence of the general public.)[68] The textbook[69] example of Buick aspirin diluting the Buick car has been debunked by Chevy for detergents, deodorants and various cleaning products.[70] Research indicates that milliseconds are involved and, as Rebecca Tushnet said, the search theory amounts to the 'use and misuse of cognitive science to explain trademark doctrines'.[71] If formulae like those used by Morrin et al[72] are required to establish trade mark dilution, the law has become *Weltfremd*—it has lost touch with reality.

Some academic theories are just as bad as judicial ones. Shahar J Dilbary[73] argues that anti-dilution laws inure to the benefit of both producers and consumers because they secure the traditional role of the trade mark owner as 'the avenger of the public'. A consumer who purchases a good bearing a famous mark receives also an intangible product (an image, emotion or any other type of psychological freight), ie, the *right* to use or enjoy the intangible psychological effect attached to the product (conveyed by the famous mark). Dilution destroys the emotional experience and the image that accompanies it and divests an article from its psychological freight (or, even worse, replaces a positive psychological association with a negative one) and renders it worthless.

How does one debunk bunkum? First, law and psychology seldom mix, especially at this level. How much emotion (except the shock caused by price) is involved in purchasing a Rolls-Royce? Second, the idea that the trade mark owner is the 'avenger' of the consumer consumes more poetic licence than Lord Byron did when he accused Time of being the Avenger. Third, laws must be capable of justification before they are adopted; any ex post justification on such nebulous grounds makes them suspect. And last, this analysis may be valid for tarnishment (all Dilbary's examples fall arguably within that category) but it does not justify anti-blurring laws.

[67] *Lucas Bols v Colgate-Palmolive* (1976) 7 IIC 420, 423 (Benelux Court of Justice).

[68] See in general B Beebe, 'Search and Persuasion in Trademark Law' (2005) 103 *Mich LR* 2020.

[69] Eg BA Jacobs, 'Trademark Dilution on the Constitutional Edge' 104 *Columbia Law Review* 161.

[70] Referred to in the opinion of AG Jacobs in *General Motors Corporation v Yplon SA* (ECJ Case C 375/97).

[71] R Tushnet, 'Gone in 60 Milliseconds: Trademark Law and Cognitive Science' (2008) 86 *Texas Law Review* 507.

[72] M Morrin, J Lee and GM Allenby, 'Determinants of Trademark Dilution' (2006) 33 *Journal of Consumer Research*.

[73] SJ Dilbary, 'Famous Trademarks and the Rational Basis for Protecting "Irrational Beliefs"' (2007) 14 *George Mason Law Review* 605.

Absent an identifiable public interest dimension, courts naturally would not be too keen to make factual findings that fail to serve such (or any) real interest. As Jason Bosland said:[74]

> Just because a trade mark is commercially and culturally valuable due to its 'effervescent' qualities or its 'commercial magnetism' should not, of itself, be sufficient reason to recognise dilution protection. Like all intellectual property rights, the protection against dilution must serve a *tangible public interest*'.

Furthermore, if Schechter is to be taken at face value, any use of the name Rolls-Royce would affect its uniqueness and amount to blurring. Since it would in his scheme of things mean that the mark would 'disappear',[75] any use would be unfair or detrimental. It would then logically follow that once the word has been used, the inquiry should be at an end. Dutch commentators, by the way, are of the view that courts have in effect created a trade mark right similar to a copyright or patent right.[76] It is at this point that most courts tend to baulk at the consequences of the doctrine.[77] They are instinctively aware of the two ironies: (a) 'that the very marks which are so famous as to deserve anti-blurring protection already receive the same scope of protection from source-confusion-based anti-infringement protection'; and (b) 'that the very marks which are so famous as to deserve anti-blurring protection are essentially immune to blurring on account of their overriding fame'.[78] And unless they are able to discern some measure of confusion, they fail to see any degree of unfairness or measure of detriment.

TARNISHMENT, T-SHIRTS AND LAUGHTER

President Sarkozy is upset about a T-shirt that has his name written in large letters across the chest with a gun target replacing the letter 'o' in his name. Above his name is the French national motto 'liberty, equality, fraternity' splattered with blood. The Chicago Cubs are upset about a racially offensive T-shirt being sold that targets one of its players of Japanese origin, Kosuke Fukudome, using the Cubs' cartoon-logo bear face but

[74] J Bosland, 'The Culture of Trade Marks: An Alternative Cultural Theory Perspective' (n 1). I do appreciate that the statement may have been taken out of context.

[75] This may be related to the principle that a trade mark may lose its distinctiveness by becoming a generic term. WJ Derenberg, 'The Problem of Trademark Dilution (n 35).

[76] D van Engelen, *Prestatiebescherming en ongeschreven intellectuele eigendomsrechten* (dissertation, Leiden, 2003) (Deventer, Kluwer, 2003). I have used the web version.

[77] About the overlap of IP rights, see D Vaver 'Canada's IP Laws Amiss and a Mess' on IPilogue, 12 October 2008: http://www.iposgoode.ca/2008/10/canada%e2%80%99s-ip-laws-%e2%80%93-amiss-and-a-mess/ and the case law there discussed.

[78] Beebe, 'A Defense' (n 25), 1161–62.

with slanted eyes and oversized glasses, surrounded by the words Horry Kow (apparently Fukudome's nickname). Starbucks failed in its attempt to stop Mr Charbucks.[79] Wal-mart was not amused by Mr Smith's parody of its name, using the names Walocaust and Walocaust designs, and Wal-Qaeda. And SA Breweries was not amused when Mr Nurse used a parody or satire[80] of the Black Label trade mark on a T-shirt which conveyed the message that since time immemorial, the company has exploited and still is exploiting black labour, that it has or should have a feeling of guilt and that SA Breweries worldwide could not care less.[81] As PJ O'Rourke said about the ever-present T-shirts, 'If Martin Luther were a modern ecologist, he would have to nail ninety-five T-shirts to the church door at Wittenberg.'

At the time of writing I had to rely on newspaper reports about President Sarkozy and the Cubs. Walmart, however, lost it case on tarnishment because Mr Smith primarily intended to express his strongly adverse opinions about Wal-Mart with his Walocaust and Wal-Qaeda concepts and because he was not interested in profit. His designs were found to be successful parodies, to be non-commercial speech, and therefore not subject to Wal-Mart's trade mark dilution claims.[82] (One wonders whether this benign approach to the trivialisation of the Holocaust would have found favour with Israeli courts.) And SA Breweries (as mentioned) also lost. Sachs J thought the T-shirt to be funny. The 10 other Constitutional Court judges had other reasons.

The first instance of tarnishment that has been noted in the literature is, as far as I am aware, the '4711' case. Derenberg called it 'a rather extreme case' of dilution but did not try to fit it within any one of his dilution categories.[83] According to Derenberg (quoting *Time* magazine),[84] the owner of the famous '4711' mark for eau de cologne obtained an injunction against a manure collector who had painted his telephone number, 4711,

[79] *Starbucks Corp v Wolfe's Borough Coffee Inc* 477 F 3d 765 at 766 (2d Circuit 2007). There was a recent retrial.

[80] For a discussion of the different forms of humour: LE Little, 'Regulating Funny: Humor and the Law' (2009) 94 *Cornell Law Review* 1235.

[81] As mentioned, I wrote the judgment of the SCA. To depersonalise the article I shall refer to the judgment as that of the SCA, which it is. This was the 'message' as found by the SCA. Mr Nurse could not suggest any other meaning. The CC was not prepared to overrule this finding [65]. Mr Nurse did not suggest that this was the truth or fair comment although Sachs J held that the imputation was true [98].

[82] *Charles Smith v Wal-Mart Stores Inc* (No. 1:06-cv-526-TCB) US District Court Northern District of Georgia (20 March 2008). The surprising thing about this summary judgment case is not the result but the fact that of the 87 pages, only five dealt with dilution. The rest dealt with primary infringement, which must have been a non-starter.

[83] Derenberg, 'The Problem of Trademark Dilution' (n 35) 448 n 49.

[84] FW Mostert *Famous and Well-known Marks,* 2nd edn [1–103], (International Trademark Association, New York, 2004/2009) using a secondary reference, attributes this judgment to the German Federal Supreme Court. I have been unable to locate such judgment. Maybe the next quoted judgment is what his source had in mind.

in 20 inch (50 mm) high numerals across both sides of his horse-drawn fertiliser wagon.

Without my having access to the judgment (not that civil law judgments are always very illuminating for the ignorant outsider), some thoughts spring to mind. Was this a trade mark case or another general delict case? It probably was the latter, if regard is had to the German Federal Supreme Court's rather inconclusive judgment concerning the use by a taxi operator of the 4711 telephone number on his taxis—a case of blurring.[85] Second, why would the law wish to protect only well-known marks against tarnishment? I would have thought that a small local perfume store should equally be able to complain. Third, tarnishment is clearly not only an unfair competition matter and, consequently, not purely a trade mark issue. Fourth, would the reasonable person find this use of 4711 funny and, if so, should that affect the court's conclusion? Next, should the fact that manure collector did not use the 4711 in the trade mark sense affect the outcome? Last, was it necessary for the perfumery to prove the probability of commercial loss and, if it was, how was it supposed to do so?

The *Laugh it Off* case[86] concerned a registered trade mark consisting of a representation of Black Label stickers on the neck and body of a beer bottle. The label on the neck contains the words 'Carling' and 'enjoyed by men around the world'. The sticker for the body of the bottle is much larger and is oblong. There are two gold lines, the upper one containing the phrase 'America's lusty, lively beer' and the lower one 'Brewed in South Africa'. In a parallelogram the words 'Carling Black Label Beer' appear.

Nurse sought to apply 'ideological jujitsu' to the trade mark by using the weight of the brand against itself. In relation to the Black Label neck and body mark, the jujitsu grip consists of what may be characterised as a caricature of the trade mark used on T-shirts. It employs the general lay-out and colours of the registered mark. However, the message is different. The words 'Black Label' were replaced with 'Black Labour' and 'Carling Beer' with 'White Guilt'. The laudatory part on the label was replaced by 'Africa's lusty, lively exploitation since 1652' and 'No regard given worldwide'.

Whether the Constitutional Court ('CC') or the Supreme Court of Appeal ('SCA') was correct on the facts, ie, whether the mark was diluted, is not the debate. The decision of whether the T-shirt tarnished the Black Label trade mark ought to be a value judgment, and it is readily conceded that the SCA's value judgment may have been wrong. Whether a value judgment is a constitutional issue, especially where the CC expressly refrained from deciding the constitutionality of the anti-dilution provision in the light of the South

[85] BGH 22.03.1990 1 ZR 43/88 *'Telefonnummer 4711'* GRUR 1990 Heft 9 p 711. Ms Anja Petersen of Hoffmann Eitle, Munich, kindly provided me with the judgment.

[86] For the latest criticism: M Rimmer 'The Black Label: Trade Mark Dilution, Culture Jamming and the No Logo Movement' (2008) 5(1) *SCRIPT-ed* 71.

African Constitution, is a matter best left for constitutional experts. The same applies to the question of whether the CC's dicta on trade mark law that are not constitutional matters bind other courts.

The question proposed to be addressed is rather the effect of the judgment of the CC.[87] The main judgment was written by Moseneke J and concurred in by all the justices (including Sachs J, whose concurring judgment is not really compatible with that of Moseneke J). In its exposition of the law this judgment does not differ much from that of the SCA. However, Moseneke J concluded that the merits of the appeal turned on whether SA Breweries 'had properly demonstrated the likelihood of detriment to the repute of the marks as required by the section' (para 35) and in the event dismissed the dilution claim 'because no likelihood of economic prejudice has been established' (at para 65). The South African provision differs from that of the UK Act—it requires a 'likelihood' of unfair advantage or detriment, while the latter requires actual detriment or unfair advantage.[88] SA Breweries did not seek to prove actual loss; it sought to rely on the inference of loss.

Moseneke J held that a trade mark owner must 'on the facts, establish a likelihood of substantial economic detriment to the claimant's mark'. This factual onus, he said, applied when 'a party seeks to oust an expressive conduct protected under the Constitution'. By this, presumably, he meant that when a defendant exercises the free speech right the plaintiff must discharge this onus. It is difficult to imagine that anyone who tarnishes a trade mark by non trade-mark use is not exercising or purporting to exercise the freedom of expression. But, if the qualification is a true qualification, it would mean that a court must first determine whether the 'expressive conduct' is entitled to constitutional protection before this onus arises. However, as noted above, Moseneke J expressly refrained from making that determination because he refused to attach any meaning to the message on the T-shirt. There is, however, an indication that the onus applies in all cases because in his summing-up Moseneke J said that 'where no economic harm has been shown, the fairness of parody or satire or lampooning does not fall for consideration' (at para 65). In other words, first prove your loss and then we'll consider whether your claim impinges on the defendant's freedom of expression.

Of significance is his statement that much is to be said for the contention that 'in a claim based on tarnishment of a trade mark, the probability of material detriment to the mark ... must be restricted to economic and trade harm.' The jump in one sentence (the one quoted at the outset of

[87] Eg W Alberts, 'The Future of Trade Mark Dilution in SA Law' (2006) 1 *Journal of SA Law* 213.

[88] For a full discussion of the requirement, see I Simon, 'The Actual Dilution Requirement in the United States, the United Kingdom and the European Union: A Comparative Analysis' (2006) 12 *Boston University Journal of Science & Technology Law* 271.

the previous paragraph) to the next from 'likelihood' to 'probability' is a quantum jump. It is the difference so well articulated by the US Supreme Court in *Victoria's Secret*.[89] Since the litigation concerned interdict proceedings, which are akin to *quia timet* proceedings (where a reasonable apprehension of harm and not on proof of actual harm is required), the statement undercuts centuries of learning.[90] *Intel* is in this regard more conventional.[91]

Limiting the requirement to cases of tarnishment, if so intended, is difficult to appreciate. Does it mean that in cases of blurring, economic and trade harm need not be shown and if so, how does one by mere interpretation dissect the same provision in the Act to have different requirements for different situations? If the judgment means what it says, one has to accept that in SA law, blurring is only possible if actual confusion can be shown, because it is not possible to envisage measurable harm without confusion, at least at the outset, since the harm caused by blurring is incremental and cumulative.

Importantly, Moseneke J held that the anti-dilution section does not protect the 'dignity' of the mark because a message that affects the 'dignity' of a mark does not affect its 'selling magnetism' (para 56).[92] In this regard he implicitly overruled the SCA which, relying on US jurisprudence based on similarly worded legislation,[93] held that a message that is likely to create in the mind of consumers a particularly unwholesome, unsavoury, or degrading association with the mark in issue, amounts to unlawful tarnishment. Likewise it must have disagreed with the approach of the SCA that:

> courts are in general not amused by sex- and drug-related 'parodies', even if they are clever or funny, simply because the prejudice to the trade mark tends to outweigh freedom of expression [and that] on the same principle, unfair or unjustified racial slurs on a trademark owner (even if not hate speech or approximating it) should in general not be countenanced, more so in a society such as ours. The whole point about reputation is that, like sanity, it operates as a working assumption—to question it is, in itself, to devalue it. [At para 31.]

This may explain the refusal to engage in a determination of the message of the T-shirt.

[89] *Moseley dba Victor's Little Secret v V Secret Catalogue Inc* (n 26).

[90] *Cf Miss World Ltd v Channel Four Television Corp* [2007] EWCH 982 (Pat) [29].

[91] *Intel Corporation Inc v CPM United Kingdom Ltd* (n 32).

[92] This paragraph of the judgment also baffled Pumfrey J in *Miss World v Channel Four Television* (n 90) [36]–[38].

[93] *Mutual of Omaha Insurance Company v Novak* 648 F Supp 905; 231 USPQ 963 upheld on appeal: *Mutual of Omaha Insurance Company v Novak* 836 F2d 397; *Dallas Cowboys Cheerleaders Inc v Pussycat Cinema Ltd* 604 F 2d 200. The SCA recognised that the position is different in the UK: *DaimlerChrysler AG v Javid Alavi (t/a Merc)* [2001] RPC 22, 842 and under US federal law: *Moseley v V Secret* (n 89).

Just as *Victoria's Secret*[94] buried dilution under the then existing US federal legislation, so did this case bury it for purposes of SA law. The Moseneke judgment did not deal with the difficulties in proving actual financial loss in trade mark cases. The CC required evidence of a reduction in sales to establish financial harm. Those with exposure to this area of the law know that damages (except in the form of notional royalties) are hardly ever recovered or even sought in trade mark infringement cases.[95]

If the judgment is applied according to its tenor, the distribution of the same T-shirt by a competitor would presumably produce the same result. But one cannot escape the feeling that what really determined the outcome was that Mr Nurse was a 'brand atheist' with no real financial interest who sought to attack a large industrial concern: a David and Goliath case. This was, in any event, the basis of Sachs J's judgment, which has attained cult status for its eloquence and broadly stated approach to matters affecting free speech and the importance of humour.[96] Sachs J's critique of the SCA judgment was based on his view that the SCA had de-contextualised the nature of the mockery contained in the message on the T-shirt and the context in which it was deployed (at para 75). Although he professed that the subjective intention was irrelevant (at para 95), he nevertheless spent quite some time in setting it out. He concluded that the 'message lies precisely in the dislocated use of the trade mark [and that] the challenge is to the power of branding in general, as exemplified by the particular trademark' (at para 102) and that the context of the message was 'one of laughter being used as a means of challenging economic power, resisting ideological hegemony and advancing human dignity' (at para 108).[97] At least one cannot accuse Sachs J of under-estimating the intelligence of the ordinary beer-quaffing T-shirt-wearing person.

The actual harm requirement in US law was the consequence of the wording of the statute, and *Victoria's Secret* exposed the weakness in the wording of the statute. The US Congress has since sought to plug the 'actual harm' hole through which many a dilution case went down the drain. Moseneke J has pulled the plug for South Africa by 'interpreting' the 'likelihood of detriment to the repute' requirement in the statute to refer to actual financial loss. The result may be palatable, but as a matter of interpretation it is difficult to swallow.

[94] Note 26.

[95] See the reservation about notional royalties expressed by Jacob LJ in *Reed Executive Plc & Ors v Reed Business Information Ltd & Ors* [2004] EWCA Civ 159 [165].

[96] Sachs J has since written about this judgment in his autobiographical work: A Sachs, *The Strange Alchemy of Life and Law* (Oxford, OUP, 2009).

[97] Pumfrey J thought that 'absent a sign which is really telling a political story, making a political point or identifying some matter of public importance', the idea that use of a trade mark can of itself generally engage free speech provision is difficult to imagine: *Miss World v Channel Four Television* (n 90) [47].

With or without the plug, tarnishment cases will still run down the drain if the objectionable use is non-trade mark use (ie badge of origin use), as is the case of a brand atheist who does not compete with the trade mark owner, because then the freedom of speech defence kicks in. US law is in this regard unsympathetic to commercial use, but that may be too narrow a view. Stacey L Dogan and Mark A Lemley are probably right when they say:[98]

> The trademark use doctrine offers the only reliable safeguard against dilution law's slippery slope. Dilution law, properly conceived, protects famous marks against uses that interfere with their *function* as source-identifiers. It should not reach every use that affects a mark's *meaning*, lest it turn into an *über*-right that would defeat the very purpose of trademark laws.

Moseneke J's judgment, in pulling the plug, did not consider the trade mark use cases such as the well-known condom cases, namely, the American Express charge card and slogan 'Don't leave home without it',[99] Mars and its slogan that 'it will liven you up',[100] and Visa condoms.[101] On Moseneke J's judgment, infringement required proof of actual financial loss, but on Sachs J's judgment the credit card companies and Mars simply have to laugh it off. Practically speaking, Sachs J is probably right. Other companies, which were subjected to Mr Nurse's ridicule, grimaced and rode the tide and the joke grew stale, while the skit on Black Label will go down in history.

CONCLUSION

Maybe I should admit that my conclusion is inconclusive. Dilution laws may tend to be monolithic, but with judges and academics chipping away at the rock, not much is left. As George Bernard Shaw did, one may use Ibsen's simile of the machine-made stitch, which unravels the whole seam at the first pull when a single stitch is ripped. Alternatively, one may say that the dilution theory was more egg-like than rock-like. Like Humpty Dumpy, dilution had a great fall, having been pushed off the wall by the judiciary. It is unlikely that the judiciary will put it together again. Courts doubt its parentage; they find it difficult to justify on public policy considerations;[102]

[98] SL Dogan and MA Lemley, 'The Trademark Use Requirement in Dilution Cases' (2008) (n 49).

[99] *American Express Co v Vibra Approved Laboratories Corp* 10 USPQ 2d 2006 (SDNY 1989).

[100] Case I ZR 79/92, 1995 [26] IIC 282 (Germany).

[101] *A Sheimer (M) SDN BHD's Trade Mark Application* [2000] RPC 13, 484.

[102] Bone, 'A Skeptical View' (n 54) 198: 'Legal protection should be given only when it is *clearly* justified on policy grounds, and this means we should err on the side of a narrow statute rather than a broad one that has flimsy support.'

they are not keen to humour the paranoia of trade mark owners; and they find it impossible to apply sensibly or consistently.

Why the difference between civil courts such as the German courts and the common-law courts? Maybe it is a difference in judicial culture. Civil courts tend to concentrate on *das Prinzip* (and if they do not have a legal theory they'll create one as Kurt Tucholsky once said: although the Germans did not invent gunpowder they were able to discover its philosophy), while common law courts tend to be more pragmatic. There is also the undercurrent in the civil systems of the *droit moral*; the definition of a delict is open-ended and, depending on the court's understanding of the commercial morals of society results may differ from case to case. The social philosopher, Max Weber, I have since submitting this piece discovered, was able to pinpoint the difference in these terms: he classified the civil approach as logically rational based on generic rules (a jurisprudence of concepts) while, on the other hand, the common law method of thought approximates the substantively irrational type because it is based on reasoning by example.[103] But courts are not programmed. The animated 'adult' film, *Tarzoon, la honte de la jungle* (*Tarzoon: Shame of the Jungle*), survived the French courts but not the wrath of the US courts!

A final word from Graeme B Dinwoodie and Mark D Janis, speaking about the recent US Trademark Dilution Revision Act:[104]

> Until independent policy rationales for dilution are articulated more precisely and connected to the contours of the implementing doctrine, it is likely that courts will receive the new version of dilution with the same overriding skepticism that led them to eviscerate the old law (and some state dilution laws before that).

R.I.P.

Postscript: Since submitting this article, dilution's bones have rattled in its grave. This time it was due to the ECJ in *L'Oréal*.[105] The case, as far as this article is concerned, is about the taking of unfair advantage of a well-known mark by a competitor without blurring or tarnishment. The Court explained:

> As regards the concept of 'taking unfair advantage of the distinctive character or the repute of the trade mark', also referred to as 'parasitism' or 'free-riding', that concept relates not to the detriment caused to the mark but to the advantage

[103] All this is explained by Max Rheinstein in his Introduction to his edition of *Max Weber on Law in Economy and Society* (New York, Simon & Schuster, 1967) (first paperback printing) xl–lv.

[104] GB Dinwoodie and MD Janis, 'Dilution's (Still) Uncertain Future' (n 11).

[105] *L'Oréal SA, Lancôme parfums et beauté & Cie SNC, Laboratoire Garnier & Cie v Bellure NV, Malaika Investments Ltd, trading as 'Honey pot cosmetic & Perfumery Sales', Starion International Ltd* Case C-487/07 (18 June 2009).

> taken by the third party as a result of the use of the identical or similar sign. It covers, in particular, cases where, by reason of a transfer of the image of the mark or of the characteristics which it projects to the goods identified by the identical or similar sign, there is clear exploitation on the coat-tails of the mark with a reputation. [At para 41.]

This appears to amount to the introduction of general principles of unfair competition via trade mark law—blurring the two and tarnishing both.

Conclusion

18

Postscript

Was There *Ever* a Common Law of Intellectual Property?

LIONEL BENTLY, CATHERINE W NG
and GIUSEPPINA D'AGOSTINO

WE WANTED TO close this collection of essays with a provocative thought: *are the divergences that now exist between the common law jurisdictions in fact any greater than they have been?* In order to answer this question, we need to make a brief historical examination of the laws of intellectual property in the common law countries. We will focus on the late nineteenth century. Doing so, we will see that the intellectual property laws of the common law countries *always* contained variations. The idea that there ever was uniformity is largely a myth, born out of an assumption that the colonial origins of the laws necessarily meant that they were imposed by Britain—an assumption that informs what Bowrey refers to as the 'considerable scholarly neglect of colonial legal history'.[1] As legal historians begin to remedy this neglect, it is becoming clear that there were significant divergences of approach and detail in the nineteenth century, just as there are today. Indeed, the essays by Bowrey and Monotti explicitly recognise that, historically speaking, there never was uniformity even amongst the British colonies, let alone within the common law family as a whole. Of course, the causes of divergences and their specifics have altered. So this postscript does not cast doubt on the usefulness of the argument made and the analyses offered by the other contributors to the collection.

The oft-assumed idea of imperial law being imposed from the metropolis on the colonies is false. Colonial law-making was typically devolved (if subject to certain control, via the bureaucrats at the Colonial Office and

[1] Bowrey, ch 3, 52.

the judges of the Privy Council).[2] All colonies were given some capacity to legislate, though the structures by which such legislation was to be adopted varied amongst the colonies as well as over time. The mode of devolution differed as between different types of colonies: some having bicameral legislative organs, others much less sizeable councils offering advice to the Governor General. As an inevitable consequence of this devolution, as well as different types and levels of representation, legislation in the British colonies was varied, complex and messy.[3] Colonial law-making was subject to imperial control, at least in so far as it could be disallowed as 'repugnant', but the 'legal doctrine of repugnancy' was, according to Frederic Rogers who had to make such determinations, 'in a very uncertain, perhaps I should say shifting state'.[4]

In so far as co-ordination of legislation with the colonies was thought desirable, this was often achieved (particularly from the latter part of the nineteenth century) through co-operative frameworks and informal networks. A circular issued by the Colonial Office might 'inform' a colony of a particular change in British law, 'inspiring' perhaps a local legislative response, or request information on the protection available to a British citizen, thus suggesting, perhaps, that such protection was necessary or desirable. But even informal practices that purported to create uniformity were not always encouraged. Colonial historian DB Swinfen describes the views of the lawyers, Sir James Stephen and Frederic Rogers (later Lord Blachford), who reviewed the colonial legislation in the first half of the nineteenth century. Stephen was sceptical about the wholesale copying of English law into the laws of the colonies where it might not be appropriate.[5] Swinfen concludes:[6]

> Uniformity of law within the Empire was, therefore, only encouraged in certain matters of personal status, and there was never any intention on the part of the British authorities to erect a common body of law for the Empire as a whole. Such a project would have been wholly unrealistic, and attempts to force uniformity on colonies of such differing origins as, say, the Cape and Lower Canada, would certainly have failed if only ... on account of the opposition which would certainly arise within the colonies themselves. The most that could be hoped for would be

[2] DB Swinfen, *The Imperial Control of Colonial Legislation 1813–65* (Oxford, OUP, 1970); DLM Farr, *The Colonial Office and Canada, 1867–87* (Toronto, University of Toronto Press, 1955).

[3] T Richards, *The Imperial Archive: Knowledge and the Fantasy of Empire* (London, Verso Books, 1993) 3 ('I have found that historians have tended to confer a lot more unity on the British Empire than is justified. Most people during the nineteenth century were aware that their empire was something of a collective improvisation.').

[4] CO 323/87, South Australia; Rogers to Merivale, 5 May 1858 cited in Swinfen, *Imperial Control* (n 2) 62.

[5] CO 209/14 fols 360–67, Stephen to Stanley, 29 Sept 1842 (on the wholesale adoption of English law in NZ).

[6] Swinfen, *Imperial Control* (n 2) 76.

that legislation enacted since the colonies' inclusion in the Empire would conform to the English model.

Only rarely, therefore, did Parliament in London legislate for the whole Empire.

PATENTS

Although English patents,[7] as exercises of the Royal Prerogative, were sometimes expressed to extend to the 'His Majesty's Colonies and Plantations Abroad',[8] evidence to the Select Committee of 1829 suggested that such rights were of limited value and, in many cases, no legal effect.[9] When in the 1850s the reform of the process for patent grant was being widely discussed, Thomas Webster proposed that the colonies, dominions and possessions abroad should not be included in any British grant, but subject to special grants by the Crown or local legislature.[10] Canada had already adopted patent laws that gave local rights cheaply and efficiently,[11] and Webster thought that the colonies were in the best position to choose for themselves whether to grant such rights, and if so, their scope.[12] There was a real consciousness that this was an important matter of local policy, and that if the colonies were bound by British patents, their industries might be

[7] On Scottish patents prior to 1852, see MacQueen, ch 2.

[8] See the examples at *Report of the Select Committee on the Law Relative to Letters Patent for Inventions* (332) 1829, 173–75, and the forms at 213–16.

[9] *Select Committee*, 1829 (n 8) 17–18. (John Farey, for example, gave evidence that where the colony had its own legislature, an express Act of that legislature was required before the patent, granted in England, would be enforceable. Farey gave one example of where this had occurred, namely in respect of Hague's patent for expelling molasses from sugar. There were practical difficulties with enforcing an English patent against infringement in the colonies: Farey thought enforcement would need to be in an English court, so such an action would be attended by the extra expense of bringing witnesses from abroad.)

[10] *Report and minutes of evidence taken before the Select Committee of the House of Lords appointed to consider of the bill, intituled, 'an act further to amend the law touching letters patent for inventions;' and also of the bill, intituled, 'an act for the further amendment of the law touching letters patent for inventions;' and to report thereon to the House* (486), 1851, 18 Parliamentary Papers, 18 (Q 67). See Henry Cole, 270 (Q 1919); MD Hill, 281 (Q 2013) (indicating potential problems with non-working); Lieut-Col Reid 305–06, QQ 2268–9; R Prosser, 318 (Q 2388); JPB Westhead, MP, 344 (Q 2591).

[11] Evidence of PR Hodge to *Select Committee*, 1851, 98 (Q 618 ff). Lower Canada enacted a law modelled on that in the United States in 1824, and Upper Canada followed the lead of Lower Canada in 1826. William Hayhurst QC, *Intellectual Property Laws in Canada: the British Tradition, the American Influence and the French Factor*, Canada House Lecture Series No 58 (London, 1995) 9 ('a virtual copy of the U.S. Patent Act of 1793'). Nova Scotia passed an Act in 1833, New Brunswick in 1834, Prince Edward Island in 1837.

[12] See *Select Committee*, 1851 (n 10), per Henry Cole, 270 (Q 1919) ('the colonies can do their own legislation much better than we can.') Two decades later Webster indicated that this was his own position: *Report from the Select Committee on Letters Patent; together with the proceedings of the committee, minutes of evidence, appendix and index* (368), 1871, 85 (Q 969–70).

placed in a worse position than competitor colonies where no patents were in operation.[13] Nevertheless, Webster's view, though influential, was not the only position. William Carpmael, in contrast, saw no reason why patents should not apply in the colonies and expressed the view that the colonies would benefit from such a regime.[14] Others agreed that it was right that the patent should apply throughout the Empire, and saw dangers if a colony, without having to pay a royalty to a patentee, could undercut a business in Britain.[15] In the end, Parliament left the matter undecided, leaving the Patent Office empowered to extend patents to the colonies.

Following the passage of the 1852 Patent Law Amendment Act, which transformed the archaic and expensive system of grant of multiple patents in England, Scotland and Ireland into a streamlined and cheaper system for the grant of a single British patent, discussion occurred within the Patent Office as to whether these patents should be extended to the colonies. On this occasion, Webster's arguments won the day, and it was decided that, in the light of the fact that many colonies had their own patent laws, that British grants should not be extended. None was.[16]

The Lord Chancellor, Lord St Leonards, sent a circular to the colonies asking for information concerning local laws. Many responded, bit by bit, by formulating such law 'taking the English Act of 1852 as their model', so that by 1864 17 British colonies had patent laws.[17] Patents Acts and Ordinances were adopted, for example in New South Wales and Barbados in 1852,[18] Victoria in 1854,[19] India in 1856,[20] Jamaica in 1852 and 1857,

[13] See *Select Committee*, 1851 (n 10), per Lieut-Col Reid 305–06 (QQ 2268–69) (indicating that colonies should have the freedom to adopt British patent law, modify it or not have it at all, in response to their own conditions).

[14] *Select Committee*, 1851 (n 10), 43 (Q 241); 65–66 (QQ 387–399). See also John Fairries, 149, (Q 954); Robert MacFie, 151, (QQ 980, 997) (although he famously opposed patents altogether). Financial Reform Tracts, No 22, *Laws for the Protection and Encouragement of Invention* (1849) (proposing patent applicable throughout Empire).

[15] *Select Committee*, 1851 (n 10), Robert MacFie, 151 (QQ 980, 997); a view he reiterated in 1864, *Report of Commissioners*, (n 16) 119, Q 1992.

[16] See *Report of the commissioners appointed to inquire into the working of the law relating to letters patent for inventions* (3419), 1864, 19 Parliamentary Papers, 30 (Lewis Edmunds).

[17] Edmunds, ibid.

[18] On differences between the New South Wales statute and the British law, see *Moorewood v Flower* in JG Legge, *A Selection of Supreme Court Cases in New South Wales: From 1825 to 1862, Volume 2*, (1896) 1109.

[19] For cases on the Victorian Act, see *Patent Composition Pacement v Richmond*, 1 VLR 50; *Ellis v Geach* 4 AJR 163; *M'Lean v Kettle* 9 VLR 145.

[20] R Sagar, 'Introduction of exclusive privileges/patents in colonial India: why and for whose benefit?' (2007) *Intellectual Property Quarterly* 164 (arguing that the replacement of the 1856 Act with another Act in 1859 reflected imperial interests, and undermined the orientation of the 1856 Act towards the encouragement of technology transfer into India. More specifically, Sagar charts the manner in which a local, Indian, novelty test was devised in order to encourage importation of inventions into India, including from Great Britain, by Indians, and that the 1859 Act modified these standards to undermine this goal and in a way which made it easier for British patentees to gain protection in India.)

Tasmania in 1858, Ceylon and South Australia in 1859, New Zealand and the Cape of Good Hope in 1860, British Guiana in 1861, British Honduras in 1862, Trinidad in 1867, New Zealand in 1870, Fiji in 1877. But, reflecting Webster's vision, these laws varied enormously. The variations in the colonial patents can be exemplified by a brief review of the contents of the patent legislation (though doubtless further variations operated at the level of practice).[21] Variations existed in all aspects of the law, from the definition of patentable subject matter, duration, scope of rights, procedure, grounds of opposition, grounds of invalidity, definitions of novelty, disclosure requirements, requirements of working and compulsory licences. Most colonies had their own application procedure and law, but a few merely extended the operation of British law to the colony.[22] Some specifically provided for local law as an alternative to any British grant that had explicitly been made applicable to the colony,[23] while others indicated that British grants made after the introduction of the colonial law to be of no effect unless they complied with the conditions under the local law—specifically indicating that colonial law was sovereign.[24]

The variations in the treatment of subject matter seem to have been at least as extensive as those described by Piper and Dutfield in relation to today's laws. The British law, both that of 1852 and 1883, operated with the definition of patentable subject matter derived from the Statute of Monopolies, and most colonies followed this lead.[25] There were, however, many variants. The New South Wales Act of 1852 allowed for the grant of exclusive rights to the author or designer of any 'inventions and improvements in the arts and manufactures,' a definition which suggests something broader than 'manners of new manufacture.'[26] India and Ceylon permitted the patenting of 'any new manufacture',

[21] Many of the laws allowed for examination, with the assistance of scientific advice, but the legislation rarely indicates the extent of such examination, in particular whether it included examination on grounds of novelty.

[22] An Ordinance for Granting Patents for Inventions within this Colony, No 14 of 1862 (Hong Kong) allowed applications based on 'English' grant, extending right to HK 'as fully as if the same had been granted with an extension thereof to this Colony by Her Majesty.' See also Ordinance No 3 of 1872 for the Extension to this Island of Letters Patent granted under the Great Seal of the United Kingdom of Great Britain and Ireland (St Helena).

[23] British Guiana s 19. ('Nothing herein contained shall extend to prejudice or affect any Letters Patent heretofore granted in the United Kingdom and made applicable by the tenor thereof to this colony.')

[24] British Honduras s 44; An Act to provide for the granting, in this Colony, of Patents for Inventions, 1860, s 14 (Cape of Good Hope) s 35 (entitled 'English patents subject to this Act').

[25] The Patent Law Amendment Act 1862, 26 Vict c 2 s 45 (British Honduras); Act to provide for the granting, in this Colony, of Patents for Inventions, Act No 17 of 1860 (Cape of Good Hope) s 1.

[26] An Act to authorise the Governor General, with the advice of the Executive Council, to grant letter of registration for all inventions and improvements in the arts or manufactures, to have the same effect as Letters Patent in England, so far as regards this Colony, Act No XXIV, 6th December 1852.

which was described as including 'any art, process, or manner of producing, preparing or making an article, and also any article prepared or produced by manufacture.'[27] Fiji allowed for the patenting of 'any manner of new manufacture' but 'also every new process of manufacture, and every new method of application of known processes, and improvements in any known process.'[28] Other laws seemed to have been influenced by the United States' definition of subject matter as 'any new and useful art, machine, manufacture or composition of matter, or any new and useful improvement thereof.'[29] The Jamaican law (1857), for example, related to 'some new and useful art, machine, manufacture, or composition of matter, not theretofore known or used within this Island, or some improvement in any invention or discovery'.[30] Newfoundland, similarly, offered patents to those who discovered or made 'any new and useful art, machine, manufacture or composition of matter not theretofore known or used.'[31] Perhaps most interestingly, the Canadian law contained specific exclusions from patentability: 'no patent shall issue for an invention having an illicit object in view, nor for any mere scientific principle or abstract theorem.'[32] Many laws permitted annulment of patents whose operation proved contrary to the public interest (or, echoing the Statute of Monopolies, 'generally inconvenient'),[33] and a number specifically required a demonstration of 'utility'.[34]

Most colonies required that the invention be new to the colony. In some cases an invention was treated as novel if it had not been 'publicly used' in the colony.[35] This was clearly a very low threshold. In contrast, India required the invention to be new in the sense that it had been neither used

[27] Act No 15 of 1859 s 1, s 38 (India); An Ordinance for Granting Exclusive Privileges to Inventors, 1859, Ord No 6 ss 1 and 36 (Ceylon). In 1872 the Indian Patent law was extended to include 'any new and original pattern or design, or application of such pattern or design to any substance or article of manufacture', though with a term of only three years: Act No 13 of 1872 (adding ss 1a and 4a to the 1859 Act).

[28] Ordinance No 3, 1879, to repeal Ordinance No 24 of 1877 and to make other provisions in lieu thereof for the issue of Letters Patent, s 2 (Fiji).

[29] Title LX, Rev Stat, c 1 sec 4886 (US).

[30] An Act for amending the Law for granting Patents for Invention (1857) c 30 s 1, First (Jamaica).

[31] Title XV, c 54 sec 1 of the Consolidated Statutes of Newfoundland.

[32] An Act respecting Patents of Invention, Act of 14 June 1872, 35 Vict c 26 s 6 (Canada).

[33] Act No 15 of 1859 s 16 (India) ('mischievous to the state, or generally prejudicial to the public'); An Ordinance for Granting Exclusive Privileges to Inventors, 1859, Ord No 6 s 25 (providing for orders that a privilege cease where 'the [privilege], or the mode in which it is exercised, is mischievous to the State, or generally prejudicial to the public') (Ceylon); An Ordinance to Regulate the Granting of Patents in this Colony, 1861, Ord No 13 s 11 ('contrary to law, or prejudicial or inconvenient to Her Majesty's subjects in general') (British Guiana); Ordinance No 3, 1879, to repeal Ordinance No 24 of 1877 and to make other provisions in lieu thereof for the issue of Letters Patent, s 18 (if proved to be 'prejudicial to the public interests') (Fiji).

[34] Act No 15 of 1859 s 15 (India); Ordinance No 3, 1879, to repeal Ordinance No 24 of 1877 and to make other provisions in lieu thereof for the issue of Letters Patent s 4 (Fiji).

[35] An Ordinance for Granting Exclusive Privileges to Inventors, 1859, Ord No 6 s 17 (Ceylon) (with an exception for use in breach of confidence).

in Great Britain nor India, and had not been made publicly known in either Great Britain or India—a much higher threshold.[36] Nevertheless, the law in India specifically excluded the possibility of invention by 'importation' of an invention (unless the importer was actually the inventor).[37] Canadian law provided that an invention was patentable where it had not been 'known or used by others before his invention thereof' and, so long as it had not been 'in public use or on sale for more than one year previous to' the application in Canada. These variations seem to have been as extensive as those described in Monotti's chapter in this collection in relation to Australia and the UK today.

The provisions on 'disclosure' and 'sufficiency' also varied—again, as much, if not more than those identified by Thambisetty. British law required a description and title, but had no requirement of best mode. A number of colonies too seemed only to require a specification, describing and defining the invention.[38] One specified that this was to be a 'clear and copious statement in writing ... particularly describing and ascertaining the nature of the same invention and in what manner it is to be performed ...'[39] However, many of the common law countries required the use of drawings and the deposit of models. Canadian law, for example, required delivery of 'a neat working model of [the] invention on a convenient scale, exhibiting its several parts in due proportion, whenever the invention admits of such model.' One colony's law, that of Jamaica, specifically created an exemption from the requirement to deposit models for 'ingenious but poor' applicants.[40]

Finally, it is worth noting the variations in term. Most of the patent laws followed the Statute of Monopolies in giving 14 years,[41] but the New South Wales Act authorised grants of between seven and 14 years, while Canada offered 15 and the United States 17 years.[42] In many cases, the possibility of extension was provided for: in Britain, Ceylon and Cape of Good Hope, potentially for a further 14-year term.[43] Many colonies were concerned that the operation of a patent in the colony would not prejudice trade there, compared with the position in other countries: so many laws provided that,

[36] Act No 15 of 1859 s 19 (India).

[37] Act No 15 of 1859 s 17 (India).

[38] Act No 15 of 1859 s 6 (India); An Ordinance for Granting Exclusive Privileges to Inventors, 1859, Ord No 6 s 8 ('in writing ... and shall particularly describe and define the nature of the said invention, and in what manner the same is to be carried out') (Ceylon).

[39] An Ordinance to Regulate the Granting of Patents in this Colony, No 13 of 1861 s 12 (British Guiana).

[40] An Act for Amending the Law for Granting Patents for Inventions (1857) c 30 s 4 (Jamaica).

[41] Great Britain (1883) s 17; Jamaica, British Guiana (1861) s 9; Natal (1870) s 2.

[42] An Act respecting Patents of Invention 1872 s 17 (Canada).

[43] Patents, Designs and Trade Marks Act 1883, 45 & 46 Vict c 57 s 25(5); An Ordinance for Granting Exclusive Privileges to Inventors, 1859, Ord No 6 s 6; An Act to provide for the granting, in this Colony, of Patents for Inventions (1860) ss 21, 25 (Cape of Good Hope).

with respect to inventions from outside the colony, any patent granted was to expire when the first foreign patent for that invention expired.[44]

All this variation suggests that British colonies had quite some freedom in legislating as to patents. As Monotti explains, in relation to New South Wales and Victoria:

> A brief review of the pre-1952 common law position demonstrates both the close connections between Australian and UK patent law at this time and the *relative independence that the young colonies and then the Commonwealth exercised.*[45] (Emphasis added.)

To the extent that the colonies modelled their laws on those of Britain, Monotti suggests, this was done for a number of reasons, including, for example, because of the historical ties to Britain, to take advantage of the jurisprudence of the British courts, or in order to facilitate local harmonisation as local inventors and advisers need not have been troubled with differing laws.

LEGISLATIVE PROVISION IN RELATION TO TRADE MARKS

Similar factors seem to have operated in the field of trade marks, though generalised (rather than trade-sector specific) legislation in this area came much later than in relation to patents or copyright. This may be in part attributable to the more fluid common law which was applicable to trade mark governance and which had emerged in Britain, with an efflorescence of cases in the mid-nineteenth century. This common law, discussed later in this chapter, served to regulate trade mark use and alleviated the urgency to take statutory steps.

Calls for reform of the common law relating to traders' marks emerged in Britain in the 1850s, with proposals both for criminalisation and the introduction of a register. The matters were considered by the Select Committee of 1862,[46] where there was a clear sense that the colonies were victims to a lot of counterfeiting of products by Britain's European competitors, particularly Germany. Various merchants testified that British labels were attached to non-British goods and sent to the colonies.[47] Some traders testified that trade mark registers were already in place in some states of America and that their trade mark rights were enforced more efficiently and

[44] An Act to provide for the Granting, in this Colony, of Patents for Inventions 1860 s 14 (Cape of Good Hope); Ordinance No 3 1879, to repeal Ordinance No 24 of 1877 and to make other provisions in lieu thereof for the issue of Letters Patent s 15 (Fiji).

[45] Monotti, ch 9, 181.

[46] *Select Committee on Trade Marks Bill and Merchandize Marks Bill, Report, Proceedings and Minutes of Evidence* (1862) 12 Parliamentary Papers 431.

[47] *Select Committee*, 1862 (n 46): R. Gilpin, 91 (Q 1939); H Browning, 113, (Q 2465); Rodgers, QQs 481–96.

expeditiously under these registers than under common law in Britain.[48] Ultimately, however, the Committee recommended the adoption of criminal law prohibitions only, in the Merchandise Marks Act 1862.[49]

There was no call for British law to apply or extend to such colonies. Rather, in so far as one of the Bills suggested otherwise, William Hindmarch sought its correction so that it did not 'interfere with the legislatures in the colonies'.[50] As in 1852 with patents, so too with trade marks, the adoption of intellectual property laws was a matter for the local government in each colony. Lord Newcastle nonetheless circulated to the colonies a copy of the British Merchandise Marks Act 1862 with a request for information regarding any then existing colonial trade mark laws in 1863. Most of the colonies promised to consider the issue, with many (including, for example, Natal (1864), Leeward Islands, Barbados (1864), British Guiana (1864), Ceylon (1865), Newfoundland (1880)) choosing to adopt similar legislation.[51] Western Australia declined, on the basis of its limited population and trade at that time,[52] and, perhaps for the same reason, no specific law was adopted in many colonies for some time.[53]

Although the British Government had, in 1862, rejected the idea of a trade mark registry, many colonies in addition to some states in America led the way. More specifically, Canada adopted a trade mark registration Act in 1861,[54] Hong Kong and South Australia in 1863, Queensland and Tasmania in 1864, New South Wales in 1865, New Zealand in 1866, New Brunswick in 1867 and Mauritius in 1868.[55] It was not until 1875 that Britain itself would make such a move, and it seems likely that the experiences of the colonies provided evidence that the benefits of such registries outweighed their perceived dangers.[56] Thereafter, perhaps not surprisingly, other colonies followed the lead of the Imperial Parliament.[57] Victoria, for example, established a trade marks register

[48] *Select Committee*, 1862 (n 46) Q 52 (R Jackson); QQ 384 ff (Mappin).

[49] Merchandise Marks Act 1862, 25 & 26 Vict c 88.

[50] *Select Committee*, 1862 (n 46) 141 (QQ 2971–75).

[51] See the survey by GGH Hardingham, *Trade Marks: Notes on the British, Foreign and Colonial Laws Relating Thereto* (London, Stevens & Sons, 1881).

[52] J Finn, 'Particularism Versus Uniformity: factors shaping the development of Australasian intellectual property law in the nineteenth century' (2000) 5 *Australian Journal of Legal History* 113.

[53] Hardingham, *Trade Marks* (n 51) indicates that, as of 1881, there was no law directed at the protection of marks in Gambia, Gold Coast, St Helena, Sierra Leone.

[54] Trade Marks and Designs Act 1861; Trade Marks and Designs Act 1879. See Hayhurst, *Intellectual Property Laws in Canada* (n 11) 27.

[55] DR Shanahan, *Australian Law of Trade Marks and Passing Off*, 2nd edn (Sydney, Law Book Co, 1990) 6.

[56] Trade Marks Registration Act 1875, 38 & 39 Vict c 91 (UK).

[57] Henry Reader Lack would later tell the Herschell Committee that 'Most of the colonies have adopted the Trade Mark Act, 1875 in some shape or another.' *Report of the committee appointed by the Board of Trade to inquire into the duties, organisation, and arrangements of the Patent Office under the Patents, Designs, and Trade Marks Act, 1883, so far as relates*

in 1876,[58] Cape of Good Hope in 1877,[59] Natal in 1885, Ceylon in 1889, Transvaal in 1892. Edmund Johnson observed in 1888 that the law adopted in the Cape and in the Australian states was 'practically … our own law' but that 'Canada is more independent'.[60] South Africa had followed the British reforms with various provincial enactments, and later with its Union Act 9 of 1916, enacted the Patents, Designs, Trade Marks and Copyright Act based on the British Act of 1905.[61] However, it is notable that India remained without a registration system until 1940, despite attempts to introduce such laws in the late 1870s and first decade of the twentieth century.[62]

COPYRIGHT

The one exception to the general devolution of statute-making related to copyright is books. In 1814 the Statute of Anne was extended—without any justification, and probably with very little thought—to give authors and their assignees rights in any 'part of the British Dominions'. Although this seems to have prompted very little reaction,[63] this changed with the passage of the Literary Copyright Act of 1842. Under this Act, if a book was first published in the United Kingdom by an author who was a resident in one of the British possessions, the book would benefit from copyright throughout the British dominions, defined as 'all parts of the United Kingdom of Great Britain and Ireland, the islands of Jersey and Guernsey, all part of the East and West Indies, and all the colonies, settlements and possessions of the Crown which are now or hereafter may be acquired.'[64] The effect of this was that if a book was published in Great Britain and registered at Stationers' Hall in London,[65] protection was secured for the imperial market.

to trade marks and designs; together with minutes of evidence, appendices, &c., C 5350, 81 Parliamentary Papers 37, 7 (Q 137).

58 Trade Mark Registration Act 1876 No 539 (Victoria). Considered in *Wolfe v Hart*, 4 VLR 125 (where the plaintiff had registered various labels, reproduced in the report); *Re Rowley & Pyne ex p Dalton* (1883) 9 VLR L 307, *Re Eno's Trade Mark* (1883) 9 VLR L 335 (with colour illustrations of competing marks).

59 Act No 22 of 1877 (Cape of Good Hope).

60 1888 *Report into Patent Office* (n 56) 7 (Q 137).

61 GC Webster and NS Page, *South African Law of Trade Marks* 4th edn (LexisNexis, binder Issue 12, 31 August 2008) [1.3] ('The provisions of the 1916 Act were based on those of the British Act of 1905, being in many instances couched in the identical terms.').

62 AK Bansal, *Commercial's Law of Trade Marks in India* (New Delhi, Commercial Law Publishers (India) Pvt Ltd, 2001) 35–40.

63 Act to Amend the Several Acts for the Encouragement of Learning, 1814, 54 Geo. 3, c. 156 (Great Britain Empire).

64 Literary Copyright Act, 1842 5 & 6 Vict c 45 (Great Britain Empire).

65 This was required as a preliminary to bringing an action: Literary Copyright Act 1842 s 24.

The colonial response to the 1842 Act was intense.[66] The Canadian colonies led the way. In 1845, the legislative Assembly of Nova Scotia raised concerns that, as a consequence of the 1842 Act, the cost of books had increased because the supply was now restricted to that from the British publishers.[67] It contrasted the prices of books in New York, London and Halifax: Byron's poems, for example was 7 shillings and 6d in New York, £1 in London, and £1 and 6 shillings in Halifax: a ratio of 1:3:4.[68] While it might be acceptable in the United Kingdom that book prices were so high because of the 'wide establishment of circulating libraries, clubs and reading societies, by which a command of fresh literature is obtained on cheap and easy terms', the impact was altogether more serious on a sparsely distributed population with no circulating libraries. In short, the operation of the new Act was detrimental to 'the advancement and refinement of the provincial mind'.[69] Moreover, because of Canada's proximity to the US, where the rights of British copyright owners were not applicable, American reprints were introduced 'in large quantities', the new law was likely 'to encourage an illicit trade, while it yields no protection to the British author or publisher.' Overall, the Nova Scotia House of Assembly objected that 'public feeling is against it ... it is regarded as oppressive and impracticable in its provisions.' The United Assembly of Canada, too, had in 1843 declared that 'a law so repugnant to public opinion cannot and will not be enforced.' Consequently, the Imperial Parliament passed the so-called Foreign Reprints Act 1847, which allowed the suspension of the operation of the 1842 Act as regards 'foreign reprints' where a colony made, by local law, reasonable provision for the protection of British authors.[70] Nineteen colonies took advantage of the Act,[71] typically allowing the imports of

[66] The lack of clubs, book societies and circulating libraries in the colonies meant the high prices had a real impact: *Report of the Royal Commission on Laws and Regulations relating to Home, Colonial and Foreign Copyrights with Minutes of Evidence*, C 2036, 24 Parliamentary Papers 163 [185]. For an exhaustive account of the early period see JJ Barnes, *Authors, Publishers And Politicians: The Quest For An Anglo-American Copyright Agreement, 1815–54* (London, Routledge, 1974) ch 7.

[67] *Colonial copyright. Copies or extracts of correspondence between the Colonial Office, the Board of Trade, and the Government of Canada, which preceded the passing of the Act 10 & 11 Vict. c. 95; and, of any recent correspondence on the subject of that act and of proposals for amending or extending the same, including the letter of the 27th day of July 1869, no. 687–69*, (339), 1872, 43 Parliamentary Papers 277, Disp No 1, 1–6.

[68] For a comparison of prices, see *Royal Commission Evidence* (n 66) 373 (Appendix XI G) (eg the British print of Trollope's *The Prime Minister* was selling at $6.30, compared with the US reprint at 75 cents).

[69] Disp No 1, *Colonial copyright* (n 67) 1–6.

[70] An Act to amend the law relating to the protection in the colonies of works entitled to copyright in the UK (1847) 10 & 11 Vict c 95 s 1.

[71] For the list of colonies, Acts and Orders in Council see: *Copyright (Colonies)*, House of Commons paper, Aug 25, 1857 No 303 (sess 2), (1857) 28 Parliamentary Papers 113. The colonies were: New Brunswick, Nova Scotia, Prince Edward Island, Barbados, Bermuda,

reprints on payment of a 12.5 per cent royalty.[72] Consequently, colonial readers could obtain (unauthorised copies of) books from the US, at considerably below the published price (of authorised copies) in Great Britain.

The 1814 Act related only to 'books', and the 1842 Act was confined to the protection of literary and musical works. Other Acts, giving copyright in engravings and sculpture, had not been extended to the Empire and, in 1862, UK law gave copyright in paintings, drawings, and photographs, but through national rather than imperial legislation. The reason for the decision to confine protection to British shores was not made clear, though experiences with the 1842 Act (and its 1847 derogation) may well have been influential.

Some colonies passed their own legislation on literary works or more generally on other types of works. In fact, in 1832 Lower Canada had already passed a copyright law in 1832,[73] modelled it seems on the US Act of 1831. This covered any 'book or books, map, chart, musical composition, print, cut or engraving', but only conferred copyright where the author was a person 'resident in this Province.' Protection lasted for an initial 28-year term (from recording of the work's title with the Superior Court), but with the possibility of renewal for 14 years if the author was alive at the end of that period, and resident in the Province, 'or being dead, shall have left a widow or child or children, either or all then living.'[74] Protection was conditioned upon registration of title before publication, and inclusion of notice of published copies.[75] Perhaps interestingly, the Act also conferred explicitly a right of first publication of a manuscript in the Province.[76] Nova Scotia produced a similar Act in 1839,[77] though only expressly covering maps, charts, books and prints (and thus not musical compositions, though this may have been implicit), and giving a more limited term of protection of 21 years from recording of the title in the office of the Secretary of the Province, with a possible 14 years renewal if the author 'shall be living, and resident within this Province' (no renewal being provided for 'a widow or child'). As in Lower Canada, protection was conditioned on registration and notice, but in contrast with the Act in Lower Canada, Nova Scotian

Bahamas, Newfoundland, St Christopher, Antigua, St Lucia, Canada, British Guiana, St Vincent, Mauritius, Grenada, Jamaica, Cape of Good Hope, Nevis, and Natal.

72 (1850) 13 & 14 Vict c 6 (Canada), approved by the Order in Council of Dec 12, 1850. By the time the Canadian Act was accepted, measures had already been passed—requiring payment of a duty of 20%—in relation to Nova Scotia, New Brunswick, Prince Edward Island and Newfoundland.

73 An Act for the Protection of Copy Rights, 2 Wm IV c 53 (1832) (Lower Canada).

74 Ibid s 2.

75 Ibid s 3 (publication of renewal in newspapers for 4 weeks); s 4 ('deposit a printed copy of the title' with Superior Court); s 5 (notice 'in the several copies of each and every edition').

76 Ibid s 9.

77 An Act for securing Copy Rights, 2 Vict c 36 (1839) (Nova Scotia).

law required publication of the registration in a newspaper for 12 weeks, and (but not, it seems as a condition) deposit of one copy with each of the two legislative bodies, the House of Assembly and the Legislative Council. The Act also contained a provision protecting manuscripts from unauthorised publication in the Province.[78] When the provinces of Upper and Lower Canada were united in 1840, a new copyright law was adopted in 1841, in almost identical terms to that which had previously been operative in Lower Canada.[79] Following confederation in 1867, Canada re-enacted its copyright law, extending its scope to cover artistic works.

New Zealand adopted a local copyright law for books,[80] modelled on the British Act of 1814: the author was given an initial term of 28 years from publication of a book, but if he was living at the end of that period the right was to continue for the residue of his natural life. The Act contained no explicit restriction on residence, and provided for the payment to a copyright owner who successfully brought a suit against an infringer of double costs (as well as a fixed sum of £50 to be paid to the government). India introduced a Literary Copyright Act in 1847, this time modelled on the British Literary Copyright Act of 1842.[81] Moves to add artistic copyright in India, first in 1864 and then later in the 1870s and 1880s, were unsuccessful.[82]

In 1869, the Victorian Government adopted its own copyright law, and in the 1870s New South Wales and South Australia did likewise.[83] All the Australian Acts protected literary, dramatic and musical productions published locally, as well as artistic works, and designs. Introducing the Bill into the Victorian Legislative Assembly, G Paton Smith, the Attorney General, explained that he did so in response to lobbying by a deputation of creators. The law was needed because the Imperial law had 'no force here, owing to the machinery for carrying them into effect being most expensive and unsatisfactory'. All that was intended to be achieved was to replicate the British

[78] Ibid s 8.

[79] An Act for the Protection of Copy Rights in this Province, (1841) 4 & 5 Vict c 61 (Canada).

[80] An Ordinance to Secure the Copyright of Books to their Authors of Mar 15, 1842 (New Zealand) reproduced in (1844) Parliamentary Papers.

[81] An Act for the encouragement of learning in the territories subject to the government of the East India Company, Act XX of 1847. Documents explaining the background to the Act can be found in the India Office Library (IOL, F4/2256 Board's Collections (1847–48) Vol 2256, 113858–114023, at No 113864).

[82] In 1864, the Government of India was urged to take steps for the improvement and extension of copyright. A bill was drawn up proposing 'that facilities be given for the protection of copyright in pictures, engravings, prints and other similar productions' but was not adopted. Statement of Objects and Reasons: Indian Copyright Bill 1885, from the Gov't of India to the Sec'y of State (June 5, 1885) (IOL, L/PJ/6/156 file 1137 para 1).

[83] Victoria, Copyright Act 1869, 33 Vict No 350; South Australia, Copyright Act 1878, 41 & 42 Vict No 95; and New South Wales, Copyright Act 1878, 42 Vict No 20. See Bowrey, ch 3.

law, and he described the Bill as 'merely a transcript of the English Acts, with the addition of such provisions as will give speedy and inexpensive remedies to persons whose rights are infringed upon.'[84] Even though there was much in the Act that was derived from British laws, there were also considerable variations and the characterisation of the Bills as 'a transcript' of the British laws should be recognised as a rhetorical strategy designed to ease the passage of the Bill through the legislature. Paton Smith acknowledged that the periods of protection given by the Bill differed considerably less than that in the UK, 'so I don't think that the operation of the measure will affect injuriously the interests of the general community.' Books 'first published in the colony of Victoria' were to be protected for 42 years from publication or for the life of the author plus seven years (reflecting the term of the UK's 1842 Act),[85] designs for two to three years,[86] but a painting, drawing, sculpture or engraving by a British subject or author resident in Victoria was only protected for 14 years and a photograph for only three years (the latter two terms being considerably less that that of life plus seven years provided in Britain by the Fine Art Copyright Act 1862).[87] In addition, engravings and sculptures, like other works, were required to be registered,[88] and a unique provision allowed for copying of any painting, drawing, work of sculpture or photograph 'in or belonging to the Museum of Industry and Art, the National Gallery or the Melbourne Library'.[89] The Victorian Act was followed quite closely in South Australia in 1878.[90] The New South Wales version, passed in 1879, had similar coverage but was differently organised (designs placed third, rather than first).[91] Western Australia did not adopt an equivalent substantive law until 1895.

The Cape of Good Hope Act of 1873 had its own peculiarities.[92] For one, it had a preamble explaining its purpose, namely 'to protect the rights of authors in this Colony in respect of their works and to afford encouragement to the production of literary works of lasting benefit to the Colony.' The Act conferred protection ('the sole and exclusive liberty of printing or otherwise

[84] (1869) 8 *Parliamentary Debates (Victoria)* 1005 (June 9, 1869). See also at 1837 (second reading). Paton Smith seems to have been particularly concerned that protection be afforded to designers, but also referred to cases of 'piracy' of plays.

[85] Victoria, Copyright Act 1869, 33 Vict No 350 s 14.

[86] Ibid s 3.

[87] Ibid s 32.

[88] Ibid s 38.

[89] Ibid s 56.

[90] One variation related to the term of copyright in designs. In addition, the South Australian Act contained no exception relating to the copying of works in the state galleries.

[91] New South Wales, Copyright Act 1878, 42 Vict No 20. It contained, in s 55, a similar exemption from liability for copying 'any painting drawing work of sculpture or photograph in or belonging to the Museum Academy of Art or any art gallery wholly or partly endowed from public funds or to the Free Public Library or the Library of the University of Sydney.'

[92] Act to Protect and Regulate the Rights of Authors in Respect of their Works, No 2 (1873) (Cape of Good Hope).

multiplying copies of any book') on the author and his assigns for the period of the authors life plus five years, or 30 years. For works first published after the author's death the term was 30 years, the rights to be 'the property of the proprietor of the author's manuscript'.

The variations in copyright operative in the various self-governing dominions in the second half of the nineteenth century thus reveal considerable variations. Compared to the sorts of variations in modern copyright law discussed in this volume by Ong, Ricketson and Zemer, the variations in breadth (whether covering just books, as in India and the Cape of Good Hope, or other works, as in South Australia, Victoria and New Zealand), and term (from fixed periods of three, 14, 21, 28, 42 years, possibly with renewal, to life plus five, and life plus seven) seem significant and substantial.

CASE LAW: PASSING OFF

In the fields of the common law, in the sense of the law developed by the courts, divergences are less easy to identify. The most important of the common law actions in the late nineteenth century was the action that has come to be known as the action for 'passing off', the core principles of which were established in the case law of Lord Langdale MR in the 1830s and 40s, but which developed in earnest only after 1850. Here, it seems, that most of the British colonies soon after recognised such an action, and drew heavily on case law from the English courts. The Irish courts did so at least from the 1860s,[93] some of the Canadian courts from at least 1867,[94] the Indian courts from 1865,[95] and the Victorian courts from 1870,[96] and even did so when it came to applying passing off rules to the trade mark

[93] *Kinahan v Bolton* (1863) 15 Ir Ch 75; *Foot v Lea* (1850) 13 Ir Eq R 484.

[94] *Davis v Kennedy* (1867) 13 Gt 523 (Court of Chancery of Upper Canada). In *Canada Publishing Co v Gage* (1885) 11 SCR 306 an Ontarian case involving the law of passing off in which counsel relied on English precedent (though not directly on passing off) and *Sebastian on the Law of Trade Marks,* and the Supreme Court of Canada too drew on English precedent (on passing off).

[95] *Orr-Ewing v Chooneeloll Muliick* (1865) Cor 150; *Graham & Co v Kerr, Dods & Co* (1869) 3 Beng LR App 4; *Ralli v Fleming* (1878) ILR 3 Cal 417 (Calcutta Appeal Court). In *Ralli*, for example, the Court found trade mark infringement where the defendant sold cloth bearing the mark '2008' which had been used by the plaintiff in such a way that the cloth was known in the market as 'do hazar ât'. All the case law cited to the court—some 35 cases—was English in origin, though neither judge found it necessary to cite any authority.

[96] *Hostetter v Anderson* (1870) 1 VR Eq 7 (holding defendant liable for re-selling its bitters in bottles marked with the plaintiff's name, Hostetter, in the glass. Although the bottles were probably sold by the plaintiff, and the defendant used a label, nevertheless—'though with some doubt'—Molesworth J granted relief on the basis of *Welch v Knott* (1857) 4 K & J 757, 4 Jur NS 330); *Wolfe v Hart* (1878) 4 VLR 125 (combination square bottle (with raised letters) and labels in blue ink, wrapped in paper of an identical shade of yellow with a label in red ink attached, produced 'striking similarity').

registration system.[97] In 1873, Ludlow and Jenkins had written that '[t]he English law of trade-marks is the parent of the law of Scotland and the United States'.[98] Contemporaries clearly perceived the English law of passing off as establishing the principles operative throughout all the common law jurisdictions.[99] Clearly, there was access to the relevant law reports, as well as frequent citations to texts published in England (particularly after 1870), such as Adams,[100] Sebastian (1879),[101] and later Kerly (1894).[102] Sebastian's *Digest* itself was a digest not just of cases from the English courts, but also those of Scotland, Ireland, the United States and 'the colonies'. A decision of the Trinidad Supreme Court from 1874 even made its way into Sebastian's *Digest*.[103]

Despite the common approach, and the tendency to cite English authorities, it would nevertheless be dangerous to assume that the laws were uniform. Because of the way that 'common law' develops over time (and at this stage it was developing quickly in England), it is hard today to appreciate the nature of any differences that might have been perceived between common law countries at any particular point in time (synchronically). But we suspect, as we sense Bowrey does in her contribution,[104] that the 'methodology' of the common law was so imprecise as to enable colonial courts to 'discover' versions of the common that were (within a range of limits) in accordance with local conceptions of what was appropriate, even if lip-service was consistently paid to the notion of precedent and the idea of a unitary common law. It is clear, however, that in some cases, the colonial courts developed the law, and, in doing so, were willing to distinguish English authority. So, for example, in *Hennessy v White*,[105] the Victorian Supreme Court held that

[97] *Re Eno's Trade Mark* (1883) 9 VLR L 335 (applying *Johnston v Orr-Ewing* 7 App Cas 224). Following federation in 1901, early Australian High Court cases, such as *WH Burford and Sons Ltd v G Mowling and Son* (1909) 8 CLR 212 (HCA) and *Henry Clay & Bock & Co Ltd v Eddy* (1915) 19 CLR 641 (HCA) relied heavily on English case law.

[98] H Ludlow and H Jenkins, *A Treatise on the Law of Trade-Marks and Trade-Names* (London, W. Maxwell, 1873) iv, and 80 ('The law as to trade-marks in Scotland is substantially identical with that of England, and the authorities cited in reference to such cases in the Scotch courts are almost entirely English.'). The Scottish position on this is discussed later in the Chapter.

[99] For New Zealand, see *Littlejohn and Son v Mulligan* (1885) 3 NZLR 446 (Richmond J) (Supreme Court, Wellington).

[100] FM Adams, *A Treatise on the Law of Trade Marks* (London, 1874), referred to in, for example, *Barsalou v Darling* (1881) IX SCR 677 (Supreme Court of Canada).

[101] LB Sebastian, *A Digest of Cases of Trade Mark, Trade Name, Trade Secret, Goodwill etc* (London, Stevens & Sons, 1879), cited by counsel, for example, in *Re Rowley & Pyne ex p Dalton* (1883) 9 VLR 307, 309.

[102] DM Kerly, *The Law of Trade-Marks and Trade Name, and Merchandise Marks* (London, Sweet & Maxwell, 1894) (with further editions in 1901, 1908, 1913, 1923 and 1927).

[103] *Siegert v Ehlers* (1874) (Trinidad Supreme Court) in Sebastian, *A Digest of Cases of Trade Mark* (n 101) [432], [259].

[104] Bowrey, ch 3, 46.

[105] *Hennessy v White* (1869) 6 WW & a'B, Eq 216 (Supreme Court of Victoria).

the defendant was not to use a similar get-up to give the impression it was selling a brandy manufactured by the plaintiff that was the same quality as brandy made and bottled by the plaintiff. The Court boldly distinguished English authority,[106] adopting a line which would ultimately be affirmed by the English House of Lords famously in the case of *Spalding v Gamage*,[107] 40 years later. In another case concerning Hennessy brandy,[108] Molesworth J distinguished the English case of *Williams v Osborne* on the basis that it was reported in the Law Times and so did 'not bear the same stamp of authenticity as the contemporaneous reports.'

For the jurisdictions which did not operate exclusively with the common law, Quebec, Scotland, Ceylon and South Africa, the apparent uniformity may have disguised latent divergences. In bi-jural Canada, the laws of passing off were inevitably influenced not just by English but also French law.[109] Although the Canadian Supreme Court[110] embraced English authorities, in *Brasalou v Darling*,[111] hearing an appeal from Lower Canada, Taschereau J relied on both French and English authorities.[112] While, as we have already noted, Ludlow and Jenkins saw the law in Scotland as a mere 'derivative' of English case law, in truth the Dutch-Roman origin of Scottish law gave it a different flavour.[113] As MacQueen has noted in this volume,[114] although the Scots law of passing off would largely produce the same result as its southern neighbour, Scots law is grounded in personal rights and may be attributed to Stair as early as 1681 in his *Institutions of the Law of Scotland*.[115] Dutch-Roman tradition also informed the law

[106] *Farina v Silverlock* (1855) 1 H &M 259.

[107] *Spalding v Gamage* (1915) 32 RPC 273.

[108] *Hennessey v Hogan* (1869) 6 WW & a'B Eq 225 (defendant not entitled to utilise plaintiff's labels on goods that came from plaintiff in bulk but which defendant was bottling). The *Williams* case, which Molesworth J distinguished, was reported at 13 LTNS 498.

[109] In the province of Quebec the law relating to property and civil rights is derived from the French civil law tradition: Quebec Act of 1774, 14 Geo 3 c 83 arts VIII–X. Nevertheless, something similar to 'passing off' can be found in the general liability provision of the Civil Code of Lower Canada (Quebec) and its associated French and Quebec authorities including case law: Art 1053: *Lambert Pharmacal Co v Palmer & Sons Ltd* (1912) 21 Que KB 451, 2 DLR 358 [56]. Art 1457 of the current Code—*Husqvarna Corporation inc c Service de jardin et forêt enr* (2009) QCCS 283; Nadeau and Nadeau, *Traité pratique de la responsabilité civile délictuelle* (Montreal: Wilson Lafleur 1971) 221 as cited in *Ciba-Geigy Canada Ltd v Apotex Inc* [1992] 3 SCR 120 [37].

[110] The Supreme Court was created in 1875 as a general court of appeal for both common and civil law jurisdictions.

[111] (1881) 9 SCR 677.

[112] Although the case involved a registered trade mark, Henry J argued that the Canadian statute which provided for the registry of trade-marks was 'but an affirmance of the common law on the subject'.

[113] Eg: Q Stewart, 'The Law of Passing Off—a Scottish perspective' [1983] 3 *European Intellectual Property Reports* 64.

[114] Ch 1, MacQueen, ch 2, 42–43.

[115] Sir James Dalrymple of Stair, *Institutions of the Law of Scotland* (Edinburgh 1681) 1.9.4.

of delict in South Africa.[116] 'Passing off' cases there were located within the general liabilities principles of *lex Aquilia*[117] and the law of 'unfair' or 'unlawful competition' would be left deliberately unconstrained by any fixed boundaries.[118] Although the terminology of 'passing off' was utilised in South African jurisprudence,[119] which often drew on case law from the common law,[120] it would be strange to think of a legal system which *also* recognised 'unfair competition' as anything but different in scope from English common law.

CALLS FOR UNIFORMITY

These divergences in the intellectual property laws of the various British colonies in the nineteenth century gave way, in the late nineteenth and early twentieth centuries, to calls for uniformity. In contrast with the traditional story of gradual movement towards independence, we see paradoxically greater interest in uniformity towards the end of the nineteenth century. This is rather surprising, given the miserable experience of Imperial copyright law between 1842 and 1911. Nevertheless, as the nineteenth century drew to a close, increasing interest was expressed in aligning the laws of Britain and the colonies in other fields of intellectual property. If in 1852, devolution of law-making was, according to Thomas Webster, a 'judicious arrangement', by 1900 it was increasingly viewed as 'anomalous'. Speaking of diversity in patents, Gerald Balfour, president of the Board of Trade, would remark in 1901 that '[t]he extraordinary multiplicity of colonial patent laws forms one of the most curious anomalies of the British patent system.'[121] The assumption that the colonial laws were part of the 'British patent system' represents a telling shift.

In 1887 the first of a number of periodic colonial conferences was held, with representatives from the 'self governing dominions' of Australia, [Cape of Good Hope] and Canada, as well as from New Zealand.[122] Alfred

[116] Taken to the Cape of Good Hope in 1652 by the colonists of the Dutch East India Company.

[117] *Atlas Organic Fertilizers (Pty) Ltd v Pikkewyn Ghwano (Pty) Ltd* 1981(2) SA 173 [TPD].

[118] *Geary & Son (Pty) Ltd v Gove* 1964 (1) SA 434 (A); *Dun & Bradstreet (Pty) Ltd v SA Merchants Combined Credit Bureau (Cape) (Pty) Ltd* 1968 (1) SA 209 (C); PQR Boberg, *The Law of Delict* (Cape Town, Juta & Company Ltd, 1984) vol 1, 149; *Schultz v Butt* 1986 3 SA 667 (A); GC Webster and NS Page, *South African Law of Trade Marks* (n 61) [15.2] et seq.

[119] Eg: *Policansky Bros Ltd v L & H Policansky* 1935 AD 89; *Lorimar Productions Inc v Sterling Clothing Manufacturers (Pty) Ltd* 1981 (3) SA 1129(T).

[120] Eg: *Pasquali Cigarette Co Ltd v Diaconicolas & Capsopolus* 1905 TS 472; *Patlansky & Co., Ltd v Patlansky Bros* 1914 TPD 475.

[121] *The Times*, 29 August 1901 6.

[122] WK Hancock, *Survey of British Commonwealth Affairs* vol 1, *Problems of Nationality, 1918–1936* (London, OUP, 1937), 30 (describing the 1887 conference as 'A motley assembly of 121 delegates').

Deakin, future premier of the Australian Commonwealth, and then Chief Secretary of Victoria, spoke in favour of a uniform patent law, so that a patent could be granted in one colony and be applicable throughout the Empire. Although little progress was made immediately with patent reform, the matter returned to the agenda early in the twentieth century when Gerald Balfour responded to a Parliamentary question on patent reform by bemoaning the 'legislative fecundity' that had given rise to a different patent law in every colony and urging reform of the situation 'which clearly calls for redress'. Although it might not be immediately feasible, he (like Deakin before him) suggested 'the ideal obviously to be aimed at is an Imperial patent covering the whole Empire'.[123] This would give 'practical expression to the desire for closer union among the scattered units of the empire.'

Balfour's idea was discussed further at the Colonial Conference of 1902 and with greater attentiveness in 1907. The 1907 Conference resolved that 'it is desirable that His Majesty's Government, after full consideration with the self-governing Dominions should endeavour to provide for such uniformity as may be practicable in the granting and protection of trade marks and patents.' Further supportive resolutions followed in 1911, but it was not until after the First World War that the matter would receive serious consideration, at a conference in 1922. The progress of the idea of an 'Empire patent', and its ultimate failure, has been thoroughly described by Chris Wadlow in an article in the *Intellectual Property Quarterly*.[124] For present purposes, the initiative is of interest in that it indicates a desire for greater uniformity precisely at a time when the self-governing dominions had increasing independence.

Attempts at gaining uniformity in copyright law were more successful. After years of stagnation with domestic copyright reform, the 1908 Berlin Revision of the Berne Convention presented Britain with a choice amongst parting from the colonies, parting from the international copyright, and finding some sort of agreement with the colonies that would enable ratification. In 1909 a Committee reporting to Parliament under the chairmanship of Lord Gorell approved the provisions of the revised Convention. It 'recommended the passage of a consolidating and amending Act covering the whole subject of copyright' stating that 'it would be a great advantage if the British law were placed on a plain and uniform basis, and that basis were one which is common so far as practicable to the nations which join the Convention.'[125] The Gorell Committee simultaneously emphasised the desirability of uniformity through the Empire. A conference of colonial representatives was summoned to London and in 1910, conference agreement

[123] *The Times*, 29 August 1901.

[124] C Wadlow, 'The British Empire Patent 1901–1923: the Global Patent that never was' (2006) IPQ 311.

[125] *Report on the Committee on the Law of Copyright*, Cmd 4976 (1909) 7.

was achieved that paved the way for reform. Uniformity of copyright was no longer to be imposed: the dominions at least were to be free to choose whether or not to adopt what would become the 1911 Act with (or without) modifications.

Robert Burrell has examined Australia's pivotal role in the Colonial Conference of 1910, and questioned why the Commonwealth government should have been so keen to support the notion of imperial unity in copyright. Amongst the several reasons he offers, including the idea that many Australians identified with Britain (so-called 'Australian-Britons'), is the widespread support for 'imperial federation'. Key figures in Australian copyright politics—Alfred Deakin, Lord Tennyson (Australia's representative at the colonial conference) and Harrison Moore, Dean of the Law School at Melbourne—were members of the Imperial Federation League, established in 1884.[126] Deakin, we have already noted, proposed the idea of an imperial patent in 1887, so it is entirely unsurprising that two decades later he should back proposals for an imperial copyright regime.

CONCLUSION

This inevitably rather superficial and positivistic overview suggests that, at least in the late nineteenth and early twentieth century, at the high water mark of British colonialism, the intellectual property laws in the common law countries were anything but uniform. The common law of intellectual property was not then—and probably was never—monolithic. There were attempts at agreed uniformity amongst those within the British Empire, the most successful being the Copyright Act 1911, which the self-governing dominions adopted (in Australia and Newfoundland in 1912; New Zealand in 1913; in India, by proclamation in 1912 but with variations, in 1914; in South Africa in 1916; and in the case of Canada, in 1924 (though retaining a voluntary registration system and compulsory licensing of foreign works)).[127] Outside the field of copyright, there was certainly a tendency to copy the British law, but there were many examples of deviation. And there were cases where colonies copied from one another (where there was no British model) and even where the British government was urged to copy from the colony.[128] These processes of copying were informed by shared

[126] 'Imperialist federationist argument, therefore, was a constant background to the imperial conference' : WK Hancock, *Survey of British Commonwealth Affairs* Vol. 1, *Problems of Nationality, 1918–1936* (London, OUP, 1937) 35.

[127] On the Canadian variations, see S Bannerman, 'Canada and the Berne Convention 1886–1971' (PhD Thesis, Carleton University, Ottawa, 2009) 258–78.

[128] J Finn, '"Should we not profit from such experiments when we could?": Australasian Legislative Precedents in British Parliamentary Debates' (2007) 28(1) *Journal of Legal History* 31–56.

language, shared legal traditions, access to common legal resources (in the form of law reports) and operated through dense networks of bureaucratic, social, educational and commercial connections. Ideas of legal protection would migrate from one place to another, as a result of Colonial Office circulars, telegraphic despatches, the movement of colonial officials from one colony to another, through newspaper networks, publications and journals, legal textbooks, case reports, learned societies, professional associations, chambers of commerce, as well as the migration of individuals, back and forth. And, of course, once one country had given the matter consideration, others often followed the lead. Sometimes such copying led courts to defer to authorities from elsewhere, particularly the United Kingdom. For example, in interpreting the Trade-Marks Act 1940, the Indian Supreme Court found 'the law of Trade Marks adopted in our Act merely reproduces the English law with only slight modifications, a reference to the judicial decisions on the corresponding section of the English Act is apposite and must be helpful.'[129]

The divergences in intellectual property laws amongst the common law countries today might seem no more extensive than the divergences that existed in the colonial era, particularly the late nineteenth century. Of course, politically and legally, the relationships between most of the countries in the common law system have changed radically. Most of the countries have been for some decades independent politically, and fewer and fewer countries look to the Privy Council as the ultimate appellate court. But the famous 'winds of change' seem to have produced less divergence, at least in the field of intellectual property, than one might have expected. In the introduction, we have tried to draw out reasons from the essays in this collection for the limited divergences that have emerged, particular in the last 50 years.

[129] *Registrar of Trade Marks v Ashok Chandra Rakhit Ltd* AIR 538, AIR 1955 SC 558 (2) SCR 252.

David Vaver: Curriculum Vitae

Born:	28 March 1946, Czech Republic
Education etc:	Auckland Grammar School, Junior University Scholar 1963; BA, French, 1968, University of Auckland
	LLB (Hons), 1970; University of Auckland (Fowlds Memorial Prize for top graduating law student)
	JD, 1971, cum laude, University of Chicago (Fulbright & Commonwealth Scholar & New Zealand Postgraduate Scholar)
	MA, 1998, University of Oxford
	Admitted as barrister & solicitor, New Zealand, 1970; non-practising since 1978

TEACHING POSTS

1968	Tutor in Law, University of Auckland
1972–78	Lecturer in Law (1972–74), Senior Lecturer in Law (1975–78), University of Auckland
	Research Director, then Director, Legal Research Foundation Inc
1978–85	Associate Professor of Law, University of British Columbia
1985–98	Professor of Law, Osgoode Hall Law School of York University, Toronto
1998–2007	Reuters Professor of Intellectual Property & Information Technology Law, University of Oxford
	Director, Oxford Intellectual Property Research Centre (OIPRC), St Peter's College
	Professorial Fellow, St Peter's College

2008–	Emeritus Professor, University of Oxford
	Emeritus Fellow, St Peter's College
2009–	Professor of Intellectual Property Law, Osgoode Hall Law School of York University, Toronto

OTHER POSTS

1968–70	Russell, McVeagh, McKenzie, Bartleet & Co, Barristers & Solicitors, Auckland: law clerk, then barrister & solicitor
2008–	Associate member, Chambers of Michael Silverleaf QC, 11 South Square, Gray's Inn

VISITING POSTS

1971–72	Visiting Assistant Professor of Law, University of British Columbia
1982–83	Visiting Professor of Law, Osgoode Hall Law School
1988	Visiting Professor of Law, Monash University
1990	Parsons Visiting Fellow in Law, University of Sydney
2000	New Zealand Law Foundation inaugural Distinguished Visiting Fellow at the Universities of Otago, Canterbury, Victoria, Waikato and Auckland
2005	Yong Shook Lin inaugural Visiting Professor in Intellectual Property Law, National University of Singapore
2007	James L Lewtas Visiting Professor, Osgoode Hall Law School

JOURNALS

Intellectual Property Journal, Founder & Editor-in-Chief (1984–98, 2010–); Consultant Editor (1998–2008)
University of Oxford Commonwealth Law Journal, Faculty Advisor (2001–08)
IP&IT Law, Editorial Board (2003–)
International Journal of Intellectual Property Management, Editorial Board (2006–)
Journal of Law & Information Science, Editorial Board (2007–)
Intellectual Property Quarterly, Editorial Board (1998–2000)
Supreme Court Law Review [Canada], Contributing Editor, Contract Law developments (1985–87)
New Zealand Recent Law, Assistant Editor (1973–78)

SOCIETIES, COMMITTEES, ETC

Intellectual Property Advisory Committee reporting to UK Minister of Trade & Industry, then Minister of Science, Member (2001–05)
Intellectual Property Institute, Member, Council of Experts (1998–); Board and Council member (2001–)
Royal Society Working Group on Intellectual Property, Member (2001–03), producing Royal Society Report, *Keeping science open: the effects of intellectual property policy on the conduct of science* (April 2003)
Creative Commons, UK Legal Advisory Board, Member (2004–05)
Oxford Internet Institute, Management Committee, Member (2001–05)
Intellectual Property Advisory Group, University of Oxford, Member (1998–2002), Chair (2002–07)
Canadian Bar Association/Patent & Trademark Institute of Canada, Joint Sub-committee on Copyright Legislation, Member (1986–98)
Uniform Law Conference of Canada Sub-committee on the Uniform Sale of Goods Act 1982 (adopted by the Uniform Law Conference of Canada), Member appointed by British Columbia Law Reform Commission (1979–81)
Auckland District Law Society, Public Issues & Law Reform Sub-committee, Member (1974–76)
Chartered Institute of Patent Agents, Associate Member (2000–07)
Intellectual Property Institute of Canada (formerly Patent & Trademark Institute of Canada), Academic Member (1986–)
International Trademark Association, Academic Member (2005–)

CONSULTANCIES

Advisor to the Department of Canadian Heritage on Copyright Law Revision (1988–98)
Consultant to Canadian Department of Industry on reform of Patented Medicines (Notice of Compliance) Regulations (1997–98)
House of Commons (Canada) Standing Committee on Industry. Moderator of submissions on a Review of the Patent Act in respect of Patented and Generic Pharmaceutical Drugs (1997)
Department of Industry (Canada), Advisor on Quinquennial Report on future copyright policy & planning, *Supporting culture & innovation: report on the provisions & operation of the Copyright Act* (2002)
Commissioners of Competition and Patents and Departments of Canadian Heritage and Industry: Co-editor (with Michael J Trebilcock & Marcel Boyer) of *Interface between competition law & intellectual property* (2006–08)

PUBLICATIONS

Books

Competition Policy and Intellectual Property Law (Toronto, Irwin Law, 2009), co-edited with Marcel Boyer and Michael Trebilcock

Intellectual Property Rights: Critical Concepts in Law (London, Routledge, 2006), 5 vols (sole editor)

Intellectual Property in the New Millennium (Cambridge, CUP, 2004), co-edited with Lionel Bently

Principles of Copyright Law (Geneva, World Intellectual Property Organization, 2002), co-edited with Pierre Sirinelli and Hossam Loutfi (plan conceived by Victor Nabhan)

Copyright Law (Toronto: Irwin Law, 2000)

Intellectual Property Law: Copyright, Patents, Trade-marks (Concord, Ontario, Irwin Law, 1997)

Articles

'Being Old and Obvious: Apotex v Sanofi-Synthelabo in the Supreme Court' (2010) 3:1 Osgoode Hall Review of Law and Policy 3; www.ohrlp.ca;

'Recent Copyright Developments' (2010), Intellectual Property Journal (forthcoming);

'To Serve and Protect: The Challenge for Intellectual Property Law', in L Boy, J Drexl, C Godt, R Hilty and B Remiche (eds), Technology and Competition — Technologie et Concurrence: Contributions in Honour of Hanns Ullrich (Brussels, Larcier, 2009) 379; earlier version available at http://www.chathamhouse.org.uk/files/13936_il230409pdf

'Reforming Intellectual Property Law: An Obvious and Not-so-obvious Agenda: The Stephen Stewart Lecture for 2008' [2009] Intellectual Property Quarterly (Issue 2) 143; abridged version (2009) 38 CIPA Jo (No 1) 25; available at www.iposgoode.ca/events-archive/; www.ip-institute.org.uk/

'Does intellectual property have personality?' in R Zimmerman and N Whitty (eds) *Rights of personality in Scots law: a comparative perspective* (Dundee, University of Dundee Press, 2009) ch 8

'Chocolate, Copyright, Confusion: Intellectual Property and the Supreme Court of Canada' (2008) 1 Osgoode Hall Review of Law Policy 5, www.ohrlp.ca; webcast mms://media.osgoode.yorkuca/events/LewtasLecture-Oct242007wmv

'Brand culture: trade marks, marketing and consumption'—responding legally to Professor Schroeder's paper', in L Bently, J Davis and J Ginsburg (eds), *Trade Marks and Brands: An Interdisciplinary Critique* (Cambridge, CUP, 2008) ch 8

'Copyright and the Internet: From Owner Rights and User Duties to User Rights and Owner Duties?' (2007) 57:3 Case Western Law Review 731; based on webcast at www.law.case.edu/centers/lta/webcastasp?dt=20061110&type=wmv&a=1

'Does the public understand intellectual property law? Do lawyers?' in *Meredith Lectures 2006: Intellectual Property at the Edge: New Approaches to IP in a Transsystemic World* (Y Blais & Faculty of Law, McGill University, 2007), ch 1; reprinted in K Grau-Kuntz & D Borges Barbosa (eds), *Ensaios sobre o Direito Imaterial: Estudos Dedicados a Newton Silveira (Essays on Immaterial Right: Studies Dedicated to Newton Silveira)* (Rio de Janeiro, Editora Lumen Juris, 2009) 375

'Popping Patented Pills: Europe and a Decade's Dose of TRIPs' [2006] European Intellectual Property Reports 282 (with Shamnad Basheer); in French translation as 'Overdose de medicaments brevets: l'Europe dans un "TRIPS" depuis dix ans' in Bernard Remiche & Jorge Kors (eds), *L'Accord ADPIC: dix ans après* (Brussels, Éds Larcier, 2007) 129

'Recent Trends in European Trademark Law: Senses, Shapes and Sensation' (2005) 95 Trademark Reporter 895

'Unconventional and Well-Known Trade Marks' [2005] Singapore Journal of Legal Studies 1; reprinted in Dr AV Narsimha Rao (ed), *Trademarks: Concepts and Contexts* (Hyderabad, ICFAI University Press, 2009) 1

'The Problems of Biotechnologies for Intellectual Property Law' (2004), Cahiers Prop Intell (Hors Série: Mélanges Victor Nabhan) 375

'Le concept d'invention en droit des brevets: bilan et perspective', in M Vivant and J-M Bruguière (eds), *Protéger les inventions de demain: Biotechnologies, logiciels et méthodes d'affaires* (Paris, Institut National de la Propriété Industrielle, *la Documentation française*, 2003) 271

'Canada's Intellectual Property Framework: A Comparative Overview' (2003), 17 IPJ 125; available at http://strategis.ic.gc.ca/epic/internet/inippd-dppinsf/vwapj/01-EN%20Vaverpdf/$file/01-EN%20Vaverpdf

'Defining and rewarding invention: a review and a modest proposal for patent law', in P Mirfield and R Smith (eds), *Essays for Colin Tapper* (Lexis/Nexis, 2003) 182, slightly revised as 'Invention in Patent Law: A Review and A Modest Proposal' (2003), 11 IJLIT 286

'Need Intellectual Property Be Everywhere?: Against Ubiquity and Uniformity' (2002) 25 Dalhousie Law Journal 1

'The Copyright Mixture in a Mixed Legal System: Fit for Human Consumption?' [2002] Juridical Review 101; (2001) 5:3 Electronic Journal of Comparative Law www.ejcl.org/52/art52–3html

'Creating a Fair Intellectual Property System for the 21st Century' (2001), 10 Otago Law Reports 1; modified version, 'Recreating a Fair Intellectual Property System for the 21st Century' (2001), 15 IPJ 123

'Intellectual Property Law: The State of the Art' (2000) 116 LQR 621; republished in (2001), 32 VUWLR 1 (Special Issue on Intellectual Property) and S Frankel and G Smith (eds) *Essays on Intellectual Property Law and Policy* (VUWLR, 2001), 1, wwwnzliiorg/nz/journals/VUWLRev/2001/2html; published in Chinese translation (trans by Li Yufeng) in (2007) 4:100 Intellectual Property 88

'Copyright in Europe: The Good, The Bad and the Harmonised' (1999) 10 Australian Intellectual Property Journal 185; slightly modified as 'Copyright Developments in Europe: The Good, The Bad and the Harmonized' in Niva Elkin-Koren and Neil W Netanel (eds), *The Commodification of Information* (Kluwer Law Int'l, 2002), 223; translated into Ukranian in Y Kapitsa (ed), *Copyright and Related Rights in Europe* (2008)

'Moral Rights: The Irish Spin' (1999) 3:3 Irish Intellectual Property Review 3

'Moral Rights Yesterday, Today and Tomorrow' (1999) 7 IJLIT 270; http://eprintsoulsoxacuk:81/inttec/hdb/Volume_07/Issue_03/abstracts/070270sgm

'Copyright Law: Recent Canadian Developments' (1998) 16 Australian Business Law Reports 412

'The Copyright Amendments of 1997' (1997) 12 Intellectual Property Journal 53

'Copyright in Canada: The New Millennium' (1997) 12 IPJ 117; in French translation (by Élisabeth Guéry) as 'La loi sur le droit d'auteur au Canada: le troisième millénaire' (1997) 10 Cahiers Prop Intell 91

'Copyright and the State in Canada and the United States' (1996) 10 IPJ 187; earlier version www.lexum.umontreal.ca/conf/dac/en/vaver/vaverhtml

'Rejuvenating Copyright' (1996) 75 Canadian Bar Review 69

'Rejuvenating Copyright Digitally' in *Symposium of Digital Technology and Copyright* (Ottawa, Ministry of Public Works and Services, 1995) 1

'The Exclusive Licence in Copyright' (1995) 9 IPJ 163

'Abridgments and Abstracts: Copyright Implications' [1995] European Intellectual Property Reports 225

'Limitations in Intellectual Property: 'The Time is out of Joint'' (1994) 73 Can Bar Rev 451; www.cba.org/cba_barreview/

'Translation and Copyright: A Canadian Focus' [1994] EIPR 159

'Report on Moral Rights: Canada' in Association Littéraire et Artistique Internationale *Le droit moral de l'auteur/The moral right of the author* Congress of Antwerp 19–24 September 1993 (Paris, ALAI, 1994) 207

'Copyright in Legal Documents' (1993) 31 Osgoode Hall Law Journal 661

'Unsettling Insurance Settlements: Of Unconscionability and Other Things' (1992) 50 The Advocate 749

'Keeping Secrets Legally Speaking' (1992) 13 Advocacy Quarterly 334

'Can Intellectual Property be Taken to Satisfy a Judgment Debt?' (1991) 6 Banking and Finance Law Review 255

'Dramatic and Musical Reproductions and Performances: Copyright and Performers' Rights and their Implications for Educators' (1991) 6 IPJ 239

'Copyright Phase 2: The New Horizon' (1990) 6 IPJ 37; in French translation as 'Le droit d'auteur phase 2: De nouveaux horizons' (1989) 2 Cahiers Prop Intell 83

'Intellectual Property Today: Of Myths and Paradoxes' (1990) 69 Can Bar Rev 98; slightly modified as 'Some Agnostic Observations on Intellectual Property' (1991) 6 IPJ 125; reprinted in P Drahos (ed) *Intellectual Property* (Dartmouth, Ashgate, 1999) 485 ff

'What is a Trade Secret?' in RT Hughes QC (ed) *Trade Secrets* (Toronto, Law Society of Upper Canada, 1990) ch 1

'Canada Starts Reforming its Copyright Law' (1989) 10 Journal of Media Law and Practice 58

'Canada' in MB Nimmer and PE Geller (eds) *International Copyright Law and Practice* 2 vols (New York, Matthew Bender, 1988 with annual releases 1989–98)

'Authors' Moral Rights and the Copyright Law Review Committee's Report: W(h)ither Such Rights Now?' (1988) 14 Monash University Law Review 284

'Unconscionability: Panacea Analgesic or Loose Can(n)on?' (1988) 14 Canadian Business Law Journal 40

'Developments in Contract Law: The 1985–86 Term' (1987) 9 Supreme Court Law Review 181

'Authors' Moral Rights — Reform Proposals in Canada: Charter or Barter of Rights for Creators?' (1987) 25 Osgoode Hall LJ 749

'Copyright in Foreign Works: Canada's International Obligations' (1987) 66 Can Bar Rev 76

'The National Treatment Requirements of the Berne and Universal Copyright Conventions' (1986) 17 IIC 577 (Part I) 715 (Part II); in German translation (by Thomas Dietz) as 'Die Inländerbehandlung nach der Berner Übereinkunft und dem Welturheberrechtsabkommen' (1988) GRUR Int 191

'Developments in Contract Law: The 1984–85 Term' (1986) 8 Sup Ct LRev 109

'Chief Justice Laskin and the Law of Contracts' (1985) 7 Sup Ct LRev 131

'Summary Expungement of Registered Trademarks on the Ground of Non-Use' (1983) 21 Osgoode Hall LJ 17

'*Snow v The Eaton Centre:* Wreaths on Sculpture Prove Accolade for Artists' Moral Rights' (1983) 8 Can Bus LJ 81

'Authors' Moral Rights in Canada' (1983) 14 IIC 329

'What's Mine is Not Yours: Commercial Appropriation of Personality under the Privacy Acts of British Columbia Manitoba and Saskatchewan' (1981) 15 University of British Columbia Law Review 241

'Civil Liability for Taking or Using Trade Secrets in Canada' (1981) 5 Can Bus LJ 253

'Trade Secrets: A Commonwealth Perspective' [1979] EIPR 301

'What's In a Name? Rights in Respect of the Commercial Exploitation of Real and Fictional Characters' [1979] Annual Industrial Property Law 211

'New Zealand' in HL Dawid (ed) *Pinner's World Unfair Competition Law: An Encyclopedia* (Alphen aan de Rijn, Sijthoff & Noordhoff, 1978) 4 vols

'The Protection of Character Merchandising—A Survey of Some Common Law Jurisdictions' (1978) 6 IIC 541

'Contracts for the Sale of Land: Recent Developments' [1978] NZ Recent Law 78 124 163 202 235

''Without Prejudice' Communications—Their Admissibility and Effect' (1974) 9 UBC LRev 85

'Medical Privilege in New Zealand' (1969) 1 Auckland University Law Review 63

Shorter articles and notes

'Ownership of Medical Images in e-Science Collaborations' (with Tina Piper) in WH Dutton and PW Jeffreys (eds) *World Wide Research: Reshaping the Sciences and Humanities* (Cambridge, MIT Press, 2010)

'Le Cas "Swizzle": IVe concours oxonien de la plaidoirie en matière de propriété intellectuelle' 2007–1 Revue de la Recherche Juridique: Droit Prospectif (vol 32:117) 521 (trans D Lefranc)

'Advertising using an Individual's Image: a Comparative Note' (2006) 122 LQR 362

'Publishers and copyright: rights without duties?' (2006) 40(6) Bibliotheksdienst 743 (wwwzlbde/aktivitaeten/bd_neu/heftinhalte2006/Recht020606pdf); in French trans (E Mackaay) as 'L'image publique des éditeurs et du droit d'auteur' (2007) 19:1 Cahiers Prop Intell 303

'Taking Stock' [1999] EIPR 339

'Issues of Current Concern in European Intellectual Property Law' in English and Japanese translation in Institute of Intellectual Property and St Catherine's College, Oxford, *Issues of Current Concern in European and Japanese Intellectual Property Law* [English translation of Japanese] (Tokyo, 1999)
'Commentary' in *Proceedings of the Colloquium on The Collective Administration of Copyright* (Ottawa, Copyright Board of Canada, 1995) 161
'Copyright Inside the Law Library' (1995) 53 The Advocate 355
'Record and Software Rentals: The Copyright Spin' (1995) 10 IPJ 109
'Tripping through TRIPs: Canada and Copyright' (1994) 22 Canadian Law Newsletter 53 Summer 1994 (ABA, Canadian Law/Section of International Law & Practice)
'Clipping Services and Copyright' (1994) 8 IPJ 379
'Intellectual Property: Copyright and New Technologies' (with Victor Nabhan) in Canadian Comparative Law Association/Institute of Comparative Law *Contemporary Law/Droit Contemporain: Canadian Reports to the 1990 International Congress of Comparative Law* Montreal 1990 (Québec, Yvon Blais, 1992) 361
'Contracts for the Sale of Goods in Canada' (1982) Juristo (No 762) 119 (in Japanese translation)
'Infringing Copyright in a Competitor's Advertising: Damages 'At Large' Can Be Large Damages' (1984) 1 IPJ 186
'"Battle of the Forms": A Comment on Professor Shanker's Views' (1980) 4 Can Bus LJ 277
'Law Reform: Professional Privilege in New Zealand' [1977] NZ Recent Law 336
'Sale of Land to Purchaser or his Nominee' [1974] NZ Law Journal 531
'Contracts—Validation of Illegal Contracts' [1974] NZLJ 149
'Real Estate Agent—Agent for Whom?' [1974] NZLJ 57
'Copyright in the Commercial World' [1974] NZ Recent Law 20
'Copyright—Literary Work' [1974] NZLJ 515
'Motor Vehicle Accident Insurance—A Question of Safety' [1974] NZLJ 58
'Illegal Contracts—Validation' [1973] NZLJ 383
'Real Estate Agent—Commission' [1973] NZLJ 287
'Car Leasing—Those Hire Purchase Regulations Again!' [1973] NZLJ 156

Book reviews

M Bridge *Sale of Goods*: (1990) 5 Banking & Finance LRev 387
M Blakeney and J McKeough (eds) *Intellectual Property: Commentary and Materials*: (1988) 3 IPJ 347
H Beale *Remedies for Breach of Contracts*: (1981) 19 University of Western Ontario Law Review 394
C Boyle and D Percy (eds) *Contracts: Cases and Commentaries*: (1979) 17 University of Alberta Law Review 567
D Falconer W Aldous and D Young (eds) *Terrell on the Law of Patents* (12th edn): (1974) 5 NZ UniversityLaw Reports 410

Working or unpublished papers

'The Enforcement of Copyright and Related Rights under the TRIPs Agreement' and 'The Dispute Settlement Mechanism of the World Trade Organization', *Working* Paper No 1, April 2000 (Oxford Intellectual Property Research Centre)

'Venturing into Intellectual Property Jointly and Confidentially' (WP 02/99), OIPRC E-Jo IPR, www.oiprc.ox.ac.uk

Introduction to Issues of Current Concern in European Intellectual Property law, W(P 08/99), OIPRC E-Jo IPR, www.oiprc.ox.ac.uk

'The Future of Intellectual Property Law: Japanese and European Perspectives Compared', WP 09/99, OIPRC E-Jo IPR, www.oiprc.ox.ac.uk

'Intellectual Property: Where's the World Going?', OIPRC Seminar Paper No S01/99, OIPRC E-Jo IPR, www.oiprc.ox.ac.uk

'Internationalizing Copyright Law: Implementing the WIPO Treaties', OIPRC Working Paper No 01/99 (Nov 98), www.oiprc.ox.ac.uk

Index